Brian

Many blessings

Le Carré

Our Inner Ocean

A WORLD OF HEALING MODALITIES

LeCain W. Smith

BALBOA.
PRESS
A DIVISION OF HAY HOUSE

Balboa Press books may be ordered through booksellers or by contacting:

Balboa Press
A Division of Hay House
1663 Liberty Drive
Bloomington, IN 47403
www.balboapress.com
1 (877) 407-4847

ISBN: 978-1-4525-1868-8 (sc)
ISBN: 978-1-4525-1869-5 (e)

Library of Congress Control Number: 2014912678

Printed in the United States of America.

Balboa Press rev. date: 8/12/2014

To Pandora and Jazmine, who bring "Papa Lee" such joy

Contents

Acknowledgments   ix

Preface   xi

Introduction   xiii

Part One — Practitioner-Applied Bodywork   1

1. Health, Healing, and the Power of Touch   3
    Becoming More Embodied
    The Role of Bodywork
    The Results

2. Considerations Before Bodywork   9

3. The Bodywork Session   13
    Before a Treatment
    During a Treatment
    After a Treatment

4. The Skilled Practitioner   19
    Considering Competence
    The Practitioner and the Healing Process

5. The Art of Being a Good Recipient   25
    Preparing for a Session
    During a Treatment
    Follow-Up Care

6. A World of Applied Bodywork Modalities   31
    I. Structural Therapies   35
    II. Functional Reeducation Therapies   65
    III. Substance- and Implement-Assisted Therapies   77
    IV. Aquatic Therapies   93
    V. Spinal Therapies   109
    VI. Abdominal Therapies   123
    VII. Trauma-Centered Therapies   131
    VIII. Energy-Based Therapies   145
    IX. Energy Field and Spiritual Therapies   209
    X. Special Therapies   261
    Some Final Thoughts About These Modalities

7. Progressive Body-Mind Psychotherapies   303

Part Two — Self-Directed Healing Practices   321

8. Breath Is the Way   323
    Some Basics About Conscious Breathing
    Enhancing Breath Awareness
    Six Types of Breathwork
    Four Phases of the Breath
    A Compilation of Breathwork Therapies and Practices
    A Collection of Specific Breathing Techniques
    Breathe in the Wind

9. Energy Flow Is the Key   363
    Awakening Awareness of the Vital Life Force
    The Divine Cosmic Connection
    The Manifestations of Energy
    Energy Fields and Energy Bodies
    The Human Energy Anatomy: Centers, Pathways, and Points
    Working with Energy
    Bodywork and Energy
    Two Powerful Ancient Practices
    Final Thoughts

10. Making a Shift in Consciousness   391
    Struggles and Obstacles
    Awakening Through Change
    Making the Shift Through Meditation
    The Practice of Meditation
    Some Forms of Meditation
    Finding Wholeness

11. A World of Self-Care Healing Practices and Exercises   409
    Aerobics to Yoga

12. Ripples From My Inner Ocean   461
    Our Life's Work
    Obstacles As Opportunities for Transformation
    Bringing It All Together with the Fabulous Five
    Seeking Happiness
    A Final Blessing

Appendix: Complementary and Alternative Health Care Resources   471
Index   475

Acknowledgments

This book would still be an ambitious dream without the assistance and expertise of a great many people, who all were most generous in providing me with experiences, information, support, and inspiration. I am truly indebted to them all for their help.

First and foremost, I want to express the utmost gratitude and appreciation for the diligent work of Sheila Moir, whose patience was undeniable when it came to the editing and proofreading of this book. Without her contribution, this book would be twice as long and half as readable. In addition, the editorial services of Laurel Robinson helped me fine-tune the manuscript. I am also very thankful for the secretarial services of Bahia Yackzan and the last-minute proofreading done by Martha Jordan.

Special thanks go to Jim Kosinski for putting together the wonderful images on the front and back book cover and enhancing a number of my photographs. I greatly appreciate the hard work of Linda Deming in preparing the artistic renderings of the line-art illustrations. Many thanks also go to Trond Andersen, Shelor Duffee, William Geisler, Ron Lavin, Wendy Sichel, and Jonathan Tripodi for their photo contributions. When I needed models for photographs, Steve Ahola, Zuzonna Hout, Lari Luehman, Michael Maynard, Faith Perkins, Vickie Pollard, and David Walker generously answered the call.

I must first honor the talented and intuitive bodyworkers who provided me with the transformative healing experiences that set me on the path that led to the creation of this book. They include David Disney, Daisy Kallop, Brennan Murphy, Martha Ohrenberger, Gayle Perkins, and Karen Rowan.

Developers of modalities and the staff of bodywork institutes helped me over the last few years by providing interviews and reviewing the descriptions of their work. I extend my grateful thanks to: Pietro Abela of the ARC Institute, Laurie Adato of the Hakomi Institute, Naisha Ahsian of the Crystalis Institute, Anne Angelheart of Zenith Omega, Judith Aston of Aston Kinetics, Alianna Boone of Kentro Body Balance, Catherine Brady of Trauma Touch Therapy, Howard Brockman of Dynamic Energetic Healing, Mary Jo Bulbrook of Energy Medicine Partnerships, Igor Burdenko of the Burdenko Water & Sports Therapy Institute, Lynda Caesara of the Berry Method Institute, Joanne Callahan of Callahan Techniques, Ltd., Lilia Cangemi of Dolphin Dance Healing, Roger Cloutier of Massage, Posture, and Movement, Sue Conlin of the Therapeutic Touch International Association, Cheryl Coull of Shinso Shiatsu International, Patricia Cramer of Vibrational Healing Massage Therapy, Theresa Dale of the Wellness Center for Research & Education, Inc., Stephen Davidson of Healthabounds, Judith DeLany of the Neuromuscular Therapy Center, Maciej Dluski of Yumeiho Therapy, Stephen Dubro of Energy Extension, Inc., Louisa Dyer of WOW Processing, Diane Ealy of Physiohelanics, Ellen F. Franklin of the Kairos Institute of Sound Healing, LLC, Bob Frissell of Breath of Life, Michael Reed Gach of the Acupressure Institute, Alice Brown Gagnon of the Core Healing Center, Jill Geiger of the American Society for the Alexander Technique, Alexander George of Healing Dance, Rebecca Goff of Aquacranial Therapy, Mika Gonzalez of the Vitality Center, Neil Gumenick of the Institute of Classical Five-Element Acupuncture, Inc., Dallas Hancock and Flo Barber-Hancock of CranioStructural Integration, Janice Hayes of Delphi University, Beloved Heartsong of the LaHo-Chi Institute of Energy Healing, Paul Hughes of Vivation International, Oscar Ichazo of the Arica Institute, Carolyn Jaffe of the Health & Wellness Integrative Medical Center, Chris Jorgensen of Heartland Attunement, Doreya Karim of BioGeometry, Donald W. Kipp of the Body Awareness Institute, Beverly Kitaen-Morse and Jack Rosenberg of the Integrative Body Psychotherapy Central Institute, Tedd Koren of Koren Specific Technique, Tekla Kosa of Autogenic Training, Judith Kravitz of the Transformational Breath Foundation, Mark Lamm of the BioSync Research Institute, Sama Laskow of Holoenergetic Healing, Penny and Ron Lavin of One Light Healing Touch, Betty Jane LeClair of the Center for Neuroacoustic Research, Shar Lee of Tibetan Cranial, Dennis Lewis of Authentic Natural Breathing, Paul Linden of the Columbus Center for Movement Studies, Bobby Lott of the Theta Healing Institute of Knowledge, John Loupos of the Association for Hanna Somatic Education,

Lisa Loustaunau of the Institute of Core Energetics, Benjamin Marantz of AcroSage, Dirk Marivoet of the International Council of Psychocorporal (Bodymind) Integration Trainers, Dorothy Martin-Neville of the WISE Method, Terry Matthews of Jin Shin Jyutsu, Inc., Sharon Metzger of Neuro Cranial Restructuring, Stephanie Mines of the TARA Approach for the Resolution of Shock and Trauma, Mary Molloy of the Gerda Boyesen International Institute of Biodynamic Psychology and Psychotherapy, Pierre Morin of Creative Healing, Jim Mutch of Soul Lightening International, Richard Pavek of the SHEN Therapy Institute, Theresa Pettersen-Chu of the International Association of Rubenfeld Synergists, Tobin Rangdrol of the Arcata School of Massage, Victoria Ross of the International Institute for Corrective Muscle Therapy, Inc., Kay Sassani of Matrix Energetics International, Diane Shewmaker of Celestial Wellspring Publications, Mary T. Sise of the Energy of Belief, Rebecca Skeele of Noetic Balancing, Jacquelyn Small of the Eupsychia Institute, Justin Snavely of the Trauma Institute, Ruth Sova of the Aquatic Therapy and Rehab Institute, Bell Tam of the Tom Tam Healing System, Jennifer Taylor of Quantum-Touch, Inc., Iona Marsaa Teeguarden of the Jin Shin Do Foundation for Bodymind Acupressure, Angelika Thusius of Kentro Body Balance, Jonathan A. Tripodi of Body Memory Recall, Susan Walker of Hellerwork International, Preston Walters of Imago Relationships International, Dan Watson of the LaHo-Chi Institute of Energy Healing, Ric Weinman of Vortex Healing, Cameron West of Aquatic Integration, June Leslie Wieder of Song of the Spine, Susan Winter of the Rolf Institute, Amanda Wongsonegoro of the Hendrickson Method Institute, Gina Wrinn of the Institute of Integrative Manual Therapy, Michael Young of the Muscle Release Technique, and Cynthia Zaal of the Myopractic Institute. Working with them made the project most enjoyable.

Likewise, I give thanks for the experiential teachings, feedback, and support provided by the professional bodyworkers, therapists, and healers who have guided me over the last decade and reviewed material for the book. They include Duffy Allen, Suzanne Blackburn, Carol Borsello, Jane Burdick, Brenda Colfer, Charlene Crane, Terry Conrad, Connie Curtin, Charlotte Davis, Dede Eaton, Benjamin Fox, Jeannie Gaudette, Laura Handler, Nora Hebich, Kathie Keane, Rocco Laptenca, Eileen Mielenhausen, Brennan Murphy, Jan Nash, John Penkalski, Faith Perkins, Gayle Perkins, Anne Perry, Claudia Ragonesi, Karen Rowan, Johanna Schwarzbeck, Wendy Sichel, Sheila Thompson, Dick Tryon, David Walker, Paul Weiss, Diane Whiteside-Peck, and Janet Willie.

In addition, I must thank those instructors and mentors who provided me with training in self-care practices that brought me further insight and well-being. They include yoga teachers Gabriel McCormick, Tim Miller, Donna Davidge, and David Walker; Holotropic Breathwork facilitators Elizabeth and Lenny Gibson; Transformational Breathwork teacher Judith Kravitz; sound healer and chant master Jill Purce; qi gong master trainers Paul Weiss and Michael Winn; embodied meditation teachers Tara Brach, Lama John Makransky, Lama Willa Miller, Anam Thubten, and Tenzin Wangyal Rinpoche; and traditional African healer Sobonfu Somé.

Last but certainly not least, I must express my deepest appreciation for the wisdom transmitted by people I've never met. At different times in my life, their teachings and examples have inspired me on my quest for self-realization and compassion. Many thanks to Meher Baba, Ram Das, Pema Chödrön, His Holiness the Dalai Lama, Osho (Rajneesh), Reginald Ray, Rumi, Robert Thurman, and Chogyam Trungpa Rinpoche. I feel blessed by the insight they have provided.

I can't close without a bow of gratitude to the many friendly people and healers in the Polynesians islands of the Pacific Ocean, who have the natural ability to share their heartfelt joys and sorrows.

Preface

When speaking of the inner ocean, many images come to mind. Like the watery home in which life first evolved, we may see it as the place of origin from which consciousness arises. It may suggest a place of great depth at the core of our being, a world of mystery that lies beneath the surface of awareness. It can be imagined as a great body of energy that is not only contained within each of us but also spreads out into limitless space, connecting everything and everybody. Perhaps everything we perceive is just a holographic representation of this larger universe from which all things originate. Can any of us really know what magnificent wonders await us when we plunge deep within and touch upon the vital force responsible for our existence?

To most of us, the word *ocean* stands for something vast, fluid, all encompassing, and full of life. Over the centuries, questions about what lay beyond the waves lapping at the shore fueled great discoveries as those who were able to get past their fears ventured forth to explore beyond the horizon. But with discovery came the problems facing us and our world today. Perhaps it is time to explore the ocean of life within each of us, a boundless sea of immense potential flowing with energy and full of mystery. It could contain a new dimension of awareness without boundaries from which our true self can surface and become recognized as an integral and well-loved part of our being. We might discover great depths of wisdom that can help us understand our true nature and the reality of our world. With this, we can surrender a previously limited identity and release capabilities that allow us to live with a new sense of openness, healthy and at peace.

When I was young, struggling to live harmoniously with my family, friends, and neighbors, I turned to nature as my guiding star, exploring the woods on handmade trails that led to secret campsites. My home was right on the ocean, and I woke up every morning with the sound of the harbor channel bell buoy in my ears. My imagination was always tantalized by what lay beyond the horizon. As the years passed and my time at school ended without my feeling any real professional call from the land, I realized my future lay upon the ocean—the outer ocean. As fate would have it, that summons from the sea became my saving grace. With strong intention, dogged determination, and, of course, some twists of fate, I was able to actualize my destiny, becoming captain of my own ship. I spent many years voyaging on the water and ultimately circumnavigated our globe.

A thousand miles from land, the meditative quality of being at one with the open ocean took hold of me in a new way. I felt a strong sense of accomplishment, wonder, and aliveness while adventuring with the elements, but my heart still yearned to be part of something greater than myself. It was as though the spirit and sacredness of something larger was calling, something that could benefit my well-being and that of others. As I reflect upon the transitions that followed, I realize that life is a continual unfolding in which each step of the path must be honored in a way that allows for constant awakening. Sailing around the world was only a precursor to the even more spiritual endeavor of exploring the inner ocean of my being.

When I first returned from my grand world cruise, I was mystified when I thought about what I should do next. How could I top such a great experience? What could make me that happy again? Looking more deeply, I realized I hadn't been that happy after all. In many ways, I had always seemed to be striving to complete that next crossing to another distant isle while fleeing the world of human discourse I had never quite been able to handle. Even though I had been present to the sea, the ship, and the adventures they brought me, I hadn't been totally present to my own true nature. My efforts needed to take a new direction. It had become apparent that the boundless sea at the heart of our existence is where the answers and solutions to the problems of our life reside. And so I embarked on the exploration of the inner ocean of my own being on a quest to discover the innate abilities and wisdom within that could heal and transform.

What I can fathom about this inner ocean depends on the level of my perceptions at any given time. Sometimes my vision is limited to the immediate horizon; sometimes my awareness expands to an infinite depth. We all have moments in life when we are able to perceive things on a deeper, more soulful level. Something has been altered in a way that causes us to feel as if our body, mind, emotions, and spirit are unified in a wise and healthy way. For me, these moments often come through bodywork, and especially through experiences with the breath. Taking a closer look at the body means recognizing not only its physical aspects, but its interconnection with thoughts, feelings, spirit, and soul. It seems quite possible that the wisdom that lies within our own bodies, contained within the inner ocean, can shift us into a state of openness and harmony in which we recognize the inseparability of ourselves and others. Such a state reduces the stresses of human interaction that so often not only lead to disease but escalate to conflict and war.

One thing I learned from my world cruising experience is that when you live close to nature in simple, relaxed environments such as I found in those remote South Pacific "paradise" islands, you seem to be living in a way that is more fully present. This is particularly true when you dive down deep into the sea, for in the presence of the unusual and unknown, you have to be fully conscious, aware, and open to the unexpected. I have since often found it helpful to try to embody this state of mind when driving in city traffic or doing some other hectic or stressful activity here on land. Maintaining this healthy state of being is not always easy when living with the stresses of the fast-moving, driven pressures of modern living. It seems that to alleviate the suffering caused by these stresses, we all need to remember what it's like to feel in harmony, in love, or in a some other state where the whole body resonates with good feelings. The key element seems to be taking a pause. When you have a chance to stop and let the body and mind remember what is really important in life, then it is possible to intuitively know in our heart of hearts what is best for us. What better way to create this pause than through bodywork, conscious breathing, energy medicine, and self-care exercises such as meditation or yoga.

Looking inward is like diving into the depths of our own being, into that inner ocean, to see what we can discover. May this publication help all beings recognize new powerful options for achieving optimal physical, mental, and spiritual health.

Introduction

If you look around at our world today, we seem caught in a maelstrom of war, disruption, civil strife, environmental disasters, pollution, and competition, all contributing to agitation, emotional problems, stress, and ultimately disease. Stress, whether caused by worries about global or local events or simply the difficulties of making it day to day, undermines the body's natural ability to ward off disease. The fast pace of modern life causes us to make unhealthy choices about things such as proper rest, exercise, and nutrition, all of which are vital to maintaining a healthy body. The rise in toxic environmental pollution weakens our immune system, preventing individual cells from doing their jobs effectively. The emotional side of things is no brighter. Many of us feel separate and alone, unable to connect with anything that is really meaningful. Our internal world is often devoid of the feeling and insight that bring us into a more integrated and balanced way of being.

During the Renaissance and the Scientific Revolution, the Western world left mythology and superstition behind to embrace a more rational perspective. With the Industrial Revolution, we mechanized our work and clustered people into cities where services could be offered more efficiently. By now, we've been to the moon, found ways to prevent diseases that were fatal not long ago, and created the Internet, which allows us to communicate instantly with people far away. But by and large, we have concerned ourselves with improving only material comfort, safety, security, and control. We've relegated spirituality to church on Sundays, lost our ancestors' day-by-day connection with the natural world, and become detached from our true feelings. Overvaluing intellect and reason has divided us into separate, nonintegrated parts, masking the wisdom of our bodies, much to the dismay of our hearts.

So how have we responded to all these pressures on our bodies and minds? By developing our modern allopathic health care system. Okay, it's technologically advanced with plenty of amazing equipment, but thanks to the efforts of rapacious pharmaceutical companies and greedy for-profit businesses and corporations, the very latest (and most expensive) drugs and equipment are foisted on an unsuspecting public, increasing the already high cost of health care. Ads offer miracle cures on every television channel, in spite of the risk of side effects and drug interactions. Of course, we've brought some of this on ourselves by our desire for a quick fix, our fear that we can't help heal ourselves, our propensity for filing malpractice lawsuits, and our conviction that new, expensive medical care, even if it has not passed the test of time, is the best way to go. Not only that, but many dedicated health care professionals cannot spend enough time with patients to truly address their problems. Modern allopathic health care is a complex system in which specialists work in compartmentalized ways; each holds a narrow, symptomatic focus that does not permit seeing the whole person. But to simply treat symptoms without addressing the root cause is like applying a Band-Aid when CPR is needed.

Health care, especially preventive care, existed long before there was ready access to doctors, but the reliance on institutionalized medicine has unfortunately marginalized these more natural alternatives. In earlier times, shamans used potions and trances to drive out disease, sometimes successfully. Throughout the centuries, wise women in local communities offered herbal treatments that are now being vindicated. Midwives delivered babies as a community service, without drugs or worrying about malpractice insurance. Every mother had a treasured recipe for spring tonic. And if we had to see a doctor, it was often someone who had known us since we were born, who could view our illness in the context of our life and family. Our very lifestyle tended to promote better health. Before cars were epidemic, people—especially kids—actually walked. Before refrigeration and refrigerated transport were taken for granted, we relied on seasonal foods, growing produce ourselves or buying from farmers who produced it without using pesticides or chemical fertilizers. We took more personal responsibility for maintaining good health. But nowadays, many people feel they can do or not do, eat or not eat anything they like, because a magic pill will restore the good health they have not cared for.

The time has come to make a significant shift and look at health and health care in a more comprehensive and holistic way by acknowledging that a human being is a dynamic organism in which the body and the mind (with all of its thoughts, feelings, and emotions) are completely interconnected and that dysfunction can manifest in unexpected ways. Creating the optimal functioning that we call good health depends on applying appropriate remedies to each and every part of this whole that requires attention. This kind of approach is necessary now more than ever. We need something that encourages individuals to slow down, be present in the moment and in their bodies, and become more self-aware and complete.

Today, you often hear the expression *complementary health care*. It embraces a substantial array of holistic therapies, practices, treatments, and preventive care that support the reality of a deep interconnection between the body and mind. This concept is often referred to as the body-mind and sometimes the heart-mind. These terms reflect the recognition that the physical body, heart, mind, sensations, emotions, thoughts, soul, and spirit are interdependently connected in ways that go deep below the surface of our everyday awareness. Then there is the energy that flows in, through, and beyond each being and makes all possible. Recent studies and scientific research are proving that there is even an energetic interconnection between the cellular and the cosmic. Some ancient medical systems, especially those in Asia, have long acknowledged these relationships and have developed natural, integrative treatments that go well beyond the scope of conventional medical practice. Acupuncture, yoga, and qi gong, as well as macrobiotics, naturopathy, osteopathy, homeopathy, herbology, and a vast assortment of therapeutic movement exercises, breathing practices, and self-care methods, all recognize the importance of treating health issues and their interconnected causes by inspiring and promoting a profound awareness of the body-mind connection. It is in the complementary and alternative therapies that the inner energies of the body, personal feelings, and spirit are honored as equal partners in health, because when all aspects of our being are integrated, we can truly attain a level of optimal functioning and health.

The Scope of This Book

When I first started work on this publication, my intention was to focus on the various modalities of bodywork that a practitioner can offer to a recipient. But over time, I came to realize that self-care methods

of bodywork were the other side of the coin, equally important for enhancing overall well-being and crucial if we want to be of service by helping others improve themselves. One significant experience was instrumental in precipitating this recognition.

A few years ago, I was participating in a Holotropic Breathwork workshop. During the sessions, participants lying on floor mats practice specific deep breathing techniques for about four hours, during which time ecstatic music is played at a fairly loud volume. The overall intent is to promote a kind of altered state in which some form of cathartic release or personal transformation can take place. Each participant is supported in the process by a nearby sitter who tends to their basic needs, while experienced professional facilitators circulate through the group and provide additional therapeutic assistance through verbal inquiry, movement of the participant's body, or certain ways of touching. It is not unusual for many of the participants in the large room to express themselves with all sorts of spontaneous sounds and body movements.

For most of the session, my experience was not particularly dramatic, though I was definitely more aware of the feelings inside my body and noticed that certain music made my skin tingle and vibrate in a way that mostly felt very soothing. However, when my expectations had ebbed to a low point near the end of the time, something shifted. I believe that this was caused in part by powerful, deep-toned chanting music that was playing just as one of the facilitators began doing some bodywork on me. My back had begun hurting, and I had just sat up straight. Typical of the bodywork done in a Holotropic session, the facilitator was applying deep pressure to the pain, which was rapidly intensifying in my back. In addition, she sandwiched her hands around my heart chakra. The pain in my back was getting intense, and I was directed to continually breathe into it. It's hard to describe what happened next as the whole of my being was peaking into an intense experience. The pain eventually exploded into a significant release in which I was simply transformed into pleasure and joy. At the same time, my body alternated between wanting to relax and receive the nurturing and wanting to sit up and be more energetically active by doing something like yoga. Each of these responses represented two seemingly opposite ways of dealing with a painful issue. One is the avenue of receiving healing through surrender, whereas in the other, you find healing through your own activity. My body fluctuated between these two kinds of healing, and I continually shifted between lying down and sitting up until I came to a midpoint in which the two extremes became the integrated state of being fully present. Energy was then flowing throughout me so strongly that I melted into a condition in which overwhelming visions and feelings carried me into a state of blissful awareness and oneness. Tears and laughter poured from me as my body vibrated with what I can only call a deep sense of insight and inner wisdom.

This experience demonstrated to me that there are two sides to the golden coin of healing, so these two approaches became the two parts of this book. In one part are the practitioner-applied therapies in which a person lies down and surrenders to receiving; the second part looks at the more active self-care healing and rejuvenating practices such as meditation, yoga, and qi gong. Since each is simply a different side of the same coin, either can contain elements that support the other. Therefore, this book about our inner ocean, which is a space of all possibilities, became a compilation of all the therapeutic forms of bodywork and transformative healing practices found around the world today that honor the deeper inner connections among all aspects of a human being. Even though many have proved themselves over many years, sometimes for millennia, most have not attained the recognition they deserve from Western medicine. I hope to give you information that will help you recognize how these complementary modalities can provide a more integrated sense of health and well-being either alone or in combination with other forms of health care.

The Organization of the Book

Part One covers practitioner-applied bodywork in which a trained professional uses varying degrees of physical or subtle touch on a client to promote health and healing. These bodywork modalities are divided into ten categories according to primary focus or approach to healing to help provide a better understanding not only of how each is used but also of how they relate to one another. These categories are: structural therapies; therapies that use movements, manipulations and adjustment of alignment to reeducate the body; therapies that address the spine; therapies that focus on the abdomen and internal organs; therapies that incorporate separate materials, implements or substances; aquatic or hydrotherapies; therapies that work with emotional and mental

trauma that have created chronic dysfunctions; therapies that work with the energy in the body; therapies that heal through manipulation of the surrounding energy fields; and special therapies that contain a unique method or location of application, that are carried out for a distinctive purpose, or that use an uncommon mix of modalities. In addition, there is a chapter on progressive forms of psychotherapy, counseling, and training that incorporate a strong recognition of the body-mind connection in the treatment of mental or emotional issues. These include practices that work to improve communication skills, change core beliefs, and improve individual quality of life.

Part Two examines methods by which you work on yourself through specific practices or exercises. Though performed alone, they most often require some initial training or guidance. These practices include such things as breathwork, energy work, meditation, rejuvenating movement practices such as dance, aquatic exercises, and transformative practices such as Aikido, Tai Chi, qi gong, and yoga. The effects of some of these therapies can be experienced immediately, although perfecting many of them requires years of discipline. Part Two also contains chapters that discuss breath, energy, and meditation, mainly because they play a key role in all healing practices, especially when it comes to releasing blockages, inhibitions, and dysfunction and encouraging the growth of self-awareness and the evolution of the spirit.

This separation into practitioner-applied and self-care modalities is somewhat arbitrary, since they are complementary to one another; bodywork modalities found in Part One often have related practices in Part Two. For example, the practitioner-applied modality of Bremma Bodywork has self-care practices that a person can perform at home, and Kunye Massage Therapy has its own yogic self-care counterpart. The Trager Approach gave birth to Mentastics exercises. The same is true for many others. The opposite is also true, since certain types of hands-on bodywork arose from elements of self-care practices such as qi gong and Yantra Yoga. Additionally, practitioners often recommend specific self-care practices as an adjunct to bodywork therapies. The dividing line here is that one type requires a separate practitioner and the other doesn't.

The Coverage of the Book

The therapeutic modalities discussed in this book have diverse origins. Many can be traced back to shamanic healing practices or the principles and practices of health care found in the Vedic-Hindu, Buddhist, Tibetan, and Chinese Taoist traditions. These ancient forms are based on the holistic approach of relating physical health to the universal life-force energies that bind us all together. The seeds they planted have sprouted and grown into many branches, both well known and obscure. Some healing practices are a synthesis of these older therapies and new ideas; some may offer a unique combination of methods from other therapies. Others have been made possible through recent technological advances. There are also modalities that are most often combined with other types of therapy. And then there are the modalities that are waiting to be born or still at the teething stage. In bodywork as in life, all is subject to change and evolution. The aim of this guidebook is to help increase awareness of these complementary therapies by presenting a basic overview of many (though unquestionably not all) of the established forms of therapeutic bodywork and holistic self-care methods presently available.

I had to develop some personal standards about which modalities to include. Words like *useful*, *significant*, *authentic*, and *worthwhile* were the ones that guided me. I tried not to allow popularity or availability to affect my decision-making. Some that you will read about are part of the mainstream of complementary and alternative medicine. Others, especially those more recently developed or practiced in remote areas, may have many virtues, but have not been tested by time or found wider usage. In addition, it was sometimes difficult to discern whether a modality was a distinct form of treatment, even some that are trademarked and well established. Many forms of bodywork are not only closely related in terms of their principles and approaches, but use similar methods and techniques. They may be based on older methods, but have evolved as new research, new technology, and new insights have cross-fertilized with a practitioner's experience. They may be something completely new, prompted by a developer's personal experience. If I have included something, it's because, even though it may appear similar to another, I believe there are elements in it that make it distinct. However, I have tried to omit those that are essentially copies or imitations of others.

Considering the number of different modalities (more than 500 forms of bodywork and 200 methods of

self-care) discussed here, it would be impossible to cover each of them in depth, so I have chosen to focus mainly on guiding principles and purpose, while also describing what actually happens during a treatment session. When appropriate, I have also discussed the energy aspects of each bodywork therapy, since that is an integral part of the healing process. Many developers and practitioners of modalities mentioned here have created their own institutions, associations, seminar programs, and training schools to further perpetuate the use and spread of their work. The web sites below listings usually provide this information, as well as details about the modality itself.

Although web-site addresses were correct at the time of publication, they do seem to change frequently, and they are certainly not the only source of information about a modality. Some of the best descriptions of modalities are found on the web sites of individual practitioners, but their inclusion here is not an endorsement of any particular individuals, except to salute them for making clear to the public what it is that they offer. When possible, web addresses with general information are what is provided. In any case, you may want to carry out additional Internet searches for further details and practitioners near you. Please realize that the inclusion of any web site is not meant to imply that the information contained there is correct or complete. The Appendix at the end of the book also contains the names of some useful organizations related to bodywork and complementary medicine as a whole.

Although I do make some basic comments about the primary intended effects of a modality, I have tried not to elaborate, except in some minor ways, upon the benefits and the results—either claimed or expected—of a treatment, since this is so subjective and depends on the particular practitioner and the condition of the recipient at that moment in time. Advertising superlatives are often not related to real-life experiences, but I am convinced that powerful and positive effects on the whole being can come through the hands of a skilled practitioner or the intention of a dedicated seeker.

If there are contraindications to a particular modality, I have tried to include them. Contraindications are considered to be existing problems that make certain forms of bodywork inappropriate for an individual. What constitutes a contraindication varies from modality to modality and in many instances, it may apply only to people with some substantially limiting condition. Anyone who is concerned about how a particular modality might interact with existing conditions should consult a health care practitioner and discuss the situation frankly with the bodyworker.

The information presented for each modality generally includes the name or names of the modality, its place within a larger medical system (if applicable), historical background (who created it and how it was developed), the basic approach and intention, the essence of a treatment session with details of the bodywork techniques, and some conclusions. Actions that the recipient can take after a treatment are also included when offered by a particular kind of therapy. In addition, there may be information on closely related modalities and those that evolved out of the original. Ancient modalities, whose origins are often clouded, matured over a long period of time with input from a number of different people. In other instances, a developer took something ancient and reestablished it with new insights, language, and parameters. Sometimes, the form was the work of a single person. Though this historical information is always interesting, the focus here is helping the reader understand and compare all of the possibilities.

The information about each of these modalities was acquired from a variety of sources, not the least of which was decades of my own personal experiences and involvement with alternative therapies. (No, I have not yet experienced them all, but maybe I will be lucky enough to do so before I die.) My own life changes through travel, retreat experiences, meditations, altered states of consciousness, and energetic practices such as yoga and qi gong also contributed immensely to my perceptions and knowledge about many of these healing therapies. In addition to years of study and research, I carried out numerous interviews with developers, founders, and practitioners, who were often kind enough to critique what I had written or add new insights. In the end, what is detailed here is a synthesis of the ideas and understandings that I gained. But I firmly believe that to really know the essence of something requires experience. You can read hundreds of books on sailing, but without getting out on a boat on the water you will never really learn how to sail. Since I am the kind of person who always likes to accomplish things and experience life to the fullest, I am passionate about exploring the inner ocean. If you're anything like me, this voyage of discovery is taken even more to heart when your interest is piqued by the amazing rewards that come from doing something you love and getting remarkable results from the spiritual realms that have a powerful way of hitting home.

The descriptions of some forms of treatment may be more detailed and specific than others because of a combination of factors, primarily my own experiences and familiarity, the amount of information available, and the complexity of the modality. Some methods are simple enough to negate the need for lengthy discussion, whereas others are more involved and part of a larger system of healing. I will also be the first to admit that to a certain extent some of the modalities discussed have been presented more extensively because they are closer to my own liking and reflect what I have personally valued and experienced the most. However, the amount of information presented does not reflect any judgment on my part on the credibility or value of any modality.

Unless specifically requested by a practitioner or developer of a modality, I have not included the initials after their names that indicate licenses or certificates. This in no way reflects on their expertise, and the information can be found on the web sites listed for these modalities.

All specialized fields in time develop their own jargon and specialized language, often not clear to laypersons. Bodywork is no different, but when possible, I have tried to explain technical terms in simple language. For modalities that originated in non-English-speaking countries, I have chosen to use the spellings that are most prevalent in present-day English or in the discipline itself. For example, you will not see *chi gong*, but rather *qi gong*. *Daoist* becomes *Taoist*. The life-force energy that permeates many of the practices is called by different names in different countries; for simplicity's sake, this energy is usually called chi throughout the book. You will, however, find variations from these general rules depending on the kind of explanation needed for a specific practice.

It's probably also helpful to clarify certain terms that are used repeatedly throughout the book. A *system* of healing is bigger than any single modality and usually includes both bodywork and other therapeutic practices based on specific beliefs about the nature of healing. The terms *modality*, *method*, and *therapy* are used synonymously to indicate a form or type of bodywork. A *technique*, on the other hand, is usually a particular practice or element that is incorporated in a modality, though some techniques are powerful enough to be considered modalities in themselves. I most often refer to the person who established a modality as the *developer* or *founder*. In some cases, this can be a bit misleading, since the roots of the therapy may have originated in ancient times, and the developer really is someone who was instrumental in establishing the present-day usage of this therapy by reviving, redeveloping, or promoting the original, as well as creating new variations on it. And finally, the word *recipient* may be exchanged with *client, patient,* or even *partner.* In any case, you know who you are.

And finally, there is the issue of gender bias in language. In this day and age, *he* is no longer the automatic personal pronoun, nor is *his* or *him.* The English language has not caught up with the indisputable fact the men and women are equal partners in the game of life. Perhaps some day, *their* will become a singular pronoun, but that day is not yet here. Rather than fumbling with *he or she* or *he/she* or *s/he,* I have chosen to alternate *she* and *he* as best I can. Chapters contain one or the other usage throughout; listings of modalities alternate them. You will undoubtedly find some slipups, but the goal has been equality.

It is not necessary to read this book in any particular order. You can start at the beginning or go right to any chapter that calls you. However, browsing through the entire work will give you a better understanding of its organization and where specific information can be found. You might even discover something unexpected and suddenly inspiring. Anyone looking for a specific modality or practice, an important historical figure, or the developer of a modality and people who played a role in its development can use the index to find this information quickly.

Each of us has many choices to make in life, and making the healthy ones that will improve our lives is not always easy. Optimum health is not an unreachable goal, and it is heartwarming to note that so many effective measures can be incorporated into our lives, whether to resolve ongoing problems or prevent such difficulties from arising. To choose correctly, we must be guided by our intuition and informed by our wisdom. It is my aspiration that this book will add to that storehouse of wisdom.

True healing is not only the recovery from a dysfunction, but an ongoing life process in which a person strives for the fullest level of functioning and fullest potential as a human being. Long-lasting change can take place in minutes or develop slowly over time, but, with the assistance of integrated bodywork and self-care practices, we can maintain healthy lifestyles that minimize stress and keep us in a balanced relationship with our natural environment. It may not be just a matter of living longer, but of living well right up to the point when we leave our bodies behind and go joyfully without worries into the vast, unknown ocean beyond. May you all have a happy journey.

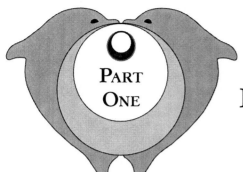

Practitioner-Applied Bodywork

Every human being is a miracle composed of interconnected and interdependent parts—body, mind, emotions, energy, and spirit—that waltz together in the dance of life. The heartbeat is the rhythm section, and the melody is played as the human organism pulses and vibrates with life-force energy. It's also a mystery, because much of what goes on within the body takes place without our even being aware of it. Skin cells are constantly being born, maturing, and dying. The blood is continually delivering nutrients to the cells, and carrying off waste products. Emotions seem to have a life of their own. But what happens when the dance is interrupted, when any of the partners falters and can't perform properly? We can just put up with it, or—better yet—we can seek some form of healing therapy to get us dancing joyfully again.

In this first part of the book, we'll take a look at the many different modalities of practitioner-applied bodywork that can be called on to get us back in our groove, every part listening closely to the body's wisdom. These holistic practices rely on the body-mind connection, so there's also information about some psychotherapeutic programs that focus on rectifying mental or emotional imbalances by addressing them through somatic practices.

Chapter 1 considers the meanings of health and healing and examines how bodywork, healing touch, and the body's wisdom can become our allies. Chapter 2 reflects on questions and concerns people might have about the experience of bodywork, including deciding which modality is the right one. The treatment session itself is covered in Chapter 3, with information on what to expect during a session. Chapter 4 discusses the training and qualities that come together to create a skillful practitioner. The art of receiving bodywork is the topic of Chapter 5. It includes information about necessary preparations and some ideas about what may be helpful during and after a session. Chapter 6 is a big one, because it covers the multitude of different bodywork modalities available around the world today. The choices are divided into ten categories, each of which represents a primary focus and approach to healing. This chapter ends with some reflections on information in this chapter. Chapter 7 goes beyond practitioner-applied bodywork to look at progressive training programs, psychotherapies, and counseling therapies that emphasize how the body, mind, and emotions are connected and how they contribute to a person's well-being and enhanced personal development.

CHAPTER 1
Health, Healing, and the Power of Touch

When discussing health and healing, it may first be helpful to define disease. Basically, a person with a disease is without ease (dis-eased), meaning the body is not functioning effortlessly, as it should. Disease can also be seen as an imbalance or lack of harmony within the body system, which is an interconnected whole in which a problem in any part affects all parts and can show up anywhere in the body with the indicators we call symptoms. Some say that disease is hereditary and caused by particular genetic codes found in our DNA. External factors such as viruses, bacteria, toxins, infectious substances, electromagnetic disturbances, chemicals, pollution, and bad weather have been posited as its origin; however, in these cases, the real cause is often the body's inability to muster its defenses against these invaders. Disease may be linked to internal blockages created by injuries, traumatic events, inappropriate beliefs, disturbing emotions, disappointments, and the stresses of modern life that have become locked in our bodies. These obstructions can prevent the free flow of natural healing energy and play havoc with our body's ability to respond in a healthy way.

Health is really an ongoing process as we strive to attain the highest level of functioning and our full potential as human beings. Unfortunately, it sometimes seems like this kind of life is unattainable. We settle for thinking that we are "just fine," especially in comparison with others who obviously are not. But if we open our eyes and see the unlimited possibilities in front of us, we realize that no matter how together we might seem, there is always more that could be changed and improved. Each of us has the ability at any time to make choices that bring positive change and the opportunity to break free of limitations, but we may not always believe it. And that's where healing comes in.

So what then is healing? At first glance, the word seems to imply that something is wrong with us, that we need fixing. Although this may indeed be the case if there are specific physical or emotional manifestations of inner disturbances to the healthy functioning of the body or mind, this notion can diminish our self-image

and even increase our resistance to improving ourselves. Healing can more properly be thought of as something that helps us improve our health, actualize our full potential, and expand our inner and outer horizons. Healing can change the heart and inspire joy. It is the love of truth and the truth of love in our lives. Indeed, in some situations where people cannot be cured, they can nevertheless be healed. Healing can address problems that arise from subtle shifts, dramatic changes, or traumatic events that occur in our lives and eventually show up in some part of the body; if left uncorrected, they can lead to further dysfunction, disease, a chronic condition, or even death. But if these disturbances are caught early, healing can be preventive rather requiring us to take on the heavy restorative work that will be necessary later. Like health, healing is not a destination but an ongoing process that involves ups and downs and the daily death of that which does not lead to well-being.

True healing may involve a series of changes that at first don't appear to resolve the issue in a straightforward way. A problem may actually seem to get worse, or the symptoms can change or move to another area of the body. The course that healing takes may force a person to face issues that she wasn't aware of and that weren't immediately apparent. And beliefs, predispositions, and the degree of readiness for healing can be why people with the same symptoms experience different results from the same practice. Indeed, the path to true healing may have more to do with the personal work done between treatments than on the effectiveness of a particular modality.

The role of the mind in healing may be somewhat analogous to the placebo effect. Scientific researchers have undertaken experiments in which a simple glass of water is given to patients who believe they are receiving a golden elixir that will truly take care of their problem. These experiments frequently yield positive healing results that are very perplexing to the researchers. What these studies really reveal is that what enables healing is often the patient's mental and emotional state. The effectiveness of a particular practitioner or modality may depend on the client's belief that the treatment will be successful. It's also a fact that healing may be happening even if it seems that nothing remarkable has occurred; the benefits may not be apparent until much later. Healing can be very obvious or very subtle and mystifying, and often the recipient becomes aware of any changes only through her own interactions with her world.

Becoming More Embodied

The body could be said to have a mind of its own, full of wisdom. It is not a frozen anatomical structure but a river of energy, with messages from each system flowing out to all the others all the time without our conscious direction. Knowledge and memory, both physical and emotional, reside in the body itself, often deep within the layers of each of our organs, right down to the cellular level. Our cells are constantly being spoken to by this flow of energetic intelligence, and in response, they offer their own wisdom. If we allow it, even every cell can become a little powerhouse of healing.

True healing can be difficult if we avoid the physical and emotional pains in life, but if we meet them head-on, we may discover the truth about their causes. Symptoms are the body's way of telling the mind that it's time to get help. However, many forms of dysfunction or disease, especially in their early stages, may not present serious symptoms. It is important to go inward and listen to what the body tells us about the cause and true location of the pain. It might even say that it's time to see a medical doctor. But if the body is led by a mind that does not listen to it, then dysfunctions can arise that are beyond the body's ability to control or heal. The more we can be a witness to subtle patterns of behavior and become aware of the internal processes occurring in the body, the better chance we have of preventing a problem from arising or healing an existing one. We can develop an inner sense of who we are and what we need by listening to the body's wisdom as the body speaks its truth and gives us the right feedback. When the inner doors of perception open, we can experience a flood of information and energy rising to the surface.

We all have a natural desire for optimal functioning and an instinctual drive toward wholeness, and we each have within a great potential for awareness, especially awareness of both the body and the spiritual dimensions underlying it. When we wake up and allow awareness

to speak to us, we can tap into wisdom and become our own healers. Each of us is the expert on our physical and mental health. When we don't acknowledge this, we are less than we can be, but when we dive into the vast ocean of awareness inside us, we evoke the potential to melt away many of the troubling issues we encounter in life.

The time has come for each of us to be overwhelmed by the magic of our bodies and our own power to heal. It's all a matter of becoming more embodied, more connected to all the sensations, energies, and subtle vibrations within our physical form. It means becoming truly alive. The body's wisdom, supported by a caring and intuitive bodyworker, can be your ally on the path toward healing. And by becoming friends with your body through bodywork, you can give it that extra loving support that is so important when it just can't cope alone with some of the more overwhelming life situations that cause dysfunctions to occur.

The Role of Bodywork

Expanded self-awareness and healing can come spontaneously through some event, as if life experiences are our teachers. But the path to good health has many pitfalls. Life's changes and tragedies can sometimes throw us out of balance and wholeness. A lost job, the death (or birth) of a relationship, an accident, the passing of a dear friend, the sinking of a ship—their effects can be detrimental in many ways and, if not cared for, remain dormant as self-limiting factors for many years. It is wise to find solutions early on before the trauma becomes ingrained in the body on a cellular level as a chronic problem. Even if we've let things go on a little too long, the natural impulse to make a change for the better can work to our advantage. Many of us need a helping hand at different times through our lives, and bodywork is just that.

Bodywork, as it is used in this guidebook, has a very broad definition. Human beings are not a collection of different unrelated parts, but a complex of totally interconnected and interdependent elements—physical body, mind, energy, and spirit. So *bodywork* means any form of healing therapy that improves health, performance, quality of life, and well-being. Though touch or some form of physical manipulation by a skilled practitioner is often involved, bodywork treatments sometimes depend instead on healing energy directed by various means to the recipient. In some cases, healing is possible just by being close to energies that vibrate at a higher frequency. Bodywork also includes the self-care practices in which people take personal action to change or maintain their states of health. Most modalities of bodywork have a primary area of focus, but many have the potential to affect all areas of the body and all levels of being to some degree because of the interconnections among all parts of the body. Although some are scientifically based and work primarily to treat symptoms that show up in the body, many are more holistic and recognize the need to integrate the physical with the mental, emotional, etheric, and metaphysical.

Touch is a major part of most forms of practitioner-applied bodywork and can range from light, exploratory palpations to pressure applied to progressively deeper layers of the body. From the time we are born, touch is one of the simplest ways of connecting with another person; it is the oldest form of communication. Touching, caressing, and stroking the body is vital to our physiological and emotional well-being. When done in a sensitive and tender manner, as can be the case in bodywork, touch can fill our fundamental need to be loved and accepted and can awaken our own ability to love. It can warm our hearts. This is powerful medicine, especially for those who need support. Of course, we all know that touch is involved in physical lovemaking. Through bodywork, we can experience the nurturing and energizing rewards of physical love without the sexual act. Touch can also be therapeutic: releasing tension, relieving pain, and stimulating the flow of energy. The skin is our largest organ and has millions of tiny receptors. It keeps us in constant contact with our surroundings and sends a multitude of sensations via the nervous system to the brain. The brain can then signal a response that can affect any other part of the body. All this from a pair of skilled and loving hands!

The work done by these hands is what we call bodywork. Some bodywork is done simply to provide a relaxing, pleasurable experience. Other modalities work with movement and manipulations to reeducate and expand a person's functioning. Some deal therapeutically with specific problems or dysfunctions. Others focus on a certain area of the body such as the feet, spine, head, or abdomen. Many are directed at working with physiological components and systems, such as the skin, fascia, muscles, joints, bones, organs, and nerves. Some forms of bodywork provide ways of processing emotions or

dealing with trauma, detrimental attitudes, or limiting belief systems. Bodywork can also focus on the energy in our body or on the etheric or spiritual realms.

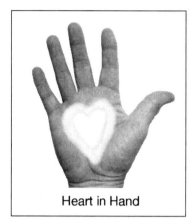

Heart in Hand

Hands convey the loving intention of the heart.

The various forms of bodywork approach healing from many different perspectives; they can therefore help us deal with the vast array of physical, mental, and emotional disruptions we face every day and help prevent us from slipping into conditions that are unhealthy. When our bodies, minds, and emotions are in a balanced state of good health, the effects can spill over to promote the health of our family and community. Alternative healing therapies, many of which have been practiced for thousands of years in cultures that understand the spiritual connectedness between our inner nature and the nature of the universe, can smooth our paths.

Bodywork can be said to have two distinct purposes—prevention and correction—but each recognize the importance of addressing the underlying cause of a problem and supporting the recipient's innate capacity to heal. The key to prevention is disarming potential problems before they can cause trouble. In this case, bodywork is often part of a regular maintenance program. We can cooperate with this effort by maintaining a lifestyle that minimizes stress and includes a good diet, proper energetic exercise, heartfelt exchange, and a balanced symbiotic relationship with our natural environment. The second approach is to correct an existing problem as soon as possible so that its effects won't become entrenched in the cells and systems of the body. Holistic therapies will address the underlying cause, the root problem, rather than simply relieving symptoms. It might be necessary to employ a therapeutic modality that targets the problem in a very direct manner, and if a chronic condition has developed, more extensive intervention may be necessary. When the causes of the problem are not clear, we may need the assistance of a professional who can guide us and help determine the form of therapy that is most appropriate for resolving the issue. A psychiatrist will probably not have much luck correcting spinal misalignment. A Swedish massage will not be able to alleviate the effects of a major trauma, nor will a foot massage change core beliefs.

The list of potential physical benefits of bodywork is long and varied: reducing stress, relaxing and calming the body and mind, improving the functioning of the body systems and internal organs, stimulating tissue, removing metabolic waste, correcting structural imbalances and increasing flexibility, improving muscle tone and range of motion, alleviating sensitivities and anxieties, removing soreness or pain, promoting better circulation of body fluids and energy, balancing the nervous system, stimulating the immune system, and providing a stronger sense of whole-body awareness and well-being. A multitude of techniques can be directed to treating the skin, muscle tension, sports injuries, spinal problems, structural imbalances, and the digestive system. Many of the different modalities not only focus on apparent dysfunctions, but work to improve the condition and potential within every body system, whether it be lymphatic, circulatory, respiratory, nervous, glandular, digestive, skeletal, muscular, or energetic. And through work on the physical body, healing on a more subtle level can also be initiated—clearing emotional trauma or altering limiting core beliefs and habitual patterns.

By approaching the healing process from the energetic dimension, bodywork can have a wide range of effects that provide changes not only in the physical body but also in the emotions, mind, and spirit. Ancient holistic medical systems, such as Traditional Chinese Medicine or Ayurveda from India that concentrate on the invisible vital life-force energy that is the basis of all physical matter have recently gained much attention, and recent studies and research, especially within the realm of quantum physics, are proving the interconnection between the cellular and the cosmic. Energy therapies work with pressure points, meridians (pathways of energy), energy centers or vortices (such as chakras), the surrounding auric energy biofields, or other universal

spiritual realms. The key premise of energetic forms of bodywork is that removing any existing energy blockages and balancing the flow of energy both within and around a person can enhance overall health.

When assistance is needed in overcoming dysfunction in the body or mind, practitioner-applied bodywork recognizes the innate body intelligence and brings it to bear on the root cause of disease in natural and noninvasive ways that also strengthen the recipient's ability to prevent problems from occurring or getting worse. Each modality has a particular focus and a specialized set of processes and techniques. Some work on a particular area of the body or follow a strict protocol, whereas others are more open ended and flexible, often guided by the client's discoveries and wishes. A vast assortment of these techniques can be incorporated into bodywork, and they are all useful for removing problems that reduce the ability to function properly. These can include physical obstructions and energetic blockages; stress, strain, tension, and anxiety; pain, soreness, agony, grief, emotional suffering, feelings of unworthiness, and premature aging; disorders, dysfunctions, ailments, maladies, illness, and mental neuroses; and abuse, injury, trauma, and chronic conditions.

But it's not only about eliminating the negative. Therapeutic touch can also produce positive results such as finding a sense of well-being, happiness, and love; connecting to the inner life force and the soul's purpose; improving posture, alignment, balance, organ function, digestion, circulation, inner sensitivity, sensory perception, self-image, memory, and personal relationships; increasing physical skills, physical pleasure, the power of the senses, personal power, and body wisdom; creating personal awareness, freedom, and a sense of harmony in life; enhancing mental processes, the flow and balance of energy within, and the potential for longevity; stimulating body strength, the immune system, and the body's innate intelligence; transforming negative habits, limited emotional states or thought patterns, and belief systems into a truthful state of open acceptance; and integrating or reestablishing a more connected sense of self-awareness and empowerment by becoming more embodied, more consciously present in our bodies.

Because it often feels good, bodywork can become a gateway that makes alternative treatment more accessible for people who may be afraid of venturing beyond the physical exam and prescription medicine that they're used to. At the very least, good feelings help relieve stress and may open a person up to recognizing the true energetic nature of existence, a state in which the actions and energies required to maintain health are seen as simply the natural path to take.

This knowing can lead to the transformation of the quest for health into one in which a person takes responsibility and participates fully in stimulating the body's own innate intelligence and immune system through things such as yoga, healthy eating, good exercise, nature walks, and meditation. The many different modalities discussed in Part Two allow us to have a direct, personal effect on our health and healing. Although some may require training from a practitioner, they all demand strong intention and diligence.

The Results

Although a bodywork treatment can be very beneficial, it is not meant to be a quick fix. If you just have a few aches and pains or simply want to relax, the occasional session may be enough. In some instances, a particular issue can be resolved quickly, sometimes in just minutes, but a series of treatments may be required for chronic problems, deep-seated dysfunctions, or to fulfill the desire for significant spiritual healing. This series of treatments will still be less intrusive and less expensive than letting an illness develop and having to enter the world of drugs with strange side effects or even surgery. However, true health is really up to each of us and requires a lifestyle that is healthy in itself, a lifestyle in which the body, mind, and spirit are all engaged in change, supported by preventive bodywork.

It's hard to describe what the results of a treatment might be because so much depends on a person's particular condition and on the strength of her intention to heal. Healing is not always immediate. In fact, sometimes after a treatment, the condition may get worse, since the elements that caused the problem must be flushed out before the body can fully restore itself to a more integrated state of being. It is usually best to try to be free of expectations. Then the results will be a happy surprise. But holistic bodywork can generally be expected to reduce symptoms by addressing their cause.

When it comes to true healing, love—especially self-love—is really the primary ingredient that makes it possible. Most of us know this intellectually, but we have a hard time actually feeling loved. Life experiences have made us fearful, and all that fear has kept us bundled up under protective armor so that love can't find us and we can't find love. Maybe the purpose of life is simply to learn and remember what love is. This love is not the desire found in the throes of passion, but an all-encompassing love of creation and consciousness. It is this love that gives the body the power to release the fear and heal. Any form of bodywork will bestow great blessings when love and compassion are combined with touch.

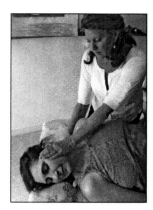

Loving touch in action.

CHAPTER 2
Considerations Before Bodywork

People who are approaching bodywork for the first time may have concerns and questions about bodywork itself or about choosing a modality and a practitioner. The next chapter will look at what happens during a bodywork treatment, but first it might be wise to clear up any hesitation about committing to such a session. For those who already have experience with practitioner-applied bodywork, the practical information may still be a valuable refresher course.

If bodywork will be a new experience for you, the first thing to contemplate is your motivation. Do you have a particular problem that a friend said could be helped by bodywork? Are you a person who likes touch and has always wanted a massage? Do you feel stressed, fatigued, and in need of something to help you relax and feel more in harmony with your world? Do you have a particular physiological issue such as a painful back or are you trying to recover from surgery? Are you looking for something energetic or spiritual? Any of these reasons and many more can inspire a person to consider bodywork. When I was getting ready for a long ocean crossing, I liked to get a nice massage as part of the send-off so that I would be relaxed, energetically balanced, and in good spirits. After returning from a rough crossing, my body, mind, and soul often craved a bodywork treatment that would wash away the residual tension.

No matter what your own situation is, bodywork can serve you well. However, those who are not familiar with this type of experience may have some resistance—some personal obstacles to bodywork. There are people who are uncomfortable with physical contact and don't like to be touched. The reasons are numerous. Many of us grew up with parents who never showed us affection in a physical way, never hugged us, never touched us. In cultures where intellect rules, feelings are often so discredited that some people feel compelled to hide their emotions; they worry—and rightly so—that physical contact might open them up to parts of themselves they have been busy avoiding and will cause them to lose control. For a victim of abuse, the aftermath is often shame

about the body and feelings of anger, fear, and grief that, held in the body, replay themselves over and over again. Religion has also played its part in alienating people from their bodies with its ideas about sin and touch, which inevitably instills a sense of guilt; this hasn't been helped by negative publicity about sex workers masquerading as massage therapists. Low self-esteem (perhaps caused by being out of shape or being labeled "fat" or "not pretty"), self-blame, and feelings of unworthiness can also lead to mental attitudes that deny the wisdom that the body holds. In all these scenarios, emotions are not only preventing us from drawing on the body's wisdom, but can become so ingrained in the mind and body that we view the whole world from a place of fear and resist trying something new, such as bodywork, that offers a way of transforming or breaking free from these limitations. Many people live their whole lives in a state of limited possibilities. Others search for solutions only when their condition becomes so detrimental that they are forced to consider alternatives.

Breaking out of limiting patterns based on fear first requires that we become aware of its hold so that the light of recognition can dispel its darkness. One way to do this is through some sort of controlled opening and release, carried out in a safe place in which we are surrounded by love and compassion so that the fear cannot overwhelm us. This can often occur through bodywork as it coaxes our physical being to untie the knots that trauma and emotions have fastened in the body. When the body is functioning at its highest level and the mind acknowledges the beauty and goodness of the body rather than seeing it as a source of unworthiness, we can begin to take on the responsibility of healing ourselves through the power of this union. We reclaim this power by loosening our attachment to fear and by listening to what our bodies have to tell us. The many holistic and complementary bodywork therapies offer us the opportunity to enter into this kind of space.

Hands-on bodywork therapy may not be suitable for everyone. If a person can't relax because she is uncomfortable or embarrassed, then it will be difficult for the practitioner to achieve the desired effects. It might be better to pursue some form of integrative psychotherapy or the energy-based forms of bodywork in which there is no physical touching. There is also the possibility that some people who are resistant to touch are simply introverted and shy and will need a gentle introduction to bodywork through forms that are used for relaxation and the relief of minor aches and pains. Even in these less intense methods, bodywork will support a person's journey toward oneness and harmony. There are many choices presented in this book for treating many kinds of dysfunction, but the key element to them all is the recipient's willingness to explore her own potential and to participate fully in the healing process. If a person refuses to get better, then no matter the kind of therapy, there is little chance of success.

There is one consideration that constitutes a valid reason not to undertake a particular form of bodywork: the existence of certain contraindications. These are physiological or psychological conditions that would either interfere with the bodywork or make a bodywork treatment inappropriate by causing further problems detrimental to the health of the recipient. The list of possible contraindications can be short or long, depending on the type of bodywork involved. Because of the number of dysfunctions and diseases that exist today, it would be impossible to provide an all-inclusive list of possible contraindications, but some of this information is included in the discussion of certain modalities. If you have any existing medical problems, it would be wise to have a frank discussion with your health care professional before trying any form of bodywork; the practitioner of a modality you would like to sample can also advise you about possible complications. A preexisting condition does not necessarily mean that you will not be able to have the healing experience of bodywork, since there are many forms of bodywork that have few contraindications, but it's always better to be safe than sorry.

To decide which modality to use, you first have to take an honest look at your particular condition, problems, and needs and the results you desire. Then you can compare the features of care that you are seeking with the information provided for each of the modalities in this book. Your decisions also depend on your experience with bodywork. If you are new to massage, the best introduction might be a simple, relaxing treatment such as Swedish or Esalen Massage. Those who have explored other modalities may follow a lead or their noses to new avenues of healing. Choosing the right modality may require trial and error; each individual is a unique combination of physical and emotional elements, and each form of bodywork offers possibilities that in practice may or may not effectively address your particular issue.

Some individuals are concerned with overall well-being, and some just want to be soothed, but if you have a specific physical condition, an injury, or an illness that you want treated, you will need to look for an appropriate modality and a practitioner who is familiar with that type of problem and knows what would be most suitable for treating it. Although many different kinds of bodywork can be helpful in a general way, people with a specific condition often require treatment that will attend to it directly and thoroughly. For instance, if you have a backache, it would be more appropriate to locate someone who does spinal therapy than to contact a practitioner who addresses stomach problems. But if you suffer from irritable bowel syndrome, you'll want that abdominal work. Certain types of bodywork can also be quite beneficial as a form of complementary therapy when you are undergoing or recovering from conventional forms of treatment, such as surgery or chemotherapy. With all of the holistic bodywork now available around the world, there really is something for everyone. And it doesn't always matter which modality you choose as long as you resonate with it. It can be hard to know intellectually what really serves you best, and, since all bodywork heals on different levels in different ways, the results may be much more beneficial than you or the therapist predicted. Over time, your choices will inevitably change as you evolve and become more tuned in to your own needs. The range of bodywork is vast, and you can take years exploring all the available options. It's a journey worth taking.

Many people have complex or mystifying conditions that are not easily resolved. Frustrated, they tend to roam around in search of the right remedy, trying out different modalities, hoping to find one that does the trick. Some give up, but many persevere in the quest for health and balance. It may be that the way a chosen practitioner diagnoses the cause and decides which techniques to apply is not effective. Another practitioner might have the intuitive ability to properly recognize a difficult problem or to treat it differently. In fact, many modalities were actually created by individuals who had fruitlessly explored the existing options without finding a successful solution. Whether or not in the end they were able to create something new and useful depends on the extent of their own research and experience. Just keep in mind that if the root cause of a problem is complex or tricky to clearly identify, it may take some time to find the right combination of modality and practitioner to treat it effectively. As is always the case, a strong intention to change ultimately leads to healing.

Once you have chosen a particular modality, the next step is to find a practitioner. Depending on where you live, local choices may be few or many, but in recent decades, there has been a definite increase in the number of practitioners and modalities available in this growing field of complementary medicine. Not long ago, you might have been able to find only a Swedish Massage bodyworker or a neuromuscular therapist practicing nearby. Now, even in many small towns, there are far more options available. In addition to the bulletin boards at local food co-ops and the assortment of health-oriented publications, Internet searches can make it easy to find resources. Bodywork schools, local clinics, and holistic health centers are also a good source of information. Personal recommendations from friends are often helpful for people who have little knowledge of the various modalities (and who have not yet read this book). However, everyone is unique, and what works for one person may not have the same benefits for another. Still, if one practitioner is highly recommended by a number of people, then the chances are good that she can be trusted. But even if the practitioner receives enthusiastic recommendations, you must use your own judgment and intuition when making your decision.

There may be variations in techniques and approaches among practitioners working in the same modality because of differences in background and training and because different schools of thought may have developed within that method of healing. However, these differences are generally not significant. Many bodyworkers are experienced in a number of modalities and can design a treatment plan to fit your specific needs by integrating elements of different treatment methods. But a practitioner very skilled in just one modality can serve you well if the approach really addresses your problem. Even if a therapist has a number of skills and is proficient in a variety of modalities, you can always

request that she stick to just one particular modality, if that is what you want. No matter what approach is used, the critical factor is the quality of the practitioner's execution of the techniques and her sensitivity to subtle perceptions about the recipient's needs.

When you are making an appointment with a practitioner on the phone or by e-mail, take the opportunity to ask a few pertinent questions. You'll want to begin by covering things such as the following. What are your credentials? How long have you been practicing? What experience do you have working on someone in my condition? What modalities do you primarily use? How many modalities does your work draw on? If you don't feel your work is appropriate for me, whom would you recommend? You may want to add your own personal concerns to this general list. After the conversation is over, other questions will undoubtedly come up. These can be discussed before your session begins. Of course if you are more experienced with bodywork, you may have a different set of questions.

You would also want to ask about the price, the length of a session, clothing protocol, the setting, and, if necessary, the possible length of a treatment plan. This is important, since some modalities adhere to a protocol that may include a long and costly series of sessions. However, the actual number of sessions preferred or required may not be determined until the extent of your problem is discovered during the initial meeting. If you are seeing a bodyworker simply to reduce stress or for relaxation, then the number of sessions is not a particular concern, since you yourself can decide when you would like another treatment. But if you have a chronic condition or need to release a deeply ingrained emotional issue, it's more likely that you'll need a series of sessions to completely resolve it.

It would also be wise to inquire about the kind of work that will actually be done in the first session, especially if you want to experience a particular technique that has piqued your curiosity. I once signed up for a modality that was reported to include some unique gentle spinal adjustments that I felt could be very useful for alleviating a nerve impingement and was never informed that the first session would involve only a series of computer analyses without any hands-on adjustments to my spine. Considering the cost of finding out what, for the most part, I already knew was wrong without getting any therapeutic adjustments, I was disappointed, to say the least. In the end, I had only myself to blame for not inquiring beforehand about what was to happen.

The length of a session is often determined by the practitioner, though you can influence this according to your desires and available funds. Practitioners frequently offer one-hour treatments, but many of us (including me) feel that ninety minutes is more appropriate since that provides enough time to enter a deeper level of receiving, which will allow a significant release of tension or other restrictions, and to awaken a deeper sense of well-being. This is a special time for you to relax and let go of worldly issues and concerns. Why limit the time for enjoying something so precious? Practitioners of certain modalities also agree that a longer session provides a better time frame for them to properly complete the treatment.

Many of us find it difficult to afford regular bodywork, but when compared with the cost in terms of money or side effects from drugs or clinical treatments in a hospital, therapeutic bodywork really is quite reasonable. Because things are always changing, I have not specified costs when discussing the different modalities, but in general, most forms of bodywork today will cost between $60 and $90 a session, with more specialized and clinical forms of treatment costing up to and maybe more than $150, depending on where you live. Some practitioners give discounts for an initial consultation or if you sign up for a series of treatments. Some offer a sliding fee scale based on income. It is also possible to get a lower-priced session at a clinic or school from students who are still in training. If you're lucky enough to have a bodyworker friend, maybe you can organize a trade of services. If this kind of healing is seen as a preventive measure, the cost is a minor worry when compared with the expense of treating a more advanced condition in the hospital at some time in the future. In fact, regular bodywork could be seen as a preventive form of health insurance.

Many of us, particularly in the United States, question why health-insurance coverage is not extended to complementary therapies. You would think that insurance companies would recognize that, in the long run, they'd save money when people are healthier, without worrying about how that health is achieved. This bias may be caused by a dearth of hard research on the effectiveness of most of the vast number of complementary therapies; it may also be the result of complicated issues within the allopathic system of health care. Things are changing, though slowly. Coverage available from both Medicare and many insurance companies now include some therapy provided by chiropractors and physical therapists. Although in a few cases, acupuncture treatments may be covered by some companies, most of the other forms of complementary and alternative medicine have not yet been acknowledged. But as consciousness of the value of these kinds of therapy grows and as more research is done, perhaps insurance companies will wake up and smell the massage oil.

Many people (like me) try to get some type of bodywork on a regular monthly or weekly basis as part of their primary health care. Though some "massage junkies" may bounce around between different practitioners and different modalities, depending on how they feel at any given time, establishing an ongoing relationship with a practitioner can have definite benefits. It allows the therapist to really get to know your issues and your reactions to treatment and enables you to develop the trust that may allow the treatment to heal at a deeper level. However, it may happen that you grow out of a particular modality. You may start out using Neuromuscular Therapy or Lomi Lomi to relieve some restrictions but, over time realize that energy medicine or energy-field work will provide a deeper release and a more integrated and balanced state of being. Changes in your condition or the arising of a new problem may also require the shift to a more appropriate modality. Each of us must develop and use our intuition and wisdom to choose what is best for us at any one time while accepting that change is inevitable since impermanence is part of life.

You should not rely only on practitioner-applied bodywork to guarantee good health. There are other exercises and practices that you can do to enhance your capacity to be all that you can be physically, emotionally, mentally, and spiritually and to strengthen your own self-healing capacity. You can learn to do these practices—yoga, qi gong, and many others—at home, which is a very sensible and economical way to better health. Many bodyworkers also provide instructions for healing exercises or practices that will sustain the good effects of treatment.

CHAPTER 3
The Bodywork Session

Have you ever seen someone after he has just had a massage or some other form of applied bodywork? If so, you probably noticed how relaxed, mellow, contemplative, and possibly slow-moving he was. Although external appearances never tell the whole story, you could definitely sense that he'd had a significant experience by the look in his eyes, which are considered to be windows on the consciousness. Most professional holistic bodyworkers believe that our bodies know the truth, and when that truth is blocked or restrained within, the squeezing, stretching and manipulations of touch therapy can draw the physiological or psychological truth to the surface and into the light of conscious awareness. So when the eyes shine, it means that the body, mind, and heart are also shining.

Today, there are hundreds of different kinds of practitioner-applied bodywork in use around the world. Many are based on physical contact with the recipient's body, whereas others rely on transmitting healing energy through the energy fields without actually touching the body. Regardless of whether or not direct physical contact is actually made, the common element in almost all forms of bodywork is the use of the hands to initiate and sustain the healing process. Even though there are some modalities in which the arms, elbows, feet, implements, or other substances are employed, the hands are considered to be the primary conveyors of the healing energies. The loving hands of a therapist are a conduit, not only providing the proper stimulation that can alleviate a host of physical, emotional, or mental disorders but also replacing what has been released with a fresh, integrated sense of well-being. However, the success of any bodywork modality and the rate at which any healing occurs also depends on the intention and willingness of the recipient to address a particular issue, his desire to be more complete and free of restraints, and the strength of his motivation to integrate transformative changes into his body, mind, and spirit. In many respects, the practitioner is simply acting as the catalyst to activate the client's innate healing abilities. The actual course of this healing process is not always predictable, and its path can take many turns.

When you consider the full spectrum of modalities from Abhyanga to Zero Balancing, you will find that the actual sequence of events and procedures can vary greatly among all forms of applied bodywork, especially those that go beyond basic massage. Even within a single modality, the therapeutic process may differ not only from culture to culture and country to country but also from practitioner to practitioner. Each individual modality is continually evolving and growing, and some of its elements will change over time. In addition, practitioners who are skilled in a number of different modalities may incorporate an assortment of methods in a treatment session. With so many variables, making generalized statements about the details of an individual session can be a bit difficult.

It's also hard to make any broad statements about the actual experience. Since every practitioner and every recipient bring their own personalities, perspectives, insights, and energies into a session, the experience will be unique for each client. And the initial experience and results of following sessions will likely change, since we ourselves are constantly changing. We all have good days and bad days, and even though the professional bodyworker has been trained to clear away his own issues and to focus only on what is most beneficial for the recipient, he is, above all and like all, a less-than-perfect human being. Likewise, on a particular day, the client may be tired, not in a receptive state, or unable to easily express himself. There may be a personality mismatch between the healer and the patient, or the modality may not be providing what the recipient had hoped. On the other hand, a bodywork session might provide unexpected and wondrous results, whether or not we're consciously aware of what we really need. You can only try to learn from each experience and, if intuition tells you it's not working, try a different practitioner or a different modality.

A bodywork treatment can take place at either a practitioner's office, the client's or practitioner's home, or, as is often the case, in a healing center shared by similar holistic therapists. Many spas and retreat centers also provide space for massage and other forms of bodywork to be performed. If you are going for an aquatic form of therapy, you could find yourself in a swimming pool, a special type of bathtub, or even in a natural thermal spring. Some retreat centers provide beautiful outdoor locations close to nature in a garden, by a waterfall, or on an open deck on a hillside. When traveling overseas, especially in less-developed countries, you might find yourself getting a treatment on the beach or in a hut in the jungle. When we were cruising around the world, we found a bodyworker who did sessions on a boat. (This works well only if the boat is at anchor or is a stable vessel like a multihull. Otherwise the process would require a gimbaled bodywork table to keep the recipient level and an especially limber practitioner.) The setting used for a session is designed with comfort in mind. Sometimes it's a small room whose décor is aesthetically pleasing and artistically soothing or inspiring, though if you're seeing a physical therapist, for example, the room may be somewhat more clinical in appearance. However, most locations provide a homey atmosphere, often with touches of spiritual and meditative art that reflect the nature of the modalities being used. In any case, the general ambience is usually intended to enhance relaxation, which is always key to the success of a treatment.

Although in some cases bodywork may be accomplished in a massage chair or on a floor mat, the hands-on contact during a session usually takes place with the recipient lying on a massage table, which is actually a customized bed. There are even special massage tables that can be modified to accommodate pregnant women. Chiropractic sessions may be carried out on special traction tables that have separate movable parts. If you are going for an Ayurvedic Swedana session, you will likely find all but your head enclosed in a steam casket. In some modalities, the table is covered with special pads that contain crystals, magnets, or other elements that help produce a desired or specific effect. Modalities that use biofeedback may have you sitting in a chair hooked up to electrical equipment. Applied Kinesiology sessions may have you standing while muscle testing is performed. During a Watsu treatment, you may be spun around in a warm-water pool.

Many bodyworkers accompany a treatment with soft, pleasant music to help the client let go of any stress and attain a deeper level of relaxation. In most forms of bodywork, the client has the final say on whether any music is to be played; however, music may be an intrinsic part of some processes. Sometimes the practitioner prefers something more evenly tonal that will register as a neutral sound that does not affect the client's mood or feelings or divert his attention from what is happening inside. Music may be considered a distraction rather than an enhancement for those modalities that require deep listening, observation, or analysis of the more subtle aspects of the client's condition by the practitioner and or the recipient. This is also true if the therapy involves a fair amount of verbal discussion.

What you wear during a session depends on the type of bodywork being performed. Modalities that require the practitioner to have good access to the skin, tissues, and muscles for resolving physiological problems are more effective if you have removed most or all of your clothing. The therapist will then drape sheets or towels over your body to protect your privacy and will perform the treatment with great respect for your personal boundaries. If you are sensitive to exposing yourself like this, some form of compromise can probably be reached, but if it would make you so uncomfortable that you couldn't relax, perhaps you should choose a different modality. Many treatments do not require the removal of clothing. For these, it would be best to wear something simple, loose, light, and, above all, comfortable. In most instances, you should remove accessories such as watches and jewelry so that they don't interfere with the treatment. Be sure to inquire about the clothing protocol when you make the initial appointment with a therapist so that there are no surprises.

Hands-on bodywork may include props such as pillows, cushions, or tools to assist with the therapy. In modalities in which direct contact is made between the practitioner's hands and the recipient's body, the practitioner often uses aromatic lotions or lubricants so that the hands can glide smoothly. This is particularly true with Ayurvedic treatments in which herbal ointments that provide soothing, cleansing, and detoxifying effects are an integral part of the therapy. For those with dry skin, lotions can definitely be a blessing. Aromatherapy with different natural fragrances may invite the sense of smell to participate in the healing process. If you are sensitive to particular lotions or fragrances, you will want to discuss this with the practitioner ahead of time. As you will see in the discussions of specific modalities, many different implements and substances such as electrical devices, needles, divining rods, stones, crystals, herbs, and grains can be used to provide certain therapeutic effects. The client is usually informed about the use of these sorts of things before the session begins.

Before a Treatment

Just before a treatment begins, both the practitioner and the client should take a few minutes to get centered, clear their minds, and relax. Practitioners of energy-based or spiritual modalities may have already carried out their own daily practice, or it may be done as a ritual or invocation during the initial stage of a session. Clearing the mind and connecting deeply within and with the surrounding energy fields is an integral and often essential part of many holistic therapies. Indeed, any form of therapy will call on as many ways as possible to activate and enhance the healing process. If the session is to really be an opportunity for growth, all involved should be open to change. It is not a time to hide from issues that trouble you. Rather it is a time to embrace those things that seem limiting or detrimental so that their significance can decrease as they melt away into the larger picture of who you really are. If you can surrender and take some risks by letting go of the ego and its impulse to control, there is a better chance that you can remain open hearted, accept any limitations, and allow any suffering to dissolve in the light of your inner truth. Quite often, the change will happen as soon as the practitioner's hands do their magic.

Although all of this doesn't appear to be relevant to simply getting a relaxing Swedish massage, the right state of mind can elevate any form of bodywork to a more expansive level and create a more worthwhile experience. Simply relaxing and releasing can often allow the true sources of problems to come to the surface, no matter how deeply rooted they may be. The practitioner is there to activate and hold a space that will allow new insights to arise from the innate healing ability that resides within each of us. We are really the ones responsible for our own healing and growth, and the practitioner is there to assist and guide us in this process and to remind us that our bodies have their own wisdom. What we have to do is tune in, listen, and allow.

During a Treatment

The actual bodywork session usually begins with a sitdown discussion between the practitioner and the client

about needs, desires, concerns, or problematic issues that the session should address. In many instances, the client fills out a medical history form, which the practitioner immediately reviews. Sometimes this history-taking is done ahead of time so that the bodywork can start as soon as the client arrives.

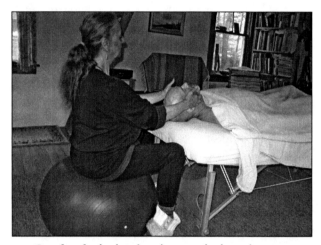

Comfort for both is key during a bodywork session.

In the West, allopathic medicine employs extensive diagnostics, but the depth and nature of this analysis is often limited to symptoms. A major advantage of complementary medicine and bodywork is that the diagnostic process captures a more inclusive, holistic view of the client that takes into account the deep interrelationship between the body, mind, emotions, and spirit. This is especially true for Eastern therapies, in which a great deal of time is devoted to preparatory analysis. However, the initial examination varies considerably with each modality. The diagnostic phase for a relaxing massage will probably be minimal, but if you're there for a spinal adjustment, the practitioner may have you stand erect to analyze your posture and alignment or hold certain positions to gain visual insight into how you are holding your body. If you are undertaking a form of movement therapy, the therapist may ask you to move in ways that reveal your range of motion or to assume revealing positions. If you've come with a specific injury or painful place, the therapist may explore the area with touch. When beginning acupuncture or meridian therapy, you may offer your wrist for a pulse reading, show your tongue, or even have your urine tested. A practitioner of a modality that works on a person's DNA or is spiritual in nature will be focusing more on etheric aspects. The approaches used for diagnosis vary with each modality, but all require the practitioner or healer to be a good observer and listener. After the diagnostic measures are completed, the practitioner decides what protocols, techniques, or sequence of procedures will be necessary during the session and shares this information with the client.

Analysis actually takes place throughout the treatment, especially when working on a particular issue or dysfunction. This is particularly true for various forms of Eastern energy medicine in which observing with all the senses is considered very important and may even be the most significant element in a healing session, although many holistic Western therapies now incorporate this kind of noticing. Sometimes certain types of analysis, for instance, muscle testing, are repeated at different points during a session to see how the bodywork or therapy is progressing. The feedback gained can often dictate a change in the procedures employed or their sequence.

As the treatment itself begins, it is best for you to simply relax and rest in a state of allowing, so that a release and any subsequent healing can easily take place. Relaxation is practically synonymous with the release of tension, so they often go hand in hand. As the practitioner executes the modality's techniques, nothing should be forced, and each technique or method employed should be done without expectation of a desired result.

The actual way a person heals is very subjective and unique to the individual, so there is no fixed rule of thumb that says exactly what has to happen as any healing takes place. Quite often, what really works for a recipient will be revealed as the session progresses to a deeper level. When a release does occur, the therapist honors it and resists making any judgments about its quality or the response from the client. Knowing that when one thing is released in the body there is often more to follow, the practitioner simply continues to allow issues to surface and supports whatever responses arise from the healing wisdom within the client's own body. In this way, the practitioner allows any and all changes to occur. Emotions and feelings often emerge when any protective armor is released. The practitioner's job then is to be fully present and to support and empower the client to integrate the experience on all levels and gain a new sense of wholeness. This may include such things

as the practitioner guiding the client through special movements, stretches, exercises, and breathing patterns during certain segments of a session. When the changes seem complete and nothing more seems to be forthcoming, it is appropriate for the practitioner (and the client, for that matter) to accept what has transpired as sufficient for the moment and give thanks.

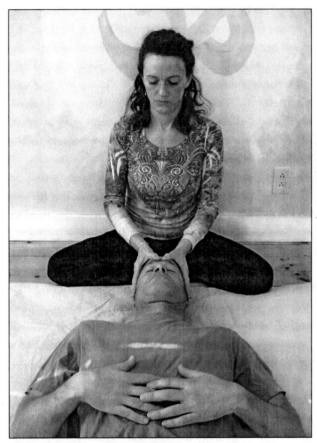

A peaceful moment on a floor mat.

At certain times, especially when a significant release or change occurs, it will be necessary for the practitioner to take things slowly. A muscle may need to become accustomed to being in better condition. An organ may need a moment to realize it is now without constriction. A new emotional feeling may need time to be honored and integrated. The brain may have to realize that it can send different signals through the neurons to the nervous system. The trick is not to lose what has been gained by falling back into a previous habitual or limited state of being. In fact, the success of a particular session is often gauged by this forward motion, although some issues may require a number of sessions to provide a complete healing or the restoration of optimum functioning.

As a session nears completion, the practitioner will often use a final sequence to help bring the treatment to a close. If the modality is a very physical one, there could be a series of gentle and slow movements. Many modalities of energy medicine employ the steady holding of certain grounding points on or off the client's body or a process of sweeping the energy. Some spiritual modalities include a prayer or blessing that helps release the client from the bond that was established during the session and gives closure to the shared time. These closing moves help bring the client back to a more grounded state of awareness in which *normal* is newly defined. If the client is disturbed by feeling spacey, unsettled, and not grounded, he should be given permission to express this so the practitioner can do something about it before the session ends.

After a Treatment

When the session is over, the practitioner may gently touch your arm or shoulder or offer a comment that lets you know he is finished. Usually, he will then leave the room and allow you some time alone. The process of returning to the world should not be rushed, but instead done in such a way that whatever goodness and healing has been provided by the session can stay with you. Don't be surprised if you don't feel normal, for you might just feel abnormally better. When you are ready, slowly sit up, get dressed if necessary, and make yourself comfortable in whatever way feels right. You may want to relax or move your body in simple ways that helps you explore what subtle changes have occurred. The practitioner will probably knock on the door to find out if you are ready for him to return. After the practitioner joins you in the room, there should be time for some discussion about the experience. Each of you can, if you wish, ask questions and share whatever feelings seem necessary. The practitioner may make recommendations about further treatments, home exercises, lifestyle changes, or any other actions that he deems worthwhile for you to undertake. Taking part in self-care activities will not only complement a bodywork session but may help allow for a fuller release in the next treatment.

With any luck—actually, it's much more than luck—you'll walk away from a bodywork session with renewed vitality and a sense of harmony and balance. Your time on the table has been a chance for the innate wisdom of the body to make itself heard, for the vital life-force energy to be recharged, and for you to face any difficulties in the safe space that the practitioner has created.

CHAPTER **4**
The Skilled Practitioner

Any form of applied bodywork is a partnership between two people: the giver and the receiver. (Of course, with self-care practices, these two are rolled into one, and that one is you.) A number of words can be used to refer to the giver—*practitioner, therapist, healer, bodyworker*—and they are used interchangeably in this book. However, some have connotations that are not particularly relevant here. *Practitioner* is very general and would seem to cover all the bases; it merely refers to someone who performs—in other words, practices—certain techniques that promote better health. The term *therapist* suggests someone who is specifically trained in methods that restore health by treating physical, emotional, or mental dysfunction, but this term could also cover people who carry out the many forms of bodywork aimed at awakening innate abilities or enhancing well-being, since this is restorative work of a different sort. As it is used in this book, *therapist* does not imply an advanced degree in the contemporary allopathic sense. The word *healer* hints at someone with energy-transforming or spiritual capabilities, but if you consider the definition of healing, it can apply to anyone who helps another overcome impediments to good health. Then there's the word *bodyworker*. It seems to assume physical contact with the receiver's body, but because of the strong connections between body, mind, and spirit recognized by holistic methods, the physical body can be affected even without being touched. In any case, all of these words suggest a certain degree of professionalism, specialized knowledge, and skill, as well as the understanding that it is only in service to others that we become fully human.

When I think of a figure who is required to have certain skills and is responsible for the welfare of others, a ship's captain quickly comes to mind. This position requires a level of competence and knowledge that must be equal to the task of handling any life-threatening situation that arises. Besides having expertise in seamanship and navigation, a captain must have the confidence to make the decisions that will ensure the survival of not only the ship but also its passengers and crew. Storms, groundings, encounters with pirates, and a myriad of other problems can test the resolve of the captain, who must direct the crew to act in the best possible way for their safety and health. If the ship is considered a metaphor for the human body, the bodywork practitioner is similar to the captain, who must unite all on board into a smoothly functioning ensemble. This captain may need to resort to firm, flexible, or even unorthodox methods of dealing with individuals when stress causes dysfunction.

An example of this occurred when I was the captain of a ship sailing through a gale off Cape Fear (yes, that is its real name) with a crew of six plus the ship's cat. A day into the gale, we were running downwind with heavy seas building and crashing behind us. The ship was rolling excessively, and the crew was getting grumpy. In fact, as time passed, each crew member's usual demeanor altered in ways that compromised our ability to work as a team. One was quite seasick, and another got very angry. Two crew members who were trying to cook greeted the pot of soup rolling off the stove with tears. Another crew member became very frightened, and the last would do nothing but lie in his bunk. We couldn't change course to make the ship's motion more comfortable without ending up shipwrecked on the cape, so at one point during the night, after I had been at the helm for far too long and the members of the crew were nearing the breaking point, I decided it was time to take action in a way that would be in the best interests of all concerned. The situation required clear but compassionate orders dictating what each crew member had to do for us come out alive. The seasick crew member was placed where he could get some fresh air without struggling to hold on to the ship. The angry crew member was bluntly told to stop acting out and help the others. The two cooks were given hot tea and words of love and sympathy. I helped the frightened crew member stay calm by keeping him active and focused on certain duties so that he wouldn't keep imagining his possible demise. The lethargic crew member was secured at the wheel and given simple instructions for keeping the ship on course. When the storm abated the following morning, the crew felt as if they had passed through some initiation orchestrated by Neptune and celebrated their newfound abilities. Each of them had played a role that they recognized as being beneficial for all.

Considering Competence

Each healing therapy is carried out by a practitioner who is presumed to be skilled in that particular modality. One way to turn that presumption into certainty is to examine whether or not the practitioner has some kind of professional certification, often demonstrated by a set of initials after her name. Over the years, developers of a number of distinct modalities have created professional organizations to provide training and testing, as well as their own certification programs, often based on a required level of training and adherence to professional standards. Examples of certified status are such titles as PT (Physical Therapist), APP (Associated Polarity Practitioner), CCST (Certified Craniosacral Therapist), and CRP (Certified Reflexology Practitioner). There are many more, so if a therapist does have letters after her name, it may be worthwhile to inquire what they stand for. Certain modalities still have no written standards of their own, but as the number of modalities increased and the need for some kind of regulation became a concern, additional professional groups and government organizations were formed to guarantee therapy content and safeguard potential consumers.

The regulation and legal status of complementary and alternative medicine therapies varies for each modality from state to state in the United States, and changes in requirements, registration, and certification are constant. Each state has different regulations for the licensing of massage therapists and sometimes even for those practicing forms of therapy that do not necessarily include hands-on work. Some states require massage therapist to register, and they classify practitioners as a registered massage therapist, or RMT. States that demand a license that defines the scope of the practice and recognizes a specific level of professional education designate the massage therapist as a licensed massage therapist, or LMT. In some states that do not have any regulations at all and don't require official credentials, a massage therapist might use MT just to indicate her profession. The level of education needed varies not only among the states but for each specific modality. Certain

national certification boards provide their own credentials, requiring that the therapist pass exams to show she meets standards of proficiency. Then the therapist can, for example, use the title NCMT (national certified massage therapist). The National Certification Board for Therapeutic Massage and Bodywork designates accomplished therapists by the legend NCTMB, showing that the practitioner has completed board examinations for licensing and shows an advanced level of competency. Other umbrella agencies provide accreditation for work within systems of holistic care, such as the National Certification Commission for Acupuncture and Oriental Medicine and the American Organization of Bodywork Therapies of Asia.

Evaluating the real significance of a practitioner's credentials can be confusing and should not be the primary indicator of the quality of her work. Recently developed or less-well-known modalities, particularly those that are energy-based, often have no certification process, even those that have been used since ancient times. European countries have their own systems for providing credentials, but when traveling in more remote regions of the world, you probably won't be able to determine the proficiency of a practitioner by credentials, so you must rely on intuition and referrals. Although they are worth noting, a greater number of licenses or certifications doesn't necessarily mean that you will get a better session. It can take time and experience for a therapist to develop skill in delivering her knowledge, so finding a good bodyworker may be a matter of looking at how many years she has practiced as well as what licenses she holds. This is especially important for practitioners of modalities that are more advanced clinically, energetically, or spiritually than methods such as Swedish Massage that mainly offer relaxation and stress reduction.

You may encounter bodyworkers who advertise proficiency in a number of modalities. As a therapist's career develops, she may be drawn to training in a number of different types of therapeutic bodywork or forms of energetic healing, and her work then becomes a composite of multiple healing techniques, allowing for a variety of options for improving a client's health. However, a practitioner who is truly a master of only one modality can provide outstanding results, and it can be counterproductive to mix some therapies

Besides proper training and experience, a therapist should have personal qualities that make her a good instrument for enhancing the client's healing process. Good intention is a great place to start, but there are other qualities you should look for when choosing a practitioner. Of course, personalities vary and compatibility is very subjective, but there are still some specific traits worth considering.

Above all, a therapist should be genuinely concerned for her client's well-being and completely free of any impure intentions that might lead to sexual or emotional abuse. It is crucial that the practitioner evoke a sense of trust and be clear in communicating her intentions, especially when working on sensitive parts of the body. Combining this trust with her own empathy and compassion, she will be able to create a safe space in which the recipient can make whatever subtle shifts are necessary for healing.

The practitioner must be energetically fit and work from a centered and balanced state of mind that is clear of her own personal issues or agendas so that she is alive to the insights coming from her inner voice of wisdom—knowledge that will help her facilitate true healing. To reach this state, a therapist will often use special meditations or rituals before a session begins. From this open and aware space, the practitioner will be able to listen with both hands and heart to the client and follow the client's positive or negative reactions to specific manipulations. Even though it's difficult to be totally free of expectations, the aspiration of the practitioner to provide a full healing should be balanced with allowing things to proceed in their own way, even if she must deviate from her plans. A treatment is a flexible, delicate dance between two partners with the underlying intention of first doing no harm.

The Practitioner and the Healing Process

Many forms of Eastern bodywork suggest that healing actually begins with the diagnostic process, when the root cause of a problem is brought to awareness. But no matter what the modality, thorough assessment is crucial in determining the source of dysfunction and the most effective treatment plan. Analytical methods such as interviews and discussion can be used to examine a person's life history, environment, lifestyle, previous health problems, and other contributing factors, but the practitioner's own observations are equally important. What does observing actually mean? It means using all

the senses (looking, listening, touching, smelling, and, in some cases, tasting), intuition, and even extrasensory perception to paint a picture of the whole person. The therapist must continue this kind of active observation throughout the treatment session to judge the effectiveness of the methods used.

For healing to occur, the recipient must feel secure enough to let whatever happens happen. A strong connection with a trusted bodyworker can create this safe space in which all can be welcomed. This partnership can be strengthened if the practitioner listens deeply to all of the client's concerns, knowing that what is said may not be the whole story, that there are worlds below the surface manifestations. The practitioner can also help strengthen the bond by acknowledging the recipient's strengths and helping the recipient notice them rather than focusing only on what is wrong. The practitioner knows that the more relaxed a person is, the better the chances of healing are, so she strives to put the client at ease, supports whatever is being experienced, and encourages a sense of lightness so that nothing is taken more seriously than it needs to be.

Caduceus

The Western symbol for healing shows similarities with the Vedic portrayal of serpents of energy rising up through the central channel around the chakras.

When bodywork touches on physically painful areas, that same heartfelt, loving connection can empower the client, giving her the courage to look into the true source of the pain and to notice any self-limiting reactions. Tender areas can be approached in special ways that allow any underlying fear and anxiety to simply soften and dissipate, giving way to a renewed sense of well-being. The practitioner's gentle encouragement can help dissolve any resistance to the process of transformation. Great respect, reverence, and freedom must be given to both the body and the emotions of the client, and this attitude will communicate an atmosphere of safety louder than words could ever do.

A person's ability to function well depends in large part on the soundness of her body's systems and structure, but healing does not originate only in the physical body, for that body is part of the body-mind continuum and is therefore strongly affected by thoughts and emotions. When stressful emotions become locked deep inside the nervous system or become lodged in the body (often on a cellular or molecular level), they can have devastating effects on any bodily functions. Any part of any bodywork procedure can give rise to all kinds of emotional reactions as constrictions and trauma held in the body are set free; release can also come spontaneously and unexpectedly from the unconscious level. There are no set rules about how a person will respond during any type of treatment, no matter what the focus of the work, and there is not necessarily any correlation between the location of the work and its effect. Work on the feet could release a headache. A spinal adjustment might bring on tears. Responses can include changes in breathing, sighing, crying, laughing, twitching, burping, or farting. The practitioner needs to allow these responses to occur naturally and also to needs realize that they can be interpreted in many ways. For example, tears can indicate joy as well as pain. Sometimes a practitioner might misinterpret those responses and reactions that are beyond the scope of the modality that she is trained in, but a strong connection between the therapist and the client may direct the bodywork to where it is needed, regardless of any set protocols.

An excellent hands-on bodywork practitioner may or may not be adept at working with emotional or spiritual issues, because some modalities focus simply on the tissues, muscles, or specific physical injuries, and some are concerned only with gentle relaxation. But since a deep emotional release can be stimulated even by simple soft-tissue work, any bodyworker must be ready for the unexpected and must react carefully when an emotional release occurs, especially if the client did not expect to confront these personal vulnerabilities during a session. Although the practitioner may sometimes have to put on the mantle of counselor, the situation must be handled delicately and without digging too deeply. Not

every practitioner is qualified to deal with psychological issues and may not even realize that a client is leaving in a state of confusion or distress. A good practitioner should know her limits and resist engaging in activities that are outside the scope of her particular therapy. If the client is in crisis, a referral to a more appropriate form of therapy may be the answer, especially for someone who exhibits mental health problems.

If the therapist is observing carefully, she will be able to sense internal changes in the client, especially as blockages are removed. A sensitive practitioner will become aware of the floodgates opening in a person by tuning in to changes in the client's breathing, behavior, and other clues to the release of emotions. When this happens, no matter what protocol is being followed, she can give the recipient time to absorb and integrate the reshaping of the emotion by slowing down or pausing. In these moments, the practitioner's role is not to try to solve the problem but instead to support the client as the feelings are experienced and, if possible, understood. She may simply acknowledge the emotion and support any spontaneous reactions, or she may use gentle, compassionate questioning such as "What are you feeling?" to help the recipient connect with what is happening. The client will be vulnerable as the release is occurring, so it is essential that the practitioner remain nonjudgmental and not lead the person into a particular response. Neutrality is the best policy at this point, as is sparing the recipient a bunch of psycho-babble or personal interpretations. And if the client doesn't want to talk, the therapist should respect that wish. When the client settles down from the release, the practitioner can help facilitate the recipient's becoming integrated and grounded in a new, more insightful way of being. On the other hand, when a release happens, it is possible that instead of the surfacing of troubling emotions, there will be a cascade of joyous and blissful feelings. A true healer will celebrate right along with the client.

Many therapists, particularly those who work in psychological or spiritual healing modalities, are familiar with emotional release and have many unique ways to rectify core beliefs and to assist in attaining and integrating a new, more fulfilled sense of internal awareness and increased vitality. Deep emotional sensitivities can present themselves as physical pain in places that cannot be touched directly by a practitioner, but there are many creative ways to get there indirectly. In one such technique, known as entrainment, the practitioner enters into an altered meditative state in which she acts as a channel for "higher" vibrations. Because of the laws of resonance, the client who is at a "lower" level of vibration will naturally and automatically shift into resonance or harmony with the vibrations of the practitioner.

As any treatment session comes to a close, the practitioner should let the client know the work is finished by touching her gently or speaking softly to her. Depending on the particular modality, a certain period is necessary to allow the client to ground herself and shift into coming back into the apparent reality of this world. A treatment also needs to be concluded in a way that gently releases the recipient from any connection to the therapist so that the client can move forward on her own with a more positive approach to health and healing.

Every modality and every practitioner of the same modality bring their own perspectives and training to a decision about the root cause of a particular issue. If a client shows certain symptoms or signs of dysfunction, she might get a wide range of responses from different practitioners about the true cause of that problem. Considering the interconnections between body, mind, emotions, and spirit, each different interpretation would probably contain an element of truth, even if they appeared to be quite different at first. For instance, a client who has a sore shoulder might go to a neuromuscular therapist and be informed that the muscle has been strained by some myofascial binding. If she goes to a chiropractor, she might be told that the cause is a nervous system impingement caused by a spinal misalignment that put a strain on the shoulder. If she talks to a practitioner of energy medicine, she might be advised that it is caused by a blockage of vital chi energy in a particular meridian. An Emotional Freedom Technique therapist might say she is holding some emotional trauma from childhood. In fact, any one symptom can have similar or multiple causes; an emotional issue can become an energetic blockage that can manifest as a misalignment that puts a strain on the fascia that causes a pain in the shoulder. Each of these modalities could provide some benefit, but the most effective and long-lasting remedy may come only from the one that deals most directly with the underlying problem, and finding it may require a search.

The unfolding of healthy change is not usually accomplished by one treatment but by a series of sessions, driven by the desire to awaken the infinite possibilities that are part of our innate ability to live in a more complete and conscious way. In the end, there will always be a degree of trial and error when choosing the most effective and proficient practitioner, but the beauty of most forms of holistic therapy is that even if an issue is not fully resolved, whatever bodywork was performed is not only unlikely to do any harm but also will very likely do some good. The wisdom of the body is the best guide, and over time, its advice will lead the way to the most effective therapist.

As you will see in Chapter 6, there are a multitude of techniques for awakening a healthier, integrated sense of well-being. The whole process can have beautiful results, much like a spiritual rebirth, although much depends on the true intention of the recipient and how ready she is to change. However, this type of subtle healing can't be forced, even if it is what the practitioner or the recipient is seeking. True healing comes in stages and only when the right combination of subtle factors is present. It's sort of like making a soup and putting the right ingredients in it to make it tasty. But the primary ingredient is the willingness to heal, not only on the part of the client but also as the intention of the practitioner. The partnership created in a bodywork session can open up the package that contains this precious gift of health.

CHAPTER 5
The Art of Being a Good Recipient

The ability to relax doesn't always come naturally, so bodywork practitioners will do all they can to encourage it during a session. But people sometimes think that when they go for a treatment, all they need to do is relax and let someone else do the work. Relaxation *is* the primary prerequisite both for releasing tension and for allowing healing, and if you're getting a simple sports massage or are too sick or low in energy to do anything but lie there, it may be enough. However, if you are really intent on achieving better health, recovering from dysfunction, or experiencing personal transformation, there is much you can do besides relaxing to help the process along. When the receiver becomes more engaged in the healing process, the therapist is better able to provide a deeper measure of healing. This does not mean that you have to actually do something physically active while receiving bodywork. What we're speaking about here is becoming "actively receptive," a state in which you are attentive to all the physical, mental, and emotional changes taking place within, while at the same time surrendering your judgments and your attachments to limiting patterns, and recognizing your role in the healing process. Becoming acquainted with your inner power (which can be considered synonymous with courage or self-worth) is the first step toward identifying and releasing the problems that limit your full potential.

We each have the innate ability to heal and to function in the best possible way if only we can gain access to it. This may simply require the gentle jolt of reawakening that bodywork and self-healing practices can provide. But healing can only be offered, not imposed. Although the spirit may unconsciously long for healing, regaining health is best accomplished when you consciously decide that this is what you need and give permission for it to manifest. Many bodyworkers cultivate this intention, and a more spiritually oriented practitioner may even ask your spirit for permission to work and request help in alleviating any of your fears about the process. But the practitioner is really only acting as a catalyst to allow you, the receiver, to open energetically and make the necessary shifts to awaken your own abilities.

Symptoms of a problem are not obstacles to be eliminated through drastic measures but may be signs of the need for real change. Very often the body knows what is needed, and the mind just needs to permit the wisdom held in the body to surface. This can happen regardless of the particular technique employed, because bodywork in essence provides a loving space in which the message of the body can be heard. True healing is a never-ending journey of recognizing and releasing any limitations and filling those spaces with health, love, and boundless energy. What transpires during this process can bring pain and discomfort as well as pleasure and joy, but what happens within can have far-reaching results.

Even when an action or a feeling causes pain, human beings seem reluctant to change, fearing that what will come may be worse than what already is. Somehow, the status quo appears safer. Many people insulate themselves from their true feelings, and the idea of confronting them can be daunting. However, once you realize it is better to welcome a change in which unresolved feelings are nurtured and released, it's easier to embrace the idea of surrender. Surrendering to what initially seemed like chaos can be a blessing in disguise as you stop wasting energy trying to control and cover up your deepest needs and fears. The need for the false sense of security that this self-limiting control provides can melt away when openness, honesty, balance, and acceptance become part of your life instead of resistance, anger, fear, or denial—the agents of control. Making this choice can require lots of work and commitment, but the actual moment of healing can effortlessly fill you with positive energy. It's as if you have come home to the place your body and mind had always longed to be, and they thank you for this by working harmoniously together. Whatever kind of release happens once control is relinquished will be supported by a bodyworker and held in strict confidence, so you can feel free to fully experience whatever occurs. Sometimes nothing phenomenal happens. If all your body asks for at a certain session is the simple release of a pain in your arm rather than some major emotional transformation, that alone makes the time special, because the body is expressing its needs, and you and the bodyworker are listening to it. Appreciating whatever transpires makes it all valuable.

Ideally you have used the information provided in the preceding chapters to make some decisions about the kind of bodywork you think will have the best chance of meeting your goals, whether they are physical, emotional, mental, energetic, or spiritual in nature. Perhaps you're just curious about a new modality. Whatever your choice, the results may not be what you wanted or expected, but if you're open to the possibilities, they will likely be what you really needed or were ready to receive. When you have become more familiar with the different modalities and more aware of your own needs, the choice will better reflect your specific condition at a given time. At some point, you may feel that your muscles need attention, whereas at another time, you may want to focus on some energy work. Many experienced recipients get to the point where they intuitively know what is best for them at any given time. However, for those with deep troubling issues, it's essential to choose a practitioner who can handle whatever comes up or is willing to direct you to someone who can—a qualified counselor or psychotherapist.

No matter which modality you choose, all types of bodywork have some experiential things in common. Good practitioners understand that each patient is unique, so they adjust their techniques to suit each person's needs and condition. In modalities that use physical touch, the intensity can be tailored to individual tolerances. If the recipient has a sore spot or some swelling, certain types of manipulation, such as rubbing or pressing, will be avoided and replaced with some light compression. If the client is ill, the treatment might be shorter and lighter. If the recipient is an athlete whose muscles need loosening, the manipulations might be more vigorous. If a pregnant woman is being treated, certain areas will be avoided while others are nurtured. Physical pain will not be a particular concern when experiencing a modality such as Reiki or Auric Healing that works on the surrounding energy fields and does not use much, if any, physical contact. However, various forms of energy medicine can cause a different kind of pain by awakening uncomfortable issues that may cause a period of physical, emotional, or spiritual discomfort, a sense of disconnection, or a feeling of vulnerability

until they are fully released or resolved. It is always your right to inform the bodyworker about your needs, any problem areas, and how deeply you want the work to go. But sometimes, rather than avoiding pain, it is wise to simply allow it to take its course and become transformed into pleasure.

If a client does not arrive with any specific dysfunction, the approach to the treatment is left up to the practitioner's intuition, although the recipient can take the initiative at any time during the session to indicate his wishes. As a person becomes more familiar with a particular modality, he will bring more of his own wisdom into the process and can make specific suggestions or let the practitioner know about issues that are coming up during the treatment, perhaps as a body memory is triggered. Just as in daily life, issues constantly change, and so will each moment during a session or in any successive treatments, even if the same modality is used. Practitioners are trained to be very sensitive to the needs of the person on the table and often recognize something happening before the client does. We learn and grow from change.

Preparing for a Session

The preparation for a treatment is fairly simple once you have decided which modality and practitioner you are going to use and have made an appointment. When you first contact the practitioner, tell him about your intentions and your basic issues, including any chronic conditions, and ask about the treatment itself, location, duration, cost, clothing requirements, and any other concerns. If you're under medical treatment, it would be wise to contact your regular health care provider to discuss your plans. It is equally important to talk with the bodyworker about any possible contraindications that would make the bodywork inappropriate for you, especially if you have had recent surgery or are taking certain prescription drugs. If this form of treatment is not appropriate, he may be able to suggest something else.

As the day of your scheduled treatment nears, it is time for you to make some simple preparations. First, get plenty of sleep the night before so that you are well rested. During the few hours preceding the treatment, you probably shouldn't eat much, but be sure to drink plenty of water so you're not dehydrated. Before going in for the treatment, take a shower or nice bath, clear your sinuses, and use the toilet. (Of course if you have a long drive to the treatment center, you may need to quickly use the facilities before the treatment begins.) Mentally plan to have a good time and contemplate what you want from the treatment, but try not to build up any particular expectations or overthink it. When you arrive at the site and are no longer driving in a car and possibly fighting traffic, take a few deep breaths and focus on slowing down and being more present in the moment. All of these steps will help you walk into the treatment room with an open heart and mind, intent on having a relaxing, healing experience in which your body, mind and spirit receive the attention they have been craving from the bodyworker and your own healing power.

During a Treatment

A huge number of healing approaches, techniques, and methods have been developed over many years and are part of a vast assortment of modalities. Additionally, although the practitioner of a given modality generally works with a specific set of techniques and procedures, he may find it necessary to make changes in his usual course of action according to what he encounters in a particular client's body. Since there are so many variables, it is difficult to convey what a typical treatment entails or how the experience will be for the recipient. The answer to this is best provided by looking at what is involved with each individual modality, as you will find in Chapter 6.

Probably the best way to experience a bodywork session is to treat it like a vacation or a birthday party. Initially, most practitioners invite you to discuss any particular issues and, if it's your first time, have you fill out an evaluation or case history form if you haven't already done so. It's important to be as honest as possible about any personal issues, since the practitioner is there to help you and will hold everything you share in strict confidence. This is also the time to agree on what clothing will be necessary and any places you don't want touched or any physical manipulations you wish the therapist to refrain from. It is wise to take care of any questions during this initial phase of the treatment so that you can focus more on simply receiving when the actually bodywork begins, but if some significant question arises during the session, feel free to ask it.

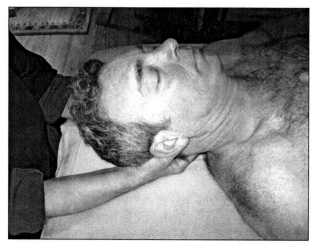

Relaxing while receiving.

This discussion time is also when the two of you can agree on the way you will let the practitioner know about any discomfort you may feel during the treatment, so that you don't have to worry about whether or not he's aware of any problems. You can agree on certain simple sounds, groans, or hand signals if you'd rather not talk. Once the real work begins, the need for verbal communication often disappears. There are no hard-and-fast rules about talking during a treatment, since spontaneous expression is not only acceptable, but in certain instances preferred. Some modalities use dialogue in the therapy protocol, whereas others that emphasize listening to the body depend on silence. Since I personally often find it difficult and rather distracting to talk during a session, I have developed a system of simple and naturally occurring sounds to signify how I feel. If the practitioner applies pressure that is too intense, I respond with an "Ow" sound. If it feels just right, I use an "Ah." There are many other tones in between, and the bodyworker often quickly understands the significance of each one. The loudness and pitch of each sound can also be used to convey an explicit message, causing the practitioner to make the necessary adjustment in contact or pressure. Even if you don't use some form of signals, a good therapist can often read the response in your body.

Certain modalities also use this period at the beginning of a treatment to make a visual or intuitive analysis of your condition or carry out specific diagnostic testing to determine what the core of a problem may be and which procedures and techniques will best help you. This may include pulse reading, muscle testing, electronic biofeedback, and an assortment of other evaluation techniques. Some modalities may use a large part (or all) of an initial session for this purpose; ideally the therapist will have let you know that the first session will be mainly diagnostic. Modalities that are primarily forms of massage often do not include this period of analysis in the treatment, instead gaining information as the practitioner makes contact with your body. Forms of spiritual healing may take this initial period to carry out some sort of ceremony, speak a special blessing, or invoke spirit helpers.

After the initial period of discussion and analysis, most practitioners will briefly leave the room and allow you to get undressed, if necessary, and relax in the proper position for the treatment. Once you have settled into the space on the massage table, floor mat, or any other apparatus that is used and are waiting for the therapist's return, try to tune in to your inner self, stretch out your body, and take a few conscious, deep, slow, full breaths to clear your mind. However, don't be overly concerned with breathing in any particular way. Let yourself breathe slowly and naturally, but try to do so consciously. If you are experienced in some sort of yoga, pranayama, meditation or internal qi gong, it is fine to incorporate some of that during this initial stage or at any other time it feels useful or necessary during the treatment. All of these subtle ways of enhancing self-awareness can allow the mind's "monkey chatter" to subside and help you enter a state in which energy can flow freely through your body to stimulate the release of blockages. Although you may find that you naturally enter a relaxed, healing space at some point later in a session, inviting the possibility early on can be very helpful. Depending on the particular therapy, the practitioner may also ask you to make some adjustments in your breathing pattern or to take a deep breath at certain times during the treatment. This can also happen spontaneously when you have a release.

Though the intention to heal is key to the success of a treatment, something more may be needed. Achieving a calm, meditative state during the treatment will allow you to move beyond good intentions and enter a space in which you can turn your attention inward to the place where the remedies lie. It's like looking beneath the waves of mental activity to find your true nature deep within your inner ocean. You may discover qualities that will help your desire to heal come to fruition, inspired by the wisdom and compassion that have always been

yours, even if dark shadows have hidden them from your conscious eyes. Things like permitting anything to happen, giving and receiving thanks and recognition, really taking care of yourself, or choosing acceptance over suffering can be found, cultivated, and used to heal yourself and others. By integrating attributes like these into all your thoughts and actions, you will be able to swiftly go beyond all that limits your true potential.

The treatment itself can be compared to opening a birthday present: you never know what you'll find inside, but you're glad to get it. Once the practitioner returns and the treatment commences, you should try to let go of all your concerns, thoughts, and everyday issues so that your body's natural intelligence can take over. When the therapist creates a new, safe healing space that is full of love and trust, you can feel free to groan, moan, cry, laugh, fart, or stretch whenever the urge comes naturally. All these responses can provide useful feedback for the practitioner, so feel free to respond as you wish. As the session unfolds, simply try to let go and relax, but at the same time, pay attention to any feelings and sensations that turn up. You may find that these sensations increase as you become more relaxed, reflecting the inner wisdom arising from your body. These feelings can be discussed at any time, although it is often more possible and preferable to speak after the session is over, when you are more grounded and have had time to process and integrate what transpired. Silence can really be beneficial, primarily because it allows for better listening. In some cases, you may become so relaxed that you fall asleep. Though this is not the best time for that, in many cases the healing process still proceeds. But most often, when some new awareness of your self arises from within, it will grab your attention so strongly that sleep seems not only inappropriate but boring. The responses that arise to what unfolds, whether pleasant or painful, are all part of the releasing process.

Whether a release is quiet or dramatic, there are bound to be certain changes in how you feel physically. Sometimes sensations can pop up that prompt you to ask the practitioner to focus his attention and manipulations on a particular part of the body that is calling for more attention. At certain times, the therapist may also direct you to reposition your body to give him better access so that the treatment can go more smoothly. If the move seems difficult, the practitioner can help you. If at any point you do need a drink of water or to use the bathroom, let the practitioner know, and he will help you with it.

Your comfort is an ongoing concern, and holding any tension may make it difficult for a true release to occur. Of course, certain types of treatment work close to the recipient's pain threshold, and that can be intense at times. But some pain can hurt good rather than hurt bad when it is part of a release process. Your intuition is your best guide, and when intense feelings arise, your mouth is the tool to communicate any overwhelming distress to the practitioner. As you become more familiar with certain therapies and the techniques they use, the thresholds of pain or discomfort will become more familiar and bearable, and a good therapist will offer suggestions for dealing with it, such as breathing into the pain. He may also use techniques to increase your tolerance so that the work can go deeper. Practitioners will often slow down when working on a sensitive or tense area of the body, especially when it elicits a significant response from the client. However, this often suggests that this spot needs more attention. In many forms of bodywork, this feedback will cause the therapist to leave a painful area of the body and work on a distant but related point; some modalities also deal with pain by focusing on what is working well in order to ease problems away by enhancing strengths.

Many people enter into bodywork without realizing that they carry emotional wounds. There may come a point in a session where you begin to feel vulnerable as the treatment opens up the deeper layers of consciousness that contain unresolved emotions. You may reexperience the situations that caused these feelings. Disturbing sensations may result in uncomfortable physical reactions, and anxiety levels may rise. The practitioner's empathy and compassion can help you feel safe and nurtured, and using the breath to release physical tension may signal the mind to relax. If you are willing to embrace your vulnerability rather than letting it choke off your feelings, chances are good that insight will appear, if only as a tiny point of light. Resolution may not come in only one session, and you must protect yourself by making sure that the practitioner leaves you in a grounded state, shielded from any harm.

Most bodywork treatments are concluded with a soothing smoothing-out and settling period in which the practitioner calms the energies and grounds the recipient. Any closing manipulations and hands-on contact are orchestrated to help the client separate from the physical, emotional, mental, and spiritual bond that has been created throughout the session. Certain sweeping moves may be made to cleanse and calm the energies, and some modalities employ hands-on work on strategic points, chakras, or other places that help the recipient settle and integrate all that has occurred. The party may be over, but the celebration has just begun.

Follow-Up Care

After the treatment has ended, the practitioner will leave the room and allow you some time to rest, become integrated, and reflect on all that has happened. For those familiar with yoga, this time is similar to that period at the end of your asanas when you lie in the corpse pose with all the subtle life-force energies vibrating ever so sweetly through your body. Sometimes, after a "heavy" treatment, it may take some time to come back to everyday reality. Reactions to a session can vary immensely, and recipients may feel full of energy, very relaxed, just mellow, tired, agitated, or simply fall asleep. When you feel grounded and ready, you can collect yourself, get dressed, drink some water, and go to the bathroom if you need that form of release as well. The practitioner will then return and allow some time to sit and discuss what transpired during the treatment and any issues that remain. Depending on the principles of the modality, he may tell you about any follow-up therapy, exercises, diet, herbs, or activities that would help you retain the benefits derived from the treatment. If you have any chronic issues, you can make arrangements for further sessions.

For the remainder of the day, certain measures will help you retain the blessings gained from the session. The most important is to drink plenty of water to help expel any toxins that have been released. Even though you might be hungry after the treatment, it is best to wait for an hour or so, and when you do eat, to try to have a good, wholesome, organic meal. Above all, be open to any inner voices that have been awakened by the treatment so that whatever has shifted becomes integrated and absorbed by your body, mind, and spirit.

Even if the initial results seem inconsequential, the treatment may have a strong, subtle effect on you in more ways than you suspect. How you feel can change slowly in the ensuing days. The body's innate intelligence has been stimulated to kick in and aid the healing process in ways that you might not initially recognize. It is also possible that your condition may even worsen before changing for the better, because what caused any imbalance, dysfunction, or disease needs some time to be flushed out before your body can be restored to a state of harmony and balance. It may also be that your conditioned habitual patterns have been disrupted and your body and internal systems need time to adjust to the new, better-aligned you. In any case, your sensitivities will undoubtedly have been increased, so be careful not to attempt vigorous activity or any stressful endeavors, at least during the hours after a treatment. If possible, it's very important to avoid driving a car for long periods, as this can make your body rigid and stiff, thereby destroying many benefits you gained from the treatment. (This may require you to consider your travel plans before your treatment.) The bodywork can also make you more sensitive and vulnerable to your immediate environment, so stay warm, be comfortable, take it easy, and spend your time in the sanctuary of your choice. This is particularly true in the winter, when a cold or flu could catch you in a susceptible condition.

Whether you feel better or worse immediately after a treatment is not always important. You may not recognize any healing or change until it becomes apparent later that the symptoms have disappeared or that you've experienced an inner shift. On the other hand, if after a few weeks, it doesn't seem the session was successful in meeting your goals, you might need to reconsider the modality or practitioner. Life is full of the unexpected, and we all learn something from our mistakes. In any case, it is good for you to be flexible, keep your expectations reasonable, and not make hasty judgments.

It may happen that you grow out of a bodywork modality when the problem that brought you to it in the first place is healed. Inevitably, other concerns will crop up that may require a different form of bodywork, especially if you are using it to maintain health and prevent disease. As your condition changes over time, you will probably develop the ability to discern the right therapy and the insight to let go of what no longer serves you. As with anything in life, there will always be some trial and error, since certain conditions can arise that leave you mystified about their real root causes. The journey of transformation and true health is really a lifelong process. It is best to simply enjoy the journey, take time to be appreciative, and continue to explore the unknown.

If all this sounds like just too much for you to deal with, don't worry. Healing will come on its own when and as it is meant to. All it takes is your decision to allow some form of bodywork to open the door.

CHAPTER 6
A World of Applied Bodywork Modalities

This chapter is a compilation of information about more than 500 forms of practitioner-applied bodywork available today, not only in the United States but also around the world. The methods and modalities grouped here demonstrate that there are many ways in which a skilled practitioner can provide a healing experience. It may be through physical contact or with subtle, touch-free, energy-based work. It may involve the use of specialized tools, therapeutic substances, or sound vibrations. Verbalization, visualization, energy transference, and an assortment of etheric processes may also play a role. Though the bodywork methods are varied, what is common to all is the skill and intention of the trained practitioner.

The modalities found here run the gamut from hands-on massage to those that work with the energy fields interconnecting the physical, emotional, spiritual, and cosmic realms. Most are holistic in nature, recognizing the body-mind connection, the interrelationship of all systems of the body down to the cellular level, and the necessity of finding the root cause of a problem rather than just treating symptoms. Each method has its own perspective on how to maintain or restore health, its own approach to how, where, and why the healing contact is made, and its own vision of what can be accomplished. The majority of these forms of therapy incorporate noninvasive methods that are by nature preventive, restorative, and integrative and that bring the recipient greater balance and harmony and awaken innate healing abilities. Many of these modalities can also be considered complementary to the more conventional medical practices of allopathic health care. Some of the bodywork modalities listed are part of ancient systems of healing such as Ayurveda or Traditional Chinese Medicine that are based on the conviction that true health and longevity depends on the universal life-force energy running in and through us all. Many of the more contemporary healing practices contain a portion or a synthesis of these older traditional therapies, whereas others have been developed through recent scientific research, state-of-the-art technologies, and discoveries about new

ways of healing that may represent the cutting edge of what is to come. We can still call those that do not include hands-on techniques "bodywork" because all communicate healing to the physical or energetic bodies; some healers even treat clients from a distance.

As mentioned in the introduction, these bodywork modalities are divided into ten basic categories that are my attempt to organize the material in a logical and useful way. Rather than grouping the therapies by symptoms or results, I've organized them so that each category represents a particular focus of practice in which can be found an assortment of modalities that approach healing from this vantage point. For instance, a treatment intended to provide emotional release of a past trauma is quite different from one that works to loosen muscles, so modalities that address emotions are placed in a different category than those that deal with structural issues. Modalities intended to provide better balance and alignment through movement are placed in the Functional Reeducation section, for example, whereas those that deal directly with the vertebrae and cranium are in the Spinal Therapies section.

The different forms of bodywork are organized by area of focus because the interrelationship of all the systems of the body-mind means that many different results can ripple out from a single therapeutic practice, making it difficult to look at the modalities in terms of the benefits they might provide. A type of bodywork that seems to be primarily physical can also affect a person's emotions, mind, heart, spirit, and energy. Work on energy fields can affect a person's physiology. A modality intended to deal with trauma can open the body to moving in new ways. In a sense, there is really no clear-cut line to be drawn between the different systems of the body, as all are related in so many ways, but I wanted to give the reader a framework from which to approach the material. In addition, each person will have a unique and subjective reaction to any experience, so I did not want to make this book into a medicine chest for specific ailments. In some cases, it was a bit difficult to decide where to put a particular practice, but I tried to look at the most prominent area of focus. I hope this method of grouping the many available modalities will make it easy for people looking for those most appropriate for transforming their problems into good health and then maintaining that vitality.

There were practices that just wouldn't fit into any specific category but were worthy of discussion. Therefore, the Substance- and Implement-Assisted Therapies section speaks of natural substances and innovative tools or equipment that sometimes stand alone but often act as adjuncts to other forms of bodywork. The Special section is home for those therapies that defy categorization because of their mix of elements and applications or because a specific condition, for example, pregnancy, requires their use.

The category of Aquatic Therapies is unique in that it does not focus on a particular aspect of the body or mind but has more to do with the medium in which the therapy is experienced. I offer no apologies. Water has always been important in my life, and I believe that treatments carried out in water have a magic all their own.

Below is a list of the ten categories of bodywork modalities that are covered in this chapter:

1. Structural Bodywork Therapies: those that primarily use hands-on massage and manipulation techniques on the skeletal structure, joints, tendons, ligaments, muscles, soft tissue, skin, and nerves for effects ranging from relaxation to restoration of function and relief of pain.

2. Functional Reeducation Therapies: those that use movement and body reeducation techniques to change self-limiting movement patterns affecting balance, range of motion, alignment, and function. They include only limited hands-on manipulation.

3. Substance- and Implement-Assisted Therapies: those that predominantly use things other than the hands or other parts of a practitioner's body; they include natural substances and an assortment of tools and equipment.

4. Aquatic Therapies: those that are performed in or with water.

5. Spinal Therapies: those that are specifically directed toward the sacrum, spine or cranial cavity.

6. Abdominal Therapies: those that work on the abdomen and the internal organs.

7. Trauma-Centered Therapies: those that deal with mental and emotional problems that affect health and the ability to function.

8. Energy-Based Therapies: those that correct and enhance the balance and flow of energy anywhere within the body.

9. Energy Field and Spiritual Therapies: those energy-based modalities that extend their focus beyond the physical to the energy bodies, energy fields, and spiritual realms.

10. Special Therapies: those that don't fit into any other category because of the unusual way they are applied, their unique focus, or the special circumstances under which they are used.

It is often the case that modalities with roots in ancient times—Acupuncture, Reiki, and qi gong, to name but a few—have many offshoots that have evolved either recently or over a number of years. Treatments may now combine new techniques with the old or offer variations from the standard method, but they still have a close relationship to their progenitors. Rather than being listed separately, they are grouped under the primary type of bodywork. For example, the different kinds of Acupuncture are all found under that heading, just as the various styles of Reiki are listed together. A modality may have been created by adding new therapeutic methods to an established one—certain forms of physical therapy now contain related practices that focus on body movements. These reconfigured therapies are also listed under the primary type, as are those in which developers of original forms of therapy have expanded on their earliest ideas to create something new with the same basic intention as the original. For instance, a modality that once dealt with emotional trauma purely through bodywork may now include a body-mind psychotherapeutic component. There are also modalities, such as sound healing, that can naturally be grouped together but differ in approach.

If in doubt about where to find something, please consult the index.

As mentioned in the introduction, the description of each modality includes information about its origins, its historical development, essential theories, and goal, along with details about the techniques used during a session of bodywork. Since change is a constant in life, I have generally refrained from including details about the location of practitioners, session costs, clothing requirements, duration of particular treatments, or the need for multiple sessions, except where they are essential to the description. Once you decide to pursue a particular modality, this information can easily be acquired online or through consultation with a practitioner. The web sites listed as contact resources for a modality will also help you find what is available, either nearby or far away.

The size of this encyclopedic compilation shows that not only are there "different strokes for different folks," but that the possibilities can be a bit overwhelming. Even within categories, each modality has a slightly different emphasis, which can translate into distinctive ways of affecting the body as a whole. The descriptions are intended to help people sort through the options and make informed choices, and I hope that the information provided here will help you discern which ones speak to your intuition, body, mind, and soul.

When sifting through the modalities in search of what resonates, you'll have to proceed with an open and honest look at your own condition and needs, even if all you want is a relaxing massage. If you want to improve your ability to dance or perform as an athlete, you might start by looking at forms of movement therapy. If you have an emotional or physical impairment caused by past trauma, you might begin with that category. However, it's important to remember that the true cause of a problem can be complex and isn't always apparent. Through a healing response to one form of treatment, other issues may be revealed that require a different therapeutic viewpoint. Someone who suffers from a pain in the shoulder may start with deep-tissue therapy. When this doesn't resolve the issue, the person may find that the underlying cause is nerve entrapment or even energetic blockages in meridians. It may take further exploration to find a solution. Fortunately, many practitioners are trained in more than one therapeutic modality and can approach a problem from different sets of principles and procedures to provide an integrative healing session. The thing to keep in mind, though, is that the client is ultimately the one who does the actual healing; the practitioner simply acts as a catalyst to help awaken the recipient's true potential. In most instances, the give-and-take, the sharing, and the exchange of energy between the giver and the receiver of bodywork create a joyful journey on the path to healing. My hope is that each of you experiences this as you explore these forms of bodywork.

I. Structural Therapies

Any vessel needs a strong, sound hull to stay afloat. During a sea voyage, a ship can encounter storms, reefs, rocks, and rough conditions that stress the hull and may threaten the integrity of the vessel; when damage does occur, an overhaul may be required to make structural repairs. Regular maintenance and upgrades are also necessary to prevent potential problems that could jeopardize safety and performance during future voyages on the open ocean. The same concepts apply to the human body: it needs preventive and restorative care. If the body-vessel is not sound, any one of its interconnected components—physical, mental, emotional, or spiritual—could be at risk. Common sense dictates that we shouldn't let things get to this point. Good health can be encouraged on a daily basis through proper diet, exercise, and adequate rest, but when things get out of balance, additional corrective measures are required. Just like a ship, the body is only as strong as its weakest link.

The forms of bodywork discussed in this section focus primarily on physical structure. Some are simply intended as soothing, nurturing, and relaxing treatments to help improve the overall functioning of the body and enhance general performance, whereas others deal with specific physical dysfunctions that may have far-reaching consequences. It's worth noting that even though the aim of these forms of bodywork is to cause positive changes in physical structure, their effects can extend beyond structure to other body systems. A simple muscle release can have a profound effect not only on the nerves and the circulation of fluids, but on the emotions and mental outlook of the individual.

Each of the following bodywork therapies has its own approach, but most employ hands-on techniques that gently or powerfully manipulate the skeletal structure, joints, tendons, ligaments, muscles, fascia (connective tissue), skin, and nerves. Remedial measures include techniques such as rubbing, pressing, cross-fiber friction, compression, palpation, percussion, lengthening, corrective stretching, and various forms of active release. Most often, the practitioner uses the fingers, thumbs, and palms, but the elbows, forearms, and even the feet can be called on to assist in the healing process. Some

modalities are based on the belief that the structures of the body know inherently how to function optimally, and these methods work to restore cellular memory by using traction and other supportive techniques.

When it comes to understanding the true source of pain brought on by an injury, you will find there are many interpretations and approaches, since each form of structural therapy has its own focus and methods. For example, isometric contractions performed against resistance may point to the source of the problem, as can Trigger Point Release Therapy, which relies on information from certain painful points. However, from the perspective of orthopedics, trigger points are a secondary phenomena and do not indicate the primary source of the problem, especially if it's a torn ligament. Practitioners of any modality must be open to the possibility that the problem may involve not only muscles or soft tissue (as in the case with spasms, strains, or adhesive scar tissue) but perhaps ligaments, tendons, joints, or nerve roots as well. The client must sometimes be patient, since as one condition is rectified, another painful area may become evident, symptom following symptom on the path to the source. Tracing the root cause of pain can also be difficult when the source is at a distance from the place where the symptom shows up. Completely diagnosing and resolving a problem may take time and a series of sessions; the client may also have to carry out prescribed exercises at home. But when it comes to physical damage, it is important to begin the healing process before scar tissue creates weak adhesions that make a person vulnerable to further injury.

Certain structural modalities that use deep strokes and heavy pressure can aggravate wounds or existing conditions. Such things as acute infections, inflammation, tumors, broken bones, fractures, rashes, hernias, torn ligaments, contagious illnesses, and a variety of other physical issues could be considered contraindications that might rule out this type of hands-on bodywork. It would be wise to consult your primary health care provider and also to let the bodywork practitioner know about any particular physical issues before a treatment. Most professional therapists will know how to avoid these areas, make modifications, or work around them, so you don't have to deny yourself the experience of an enjoyable form of touch therapy. Of course, if your condition is too extreme, a professional practitioner may recommend some other form of touch-free therapy to aid in the healing process.

Active Release Techniques® (ART)

Originally called Myofascial Release, this method of relieving soft-tissue dysfunction, developed by chiropractor Dr. Michael Leahy, combines hands-on work with movement to treat problems with muscles, tendons, ligaments, fascia, and nerves that may be caused by over-straining or overuse. It is based on the principle that by reducing adhesions, which are bands of fiber that cause fascial surfaces to stick together, free motion and proper functioning can be reestablished. When working with the muscles and fascia, the primary focus is on softening binding scar tissue, breaking up adhesions, and healing muscle tears.

A session begins with an evaluation of the problem area, carried out by the practitioner's trained hands. The therapist then has a choice of more than 500 treatment protocols in which hands-on work on areas of tension is combined with specific movements of the client's body. Since there are no friction-producing components such as rubbing in the deep manual contact, no lubrication is required during a treatment. The process generally is not painful, but when work is done directly on the adhesions, the client may find that it "hurts so good." Contact: www.activerelease.com

Balinese Massage / Boreh / Indonesian Massage

When traveling to other countries, it can be very worthwhile to experience indigenous forms of bodywork. Unlike other islands in Indonesia, Bali is predominantly Hindu, and traditional Balinese Massage is closely related to ancient Indian Ayurvedic forms of massage. Balinese Massage uses a combination of gentle stretches, Acupressure, and Reflexology techniques, along with essential aromatic oils, to bring about deep relaxation while stimulating the flow of blood, oxygen, and life-force energy throughout the body. The intention is to soothe the body in every possible way as the therapist uses long, gentle strokes to relieve stress and improve circulation. Depending on the client's condition, treatments can also use firm and deep massage techniques that include thumb walking, palm pressure,

gentle stretches, and a variety of other actions such as skin rolling, kneading, and stroking. In addition, especially deep pressure may be applied to knotted tissue or damaged muscles. The treatment is usually performed on a soft floor mat, but can be done on a massage table or with the client seated in a chair. At the end of the massage, the therapist usually smooths scented oils such as coconut oil on the body.

Indonesia is home to many aromatic spices—sandalwood, ginger, cinnamon, turmeric, eucalyptus, clove, and sesame—as well an assortment of fragrant flower petals and rice powder, so it stands to reason that they would be used in many forms of bodywork and in the popular purifying body baths or wraps. Many of the Indonesian "spice islands" have fashioned their own special forms of bodywork for both physical and spiritual purposes that intermingle ancient traditions. In Boreh, created by Balinese rice farmers, an exfoliating paste of ground spices and herbs mixed with rice powder is applied to the recipient's skin and produces a heating sensation. After it is left to dry for a period of time, the residue is rubbed off, and natural moisturizers are spread onto the skin to replenish it. In Java, a massage ritual is often performed so that a woman will look beautiful on her wedding day. This traditional exfoliating and cleansing treatment involves the use of herbs soaked in water to create a paste, which is blended into a scrub and then massaged all over the body. After the paste has dried for a while on the skin, it is washed off, leaving the skin soft and clean. The people of the island of Lombok have their own version of a full-body massage that includes a body scrub with ground coffee and sea salt. Other Indonesian treatments use purifying body baths in which the client soaks in goat milk or yogurt, though modern herbal formulas that soften the skin without leaving a pungent smell are replacing this practice. There is also a special treatment in which a large herbal body wrap with specific rejuvenating ingredients is secured around a postpartum woman's abdomen to help her regain her figure after giving birth. Contact: www.balinesespa.com

Benjamin System

This form of orthopedic massage therapy was developed in Austria around 1967 by Ben Benjamin, who was influenced by the therapeutic work of Wilhelm Reich, James Cyriax, and Frederick Alexander. A form of muscle therapy that combines bodywork treatments with body reeducation, the method's goal is to precisely locate and treat chronic pain or tension in a way that prevents its reoccurrence. The problems may have been created by injuries, accidents, surgery, occupational hazards, poor movement habits that affect structural alignment, and detrimental environmental conditions. The therapy emphasizes a full assessment that analyzes every aspect of the body before employing any hands-on techniques and then focuses on the parts of the anatomy that will have the most significant effect on a specific issue.

The treatment primarily addresses complex injuries and works with joints, ligaments, and tendons as well as the muscles. The bodywork itself uses connective-tissue massage with deep hand work along with self-help exercises and postural alignment work to reeducate the body for optimum functioning. Several hundred specific movements are available to release tension and address specific physiological conditions. Although the therapy is very useful for relaxation and the reduction of emotional and mechanical stress, it is most appropriate for treating a wide variety of preexisting painful dysfunctional issues.

Contact: www.benbenjamin.com/therapy.html

Berry Method®

The Berry Method is a system of manual therapy that was created during the 1940s by Lauren Berry. As a young man, Berry learned Swedish gymnastic techniques that he was able to use to heal his mother. As time passed, his fascination with the structure and intelligence of the human body continued to grow. The foundation of his approach to manual therapy was formed during his anatomy studies in the coroner's office in Oakland, California. Berry continued to study a variety of healing modalities, including those used in Mexico and Tibet, and was often told that his work closely resembled old-style Osteopathy. When it came to therapy, Berry simply considered himself a mechanic, and his approach resembles that of a structural engineer, which he was by profession. Although primarily based on correcting distortions and returning balance to soft tissue, his method includes visceral components, alignment work, and extensive lymphatic work. He also devised a system of stretches that can have a positive effect on fascia, cartilage, and joints.

The treatment uses deep-tissue massage and soft-tissue manipulation techniques that are intended to correct imbalances, smooth the muscles of the organs, and release distortions, adhesions, and spasms. Crucial to the Berry Method is the importance of the position of muscles, tendons, ligaments, and organs to an individual's health and pain-free functioning. Any distortion may be the body's natural adaptation to a primary imbalance, and this approach includes a soft-tissue positioning technique that shifts displaced parts of the body back into their proper places. Berry understood that the body has a memory and that, with a little encouragement, the organs and structural components will want to return to their normal positions. The pelvis is the natural center of gravity and key to the body's balance, so if it is out of balance, the rest of the body above and below this center may become distorted in ways that interfere with proper functioning and the body's innate ability to self-correct. By focusing the bodywork on the pelvic girdle, the visceral cavity, and the connecting muscles, ligaments, joints, and fascia, these distortions can be eliminated. Much like his contemporaries—Trager, Feldenkrais, and Rolf—Berry brought a distinctive approach to manual therapy that continues to be taught through the Institute of Integral Health, Inc.

Contact: Berry Method Institute of Integral Health – www.theberrymethod.org/institute

BioSync / Lamm Therapy

Biosync combines both Eastern and Western healing techniques to treat a wide range of physical and emotional dysfunctions that may manifest as pain, soft-tissue injuries, structural anomalies, or limited range of motion. An important element of the method is the energetic connection between the practitioner and the client. Like many other holistic therapies, Biosync holds the belief that healthy living requires that an individual attain balance between mind, body, and soul. Also foundational to this work is the focus, flow, and directed use of the vital life-force energy. Mark Lamm, a Kundalini Yoga instructor who developed the therapy, believes that the body contains the history of all traumatic experiences that have occurred during a person's life. These experiences include everything from genetic predispositions to the physical effects of aging to traumas that have literally become frozen into the body. This form of therapy uses hands-on movement education and deep-tissue and neuromuscular techniques to address the accumulated issues held within the body. The aim is to increase flexibility, elasticity, and functional harmony, while restoring healthy well-being.

The healing session incorporates an intuitive three-step process to provide a deep release of connective soft tissue that has become compressed or hardened. Nerve impingement in twisted connective tissue is recognized as a major cause of chronic pain, and the therapy works to release this cross-linking by unwinding the connective tissue and addressing any locked or hardened strands in the muscles. Techniques include forms of physical intervention such as the penetration of soft tissue, the lengthening of tissue through manual traction, and the unwinding of cross-linked connective tissue in a unique spiral fashion. Biosync has been used for a wide range of muscular and trauma-related disorders and is complementary to other clinical forms of therapy.
Contact: BioSync Research Institute –
    www.biosync.com

Bowenwork®

Bowenwork, also known as the Bowen Technique, is a holistic style of therapy that combines gentle hand movements with soft-tissue manipulation. It was developed during the 1950s in Australia by Thomas Bowen as a way to improve the structure and function of the human body. The therapy integrates elements of contemporary Western massage, Asian bodywork, and Osteopathy into a series of procedures carried out in a specific sequence. Instead of forceful adjustments and massage techniques such as deep probing, pounding, stroking, and rubbing, Bowenwork uses light, delicate pressure across muscles to spark a neuromuscular reflex that brings about a corrective response in the body. This system of subtle and precise procedures uses the minimum number of manipulations necessary to trigger the desired healing response and balance tension patterns in the body. Bowenwork can be used to treat numerous types of physiological dysfunction, including stiff joints, painful trigger points, body tension, strains, and limited range of motion.

A typical session starts with three basic sequences to rebalance the lower back, sacrum, upper back, and neck. Other specific mobilization procedures address specific problems but without deep probing or other actions that would shock the system. In synchronization with the client's breathing, the practitioner's thumb and fingers are used in a progression of stretching and rolling motions over the spinal area and across superficial muscles, fascia, nerves, tendons, and other areas. Aided by the inherent slack in the skin, the thumb gently presses laterally and downward through the skin toward the core of a muscle. This momentarily slightly stretches and compresses the muscle, which springs back into a natural position after the thumb is removed. The nervous system is alerted by these moves and responds reflexively, thus reorganizing the musculature and structure at a deeper level. The therapist encourages a client to sigh while exhaling and provides a pause between movements so that the client can absorb the changes. It is considered best for a recipient not to immediately use any other manipulation modalities that might interfere with the body's self-adjusting healing process, which can continue for several days after treatment.
Contact: Bowenwork Academy USA –
    www.bowenworkacademyusa.com

Budzek Medical Massage Therapy™

This form of therapeutic bodywork, developed by nurse Jeffrey Budzek, combines a number of therapies designed to relieve many forms of acute and chronic pain that originate from contracted muscle spasms, hypersensitive nerves, fascial constrictions, adhesions (scar tissue), joint problems, and a variety of other physical issues. This form of therapy can be used to enhance post-surgical recovery, release fascial restrictions, increase range of motion, and reduce complications in the area of the spine.

During a treatment, a synergistic sequence of manipulations is carried out according to a seven-point protocol, with twelve different bodywork modalities (including Swedish Massage, Deep Tissue Massage, and myofascial bodywork) being used in a specific order to simultaneously address eight key aspects of the musculoskeletal pain cycle in the body. Its effectiveness in relieving painful conditions can be beneficial for active individuals such as athletes and is also useful for elderly people who are prone to joint disorders and other forms of deterioration caused by age.
Contact: www.thestressreliefcenter.com

Clinical Flexibility and Therapeutic Exercise (CFTE)

CFTE is a protocol that works with the body's soft tissue to improve blood flow and the body's structure through a process that focuses on the solution rather than on the pain. The goal is to help clients understand their problems while the treatment is occurring so that the therapist can teach the recipient why the pain exists and how to prevent further injury. CFTE uses a series of flexibility exercises and some manual therapy to open soft tissue, increase range of motion in the joints, and strengthen the muscles.

Treatment starts with muscle testing and a verbal and visual assessment of restrictions, followed by an assortment of physical movements to restore flexibility. There are more than fifty different actions for enhancing flexibility and strengthening muscle tissue to choose from; the one known as active isolation stretching is often used. In each technique, a stabilization belt keeps the pelvis anchored while a position is held for just a couple of seconds. Compromised muscles and ligaments are known to skew the pelvis, which can cause problems in the entire body, so proper stretching of the ligaments, particularly around the hips, is considered essential for releasing contractions. Rather than moving parts of the recipient's body, the practitioner directs the client in carrying out physical actions throughout the session. The protocols of CFTE are adjusted to each individual and are often used to address painful back and hip problems. Contact: www.downeastschoolofmassage.net/cont-ed/cfte2.htm

Connective Tissue Massage (CMT)

CMT is a massage therapy, formerly known as Bindegewebs Massage and sometimes called a nerve massage, that originated in Germany in 1930s with physiotherapist Elizabeth Dicke. She created this method after being faced with amputation because of an infection in her leg. With the help of a colleague and by using self-massage on specific areas of her body, she was able to get rid of all her symptoms. After another decade of research, she created a body map of skin reflex zones that correlate to internal organs and that can be used as part of a treatment plan. These reflex zones are present because many nerve endings are embedded in the fascia, the connective tissue that lies just beneath the skin but is also widely distributed and interconnected throughout the body. Because of this interconnection, a massage on one part of the body may have a powerful effect on many other areas. Dicke's method resulted from the recognition of this strong connection between the connective tissue and the nervous system and internal organs.

CMT uses reflex zones to locate and treat problem areas in the body and eventually became a common adjunct therapy for the treatment of organ and musculoskeletal disorders.

The bodywork uses specific techniques that work with just the surface layers of fascial tissue rather than by going as deeply as in some other ways of releasing myofascia. The session begins with the sacral-pelvic area, since it is considered an essential location for energizing the nervous system. The practitioner then gradually proceeds up the torso to the neck, working with reflex zones that influence the spinal nerve endings. The hand work on the connective tissue under the skin is done by pulling and dragging the tissue under the fingers. Using movements such as fanning, hooking, smoothing, and stroking also can also send sensory stimulation to the nerves. Since no oil is used during the treatment, the strokes can feel like scratching; however, it is not painful. The treatment is primarily done with the client in a sitting position, although work on the legs is done with the client lying down. This form of massage is recognized and prescribed in Europe for treating disorders related to circulation, respiration, and a variety of other physiological conditions. Contact: www.ctm-bindegewebsmassage.com

CORE Myofascial Therapy

This form of bodywork, also known as Core Structural Integrated Therapy, was developed by George Kousaleos, founding director of the CORE Institute, as part of its advanced structural integration program. A full-body approach that is intended to mobilize the myofascial network and thus improve body alignment, resiliency, flexibility, balance, and awareness, this therapy is helpful in treating chronic pain. It involves bodywork that combines myofascial and craniosacral techniques, joint mobilization, and exercise to access core issues (traumas) held in the body. CORE Myofascial Therapy is a systematic, four-phase process that slowly follows a particular road map of the fascia network and focuses on balancing progressively deeper layers of connective tissue, muscles, and soft tissue.

The web of fascia envelop and connect every part of the body, as well as integrate and support most of its physiological systems. An extensive network of nerve endings are found in there, and as people age, the accumulation of life stresses in the fascial structures can cause them to contract, become less elastic, and produce pain. In addition to limiting range of motion and affecting balance, there can be an increasingly detrimental effect on cartilage, bones, and posture. To reverse or limit these effects, it is necessary to increase fascial resilience.

The bodywork techniques used in CORE Myofascial Therapy include the unwinding process of myofascial spreading; joint mobilization through arthrokinetics; slow, deep, and specifically directed pressure applied across the muscles of the shoulder, back, and hip; cross-fiber techniques for core release in the spinal area; and finishing work using techniques to reposition and relax the upper body between the abdomen and face.

The complete process may require a total of ten sessions, and is arranged in four phases organized according to which layers of fascia, muscles, and supporting tissues are manipulated. Each phase works with the breath and postural balance while progressing into deeper fascial layers. CORE Massage mobilizes the superficial fascia to provide fluidity, balance, and resilience to the structure. The practitioner's job is to feel subtle restrictions in the fascia and to sense the letting go or melting that occurs as they become more pliable. CORE Extrinsic Therapy (fascia opening) addresses posture and balance around the pelvis, as well as improving breathing. CORE Intrinsic Therapy (lengthening, balancing, and releasing) works on the deepest fascial layer with an emphasis on organizing the legs, pelvis, thorax, neck, and head. The final phase, CORE Integration, aims for the structural integration of deep tissue when the body is in a natural state of alignment. Under the direction of the practitioner, isometric exercises are taught so they can be used later to reinforce positioning and structural alignment, increase awareness of the five basic segments of the body, and support long-term improvement.
Contact: www.coreinstitute.com

Deep Tissue Massage

The rejuvenating process of deep muscle and tissue massage is carried out for the purpose of relieving muscle tension that may be caused by strains, injury, overuse, repetitive stress, or past trauma that is held in the body. This form of bodywork was created in part by Will Green, a Canadian who studied the work of Therese Pfrimmer, Joseph Pilates, Ida Rolf, Samuel West, and Debra Smith. The aim of the bodywork is to release the pain that is present in the body in the least painful way, adjusting the treatment to

the client's individual level of pain tolerance. The massage therapist uses a number of techniques and tends to focus on specific contracted areas of the muscles and fascia, such as those that require the softening of scar tissue.

During a session, various strokes are used to break up chronic patterns of muscle tension layer by layer and to work out the strains and adhesions. In order to effectively perform Deep Tissue Massage, the muscles must first be relaxed. Firm pressure and long, slow strokes that either follow or go across the fibers of the muscles, tendons, and fascia are used to relax and loosen the muscles and to break up adhesions. As the tightness is diminished, the therapist can go into deeper layers of the muscles, lengthening them and reorganizing the surrounding fascia into optimum patterns. Developments in the application of deep-tissue work have also come to include forearm techniques that help the practitioner avoid overstressing the hands.

The massage is also meant to provide the client with an awareness of tension and holding patterns within the structure so that the body and the mind can become synchronized while opening up to the release of tension. Since deep-tissue work is usually carried out on an already painful area, there is some element of discomfort involved no matter the depth at which the practitioner is working. Rather than simply being used for relaxation, Deep Tissue Massage, which incorporates elements of Swedish Massage, is considered a form of remedial therapy and can be the precursor to other forms of deep-tissue work such as Rolfing Structural Integration.
Contact: www.freemassagecourse.com

Esalen® Massage

Bernie Gunther, a leader at the Esalen Institute in Big Sur, California, formulated this method of massage in the 1960s; Charlotte Selver, who helped Gunther start the institute, assisted in its creation. The bodywork, which is based on the principles of sensory awareness and nurturing, uses a modified method of Swedish Massage that emphasizes strokes that are long, slow, rhythmic, flowing, lengthening, sedating, and nurturing. Gentle rocking, stretching, sculpting, and assisted joint movement help the recipient relax and can also release any physiological blockages and restrictions in the body. When done at this seaside institute, a complete session often includes time in a sauna to further soften and cleanse the body. There is liberal use of herbal oils during the treatment, which is set apart from Swedish Massage by its emphasis on the practitioner's sensitive, empathetic healing attitude. Chinese acupoint work is also sometimes incorporated.

Since its inception, variations of Esalen body work have also been established elsewhere. Dayana is a special type of Esalen work, formulated by a woman of that name, that uses a combination of Esalen bodywork, Myofascial Release, Lomi Lomi, qi gong, and other energy work. Heartwood is another variation established at the Heartwood Institute in California that combines elements of Esalen Bodywork with Swedish and other forms of massage.

Contact: Esalen Institute – www.esalen.org

HEMME Approach

A form of soft-tissue therapy developed by Dave Leflet in 1986, this approach to healing is based on the principles of Physical Therapy, Osteopathy, Chiropractics, and Medical Massage Therapy. It is generally offered by practitioners in a clinical setting that emphasizes treatment with manipulations rather than more invasive practices such as surgery. HEMME stands for history, evaluation, modalities, manipulation, and exercise; history represents part of the initial evaluation process in which the practitioner establishes the client's condition and the extent of any problems. Based on these findings, modalities that include the most suitable physical manipulations and exercise are chosen.

During a session, a series of constant feedback procedures are employed to ensure that the therapeutic process is headed in the right direction. If the feedback is negative, then the appropriate changes in procedure are made. The bodywork focuses on restoring body alignment, improving myofascial function, and treating conditions caused by injury. This approach is especially suitable for those individuals suffering from chronic low back pain and soft-tissue injuries.

Contact: www.hemmeapproach.com

Hendrickson Method®

The Hendrickson Method is a system of massage and manual therapy intended to relieve pain and restore function in a large number of orthopedic conditions. A practitioner uses principles of Tai Chi to focus internal energy, move fluidly, and effortlessly achieve profound results with no strain on her own body.

Dr. Tom Hendrickson, a chiropractor specializing in musculoskeletal disorders, developed this treatment system in the 1980s after extensive training in the healing arts, including an apprenticeship with Lauren Berry, the creator of the Berry Method. Hendrickson's experience culminated in the creation of this treatment system, which he has been teaching through the Hendrickson Method Institute for more than thirty years. This structural therapy brings together a combination of precise massage, mobilizations, and neuromuscular reeducation techniques that are blended with Eastern energy practices to enhance optimal functioning.

The signature technique of this method is called wave mobilization. A client lies fully clothed on her side, comfortably positioned with pillows as the practitioner performs the strokes in a rhythmic, rocking motion. The client is able to deeply relax while the practitioner is penetrating thickened soft tissue and realigning the fibers. The mobilization strokes are interspersed with the Muscle Energy Technique of contracting and relaxing, which resets a muscle's resting tone, lengthens fascia, and engages inhibited muscle fibers. Joint mobilization reintroduces normal movement patterns and joint play. This form of rehabilitation massage is suitable for many dysfunctional conditions, including lower back pain, whiplash, or spinal injuries.

Contact: Hendrickson Method Institute –
www.hendricksonmethod.com

Integrative Manual Therapy™ (IMT)

A systems approach to structural rehabilitation, IMT acknowledges the complexity of the interrelationship of the emotional, mental, and spiritual aspects of a person's pain or dysfunction, as well as the connections between that pain and all systems of the body. Dr. Sharon Giammatteo created this holistic health care practice to deal with dysfunction at the cellular level by supporting the client's inherent healing wisdom. It is based on the premise that there is often no one single problem causing a person's ailments and that health can be influenced by any number of emotional, mental, and spiritual factors. IMT blends a number of therapeutic techniques to correct the biomechanics of the skeletal system while improving the functioning and integration of the muscular, nervous, visceral, lymphatic, and circulatory systems of the body. The practitioner must have a thorough understanding of anatomy and uses gentle palpation and myofascial mapping techniques for both diagnosis and treatment; the priority and order in which each system will be treated are determined by the initial diagnostic findings. It is considered possible that when the blockages are manually removed, the body's natural lines of communication will be opened.

After the practitioner completes the diagnostic phase by carefully using his hands to listen to the body rhythms, he proceeds to a variety of manual modalities and techniques to address any recognized physical pain, dysfunctions, disabilities, or disease. Generally, gentle manipulations are employed to promote tissue repair, normalize the body structure, and restore proper functioning. In addition to working on the integrity of joints in the pelvis, sacrum, and spine, certain manual adjustment techniques—Muscle Energy Technique, the Strain & Counterstrain Technique, compression syndrome techniques, fulcrum techniques, visceral mobilization, advanced neurological techniques, tissue and joint unwinding techniques, and methods of core stabilization—are often used to promote healing. IMT also integrates customized nutrition programs. This form of therapy is often used by physical therapists, massage therapists, and bodyworkers. Giammatteo and a core team of IMT practitioners are continually developing new techniques that provide more permanent pain relief. Contact: Institute of IMT – www.instituteofIMT.com

Isometric Muscle Balancing

Isometric Muscle Balancing, also referred to as Isometric Massage Therapy, is a gentle kinesthetic reconditioning exercise that was developed by Charlotte Vandergrift. It is helpful in both preventing injury and increasing the rate of recovery from injuries that have caused symptoms of the muscular imbalances referred to as somatic dysfunction. Working with the principle that a muscle that has tightened up and doesn't release after contraction will cause the opposing muscle to become overstretched, this simple therapy's goal is to restore proper balance to an individual's musculoskeletal system by retraining contracted muscles to release and stretch. Balancing the muscles is particularly beneficial for those with back pain, muscle fatigue, muscle spasms, bad posture, and pinched nerves.

Clients learn a series of gentle, isometric muscle-balancing techniques that teach them how to tighten and release the problematic muscle without moving the adjacent joints. As the contraction is released, the muscle is allowed to reset and lengthen, over time allowing that muscle and any others that it impacts to return to normal. In a clinical setting, a practitioner can influence this process by placing a constant and equal force on a muscle shortened by contraction while the recipient remains completely still. This activation process helps tone the muscles of the whole body and improves overall mobility. The practice of isometric balancing also includes a technique that calls on muscle reflexes to help improve mobility in the joints through a process of contraction, release, relaxation, and stretching. The therapy is initially done with the assistance of a practitioners, but afterwards can be done by the client anywhere without any special equipment.
Contact: www.medicalmassageiso.com

Kinesis Myofascial Integration (KMI)

KMI is a form of structural integration that evolved from the work of Dr. Ida Rolf and Moshe Feldenkrais. Thomas Myers was instrumental in the development of this form of hands-on therapy, which uses a special anatomy trains map that describes the connective-tissue patterns in the body. The connective tissues play an active role in transferring and distributing kinetic energy throughout the body, and KMI treatments are designed to free constrictions in the fascial network to reeducate the body and address complex and restrictive patterns of posture and movement resulting from tension, trauma, repetitive actions, and other stresses. KMI is similar to Myofascial Release in that it deals with connective tissues, their imbalances, and the removal of adhesions that may cause restrictions in the tissues and thus interfere with movement.

The bodywork is accomplished through a series of up to twelve sessions, depending on the severity of the condition. The recipient either sits on a stool or lies on a massage table, and the practitioner prefers that the client be minimally clothed so that there can be direct contact with the tissues that are restricting the free flow of movement. After an initial discussion and analysis of the client's health history and postural patterns, the therapist will make contact with the tissues and gently proceed to work as deeply as possibly within the client's comfort level. The recipient will be asked to move in ways that encourage the tissues back into the place they were inherently designed to be. Sessions progress by working on freeing each area of the body, from the more superficial level to the deeper core muscles closer to the spine. The last few sessions are designed to integrate all of the work in a way that provides lasting change with freedom from habitual patterns. KMI is suitable for inclusion in a number of related integrative bodywork modalities.

Contact: Anatomy Trains – www.anatomytrains.com

Kripalu Massage

Kripalu Massage is a form of bodywork developed at the Kripalu Center for Yoga and Health in Lenox, Massachusetts, that combines elements of Swedish Massage, Polarity Therapy, energy balancing, and intuitive awareness. Although the massage is very physical and firm, the manipulations themselves are gentle and soothing and make full use of the practitioner's palms, fingers and thumbs. Muscles are massaged with a variety of full strokes, pressure, and kneading, alternating fast or slow movement carried out in a fluid, flowing motion while the recipient's body is fully supported. The recipient is guided into a deep state of relaxation and meditative awareness as each body part is loosened. The practitioner's intention is to stay fluid, centered, and energetically balanced, and the recipient is encouraged to breathe deeply and consciously at various times throughout the session.

Contact: Kripalu Center for Yoga and Health –
        www.kripalu.org

Kured® Therapy

Kured Therapy, also known as **Kurashova Re-education**™, is a well-established and integral part of the medical massage system used for rehabilitation in Russian clinics. Its developer, medical professor Zhenya Kurashova Wine, introduced this therapy to the United States when she immigrated in 1986. Although it induces relaxation and promotes rejuvenation, Kured is primarily carried out to treat a wide variety of physiological dysfunctions and neurological disorders. It is based on the idea that the nervous system and its connections to certain areas of the brain can be used to educate the body about how to perform. Specific forms of touch cause the central nervous system to generate signals that produce a chain reaction of positive healing reflexes, and these hands-on stimulations are repeated until the brain makes the reaction part of its own functioning.

It is therefore essential that the practitioner know what kind of touch produces what kind of reaction in the body. The primary intention is to restore the body's self-regulating processes in order to effectively change restrictive patterns of the mind and body. This form of bodywork helps with inflammatory conditions, muscle tone, nervous system disorders, and is often used to treat significantly disabling conditions.

Even though Kured Therapy emphasizes affecting the nervous system, it addresses the muscles in great detail and evaluates eighteen recognized tender points on the body. The techniques used are similar to Swedish Massage, but employ more precise and clinical manipulations and movements tailored to a client's individual rehabilitative needs. One distinctive aspect of this treatment is the practitioner's use of elbows and shoulders instead of the hands when performing deep-tissue work. The bodywork focuses not only on muscles and joints but also on injuries such as sprains, strains, and tears caused by overuse of certain muscles. The massage commonly makes use of techniques such as effleurage, petrissage, and vibration, along with friction and raking strokes, and palpation on connective tissue and nerves. More than one hundred strokes that work as deeply on a client as necessary in an essentially painless way are used; the choice depends on the client's condition. When working with second-degree muscle strains, the primary goal is to reduce pain and swelling. Once this has been accomplished, the bodywork focuses on improving the elasticity of the tissues. Although all of the touch techniques are designed to go deep but not hurt, it is possible that some individuals' conditions may become temporarily aggravated during a session as restrictive patterns are opened up and body fluids start to move freely. Kured Therapy has been effective in alleviating a variety of disorders, particularly fibromyalgia. It also involves a reeducation process that will enable an athlete to prepare for the stress of competition and prevent the most common injuries from becoming a long-standing problem.

Contact: www.ggrantmassage.com/offer.html

Looyenwork

Looyenwork is a form of deep-tissue therapy that was introduced by Ted Looyen in 1985 after he suffered a serious back injury. His creation of Looyenwork was motivated by the desire to find a gentle alternative to deep-muscle work so that the client would be more comfortable physically and therefore better able to process the release of intense emotions. The principal aim of this therapy is to release back pain, body tensions, and habitual patterns of holding in order to achieve permanent structural alignment, without causing the repetition of any initial trauma.

The treatment uses a combination of the restructuring techniques found in Rolfing Structural Integration, Postural Integration, Feldenkrais, and Aston Patterning. The bodywork is considered a painless approach in which the practitioner uses deep-tissue therapy to release and separate adhesions in the muscles and fascia. Varying levels of pressure release physical tension, and the practitioner helps the client work through any emotional issues that might arise. Elements of this therapy have been incorporated into other forms of therapy, such as prenatal massage.
Contact: www.realmagick.com/looyen-work

Lypossage

A noninvasive technique that decreases cellulite in the fibrous connective tissue and reduces sagging of the skin, Lypossage, developed by Charles Wiltsie, works on the lymphatic and myofascial systems of the body. It is essentially a detoxification treatment that uses a body-contouring massage and a combination of deep-tissue work, lymphatic drainage, and Rolfing Structural Integration to break down adhesive fibers that hold fat in uneven patterns and to help tone the muscles. A special liposuction machine may also be used. This form of bodywork is often part of Spa Therapy and generally requires a series of sessions to be truly effective.
Contact: www.lypossage.net

Medical Massage

A clinical treatment similar to Swedish Massage, Medical Massage is primarily used for rehabilitation after an injury, an illness, or a surgical procedure, rather than simply for relaxation. The therapist may work in a hospital setting or on referral from a physician and must be trained to treat a variety of common pathological conditions with a good understanding of the effect that other medical conditions and drugs may have on the treatment process. Although the massage is focused on a specific problem area, adjoining areas may also be treated to improve circulation to and from the problem area. A gentle touch (or no touch at all) may be required when dealing with extra-sensitive areas or wounds. Because it is not a full-body treatment, a typical session is shorter than a regular Swedish Massage.

Post-Surgical Therapy is a form of Medical Massage that uses special hands-on bodywork to encourage the healing process after injuries or surgical work. These treatments must be done with care. The aim is to speed up healing and resolve any traumatic issues.
Contact: www.medicalmassage.com

Muscle Energy Technique (MET)

The Muscle Energy Technique was designed for people who suffer from somatic dysfunctions, such as muscle spasms, joint stiffness, or restricted mobility. It was created by osteopathic physician Dr. Fred Mitchell for the purpose of restoring proper physiological functioning to stiff joints by using the principle of reciprocal inhibition, which explains how muscles relax and contract in relation to applied pressure. MET rapidly normalizes joint motion through a very gentle process that quickly covers the entire body. Proper evaluation and attention to the lumbar spine, pelvis, sacrum, and hips are considered essential for a successful treatment because of the significant effect these areas have on relieving symptoms in the extremities.

During a session, the patient first undergoes a full-body screening to help the practitioner determine the principal areas of restriction or dysfunction that limit mobility. MET then uses the muscle motion barrier concept in which the client is placed in a certain position that will engage a restriction and is then asked to perform a gentle isometric contraction against a precise counterforce applied by the therapist's hand. As the client resists this barrier, the therapist rhythmically intensifies and slackens pressure to enhance further mobilization. After contracting the muscle for a few seconds, the client gently stretches it in the opposite direction to open up any restrictions. After treating all the joints of the body that need attention, the session is concluded with a final screening to assess the outcome of the manual techniques. The intention of this type of osteopathic manipulation is not only to mobilize restricted joints but also to lengthen and strengthen weak muscles and fascia, restore proper neuromuscular activity, and improve spinal mobility without the use of manipulation. Because MET is gentle, it is appropriate for patients with back pain, headaches, hip issues, or serious physical injuries.

Contact: www.massagehealththerapy.com/
massage-techniques/muscle-energy-technique

Muscle Release Technique™

Designed to supplement a physical therapy program, the Muscle Release Technique focuses on injuries to muscles caused by trauma and repetitive strain. It recognizes that the body must be addressed as a whole in order to provide real long-term relief and increased flexibility. The basics of this treatment modality were developed in Europe by Stuart Taws of British Sports Therapy. Taws is a sports rehabilitation therapist from England now living in California, the innovator and designer of a dynamic therapy called Soft Tissue Release Training (see later in this section). Michael Young, a certified massage therapist and injury and rehabilitation specialist, was fortunate to learn the fundamentals for his work—the Muscle Release Technique—from Taws at a time in his career when his own body was suffering the effects of a repetitive strain injury. Applying Taw's soft-tissue release work to his own tendonitis, Young was able to rid himself of the problem. After spending hundreds of hours helping clients in his local community, he found ways to simplify the technique he had learned, providing a more efficient way to work, and ways in which to offer long-term and permanent relief for a multitude of chronic pain issues. He approached his teacher, Stuart Taws, with the idea of working together to build and grow a protocol to reach as many professionals and pain sufferers as possible. Taws was busy with his career and asked that Young rename his work so as not to confuse the public. This is how the Muscle Release Technique was born.

The technique focuses on pain relief caused by scar tissue, adhesions in the muscles, and nerve entrapment. Instead of using cross-fiber work or deep-tissue techniques, the client is placed in a position from which the muscle can be stretched with moderate pressure rather than force. During a session, the practitioner first identifies areas of the body in need of attention. This is done through visual observation and assessment of the client's complaints. Once the practitioner starts the hands-on work, he can feel tension in the muscles causing pain to the client. This hands-on technique integrates compression, specific movements, and muscle extension in combination with breathwork, all for the purpose of releasing muscle tension and pain in the body. This muscle work also includes various methods to normalize joint dysfunction and increase range of motion. After the session, the practitioner teaches the client what to do at home to keep the muscles lengthened and his pain at ease. Young's goal is to empower his clients to take charge of their own health. The Muscle Release Technique is often able to help a client in one treatment, although several sessions may be necessary for those clients with significant injuries.

Contact: www.mrtherapy.com

Myofascial Release (MFR)

Although the principles of Myofascial Release were recognized in Osteopathy many years ago, it was physical therapist John Barnes who developed the therapeutic form known today as Myofascial Release. The fascia create a three-dimensional web of connective tissue that protects, supports, surrounds, interpenetrates, and interconnects the whole body. The superficial or subcutaneous fascia lies just under the skin and allows it to move independently from the tissue below. Muscles, muscle groups, tendons, and ligaments are covered by the deep fascia. The subserous fascia is the deepest level; it shields blood vessels, nerves, and the lymphatic system, and lines the body cavities to protect the organs. In its different forms, connective tissue absorbs shock, allows adjacent surface to slide smoothly over each other, transmits movement, provides lubrication, and protects the physical structure of the body, the organs, and the cells. Fascia is composed mostly of collagen, a body protein, and hollow microtubes of collagen create its fibrous structure. The space outside the cells and protein fibers is filled with a substance whose consistency differs in different parts of the body from fluid to gelatinous. This ground essence, when in good condition, provides a reservoir from which the circulatory and lymphatic systems can draw nourishment and eliminate waste and also allows cellular communication throughout the body. For many reasons, including dehydration, illness, physical injury, habitual poor posture, or emotional stress, this fluid medium can solidify and create restrictions and blockages that can affect joints, muscles, tendons, ligaments, and bones and inhibit the flow of energy. Since fascial tissue acts as a conduit for cellular communication, the flow of vital life-force energy, and even the flow of consciousness, Myofascial Release may also have a quantum energy effect, restoring the vibrations, resonance, and flow of subtle information that will enable a person to achieve a significantly healthier quality of life. Myofascial Release has also been found to be closely associated with the meridian energy channels, since pressure-point bodywork will stimulate a spontaneous reorganization in the fibers.

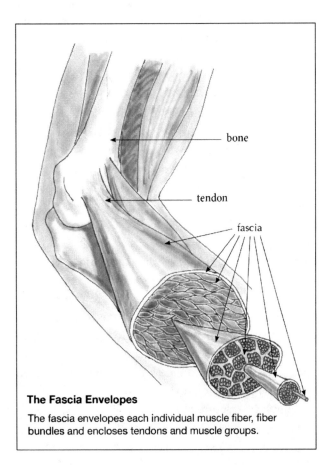

The Fascia Envelopes

The fascia envelopes each individual muscle fiber, fiber bundles and encloses tendons and muscle groups.

Myofascial Release therapists are conscious of the fact that problems rooted in the fascia can show up as pain or constriction in many different body systems, but that proper treatment can have beneficial results. Most MFR massage works primarily with all layers of the connective tissue, and its effects can be felt throughout the body. MFR is based on the principle that the recipient's body will give the practitioner feedback on the areas that need work and the amount of stretching needed and that the fascia will release at its own rate.

The treatment, often performed in concert with the recipient's breathing cycle, uses both gentle and more forceful pressure applied by fingers, elbows, or forearms in the direction of recognized areas of fascial restriction to move, elongate, and slowly sculpt the tissue. This process also warms and hydrates the fascia, making it more pliable. The practitioner waits for the tissue to relax and then increases the stretch. The process is repeated until the tissue is fully relaxed before moving on to another area. Broad, sustained strokes stretch the elastic fascia and slowly open the adjacent muscles. Vertical or transverse motions across the grain of muscles, tendons, and fascia organize the fascia for a higher level of functioning. A gentle form of unwinding by using sustained pressure and stretching of the tissue can alleviate pain in those places that hurt. A rebounding technique uses gentle, rhythmic rolling to release fascial restrictions and subconscious holding patterns while accessing the tissue memory that created the constriction. Palpation, trigger-point work, soft-tissue massage, and craniosacral therapy are all adjuncts to Myofascial Release Therapy, and some of the MFR techniques are incorporated into various kinds of structural massage to release chronic patterns of tension. Since working on connective tissue can improve the structure and stimulate the functioning of multiple body systems, MFR can result in a well-balanced, symmetrical, pain-free, and mobile body.

Contact: Myofascial Release Treatment Center
(Eastern Center) – www.mfrcenter.com or
www.myofascialrelease.com.

Active Isolation Stretching, or the Mattes Method, is a form of myofascial work, developed during the 1970s by kinesiotherapist Aaron Mattes, that incorporates efficient stretching and work on the fascia to help restore flexibility and healthy function ning. Proper techniques that stretch the muscles or fascia increase performance, ward off the stiffening caused by atrophy and aging, and enhance longevity and wellness by rehabilitating past trauma or muscle overuse. The process also promotes blood flow that increases oxygen in the body, stimulates the circulation of lymph, breaks down adhesions in the tissues, revitalizes the nervous system, and helps remove toxins.

Before a session begins, bilateral palpation is often employed to analyze the posture for tension and limitations in the range of motion. This involves applying light pressure to the same area on each side of the body

to compare differences in tightness. Next, an advanced technique called phasing is used to accurately identify specific areas of restriction before any stretching or massage begins. Then, precise movements of the client's body are used to stimulate specific areas of fascia and tissue that have been compromised by overuse or injury or have become tight, inhibited, contracted, disrupted, inflamed, or full of painful trigger points. Stretching is done by the therapist, not the recipient, and each stretch is held for only a few seconds. A stabilization belt is used as needed to keep the pelvis in a fixed position. Clinical Flexibility and Therapeutic Exercise, Soft Tissue Release, chiropractic work, and various other therapies also employ Active Isolation Stretching as a method to open soft tissue.
Contact: www.stretchingusa.com

Neurofascial Therapy (NFT), developed in Europe in the 1920s, is one of the diverse developments in the realm of myofascial therapy that is becoming a standard component of chiropractic bodywork. This form of manual therapy consists of a series of transverse pulling strokes delivered with the tip of the practitioner's third finger, which glides across zones or segments of the body to create friction in the fascia and stimulate neuroreceptors, eliciting a local reaction of cascading reflexes that can be beneficial for neurological functioning. A specific pattern of strokes is used, depending on the particular organ, painful area, or dysfunction that is being treated. For example, in the spinal and pelvic areas, which are often treated in the initial phase of care, strokes have a strong effect when they begin close to the spine and then move away from it. The process is quite gentle, though the recipient may experience a sharp, cutting sensation. The client's feedback on the sensations caused by the gliding strokes acts as an indicator of shifts in the internal condition. The therapy has been used to treat a variety of painful trigger points, dysfunctions, and chronic conditions and is particularly appropriate for elderly clients who may need a gentle approach.
Contact: www.neurofascial.com

Myopathic Muscular Therapy

This method of muscular manipulation is designed to relax areas in which there is progressive or residual tightness from muscle or nerve strain, sports injuries, accidents, infections, or years of declining health. It is a gentle therapy that is based on the osteopathic principle that normal body function depends on normal body structure. This form of therapy was created by osteopath Dr. Claude Heckman to reduce inflammation, pain, and residual tension while restoring normal blood supply and nerve functioning through a systematic process of relaxing the muscles. This is accomplished without the use of oil, cream, powder or lotion through progressive application of rest, heat, and a myopathic treatment in which the hands, fingers, and elbows work with muscles that are strongly contracted.
Contact: Myopathic Muscular Therapy Association – www.myopathictherapy.org

Myopractic® Muscle Therapy

Myopractic Muscle Therapy is a form of myofascial bodywork that focuses primarily on misalignments in the lower body. It is used for rebalancing posture, releasing tension, clearing soft-tissue obstructions, and releasing adhesions. This form of deep, hands-on therapy was developed in the late 1980s by Robert Petteway after he had worked for decades with individuals suffering from chronic pain. Its primary goal is to identify misalignments in the structure, especially in the lower body, that cause chronic pain and then to realign them. These corrections in turn will often relieve tension in the upper body.

This therapeutic method works to increase the integration of the muscles, fascia, and body structure by combining three basic techniques. Compression stretching is employed to relieve muscle tension and holding patterns so that the patient can relax. Clearing methods using covered thumb and framing techniques are used to clear obstructions from soft tissue. Separating techniques are then used to release the adhesions and balance the muscles. A spot therapy that focuses on an area that causes particular problems for an individual is also used. Myopractic work integrates various styles of bodywork and focuses on neuromuscular trigger points, scar tissue, muscle bundles, and old bruises. The therapist uses her own body weight to create leverage during the session. One unique thing about this therapy is that it uses vibrating power tools, such as automobile buffers normally used to wax cars, that are not usually applied to humans.
Contact: Myopractic Institute – www.myopractic.com

Naprapathy Treatment

Naprapathy is a form of hands-on health care that focuses on the diagnosis, evaluation, and treatment of conditions and disorders involving the connective tissue and neuromusculoskeletal system. It is based on the principles of the osteopathic and chiropractic work that were developed during the early 1900s. Diagnostic evaluations use a combination of a person's medical history, anatomical evaluations, muscle testing, ultrasound work, and neurological analysis. Existing pain is often caused by imbalances and distortions caused by trauma, repetitive motion, faulty posture, or injury from accidents, and the bodywork is carried out to provide pain relief through manipulations of the ligaments, muscles, fascia, cartilage, and tendons.

During a session, the practitioner uses palpation to explore the connective tissue while looking for rigid, contracted areas of the body. This is followed by repetitive rhythmic thrusts to gently stretch the contracted connective tissue in order to alleviate existing pain. Sessions often focus mainly on the ligaments near the spine, and gentle manipulations of the vertebrae are used to stretch connective tissue that may be irritating the nerves where they exit the spinal column. Joint mobilization techniques are used on restricted joints along with special chiropractic articulations to increase range of motion. Botanical medicines, nutritional supplements, and corrective exercises for the client to perform at home are often included as an adjunct to complement the manual treatment. Sometimes traction, hot and cold packs, infrared rays, electrotherapy, and orthopedic appliances such as belts, supports, and pillows are included. Naprapathy is appropriate for the treatment of a number of physiological issues and is often used in combination with other modalities.

Contact: www.naprapathy.us

Nerve Mobilization

Individuals with neurological symptoms such as tingling and numbness usually have nerves that lack elasticity, are shortened, or resist stretching because they are irritated by constricting myofascial tissue. This form of therapy focuses on neurological dysfunction and uses an assessment method that determines the length, elasticity, and irritability of the peripheral nerves in the body. Tension testing may also be used to find impingements caused by tight muscles pressing on nerves.

Developed by Doug Alexander, Nerve Mobilization employs a combination of hands-on myofascial, lymphatic, and muscle release techniques to normalize nerves and tissue function, particularly down the arm from the neck to the hand. A number of interventions and mobilization techniques are directed toward the irritated nerves. One of these milks the inflammation away from the nerve at various points along its length. Another is an osteopathic traction technique that works to decompress the surrounding tissue, allowing the nerve to be released. Nerve Mobilization also incorporates a gliding method of direct nerve stretching along with a number of assisted movement exercises to relieve underlying issues.

Contact: www.integrativehealthcare.org/dougalexander

Neuromuscular Massage Therapy (NMT)

Neuromuscular Massage Therapy provides the systematic examination and treatment of muscular and postural disorders such as soft-tissue problems, tight muscle bands, structural imbalances, work and recreational injuries, nerve compression or entrapment, and other physiological problems or dysfunctions. It was during the 1930s in Europe that osteopaths Stanley Leif and his cousin Boris Chaitow were instrumental in the development of the European form, referred to as Neuromuscular Techniques (NMT). Slightly different versions of this therapy have since evolved in the United States through the influence of a number of osteopaths, chiropractors, and naturopaths, yet all work primarily to prevent the hardening of connective tissue and to improve physical functioning. Since the true cause of a problem can be caused by multiple factors, precise and thorough assessment of the sensory motor reflexes is beneficial and informative if used before any manipulations are applied. A series of protocols is used to examine specific muscles in areas of the body that are tight, painful, or have limited range of motion, spasms, and nerve impingement. This will include muscles that are closely related to or surround the affected area.

The basic hands-on process involves muscle-by-muscle examination using soft- or deep-tissue manipulation that is applied with the fingers, thumbs, palms, forearms, or treatment tools. The applications are focused on muscle fibers first, in an effort to increase blood flow and decrease tension on the tendon insertions. In some cases, carefully applying pressure to specific muscle attachments may be included. Joint decompression may be an added benefit, particularly if decompression techniques are included. Reducing intrajoint pressure may help release muscle tension, and may also influence neural hyperactivity that involves the central nervous system and musculoskeletal system. Surface tissue is usually addressed before working on deeper layers, and areas more distant from those related to the primary symptoms are dealt with later. A variety of manual techniques are used to relieve problems in the tissues by easing the existing stiffness that has developed over time with disuse and abruptly with trauma. Initially, slow-paced thumb drag methods or medium-paced thumb and finger gliding strokes are used to increase blood flow and soften the fascia. Once the tissue or fascia is softened, the practitioner applies further manipulations that include the bending and lifting of the fibers and the palpation of the tight bands in which fibers are locked into a shortened position. Pressure is applied to painful trigger points in the muscles to deactivate them and to reduce their referral patterns. The appropriate degree of pressure is sustained for only a short period, averaging ten to fifteen seconds, until a release is felt within the constricted area and the referral pattern is reduced. This pressure-release technique can be repeated for each trigger point a number of times during a session, always with the most appropriate level of pressure. The final part of a treatment employs passive or active stretches that lengthen the fibers. When signs of tendon inflammation are present, manually applied methods that lengthen the fibers without putting stress on the attachments are used. Stabilization of the pelvis, correction of foot dysfunction, such as pronation, and corrections to overall posture and habits of use are also integral to the process. Client feedback is an integral part of this work, so increasing the client's body awareness is also an important element of the complete therapy. NMT also emphasizes that home self-care stretching and exercises, not just practitioner-applied bodywork, are important for the real resolution of problems.

Unlike Swedish Massage, where the focus is primarily relaxation, Neuromuscular Massage Therapy is intended to address physiological and biomechanical disorders that often require the practitioner to fully understand anatomy and physiology, and to have knowledge and experience in a variety of techniques. Although many of the following modalities use similar techniques,

it is often how and where they are applied, for how long, and in what order that differentiates one from another. Contact: NMT Center – www.nmtcenter.com

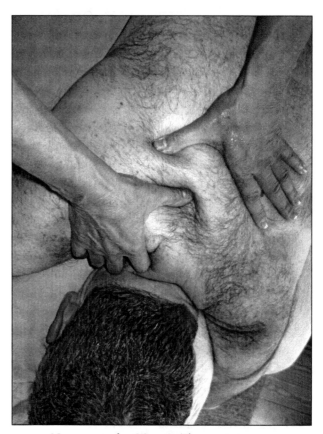

Neuromuscular Massage Therapy in process.

Neurosomatic Therapy (NST) is an integrative neuromuscular approach to pain relief that is based on locating improper structural and biomechanical patterns in the patient's body that may be hidden sources of pain. The therapy is based on the idea that form follows function and that a distortion in the form of the body often correlates with improper functioning of the body. Paul St. John, a student of Raymond Nimmo, developed this approach as a way to analyze and chart dysfunctional postural patterns and correct them through a comprehensive program with five stages of rehabilitation. It includes methods to eliminate muscle spasms, restore flexibility and proper biomechanics, and increase muscle strength and muscular endurance. The goal is not only to eliminate pain but also to educate the client on ways to prevent a recurrence of the symptoms. St. John taught others and developed another neuromuscular method that bears his name (see below).

Contact: www.neurosomaticeducators.com

Neuromuscular Reeducation™ (NMR) is a hands-on approach to the evaluation and treatment of soft-tissue injuries and musculoskeletal problems that was developed by chiropractor Dr. Gary Glum in the 1960s. When Glum retired during the 1980s, Dr. Peter Levy took over the practice and made some modifications. The aim of this therapy is to treat muscles and joint problems by focusing on the less elastic adhesions or scar tissue that the body naturally creates after an injury. The adhesions that form in a damaged area create both muscle weakness and limited range of motion. This therapy works to locate the adhesions and then take the muscles and joints through a functional range of movements while using deep manual pressure to break up the adhesions. Treatments may also include balancing exercises such as standing on one leg, the use of a wobble board, or exercises involving changes in posture, all used to evaluate and treat problems with physical instability. The overall intention is to reduce pain and improve muscular movement, coordination, balance, and posture.

Contact: The Levy Approach to NMR – www.nmrseminars.com

Neuromusculoskeletal Therapy is a form of hands-on bodywork often practiced by osteopaths and chiropractors, that is used to alleviate musculoskeletal pain, be it mild or chronic in nature. Though not a specific modality in itself, this approach was influenced by the work of American chiropractor Dr. Raymond Nimmo and is based on the belief that imbalances in the body's nervous system, blood vessels, muscles, and skeletal framework of the body can cause disorders and disease. Practitioners use a combination of manipulations, chiropractic adjustments, and physical therapy in their treatments. The many techniques employed range from the high-velocity adjustments often used by chiropractors to slow or soft techniques that involve massage or client-initiated muscle movements. (See more under Nimmo Receptor Tonus Method under Chiropractic in the section on Spinal Therapies in this chapter.)

Contact: The Neuromusculaskeletal Research Center – www.health.usf.edu

Neuromuscular Therapy St. John Method is an approach to managing pain that works on balancing the nervous and muscular systems in a way that interrupts the stress and pain cycle. This method, as its name suggests, was developed during the late 1970s by Paul St. John after he studied with Raymond Nimmo. It uses massage to relax the muscles, release muscle constrictions, and increase blood flow in order to regain muscular integrity. The neuromuscular bodywork focuses on biomechanics, trigger points, soft-tissue pain, postural distortion, and nerve entrapment and compression. Attention is also given to hormonal balance, nutrition and the elimination of toxins. Although this method often stands alone as a treatment, it can be used as an adjunct to other modalities.

In 1989, one of St. John's associates and the first approved instructor besides himself, Judith (Walker) DeLany, went on to create NMT American Version™ (see below) and later established the NMT Center, in which integrative advances in this field continue to this day. In 2005, St. John developed Neurosomatic Therapy (see previous discussion), which retained strong components of his former NMT material. He sold NMT St. John Method seminars to a new owner, who no longer teaches the method. Although, NMT St. John Method is no longer being taught, thousands of previously certified practitioners are enjoying success in a variety of practice settings.

Contact: www.neurosomaticeducators.com or www.nmtcenter.com

Neuromuscular Therapy American Version™ was developed by Judith (Walker) DeLany in the early 1990s. DeLany combined techniques learned from Paul St. John, including Dr. Nimmo's original protocols, with osteopathic concepts shared by her co-author, Dr. Leon Chaitow, nephew of Boris Chaitow. NMT American version evolved considerably during the next two decades and now comprehensively addresses biomechanical, biochemical, and psychosocial factors that influence the state of health of the tissues, as well as of the person as a whole. Additionally, consideration is given to static and dynamic posture, habits of use, and perpetuating factors, such as nutrition, chemical exposure, and emotional stress. The client participates actively in the treatment process, particularly in the development of a home care plan that fits the person's lifestyle.

Chaitow and DeLany's collaborative writing resulted in significant alteration of the foundational platform of NMT and produced the first comprehensive academic textbooks on NMT, which combine European NMT and NMT American version™ as an integrated model. Both actively teach and write about Neuromuscular Therapy and the treatment of chronic pain.
Contact: www.nmtcenter.com or
www.leonchaitow.com

Neuro-Structural Bodywork (NSB)

The main purpose of this bodywork therapy is to extend range of motion by restoring sensory perception; making breathing more even; providing fascial release; balancing the musculoskeletal, nervous, and energetic chakra systems; and improving body control. Combining a variety of techniques, including Myofascial Release, Neuromuscular Reeducation, craniosacral adjustment, and breathwork, it works on the deepest level of connective tissue using gentle neural touch techniques and other subtle osteopathic procedures. This somatic therapy is directed at both acute injuries and chronic conditions caused by problems such as disc disorders, locked shoulders, headaches, and fatigue syndrome. NSB is intended to provide a possible alternative to more invasive treatments or surgery. This form of bodywork was developed primarily by Nancy DeLucrezia as a means of stimulating and supporting physical and emotional release and as an adjunct to other physical and psychological integration therapies.
Contact: www.kaliinstitute.com

Onsen Technique®

After years of studying deep-tissue work, Swedish Massage, and Polarity Therapy, Richard Phaigh concluded that the only way to provide long-term relief from pain was to correct its structural source. He developed the Onsen Technique, also known as Onsen Muscle Therapy, as a way to assess and correct structural and functional imbalances that cause stress and pain, as well as affect a client's peace of mind. *Onsen* is actually a Japanese word that means "to rest or be at peace."

Once the initial assessment is completed, three treatment techniques are combined into a protocol that strives to strengthen, lengthen, and balance the body's soft tissues. The three main components are Muscle Energy Technique (discussed earlier in this section), post-isometric relaxation exercises, and transverse friction massage of soft tissues. The latter two complement the skeletal alignment work of the first. The Muscle Energy Technique includes gentle skeletal repositioning, methods for addressing individual spinal segments, manual corrections of spinal curves, and other corrective techniques that focus on specific joints and the sacrum. The Onsen Technique has been gaining popularity with osteopathic physicians and physical therapists, especially for treating clients who have significant twisting or deformations in the body.
Contact: Onsen International –
www.onsentherapy.com

Orthopedic Massage

Orthopedic Massage is actually just one of many practices found under the umbrella of Orthopedics, a specialized form of health care that incorporates a comprehensive physical-therapy approach for dealing with the prevention and correction of disorders involving the soft tissue, muscles, joints, fascia, bones, ligaments, cartilage, and nerves. Along with any dysfunction or injury that restricts movement, the therapy addresses painful musculoskeletal problems, adhesions, entrapped nerves, myofascial trigger points, and many other issues through an assortment of rehabilitative techniques.

The principles of Orthopedics were formulated in London in part by Dr. James Cyriax during the 1930s at a time when physiotherapists had limited success in the rehabilitation of their injured patients. Cyriax was frustrated by the limitations of existing techniques for alleviating the conditions of patients suffering from a variety of physiological issues. He spent more than a decade in search of a clinical solution that would reduce the need for surgery. Considered the father of Orthopedics, he was the first to create a methodical method of diagnosis and assessment of injuries and the hands-on technique of cross-fiber friction. Since that time many practitioners in this field of care, such as James Walaski, Ben Benjamin, and Whitney Lowe, have made great strides in developing an assortment of specific and functional clinical assessment tests and a wide range of techniques to relieve pain and restore full range of motion.

Orthopedic bodywork is most appropriate for a client who is seeking relief from pain, injury, or chronic conditions. The list of identifiable and treatable conditions is quite extensive and includes physiological issues such as a pulled muscle, displaced pelvis, strained ligament, failed back surgery, tennis elbow, groin injury, bursitis, or various soft-tissue sprains and lesions. One of the basic concepts of Orthopedics is that simply treating symptoms will not lead to permanent resolution of a problem. It is the root cause, whose location may be entirely different from that of the actual pain, that must be determined and remedied, a process that may unfold over a series of sessions.

Proper knowledge of the interconnection of all parts of the physical structure and a complete evaluation of the patient's condition are emphasized and considered necessary for developing the most effective treatment plan. A correctly orchestrated protocol with the techniques that are most appropriate for the unique needs of the individual patient is then used to address the dysfunction. The initial evaluation can include both active and passive analysis of range of motion, testing the ability to resist force, and a detailed assessment of specific areas of the client's body. It often reveals whether and when massage or some other form of physical therapy is suitable. Finding the solution to chronic conditions that have been held for a long time in the body will require a more involved assessment. Therapists need to be well trained in all aspects of physical injuries and the variety of techniques that would be useful for rehabilitation.

If Orthopedic Massage is indicated, there are many forms that can be used to remove tension and restrictions held tightly in the body while balancing and lengthening the fascia and increasing pain-free range of motion. The actual bodywork is not limited to any one modality, but may incorporate elements of Myofascial Release, Neuromuscular Therapy, the Berry Method, Craniosacral Therapy, Trigger Point Release Therapy, transverse friction techniques, scar tissue mobilization techniques, or myoskeletal alignment work. No matter the approach used, the quality of attention given by the practitioner is a key element. Although there is no such thing as a typical treatment, a hands-on session can use pressure, friction, heat, an assortment of muscle manipulations, and gentle movement techniques that employ slow isometric stretching, along with movement repatterning to improve range of motion. Some breathing exercises may also be included. In addition, clients can be instructed in types of stretching and strengthening techniques that they can use at home.

Contact: www.orthomassage.net,
www.benbenjamin.com,
www.omeri.com, or
www.carlsoncollege.com

Osteopathic Manipulation Therapy (OMT)

OMT is a practice within the system of osteopathic medicine, an approach to healing developed in the mid-1800s by American Dr. Andrew Still that is dedicated to treating the patient as a whole. Osteopathy goes beyond conventional medical practices to include an emphasis on the systematic assessment of all the body's physical restrictions and the structural balance of the musculoskeletal system as a whole, but with a particular focus on the spine. The osteopath's job is to help a person regain structural integrity, thus allowing the freedom of movement that ensures that all body systems are free to self-correct. The underlying principle is that a patient's history of illness and physical trauma can be seen in the body's structure because of the connection between the organs and the musculoskeletal system. Osteopathic manipulation not only treats joints, muscles, and tendons but also helps alleviate headaches, breathing disorders, and digestive problems.

During a treatment, the osteopathic physician gently applies a precise amount of force, either at the surface or at deeper levels, to promote healthy movement of tissues, to eliminate abnormalities in body movements, and to release compressed bones and joints. Gentle manual pressure is used to palpate the fascia in order to change the intercellular matrix, release muscular restrictions, loosen the surrounding connective gel, and soften the body. Manipulations and thrusts are only as forceful as required and are usually applied in the direction of the restriction. The techniques used may include joint mobilization, articulations, cranial manipulation, methods of functional and positive positional release, lymphatic pumping, and muscle energy work. Nutrition, postural corrections, and relaxation techniques may also be incorporated. Treatments can result in some soreness caused by the work on painful areas, but most clients find the process relaxing.

Contact: www.osteopathy.org.uk

Cranial Osteopathy is based on the work of Dr. William Sutherland, who took the principles of Osteopathy into work on the cranial field. After a full-body evaluation, a refined and subtle type of osteopathic treatment that encourages the release of body stress and tension especially in the area of the cranial cavity, is employed. Most of the work is performed on the sutures of the skull as the osteopath cradles the head. Practitioners are trained to feel the faint cranial rhythms present in all body tissues, which requires a finely developed sense of touch, since the movement of cranial fluid is very subtle. Only minor manipulations with slight twists or pulls are used, and often the touch is so gentle that it seems like not much is happening. These techniques can also be used for the internal organs of the body. Cranial Osteopathy is considered effective for treating a wide range of physiological conditions for people of all ages, including children and babies. It is especially useful for treating sports injuries such as the concussions suffered by football players and other athletes. (See more under Craniosacral Therapy in the section on Spinal Therapies in this chapter.)

Contact: Sutherland Cranial College –
www.cranialosteopathy.org

Mechanical Link is a form of osteopathic treatment, developed by French Dr. Paul Chauffour in the late 1970s, that works on the entire body and its systems by treating the sources of impaired body function known as lesions. These lesions are restrictions found within fascia caused by a combination of physical and emotional traumas that can occur anytime in a person's life. Mechanical Link was developed as an efficient method of evaluating and treating the primary lesions of the entire body within a single session. Treatments use gentle palpations to determine where lesions are located. With a technique called inhibitory balancing, the practitioner determines which lesions are the primary ones and targets the treatment at them. Once a lesion is isolated, a recoil technique is used to release it by manually applying vibrations at a precise speed in a specific direction. This triggers a reaction through the central nervous system that creates a response that frees blockages and provides a release in other affected areas of the body.

Contact: www.mechanicallink.info

Neurofascial Release Therapy (NRT) is a type of osteopathic manipulation that was developed in 1987 by osteopath Dr. Stephen Davidson based on the fundamental concepts established by Andrew Still. The process is begun by first identifying subtle or significant strain patterns in the fascia and then using very light pressure to release tension at those release points related to the tightness in the connective tissue. The intention is to unwind strains caused by twists and pulls in the fascia that were caused by poor posture or previous trauma; it often happens that there is an emotional release because of body memories that have been held in the connective tissue. Even though force is not used in the treatment, some soreness can result as a side effect. This is often a good sign that a powerful release has occurred during the treatment session, and the soreness will not last long.

Contact: www.healthabounds2.com

Pfrimmer Deep Muscle Therapy® (PDMT)

This deep form of muscle therapy was developed in 1946 in Canada by physiotherapist Therese Pfrimmer after she was able to overcome her own paralysis caused by work-related injuries. After the doctors told her she would never walk again, she was able to heal herself through deep, hands-on manipulations of her own muscles. What evolved out of this event became a therapy that works to alleviate functional impairment by increasing the flow of blood and lymph within the muscles, thus improving the oxygenation of tissues and promoting detoxification.

This corrective therapy provides rehabilitation through a process of deep kneading, mobilizations, and manipulations of all muscle layers and fascia. Over the years, a number of specialized muscle therapy techniques have been developed to help relieve an assortment of physiological issues. Most notable is the Comprehensive

Cross-Fiber Technique, also known as Cross-Fiber Corrective Muscle Therapy, in which friction is applied in the direction away from the heart to soften and loosen hardened fibers in all layers of the muscle tissue. This helps clear adhesions, relieve congestion, reduce inflammation, release entrapped nerves, and improve the flow of the lymph and blood. Most often, only the thumbs and fingers are used by the practitioner. It does not have the reputation of being painful, although some recipients have reported discomfort, especially when work is done on areas of tension. Other hands-on techniques include Cross Fiber Muscle Isolation, Gentle Fascial Release, Joint Release, Gentle Vascular Release, and the Visceral Release Technique. The Pfrimmer method of muscle therapy is continually expanding in scope and is now used by a variety of health care professionals.

Contact: International Institute for Corrective Muscle
Therapy Inc. – www.iicmt.com

Phenomenal Touch™

A form of intimate, loving-touch bodywork founded by Leslie Bruder, Phenomenal Touch relies on the quality of the touch and the manipulation offered for a successful outcome. Together, the recipient and the fully present practitioner enter a deep space, connected with the sacred spirit, in which the practitioner meets the client where she is.

One of the holds in Phenomenal Touch.

The session can include about seventy-five essential principles and more than a hundred different movements that call on the effects of gravity and momentum rather than force as the body is moved in a fluid, undulating,

rhythmic way. Three-dimensional work, which is intended to embrace the body in space, is carried out as the therapist lifts and supports parts of the body to address both sides at once while moving the body in space. A technique called body draping allows for easy movement of the recipient's body, the use of fulcrums, and improved muscle release. Seamless transitions between movement and stretching during each part of the bodywork provide flow, continuity, and integration as the session follows the needs of the individual body rather than abiding by a set order of events. Particular creative moves used in the therapy include those known as Shiva, Belly Wave, Come to Me, Rag Doll, Mermaid, Rock n' Roll, Slide n' Drool, Up n' Over, Frog, Hip Hop, and Undertow. Phenomenal Touch is described as a reverent dance that combines elements of Watsu, Trager Approach, Lomi Lomi, and Thai Yoga Bodywork with deep-tissue work.

Contact: www.phenomenaltouch.com

Physical Therapy (PT)

Physical Therapy has been an established part of professional health care in the West for many years. Its aim is to promote healthy recovery from accidents, disabilities, surgery, fractures, sprains, strokes, trauma, neurological disorders, and other physical ailments. Its scientific principles include the physiological practice of biomechanics and hands-on rehabilitation techniques. Therapists use a broad range of modalities that include Integrated Manual Therapy, exercise, massage, movement facilitation, and biomechanical therapies. Many therapists specialize in particular areas, such as pediatrics, sports injuries, and occupational disabilities.

The hands-on work covers a broad range of techniques that address fascia, muscles, and joints. When areas of restriction are alleviated, the therapist reinforces the integration of structure and function by providing new movement patterns through those specific exercises most appropriate for the client. Today, many practitioners of physical therapy are becoming more integrative by including numerous other forms of therapy such as craniosacral bodywork, massage therapy, energy work, and mental health counseling. This makes them more effective in providing a complete rehabilitation service, especially on an outpatient basis.

Contact: American Physical Therapists Association –
www.apta.org or World Confederation of
Physical Therapists – www.wcpt.org

Early Intervention Therapy (EIT) is a proactive form of occupational physical therapy that addresses discomfort and fatigue before they become chronic conditions. The goal is to prevent injuries and reduce the severity of the effects of accidents by working with the early warning signs of unhealthy behavior patterns. Since it is basically a preventive form of bodywork, massage is not a particular part of this therapy. Instead, EIT incorporates a variety of self-treatment exercises and recommends changes in habitual behaviors that often relate to the workplace. Usually, the physical therapist will meet with the client and the employer to determine which existing conditions may cause problems and then suggest corrective measures that decrease the chance of a future injury. Many such injuries are recognized as cumulative, since they can arise through the repetition of bad work habits. With early intervention, the therapist can help both the employer and the worker save time and money lost to workers' compensation claims.

Physiatrics is a branch of physical therapy that specializes in treating muscle pain and assisting in rehabilitation by using a combination of exercises, massage, and hot or cold hydrotherapy. High-tech electronic equipment often helps identify specific issues. Physiatrics may employ a team of medical professionals that includes physicians, neurologists, orthopedic surgeons, and physical therapists. Taking time to accurately diagnose the source of an ailment is considered crucial to determining the correct physical therapy treatment plan.

Proprioceptive Neuromuscular Facilitation (PNF) Therapy was developed by Margaret Knott and Dorothy Vass in 1956, based on the initial concepts provided by Dr. Herman Kabat during the 1940s. With roots in Sports Massage, the therapy plays an important role in the strength training of athletes. It can also be a comprehensive conditioning program for people suffering from various musculoskeletal injuries or dysfunction. A variety of techniques are used to promote a beneficial response within the neuromuscular mechanisms so that movement can be free of pain. PNF employs special static, ballistic, and assisted stretching techniques

for the neuromuscular system, as well as methods that encourage body-mind awareness. Specific, appropriately timed hands-on contact can facilitate and guide the client's body movements while the maximum tolerable resistance is applied. Repetitive rhythmical activation techniques are used in conjunction with applied resistance to develop a full range of motion.

During a treatment, the physical therapist stabilizes a certain part of the client's body with a hand or with his body, and his other hand offers very specific patterns of resistance while gripping one of the patient's extremities. Verbal instructions direct the patient as the therapist alternates between resistance and relaxation to activate reflexes that facilitate contraction as well as improve range of motion. Through this practice of contraction and relaxation and other isometric or slow-reversal exercises, the muscles can be relaxed and conditioned to function more flexibly. Vibration, massage, stroking, ice, heat, specific patterns of movement, postures, ultrasound, and electrostimulation may be used to enhance both voluntary and involuntary movement. Positions and postures are an integral part of the repatterning process, and once certain techniques are learned, they can be done without a practitioner. This therapy can easily be combined with other movement disciplines.
Contact: International PNF Association –
www.ipnfa.org

Postural Integration® (PI)
Postural Integration is devoted to releasing and organizing the layers of fascia that envelop the body's muscular system, while at the same time freeing the breath and emotions. Jack Painter developed PI in the late 1960s after years of exploring a variety of yoga and deep-massage techniques along with Acupuncture, Rolfing Structural Integration, Reichian therapies, and human psychology. Wilhelm Reich's work on body armor played a significant role in the creation of this integrative therapy. The armor represents internalized, unconscious, guarded feelings that show up as rigid tension held in various tissues of the body. Their presence creates habits, postures, and attitudes that have a limiting effect on the ability to develop true self-awareness and to deal creatively with life problems. This healing approach aims

to dissolve these often evasive restrictions in a deeply effective way.

Postural Integration is a step-by-step process that unifies body tissues, personal feelings, and self-awareness in order to harmonize physical movement. This systematic approach considers the needs of each individual and supports all forms of emotional expression. Because the body armor is often held deep within the layers of connective tissues and can easily avoid confrontation by shifting to new locations, this approach works progressively on releasing all layers of tissue. The whole program involves ten sessions that incorporate deep-tissue work, deep breathing, Gestalt therapy, regression work, meditation, movement awareness practices, techniques for good posture, and Acupressure into a healing process intended to help clients release ingrained habits and rigid postures that limit their potential. The first seven sessions focus on helping a recipient recognize and let go of the defensive armor held in fascia by manually working on the legs, pelvis, torso, arms, and head. The final three sessions help the client integrate a new, more truly expressive and harmonious sense of self.

Treatment sessions are divided into the three phases. The first involves mobilization methods for opening the different layers of the body-mind and improving the circulation of energy and feelings. This is followed by a process that helps the client release the subtle extensive defense patterns and deep resistance that exist on a cellular level. The final phase uses softer, flexible contact to provide the fuller integration that helps free the thoughts and feelings. Through this work, clients can understand and assimilate the changes they experience in a way that allows them to accept the old self while experiencing a new sense of the self that is more free and open.

The success of this therapy lies in the willingness of the client and the practitioner to work on many levels at the same time. During a session, the practitioner encourages the client to breathe more fully, explore physical movements, and freely express emotions or thoughts while the therapist manipulates layers of the fascia using the fingers, fists, knuckles, and elbows. Not only does this allow the body tissue to soften and become more malleable but it also permits the body to begin to open and find balance. When this opening occurs, the client's emotions can discover more creative ways of expression, often becoming free of old habitual patterns. Breathwork

is integral to the entire release process, since it is considered the key to strengthening inner vitality and power. The practitioner helps the client improve weak breathing habits by encouraging a deeper, balanced, spontaneous rhythm that enables a more significant physical, emotional, and energetic discharge during the exhalation.

Another part of Painter's therapy, called Energetic Integration® (EI), also represents a holistic approach to the body-mind connection that encourages a bond between the client and the practitioner. The process helps the client unite the tissues, breath, body movement, feelings, thoughts, and attitudes to provide more vitality and freedom. However, rather than systematically working on releasing the layers of fascia that envelop the body's muscular system, EI focuses on freeing and integrating the energy that is blocked within the recipient's body structure. It uses strategies that include hands-on work that allows the client's body-mind to melt away the bands of body armor and regulate the energy cycle. EI offers a sequence of individual sessions using breathwork and body awareness in an interactive way that enables the client's body defenses to become more open to a sense of wholeness. The practitioner, referred to as the integrator, also helps clients experience, interpret, and accept whatever they are holding within through personal dialogue in a supportive setting that allows them to discover the network of energy and feelings that can help reveal underlying aspects of themselves.

Contact: International Council of Bodymind Integration Trainers – www.icpit.info

PUSH Therapy

PUSH is a system of muscle therapy developed by Michael Takatsuno after he himself had significant experiences while studying with William Leigh, the founder of Zen Therapy. With further knowledge gained from studies in physical therapy and insights acquired from his own practice of Tai Chi, Takatsuno went on to establish PUSH as an alternative-medicine therapy to reduce pain and chronic soft-tissue muscle tension. PUSH stands for "power under soft hands," and it is used to address chronic tension that manifests particularly in the back, neck, and shoulders. This form of therapy is designed to include the client as an active participant who then becomes more self-aware and able to recognize the body's core and its alignment. PUSH uses a soft-pressure stimulation technique to release tension, get the blood flowing, and increase range of motion. Therapists are trained to adopt a relaxed stance (as in Tai Chi) while practicing this bodywork so that they can provide a more effective treatment while not straining themselves. A concept called the hanging spine, in which all the major joints are lined up, is an integral part of the therapy. Rather than using typical stretching techniques, the therapy proposes that chronic pain is better eliminated when the muscles rest without tension.

The treatment begins with body readings to assess tension and misalignments in the client's body. Then very brief palpations using light fingertip pressure are employed to identify the areas in need of treatment and to explore the superficial layers of tissue. The therapist proceeds by using the elbow or a handheld tool to stimulate problem areas with stationary pressure. The practitioner's hands apply soft pressure that sinks into the tissue until reaching a sensitive layer that indicates tension. The tissue is then engaged in a relaxed way without further pressure so that a release will occur. Practitioners may also employ special pressure-point tools during the treatment. Throughout the session, the practitioner continually communicates with the client, helping the recipient better understand the effects of tension and the way that the stimulation of muscles is creating a fully relaxed state. At the halfway point, when one side of the body has been treated, there is a rest period in which the practitioner can take a body reading and the client can observe changes and gain further insight into the effect of the treatment. Work then continues on the other side of the body and concludes with another body reading. After a few sessions, clients are taught self-treatment techniques using special tools or rollers and are encouraged to practice various posture exercises that will help sustain the effects of the treatment.
Contact: www.pushtherapy.com

Rolfing® Structural Integration (SI)

Beginning in the early 1920s, Dr. Ida Rolf was motivated, in part by her search for solutions to her own health problems, to study and experiment extensively with many systems of healing and types of manipulation. She recognized that imbalances in structure caused by detrimental life experiences put demands on the extensive network of soft tissue in the muscles, fascia, tendons, and ligaments, since the natural tendency of the body is to compensate for these imbalances in ways that distort the body. She soon became a leader in the effort to find methods by which individuals could free up their physical structure and recover their optimal capacity for easy movement by releasing their habitual constricted patterns. Looking closely at the effects of gravity and the complexity of the web of fascia that envelops and holds the body together, Rolf developed a comprehensive system of soft-tissue manipulation and movement education that affects the body's structure and improves its long-term functioning. Rather than treating specific symptoms, SI reduces compensations; provides a remedy for poor posture by improving alignment, flexibility, and resilience; and helps a person take control of physical, emotional, and spiritual health. Its effects can assist in rehabilitation from injury and the alleviation of pain. By 1971, the Rolf Institute of Structural Integration had been formed in Boulder, Colorado, and there are now regional offices in various countries around the world.

A wide range of holistic techniques are used to carry out the healing process. Initially, the therapist uses observation and gentle palpations to determine the location of imbalances in the tissues. Then, with the client lying on the table, the practitioner manipulates all the layers of fascia (the network of connective tissue that gives muscles their shape and holds bones in position). In this way, the body's restrictive holding patterns can be released as alignment and balance is improved. The manipulations can soften and lengthen the fascia and free adhesions with both slowly delivered, firm pressure and gliding strokes over fascial surfaces. Sometimes a client is directed to sit and hold a certain position on a special bench while the practitioner carries out certain manipulations. The bench allows the Rolfer to address the pelvis and spine from a different perspective, in relation to gravity, than when lying on a table.

Although at one time Rolfing Structural Integration was known as a painful form of bodywork, nowadays the amount of deep pressure applied during the treatment is more sensitive to the client's limits of tolerance, and communication is kept open between the practitioner and the client for good feedback throughout the session. However, if the existing imbalances or holding patterns are extensive, deeper and more sustained pressure may be required to release the distortions. As with any form of bodywork, the intensity of the physical experience and the emotions it brings up can reflect the effectiveness of the treatment and is often transitory.

A systematic series of ten sessions to optimize structure and function is the standard practice in Rolfing Structural Integration. Each session focuses on releasing restrictions held in the body and builds upon the previous one as deeper aspects of the body are worked on. Changes produced in one session open the possibility of deeper, more extensive changes in the next. The initial three sessions, working in concert with the breath, strive to loosen and balance surface layers of the connective tissue. Sessions four through seven examine the body's deeper core between the base of the pelvis and the top of the head. The final three sessions focus on integrating all of the previous work in a way that encourages smooth movement and natural coordination. The exact protocol with each session is orchestrated by the practitioner in a way that is unique for each individual.

The movement education component of Rolfing SI is Rolf Movement® Integration (RMI), developed to help identify poor movement patterns that create strain and to make the client aware of solutions that provide more balance and symmetry. Rolf Movement Integration may be integrated within Rolfing sessions, or it can be taught through a series of dedicated sessions to enhance higher levels of self-awareness and a sense of unity within the body. This process may explore basic movement activities, such as breathing, walking, or standing; focus on more specialized activities, such as desk work, exercise, sports, or carpentry; or concentrate on very subtle anatomical movements, such as the flexibility of each vertebrae or improving functionality of specific muscle usage.
Contact: The Rolf Institute – www.rolf.org

Rossiter System®

This approach to healing is designed to provide direct, quick, powerful, and effective pain relief through the systematic application of bodywork in conjunction with stretching coached by the practitioner. It was developed in the 1980s by Richard Rossiter as a way of allowing deeper penetration of the body tissues to release tension. Rossiter created this system after he became disappointed in the length of time it took for Rolfing bodywork to effectively relieve significant physical disorders and injuries suffered by factory workers. A key component of this therapy is giving clients the responsibility of actively communicating with their bodies and freeing themselves from pain by stretching it away while the practitioner coaches, encourages, and guides them. The

stretching techniques work to loosen all of the connective tissue to restore mobility and improve circulation.

The Rossiter System incorporates elements of several bodywork modalities such as Deep Tissue Massage and Myofascial Release. Many smooth and easy stretching techniques are applied in a specific way to each part of the client's body, and they are accomplished while the client lies fully clothed on a floor mat or positioned on a padded chair. The therapist uses the feet to anchor the client's tissues in place while calling for specific, directed stretches. This partnership allows deeper penetration and the possibility of affecting greater areas of tissue in shorter periods of time. The client is considered the person in charge, whose job is to hunt for pain or stiffness, follow it, and stretch it away. The practitioner, with knowledge of anatomy, incorporates many techniques that make use of weight, body locks, and repetitive movement, while the client, as an active participant in the recovery process, provides feedback and input. This system of healing is not for those who want only a relaxing massage but is intended for people who are motivated to take charge of their own health care and fitness.
Contact: www.therossitersystem.com

Salsa Massage

If you like lively music with your bodywork, this type of massage is the one for you, since it is carried out to the rhythms of salsa. Its roots are probably in parts of West and Central Africa, where the practice of vigorous body beating helped community members limber up before the day's work, but its music is Caribbean. It first appeared in the United States in the 1950s with the arrival of Puerto Rican and Cuban immigrants. Salsa Massage, also known as Cuban Massage, is not a modality in itself but a way in which a practitioner of any modality can enliven a session. All movements are done to the rhythm of the music, and the recipient is encouraged to gently rock the body and flex the muscles. The recipient is encouraged to feel the music and entrain with its beat as it pumps energy through the body.
Contact: www.salsa2spa.com

Sensory Reeducation

A therapeutic program originally created by Charlotte Selver, the developer of Sensory Awareness and one of the founders of the Esalen Institute, Sensory Reeducation uses sensory stimulation and education to help individuals with various forms of sensory loss or impairment recover function, prevent further damage, or learn to live better with their conditions. Sensory impairment is often caused by damage to the central nervous system caused by nerve damage, aneurysm, stroke, or nerve impingements and can also show up as sensations of numbness, tingling, or burning after surgery or chemotherapy. Sensory Reeducation can be administered on its own as a distinct therapy or as part of a wider therapeutic program.

This form of therapy begins with a complete examination and analysis of the client's medical history and current conditions, taking into account any possible contraindications before a treatment plan is implemented. The recipient is constantly monitored for further damage as a variety of therapeutic techniques are employed. They include massage, the application of pressure, vibrational therapy, biofeedback, electrical stimulation, stroking the skin with a textured object to produce friction, and the use of special modified instruments. In addition to addressing the loss of feeling caused by nerve damage, Sensory Reeducation can deal with other forms of impairment, such as a field of vision that has been compromised by a stroke. In addition to retraining neural pathways in order to restore sensory perception, the educational component of the modality recruits previously unused neural connections to take over for the damaged pathways The reeducation process also deals with hypersensitivities represented by the patient's overreaction to mild stimulation. The patient may also be taught to either compensate for a disability until full rehabilitation is achieved or to adapt if full rehabilitation is not possible. The complete process of rehabilitation often includes a series of follow-up examinations to record and maintain progress.
Contact: www.returntooursenses.com

Soft Tissue Release (STR)

Once known as the Taws Method, this form of treatment was developed in England by sports rehabilitation therapist Stuart Taws, who worked with track teams and Olympic athletes. He now conducts training sessions and practices in the United States. This hands-on therapy is a form of sports rehabilitation that was developed to help sprinters and other athletes recover from injuries by dealing directly with soft-tissue dysfunction, nerve entrapment, and scar tissue. Based on European osteopathic techniques, STR is a structural mobilization treatment that has also been used successfully for chronic back pain, carpal tunnel syndrome, and whiplash injuries. Recent developments with simple techniques based on years of research directed at the fast-responding central nervous system show promise for the treatment of fibromyalgia patients. The therapy is closely related to some forms of craniosacral bodywork and recognizes that long-term pain conditions often have little to do with the site of the original injury.

Once the location of the injury is defined, the client is placed in a position from which the muscle can be extended in a specifically determined direction or plane, and the practitioner applies pinpoint pressure directly to the affected tissue or along a specific line of injury. A variety of gentle techniques are directed at irritated nerve endings to release pain. The client is then given verbal information about the condition of the muscles. The flowing motions of this pain-release process have been modified over the years so that they are performed with no discomfort to the recipient. This method of treating soft tissue can also be incorporated into many different types of manual therapy.
Contact: www.softtissuerelease.com

Soma Neuromuscular Integration

Soma Neuromuscular Integration, also known as Soma Bodywork or Soma Veda Therapy, evolved out of Ida Rolf's work through refinements made by Bill and Ellen Williams. They expanded Rolf's original practice to create a holistic form of therapy that synthesizes elements of Rolfing Structural Integration, Thai Yoga Bodywork, Medical Massage, yogic practices, and Chinese and Native American healing practices. A Soma Veda Institute was founded in 1978 to carry on the teachings of this therapeutic practice. The Williams refined Rolfing into less intrusive ways of entering and manipulating the myofascial tissue to remove blockages, induce integrated changes within the body, and rebalance the nervous system. A series of ten sessions, following the same sequence as in Rolfing, are usually part of this form of deep-tissue therapy. However, Soma Neuromuscular Integration incorporates additional elements such as autogenic relaxation training, a blockage-removing muscle massage technique, movement education, and dialogue, along with personal record keeping through journals, photographs, and videos.

The intention is to elevate the client's self-awareness by inducing physical, emotional, and perceptual changes. The focus is on the body's core brain, a source of chi energy located in the abdomen. A technique based on the three-brain theory is used to provide a way to understand the activity of the nervous system and human consciousness. A form of holographic body reading may be used to restore circulation.

Contact: Soma Institute of Neuromuscular
Integration – www.soma-institute.org

Sports Massage

Although its name implies that this is a massage is intended for professional athletes, performers, and dancers either before or after a physical workout, this form of bodywork is suitable for anyone who wants to enhance physical performance. The use of massage to improve or restore muscular ability has been around since the time when Greeks and Romans included it as part of their Olympic training. They recognized that sports massage was useful in preparing athletes for action, as well as a way to relieve fatigue and pain afterwards. Although this specialized form of massage had not been a common component of therapeutic bodywork, Jack Meagher was instrumental during the 1960s in promoting its use in today's sports training.

These days, Sports Massage is an integral part of fitness training, helping a person function at the optimal level while reducing the strain and discomfort associated with intense physical activity. Performance is improved and the chances of injury are reduced by increasing muscle strength and flexibility through resistance work and stretches that improve range of motion. Sports Massage is often used to reduce the pain, tension, and swelling that result from an injury; to prevent the formation of adhesions; to enhance recovery; and to allow a speedy return to further physical activity. Besides being restorative, it is beneficial in calming the nerves and promoting better awareness of how to avoid further injuries that might be caused by overuse or excessive straining.

Although some of its techniques are similar to those strokes found in Swedish Massage, the bodywork is done in a more precise and deeper way with greater use of compression and direct pressure applied to specific injured areas or muscle constrictions. Friction strokes done across the fiber are employed to separate layers of tissue, and joint and body mobilization techniques

are used to promote flexibility and structural balance. Other techniques include Proprioceptive Neuromuscular Facilitation, the Muscle Energy Technique, Active Release Techniques, and muscle squeezing. Which technique is used will depend on the particular needs of the recipient and whether it is done as a warm-up or after an event. Before participating in an athletic event, the massage can either be like a vigorous workout or a light massage done with manipulations such as light jiggling, compression, and stretching to loosen and stimulate specific muscles and warm up the body. Treatments after a competition or a period of extensive physical exertion often use longer, slower, and more sedating strokes to relax cramps, unwind the muscles, flush out metabolic waste from muscle tissue, and restore normal muscle tone. Sports Massage is often combined with cryotherapy (the use of ice) and other forms of hydrotherapy.

Contact: Jack Meagher Institute
of Sports Therapy –
www.jackmeagherinstitute.com

Strain & Counterstrain Technique

The Strain & Counterstrain Technique, also known as Positional Release Therapy (PRT), is a type of treatment that was developed by osteopath Lawrence Jones during the 1950s to treat a variety of neuromuscular issues. In 1988, the Jones Institute was formed to offer Positional Release Therapy seminars for health care professionals throughout the United States.

Strain & Counterstrain is used to restore pain-free movement by reducing tenderness in the soft tissues, decreasing protective muscle spasms, and alleviating dysfunction in the joints and musculoskeletal system, as well as enhancing the activity of the nervous system. This type of manual soft-tissue therapy is quite gentle and easy on the body. PRT has been used to effectively treat a variety of chronic physical conditions and is often incorporated into other modalities in which the body is manipulated.

After the initial assessment of painful trigger points and the identification of the related dysfunctional muscles, the technique involves placing the body or limbs in positions that just exceed the recipient's comfort zone to compress the muscles and relax the reflexes that produce muscle spasms. Light digital pressure is applied to the trigger points until the pain subsides. The pressure is usually applied for around a minute to relax the muscle, thereby normalizing the motion of the joint. Depending on the location of the source of pain, the client is sometimes asked to bend or twist into another position for further treatment. Afterward, the client is returned to a neutral position and reexamined for signs of improvement. The gentleness of this technique makes it appropriate for infants, fragile people, and the elderly. The recipient is also instructed in the appropriate home stretching techniques that will be most beneficial for the affected areas of the body.

Contact: Jones Institute – www.jonesinstitute.com

Structural Energetic Therapy® (SET)

Rather than trying to manage pain, SET addresses the physical conditions responsible for pain by using specific soft-tissue protocols and techniques that release distortion in the cranium's core to correct physical imbalances or misalignments and reduce chronic and acute pain and dysfunction. This form of therapy was developed in the late 1970s by Don McCann and since then has been continually evolving and expanding its scope. It integrates cranial structural techniques with Acupressure, Applied Kinesiology and muscle testing, myofascial unwinding, myofascial restructuring, deep-tissue work, methods of emotional energy release, postural analysis, and techniques to release scar tissue and adhesions. Its aim is to treat specific needs and problems that relate to particular injuries and structural disorders. It also works to release and unwind core distortion patterns, both cranial and structural, so that a balanced weight-bearing pelvis will support the entire spine.

After an initial analysis to determine what measures are most appropriate for treating the client, a specific sequence of techniques is employed. First the therapist addresses the primary area of discomfort using specific protocols and then releases any restrictions that cause imbalances in other areas of the body that inhibit proper body alignment. Though it often focuses on problems associated with the spine, SET has been effective in treating multiple conditions in the upper and lower body and is considered both a primary and adjunct therapy that complements other standard chiropractic and medical treatments.

Contact: www.structuralenergetictherapy.com

Swedish Massage

When people think of massage, Swedish Massage is what most often comes to mind. This is because it has been recognized for many decades as the foundation of the Western forms of hands-on bodywork most often used today. However, it was originally created as a synthesis of manual manipulations, medical gymnastics, and some Eastern bodywork traditions. Swedish Massage was first formulated and promoted in part by both Pir Heinrik Ling and the Dutch physician Dr. Johann Mezger during the early to mid-1800s. However, there is some debate about who actually did what. This therapeutic form of bodywork is primarily used to improve a person's structure and ability to function through techniques that relax, stimulate, or rehabilitate the body. The practitioner's hands are applied to the body's soft connective tissue structure with an assortment of manipulations and strokes that are intended to induce relaxation, reduce stress, increase range of motion, restore flexibility, improve joint mobility, and energize the body by stimulating circulation.

A treatment session combines hand movements and a number of different rhythmic strokes performed in a variety of ways with different parts of the hands in order to provide specific benefits. Effleurage is the use of smooth, gliding strokes carried out with varying degrees of rhythmic pressure by the palms, thumbs, fingers, or forearms; it warms the tissues, soothes the muscles, improves circulation, and relaxes the body. These strokes are generally directed toward the heart to stimulate blood flow. Friction and rubbing with circular, transverse, or linear strokes is often employed to loosen the joints and tendons. Some specific deep rubbing strokes, known as cyriax, use cross-fiber friction movements on the muscles to free them from adhesions. A series of rapid tapotements (percussive movements) that include tapping, pummeling, hacking, beating, cupping, and plucking the skin and muscles may be used to stimulate and loosen underlying tissue, but they are used judiciously to avoid damage to nerves and muscles. Petrissage, or kneading, involves the more vigorous, deep, rhythmic act of actually picking up the muscles and wringing, squeezing, pressing, and rolling them. This is done to improve blood circulation, flush out toxins, and stimulate nerve endings. Rapid vibrating movements stimulate nerves and release tightness in the muscles. A rhythmic pumping movement known as compression also helps relax the muscles and improve circulation. Passive exercising of the recipient's limbs, accomplished by manually rotating, flexing, and extending them, is used to improve range of motion. All of these techniques help flush lactic acid and other metabolic wastes out of the tissues. Swedish bodywork can not only reduce pain, stiffness and tension but also stimulate the skin and nerves while relaxing them. Except when using techniques to free adhesions or scar tissue, oils or non-sticky lotions or creams are commonly used to reduce skin friction and allow the strokes to be more smooth and flowing.

Variations of Swedish Massage using other techniques have been developed over the years. The Lifestream Massage found in California uses a deeper form of tissue release work, whereas styles such as Esalen Massage have a more flowing, nurturing approach. More clinical approaches are found in both Sports and Medical Massage.

Contact: Swedish Institute College of Health
Sciences – www.swedishinstitute.edu

Trigger Point Release Therapy / Myotherapy

Trigger points are distinct knots or taut bands of contracted fibers within muscles or muscle groups that cause myofascial pain to spread to the surrounding tissue and joints as the contracted muscles pull on tendons and ligaments. These trigger points can be activated by a variety of systemic conditions, including overuse, physical injuries, strains, infections, allergies, stress, and psychological distress. They may lie dormant for years as latent trigger points until switched on by pressure or strain. Pain can also radiate (be referred) to more distant places in the body along nerve pathways, and secondary and satellite trigger points can be activated when the primary point is palpated. When muscles are working normally, they exhibit the capacity to respond to stimuli and to contract and extend in a balanced way. But if trigger points have been activated, the muscles will not return to their normal position after a contraction. The symptoms of the dysfunction can be pain, weakness, or restrictions in mobility. There are more than 600 potential trigger points in the human body, and their pain and referral patterns are the same in most people. This has allowed therapists to create trigger-point maps that can be used in treating these points.

The therapy that has evolved over the years offers a precise neuromuscular treatment for the relief of acute or chronic muscle pain that often presents itself as spasms and cramping. Dr. Janet Travell pioneered the practice of Trigger Point Release Therapy in the 1940s after these points were first identified in Europe. Dr. Travell and later Dr. David Simons both undertook research that revealed much about the causal relationship between chronic pain and its source. Originally, injections of a saline solution were used to treat these points. In fact, Dr. Travell used injections to treat President John F. Kennedy's back pain while she was the White House physician. At that time, assisted stretching along with cooling sprays were also employed as part of the treatment.

Further development of this therapy came about in 1976 when physical therapist Bonnie Prudden began using manual pressure to release trigger points. Over the next decade, she developed a method known as Myotherapy, the umbrella system under which Trigger Point Release is now found. Myotherapy is a form of treatment that applies pressure on the painful points that may be triggering pain in other areas of the body. The complete therapy can call on a variety of bodywork methods such as Deep Tissue Massage, Myofascial Release, Proprioceptive Neuromuscular Facilitation stretching exercises, joint mobilization, electrostimulation, heat therapies, Cryotherapy, and some ancient healing methods. The primary aim of this therapy is to seek out sensitive trigger points and apply specific techniques to deactivate them in order to restore full muscle length and strength. However, sustained relief also requires resolution of the factors that caused the problem.

A key part of a Trigger Point Release session is encouraging the client to be personally responsible by communicating fully with the therapist. During a session, specific palpation techniques are used to identify trigger points within a muscle. Then these points are treated with intense, sustained pressure and compression applied by fingers, knuckles, elbows, or specially designed tools intended to prevent stress on the practitioner's body. The goal of the treatment is to break up cycles of spasm or pain and reeducate the muscles in order to return them to normal functioning. The practitioner needs to apply sufficient pressure on these points to release their chronic condition by interrupting the stress reflex. Although the amount of pressure may be uncomfortable, it should not be so strong that the muscle contracts further to protect itself. Pressure is commonly held on each point until the recipient feels the soreness dissipate, typically within five to eight seconds.

After compression, the practitioner gently stretches and manipulates the surrounding muscle tissue to further help reduce local constrictions, free the nerves, relax the muscles, and prevent further stress from reactivating the trigger points. These manipulations include lengthening strokes, stretching, spreading, and finger, knuckle, and elbow pressing. Friction strokes are also used to release any tight muscle bands that are associated with the trigger points. These help warm up the muscles, thus improving circulation and the removal of waste from the body. As the muscles relax into a natural extended position, the bones can also return to their correct position, and the body will be in proper alignment. The specific corrective measures taken vary with each practitioner, and sometimes heat or a jet of water may be used to passively stretch the muscles or an anesthetic agent may be injected into the trigger point. Trigger Point Release Therapy can also include the use of a tapping technique, in which a tennis ball is applied over sensitive spots on the spine that may align with acupressure points. In all cases, the goal of this corrective therapy is to prevent the problems from recurring. At the end of a treatment, the client is instructed in corrective self-help exercises and stretching techniques that can be practiced at home as part of a pain-management program. Since a period of muscle soreness can exist for a time after a treatment, a nice hot bath is considered a good follow-up indulgence if any pains persist. Although this form of therapy does not specifically address the release of trauma, individuals who hold significant emotional issues in their tissues may very well realize a beneficial emotional release.
Contact: American Institute of Myofascial Studies –
www.aims-llc.org or National Association of
Myofascial Trigger Point Therapists –
www.myofascialtherapy.org

Yamuna® Body Logic

Yamuna Body Logic is a form of physiotherapy that was developed in the United States by yoga teacher Yamuna Zake, who combined yoga postures with elements of Chiropractic, Orthopedics, and Acupuncture.

Its goal is to treat a wide range of musculoskeletal conditions through soft-tissue work, joint mobilization, and other forms of manipulation to relieve the whole body of a variety of limiting physical conditions or injury-related issues. Because treating all the dysfunctions at one time enhances the possibility of immediate optimal body movement, this approach is appreciated by dancers and athletes. Instead of placing attention on fascia to provide structural integrity, the focus of Body Logic is on providing body realignment by releasing muscles at their point of origin, the place where they attach to the bones. Body Logic deals with a wide range of concerns by helping remove restrictions, elongate muscles, and create space in the body, especially in the spine, chest, pelvis, knee joints, ankles, and feet. The "logic" of this practice lies in the recognition that muscles have an instinctive memory that the practitioner can work with to modify negative holding patterns. When the body remembers how it feels to move effortlessly, it can rapidly and naturally make the proper corrections.

A session starts with the practitioner stretching the recipient's body while he is standing in order to determine where limitations exist; the remainder of the bodywork is done with the client lying on a padded floor. Every part of the body receives attention. The treatment uses traction on the joints to create a space that helps elongate the muscles, and joint rotations are done without force in every possible position to help the muscles loosen and function better. Practitioners use their bodies for leverage while applying a hand hold, elbow line tracing, or thigh hook. Although the work focuses on physical structure, it pays great attention to the individual's energetic nature by incorporating chakra and spinal energy-channel work, and the whole practice is carried out in a close and intimate way. Zake also created Yamuna Body Rolling, a self-help outgrowth of this therapy, in which small balls are used in an exercise program to develop balance and control in the core muscles. (See more in Chapter 11.) In addition, she developed a related therapy called Foot Fitness.
Contact: www.yamunabodyrolling.com

II. Functional Reeducation Therapies

A well-balanced sailboat with her sails set right can perform effortlessly and hold a true course with no unnecessary strain on the helm or the hull. Likewise, when the human body is balanced, aligned, and in harmony, it functions to its optimum potential, and all movements are fluid and without stress. Although the body may encounter conditions along the voyage of life that throw it off course, staying properly aligned will allow the best corrections under the circumstances to be made. But when experiences come along that disrupt that balance in a more significant way, extra adjustments may be necessary to handle the winds of change that always seem to occur. Movement is a language in itself, and it's one that all can speak. An open, balanced, expressive body can communicate so much and allows us to express ourselves without words. When sailing around the world, I visited many countries whose words I could not speak or understand. However, I was amazed at how well I could communicate with others through body movement. In the Spanish-speaking country of Costa Rica, my first mate and I went on a jungle trek to find some indigenous animal life. We had heard there were armadillos in the area, and since we had never seen one in the wild, we stopped and tried to ask a local farmer where we might find one. Not knowing the correct words to use, I tried to express what an armadillo was through pantomime, which is really just the orchestration of body movements. The farmer enjoyed my antics so much that he decided to be our guide. Although we never found an armadillo, we did get to see a wonderful waterfall and spend the afternoon with a new friend.

If you have ever seen a spinner dolphin jump high into the air and do a dance of flips, twists, and turns before plunging back into the sea, you will never forget it, for this joyful display of movement is amazing to watch. Just as with animals, the way people's bodies move can reveal much about the way they feel and think about themselves and the world around them. Sometimes the way a stranger moves his body can bring things to light in an obvious way; a limp or hunched posture can indicate some form of dysfunction. However, many times the physical indications of a particular condition are subtle; when we call someone "uptight," we are probably responding to attitude and energy reflected in the body. We often use these kinds of visual perceptions to gain some insight into a new acquaintance. Only by recognizing how our own feelings and conditions are reflected in our movements can we understand how we present ourselves to the world. This also helps us comprehend the body language of others. Although some of these therapies don't work directly with enhancing this kind of self-awareness, it is really the essence of what these modalities attempt to provide.

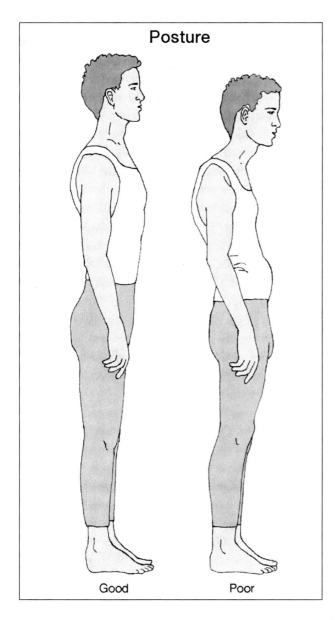

Posture

Good   Poor

The bodywork therapies in this section represent various ways the human body can be returned to optimal movement and functioning, and many aim to accomplish this by increasing self-awareness and sensory perception. These somatic therapies primarily focus on movement, mobilization, adjustments, structural integration, and manipulations of the body that will correct physical dysfunctions and improve balance or alignment. These therapies often incorporate some form of movement reeducation in order to transform old habits or patterns of movement that no longer benefit the client; active client participation is often key to the process in these kinds of treatment. Most movement therapies incorporate little actual massage, although some do use forms of manipulation in conjunction with extensive movement of body parts. Because the network of fascia is so interconnected with physical functioning and body structure, myofascial release work and tissue mobilization techniques are often employed to enhance proper alignment, balance, range of motion, and neuromuscular coordination. Some of these movement therapies also work with energy to relieve tension, alleviate physiological dysfunctions or holding patterns, and provide a new sense of ease and well-being. Others incorporate verbal coaching, sensory awareness, breathwork, fitness training, stretching techniques, and a variety of structural manipulation techniques. Although many of these modalities are intended to provide ways of managing existing pain or correcting functional issues, all are useful for people wishing to increase their level of fitness, stamina, physical performance, flexibility, and energetic potential.

Alexander Technique

The Alexander Technique takes its name from Frederick Alexander, an Australian who lived from 1869 to 1955. A Shakespearean recitalist in the days before electronic amplification, he began to have problems with his voice that interfered with his livelihood. After doctors could not find anything wrong with his vocal mechanism or ease his difficulties, Alexander reasoned that the cause must have to do with how he was using his voice. After many years of self-observation and investigation, he found that a pattern of habitual physical reaction lay at the heart of his troubles. Once he was able to eliminate those habitual patterns of tension, he not only stopped having problems with his voice but also experienced improvements in his posture, breathing, and overall coordination. Others in his community saw the changes he experienced and requested his assistance, so he began to teach what he had discovered to other actors, singers, and those interested in public speaking.

Alexander discovered from within himself what's known about the functioning of all mammals: the relationship of the head, neck, and back affects the general integration and coordination of the whole body. Any restrictions in that relationship interfere with posture, balance, breathing, movement, and overall functioning, and often results in stiffness and pain. A leading factor contributing to musculoskeletal pain (and often its underlying cause) is unrecognized patterns of excess tension. Because what he had learned is basic to overall functioning, he was able to help people with various other problems as well. As interest in his method grew, he designed a training program to enable people to teach it to others. The Alexander Technique is effective because it teaches how to recognize and unlearn these habitual patterns.

The Alexander Technique deals with common habitual patterns of tension by making adjustments that improve coordination and posture, thereby helping the client become aware of how the body is being held; how to recognize conditioned patterns of movement and stop them before they begin; and how to consciously break up old habits and institute healthier ways of moving. An important component of reaching this state of ease is work that lifts the head, lengthens the neck, and opens the back. Rather than being a form of bodywork or an exercise program, the Alexander Technique is a method of reeducating the neuromuscular system. It is taught through a series of lessons, the goal of which is the integration of principles that enable improved coordination to become second nature.

Direct experience is the cornerstone of the Alexander Technique. Overcoming self-limiting habits is the first step, and a typical sessions incorporates the gentle use of hands and verbal coaching to guide the recipient in movements that will break up old patterns of holding and stress that have built up in the muscles over the years. Using simple activities such as sitting, standing, bending, and walking, the teacher uses verbal instructions and hands-on guidance to enable people to experience movement free of excess effort and tension. Participants are then led through a process that demonstrates what a new pattern of movement would feel like. This process enhances movement awareness and teaches the recipient to consciously choose movements rather than just react to stimuli. When new ways of effortless movement are experienced and understood, the old ways lose their appeal and can be more easily abandoned.

The Alexander Technique is well known among performers and is taught in music and drama programs worldwide. In addition to musicians, actors, and dancers, it's used by athletes to improve performance in such sports as golfing, skiing, tennis, and running.
Contact: American Society for the Alexander
Technique – www.amsatonline.org

Aston Kinetics®

In 1968, Dr. Ida Rolf asked American Judith Aston to create a movement program. In 1970, Aston created Aston-Patterning®, now entitled Aston Kinetics, as a gentler alternative to Ida Rolf's Structural Integration therapy. A former movement educator for dancers, athletes, and actors, Aston had herself found Rolf's work to be of great benefit, but she saw proper alignment from a different perspective and went on to develop an integrated system that combines bodywork, movement coaching, ergonomics, and a fitness training program. Rather than Rolf's method of shaping all bodies into linear symmetry, her Aston Paradigm proposes that there is no ideal body type and that asymmetrical differences must be approached by considering necessary and unnecessary tension. Balance and alignment along with efficient patterns of dynamic movement are the key principles of this therapy. In addition, Aston's work includes fitness training that involves a comprehensive evaluation process along with a trio of gentle, hands-on techniques that address function and structure, especially patterns that are accumulated in daily activities and stored through emotional experience.

Integral to Aston Kinetics is the use of three-dimensional spiral patterns. The first technique is a specialized form of Swedish Massage that uses this pattern in surface-to-bone spiral strokes to release muscle tension and holding patterns. The next, Myokinetics, consists of a form of myofascial release work that uses spiral stretch and release strokes to liberate holding patterns in the soft tissue. The last method is Arthrokinetics, which is the deepest work, affecting joints, bones, and the junctures of tissue planes by using spiral patterns

along the bone and at joint surfaces. The massage treatment has no set series of procedures, and each session is geared to the needs of the individual. Aston Kinetics makes new movement options available, and sessions are followed with a Neurokinetics movement education lesson. This educational component is a part of Aston Fitness therapy in which manual techniques and exercises, which include vertical and horizontal loosening, toning, stretching and cardiovascular fitness, are used to create space in the body structure and to sustain positive changes.
Contact: Aston Kinetics – www.astonkinetics.com

Body Mind Centering® (BMC)

BMC is an approach to movement education that stimulates self-discovery through exploring the body's systems and enhancing awareness of movement patterns that were developed during infancy or childhood. It allows people to experience an intimate connection with their inner anatomies so that they can learn how the mind expresses itself through the body in motion. This approach was developed by occupational movement therapist Bonnie Cohen after extensive study and practice of Aikido, Zen, Occupational Therapy, Laban Movement Analysis, yoga, dance therapy, neurodevelopmental therapy, and a variety of both Eastern and Western forms of bodywork. Her early life experiences with circus performers also affected her knowledge of body movement.

BMC is based on the idea that the body is an instrument through which the mind is expressed, and its aim is to allow a more intimate experience of the body itself by stimulating deeper sensory awareness of internal organs, tissues, and body systems. The recipient is then invited to initiate all movement from this state of expanded awareness. Each part or system of the body is associated with a particular state of mind and its attendant feelings, expressions, thoughts, intuitions, expressions, or nervous energy. When the quality of its movement is altered, beneficial physiological, psychological, or spiritual changes are created in the whole being. Many habit patterns used for survival since early childhood and held deep in the body can be transformed in this way.

The practice combines hands-on bodywork, dialogue, behavior repatterning, guided imagery, yoga, music, dance, guided movements, art, psychotherapy, and elements of Aikido, along with the use of playful props such as large balls and metal bands, into a session that is customized and tailored to the needs of the individual. The practitioner uses physical contact to inspire individuals to make a shift into more thoughtful patterns of movement. When participants find a gentler, more flowing, and highly self-resonating way of moving efficiently, they can drop limiting patterns, find new strength and flexibility, and embody their fullest potential.

Contact: Body-Mind Centering Association Inc. – www.bodymindcentering.com

Dynamic Embodiment™ (DE-SMTT)

A form of somatic education and movement therapy training created by Dr. Martha Eddy, Dynamic Embodiment was devised to help individuals, especially dancers and movement therapists, relieve stress, expand body awareness, find ways to enhance expressiveness, improve physical movement, and balance the body with the psyche. Elements of Laban Movement Analysis and Body-Mind Centering are integrated into the process. The approach is very interactive and employs a variety of touch techniques, movements, and verbal directions to teach participants how to access the wisdom of the body. As a therapeutic method, Dynamic Embodiment is appropriate for working with infants, children, health care providers, cancer patients, and individuals who have lost touch with their bodies.

The practice depends on the therapist's keen observation skills and sensitive support and on the willingness of the recipient to explore different possibilities of behavior. Once trust is established, client and therapist work together to set goals. After limiting patterns of behavior are identified, a sequence of movements (known as EddyWorks), clear verbal and nonverbal communication, creative relaxation methods, expressive movement exercises, improvisations, and guided exploration of the breath are used as needed to help each individual client become more embodied and self-aware. The personal insight and self-acceptance gained through the process can create a lifestyle in which the body and mind work together to empower the individual.

Contact: www.movingoncenter.org/DynamicSMTT/

Eutony®

Eutony is an educational process designed to increase sensory awareness and develop mind-body consciousness. It is based on the principle that there is constant interaction between muscle tone and psychological activity. By releasing muscle tension and replacing it with flexibility, a more creative and spontaneous response to the physical, emotional, and intellectual demands and stimuli of life can be found. Since muscle tone can also affect the breath, it is essential to work with the inner anatomy in a way that resolves existing restrictions without interfering with the natural rhythm of the breath.

Eutony was created in Germany during the 1930s by Gerda Alexander, who had been teaching a system of self-analysis using movement and music called Eurhythmic Education. In Eutony, however, the learning process focuses on resolving musculoskeletal disorders and conditions caused by disease or injury. Intended as a method that balances tension through relaxation, Eutony re-educates the sensory motor system to improve body alignment and allow free movement. As an instructor guides participants through a variety of exercises, they learn to perceive and adjust the inner anatomy by observing how the muscles and bones feel both at rest and when moving. Experiencing the feeling of muscles moving over bone can release deep-seated tensions and lead to a more aligned, balanced, and grounded state of being. Many of the exercises are done while participants lie on a floor mat, and some include work with rubber balls. Participants are encouraged to take personal responsibility for developing the self-awareness that will lead to their being fully engaged in sensing and feeling themselves. Although there is no applied touch therapy, participants often touch parts of the body to enhance embodied awareness. Each class is unique and tailored to the needs of the individuals participating. In addition to group classes that often include partner work, it is also possible to receive a private lesson that includes some hands-on therapy.

Contact: www.thinkbody.co.uk/seminars/
Eutony-Gerda-Alexander.pdf or
www.selfholistichealing.com/eutony.html

Feldenkrais Method® of Somatic Education

The Feldenkrais Method of Somatic Education is a comprehensive approach to movement reeducation designed to restore and integrate optimal functioning through a process of releasing the compulsive, repetitive, or limiting habit patterns of movement and behavior that have become fixed unconsciously over a lifetime.

This approach of awareness through movement was developed by Moshe Feldenkrais, a Polish-born Russian engineer and judo master, during the mid-1900s. In order to avoid surgery on a knee injury that occurred while playing soccer, Feldenkrais studied alternative movement-related therapies, including Kinesiology, Acupuncture, neurology, yoga, and the teachings of Frederick Alexander and G. I. Gurdjieff. With this information, he developed a comprehensive approach that emphasizes a positive body image and the thinking-through of movement to reeducate neuromuscular awareness and the nervous system. Feldenkrais is a dynamic process that unfolds through understanding movement patterns and repeating them many times. Once a new movement is established through this repetitive sequence, the brain will recognize it as being normal and natural. By retraining the central nervous system through the skeletal system, old patterns or habits are eliminated and replaced with new ways of moving and being that improve the functioning of the body and allow life-enhancing choices. The Feldenkrais Method has two basic branches: Functional Integration® with a hands-on practitioner and a method of group practice called Awareness Through Movement®.

A practitioner of Functional Integration does not use extensive manipulations, but instead lightly touches and lifts the bones and gently guides the client through a sequence of slow, gentle movements that teach the whole body and mind how to move most effectively. Special movement sequences, often concentrated on specific body areas and joints, invite the whole body to participate rather than unconsciously overusing certain areas and underusing others. During a session, a client may be moved to different positions or rolled over while lying on a low, wide bodywork table or floor mat. Soft bolsters and a variety of foam pads may be used to support the client in a way that allows the effects of gravity to relax tension. All of the work focuses on gently and gradually bringing conscious awareness to all of the body's movements.

The Awareness Through Movement® aspect of the Feldenkrais Method is carried out in a group setting in which functional integration is accomplished through a series of movement lessons guided verbally by an instructor, rather than through hands-on work. The exercises are designed to improve the conscious choice of natural body movement and to reenergize certain areas

of the body in a way that translates to other areas; they are often enhanced with visualization practices. Rather than a form of therapy used to treat dysfunction, Awareness Through Movement could be considered more of an educational process that provides recipients with new, learned responses for simple improvement. It bestows a return to the many-faceted choices we once had in our movement—choices that have been compromised by injury, illness, surgeries, repetitive stress, and assumptions about what movement should look like—by restoring inner integrity and the sense of deep relaxation as a home base to which we can return over and over.

There is also an in-the-water version of Feldenkrais Therapy called Fluid Moves, which is discussed in the Aquatics Therapy section in this chapter.
Contact: Feldenkrais Guild of North America – www.feldenkraisresources.com

Hanna Somatic Education® (HSE)

American philosophy professor Thomas Hanna created this system of sensory awareness and muscle training during the mid-1900s after working with the Feldenkrais Method. Intended as a way to provide pain management and movement rehabilitation, this active approach encourages learning through doing rather than passively receiving. HSE is based on the idea that the body responds to stressful life trauma with specific muscle reflexes. Although these reflexes are often a natural survival response, they can become habitual as muscular contractions so deeply embedded at an unconscious level that the resulting tension comes to feel normal. When the mind and body don't remember that a muscle's normal state is relaxed, chronic conditions manifest as limited range of motion, soreness, stiffness, the inability to fully relax, and a variety of other debilitating problems. HSE was created as a way to restore healthy function by reprogramming the nervous system through hands-on table work and slow movement exercises. This active teaching approach focuses on developing a more vivid bodily awareness and better muscle control to end painful muscle spasms and restore freedom of movement without great effort or force.

Instead of the practitioner's hands doing all the work, a typical maneuver asks the recipient to voluntarily contract a muscle and then slowly and completely relax it, all the while staying mindful of the sensations produced. By the end of the movement, the recipient's muscle tone has recovered to a healthier level of relaxation than when the action began. Many of the exercises are done to activate and integrate the sensory and motor areas of the cerebral cortex involved with movement and sensation. The practitioner guides the client into different positions and gives appropriate instructions, always reminding that moving should be free of pain. If functional muscle disorders are present, the practitioner gently manipulates the muscles to unfreeze them. A continuous series of slow, controlled movements and constant sensing by the client in combination with the hands-on work by the practitioner can shift the resting set point of muscles from strongly contracted to relaxed. The goal is for the recipient to enjoy a significant and lasting improvement in muscle control, coordination, and range of motion. Results are often immediate and may be cumulative with continued rehearsal of the indicated movement patterns. This form of therapy also deals with an assortment of functional disorders such as those involving organic muscle lesions or sensory motor amnesia.

Candidates for Hanna Somatics Education can opt for clinical sessions with a practitioner or choose to experiment on their own with a number of predetermined movement-pattern series. Hanna Somatic Biokinetics, also referred to as Somatic Exercises, is a program similar to HSE that uses a combination of exercise techniques for rehabilitation through neuromuscular retraining that are designed to release chronic muscular contractions and pain patterns resulting from injury, stress, or repetitive motion. This muscle-training method teaches how to relieve tension quickly, lengthen and relax muscles, regain comfort, and restore voluntary control of the muscles. The Hanna Somatic Cat Stretch series is one of a number of transformational somatic exercise programs that are available for a wide range of conditions

Contact: Association of Hanna Somatic Education –
www.hannasomatics.com

Hellerwork®

An outgrowth of Rolfing created by Joseph Heller from Poland, who worked with Ida Rolf and Judith Aston, Hellerwork integrates bodywork with movement reeducation and verbal communication to create a three-component system of body rebalancing. The first element is connective-tissue manipulation to realign the body and release chronic holding patterns. The next is movement reeducation that increases body awareness and teaches methods of accomplishing daily activities without stress. The final component uses guided dialogue to help the client recognize the relationship between the body and the psychological and emotional issues that can arise during a treatment or at any other time in life.

The complete process consists of a series of eleven sessions that systematically addresses different physical and psychological themes. The first three sessions deal with the superficial fascial layers and with developmental issues that a person acquired early in life. The next four sessions work at the core, both physically and emotionally, to deepen the client's awareness. The last sessions revisit earlier work and integrate newfound knowledge to produce permanent and structural change. People often come to Hellerwork to address pain, and through the unique experience of bodywork, movement, and communication, the Hellerwork series is designed to create pain-free life and enhance stress-free movement in daily activity.

Contact: Hellerwork International –
www.hellerwork.com

Ideokinesis

Ideokinesis is a different approach to kinesthetic reeducation in that it is designed to provide better postural alignment and more efficiency in movement by using imagined movement. *Kinesis* is physical movement induced by stimulation, and *ideo* defines the stimulator as the mind. Ideokinesis is based on the idea that since the nervous system directs and coordinates all patterns of posture and musculoskeletal movement, improving movement requires changes in neurological activity. When the mind imagines new lines of movement through the body, new impulses along neural pathways to the muscles can be generated, thus stimulating the muscles into performing the desired motion properly.

This somatic form of neuromuscular training was formalized by Dr. Lulu Sweigard, based on previous research on the relationship between posture and speech carried out by Mabel Ellsworth Todd during the 1920s and 1930s. Sweigard's method of using imagery instead of conscious effort revolutionized the way people, and especially dancers, thought about their bodies, and she joined the faculty at The Juilliard School as a neuromuscular reeducator. Her method stresses the idea of trusting the body's inherent wisdom about how to move.

The practice uses methods that require as little physical effort as possible to reduce muscular tension or stress, which might then be held in the body. Ideokinesis uses two techniques—the constructive rest position and the nine lines of movement—to improve postural alignment and flexibility. From the rest position, which is the most relaxed position that a body can be in, participants are instructed with words and touch to visualize nine lines of movement in their bodies; these lines are designed to affect the skeletal parts involved in postural alignment. Once the nervous system is given a clear mental picture of the intended outcome, it will automatically select the most efficient way to signal the muscles to achieve the goal. Although change is possible without physical exertion, sustaining new habits of movement in the muscles may take months of diligent daily practice. Sweigard's methods as they applied to dance were taught and refined by her students and have been passed down to the present day.
Contact: www.ideokinesis.com

Kinetic Awareness® (KA)

This movement therapy is a guided experiential exploration of the fundamentals of human movement whose goal is releasing muscle tension and improving overall well-being. It was created by choreographer Elaine Summers as part of her search for a way to heal her own potentially paralyzing condition. After studying Sensory Awareness and other forms of movement therapy, she created Kinetic Awareness as a way to explore the effect of tension frozen in the body on body posture and performance. Constricted parts of the body will distort alignment and constrain movement, and Kinetic Awareness recognizes that improved self-awareness of muscle tension can be a tool for discovering and releasing these areas of discomfort.

During an initial private or group class, individuals learn how to scan and tune in to the body by examining each part in depth to observe the level of tension held there. This process is aided by placing rubber balls of various sizes underneath the part of the body being examined to focus attention on the sensations; the ball also delivers a gentle massage. Moving slowly over the ball enhances the elasticity and responsiveness of the muscles

and joints and can reveal the relationship between different parts of the body while they are in motion. The instructor and the client both pay attention to changes in the client's breathing and any shifts in comfort level. Teachers also encourage individual sharing of any emotional feelings that may arise. The awareness training also includes anatomy lessons, practices in which several body parts are moved simultaneously, exercises in which movement is carried out at varying speeds with minimal effort and quiet alertness, and methods to consciously change tension levels. The overall goal of KA is to free up the body so that as it moves, sensations are pleasurable rather than painful.
Contact: www.kineticawarenesscenter.org

Laban Movement Analysis (LMA)

During the early 1900s, Hungarian-born dancer and movement teacher Rudolph Laban created a system that improves an individual's understanding of movement. Through the exploration of a multitude of disciplines such as dance and martial arts, Laban developed a form of notation to record body movements and a system of movement analysis called Laban Movement Analysis. This system provides a vocabulary for describing movement, which, by its nature, is a form of communication without words. Because much information about emotions and feelings can be expressed through movement, once learned, this same language can be used to give voice to experiences in all areas of life.

Irmgard Bartenieff, a dance therapist and one of Laban's students, applied her physical therapy training, particularly with polio patients, to further develop this approach to somatic movement education into what has become known as the Bartenieff Fundamentals (BF). This form of movement therapy uses movement experiences to guide participants through expressive and functional changes that can improve their daily lives. The fundamentals address dynamic alignment, developmental patterns, and other somatic building blocks by using practices that support the breath and core strength. Besides improved alignment and efficiency, BF also helps enhance body awareness and increases range of movement.

Exploring the qualities of movement is the foundation of the therapeutic work. By understanding the concept of effort without exertion, the space through which the body moves, the shape of the body when changing form, and how the body is used, mobilized, and performs, it is possible to recognize new, more dynamic neuromuscular patterns. The program also works with the functional aspects of how a person uses intention, initiates movement, breathes, and shifts weight while performing a sequence of actions involving the muscles. Specific exercises are performed in a relaxed way while lying on the floor, standing, or sitting, and many are designed to help participants achieve more efficient use of deeper muscles, thus developing a wider range of motion. During each activity, fluid conscious breathing is emphasized. In addition to making movement more efficient, all the exercises are intended to ground a participant by engaging the lower body and improving the relationship to the center of gravity.

Contact: Laban Bartenieff Institute of Movement Studies – www.limsonline.org

Mensendieck Remedial Therapy System

The Mensendieck Remedial Therapy System for improving overall body functioning uses movement techniques to correct body mechanics, muscle function, and posture and to prevent dysfunctional issues from becoming a part of daily life. During the late 1890s, one of the first American-born female doctors, Dr. Bess Mensendieck, also the creator of Somatosynthesis, initially developed this form of educational therapy to help restore muscle functioning in patients suffering from paralysis. Through her research into kinesiology and functional education that works on neuromuscular coordination, she created her own series of movement exercises that require minimal effort to rebuild, reshape, realign, and revitalize the body. Mensendieck saw the body as an assembly of distinct masses connected at the joints. When each mass is properly positioned and supported, there is no strain on any muscle groups. The therapy works on the premise that if movement is executed in a correctly balanced manner, it contributes to a properly positioned and well-functioning body. Attention to breathing efficiently is a significant part of the training.

The teaching begins with personalized sessions that include instructions on the fundamentals of a well-balanced body stance, followed by different exercises chosen from among more than 200 that emphasize graceful, balanced movements. Each exercise is intended to help the client learn how to move one part of the body without overcompensating in another part, thus creating strain. Through repetition of each exercise, new patterns of movement become imprinted in the body and replace the old, ineffective habits. Postural corrections are carried out with the assistance of mirrors placed all around the minimally clothed client to give visual feedback on the way various physical movements are initiated and carried out. The Mensendieck System is designed to be helpful for a variety of stress-induced conditions, injuries, diseases, chronic pain, and recovery issues. The number of sessions required for rehabilitation depends on the extent of the particular health issues and the perseverance of the client.

Contact: www.mensendieckmoves.ni or
www.amazon.com/bessmensendieck

Mezieres Method

The Mezieres Method is an orthopedic form of bodywork developed in France during the 1940s by anatomy teacher Françoise Mezieres. It is based on the idea that, since structure determines function and stiffness in one area causes compensations in another part of the body, all connecting parts must be stretched and readjusted at the same time. In order to resculpt and reshape the body into its ideal balanced form, the practitioner makes corrections by releasing distortions and other displays of muscle dysfunction in the body through a series of intense sessions that focus on creating equilibrium between structure and function by working with precision on the fascia, muscles, viscera, and bones.

After an initial posture analysis, the treatment proceeds slowly through specific movements to reshape the body and remove imbalances. With the client lying on the floor, the practitioner places her body in precise positions and then uses her own body weight to maximize a particular stretch while she kneads the tense muscles that are involved. The process can be uncomfortable at times, but this will pass when the distortion disappears. The client is also instructed in ways to practice elements of this method at home. This method of bodywork is commonly found in Europe.

Contact: www.mezieres.eu/anglais/la_methode.php

Phoenix Rising Yoga Therapy (PRYT)

Phoenix Rising Yoga Therapy is a fusion of Hatha Yoga, bodywork, assisted movements, and elements of contemporary body-mind psychology that was developed by Australian educator Michael Lee after experiencing a significant emotional shift during his own practice of yoga. The form he originally created, in which a therapist directly assists a client in holding yoga poses and moving through different asanas, has evolved into a method that also increases the client's awareness of physical and emotional restrictions that inhibit everyday freedom of movement. In addition to releasing physical and emotional tension and helping extend range of motion, PRYT can awaken the flow of the healing life-force energy, promote deep relaxation, and enhance awareness of body and spirit through the integration of assisted yoga poses, dialogue, and breathing exercises performed in a safe, loving atmosphere.

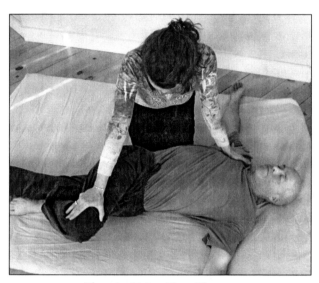

Phoenix Rising Yoga Therapy.

A pulse assessment and body scan may sometimes be done first to ascertain the client's overall condition and reveal where tightness needs to be released. After a short discussion about his condition and intentions, the client is encouraged to sit still, take a few deep breaths, and get centered and calm. Specific yoga postures are then employed to provide relief in restricted areas. Firm holding or light palpations may be used to deal with spinal curvature, constrictions, and other muscular conditions discovered during the movements. The therapist supports the recipient in the pose longer than he might be able to do on his own, gently pushing his physical limits until emotional tensions begin to surface and release. The practitioner encourages the client to explore all sensations that arise as the body is gently stretched to the edge of pain and asks the recipient to describe

how he feels physically, emotionally, mentally, and spiritually. Throughout the session, supportive verbal dialogue provides insight, awareness, and integration of the emerging emotions that are experienced. The practitioner does not follow a set sequence but, based on the client's verbal responses, intuitively chooses positions that will be most useful. The client is also free to move in any way that his body requests. Aromatherapy and visualization may also be incorporated into the session, and props are used if necessary. At the end of the session, the practitioner guides the recipient through a meditation with affirmations to reinforce self-awareness. When participating in PRYT, the recipient doesn't need any knowledge of yoga, since the therapist will help move him into the positions that are most appropriate for his individual condition.

Contact: The Phoenix Rising Center – www.pryt.com

Reposturing Dynamics

Reposturing Dynamics is a system of techniques designed by Aaron Parnell that helps restore balance and flexibility to the body, giving clients more physical flexibility and freedom from pain. This form of therapy is a participatory process in which the client integrates the breath with stretching and exercises. The rebalancing exercises help to release stress from each muscle group. The client is always in charge of how quickly and how deeply any release occurs. Reposturing Dynamics aims to increase freedom of movement in the arms and shoulders, reduce back pain, restore spinal freedom, improve lung capacity, liberate head and neck movement, and increase the recipient's body awareness. The ultimate goal is to help individual clients increase energy and stamina while naturally achieving great posture and experiencing better health and vitality.

Contact: Vitality Center – www.livingwithvitality.com

Rosen Method®

This approach to healing combining bodywork and movement was developed by physical therapist Marion Rosen in the 1950s. Rosen had been involved in movement classes as a young girl in Germany, and after studying massage, breathwork, and a number of movement therapies, World War II forced her to flee to Sweden and eventually the United States, where she became a licensed physical therapist. Soon after that, she created her own healing system combining gentle-touch bodywork, physical movement exercises, breathwork, and verbal support in order to help others resolve physical discomfort and enhance personal growth. Like many other modalities, this type of therapy is based on the idea that old forgotten memories and emotions become stored in the body in ways that are not beneficial and often lead to dysfunction. The Rosen Method maintains that illness could be prevented if people were more aware of unconscious tension in the body. It uses hands-on bodywork and physical therapy exercises to open up various parts of the body, removing barriers and conditioned habits that limit free expression and spontaneity and returning people to the natural state of openness with which they were born.

The bodywork done on a massage table emphasizes simplicity and involves sensitive, gentle, direct touch accompanied by verbal cues to help the client become aware of unconscious muscle tension. Pressure is applied slowly as it meets any resistance in tense muscles. The practitioner pays attention to shifts in muscle tension as well as changes in the breathing pattern to help guide the work. Any change in a person's breath, especially shortness or shallowness, is seen as a signal of important unconscious emotional material that needs to be released. By encouraging more relaxed breathing, the client can unwind and enter a state in which he can integrate unconscious material that causes pain now or will in the future. The practitioner then supports further emotional release by helping the client heighten body awareness.

An addition to this bodywork is movement classes using exercises that are playfully executed and set to music. Participants perform swings, stretches, bounces, and twists to loosen the muscles at the joints, expand the chest, and free up the diaphragm. All the movements are intended to promote balance and expand range of motion through pleasure rather than with strain.

Huma Somatic Psychotherapy, once called Huma Transpersonal Bodywork, is an offshoot of the Rosen Method that uses subtle touch and verbal communication not only to address physical and psychological health but also to attend to the deeper energetic and transpersonal level of the self. The bodywork integrates healing elements of both Western and Eastern traditions to enhance awareness at the core level of the inner being, allowing a significant shift in awareness from the physical to the energetic realm. Dancer and somatic

psychotherapist Louise Barrie developed this method with Marion Rosen to ease constrictions in the body and access the tranquil stillness in the energetic core. Contact: www.rosenmethod.com

Sensory Repatterning

James Stewart, a student of Milton Trager, developed this kinesthetic form of bodywork as a way to affect the nervous system through assisted passive joint movement that invites the body to explore a range of motion beyond existing patterns of limitation. Although based somewhat on the Trager Approach, this gentle method speaks to the whole person through the quality of touch and new ways of movement that evoke a heightened state of awareness, encouraging a more effective way of being and moving in the world. Through deep inner listening and experiencing new sensations, the body-mind is allowed to explore beyond existing restrictive patterns and awaken the natural healing abilities that can provide emotional peace of mind.

During a treatment, the practitioner moves the client's relaxed body in a combination of slow, gentle, rhythmic, rocking, stretching, cradling, and undulating motions so that the recipient can let go of muscular restrictions and become aware of holding patterns. The muscle tissue can then be kneaded and massaged deeply. The body-mind is invited to relax and reconnect with its core so that the client can rediscover a sense of ease and heightened awareness.

Skinner Releasing Technique™ (SRT)

Skinner Releasing Technique owes its inception to an injury during a professional dance performance when Joan Skinner ruptured a spinal disc and found herself unable to continue performing. After using the Alexander Technique to recover, during the 1960s she went on to create her own system of kinesthetic training, which draws on many of the same principles as Ideokinesis to create a transformation in movement by using imagery to release habitual patterns. Different types of imagery create metaphors for moving specific body parts and can place a participant in a disorientated state from which new patterns of movement can spontaneously arise. Releasing muscular tension and distortion can lead to the release of the preconceived ideas and habits manifested in balance and alignment, which can bring a sense of freedom and enhanced well-being.

A practice session is done with the participant lying on the floor, allowing the breath to move of its own volition, feeling the parts of the body soften and melt, and pausing frequently to shift the focus through each area of the body. Once fully relaxed, participants fashion mental images that further develop awareness of any existing tension patterns and allow new movements to emerge. Proper balance and alignment are considered to be a dynamic process in which weight is continually adjusted; a checklist of suggestions teaches how to move parts of the body in subtle ways. This process of self-discovery can be aided by a partner, who may use light touch to encourage the release of restrictions at specific points or trace three-dimensional energy patterns along the surface of the body. Traditional myofascial massage techniques may also be used as part of the learning process. Participants are encouraged to keep a journal or use tape recorders to preserve a record of their experiences. The goal of the Skinner Releasing Technique is effortless movement from a state of dynamically balanced alignment, but there are broader applications for this method of using imagery and intuition to create a release. Contact: www.skinnerreleasing.com

Structural Awareness

This form of movement therapy, which is based on the principles of Rolfing Structural Integration, was developed by family counselor Dorothy Nolte, after she trained with Dr. Rolf. The practice aims to provide participants with healthier relationships, better parenting abilities, improved family dynamics, and more effective ways of dealing with life. The process involves a variety of methods that train participants to look more closely at how their bodies move while performing daily activities. One example asks a person to observe the way she walks, noticing which part of the body leads her, and then recognize how this feels and how it affects structural alignment. A number of methods like this are used to help explore how conditioned patterns of behavior affect structure, how structure affects the mind and the emotions, and how movement influences the dynamics of relationships. Structural Awareness encourages a person to reach for the inner strength needed to express values that can be passed on to children, grandchildren, and generations to come. Contact: The Rolf Institute of Structural Integration – www.rolf.org

Trager® Approach

Also referred to as Psychophysical Integration, this form of therapy combines hands-on bodywork with a set of simple movement exercises, called Mentastics or mental gymnastics, to release muscle tension, increase range of motion, and reeducate the body. It was developed by Dr. Milton Trager between the 1930s and 1950s as a means of releasing deep-seated areas of holding and pain or dysfunction interrelated with the neurological functioning of the mind and body. After using running and gymnastics to successfully correct his frail boyhood condition, he discovered that he had the ability to restore health with his hands, and while training to be a boxer, he found that he was able to heal a number of people, including a polio victim. After giving up boxing and getting involved in dancing and acrobatics, he pursued therapeutic training to support his own growing abilities. Trager believed that all deep-seated patterns of dysfunction begin in the mind and that by using sensitive touch to communicate relaxed feelings to the brain via the nervous system, existing painful patterns can be removed. The intention of the Trager Approach is to provide a more effortless way of being by providing the body with the experience of light, easy, and free sensations.

The treatment is done in a noninvasive, meditative way without using any long or broad strokes, extreme pressure, or rapid thrusts on the connective tissue of the body. Instead, gentle and pleasurable rhythmic cradling, jiggling, kneading, shaking, pulling, rotating, rocking, stretching, bouncing, and rolling of body parts mobilize soft tissues and encourage release and relaxation, while the recipient directly experiences how it feels as different parts of the body are freed up. When the client's joints and muscles are relaxed, light, soft, free, and flexible, these positive sensations are fed back into the central nervous system to help teach muscles and joints how to move effortlessly with mindfulness of the energy within. The client remains fully or partially clothed, and no massage oils are used. Although the treatment is appropriate for a number of physiological issues, the results often manifest simply with the body feeling very loose, open, limber, and taller.

In addition, the Trager Approach includes a set of fluid, dance-like, body-educating exercises called Mentastics that use rocking, swings, shakes, eight different kinds of kicks, and stretches to provide gentle healing effects while releasing blockages in the body. Its intention is to help the recipient retain the benefits of lengthening, widening, softening, and expanding the body that were brought about through the hands-on bodywork. The exercises are also taught to the client so that they can be performed at home to reinforce the bodywork session.

Contact: United States Trager Association –
www.tragerus.org

III. Substance- and Implement-Assisted Therapies

When any part of a ship becomes damaged during a long voyage around the world, special tools and assistance may be needed to carry out unique or unusual repairs, and various implements not usually found onboard may come in handy to deal with unusual circumstances. In a similar way, therapeutic work on the human body sometimes requires more than just the hands and heart of a practitioner.

The modalities discussed in this section are not what would be considered typical bodywork, because the healing effects are primarily provided by a natural substance, a tool, or a piece of equipment rather than the action of a practitioner, though some are indeed hands-on practices or are used in such practices. The objects used include such things as stones, magnets, metals, crystals, essential oils, herbs, minerals, spices, flowers, color, light, electrical instruments, electromagnetic and electrical impulses, pendulums, negative ions, lasers, infrared rays, sound waves, and computerized apparatuses. Many are applied directly to the body; some are placed nearby to affect the recipient. Though modalities found in other categories of bodywork may use additional implements and substances as part of their process, they are intended to enhance the therapy rather than act as the source of healing.

Certain methods clearly show how recent developments in scientific research are playing a significant role in healing. In recent years, new processes have been created to excite muscles and release blockages by using electrical stimulation provided by various machines, some of which are discussed in this section. Other less technological methods, such as hot stones, have been employed for centuries by various traditions. Color and light therapy is a common supplement to bodywork modalities found in other sections of this book; under its umbrella are a variety of techniques using colored gemstones, sunlight, colored light rays, and crystals for treating disease and enhancing well-being.

Many of the therapies discussed below have strong enough effects to be considered complete modalities on their own; others have a long history as complements to forms of bodywork discussed in other sections. Various therapeutic implements (such as rubber balls, mats, props, and inversion tables) are also often employed for exercise and practices other than applied bodywork. They are discussed within the self-care practices found in Part II.

Aromatherapy

Aromatherapy has been used for relaxation and healing for thousands of years. Although its true origins are lost in the mists of time, Egyptians, Greeks, Romans, Chinese, Indians, Europeans, Aztecs, Native Americans, and various other cultures have all used scented oils and the fragrance of plants for medicinal purposes. The Egyptians extracted oils from aromatic plants as early as 1500 BCE and used them in the mummification process. Around the same time, the Chinese burned scented woods and had many applications for aromatic herbs. The Aztecs and North American Indians used fragrance in their herbal

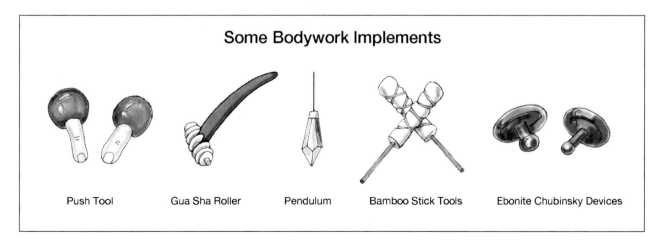

Some Bodywork Implements

Push Tool   Gua Sha Roller   Pendulum   Bamboo Stick Tools   Ebonite Chubinsky Devices

remedies. The Greeks and Romans indulged in scented baths and body lubricants. Around 1000 CE in the Middle East, the physician Avicenna treated patients by soaking handkerchiefs in aromatic oils. The use of fragrance in Western forms of therapy was brought to life again many years later, when during the 1930s, French chemist Rene-Maurice Gattefosse was instrumental in spreading awareness of the healing effects of scent. In the 1940s, French physician Dr. Jean Valnet conducted research using essential oils, and French biochemist Dr. Margaret Maury was developing massage techniques that increased the effectiveness of bodywork by applying essential oils on the skin. Through her research, she established techniques that formed the basis of modern Aromatherapy, which she brought to England in the 1950s. Today, it continues to increase in popularity and is included in many forms of bodywork and spa therapy.

Aromatherapy employs aromatic essential oils extracted from herbs, flowers, resins, wood, and roots, and numerous massage modalities use it is as an integral part of the therapy or as a sensory adjunct. The pure oils are highly concentrated essences reputed to possess antibiotic, antiseptic, hormonal, and other therapeutic properties. Most often, the essential oils are mixed with massage oil and applied to the skin, from which they can be absorbed into the bloodstream or nerve endings, but Aromatherapy can also be administered by diffusion, topical compresses, healing baths, or hydrotherapy.

During a full-body massage, oils can be applied to the whole body or to specific problem or congested areas. Applications along the spine are particularly beneficial since a large number of nerves and acupressure points with direct influence on most of the body organs are here. Besides the fact that aromas have a sensual appeal, they also act very rapidly on the brain. Inhaling these scents can stimulate childhood memories and feelings that may promote healing. This kind of sensory input also works well on the lymphatic system and is often incorporated into many other types of treatments. Diluted extracts of flowers and plants can also be used to balance the emotional and spiritual bodies; their essences are believed to heal by clearing out negativity at the level of the soul.

Contact: The Alliance of International Aromatherapists – www.alliance-aromatherapists.org or the National Association of Holistic Aromatherapy – www.NAHA.org

Bach Flower Therapy

Bach Flower Therapy was developed by homeopath Dr. Edward Bach in the early 1920s and combined his studies of immunology and bacteriology with certain principles of homeopathy. By ingesting the essence of specific plants or applying it to the skin, the healing power of these natural substances can influence the subtle energy body, which in turn can affect the physical body. The thirty-eight remedies, created by combining petals or plant parts with water and either exposing the solution to sunlight or boiling it, are offered as tinctures that can be used to address a specific mood, personality trait, negative emotion, or emotional imbalance through the transfer of vibrations, as in homeopathy. Written guides are available to assist in choosing the most beneficial remedies. The well-known Rescue Remedy is a combination of flower essences that can be helpful in stressful situations.

In a Bach Flower massage, the essences, which are quickly absorbed, are applied to the body, sometimes in areas where acupressure points or the chakras are located. At the end of a session, the therapist may recommend one or more remedies for home use. Bach Flower Therapy is often an adjunct to other modalities.
Contact: www.bachtherapy.org

Bamboo Fusion

Naturally occurring bamboo, a very light, strong, durable, and smooth-surfaced wood, has become a handy tool in the hands of a massage therapist. By applying pressure with a bamboo tool, massage therapists can greatly reduce the amount of pain in their hands, wrists, and thumbs while still offering hands-on deep-tissue work. Bamboo is a versatile and portable tool that has good antibacterial qualities and holds heat for a long period of time. The therapeutic benefits of heat have been well documented, with hot stones, heat packs, and warming oils having long been used to reduce stiffness and pain, promote circulation, remove waste from the tissues, and help the client be more receptive to deeper forms of bodywork. By using preheated bamboo for massage, a very effective fusion of these two tools is created.

The treatment uses various sizes and designs of handcrafted bamboo and rattan tools that are applied with long, soothing, rhythmical strokes. The bamboo is first heated with steam infused with essential oils

and then applied to the body using a combination of rolling, sliding, kneading, and tapping movements to relieve and renew stressed muscles. The bamboo glides easily over skin and body hair, reducing the need for large amounts of oil. The effects are considered similar to that found with heated stone bodywork; however, the various sizes and designs of the bamboo can act as an extension of the practitioner's strokes to deal with fascia and muscles. Treatments can also be performed with the client seated.
Contact: www.bamboo-fusion.com

Batu Jamu Massage

The application of stones and herbs during a massage has a rich tradition, especially in Indonesia, and Kim Collier has created a form of cleansing bodywork based on Batu Jamu, the Balinese massage that uses the synergy of smooth, warm batu (volcanic stones) and jamu (herbal remedies) for healing purposes. The bodywork actually includes a variety of Indonesian techniques with Hindu, Chinese, and European influences to create a very relaxing and energizing experience.

During the treatment, the stones are slid across the body in long, flowing, gliding strokes. They are also placed on various energy points. Sessions also incorporate Acupressure work, foot massage, percussive drumming, kneading strokes, and skin-rolling motions, done with the hands. The bodywork is rhythmic, beginning slowly and then building to a staccato pace. Coconut oil infused with spices, such as vanilla, helps enhance the effectiveness of the treatment. Traditional aromatic herbal remedies, flowers, fruit, and volcanic clay may be incorporated into scrubs, compresses, facial masks, and baths.
Contact: www.jamuspa.com or www.stonespirits.org

Biofeedback and Neuro-Biofeedback

Biofeedback equipment has been used since the early 1960s to provide real-time information to people about their physiological and emotional responses as they are learning to consciously change behavior patterns and ways of reacting in order to solve health problems. In recent decades, scientific and technological advances have allowed the definition of biofeedback to be expanded. Incorporating quantum physics theory, it now includes systems in which the equipment itself promotes changes in these patterns by sending bioenergetic signals back to the client through the monitoring system.

A variety of electronic (and now computerized) monitoring devices measure electrophysiological reactivity and allow a person to track, measure, and consciously alter autonomic bodily functions that respond to "stressful" situations. Each type of device is connected to a different area of the body to measure specific physical, neurological, or energetic conditions. The most common instruments are EMGs (electromylographs), which record muscle tension; ECGs (electrocardiographs), which monitor heart function and pulse rate; and EDGs (electrodermographs), which measure changes in the electrical conductivity of the skin as the sympathetic nervous system and the sweat glands react to changing emotions. EEGs (electroencephalographs), which provide a visual representation of brain activity and MEGs (magnetoencephalographs), which measure magnetic fields generated by neural circuits in the brain, are used in specialized neuro-biofeedback training. A number of different types of equipment can be used for other purposes.

During a typical biofeedback session, the client is seated in a relaxed position, and electronic sensors are placed on specific parts of the body, such as the fingers, head, wrist, ankles, or muscle groups, to record biological activity and identify unhealthy reactions. Changes in this activity traditionally were demonstrated by flashing lights or sounds, but a computer screen can also be used. Once the current state is established as a baseline, the practitioner guides the client to consciously alter the feedback, perhaps by relaxing certain muscles, changing a mental attitude, or breathing more deeply. A computer screen can also display images that lead to relaxation. As the client learns and applies techniques of stress reduction and body reeducation, the process can lead to better overall health through more conscious control of the involuntary nervous system and the body and emotions. Though perhaps not considered a typical form of bodywork, biofeedback can be used as a primary therapy or in conjunction with other bodywork modalities or stress-reduction therapy. It has been helpful in treating a variety of conditions such as anxiety, depression, hypertension, anger, and addiction, as well as for stress and pain management, improved muscle control, better physiological performance, and relaxation training. Urinary incontinence in children can be addressed through a system that acts as a bed-wetting alarm, conditioning the child to wake up when the bladder is full.

More advanced forms of biofeedback and quantum physics technology have recently been incorporated into such therapies as Electro-Acupuncture, Reflexology, Neurolinguistic Programming, spinal testing, and work on biorhythms.
Contact: Association for Applied Psychophysiology and Biofeedback – www.aapb.org

The **Indigo System**™ is a form of biofeedback that gently measures electrical activity with the intention of reconnecting clients to their innate wisdom, or inner knowing. Indigo refers to the color inherent in the third eye, which is recognized as the center where the higher awareness resides. This form of biofeedback uses a sensitive and sophisticated waveform generator to identify stressful reactions and then to help reeducate clients' physical and subtle energy bodies by giving them the opportunity to entrain with the harmonious energetic frequencies that will create coherent patterns of vibrations.

During a session, the client wears sensors contained in a head harness and bracelets on the wrist and ankles. The electrodes in these sensors read the electrical impulses coming from the body and send information to the monitoring computer. This reveals those areas of the body most in need of stress reduction. The device then provides more harmonious frequencies with which the client can become entrained. After the treatment, the technician works further to educate the client on managing stress. As in any procedure for relearning healthier patterns, the number of sessions required depends on how significant the existing stress patterns are and how long they have been held in the body.
Contact: www.indigosystem.com

LENS (Low Energy Neurofeedback System), also referred to as brain-wave biofeedback, was developed by Dr. Leonard Ochs as a way to help restore optimal brain function by correcting unhealthy brain-wave patterns with a very low-powered electromagnetic field. It is a noninvasive process that involves the monitoring and analysis of EEG (electroencephalogram) signals sent from electrodes placed on the scalp. As the signals are analyzed by a computer, feedback is sent to the client to affect the brain wave. Abnormalities in EEG read-outs are associated with mild to severe brain trauma that can result from a variety of injuries, and changing the amplitude of the brain wave creates a reduction of symptoms such as pain, headaches, or depression.

The various areas of the brain have been mapped out with regard to the type of activity that goes on in each segment. Depending on the symptoms displayed, electrodes are placed at the appropriate locations to determine the best healing frequency for the client's particular problem. The client simply sits, relaxes, and watches a monitor showing a series of visual images that have been programmed to elicit a certain very subtle response. The practitioner monitors the EEG and checks with the client to see what is occurring in the brain as the feedback frequency is adjusted in order to determine the optimum resonant frequency for healing. Over a series of sessions, the continual feedback of these optimum frequencies delivered through the electrodes is said to relax the nervous system, improve motor skill, and retrain the brain for better cognitive functioning.
Contact: www.ochslabs.com

Quantum Biofeedback represents one of the latest approaches that use a number of high-tech diagnostic and treatment devices to gather bioenergetic data from the body to ascertain its needs and then provide different corrective energy frequencies that neutralize destructive wave patterns. The equipment includes such devices as the EPFX, SCIO, and QXCI, which were developed by quantum physicist William Nelson. Although there is a lot of controversy and pending legal issues regarding the use of this technology, the equipment may be helpful in certain contexts. Each device has differences in design, but they have similar applications.

The EPFX (Electro-Physiology Feedback Xeroid) device is used to scan the body to find energetic imbalances, deficiencies, weaknesses or abnormalities by measuring voltage, amperage, resistance, hydration, oxidation, proton pressure, electron pressure, impedance, reactance, and phase angle on the cellular level. Once the results are known, the figures are compared against normal readings to achieve an understanding of the person's needs, dysfunctions and vulnerabilities. The device then applies a corrective resonance, which neutralizes destructive patterns and passively reeducates the muscles, helping the recipient relax and reducing tension, stress or pain. It also may detect energetic imbalances related to such things as vitamin levels, amino acids, nutrients, food substance, minerals, enzymes, natural sugars, toxins, hormone levels, muscle tone, disease, bacteria, molds, fungi, viruses, and the status of internal organs. The process works in a way similar to that of a virus scan on a computer by calculating the biological reactivity and resonance in the body. The SCIO (Scientific Consciousness Interface Operation) device works in a similar manner.

The QXCI (Quantum Xeroid Consciousness Interface) device is a high-tech diagnostic and treatment device that generates an electromagnetic pulse to perform an extensive scan of the body. This form of biofeedback therapy measures the electrical responses of the client's body and is capable of testing for allergies, deficiencies, infections, and even adverse emotions that can cause physical reactions. During a treatment, the recipient is fitted with head, ankle, and wrist harnesses so that readings can be taken. It is a completely painless process that takes several minutes to check the entire body by measuring electrical impulses and brain-wave frequencies. After the diagnosis is completed, resonance is used to treat any imbalances by feeding back frequencies that correct, enhance, counteract, or neutralize any destructive patterns in the body. The QXCI device has also been used to measure the frequencies of mental activity and map out a client's psyche and emotional state.
Contact: www.quantum-biofeedback.net

SCENAR Therapy, which stands for Self Controlled Energo-Neuro-Adaptive Regulation was developed in the 1970s for the Russian space program. The electrotherapy device is controlled by a sophisticated software program that reads changes in the skin's conductivity to determine what types of imbalances exist and then generates electrical impulses that are sent back to the skin. These signals affect fibers in the nerves that trigger the production of the neuropeptides in the brain in order to promote healing. As a stream of biofeedback information is sent back to the device, the output is continually

adjusted as conditions change. During a treatment, the device is placed on the affected area of the body or on the spine or abdomen and left there until specific signs of change are noted by the therapist. Noninvasive SCENAR Therapy can be used to treat a number of conditions, but its primary application is for pain relief and sports injuries; a number of sessions may be necessary depending on the client's particular condition.
Contact: www.scenar.info

Biomagnetic (Magnet) Therapy / Magnetic Field Therapy

The healing properties of magnets have been recognized by many ancient civilizations, including the Chinese, Egyptians, Greeks, and Romans. During the fifteenth century CE, the Swiss alchemist and physician Paracelsus became the father of modern-day magnet therapy when he proposed that illness was caused by external substances and became an advocate of using magnets to influence and support the body's energetic life force. Over the centuries, a number of researchers working in different fields, including William Gilbert, Franz Mesmer, Michael Faraday, Daniel Palmer, Albert Einstein, and Dr. Andrew Bassett provided further understanding of how certain electromagnetic fields, including that of the earth, affect the functioning of the brain, the growth of bones, the health of living tissue, and an assortment of other human activities. By the late 1900s, research had verified that certain frequencies of pulsating low-energy fields can produce magnetic resonance that stimulates positive changes in the body and brings balance and energy to the human metabolism.

Biomagnetic Therapy, also referred to as Magnetic Field Therapy, can be divided into two branches: fixed magnetic therapy and pulsed electromagnetic field therapy (PEFT). The primary principle underlying the use of magnets is that cells have an electrical nature, and therefore both negative and positive magnetic charges have a particular vibratory and resonant effect on them. There are other forms of biomagnetic therapy that work on multiple levels of the body by restoring the energy fields that surround it. By improving the condition of these auric biofields, the balance and alignment of the internal energy pathways can be affected in a positive way that will release blockages, stimulate blood flow, and hence relieve any chronic issues.

In fixed magnetic therapy, tiny, specially designed magnets are applied to the skin for specific periods of time to relieve pain, improve circulation, correct neurological disorders, and heal various ailments. For therapeutic results, magnets are placed directly on the area of the body to be treated and held in place by a special backing or bandage. Magnets can also be contained in a belt, a magnetic pad, or a blanket. Fixed magnets are often used as an adjunct to hands-on bodywork, but their correct application depends on the particular size, strength, and polarity of the magnets. Size and strength determine the force of the magnetic field created, and both the north (negative) and south (positive) poles of a magnet cause different interactions with the cells. The length of time they are left in place is adjusted according to the symptoms. Pregnant women should not use biomagnets, nor should people with pacemakers, insulin pumps, or bleeding wounds. There is also cautionary evidence that the south or positive side of bipolar magnets can cause an increase in tumor growth in people fighting cancer.

In pulsed electromagnetic field therapy, a PEMF device delivers an electrically generated magnetic pulse that penetrates tissue to the bone, thus stimulating the healing process on a cellular level and creating a polarity shift in the metabolic rate. This has been shown to improve the healing of fractures and soft-tissue damage, as well as being used to treat depression. Various research studies on biomagnetic therapy have also revealed an effect on the brain and neurological disorders. Contact: www.biomagnetic.org

Biomat Therapy

Biomat Therapy, though helpful on its own, is more likely to be used to supplement the therapeutic potential of different forms of bodywork. The biomat is a special mattress constructed with natural jade and bio-clay placed between layers of cotton, which provides thermal insulation. When the mat is heated, the jade emits beneficial negative ions and long-wave infrared rays that penetrate the body, dissolve harmful substances, and revitalize the biological functioning of the cells, the circulatory system, and the metabolism. This product can be used for personal relaxation or in conjunction with bodywork when it is placed between the recipient and the massage table. In either case, simply lying on the mat is healing because the infrared rays penetrate deep into the skin and dissolve harmful substances that may

have accumulated in the body. There are also different types of mats available that contain crystals. Since it does make a wonderful complement to most any modality, more practitioners are using mats on their massage tables. Contact: www.therapy.biomat.com

Bioresonance Therapy and Bioresonance Feedback Therapy (BRFT)

Bioresonance Feedback Therapy, a form of Bioresonance Therapy originally referred to as MORA by the developer of the first machine, uses devices to gather the frequencies of the electromagnetic oscillations produced by every component of the body and the body as a whole. The therapy recognizes that every cell has its own resonant frequency and that the frequencies in the whole body can be affected by disease. The BRFT equipment then sorts out the unharmonious oscillations (energetic wave patterns) produced by unhealthy conditions, reverses these oscillations, and sends them back to the recipient to balance the body, improve energy flow, and weaken any disease process. The instrument targets systems and organs that have been affected by allergic, inflammatory, or degenerative processes. The process also helps free up toxins so they can be released into circulation and eliminated naturally from the body through the urine or skin. The therapy works on the same principle as sound or color therapy by using resonance to release a person from factors that block the flow of energy. It also relates to ancient Chinese medicine in recognizing the connection between energy and the activity of the organs, as well as the way in which these activities are subject to rhythmic vibrations. A number of different devices can be used in Bioresonance Therapy. Although it's possible to use BFRT for many types of illness, some contraindications do apply, as extreme deficiencies of essential nutrients limit its effectiveness and certain drugs can interfere with the process.

Study of BRFT began in 1923 with the research of Russian scientist Alexander Gurwitsch on biophotons, weak electromagnetic waves in the ultraviolet area of the color spectrum. Fifty years later, technology was created that revealed that ultraviolet light waves are emitted from many biological substances. In the early 1970s, Dr. Beetz of the Max Plank Institute created a way to project the process onto the TV screen of a scanner equipped with a photo amplifier. Soon after this, German physicist Dr. T. A. Popp proved the existence of biophoton light

emissions emanating from living cells. This was followed by a series of studies by different scientists encompassing quantum field theory, electron activation, chemical reactions, electro-acupuncture diagnostics, and the way in which allergic reactions can be neutralized by means of electromagnetic vibrations with a certain frequency. This research contributed to the development of the first machine that utilized these findings to electronically rectify the vibrations of an allergen and bring strength and balance back to the body. This equipment, developed by Dr. Franz Morell during the 1970s, essentially emits alternating current through electrodes which can stimulate a change in bioresonance in the cells, thereby reversing any harmful changes. Today the equipment has been refined and is capable of isolating the effects of a pathogen and then transmitting corrective signals over the same electrodes to provide a curative effect.
Contact: www.energymedicine/bioresonance.com

Pulsating Energy Resonance Therapy (PERT) is a form of Bioresonance Therapy that was developed by a team of Russian scientists during the late 1960s as a way to monitor, measure, and stimulate the health of cosmonauts while they were in space. It recognizes that the entire universe is a sea of energy in which all matter vibrates at varying frequencies. To activate the body's own energies, PERT uses a device that influences the energy frequencies of the different organs by delivering pulsating electromagnetic fields generated by a well-controlled electric current. The compact device is programmed with different combinations of frequencies that work to sedate, stimulate, and regulate a person's energy, addressing a variety of problems. For example, the device may first record the natural force field of a healthy young person and then introduce these frequencies into the fatigued and energy-starved body of sick or elderly people, boosting body systems and enhancing the self-healing process. PERT Therapy can also be used to help prevent dysfunction from developing.
Contact: www.bio-resonance.com

VIBE Healing is a form of Bioresonance Healing that owes its genesis to Russian scientist and inventor Nikola Tesla, who did early research on powerful multiwave oscillators and high-energy electromagnetic coils. He invented several devices, such as the Violet Ray Machine, specifically for healing the body. He also helped Georges Lakhovsky develop the original multiwave oscillator device in the early 1900s. The VIBE (Vibrational Integrated Biophotonic Energizer) machine, invented during the 1930s by Lakhovsky, is one of many that have evolved as technology has advanced.

Presently, VIBE Healing uses a stand-alone electromagnetic field generator rather than electrodes hooked up to the body. The original equipment used argon gas in copper tubes as an antennae along with an electromagnetic coil, but a wider spectrum of special gases charged with high-frequency currents and more powerful multiwave oscillators are now used to enhance the client's field of energy as he sits close to the electromagnetic coil. The unit creates multiple frequencies and biophotonic light that delivers the optimal vibration and frequency for cellular development and regeneration. Basically, it establishes the correct electromagnetic charge that helps improve the flow of nutrients, supports detoxification, stimulates DNA, and eliminates the damaged cells that are responsible for health-related problems. The VIBE machine is designed to bring cellular energy to its natural state.
Contact: www.vibelife.net

Cathiodermie (Hydradermie)
Cathiodermie is a relaxing and rejuvenating skin treatment, originally developed by the French biochemist Rene Guinot, that uses galvanic and high-frequency electrotherapy to rehydrate and regenerate surface tissues. In 2001, it was renamed Hydradermie. A machine provides low-voltage doses of electricity to cleanse and oxygenate the outer layers of skin tissue.

Besides being a form of facial therapy, Cathiodermie can be applied around the eyes and on the neck, bust, and back to help minimize lines, shadows, and wrinkles and to firm, smooth, tone, and refine the texture of the skin while gently easing strained muscles. It can be used for both men and women and is helpful for oily or acne-prone skin.
Contact: www.thebodyguide.co.uk

Chubinsky Method
Vladimir Chubinsky began his career as a therapist working on Olympic athletes in Russia, following the

custom of frequently using hand tools in the practice of massage. After immigrating to the United States, he began developing more effective versions of these tools, using ebonite. Ebonite, a hard rubber, is specially formulated to release beneficial negative ions that enhance the transfer of the heat produced by the action of massage into the deeper layers of the skin and muscles. Its hard, shiny surface resists the absorption of liniments and body fluids, yet helps to facilitate the penetration of massage oils or lotions deep into the skin of the recipient, and the ergonomic design of the tools spares the therapist's hands and body. The use of ebonite tools is intended to amplify the benefits of a therapeutic massage as the enhanced heat transfer promotes the healing of skin, tissues, and muscles and increases the flow in the body's lymph and circulatory systems.

The Chubinsky Method of bodywork combines an assortment of these tools with specific hands-on techniques. Each device, resembling a circular disk with a detachable knob that fits nicely into the practitioner's hand, is designed for massage on different segments of the body. One tool is particularly intended to provide fast recovery from spinal injuries. The patterns of hand movement unique to this form of bodywork vary depending on the part of the body being treated and include circular, back-and-forth, zig-zag, and direct-line movements. The practitioner essentially guides the device like an extension of his own hand, working deep into the tissue in such a way that the client hardly realizes that the tool exists.
Contact: www.vcmassage.com

Color and Light Therapy

There are a number of therapeutic methods that recognize the healing effects of the vibratory frequencies of color and light on the body. A variety of both color and light therapies have been developed with the same goal of healing physical and emotional distress by restoring energetic balance on a cellular level. During the early 1900s, Dr. Max Luscher developed a standard method of diagnosis using a color test that shows the effect of a color on the body; it was instrumental in the development of color therapy. Color and light therapies can be complementary additions before, during, or after various forms of bodywork.

Recognizing that what the eyes and skin receive will trigger the brain to respond in a positive way, color and light therapy has been employed in a variety of modalities. Peter Mandel modified conventional Acupuncture by using color rather than needles to target certain acupuncture points on the body. Other methods use lamps, floodlights, flashlights, or computer-controlled instruments to beam colored light into the face of a recipient. Colored oils may be applied to the chakras. Other applications of color therapy involving color irradiation, color meridian therapy, color light therapy, and meditations on color have been used successfully in the treatment of various forms of dysfunction. Color therapy has also been used to improve the balanced relationship between a person's physical, astral and spiritual realms.

It is well recognized that the lack of sunshine in winter can lead to depression and lethargy and can have a significant effect on the metabolism. Light-bath therapies, which treat these seasonal affective disorders, often employ light boxes that produce full-spectrum wavelengths of natural light to which the client is exposed by sitting near the box. Healing methods with light also includes cold laser therapy, which beams low-level laser light into the cells to promote natural healing.
Contact: www.chunginstitute.com

Aura Soma Care System® is a holistic approach to color and light therapy using the vibrational power of colors, plants, crystals and natural aromas to restore the body's original balance and harmony. The treatment is based on the conviction that these vibrations can be absorbed by the skin and from there pass information throughout the body, helping restore, revitalize, and rebalance the recipient on all levels. These vibrations can also transform consciousness.

Aura Soma, which means "shimmering light body," was created in England during the early 1980s by chiropodist Vicky Wall, who was endowed with the ability to see auras. Though blind, she was guided to create a series of specially formulated equilibrium bottles in which naturally colored liquids are charged with the essence of plants, minerals, and natural substances that emit deep, vibratory healing frequencies.

The process begins with the client choosing up to four bottles from the 108 currently in existence, basing the choice on the intuition of the heart. When the contents of the bottles are applied

to chakras or other parts of the body, their vibrations are brought into a person's etheric body or electromagnetic field. This in turn brings balance to the aura of the refined light bodies. The vibratory energies are dynamic, changing as the recipient changes. The system also includes a number of essences that can be applied to the skin and the aura to strengthen the etheric field and the chakras. The bodywork is not designed to release physical tension through deep massage, but rather to allow the energies of the gently applied products to correct what is out of balance in the client. After a session is completed, clients can continue using the chosen color(s) to lead to a more insightful awareness that emanates from the inner sacred core.
Contact: www.aura-soma.net

Crystal Therapy

The essences and subtle energies of crystals and gemstones have a long history of use for clearing the energetic pathways of the body. Crystal Therapy was employed by ancient Egyptian priests, Ayurvedic medicine practitioners, and in many other traditional cultures around the world; presently it is incorporated into many forms of bodywork. Since crystals and gemstones both have been recognized to have certain vibrational healing qualities, many people wear them around the neck or as a crown on the head. Quartz, amber, moonstone, lapis, topaz, and jade are commonly used in bodywork therapy, and each stone is considered appropriate for specific body parts and health conditions. The color of a particular stone or crystal also is considered an important factor.

During a massage, crystals can be placed on certain areas of the body, such as on the chakras or along meridians. The client may even be surrounded by crystals during a healing session to provide a beneficial effect on the energy field as a whole. Crystal bowl therapy is also used to activate, tune, and charge the chakras and energy bodies by transmitting sound vibrations that resonate at a cellular level. Therapists may even use crystals stimulated by pulses of high-frequency electromagnetic waves.
Contact: www.crystal-therapy.com or
www.luminanti.com

Crystalline Therapy, a recent variation within the field of crystal therapy, uses a self-activated crystal stimulator on acupressure or reflex points. It creates an electrical stimulus as two quartz crystals inside come together into a geometric pattern. The intention is to stimulate the release of endorphins in the brain that will help block the pain receptors in afflicted areas while opening the body's energy circuits. Different mineral crystals besides quartz may be chosen as dictated by the particular needs of the client, whether human or animal.
Contact: www.crystallinetherapy.com

ElectroCrystal Therapy is a gentle method of balancing the human energy field created by biologist Harry Oldfield during the 1980s and based on advances in Kirlian photography. Using Polycontrast Interference Photography (PIP), in which a special camera that records very high frequencies of light transmits information to a computer, which then converts these frequencies into colors, a picture of a person's energy pathways and auric field is created. Each color and the pattern of colors represent the condition and level of health in the chakras and auras at that point in time. The results are then analyzed to determine the best frequency for healing any energetic problems. Next, the ElectroCrystal Therapy takes over. Crystals contained in tubes are placed on certain points on the body and attached to a generator that beams amplified electromagnetic frequencies through the crystals to the recipient. The aim is to direct a vibratory pattern back into the body to correct the imbalance created by a particular dysfunction. At the end of the session, another PIP scan is performed to see how effective the therapy has been in producing positive changes. How long the effects last is not known for sure.

Oldfield also developed an Opto-Crystal Therapy unit that emits visible light pulsed through a crystal to balance the body's energy field. The unit uses light-emitting diodes (LEDs) mounted on a headband and directed into the client's eyes to invoke a healing response.
Contact: www.electrocrystal.com

Buddha Maitreya Soul Therapy® is an application of crystals for healing, spiritual awakening, and transformation that was developed by a healer known as H. H. Tulku Buddha Maitreya. As part of his Shambhala healing process, he created a Shambhala Pyramid System that incorporates the Shambhala Healing Tools™, a particular combination of crystals, magnets, and soul-therapy music married together within a special structure. A large, sacred-geometry pyramid is constructed with specially refined, double-terminated pure quartz crystals, rare earth magnets, and copper, silver, or gold wire, and it is placed over and around a special bed. The recipient simply lies on this bed while listening through headphones to a meditative CD of sacred sounds and tones that complement the healing process. In addition to this large pyramid, which is about eight feet square with a peak eight feet high, participants can use smaller similarly designed crystal pyramids that can be held in the hand or placed on the body or chakras. Each of these tools is intended to provide an awakening of telepathic abilities that allow the recipient to come into contact with the inner buddha. The intention is to provide a very deep, calming state of meditation that will transmute negative energies by naturally stimulating vital energy and correcting imbalances.

Contact: www.buddhamaitreya.org

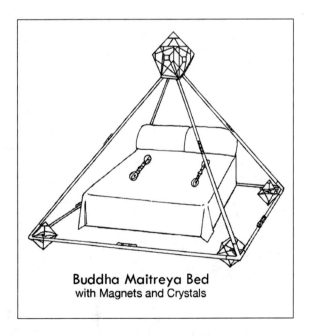

Buddha Maitreya Bed
with Magnets and Crystals

Dowsing

The ancient art and science of Dowsing is based on the relationship between matter, energy, and consciousness. It has been used not only to find water or metal but within the realm of healing to assess the energetic state of the chakras, energy fields, and a person's overall health. It is said that Dowsing will detect energy blockages with pinpoint accuracy. Dowsing also works to detect the root cause of dysfunction by determining the client's own subconscious tendencies. It has been shown to identify incompatible foods that can be the origin of disease, as well as which remedy will effectively treat a detrimental condition.

Many different dowsing instruments, in particular, pendulums made of wood or crystals, have been used, and they have been shown to react with the human nervous system and the body's internal vibrations. Dowsing with a pendulum has been used in America to detect stress and treat disease since the 1920s, and many practitioners incorporate pendulums and Dowsing in their therapy. Certain spiritual-alignment therapies also employ a special handheld metal aura meter to find imbalances in the electromagnetic field, which can then be treated with multidimensional energy work.

Contact: www.dowsinga.com or www.pendulums.com

Endermologie

The mechanical stimulation of the surface of the skin for healing purposes, referred to as Endermologie, was first developed in the late 1970s in France. The therapy utilizes computerized equipment with two adjustable rollers and controlled suction, which continuously fold and unfold the skin. The separate motorized rollers each gently pull the skin in three directions. At the same time, a lifting tool creates a wave of tissue. Its lift-and-roll action provides deep, smooth, and regulated tissue mobilization that can heal abnormalities in the underlying tissue. The stimulation of the skin's surface sends a message to cells down deep under the surface that provokes a physiological response. The suction improves blood flow and lymphatic drainage. The machine allows the therapist to cover a larger area more quickly with less effort. This form of treatment is usually found in health spas for beautifying the skin, treating cellulite, stretching tight tissue, and stimulating circulation. Although Endermologie is not a typical form of bodywork and its implementation is not very natural, it has been shown to be an effective form of treatment.

Contact: www.endermology.info

FAR Infrared Therapy (FIR)

Recent scientific research has contributed to the development of a new form of bodywork that incorporates the energy of infrared light. The basis of the therapy is that invisible infrared rays are very beneficial to human health, unlike the ultraviolet rays at the other end of the spectrum that can damage the skin and eyes. Infrared rays can come naturally from a variety of sources including the sun, but since sunlight contains a mix of rays, some of which are harmful, special equipment has been created to emit only infrared rays. These thermal rays have been scientifically recognized as capable of penetrating deep into the human body, where they gently elevate the body temperature and enhance bodily functions.

Treatments are considered useful for removing pathogens, permitting detoxification, increasing blood flow and oxygenation, repairing tissue, improving metabolic activity, and strengthening the immune system. This form of therapy employs a special device (sometimes a modified enclosed sauna box) that encircles the recipient's body. Treatments simply require the recipient to sit or lie in a relaxed position for a period of time while receiving the emitted rays; no practitioner participation is necessary. It is also possible to use infrared imaging for early detection and diagnosis of health concerns through thermography with a camera that reads and provide images of the entire electromagnetic spectrum of a client's body.
Contact: www.firheals.com

Graston Technique® (GISTM)

In 1987, David Graston suffered a multiple-ligament injury in his knee during an accident. After surgery left him with limited range of motion, Graston tried various forms of physical therapy to rectify the situation, but when he tried to correct the problem himself with extensive manual massage, his hands became very fatigued. This became the impetus to develop a new method for treating athletes with soft-tissue injuries and dysfunctions.

The therapy he created uses at least six different specially designed stainless-steel instruments to detect and treat areas in which soft tissue is inflamed in order to break down scar tissue, cross-fiber links, and fascial restrictions. When applied to the body, the tools are diagnostic, because vibrations can be felt through them.

Just as a stethoscope amplifies what the human ears can hear, this tool amplifies what the human hands can feel, allowing the practitioner to isolate and precisely treat the adhesions and restrictions. Healing is stimulated by creating small amounts of micro-trauma, often recognized by the reddening of the skin as blood rushes into the area, to which the body quickly responds. Today, the instruments are often used by chiropractors and bodyworkers because they provide improved diagnostics, decrease the overall treatment time, and prevent muscle fatigue in practitioners, since they don't use their hands extensively. This treatment is also considered a good precursor to other forms of bodywork such as the Active Release Techniques.
Contact: www.grastontechnique.com

Gua Sha

Gua Sha is an ancient Chinese method of body cleansing that uses a variety of smooth, flat scraping spoons or specially designed instruments to stimulate and rejuvenate the skin and to remove toxins and dead cells from its surface. This process can help tone the skin, activate the lymph glands, smooth out tension, improve blood circulation, stimulate pressure points, and slow down the aging process. The tools may be made of metal, porcelain, animal bone, polished plastic, or jade; besides a natural shape such as buffalo horns, their various designs include a roller, a stick, a comb, and a fish-shaped instrument. In Vietnam, practitioners often simply use the edge of a coin as a tool.

Oils, balms, and herbs that open the pores are often the first part of the cleansing process. Then the practitioner scrapes or rubs the skin with the Gua Sha tool, working primarily on the back, neck, shoulders, chest, hips, limbs, and any particular problem areas of the body. Each tool is applied to the skin with downward strokes, using moderately firm pressure without any strong friction. This action often results in the development of discoloration or a rash on the skin caused by changes in circulation and the release of metabolic waste; the condition will disappear after a few days. Areas of the body with moles, cuts, or unhealed wounds are avoided. Gua Sha can be used as an adjunct therapy by acupuncturists or in conjunction with a form of cleansing spa therapy, but it is not intended as a way to diagnose or treat any disease process.
Contact: www.guasha.com or www.guashashop.com

Kinesio Taping

During the 1980s, Japanese chiropractor Kenzo Kase created Kinesio Taping as a way in which the benefits of bodywork on acute and chronic neuromuscular and myofascial dysfunctions as well as other physical problems can be carried over between or after physical-therapy sessions. After the practitioner has completed the massage, special cotton-based elastic Kinesio Flex Tape is applied over and around the muscles, ligaments, and joints that have been treated in order to address chronic swelling, provide support, and prevent overcontraction. The tape creates space for the flow of lymphatic fluid by actually lifting the skin. It also allows full range of motion while keeping the muscles safe from further injury, as well as reducing pressure on and irritation of neural receptors. The application of the tape is relatively simple, yet considerable understanding is required for its proper positioning. The tape can be applied in two ways: without prestretching to provide a gentle form of neuromuscular reeducation or prestretched to apply a more aggressive corrective effect that may be appropriate for chronic conditions. It can be worn constantly for several days, and athletes often wear tape during competition. There are a number of other taping methods available, and each is appropriate for use in conjunction with many forms of bodywork. Since all tackle issues of inflammation and muscle fatigue, their use is becoming quite popular in the field of sports medicine.
Contact: www.kinesiotaping.com

> **Acutaping** is a form of treatment for chronic pain and injuries that uses an elastic adhesive bandage. However, in this case, the bandage is placed not only on the problem areas but on related acupuncture points or along specific meridian pathways. The therapy combines the actions of acupressure and gentle massage on an inflamed area while enhancing lymphatic drainage. Acutaping was developed by German doctors Kay Liebchen and Hans-Ulrich Hecker and is intended as an alternative to extensive physical therapy and drug use.

> **Functional Fascial Taping®** (FFT) is a rehabilitative taping technique, developed by Australian Ron Alexander, that is applied to any area of fascial dysfunction for relief of pain and to increase range of motion. Since this type of tape is rigid, it creates constant sustained tension that can help stretch the tissue for an extended period of time. The tape is applied in the locations and directions that are most suitable for the client's particular dysfunction as revealed through a hands-on fascial-tension assessment test. This form of physical therapy helps the soft tissues remain mobile for a prolonged period while the patient is active physically.

> **McConnell Taping**, developed by Jenny McConnell, is a taping method that uses a super-rigid cotton-mesh adhesive tape to brace and support areas of chronic dysfunction for short periods of time, usually up to eighteen hours. It is primarily used for neuromuscular reeducation of an afflicted area when activity is necessary. It should be removed after a short time to prevent any adverse reactions or irritation caused by the constrictive nature of the tape.

Kosmed Therapy

Years were spent in Russia developing a cheap, portable, noninvasive, universal healing device. The result is an instrument that uses electrical impulses in appropriate patterns applied directly to particular areas of the body in order to stimulate the body to activate or reactivate its own self-recovery program. A hand-held instrument with a small digital readout screen and two metal contact plates is placed on the skin and communicates through the autonomic nervous system in a biofeedback loop between the body and the device. Using information about the body's condition, the device adjusts the electrical impulse that is intended to influence the body's internal function. This tool can open energy pathways and remove blockages. There are no claims made that anything can be healed, but the goal of the therapy is the reduction and elimination of many types of pain.
Contact: Kosmed International – www.ritmcanada.ca or www.wholisticresearch.com

Laser Therapy

Laser Therapy, also known as Cold Laser Therapy or Low Level Laser Therapy (LLLT), refers to the use of the red to near-infrared wavelengths of light produced by a laser that are applied directly to an affected or irritated

area in order to reduce pain and inflammation and help heal wounds. These wavelengths from the cold part of the electromagnetic radiation spectrum penetrate the surface of the skin with no heating effect, and when the laser light is directed to the body cells, it is converted into chemical energy to promote natural healing and pain relief. When the low-level light penetrates deep into the skin, it can optimize the immune response of the circulatory system. Many acute and chronic conditions can be improved or eliminated with Laser Therapy, and sometimes cold lasers rather than needles are used to stimulate acupuncture points. This therapy originated in Hungary during the 1960s and should not be confused with the laser surgery that is used to treat some cancers. Contact: www.laserspineinstitute.com, or
www.thorlaser.com

Ozone / Oxygen Therapy

Although not commonly used in bodywork, the benefit of the supplemental introduction of small amounts of ozone, oxygen or a mix of the two into a person's body has been known for a number of years. The primary purpose is to help increase the oxygenation of body tissue. Medical Ozone Therapy basically requires a contaminant-free ozone generator that creates ozone from the pure oxygen delivered by a tank with an adjustable output. Methods of application vary and include such things as a steam cabinet or sauna, a body suit, a special bag applied to an isolated body part, an implement that irrigates the ears, a rectal insufflation instrument, or an intravenous drip of small amounts of medical-grade hydrogen peroxide and water. Contact: www.ozoneuniversity.com or
www.oxygenhealingtherapies.com

Photon Sound Beam Therapy (PSB)

Photon Sound Beam Therapy provides a full spectrum of harmonic vibrational frequencies that are used to rectify energetic imbalances while stimulating and strengthening the body. Photon energy is delivered through combining an ionized field of noble gas energy and penetrating harmonic radio sound waves, resulting in an extremely wide band of photobiotic light and sound frequencies that can depolarize and break up energy blockages and reestablish an ideal energetic state in the body that destroys pathogens. This high-tech system essentially helps detoxify the body by enhancing the flow of lymph and blood through the resonant healing effect of the photon sound beam.

The therapeutic action is accomplished by attaching tubes filled with noble gas to the skin and then sending through them the harmonics-rich output created by a radio-frequency sound probe and a vibrating crystal oscillator. The resulting combined vibrations of light and sound help stimulate the body, reestablish the optimum frequency for cellular functioning, and recharge the life-force energy. Though by far not a typical form of bodywork, this advanced technological tool can be used in conjunction with more natural health programs. Contact: www.photonsoundbeam.net

Radionic Therapy

Radionic Therapy, sometimes referred to as Psychotronics, is a form of vibrational healing that uses a special instrument to analyze disturbances in a person's energetic frequency and then send a frequency of universal healing energy to treat any disease detected. The instrument, developed during the 1930s in Europe by Dr. George De La Warr, has been used extensively there and in Canada for decades to treat a variety of problems. This electrical instrument looks like a small black box and broadcasts an intense ray of energy with a narrow band of specific vibrational frequencies in order to generate a minor electromagnetic energy field attuned to the recipient.

During a session, subtle vibrations from the client are first picked up by the Radionics instrument for the practitioner's analysis. The dials on the box are then reset to radiate the vibrational frequency that will restore the client to a state of balance and harmony. The client doesn't even have to be present, since something personal (a hair sample or a photo) can be used for the energetic attunement process. It is reported that when the recipient is present, the effects vary from subtle and mild to intense, according to client sensitivity and the extent of the problems. A complete healing release may require a number of sessions. The therapy is definitely not bodywork in the usual sense. Contact: www.radionics.org

Raindrop Therapy

Gary Young created Raindrop Therapy after he studied the electrical fields and frequencies of natural oils that he processed and distilled on his farm in Utah.

However, some suggest that this therapy originally came from the Native American Lakota tribe. In any case, the Raindrop Therapy that Young developed involves a sequence of specific essential oils being gently dropped like rain on the feet, shoulders, and back. The electrical charges of these oils are then "breathed" into the body. Specific massage techniques such as thumb walking, finger rolling, and feathering spread the oils upward on the back and outward from the spine and are followed by circular and transverse motions. A finishing oil balances out the energy. The oils used during the process may include those of oregano, thyme, coconut, olive, basil, cypress, wintergreen, birch, and marjoram, as well as a combination called valor oil and peppermint oil, which enhances all the others. A hot compress is then used to open the pores and nerve receptors. Passive stretching with vibration and flexing of both the back and neck completes the process. The therapy can be used to address defects in the curvature of the spine caused by dormant bacteria or viruses. It is best for a recipient to drink plenty of water before the treatment to help flush out the body's toxins and to stay well hydrated afterward. Some practitioners combine this therapy with Reiki energy balancing.

Contact: www.raindroptherapy.net

Stone Massage Therapy / Hot Stone Massage

The use of stones in bodywork is found in the ancient indigenous cultures of Europe, the Americas, Asia, and the Pacific Islands. The Chinese used heated stones as a means of improving the function of the internal organs and nervous system. In Japan, stones assisted the energetic treatment of acupressure points. European folk healers diminished the discomfort of menstruation with heated stones. The Romans used stones for therapy in their saunas. A variety of methods that use stones in their massage practices, including Batu Jamu (discussed earlier in this section) and the Hawaiian Pohaku Welawela, an adjunct part of the Lomi Lomi system of healing (see the section on Special Therapies in this chapter), have been developed over the years in different parts of the world. Heating an area of the body with hot stones causes more blood with fresh nutrients to flow into that area; cold stones cause the blood vessels to contract and are commonly used to reduce inflammation or to move blood out of the area. The more extreme the temperature, the stronger the response. Sometimes,

hot and cold stones are alternated, creating a pumping action that promotes healing on a cellular level by producing a rapid exchange of blood and lymph that increases oxygenation. In most instances, hot stones are preheated by the therapist, but their preparation can also be geothermal (naturally heated by the heat of the earth). Stone therapy in all of its many applications has been shown to be beneficial for the circulatory, digestive, nervous, and lymphatic systems and for the muscles and skin. Stones and minerals are also used in the practice of Lithotherapy for energetic balancing.

Which stones are chosen depends on the practice. Volcanic lava stones such as basalt are commonly used for hot stone work, and marble is ideal for cold applications. In any case, the various sizes and shapes will be smooth. Jade, limestone, crystals or gemstones can also be employed to obtain particular metabolic and emotional effects. During a hot stone massage, the client typically lies alternately on tummy and back, unclothed but covered with a large towel. Stones heated to a comfortable temperature are placed on the skin at various locations on both sides of the body so that the penetrating heat can soften the tissue, relax the body, and relieve myofascial pains. Hot stones can be stroked along the body, applied with gentle rotary pressure, or simply rested along areas such as the spine to release stagnant energy. They can also be pressed into particular locations on the body's meridians for energy balancing or on specific trigger points to release painful muscle constrictions. Sometimes massage cream or oil is first kneaded into the skin so that the stones can glide smoothly over the body.

Though the actual origins of Hot Stone Massage are lost in the distant past, the use of stones was revitalized and offered to the general public in 1993 when LaStone Massage was developed by Mary Nelson-Hannigan. She drew upon the wisdom of various ancient healers to further develop her own approach to stone bodywork, which uses alternating hot and cold stones in a specific way throughout the whole massage. This method is now used by many health spas.

Another form of stone bodywork, called Stone Therapy Massage, created by Jane Scrivner, places stones along the main chakras as well as at specific locations on the back, hands, neck, and legs. Hot natural basalt stones and specially shaped cold marble are used at different times to massage the whole body. Alternating the temperature of stones can produce a very relaxing, calming, and yet stimulating experience. Both hot and cold stones are left on the body for an extended period of time to create the strong physiological response that will help the body keep itself in balance.

Many variations of hot stone therapy have been incorporated into other types of massage such as Swedish Massage, Deep Tissue Massage, Myofascial Release, Polarity Therapy, Craniosacral Therapy, and energy-oriented chakra or meridian work.

Contact: www.experiencelife.com or
www.janescriver.com

IV. Aquatic Therapies

As the inner ocean within our own being meets the surrounding waters of the outer ocean, our bodies easily become one with water's natural, relaxed fluidity. It's as if the water that makes up such a large part of our bodies feels somehow nurtured when the body rests in a watery environment. Just consider lying flat on your back in seawater while looking at the blue sky above. Or better yet, diving down deep into the clear blue-green sea and rolling over to look up at the sunbeams streaming down to greet you. It's no wonder that transformations occur when the body is immersed in or treated with water.

Enjoyable aquatic therapy when traveling on the ocean.

The fluid quality of water has the natural ability to soften and relax the body, which reduces stress and allow us to function better. The increased resistance of water as compared with air helps strengthen core muscles during any workout, thus improving the ability to function physically. The buoyancy provided by the water eases the bonds of gravity and allows multidimensional movement without muscle strain. Just as it holds a boat sailing on its surface, water carries the human body softly. Its support allows the body freedom of movement, which enables it to fully express itself without restriction. Add to this some flow, as found in the currents of the ocean or in the energy released throughout the body when it's loose, relaxed, and open, and a great journey becomes possible.

Most of my own therapeutic experiences with water came naturally through my travels at sea. Thinking

about those times, vivid images of certain experiences come to mind. When I was sailing and got becalmed (an extended period of time when there is no wind), I would dive off the bow down deep into the clear blue water and roll over and look up to see the hull of the sailboat slowly drifting above me. Luminescent beams of sunlight radiated down around me like a glow from heaven. It definitely put a different perspective on my existence. Of course I can't forget diving on a tropical reef full of brightly-colored coral and brilliant fish moving about close to my face. This undersea world would make anyone gasp with awe (while being careful not to inhale that salt water!) and inspire great appreciation for the wonders of life. Even my many experiences with dolphins might be considered healing, because they brought such joy to my heart. Hanging low off the bow, eye to eye with these happily prancing creatures, is something I wish everyone could experience. More in the context of aquatic bodywork, I can never forget the feeling of seawater massaging my body. This is best accomplished when the boat is sailing fast downwind. You hook up a bosun's chair on the end of the main boom, climb out onto this seat, swing out just over the surface of the water, and stretch out horizontally. As the boat rolled, I would get dunked into the water as it rushed by. Every surface of my body from head to toe pulsated with the cascade of water molecules. You can get somewhat the same effect from standing under a waterfall. Give it a try sometime.

Water has always been important in ancient healing methods for purifying, detoxifying, cleansing, and rejuvenating the body and soul, often in conjunction with sacred healing rituals. The ceremonial nature of many of these activities has led not only to better physical health but spiritual transformation. In Native American and other indigenous cultures around the world, sweat lodges were a regular form of care for all individuals within a community, often incorporating the purifying and cleansing power of steam assisted by herbs, muds, or magic stones. The Greeks and Romans employed large-scale baths for relaxation and therapy. In Japan, where there are more natural hot springs than anywhere else in the world, the cleansing properties of the minerals in the water have been an integral part of the culture's energetic healing therapies for centuries. Many ancient aquatic treatment therapies are still in use today, and a number of contemporary adaptations have been developed using modern facilities and equipment.

This section discusses therapeutic methods carried out with, in, or around water. They can be divided into two broad areas: those that rely on the water itself to do the work and those in which bodywork is carried out in the water. Balneology is the ancient technique of bathing in or drinking mineralized waters, often found in natural hot springs, and it can also involve the use of organic muds, natural gases, and steam therapy. Any passive immersions in hot or warm baths, natural mineral waters, or other aquatic spa facilities could be called Balneology or Spa Therapy. Hydrotherapy originated in part from Balneology, but generally refers to modalities that rely on the motion of water at a specific temperature, for example, a whirlpool bath. It can also refer to the external application of water or steam by means of sprays, baths, showers, jets, and compresses. With all these more passive forms of aquatic therapy, the fluid joy of simply interacting with water is therapeutic in itself.

Some massage therapists have submerged their practices in warm water because it allows for the possibility of innovative forms of movement and manipulations. When bodywork is performed as the recipient is supported by the water in a pool, the practitioner is able to slide the hands in an uninterrupted motion all around, over, and under the client's body without lifting. This also does away with the need for the client to turn for access to a different side, making it easier for those with impaired mobility. In fact, the use of warm water has been shown to open up new possibilities for those having trouble moving easily. Most of these treatments are used not only to alleviate stress, release holding patterns, and cleanse the body but also to stimulate the skin and muscles, improve digestion and the circulation of blood and lymph, fortify the immune system, and relieve pain by stimulating the nervous system. Aquatic therapies can renew the vital life-force energy and bring about a powerful emotional response that can lead to a rebirthing experience as the inner child is contacted.

Aquatic therapies of all types are accomplished in a variety of settings, sometimes outside close to nature and sometimes within the confines of an aquatic healing center or spa. There are even massage treatments, known as Anthotherapy, that take place in caves heated by a nearby hot spring or in other natural settings filled with moist, hot vapor. The combination of steam and massage in a natural setting has been found to provide a very relaxing and stress-reducing form of therapy. Healing aquatic modalities can be experienced with a group or as a personal health care practice as simple as exercising in water. These therapies often include a hydrothermal massage, which combines heat, water, and aromatherapy while the client is soaking in a tub or pool of warm or hot water. In some cases, the recipient lies on a special mat filled with warm water that is kept at a constant temperature.

When warm or hot water is used, modalities are referred to as hydrothermal. These heated-water methods, either on their own or in conjunction with massage, not only improve circulation and respiration but also help remove toxins from the skin, tissues, and organs. Saunas, sweats, hot springs, or tubs are often involved. Hydrothermal facial therapy is becoming a popular method for cleansing the face and skin, and in thermotherapy, hot and cold packs are applied alternately to increase circulation. In addition, localized heat treatments can be carried out with moxibustion, compresses, and body wraps, and by inhaling steam through the nose.

Water has also led to some interesting and unique healing methods. One relatively recent example is Dolphin-Assisted Therapy, in which people swim and interact with dolphins. The dolphins' innate ability to identify dysfunctions and heal through their own form of sound therapy seems to reduce stress and provide emotional and physical healing. In Eastern Europe, there is a form of treatment in which the client immerses the feet or other parts of the body in water containing hundreds of small fish that nibble off all the dead skin. This practice is considered beneficial for fighting psoriasis and chronic skin diseases. It has been reported to be a very ticklish affair.

The following compilation includes therapies that involve water in one form or another, though some of them are not bodywork in the strictest sense. If a particular treatment includes any manipulation of the body, whether it is applied by a practitioner's hands or by the water itself, it is included here. Also listed are several other types of treatments such as spa therapy, body baths, footbaths, and body wraps, which often combine water, heat, and natural substances such as muds, salts, and paraffin and sometimes include massage. Personal movement exercises done in the water

without any applied bodywork are detailed in Chapter 11. Although most aquatic therapies have only a few contraindications, it would still be wise to first check with your health care practitioner if you have particular preexisting conditions that might be problematic.
Contact: Aquatic Resource Network –
www.aquaticnet.com or Worldwide Aquatic
Bodywork Association – www.aba.org

Ai Chi

Ai Chi is a gentle bodywork therapy created during the 1990s by Jun Konno, who is an aquatic fitness consultant and founding president of the Aqua Dynamics Institute of Japan. It is intended to promote relaxation, stability, and better health through water movement exercises in conjunction with conscious controlled breathing. The therapy embraces the traditional Asian meditative movement practices of Tai Chi and qi gong and yogic breathing techniques; it places strong emphasis on the progressive cultivation of chi. These practices are combined with assisted yoga, Watsu techniques, and Shiatsu to provide an energizing and flowing form of aquatic therapy.

A session is performed with both the practitioner and the client in shoulder-deep warm water. While the practitioner gives verbal and visual instructions, the recipient practices deep diaphragmatic breathing and carries out a slow progression of broad circular movements of the arms, legs and torso. This is usually a hands-off rather than hands-on therapy, but the facilitator may intermittently apply some touch and massage. There are different levels of practice, and the therapy is suitable for people of all ages and conditions, for it is very gentle, soothing, and relaxing. Once learned, the individual exercises can be done without a practitioner. Besides promoting health and fitness, this therapy may be useful for people with arthritis.

Jun Konno has also developed a variation of this therapy known as Ai Chi Ne that combines partner stretching and special breathing techniques with elements of Ai Chi to remove stress and tension while enhancing the body's reflex responses and flexibility.

Ruth Sova, the founder of both the Aquatic Exercise Association and the Aquatic Therapy and Rehab Institute, helped popularize the program globally.
Contact: www.aqua-gear.com, www.aeawave.com,
www.atri.org, or www.ruthsova.com

Aquacranial Therapy

Aquacranial Therapy was developed by Rebecca Goff, a massage therapist and naturalist in Hawaii, after she studied the behavior and movement of whales and dolphins. It uses a combination of yoga postures, meridian work, and Craniosacral Therapy to create the fluid, wave-like, gentle movement of sea creatures, thus improving the circulation of the cerebrospinal fluid and the functioning of the central nervous system. The client is cradled, supported (with the help of a neck pillow), and gently guided through the water while the therapist applies gentle touch and pressure on certain points on the skull and along the length of the spine in conjunction with rocking motions that help the recipient retain equilibrium. The therapist often pushes the client through the water while contacting reflex points on the bottom of the feet. This pushing also creates waves of movement that help accentuate the bodywork. Many of the techniques used were revealed to Goff by dolphins that had previously come into the deep-water treatment area and made contact with the participants.

Treatments take place either in the ocean, when weather permits, or in large natural hot springs, pools, or hot tubs. The outdoor warm-ocean environment is considered best, since the natural rhythm of the waves allows the recipient to just let go and the salt water's increased buoyancy enables easy floating. Although each person will likely have a different experience, the benefits commonly include stress relief, increased circulation, better flexibility, and relief from chronic pain. Emotional release may also occur as the recipient surrenders to this fluid, womb-like environment. The therapy is not only helpful for those with a variety of disabilities, but can provide a very sensual experience in which there may be a transformation to a peaceful altered state of consciousness. Goff has since expanded this form of aquatics to create her own special therapy, which has been likened to a rebirthing experience.
Contact: www.aquacranial.com

Aquatic Integration (AI)

Another approach to body-temperature hydrotherapy, developed by Cameron West, a massage therapist and adaptive physical-education teacher, Aquatic Integration uses warm water as a holistic therapy to encourage sensory integration through touch, communication, stillness, and movement. Rooted in Watsu and neurosomatic assessment, AI bridges Eastern and Western approaches to healing and is an effective treatment for sensory neurological repatterning and physical and emotional trauma. In addition to rhythmic movement and touch, the breath is considered the key to unifying and unlocking the highest potential for healing.

During a session, a soft collar and leg floats often support the client, allowing the practitioner to use both hands for palpating, mobilizing, and connecting with the recipient. Communication between the practitioner and client is considered essential for maintaining a trusting, healthy relationship. Aquatic Integration is particularly appropriate for restoring impaired sensory perception and increasing range of motion, though it can be used by therapists working in a number of different rehabilitation modalities.

Contact: www.aquaticintegration.com

Aquatic Integration session.

Aquatic Proprioceptive Neuromuscular Facilitation (Aquatic PNF)

PNF has evolved through various modifications since Dr. Herman Kabal originally developed it as a treatment for polio patients by in the mid-1950s. Although elements of the original therapy (such as the use of fixed external resistance) were included in the Bad Ragaz Ring Method (see in this section), further experimentation done decades later, particularly by Lynette Jamison and David Ogden, brought new movement patterns into use. This active form of aquatic movement therapy can be provided in either a hands-on or hands-off manner by the facilitator.

During a session, the client is verbally, visually, and/or tactilely instructed in performing a series of functional, spiral, and diagonal movement patterns while standing, sitting, kneeling, or lying horizontally in the water. The patterns may be performed actively or passively with resistance or assistance provided by the therapist or special equipment. The equipment includes such things as aquatic gloves, dumbbells, paddles, or bells for the upper body, and fins, boots, or specially designed shoes for the lower body. These devices can provide resistance or drag even to parts of the body distant from the device as the client is guided through a series of moves and poses. Since the resistance is not in a fixed position but moves with the client, a more fluid type of strengthening workout is provided. The therapy is most often performed in pools with the water kept above 90 degrees Fahrenheit.

Contact: www.aquatictherapist.com

Aquatic Relaxation Chamber (ARC)

In this warm-water pool specially designed by Mike and Sue Nelson, clients can soak, relax, and gain therapeutic benefits while encircled with soothing sounds, pleasant images of a beach at sunset, and tantalizing scents that stimulate well-being. It is a chamber that incorporates easy access, a water-flow control for soothing water massage, mood lighting, and aromatherapy. Among the most relaxing features of the ARC are the sound effects produced by an under- and above-water speaker system and visuals from a projector that displays life-size video images on the surrounding walls. The experience is like a virtual-reality, feel-good healing process.

Contact: www.USAswimming.org

Asclepius Therapy

This ancient healing method, named for the Greek health practitioner Asclepius, dates back to around 1200 BCE, and Hippocrates later used this particular therapy to treat athletes. It was very much influenced by the Asclepian healing protocol in which people traveled to a specific site to partake of elements of spa therapy. Asclepius is likely one of the first responsible for the use of hydrotherapy in conjunction with massage for healing, which, in this case, was accomplished at a unique snake-charming temple built around healing springs. Inside this temple, people fasted, took hot water or steam baths, and then slept in a dream-incubation chamber. Their dreams were believed to contain

remedies offered by the gods. An oracle would then interpret these dreams and devise the cures. The cult that developed from this temple healing later came to Rome and ultimately evolved into the Turkish baths and Roman sweat rooms that are still in use today.
Contact: www.asclepiusmassage.com

Bad Ragaz Ring Method (BRRM)

Originally known as just Bad Ragaz, this form of aquatic therapy, formulated in 1957 in Germany and established at the thermal pool resort of Bad Ragaz in Switzerland, is always performed in a hands-on manner. The client is verbally, visually, and physically instructed in a series of movements or relaxation patterns while positioned horizontally in the water and supported by rings or floats. The patterns may be performed in a passive mode with the therapist moving the recipient's body to induce relaxation and increase flexibility. It has evolved into a method of muscle reeducation that uses specific patterns of resistance, endurance, elongation, relaxation, muscle toning, and range of motion. In other instances, the work can be more active on the part of the recipient, with the facilitator just assisting the patterns of movement.
Contact: www.badragazringmethod.org

Body Baths and Showers

Various forms of soothing body baths and showers are often employed as part of detoxifying spa therapies. Body baths include a wide variety of healing treatments that use warm or hot water and can range from full-body soaks to just a simple ionic detoxifying hand- or footbath. Some spas and healing centers use seawater, and special baths found in Japan contain water rich in specific enzymes. Natural thermal mineral springs of varying temperatures, ranging from warm to very hot, have been used around the world for centuries. If the water is not from such a spring, it can be enriched with healing substances such as herbs, seaweed, kelp, peat moss, mud, mustard powder, whey powder (milk), oils, minerals, and oxygen. These may be combined with stone therapy, steam vapor, sound waves, and light therapy. Special showers with bubble jets, underwater pressure jets, and hot tubs with whirlpools may be used as an adjunct to bodywork such as Swedish Massage, Shiatsu, Reflexology, and Acupressure. The following is a sample of some of the more popular types of baths and showers available, each of which can be used as a form of self-care with or without professional assistance.

Brine Baths are for those who want to gain the therapeutic benefits that the natural salts in seawater can provide. Hot salt water also helps warm and soften muscles before stretching or other exercise.

Detoxifying Footbaths can be a blessing for sore, tired feet. The recipient sits fully clothed while placing the feet in a small tub of warm water mixed with a variety of soothing herbs and minerals. Today, a footbath is often part of a more extensive spa therapy session.

Douche Showers use fine jets of water to deliver a thermal aquatic massage to particular areas of the body that need attention. A douche can also be a handheld device that sends a stream of water (that may include vinegar or antiseptics) into body cavities to cleanse these areas.

Mineral Salt Baths use natural mineral salts (especially sodium chloride and sodium sulfate) taken directly from the earth and containing properties long recognized to be healing. The therapy simply involves the client soaking in a tub of water mixed with these salts for a period of time. Soaking in Epsom salts (magnesium sulfate) has been recognized as beneficial for relieving the soreness of tired or aching muscles.

Natural Hot Spring (Mineral) Therapy has most likely been around since early human history, when natural hot springs were used for enjoyment and for healing. Most early civilizations made this discovery naturally, and both the Romans and Greeks used hot springs for pleasurable social gatherings. The first European spas, usually established at natural springs, became very popular during the seventeenth and eighteenth centuries and remain so today. Japan is blessed with more than 2,000 natural springs, which were used by both royalty and laypeople as an integral part of everyday life. Although in the past, indigenous people found the virtues of these minerals through experience, modern science has confirmed their benefits through research in chemistry.

Finding heaven in a hot spring.

Each of the springs around the world contains a unique combination of assorted minerals. The most common include bicarbonates (also called salts), sulfur (mostly hydrogen sulfate), sulfates (often bonded with calcium, sodium, and magnesium), and chloride (primarily sodium chloride). In addition, other minerals, such as iron, calcium, magnesium, potassium, lithium, arsenic, and silica, along with carbon dioxide, radon gases, and peloids (thermal mud), can be found in these thermal waters. Not all of these minerals are beneficial on their own, but are helpful when found in a certain combination or quantity. Mineral springs in general have primarily been used to treat problems with digestion, circulation, respiration, and the skin, not to mention the basic soothing, relaxing, and stress-reducing qualities of the experience they provide. Some waters with an alkaline pH and specific mineral content have gained the reputation of being exceptional for drinking, and today they are available as bottled water.

Scotch Hose Massage is a form of aquatic therapy in which a practitioner uses a hose to direct strong needle-point jets of water in specific patterns on the recipient, who is standing several feet away in a large shower stall. Alternating hot and cold water or seawater is used to stimulate circulation. Reportedly, it can be an intense and invigorating treatment.

Sitz Baths are for those who like the idea of alternating between cold and warm water during a bath. Hot-and-cold aquatic therapy can be very energizing as well as beneficial for inflamed muscles.

A similar invigorating effect can be obtained by jumping into a cold river or a bank of snow after indulging in a sweat lodge or sauna. This therapy is very stimulating to the metabolism, but is not recommended for those with a weak heart.

Steam Bath Therapy is considered one of the best forms of cleansing therapies available, and it's one of the author's favorites. It is an excellent way to produce full-body sweating for the purpose of detoxification and has been found to increase the activity of immune cells, thus promoting a more effective defensive response; it also offers benefits in weight management programs. Steam therapy is particularly helpful to the respiratory system (especially the nasal sinuses and lungs) and the circulatory system, as well as for opening the pores of the skin. It is often better tolerated than dry heat by people with dry skin or sensitive nostrils.

Native American sweat lodge.

Steam has been used as a form of cleansing since early times and has a long history of use in Ayurvedic, Japanese, and European hydrotherapy traditions. In ancient times, natural hot springs were a major source of such therapy; today, many innovative facilities can be found in spas and retreat centers. Massage therapists appreciate the use of steam therapy before bodywork, because the muscles, ligaments, fascia, and tendons become more relaxed and flexible. In fact, there are practitioners who use a special steam canopy that fits over a massage table, a steam cabinet, or a steam capsule. (Steam canopies are useful for those who may otherwise suffer from dizziness or nausea, since the head and neck are outside the canopy.) Many retreat centers or spas also have inventively designed steam rooms in which groups can sweat together. Steam is also used for sacred ceremonies in various indigenous sweat lodges, such as those found among the Lakota people. These lodges provide a place where special healing practices can bring about intense physical and emotional release, sometimes leading to spiritual transformation, all of which are beneficial for the individual as well as the whole community.

Swiss Showers, as the name suggests, were developed in Switzerland, a country in which the popularity of thermal aquatic therapies has led to many innovative applications. In a Swiss shower, an individual stands in a shower stall with many nozzles that spray from various directions on all areas of the body.

Underwater Pressure Massage is a type of aquatic bodywork that uses a special tub fitted with a pressurized water hose with a variety of interchangeable nozzles. The recipient lies relaxed in a tub full of warm water, while the therapist moves the hose over various muscles and body parts in a prescribed fashion, applying an underwater stream of warm water. The pressure of this stream is adjusted as needed for client's particular conditions, and the client lies on her side while the back is massaged. Circular and diagonal motions are often used on areas such as the neck and parts of the back, and the individual's needs determine the direction in which other areas are massaged. After the massage, a cold-water effusion may be used to stimulate circulation.

Vichy Shower Massage is performed with pulsating jets of water directed in gentle or vigorous patterns primarily at the reflex zones along the spine, sacrum and legs to stimulate internal body systems and circulation. This water massage is often carried out after nourishing skin products are applied with body wraps. During the treatment, the client either stands or rests horizontally on a table in a large wet-room while water of varying temperatures is sprayed over the entire body by a number of water jets. This is often followed by an exfoliating treatment with dulse or a loofah sponge or by a salt-glow scrub.

Body Compresses

Compresses may not always be made with water (a warm castor oil compress can help relieve soreness), but they can be applied as stand-alone spa therapies or as an adjunct to massage. Compresses prepared with warm or hot water can be used on localized areas of the body to improve the metabolic rate of cells and to increase blood circulation to the area; increasing local blood flow and the influx of white blood cells will enhance the healing of an injury. Improved flexibility can also result from heating an area, allowing a better stretching of muscles and easier movement. Cold compresses help reduce inflammation and its resulting pain, though to be most effective they should be applied soon after any injury occurs. Body compresses allow a variety of healing substances to be absorbed into the bloodstream through the skin, especially when the compresses are made with warm water. Although compresses may be applied to specific areas of the body, the benefits are often transmitted to the whole body, mind and spirit.

Hauschka Body Compress Massage refers to a method developed by a German chemist named Dr. Hauschka, who also has a line of skin-care products. The treatment involves the use of a warm, scented compress placed on parts of the body. This is followed by a light, rhythmic massage (similar to Swedish Massage) with moisturizing oils. The aim is to stimulate the lymphatic and circulatory systems to help release toxins and strengthen the immune system.
Contact: www.drhauschka.com.au

A **Thai Herbal Compress,** similar to herbal compresses found in other parts of Asia, consists of a warmed mixture of therapeutic herbs and other ingredients such as fresh coconut and lime. The ingredients vary depending on what the therapist is hoping to achieve and often include camphor (for cooling), turmeric (for antisepsis), ginger (for moisturizing), and menthol (to treat the respiratory system). The compress can be applied during bodywork that uses massage strokes that include compression on problem areas or applied after a session to help alleviate any residual tension.

Body Packs / Fango Therapy

The practice of using natural muds for localized body packs or for coating the whole body has long been a part of spa therapy. Therapists have recognized that these muds help soothe and soften the skin and remove toxins from the body; they are also believed to be useful in relieving muscle pain and arthritic conditions. Sometimes a person is totally immersed in a tub of warm mud made with water from natural hot mineral springs. One form of Fango (Mud) Therapy is the Asian Rasul, which is a traditional ritual Arabic cleansing treatment. After clients shower with seaweed soap that may contain a floral cleanser, they are coated with a medicinal, mineral "magic mud" mixture. This is followed by the application of dry heat and then an herbal steam bath. This practice is meant to exfoliate the skin, open the lungs, and detoxify the system and is often done before a massage.

Body Scrubs

Though by themselves body scrubs may not really be an aquatic form of therapy, they are often employed in conjunction with aquatic spa therapies. Scrubs involve rubbing the body with a mixture of mineral salts, seaweed, and abrasives with the goal of exfoliating the body surface by removing the outer layer of dead skin cells, thus leaving the skin clean and smooth. Many of these preparations are quite exotic and include such things as salt, sugar, apricot kernels, and coffee grounds. After the completion of a scrub, the remains are wiped off with a wet towel. Polish Brossage is a scrub that uses a series of scrubbing brushes and exfoliating salts to remove dead skin and improve circulation. This skin-toning treatment is often followed with a seaweed body massage or mud mask.

Body Wraps and Hot Packs

In addition to exfoliating body scrubs, herbal or seaweed wraps and body masks are often part of skin-cleansing therapy, and hot or cold packs are used to stimulate the circulation. In an herbal wrap, blankets infused with herbal essences are placed on the skin. These herbs can then penetrate the skin to promote cleansing and relaxation. Whole-body wraps envelop the body with sheets that have been soaked in special blends of herbs, ash, or paraffin. Natural substances such as essential oils and mud are used in packs, either on the face or over the whole body, to help purify and detoxify the skin and myofascial tissue layers. Aromatherapy with particular blends of high-quality essential oils is often incorporated into body wraps and facials for the purpose of reducing swelling and stimulating the lymphatic system.

The **Indonesian Body Wrap** is an integral part of Indonesian treatment therapy. Cleaning and purifying the skin and body with baths, scrubs, masks, facials, and wraps is highly appreciated in these spice islands. In itself, the body wrap is a refreshing process intended to detoxify the body and may consist of a single application or a series of them. The purifying substances are applied in a soothing manner, which may or may not include a full-body massage. Natural substances used in the treatment may include marine algae to exfoliate the skin; a Thai coconut oil and lemongrass scrub to refresh the body; Balinese sea salts and flower lotions to purify the skin; a Java lava scrub and mask with oils and volcanic clay to detoxify the skin; and a scrub and lotion rub with coconut and vanilla oil. Spices are often blended into a mask, and the skin massaged as the mask dries. There are also a number of ritual bodywork treatments, such as the Javanese Lulur and the Balinese Boreh, that use an assortment of these natural elements in combination with massage.

Colonic Irrigation / Cleansing — See section on Abdominal Therapies in this chapter.

Crenotherapy

Crenotherapy is a general term used to describe any treatment that combines thermal mineral water, mud, or vapor to soothe muscles, reduce pain or stress, and promote well-being. Different methods encourage the absorption of this medicinal water. They include mud poultices, water massage, a mobility pool, a spray pool, and an aero bath or jet sprays. Medicinal water can also be taken internally to aid digestion and provide a laxative, diuretic, phlegm-producing, or respiration-inducing effect. This therapy is intended to be beneficial for digestion and as a boost for the immune system. Crenotherpy is very popular in Europe.

Cryotherapy

Cryotherapy is a type of hydrotherapy in which either the body is immersed in cold water or very cold

or frozen compresses or ice packs are applied to it. It is intended to reduce fever and, by causing the blood vessels to contract, also restricts blood flow, thus reducing inflammation, pain, and swelling around injuries. This type of treatment may also use a ice-cold wand to cause the skin and muscles to contract. Used alternately with heat, Cryotherapy can increase circulation and remove wastes or toxins from an injured area.
Contact: www.uscryotherapy.com

Dolphin Dance Healing

A multifaceted aquatic and subaquatic exploration, Dolphin Dance is a bodywork modality with multiple expressions, including passive receiving; interactive and alternative sessions; a series of intensive workshops teaching its healing form and principles; a movement-based group experience in warm water; and a performance tool for aquatic artists. It was developed by Lilia Cangemi, a professional dance teacher, massage therapist, Watsu instructor, and registered Healing Dance Therapist who also created Quantum Leap Healing. This modality offers individual sessions based on floating the client in warm water while applying the principles of Lomi Lomi and Deep Tissue Massage, the point work of Shiatsu, the muscle relaxation of the Trager Approach, the energetic connection of Reiki, the delicate work of Craniosacral Therapy, and the joint manipulation allowed by hydrodynamic movement impressed by the practitioner on the receiver above and under body-temperature water. The spine is naturally elongated and decompressed, while muscles and organs are massaged and invited to release toxins and habitual holding patterns. In addition, the therapy explores active ways of unwinding and interacting as underwater dance and contact improvisation become a part of the session. The whole process is designed not only to make individuals comfortable and relieve any fear of being in water, but to allow them to feel a new sense of connection with and gratitude for life.

An individual session starts on the surface of the water and then leads the receiver (upon request) into the world of the underwater universe, as nose clips enable effortless breathing between air and water, creating an easy interface between the two elements. A physiological dive reflex allows longer submersions and an almost magical breath suspension, which becomes the vehicle for deep states of relaxation and a profound healing

space. The experience can generate a state of rebirth in which a prenatal womb consciousness may become available and past traumas are nurtured and integrated. Dolphin Dance Healing further explores nonpassive individual unwinding and interactivity with the client's movement, during which the receiver is in control of her submerging and surfacing, as well as alternative kinds of sessions like the triad and couples sessions. Emotional Freedom Technique, Contact Improvisation, and subaquatic dance are part of sessions, all designed to bring the client through any fear of being uncomfortable in water.

The Dolphin Dance experience.
PHOTO COURTESY OF TROND ANDERSEN

In addition, an aquatic and subaquatic group pool experience in body-temperature water, known as the Pod Experience, leads participants into a nonverbal space filled with music in which they can express themselves and move from their emotions in free-form improvisation and dance alone, in pairs, or as a group. Decreased gravity and the embrace of water with the safety of nose clips provides individuals with a joyful exploration as a "human pod" while they dive into the three-dimensional world of the dolphins. With creative movement, profound stillness, and playful, unfolding ease, this dive into "the inner dolphin" lends itself to heart-opening intimacy and a deeper soulful connection. A special version of this experience may be done for couples on a honeymoon or anniversary.
Contact: www.aquaticdance.com

Facials

Facials are a form of therapy that, although not always strictly aquatic, works to cleanse, moisturize, and therapeutically treat and rejuvenate the skin on the face and sometimes the adjacent area of the body. Numerous types of facials using substances such as oils, herbs, vitamins, gems, stones, and muds employed with or without massage are an integral part of spa therapy. The following is just a sample of the many available.

Anti-Aging Facials are a Chinese method that uses special precious-pearl powder to soften and moisturize the skin in conjunction with an Acupressure facial massage. The powder is considered an ancient secret remedy for wrinkles and dark spots on the skin. This facial treatment is good for exfoliating and toning the skin.

Aromatherapy Salt Glow combines coarse, mineral-rich sea salts with pure essential oils in either a facial or a full-body massage to cleanse, exfoliate and stimulate circulation. It is often used to prepare the skin for herbal infusions. A variety of warm aromatic herbs oils can be applied in a facial wrap.

Belavi Face Lift Massage, also referred to as a "honey lift," is a relaxing, pampering, and healing treatment intended to help people look and feel good. It was developed by Nina Howard as an anti-aging therapy that uses Acupressure, lymphatic drainage, contouring massage strokes, chin straps, tapotement techniques, and warm-to-hot towel wraps on the face, with a focus on cleansing and exfoliating the skin. It is designed to firm the skin, stimulate the flow of blood and oxygen, release toxins, and soften lines in the face and is considered beneficial for those with sinus and allergy problems. A number of sessions are required for those with aging skin.
Contact: www.belavi.com

The **Burnham System**[SM] of facial rejuvenation, developed by Bruce Burnham, is a process of hands-on sculpting of the face, neck, and shoulders combined with Reflexology techniques on the head and nerve rejuvenation. It uses carefully patterned precision strokes in an energetic touch sequence. During the treatment, twelve major facial nerve centers are stimulated. This energetic process is intended not only to treat a person's face but also to transform the inner being.
Contact: www.burnhamsystem.com

Crystal Gemstone Facial blends gemstones, golden spoons, crystals, and facial masks of aromatic oil in an Acupressure massage. Variations employ Ayurvedic principles along with Eastern and Western massage techniques that work to uplift the face and provide a youthful appearance.

Golden Spoons Facials, based on the Kneipp principle of alternating cold and warm stimuli (see Kneipp Therapy in this section), use golden spoons to massage the face. Unlike other metals, gold does not cause allergic reactions. The treatment first uses a wet, cold golden spoon to cleanse and stimulate tired skin. After cream and lotion are applied to the face, a warm spoon is used with percussion to enhance deep penetration of the mask into the skin. A final application of the cold spoon rounds out the treatment. The process triggers a rhythmic expansion and contraction of the blood vessels, resulting in better circulation.

Kobido is a rejuvenating form of facial massage established during the 1400s in Japan that uses Acupressure, massage, and energy-balancing techniques to prevent aging by cleansing, moisturizing and energizing the face and the important meridians that originate and terminate there. Kobido represents the ancient way of beauty in which the focus is on the condition of the client's skin, but the Japanese way of restoring vitality and beauty also embraced rituals, healing, exercises, nutrition, and massage. It was the favorite treatment of the empress of Japan at the time it was developed.

During a treatment, the face, neck, and scalp muscles are systematically massaged to activate acupressure points. In addition, the stimulation of facial nerves within or beneath the surface of the skin improves blood flow. Manipulations such as percussion, kneading, circular moves and smoothing are carried out in a delicate and precise manner to help free constrictions in the connective tissue.

The massage is performed very lightly with smooth strokes and quick, light percussion, though some deep kneading may be used to unlock restrictions in the facial muscles. It can also incorporate a facial mask. Since the effects are cumulative, it is not considered a quick fix, and a number of treatment sessions are often required. Shogo Mochizuki brought this therapy from Japan to the United States in 1984.

Contact: www.kobido.com

Flotation Repatterning and Flotation Therapy

Flotation Repatterning is a form of bodywork performed in body-temperature water that allows uninhibited movement as the practitioner manipulates the client's body to release old holding patterns or energetic blockages. This form of bodywork commonly allows for a strong emotional release because of its gentle, flexible, and fluid nature. Both the practitioner and the recipient work as a trusting team as the innate intelligence of the recipient's body guides the work. Very often, two massage therapists work together on the client who simply relaxes in the warm water and is supported in a way that allows for great freedom of movement. The team focuses on the area of the neck and spine and carried out manipulations of the joints, muscles, and fascia in that region; they may also use Craniosacral Therapy. The client's body is moved through a series of stretches that encourages improved alignment while releasing tension. Flotation Repatterning is often found at spas and resorts as a form of physical therapy. It is suitable for people with a wide range of physical abilities and for all ages from young children to elderly.

Flotation Therapy, developed in the 1950s by Dr. John Lilly, takes this type of therapy a step further into the realm of sensory deprivation. Here, the recipient floats with the head supported on an inflated pillow in a small, pitch-black enclosed tank filled with extremely salty mineral water that provides extra buoyancy. This form of sensory deprivation is generally done in total silence, though some centers include music. The treatment goes beyond simple relaxation, since it is designed to allow the participant to enter an altered state. The lack of external stimulation allows the recipient to fully experience the subtle realms of her own self. The therapy can also be part of a rebirthing process.

Contact: www.thelilypadspa.co.uk

Fluid Moves (Aquatic Feldenkrais)

An aquatic therapy modeled after the Feldenkrais Method of Somatic Education, Fluid Moves is an exploratory process that follows a sequence of movements to help improve body function, balance, and symmetry. Debbie Ashton created the techniques to retrain the recipient in forgotten motor skills once learned as a baby. During the active part of a session, the client stands in chest-deep water, typically with his back to the pool wall, and is verbally and visually instructed by the facilitator to perform a slow, rhythmic combination of therapeutic movements combined with deep breathing. During the passive, hands-on component of the therapy, the practitioner carries out techniques from the Feldenkrais Method of Somatic Education.

Contact: www.aquaticnet.com

Hammam Therapy

Hamman Therapy originated in the cultures of the Middle East, primarily in the Turkish-Muslim tradition. The spread of Islam has carried this therapy to many Mediterranean countries from Arabia to Morocco. Water was always a highly valued commodity in these desert cultures, and its use in these therapies dates back to around 500 BCE, when they were part of a religious purification process. Steam rooms and baths were a significant part of this ritual therapy and served as places for social gatherings and cleansing.

The typical Turkish Bath includes three interconnected rooms; in the Ottoman Empire, hammam facilities were constructed as an annex to a mosque. First is a warm room heated by a flow of hot, dry air that encourages perspiration. Next is a hot room, which is like a wet sauna in which people can really soak up the steam; then they are splashed with cold and/or hot water. This is followed by a full-body scrub to remove dead skin; sometimes raw silk gloves are employed for this purpose. Afterward comes a wet massage, with lots of warm or hot water poured over the client, who is lying on a marble slab. In some instances, the full-body massage is carried out with a thick, foamy, soapy lather of olive oil and water. After a wash-down, participants retire to the cooling room to relax on a bed of dry, heated marble before getting dressed and having a cup of tea. Variations in the details of this process may be found at different locations. Similar facilities were used in the Roman, Greek, and Byzantine Empires, and over the centuries, numerous centers were built all over Europe simply for cleansing and relaxation.

In Morocco, these same kinds of facilities are used in a slightly different way. The Moroccan Baths treatment begins in a hot steam room, where sweating is induced, and then the recipient moves to a warm room to relax or receive a massage while lying on the floor. This traditional full-body massage is quite vigorous as the body is pummeled, stretched, and twisted. The skin is then scrubbed with a brush, and the process concludes with a rest in the cool-down room.
Contact: www.hammamspa.ca

Healing Dance

The creation of Watsu and its use at Harbin Hot Springs in northern California has influenced many therapists, including Alexander George. With a background in ballet and the Trager Approach, along with studies in WaterDance, he went on to develop his own flowing form of aquatic bodywork. Sessions use a variety of movement techniques intended to mobilize and stretch the participant's body and enable him to surrender to playful participation and awakening. The practitioner establishes an empathetic and nurturing connection with the receiver to provide a space for the dance to emerge.

A session includes stretching, massage, and broad, dynamic movements intermixed with restful pauses that allow for subtle integration. The subliminal messages within each movement are intended to awaken the receiver's own self-healing impulses. The dancer is led through more than thirty full-body waves and spiral movements along with various circles and figure eights that will open up blocked energies. The improvised wave movements are sometimes intended to disorient him and encourage the release of holding patterns. Besides providing a way to loosen the joints and alleviate spinal problems, the experience enables the recipient to expand internally into a fuller awareness of himself. Healing Dance can be beneficial for anyone, whether or not any dysfunction exists. Dancers, athletes, swimmers, or those taking any movement training may find it useful for enabling free-flowing expression. In recent years, it has been used with great success treating the physically and mentally challenged people, who delight in the freedom of movement and the nurturing holding.
Contact: www.healingdance.org or
  www.watsu-tuebingen.de

Ionization Therapy

Negative ions have been shown to have certain health benefits, primarily the removal from the body of toxins such as heavy metals, chemicals ingested with food, and overly acidic elements that have accumulated from the environment. In the cleansing process of ionization, negatively charged water molecules, created by the loss of a hydrogen atom, create an alkalizing effect on the body. Although it is possible to get this and other revitalizing benefits naturally by walking on the beach in the breaking waves or at a waterfall where the molecules are shaken up and ionized, Ionization Therapy can be delivered both actively and passively by electrically stimulating water. In an active treatment, an electrical stimulus is applied continuously during immersion, and only one person can be treated at a time. In the passive style, the water is excited before clients enter. The treatment can be given as either a footbath or full-body bath and lasts about thirty minutes. The full-body bath is usually most effective, since the energy is available to all the submerged parts of the body, and it also helps hydrate the skin. There are a number of different home-use units available.

When a footbath is used, individuals immerse their feet in a container of water ionized with negative electrons. Low-voltage direct current runs into the water to create the ions, and, through the natural process of osmosis, waste particles are pulled out through the exposed areas of the body. When the ionized water acts on a very acidic or toxic body part, the extracted waste accumulates in the water as a dirty sludge. The mucus and fat residues found in the water after this bathing process shows the extent of the unhealthy particles that have left the body during the session. The removal of acidic wastes from the body can be of great benefit to the joints, tissues, glands, and organs, not to mention its role in helping prevent disease and enhancing overall vitality.
Contact: www.healingwings.ws, www.theaquachi.com,
  or www.naturalhealingtools.com/
  product_information/Explore_
  Article_Ionization_Ther.pdf

Jahara® Technique

The Jahara Technique is an aquatic therapy that consists of micro-adjustments of the structural alignment of the body combined with a modified version of Swedish Massage performed in warm water. This

therapeutic method was developed in 1995 by Mario Jahara, a bodywork teacher and osteopath, for work on athletes, although now there are many other recipients. It involves a series of safe, gentle joint stretches and muscle manipulations that help provide proper alignment and elongate the spine. The therapist moves the client slowly through a smooth, painless series of spiral motions that takes advantage of water's ability to mitigate the effects of gravity, allowing a wider range of motion. The process is aided by a variety of supportive, flexible flotation devices and techniques for holding the client in a comfortable and nurturing fashion. This support is combined with gentle traction to help elongate the spine and decompress the neuromusculoskeletal system. Jahara Therapy is similar to Watsu, but is not as intimate, since the client is more often held farther away from the practitioner.
Contact: www.jahara.com

Kneipp Therapy

Sebastian Kneipp, a monk who is often considered the father of Western hydrotherapy, developed his own specialized form of physiotherapy in Germany during the mid-1800s after healing himself from tuberculosis by repeatedly jumping into the icy Danube River and then running home as fast as he could. The basic technique of the therapy is warming the body through exertion followed by a very short dip in cold water and then using more physical exercise to warm the body again. Much of the hydrotherapy offered at European spas is based on Kneipp's work. This holistic approach combines hydrotherapy, plant therapy, medicinal herbs, natural foods, a high-fiber diet, and aerobic exercises; it works with natural biorhythms to support a balanced lifestyle. The hydrotherapy portion incorporates alternating hot and cold water treatments on various parts of the body to, among other things, treat high blood pressure, aid digestion, enhance circulation, boost the immune system, and establish overall harmony. However, the emphasis of the treatment is most often on the cold-water aspect of the therapy. In many instances, massage with cold gloves is followed by a full-body hot wrap to induce sweating, sometimes with a pack of fresh herbs placed under the spine. Today, treatments often use a combination of massage, compresses, packs, and water jets, along with hot and cold showers and baths. Versions of this therapy are still popular in Europe and are beneficial in treating a variety of disorders and stimulating the metabolism.
Contact: Kneipp International – www.kneipp.com

Liquid Sound®

After studies on and experiences with sound in water, Micky Remann designed a special facility in which aquatic therapy and multimedia events can be enjoyed. Housed in a futuristic structure in the German town of Bad Sulza, this natural saltwater pool vibrates with sound waves that resonate through the water from liquid acoustic speakers, penetrating the immersed body of the recipient and providing an ecstatic experience. Some of the recorded sounds used are produced naturally by animals such as whales and have specific effects on human brain waves. Although its therapeutic effects have yet to be completely defined, studies have shown measurable benefits to the nervous system. The idea of sound waves enveloping and massaging a person from all sides, stimulating the senses and reaching not only the ears but the skin and bones, is fascinating. At the same time, a laser light show with a full spectrum of color illuminates the space and enhances the experience. This technology has also been introduced in other spas. Aqua Wellness, a form of bodywork which combines massage above and below the surface of the water, breathwork, energy work, joint loosening, and playful underwater stretching, is offered in the Liquid Sound pool by Liquid Bodywork, which also has other bodywork treatments available.
Contact: www.liquidsound.com or
www.liquidbodywork.com

Lyu Ki Dou

Lyu Ki Dou is a form of aquatic therapy originally from Japan that can be translated as "floating life energy pathways." The therapy was further developed in Hawaii by fitness trainer and intuitive Donna Adler as an energy-based program intended to motivate a person to access the life-giving energy source within. This energetic fitness program is a synthesis of hands-on bodywork, Ai Chi, Tai Chi, and qi gong carried out in warm water. Although the emphasis is on providing facilitators of healing modalities with a self-care program that will improve their capacity to help heal clients, anyone can attain benefits.
Contact: Aquatic Therapy Rehab Institute –
www.atri.org

Panthermal Treatment®

A Panthermal Treatment is a process developed in Italy during the 1960s in which all of the body except the head is enclosed in a metal tube through which hot, dry air and streams of ionized vapor are circulated and absorbed by the body, causing the recipient's pores to open and perspiration to result, thereby releasing toxins. The therapy is not only relaxing and stimulating for the skin and circulation, but is helpful for the reduction of cellulite and excess body weight. After simply resting in the enclosure for a period of time, the recipient is massaged with consecutive streams of warm and cold water. Soluble substances such as plant extracts and essential oils may be added for an additional cleansing effect. Contact: www.panthermal.com

Sauna Therapy

The use of warm and hot saunas for therapy, long established in Scandinavia, has gained worldwide popularity in recent years. A typical sauna is an enclosed, cedar-lined room fitted with a heater producing dry heat of 160 to 210 degrees Fahrenheit, or higher if necessary, with seating provided at different elevations. Saunas are often incorporated into spas and fitness centers and are sometimes used in combination with massage therapy. Although primarily a source of dry heat, some electric heating units are designed to produce some steam to help humidify the air inside. In wood-fired saunas, both the stove and specially chosen rocks can be doused with liberal amounts of water to provide steamy conditions that promote sweating without any burning dryness. The choice of dry or moist depends on the recipient's particular condition and predisposition. Just like a steam bath, a sauna increases body temperature, which leads to increased circulation and the elimination of toxins from the body.

Spa Therapy

Though today not all spas are strictly aquatic in nature, the word *spa* actually came from an iron-rich healing hot-springs center in southern Belgium called Espa that was discovered by the Romans. Elements of Spa Therapy have been carried out in natural hot springs or caves since ancient times, but today the term usually denotes a resort or health facility that caters to some form of therapeutic healing arts, be it aquatic or otherwise. Today, Spa Therapy is very popular in Europe,

where the connotations of the word *spa* are more holistic than in the United States, though this is rapidly changing as awareness of the health benefits of the spa retreat setting are recognized. The therapy involves more than just pampering, waxing, facials, pedicures, and manicures. Many spas, often in beautiful settings around the world, offer hydrotherapeutic methods for purifying, detoxifying, or cleansing the skin, as well as a variety of restful leisure activities. Skin detoxification and cleansing therapies have always been a significant part of spa therapy and can often precede other forms of bodywork.

Assorted spa treatments can include mud, enzyme or chemical masks; facials; inhalation therapy; steam saunas; hot stone massage; underwater massage; steam, mineral, or mud baths; scalp massage; scrubs with sea salt, pumice, oil, oatmeal, loofah sponges, dulse, or sugars that brush or polish the body surface; the pouring on of streams of water with or without pressure; warm body wraps with essential oils, herbs, minerals, vitamins, seaweed, flowers, crystals, and gemstones; body packs with mud, clay, pumice, sugar, salt, and other minerals; special showers; hot steam and herbal compresses; dry brushing; seashell therapy; compressed-air baths; oxygen therapy; infrared therapy; and paraffin treatments for the skin and joints. Some of these forms of treatment heat, cool, soften, moisturize, soothe, invigorate, exfoliate, rejuvenate, or tone the skin, whereas others work as a disinfectant or an aid to respiration and circulation. There are many types of facials and localized or full-body wraps that use muds, seaweed, steam, chemicals, powders, creams, herbs, hot stones, paraffin, essential oils, warm almond oil, hot water, iodine, brine, loofah sponges, or sea salt. These substances can be used in sequences or combined with immersions in or spraying with hot water. Facials may also incorporate the principles of alternating-temperature hydrotherapy to increase circulation and firm and cleanse the skin. Many of these types of Spa Therapy are covered individually in this section.

Many varieties of these spa therapies can be combined with other forms of bodywork, before, during, or after a treatment. The actual sequence and implementation of therapies varies greatly, and many clients, not only women, use spa therapy on a regular basis. The development and extent of spa therapy worldwide seems to be continually expanding, and many of the other aquatic therapies mentioned in this section are now found in spas. Contact: www.spafinder.com

Swedana

The Ayurvedic treatment process known as Pancha-karma has been used for thousands of years to detoxify, purify, and rejuvenate the body. Swedana is the part of Panchakarma Therapy that uses the power of steam and, like some other Panchakarma techniques, also incorporates massage. During a session, the recipient is first rubbed with oil and then enclosed, except for the head, in a cedar-lined box in which herbs have been placed. Hot steam is introduced into the box through the herbs, allowing the oil to penetrate the tissues as the pores open up, thus removing deep-seated toxins and stimulating circulation. Vital organs are sometimes covered to protect the skin from the heat. Then the skin is cleansed and exfoliated by rubbing barley flour on the body. This is often followed by a full-body massage with ample amounts of oil. It is a very rejuvenating and cleansing process that may even be completed with a great macrobiotic feast in Ayurvedic treatment centers.

Another form of Swedana is the Nadi Swedana treatment. This method uses jets of herb-infused steam directed by a spray tool onto either particular troublesome areas of the body or the energy channels called nadis. At the same time, medicated oils are vigorously massaged into the same places. Even though it is primarily intended for localized applications, especially on the face, the whole body can be treated in this way by moving from one area to the next. This specialized, highly rejuvenating technique addresses a variety of musculoskeletal disorders and is intended to relieve tension, improve circulation, stimulate the vital organs, and release toxins from the body. A variation without steam, known as Pinda Swedana, is a deep skin-cleansing treatment that uses a poultice of a pudding-like mixture of rice boiled in milk and herbs. This acts on the client's tissues and joints while causing the whole body to perspire, thereby cleansing it of impurities. Each of these therapies is often combined with other Ayurvedic massage techniques.
Contact: Hollyhock Retreat Center –
www.hollyhock.ca

Thalassotherapy / Algo Therapy

Thalassotherapy or Algo Therapy is a treatment that calls on the therapeutic benefits of seawater and the vitamins and minerals contained in the sea to restore health and vitality to the body, skin, and hair. After an initial freshwater shower, sea salt, seaweeds such as kelp,

ocean mud, algae paste, or even seashells are formed into a marine mud that is applied to the body, which is then wrapped in sheets or blankets to allow the nutrients to be absorbed. Sometimes this therapy includes a massage with seawater, done with the recipient either seated in a tub full of water with underwater jets directed at the body or in a stall with a therapist who directs a forceful stream of water from a hose.

Besides being cleansing, the purpose of these techniques is to increase circulation, improve the metabolic rate, stimulate the digestive system, and enhance the elimination of toxins. Simply breathing in sea air is also considered part of Thalassotherapy. Because of their nutritional and antioxidant benefits, ingredients from the sea are now used in everything from scrubs and body lotions to serums and facial products, as well as nutritional supplements. Using elements from the sea for healing has always been a significant part of Irish bodywork.

WaterDance

WaterDance is a dynamic aquatic pool experience, called Wassertanzen in its native Germany, that combines elements of massage, body movement, and hydrotherapy; it was created by Arjana Brunschwiler and Aman Schroter in 1987. Sessions begin with the recipient being stretched and relaxed as a facilitator cradles her on the surface of the water. Then she is given nose clips and taken entirely underwater. The client is then moved in a dolphin- or snake-like manner that owes much to the movements of Aikido, with rolls, somersaults, undulations, and inversions all done like a form of dance. The movement therapy helps a person let go of fears through the challenge of surrendering control by going underwater; it also promotes relaxation and improves breathing.
Contact: www.fluidbreath.com/water

Watsu® Therapy

This soothing, sensual, and meditative form of aquatic bodywork incorporates elements of Shiatsu, chakra work, yoga, and energy work, and Zen Shiatsu and is performed on a person floating in a pool of water heated to body temperature. The principles of the therapy originated in Japan and were modified and brought to the United States by Harold Dull, after he studied with Shizuto Masunaga and other Asian bodywork developers.

During the 1970s, Dull made it one of the leading forms of treatment at Harbin Hot Springs Resort in California.

Sessions are accomplished in an intimate way with the practitioner in close physical contact with the recipient. During this fluid, nurturing treatment, the recipient is closely cradled and supported by the practitioner while being guided through an uninterrupted, flowing, dance-like series of movements, balanced with moments of stillness. Patterns of rocking, arching, cradling, stretching, bending, and folding movements are used while the practitioner stimulates pressure points with Shiatsu bodywork. The recipient is spun smoothly around in a spiral motion, which allows more extensive stretching than is usually possible and frees up the spine. As the body is moved in this way, the recipient gains the additional subtle effect of being massaged like a piece of seaweed by the flow of water around him. The practitioner leans in with his whole body and synchronizes his movement with that of the receiver so that both the giver and receiver benefit from the increased flow of energy that is often a natural consequence of the bodywork. The totally relaxed body and state of mind evoked by the Watsu experience may allow a significant emotional release, since either painful or pleasurable memories can easily surface; all forms of release are honored. The fluid nature of the whole process may allow the recipient to reexperience the feeling of being in the mother's womb or emerging through birth into a new world.

Cradling in a Watsu session.

Harold Dull also created a form of water yoga, called Woga, that guides participants through a wave-like pattern of stretches similar to asanas. In addition, Dull established the practice of Tantsu (discussed in the section on Energy-Based Therapies in this chapter), which is a form of tantric Shiatsu that is done on land in a fashion similar to Watsu, with the body of the practitioner cradling the recipient. Some of his students at Harbin Hot Springs have also created their own versions of Watsu, as is the case with Fluidics. The primary difference between the two is that different modalities of bodywork are used.

Contact: Harbin Hotsprings – www.harbin.org

V. Spinal Therapies

The condition of a backbone—the keel of a ship or the spine of a human—is critical to the overall alignment and performance of any vessel or any body. So many of its structural parts are connected to this backbone that a ship would have no shape without it, and the human body cannot function in a balanced way if the backbone is subject to any dysfunction or restriction.

The spinal column, which runs from the tip of the tailbone to the base of the cranial cavity, is the chief physical support for the human body. But, unlike the keel of a ship, it has within it a central channel through which runs the bundle of nerves we call the spinal cord. The spinal cord carries instructions from the brain to the body and information from the body and its sensory organs to the brain. The spinal cord and the brain itself are nourished and protected by the cerebrospinal fluid that pulses through the spinal column and the cranium. This cranial pulse also represents the rhythmic flow of the subtle energy that enlivens all the organs and systems in the body. Just like the wind that blows around the globe, the strength of these pulsations is never steady but continuously fluctuates with a person's state of health. Keeping the cranial cavity, the vertebrae of the spinal column, and the neurological circuitry aligned and unrestricted is the main focus of spinal bodywork therapies. By creating the most favorable conditions within and along the spine for physical movement and for the flow of energy and fluids, health problems and associated painful conditions can be transformed.

The modalities discussed in this section focus on the relationship between bones and muscles and the integrity of the nervous system. They often involve methods designed to correct distortions in the central nervous system and the body's center of gravity. Some employ active hands-on techniques that use extensive manipulation in a somewhat invasive manner, whereas others are much more subtle and use soft, gentle touch and intuitive listening, which can provide healing on a deep level. The different therapies strive to provide proper spinal alignment free from constrictions and nervous disorders by using neurophysical therapy, myoskeletal techniques, methods of joint mobilization, and biomechanical therapy. Various forms of Chiropractic Therapy

work on the bones and discs, and craniosacral techniques ease the flow of cerebrospinal fluid. Fulcrums, rotations, rocking, and stretches can be employed to help release restrictions in the joints and skeletal system. Soft-tissue release work and adjustments to the muscle groups in the lower back are also commonly part of these spinal therapies. Although many people think of these forms of therapy as simply a means of relieving the very common problems of back pain and limited range

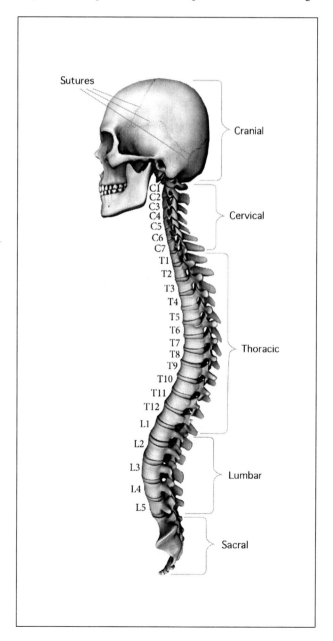

Sutures

Cranial

Cervical

C1
C2
C3
C4
C5
C6
C7
T1
T2
T3
T4
T5
T6
T7
T8
T9
T10
T11
T12
L1
L2
L3
L4
L5

Thoracic

Lumbar

Sacral

of movement, the results of these treatments can provide a much wider range of benefits that enhance the flow of energy throughout the body.

Biokinetics™

Developed during the 1980s in California by chiropractor Dr. Lawrence Newsum, Biokinetics is a form of neurophysiological therapy that incorporates a series of procedures to locate and correct areas of interference in the body caused by injuries, emotional experiences, neurochemical imbalances, and electromagnetic disruptions. The four basic types of interference to bodily function are considered to be emotional, physical, biochemical, and electromagnetic, and Biokinetics recognizes that all will cause imbalances. Since the neurological pathways that stimulate the immune system, the endocrine system, and the limbic system, which regulates emotions, are key to healthy functioning of the interconnected body systems, Biokinetics ensures the proper functioning of these pathways. This is accomplished by alleviating spinal problems that are a result of compensations, which are considered to be a natural survival response to accidents and injuries sustained over a lifetime and even during birth. This modality may also be useful for restoring optimum functioning to the glands and organs, correcting all kinds of spinal problems, improving the healing of injuries, eliminating sensitivities and allergies, removing negative emotions, balancing the body's own electrical energetic frequencies, and increasing resistance to environmental hazards.

A treatment focuses on dealing with interferences that lead to dysfunction and with physical compensations. A handheld instrument called a New-Stim is used to mechanically stimulate specific neuroreceptor contact points in order to trigger a neurological response in the brain that will help interrupt any interference. In combination with stress-correction protocols, restorative techniques are employed to correct all spinal compensations, including any cervical curves. This part of the therapy requires intensive work, and the treatment may go on for weeks or months, depending on the seriousness of the patient's particular condition. Biokinetics has been shown to reduce pain and stiffness, increase range of motion, enhance stability, relieve pressure on spinal discs, minimize arthritic degeneration, and stimulate mental and emotional functioning.

Contact: www.biokineticshealth.com

Chiropractic Therapy

Chiropractic Therapy is usually carried out through a series of manual adjustments to the joints, bones and spine in order to realign and balance the body, normalize joint motion, and reduce nerve interference. It is particularly effective in treating back problems, headaches and a variety of physical injuries. This form of therapy was originally developed by Dr. Daniel Palmer in 1895, when he opened a studio to work on finding the cause of disease. He theorized that almost all disease could be caused by problems with the vertebrae and an imbalance of tension in the nerves running through the spine. After Dr. Palmer cured his janitor by working on his back, he went on to treat many other individuals with a fairly good success rate. Eventually his son, B. J. Palmer, took over the marketing of the practice, which was not well thought of by the established medical system at the time. In fact, in 1906 both Dr. Palmer and his son were arrested for practicing medicine without a license. However, during the following decades, B. J. Palmer was able to make the practice into a successful, organized, and professional venture. Later, one of B. J. Palmer's disciples, Willard Carver, started his own chiropractic school based on new ideas that expanded the parameters of the original philosophy and scope of the practice. During the 1960s, the American Medical Association still condemned the practice, and it wasn't until the 1980s that the medical establishment granted full recognition.

Today, Chiropractic Therapy is more holistically inclusive than it originally was and focuses on the diagnosis and treatment of structural abnormalities in the spinal column and the relationship between the vertebrae, discs, and nervous system. Most often, the goal of treatment is to alleviate the root cause of pain by opening the space between the vertebrae and enhancing the flow of electrical impulses between the brain and the nervous system. A large number of chiropractic techniques have been developed over the years and are also used in many other forms of therapy.

After an initial verbal and visual evaluation, further diagnostics may include Applied Kinesiology, in which muscle testing is employed as a feedback mechanism to assess the condition of the muscles as affected by the bones. A number of kinesthetic techniques can then be applied to balance and strengthen muscles near misaligned areas. However, chiropractic work itself is considered to be primarily a manipulation therapy done to regain proper spinal alignment and balance. The practitioner palpates any vertebral displacement and makes adjustments by applying pressure to the bone in order to shift vertebrae back into place. Joint adjustments are often done with the body part precisely stretched just beyond its normal range of motion. Sometimes a high-velocity thrust is delivered to realign a segment of the spine. A technique developed by James Cyriax that uses manipulation to move a small fragment of a disc can be employed to address disc problems. Strong traction may also be used to move a small fragment of disc by separating the joint and giving the fragment room to shift. This is often done on a special bodywork table with movable sections. Other forms of manipulation and mobilization are used to alleviate pain, relieve nerve root compression, normalize joint mobility, and release soft-tissue restrictions. Procedures also include joint palpation techniques such as a toggle drop or lumbar roll, gentle vertebral release techniques, and other manipulations. Some chiropractors employ a bioenergetic synchronization technique in which certain points are pressed while the client holds her breath. Practitioners also may use a variety of implements, such as a hand roller, a torque release instrument, a vibrating bed, a snapping tool, and other handheld or electrical equipment, to help facilitate adjustments and provide proper rehabilitation. In recent years, new integrative approaches to Chiropractic Therapy have been developed in conjunction with new techniques. Some of the recent developments in the growing field are discussed below.

Contact: American Chiropractic Association –
www.acatoday.org

Bio-Geometric Integration (BGI) is an approach to Chiropractic Therapy, developed by Dr. Sue Brown, that generates a very focused and gentle release of stored tensions in the body with minimal use of traditional adjustments. The practitioner just facilitates a release process that the client actually performs on his own. Initial analysis focuses on the natural structure of the client's body in order to map out specific patterns of stored tension for further treatment. BGI gives a person an opportunity to clear out unresolved tension patterns that have built up over time inside the body. Although it is a simple

process, the complete integration of the therapeutic results may take time, especially when the client has many unresolved problems.

Contact: www.bgiseminars.com

The **Koren Specific Technique (KST)** uses a gentle, low-force, directional adjustment protocol; there are no forceful and uncomfortable manipulations (no "snap, crackle, and pop"). This new method is used by chiropractic doctors, dentist, allergists, psychologists, naturopaths, and other healers. It is appropriate for all ages from newborns to the elderly, and is safe for those with degenerative conditions. KST is used to correct dyslexia, allergies, ADD/ADHD, and nervous system stress, and is especially sought out by athletes to improve balance, hand-eye coordination and performance, and enhance healing of injuries.

The technique was developed by Dr. Tedd Koren, who searched for ten years for relief from injuries he suffered in an accident. During that time, Koren traveled all over the United States and saw forty to fifty different chiropractors, as well as osteopaths, physical therapists, craniosacral therapists, medical doctors, bodyworkers of all kinds, acupuncturists, and other practitioners, none of whom could give him lasting relief. He discovered KST by working on himself. Within a week, ten years of pain in his head, neck, hand, arm, wrist, shoulder, and other area were gone. His thirty years of sciatica was resolved after six weeks of self-care.

KST is usually practiced with a handheld device known as an Arthrostim, which delivers a precise low-impact force at a specific frequency known as the Schumann resonance. This resonance has been found to have a base frequency that promotes optimum healing within the body. This treatment can also be carried out by the hand. KST is very gentle and safe, and its focus is on ensuring that the nervous system, which is considered the most important system in the body, and the meningeal system are working efficiently and at their highest potentials.

Contact: www.korenspecifictechnique.com

The **McTimoney Method** is a holistic form of chiropractic manipulation that uses gentle techniques to achieve harmony in the body. It was developed during the 1970s by John McTimoney as an alternative to other more forceful forms of chiropractic work. This method is intended to treat the whole person in a comfortable, stress-free way.

The primary technique, called toggle recoil, uses both hands: one hand is held over the precise spot that needs adjustment, and the other hand is brought down sharply on the first with a slight twisting motion. This toggling action is intended to change the tension surrounding the joint, allowing it to be freed quickly before the surrounding muscle can react with a protective spasm. During the treatment, manipulations are made in sequence on the neck, pelvis, ankles, toes, arms, hands, and finally on the collarbone, face, and skull. There are also special techniques to treat repetitive strain injuries such as carpal tunnel syndrome. The treatment ends with a quick rubdown and any other final adjustments deemed necessary by visual appraisal.
Contact: www.mctimoneychiropractic.org

The **Nimmo Receptor Tonus Method (NRTM)** is a form of chiropractic work was developed during the 1960s through the work of Dr. Raymond Nimmo, who was one of Dr. Palmer's students. This approach focuses on the relationship between muscles and bones and their reliance on a nervous system that is working properly. Nimmo created this hands-on method to restore the integrity of the body and especially the spine by freeing the nervous system to function in an optimal, pain-free way. NRTM is a systematic approach that uses compression to release painful myofascial trigger points along with sustained pressure lasting a specific period of time (usually a few seconds) on the soft tissue. It is applied in a way that is mindful of a patient's tolerance for pain. This therapy is primarily used for different types of back pain.
Contact: www.csha.net/programs.html

Craniosacral Therapy (CST)

Craniosacral Therapy, which emerged from Osteopathy, is a very gentle, hands-on form of bodywork intended to relieve pain and restore structural integrity. Although certain forms of cranial bodywork (for example, bone setting) were found in different cultures

during ancient times, it wasn't until the twentieth century that craniosacral bodywork became a distinct therapy, when CST was developed during the early 1900s by Dr. William Sutherland, who is considered the modern father of cranial osteopathy. After studying with Andrew Stills, the primary developer of Osteopathic Manipulation Therapy, Sutherland expanded on the osteopathic concepts he had learned. He was the first to recognize that the brain moves involuntarily and rhythmically as the skull plates move and that there is a working relationship between the sacrum and the cranium. Until then, the consensus was that the sutures of the skull plates were fused and that movement of the brain during respiration could not occur. At the core of Sutherland's theory is a concept called primary respiration, which sees the breath as the foundation of metabolism and the spark that feeds the tissues. During the 1970s, osteopathic physician Dr. John Upledger extended Sutherland's work with skull plates to establish a treatment modality that considered the entire craniosacral system, which extends from the cranium through the spine to the sacrum, as well as the dura mater, the tough, fibrous outer layer of the membranes that cover the brain, the spinal cord, and the inner surface of the skull. He went on to formalize other therapies and eventually established the Upledger Institute for further research and teachings on matters outside the scope of traditional Osteopathy. Ongoing research on the interplay between cranial adjustments and consciousness has created new paradigms of craniosacral healing.

Craniosacral Therapy is basically a method for correcting cerebrospinal fluid imbalances or blockages and cranial distortions, all of which can cause sensory or neurological dysfunction; restoring balance to the nervous system can lead to improved functioning of the whole body. It works by easing restrictions in the layers of membranes that line the bones of the skull, the vertebrae, and the base of the spine in order to affect all the body's subtle vital rhythms and promote the internal stability of the system. The therapy is delivered in a delicate fashion by using light, noninvasive, subtle articulations and manipulations of both the fascia (especially the dura mater) and the bones of the spinal column to allow free circulation of the cerebrospinal fluid. This fluid is pumped through the spinal column at a certain pulse rate, which varies depending upon a number of physiological factors. The whole craniosacral system also pulsates in a unique rhythm created by fluctuations in the flow of this fluid.

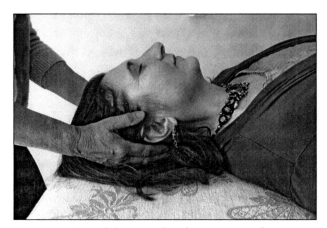

One of the many hand positions used in Craniosacral Therapy.

Analyzing and sensing the subtle rhythm and pulse of the craniosacral system is the primary part of the therapist's initial evaluation. By assessing its rhythm and a motion called the cranial wave and by detecting changes in pressure and flow rate, the therapist can identify areas of restriction in the bones of the skull or spinal column. In practice, very gentle palpations at the base of the skull and sacrum allow the therapist to connect with the patient's craniosacral system by using the fingers as fine sensors to amplify any subtle disruptions and to reveal disturbances in the rate, amplitude, symmetry, and quality of the flow. During treatment, the cranial pulse can shift, grow stronger, or even become still. The true source of a client's complaint is often revealed only during a session, since its source may lie distant from the area in which it is felt.

After these diagnostic assessments are made, various sections of fascial tissue anywhere from the head to the toes are delicately manipulated to unwind and release constrictions, since any distortion in a fascia can pull on the skin, muscles, connective tissue, and bones and affect the craniosacral system. A series of ordered techniques, known as the ten-step protocol, is often employed, though, depending on what the client's body reveals, not necessarily in an exact order. However, it is considered essential to follow the exact procedure and application of each step if possible. This ten-step technique includes stillpoint induction (creating a pause), diaphragm release, decompression work, a dural tube rock-and-glide technique, a frontal lift, a parietal lift, compression-decompression techniques, temporal techniques (with temporal wobbles, finger in the ear, and ear pull), temporomandibular joint compression and decompression work, and a CV-4 stillpoint technique. A particular procedure known as a V spread is sometimes used. This involves holding the hands on either side of a restriction and sending energy into the area. In addition, the therapist harmonizes the dura mater at the base of the skull by applying gentle compression to realign skull bones and membranes so that cerebrospinal fluid can circulate freely.

Craniosacral Therapy cannot be considered a quick fix, and many individually unique sessions may be necessary for a client. Besides being suitable for a variety of structural issues, including chronic back pain, CST can often heal past trauma and stored-up emotions. Dr. Upledger has continued to expand the frontiers of his work with other modalities such as Somatic Emotional Release and Visceral Manipulation. Dolphin Therapy is an aquatic version of CST that is also available at the Upledger Institute. Besides the following related forms of Craniosacral Therapy, there is also a modality called Visionary Craniosacral that is discussed separately at the end of this section.

Contact: Upledger Institute – www.upledger.com or www.acsta.com

Biodynamic Craniosacral Therapy (BCST), developed by Franklyn Sills, is a variation of Craniosacral Therapy that treats the central nervous system and the core of a person's being by combining gentle hands-on methods to reduce resistance with subtle energy medicine. This therapy takes over where regular craniosacral bodywork ends, gently restoring balance and resilience to both the body and mind by accessing the messages that are communicated by the rise and fall of the pulse within the body. Underlying the practices of BCST are theories about the evolution of consciousness and intelligence at the moment of conception, and the goal of the therapy is to resolve a client's deeply held resistance caused by unresolved emotional trauma or experiences held in the body. This modality was influenced by a combination of Buddhist practices and the work of Dr. Sutherland. Studies by Dr. Rollin Becker and Dr. David Bohm on the holographic concept and the tidal rhythms of the body are also incorporated.

During a treatment, the practitioner works with the slow, subtle rhythms of the body to help restore the original pattern of health inherent in it. This is accomplished through delicate, attentive touch and palpations of the cranium and spine while making a deep connection with the cranial pulse and the energetic breath of life within the client as it unfolds throughout the many layers of the body. The practitioner's attention to and relationship with the client's breath is critical to the success of the treatment. This nourishing hands-on therapy is nonmanipulative and noninvasive. The subtle positive emotional and spiritual effects of this form of energy medicine are often slowly recognized in the days after a session.
Contact: www.craniosacraltherapy.org

CranioStructural Integration® (CSI), a form of Craniosacral Therapy developed during the 1980s by Dr. G. Dallas Hancock, D.C., Ph.D., evolved from chiropractic and osteopathic therapies into a structural cranial modality. It focuses on treating chronic pain and postural distortions held in the soft connective tissue (muscles and fascia) of the head and musculoskeletal system. Evaluations include palpations, manual muscle testing, joint range of motion, and reflex techniques from Applied Kinesiology and Touch for Health.

The treatment utilizes cranial suture mobilizations and soft-tissue release techniques that help remove restrictions that limit cranial motion, perpetuate chronic patterns of musculoskeletal compensation, and further aggravate a person's condition. Practitioners use their hands to gently improve the range of motion in the many bones of the head, which in turn helps free the neck, shoulders, spine, and pelvis. Emphasis is placed on aligning the physical structure rather than on moving cerebrospinal fluid or balancing the cranial rhythm. CranioStructural Integration aims to free restrictions in the sutures of the skull that can cause not only head and jaw pain, but also habitual muscle imbalances from head to toe.

During the 1990s, this approach grew into a broader integrative and holistic form of Craniosacral

Therapy, known as CranioSomatic Therapy. Developed with his wife, Dr. Flo Barber-Hancock, L.M.T., Ph.D., founder of Facilitated Pathways Intervention, this expanded approach works to rapidly alleviate trauma-induced pain, many repetitive motion disorders, and other dysfunctions that involve the muscles and joints.
Contact: www.craniosomatics.com

Sacro-Occipital Technique (SOT) is a form of Craniosacral Therapy that combines three separate but similar procedures using the hands to sense the rhythms and movements of the cranium. It was developed by Dr. Major DeJarnette, a chiropractor who studied with Dr. Sutherland in the 1920s. The treatment employs three approaches: the sutural approach, which manipulates the sutures of the skull; the meningeal approach, which releases restrictions in the underlying membranes by working on the bones; and the reflex approach, which relieves stress by stimulating nerve endings to trigger the nervous system. This therapy is applied to either end of the spinal column to decrease or eliminate the buildup of cerebrospinal fluid.
Contact: www.sotousa.com

Dynamic Spinal Therapy

Rolf Ott of Switzerland developed this form of bodywork in the 1980s as a way to treat various physical disorders and promote better health by correcting the alignment of the spine. The therapy works with body posture using principles of Reflexology and Acupuncture and attention to the flow of life-force energy. In addition to some of the gentle and smooth techniques of Swedish Massage, the bodywork incorporates specific rotations, stretches, and rocking to help improve body alignment.

The therapy consists of three different parts. The first part involves a method of testing in which a stylus is pressed on different areas of the ear, tracing specific lines that correspond to the meridians to reveal energetic blockages and stimulate healing. The second part involves manipulating and making adjustments to the spine and pelvis by using rotations and specific stretches to improve range of motion and strengthen the connective tissue while the client relaxes first face up and then face down on a therapeutic cushion. Several methods of gentle rocking help the joints relax and loosen any impinging restrictions. In the final part of a session, the practitioner works with gentle massage to treat any specific conditions that are bothering the client. Dynamic Spinal Therapy is not only useful for relaxation and stress relief, but is also suitable for those individuals with a wide range of issues, particularly spinal and joint problems.

Contact: www.dynamicspineandrehabilitationcenter.com

Kenku Jutsu

One of the four fundamental parts of Japanese Amatsu Therapy, Kenku Jutsu focuses on cranial balancing to create harmony, mobility, good posture, and body symmetry. The head is considered to govern all spinal movement, so the principle of the therapy is that where the head goes, the body will follow. The treatment uses gentle manipulations and point work similar to that found in other forms of Amatsu therapy, but Kenku Jutsu is done primarily on the head and also on the spine and pelvis. By positively affecting spinal and cranial balance and alignment, this therapy strengthens the immune and nervous systems, as well as reducing any discomfort when the body is in motion. This gentle, cranial treatment is suitable for both young and old who have a variety of dysfunctional conditions. Kenku Jutsu treatments are found primarily in Japan and are not readily available in the West.

Contact: www.amatsu.info

McKenzie Method®

A form of treatment often used by physical therapists and chiropractors, the McKenzie Method, sometimes referred to as the McKenzie Technique, is a complete program for the assessment, treatment, and prevention of painful conditions of the spine and the body's extremities. This method of treatment was developed in the 1960s by physical therapist Robin McKenzie in New Zealand. He recognized that extending the spine could provide significant pain relief to certain patients and realized that centralizing the pain allowed it to be treated more effectively. McKenzie became inspired to teach patients how to treat themselves and manage their own pain by using exercise and other strategies.

The McKenzie Method essentially uses physical therapy and exercise to move the client's pain away from the extremities (the legs or arms) to the back, where it can be treated by extending the spine. If the pain cannot or should not be moved to the back, it is treated in a way that consolidates it in another location so that it can be more effectively treated and released with exercise and manual therapy. Once an initial assessment is completed and the pain has been moved, a number of proactive techniques are employed to rapidly alleviate the pain and allow the client to return to a level of normal functioning. Besides helping with back problems, the therapy works well with issues in the neck and shoulders. Each patient is also instructed in techniques and strategies of self-treatment that can be used whenever painful conditions arise in the future.

Contact: The McKenzie Institute International – www.mckenziemdt.org

Merudanda Spinal Massage

An integral part of the Ayurvedic system of healing, this form of Abhyanga therapy is designed to produce deep relaxation and stress reduction by working on the nerve roots along the spine. It enhances the flow of energy to the nerves and joints while also improving the movement of the spine.

A treatment session follows a specific sequence and direction from the base of the spine to the base of the skull. The delicate hand techniques most often used are forms of pressing, stroking, tapping, kneading, rubbing, and squeezing. This subtle and gentle massage treatment is often followed by a warm- or hot-oil herbal sponge bath, a combination that helps stimulate, lubricate, and provide nutrition to the spine. Merudanda Spinal Massage is appropriate for those with back problems and spinal injuries, and it also can provide the recipient with more energy by stimulating its flow within the body.

Contact: www.ayurveda.com

Myoskeletal Alignment Techniques® (MAT)

This therapeutic approach is dedicated to the treatment and management of chronic pain conditions. It was developed by Dr. Erik Dalton in the 1990s after a neck injury motivated him to study the neurological and biochemical relationship between muscles, joints, and spine. The resulting integrated approach to back and neck pain is based on the theories and techniques of Rolfing Structural Integration, Osteopathy, and related physical healing practices. The therapy recognizes that the body's myofascial and skeletal systems cannot be separated and that what affects one always affects the other. Its goal is to identify and correct unbalanced physical conditions with a variety of myoskeletal techniques.

Myoskeletal Alignment Therapy focuses on detecting and correcting strain patterns by using Neuromuscular Therapy, Rolfing Structural Integration, deep-tissue work, assisted stretching, and nonforceful spinal alignment adjustments. Mobilizing the joints through manipulating the muscles is one of the primary methods used to treat stubborn pain. Various techniques are employed to correct adhesions, spasms, and joint blockages caused by tension, trauma, and poor posture. The treatment process also incorporates techniques such as friction on the ligaments, the lengthening of tight muscles, deep palpations, tonification of weak or inhibited muscles, and diaphragm-release work.

Contact: www.erikdalton.com

Network Spinal Analysis™ (NSA)

This synthesis of chiropractic methods, quantum mechanics, and neurophysiology was created by Dr. Donald Epstein as a simple protocol with a more energy-based approach to wholeness than that used in standard chiropractic therapy and with special emphasis on the interface between energy, consciousness, and physical tissue. The word *network* in its name acknowledges the collection of different therapeutic approaches that have been compiled to help recognize and enhance the functions of the body, and *analysis* is used to emphasize that wellness, rather than simply being the antithesis of disease, is based on a person's ability to experience her own body and to make constructive, healthful choices. NSA focuses on the central nervous system, which includes the brain, the spinal cord, and the supporting intricate system of tissues and fluid. It recognizes that tension stored in the body will distort this system and that dysfunction is usually not caused by isolated conditions. The objective of the treatment is to enable the body to self-regulate and reclaim its wholeness by freeing inhibited neural pathways through various stages of therapy that connect the recipient more closely with her body.

Network Spinal Analysis is applied through a series of four levels of care based on the establishment of enhanced somatic awareness that will provide a wider range of self-empowering responses and choices. It uses gentle and specific touch, applied with precise force in a consistent sequence primarily to the upper and lower spine. The goal is to enable the client's own body to release complex patterns of tension that have accumulated from stressful life experiences and other environmental conditions by helping her to more effectively connect the brain to the body. Clinical assessments are first used to evaluate the condition of the nerves within the spine; some practitioners employ a rolling sensor hooked up to EMG (electromyography) scanning equipment to take readings along the spine that indicate excessive muscle heat caused by overwork, as well as excess electrical activity around the vertebrae. Both may be residue from previous fight-or-flight body responses. Palpations of the vertebrae, ligaments, and spinal discs are also used to determine where tension is being stored. These diagnostic methods help the practitioner determine which areas of the spine need realignment and release. Delicate, rhythmic oscillations of segments of the vertebrae, coordinated with the patient's breath, are employed to release tension. Unwinding of deeper tension is accomplished by gentle finger or hand contact on spinal gateways or access points, those places where various muscles and meridians intersect nerve roots along the neck and the lower end of the spine. This action also engages the frontal lobes and cerebral cortex of the brain. During the therapy, two healing waves can develop. One is a breathing wave that releases tension, and the other is a body-mind wave that is associated with the undulation of the spine. The complete care program provided through NSA includes a practice known as Somatic Respiratory Integration that works with spontaneous stretching and breathing to encourage greater self-awareness (see Chapter 8 for more details).

Contact: www.donaldepstein.com

NeuroCranial Restructuring® (NCR)

NeuroCranial Restructuring was initially developed in 1995 by naturopathic physician, Dr. Dean Howell. This approach is designed to treat pain at its causative, structural source without drugs or surgery. NCR works by unlocking and unwinding the body through subtle adjustments and mechanical movements of the musculoskeletal system, especially the skull, thus attaining optimal, balanced body alignment. Its success occurs because the spine and the rest of the musculoskeletal system's alignment patterns are primarily determined by the skull shape, so the positioning of the skeleton is brain-designed to stabilize and hold up the skull. Cranial asymmetries thereby strongly affect spinal alignment.

Treatments begin with deep muscle massage and external cranial manipulation, and end with a balloon-assisted movement of the sphenoid bone, which is found behind the eyes and nose, the roof of the mouth, and the temples—an area in which almost all of the twenty-eight bones of the skull connect to one other. Proprioceptive testing with very light pushes on joints throughout the body is employed to map where the sphenoid bone should be specifically released. This information is used to create the treatment pattern to be used with the endonasal balloon, which is inserted through the nostril into the throat and inflated briefly to move the skull bones in a final stabilization of the musculoskeletal structures. NCR has been found to be beneficial in treating a variety of dysfunctions such as headaches, sinusitis, learning disabilities, chronic anxiety, chronic depression, and spinal conditions such as neck, arm, and low back pain, as well as whiplash.
Contact: www.drdeanhowell.com

Seitai Bodywork

Seitai is a principal part of the ancient Japanese Amatsu Therapy that was redeveloped by Yoshida Taido (and later Dr. Kyoshi Kato) during the 1950s as a way to restore the state of perfect health by balancing the functioning of organs and their corresponding energy systems so that the body and the back are also in equilibrium. As with many other therapies, encouraging the body's self-healing capacity is key to optimum health. Seitai Therapy uses both abdominal massage and craniosacral work to gradually maneuver the musculoskeletal system back into position and to encourage body tone and coordination; adjust the alignment and symmetry of the head, spine, pelvis, and feet; and balance the meridian system.

The bodywork involves a particular tonifying type of Shiatsu that mainly uses circular myofascial rubbing, friction strokes, and light pressure-point work along the meridians to stimulate energy and bodily fluids. Treatment does not necessarily involve specific acupoints. Soft-tissue manipulation, postural and reflex patterning, ligament and muscle balancing, and stretching of the body are usually incorporated. Massage of specific points on the face can release feelings and thoughts and give a sensation of rebirthing. Seitai bodywork is usually done with the client lying fully clothed on a floor mat. This form of therapy has had a strong influence on Osteopathy, although Seitai is considered a much more gentle approach.
Contact: www.acuseitai.com/treatment-modalities/
seitai-shiatsu.html

Spinal Joint Mobilization: Maitland Mobilization Techniques and Mulligan Techniques

Without proper mobility, the body cannot function very well, and the condition of the joints, especially in the spine, is an important part of freedom of movement and range of motion. A number of joint mobilization techniques have been developed since the 1980s to treat pain and stiffness in these parts of the body. Two prominent hands-on approaches are the Maitland Mobilization Techniques and the Mulligan Techniques.

The Maitland Mobilization Techniques, developed by Geoffrey Maitland, increase flexibility and rebalance the body by improving the alignment of the spinal area. This comprehensive and holistic method includes a complete protocol for patient examination and treatment and a range of techniques that are adjusted to match the patient's condition. Hands-on oscillating manipulations are applied to the spine and vertebral joints with both gliding and rolling motions of differing intensities, determined by the condition of the client.

First, joint play and range of motion in the spine are carefully examined. This is followed by various joint mobilization techniques that focus on both the spine and the extremities of the body, along with specific manipulations accomplished in a very precise and delicate manner either within the joint's normal range of motion or close to its upper limit. Small-amplitude movements such as cervical gliding are performed on a painful joint before resistance materializes, and other mobilization techniques such as high-velocity thrusts are used when resistance to movement is encountered before pain. Treatments also incorporate myofascial-release work and soft-tissue mobilization to to relax tension in the muscles and fascia.

The Mulligan Techniques, in particular Mobilization with Movement, developed by Brian Mulligan, are similar in their intention to improve spinal alignment, but make corrections by taking a joint through a series of movements as the therapist applies resistance. These techniques are designed to deal with restrictions that are chronic rather than acute. Sustained rotations and gliding strokes are manually applied to the cervical spine as the patient attempts specific movements. Techniques generally use minimal compression and are performed with the patient sitting or standing, depending on which position prevents the symptoms from being aggravated. Mulligan has also developed the Pain Release Phenomenon Technique for the treatment of the back, neck, and limbs.

Contact: www.physio-pedia.com/Maitland's_
        Mobilisations or www.bmulligan.com

Spinal Touch Therapy

Spinal Touch Therapy was originally developed by an engineer named Dr. John Hurley in the 1920s. Initially, it was a form of gentle touch therapy based on working with the energy flowing through the spine. In the 1960s, the technique was rediscovered by Dr. LaMar Rosquist, who formalized the method into a precise technique of subtle sacral movements to balance muscles and thus correct postural irregularities. It is based on the idea that the body can be guided to realign itself with its center of gravity so that the skeletal structures can move back to their normal positions. Because it causes stress and strain, bad posture can trigger various complaints, with back pain probably the most common. The condition of the sacrum is critical to good posture because of its position at the base of the spinal column and its role in supporting the spine.

Treatments start with the use of a plumb line to determine necessary corrections. The practitioner also observes the gravitational pull on the body and the results of any distortion. During treatment of the sensitive spinal area, a precise, light touch is used on reflex points, muscle insertions, and along the meridians to encourage the release of tension and pain. At times, one of the practitioner's hands holds a specific contact point, often the sacrum, while the other hand gently rubs a long sequence of points around the center of gravity and up the spine. The recipient's experience of this therapy naturally varies, since the actual techniques are adjusted to the condition being treated. As painful blockages are freed up and alignment is improved, the release of energy can be experienced as an additional benefit. Practitioners often make suggestions about changes in habits such as posture, diet, and lifestyle that would most benefit the recipient. In some cases, padded inserts (orthotics) in the client's shoes are suggested to help alignment issues. Although Spinal Touch Therapy is best known for helping people with back ailments, it can be of benefit in a far wider range of conditions.

Contact: www.thespinaltouch.com

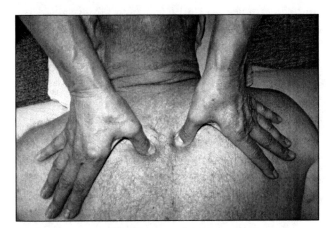

Working on the spine.

Tibetan Cranial

Pulse reading is usually thought of as interpreting the pulse along the radial artery at the wrist. However, in the Tibetan Cranial healing approach, pulse readings (over 200 are possible) are done on the cranial cavity. This ancient intuitive method of healing, based on the principle of the natural connection of mind, body, and spirit, has been passed down through generations of devout Tibetan teachers. Tibetan Cranial sees the holiness in each person and works on the body in a profound yet scientific way, as if tuning an instrument, focusing on an individual's strengths rather than weaknesses. Through a combination of techniques, the therapy fine-tunes the cranial sutures and moves the plates of the head to allow cerebrospinal fluid to flow freely and evenly, while removing any toxins or the effects of cranial trauma from the central nervous system. A deep spiritual connection is created between the practitioner and the recipient as mantras allow the practitioner to understand more precisely what the body is communicating.

After studying for years with various Buddhist masters, during the 1980s, American healer Shar Lee was blessed to receive personal training from Lama Dorje in Kathmandu. Since the lama could not speak English, all of the training was done by tactile display with no verbal communication. If she did something wrong, the teacher would tap her and make corrections by either moving her hand or by demonstrating what he meant. Her attempts to get further training from Lama Dorje failed when, after a period of absence, she returned to Nepal to find out that he had passed away. The pulses of the cranial cavity have never been mapped out and much of the healing takes place on a very subtle and intuitive level that cannot be easily expressed in language, but, with the help of other lamas and further persistent work, Shar Lee was able to develop and perfect her own experiential and intuitive style of the practice, which she now teaches in the United States and Europe.

Although pulse readings at the wrist can provide information about the organs and any trauma in the body, readings taken on the head are more complex and can provide a more extensive picture of the client's overall condition at a deeper level. It may help to compare it with a growing fetus: the head develops first and then helps orchestrate the emerging rhythms and pulse of the vital life force that creates the rest of the body. The health of both the endocrine glands and the nervous system within the spinal area is also affected by the balance of the pulse, and restoring the functioning of the brain and the nervous system can transform any chronic pain or other deep-seated issues and enhance overall well-being.

The process of Tibetan Cranial consists of three main elements: making a deep pulse analysis of the occipital area of the skull, moving the cranial bones in specific ways, and sealing the cranium at the end of the session. A wide range of sensitive and sophisticated body readings and adjustments work to increase the balance and flow of cerebrospinal fluid, blood, and subtle energies. Instead of using manipulations, the practitioner simply applies a specific amount of pressure to enable the pulse to make a subtle shift into a more balanced state, thus creating a more harmonious flow of energy on the cellular level. These techniques can even smooth out the flow of cerebrospinal fluid around any scar tissue that has been impeding its flow. Shar Lee considers the therapy as a process that is "like removing rocks from a river."

The treatment session takes place in a quiet setting with the recipient reclining on a special board rather than a massage table. The practitioner will initially read the pulse in the feet and wrist before coming up to the head and then kneels at the end of the table where the client's head rests so that her heart chakra connects with the client's crown chakra. Having been trained in meditation, yoga, and prayer, the practitioner enters into a calm, receptive sacred space that enables her to be completely open to the subtle pulse, rhythms, and movements present within the recipient. Her hands form a sacred position called a mudra and move to various vital points, different than acupoints, on the client's head, neck, hands, wrists, middle torso, and ankles to gain information from the pulse about what the systems of the client's body need. This is followed by subtle adjustments of the cranial bones along with manipulations of cranial sutures and other vital points on the skull, face, jaw, and neck. With the recipient's permission, even points on the inside of the mouth are used. Pulse readings and adjustments are repeated at intervals until the optimum possible balance is achieved. At the end of the session, the newly adjusted body and the interwoven space between the practitioner and the recipient are sealed, followed by a quiet period of integration to allow the cerebrospinal fluid to readjust to its new state of flow. A complete healing series often requires five to seven treatments to help the client fully integrate the changes and resist falling back into old limiting patterns of behavior that resulted from previous restrictions. The results of this natural healing process may be felt for weeks after a treatment. A specially designed, lighter form of Tibetan Cranial can be performed on infants to help diminish problems such as overlapping sutures caused by the birthing process. Contact: www.tibetancranial.org

Visionary Craniosacral Approach

The key to healing for many energy-based therapies such as the Visionary Craniosacral Approach is the therapist's ability to perceive deeply from within a meditative stillpoint. If the therapist is not in a balanced, centered space, free of mental chatter, then he is less able to intuitively recognize the true nature of the client's problem. The Visionary Craniosacral Approach is distinct from other forms of craniosacral work in that it relies on open-hearted awareness of the soul and its energetic connection to the physical, mental, and emotional bodies. This takes the craniosacral work beyond the usual mechanical and technical framework into the deeper realm of the energetic and spiritual biofields. Although there are protocols to follow, the practitioner must let go of any set agenda that might inhibit his ability to discover and release deep-seated issues that otherwise might remain hidden. As a client's true needs present themselves, the therapist must be flexible enough to shift his attention to those areas that are calling out to him. Techniques are considered less important than true presence, which inhabits an expanded state of consciousness, and complements analytical understanding.

Scottish osteopath Dr. Hugh Milne developed the Visionary Craniosacral Approach during the 1990s, after years of work and experiences with different forms of healing. It incorporates elements of Osteopathy, energy work, bioenergetic touch, shamanism, and Taoist healing practices, and combines sensitive bodywork with a meditation on the inner eye and ear that enables the emergence of visionary consciousness. A very gentle, meditative approach of "doing non-doing" allows the souls of the practitioner and the client to connect, which permits the recipient to express his needs through the space of stillness. The deep meditative state in which the practitioner works allows him to hold a safe space for more effective healing and to more easily perceive subtle rhythms such as the cranial wave, which is considered a signal from the soul coming through the chakras and the cranial membrane system. This wave changes constantly depending on the state of a person's health, and proper detection of its condition can reveal what the body and spirit need for true healing.

After the practitioner takes a moment to prepare himself through a centering meditation that gives rise to stillness and a heightened level of perception by the inner eye and ear, the bodywork session progresses through various stages of diagnostic inquiry to determine the client's real needs. A certain amount of verbal inquiry is usually included. The intuitive inquiry never really ends, since it continues throughout a session as the practitioner places his attention on the client's breath, body language, and energy field. In addition, the therapist uses visionary tracking of the client's consciousness, respiratory entrainment, step-by-step soul center reading, and sensitive methods of releasing any energetic restrictions. Spirit helpers may be called upon to assist in the healing process. What actually happens during a session can be a very spontaneous experience that may even include singing or chanting.

The practitioner generally acts as a silent partner and does not touch the client until they are connected by a strong sense of presence. The touch used is primarily very light finger pressure held for an extended period of time in order to activate a very small pattern of movement in the cranial bones that frees up the cranial wave. However, if necessary, deeper hands-on work may be performed on different areas of the body. This touch can be firm, vibratory, tapping, oscillating, or manipulative, depending on what is called for and can be done on acupoints and areas related to particular chakras, the chakras themselves, and the surrounding energy field. The work can have a profound effect on the recipient as deep emotional issues or transformational energies surface, and the practitioner is encouraged to offer the client periods of silence to integrate the healing that has taken place. On the physical level, the Visionary Craniosacral Approach has been found beneficial for chronic fatigue, back pains, and headaches. On an energetic or spiritual level, it provides an inner journey in which a person can become more integrated and experience an evolution of consciousness. Contact: Milne Institute Inc. – www.milneinstitute.com

Yumeiho Therapy®

An energy-based form of manual adjustment and repositioning therapy, Yumeiho focuses on returning symmetry and equilibrium to the body by removing imbalances that cause pain and that can lead to further serious problems. It is based on the premise that most people develop an incorrectly positioned pelvis soon after birth. The condition of the pelvis is considered critical for overall health, since it works as a pivot point for the whole body. The imbalances in the hips and spine caused by pelvic misalignment can lead to other forms of distortion, dysfunction, or degeneration that in turn can result in pressure on nerves, causing pain and disturbances in the internal organs. A painless form of structural repositioning that has associations with the martial arts, Yumeiho Therapy was created in 1978 by Japanese naturopath Dr. Saionji Masayuki, who was the director of the International Institute of Preventative Medicine in Tokyo. The original name of the therapy was Kotsuban Seitai Yumeiho, which means to let the life force gush out by treating the pelvis with the Japanese manipulation technique known as Seitai (see in this section). This preventive therapy is now used to treat and reduce a variety of functional disorders by creating positions that provide symmetry in the pelvic girdle.

The treatment uses rehabilitation techniques, including massage, compression, mobilization techniques, osteo-articular readjustments, and other forms of manipulations, all of which are intended to correct the position of the pelvic bones and vertebrae, thereby creating equal distribution of weight on both legs to rebalance the body. It focuses on the sacrum and the pelvis with particular emphasis on the joints and the hip bones. The manual stimulations used during a session may consist of specific body manipulations such as twists and bends, and a complete session includes any of one hundred different mobilizing maneuvers performed on the entire body. Special massage may be employed, as well as complex manual procedures, such as special corrective manipulations, passive articulations, puncto-therapy procedures, special massage techniques, stretches, elongations, posture corrections, and other exercises aimed at restoring functional balance to the body. There is also a self-care form of gymnastics called Yumeiho Taiso that uses breathing techniques and other methods for relaxation.

Contact: www.yumeiho.eu

Zero Balancing (ZB)

A body-mind therapy, Zero Balancing uses skilled touch to assess and address the relationship between energy and the structures of the physical body. ZB was developed in the early 1970s by Dr. Fritz Smith, an American doctor of both osteopathy and medicine. Smith has a diverse background and formal training in yoga, meditation, Traditional Chinese Medicine, Rolfing Structural Integration, and Acupuncture. As someone with a long-time fascination with the healing power of touch, Dr. Smith has been a pioneer in the field of integrative medicine.

Zero Balancing is a noninvasive, hands-on therapy that works with deep energy currents flowing through the skeletal system, with special emphasis on the foundation and semi-foundations joints—the cranial bones, sacroiliac joint, tarsal (foot) and carpal (hand) bones, pubic symphysis, and the attachments of the ribs to the vertebrae and sternum—where emotional and physical trauma that have settled into the body can block energy. Although ZB recognizes the surrounding energy fields, it focuses on improving the flow of energy through the skeletal system and on ways to correct imbalances between energy and structure.

Zero Balancing recognizes that the internal flow of energy exists on three different levels within the body. On the deepest level, energy moves through the bones. On the middle level, a flow involves the soft tissue, muscles, fascia, tendons, ligaments, and organs. On the superficial level, there is a flow of energy just beneath the skin. Although most of the work done in ZB focuses on the deep layer of bone energy, tension and blockages are released on the middle and superficial layers as well.

The therapeutic process begins with a seated assessment, followed by a treatment protocol that works with bone energy to correct imbalances throughout the body. The person receiving a ZB session remains fully clothed, lying on her back throughout the treatment. The working tool that the practitioner uses in ZB is referred to as a fulcrum, which is a specific field of tension that is created through gentle, noninvasive touch. Any field of tension can create a fulcrum—lifting, bending, sliding, pushing, pulling, twisting or compressing. The ZB practitioner uses all of these movements to create a stillpoint in which everything can rest, allowing the body itself to establish balance in that stillness between physical structure and the flow of energy through the structure. The sequence of assessing and applying fulcrums is repeated in different areas to affect the whole body. In addition, the painless technique of joint balancing is used to allow energy to move freely. The practitioner's constant, subtle visual observation and concentration assists in strengthening the recipient's energy field, often resulting in an expanded state of consciousness. Telltale relaxation responses such as sighs and changes in breathing show that a new level of connection and integration between structure and energy is occurring. These guiding signs are key to maintaining the connection between practitioner and client and to directing the work of the practitioner throughout the session.

Although ZB doesn't specifically diagnose disease, it is beneficial for dealing with lower back pain, hip or neck issues, headaches, and a variety of other physical symptoms that may be caused by stress or structural imbalances. When a session is complete, clients often report feeling lighter, more integrated in their bodies, and able to stand more erect and move in a flowing manner. In addition to balancing the body structure, resolving musculoskeletal problems, and reducing stress caused by imbalances, this form of bodywork can provide a deep feeling of harmony and connectedness and a greater sense of well-being. Zero Balancing is often incorporated into Acupuncture and other healing modalities.

Contact: Zero Balancing Health Association – www.zerobalancing.com

VI. Abdominal Therapies

It says in the Bible that Jonah went down deep into the belly of a whale, but it never mentions the metabolic wastes he encountered. Did he get thrown about by the undulations of peristalsis? What kind of digestive problems did the whale have when that alien lump landed in his stomach? Like him, humans swallow things that don't serve them well, especially if they are not gotten rid of properly. And what about Jonah himself? Was he too nervous or upset to properly digest all that had happened to him?

The abdomen and the viscera (the organs held within it) may contain much that has not been fully assimilated. Often, our attention is drawn to the tummy after eating the wrong kinds or quantities of food, but it's not only physical material that may be difficult to digest. When you get excited, you may get "butterflies" in your stomach. When an emotional experience gives you a "gut feeling," it should not be denied, since it can affect the internal organs and, if held in there, create constrictions or energy blockages that can influence the flow of energy and lead to disease. Sometimes we just need to pump the bilge and revitalize the abdominal area.

Recent studies attest to the likelihood that the digestive system has its own primordial nervous system and that there is a "brain" in the belly with neurotransmitters similar to those found within the brain in our heads. What is most evident is that with all the emphasis on the brain in the head, our understanding of and sensitivity to the belly has been very limited.

Many forms of bodywork never touch the abdomen, as if this area is considered out of bounds because it's too sensitive. But with the present-day resurgence of more holistic approaches to healing, abdominal therapy is being recognized as an integral part of healing the whole person. Touch to the tummy definitely requires deep listening, significant skill, and tender sensitivity on the part of the practitioner, as well as the willingness of the recipient to open to deeper levels of work. Regular attention to this area can provide both therapeutic and preventive benefits by reducing or eliminating the accumulation of toxins that can lead to many types of dysfunction.

The correlation between the nervous system, emotions, and digestive disorders seems to be a close one. Consider that when we feel upset, we often lose our appetites, and anxiety can be both the cause and result of digestive problems such as irritable bowel syndrome. For the recipient, abdominal work can be very emotional as unprocessed feelings manifesting as blockages and tensions are released.

Massage of the abdomen often makes use of very sensitive yet powerful and sometimes deep manipulations that rely on specific movements around and on each internal organ. These techniques are primarily intended to release restrictions, cleanse the body of toxins, and stimulate the optimal functioning of all the interdependent internal organs, while supporting the circulatory, digestive, nervous, and immune systems. Abdominal therapies can promote a more harmonious relationship between the organs and the body-mind by relieving the compensations the body has made to cope with dysfunctional conditions, which can result in physical and energetic imbalances.

Various forms of abdominal work were part of ancient systems of health care. In Europe and precontact North America, folk healers manipulated internal organs, and many traditional and indigenous cultures in the Pacific islands, Central America, and East Asia recognized the value of this form of bodywork. Both Ayurveda and Traditional Chinese Medicine have incorporated abdominal therapy since early times, and Tibetan medicine even recognizes the existence of a subtle form of intelligence in the area of the navel. The following modalities are a sampling of the variations that are readily available today, and although most of them constitute a complete form of bodywork on their own, it is possible to find elements of some included by practitioners working in other modalities.

There are definitely certain contraindications (existing conditions that could make the therapy inappropriate for the client) that apply to most abdominal treatment therapies. Generally speaking, they include such things as the presence of infections, acute pain, intestinal tumors, hernias, fevers, and usually pregnancy. It would be wise to check with your health care provider and the professional practitioner of a particular modality about any significant issues or dysfunctions before taking advantage of any one of these treatments.

Arvigo Technique of Maya Abdominal Therapy™ (ATMAT)

The indigenous Mayan Indians of Central America included a form of bodywork known as Talladas in their comprehensive system of energetic healing. Although much of this knowledge has been lost, one ancient technique for working on the abdominal organs was preserved and passed down through the generations by midwives, healers, and shamans. The technique was further developed during the 1990s by Dr. Rosita Arvigo after she apprenticed in Belize with Don Elijio Panti, one of the last traditional Mayan shamans in Central America. Arvigo combined Don Elijio's teachings with her Western naprapathic and herbal training to develop her own form of therapeutic treatment known as the Arvigo Technique. This holistic modality uses knowledge from science and traditional healing, including anatomy, physiology, herbal medicine, nutrition, and emotional and spiritual healing. The Arvigo Technique is a noninvasive way of using the hands to guide dislocated internal abdominal organs into their proper position and of improving blood flow to digestive organs.

The goddess of Maya Abdominal Therapy.

Although the techniques are generally intended to improve organ function for everyone, Maya Abdominal Therapy is most often used to address dysfunctions of the female reproductive organs, such as painful periods, irregular menstrual cycles, ovarian cysts, uterine fibroids, endometriosis, fertility, and menopausal discomfort. It is also helpful for men addressing prostrate

health and for digestive problems such as irritable bowel syndrome and gastritis. The method works by relieving physical and emotional congestion and blockages to improve the flow of energy and fluids that provide support to the digestive, reproductive, circulatory, lymphatic, and nervous systems. Besides working with the organs, the Arvigo Technique focuses on the alignment of the spine, sacrum, and hips and may incorporate the use of wraps, castor oil packs, and traditional vaginal steam baths. Additional self-care techniques and consultations on lifestyle changes are also provided.

Practitioners are licensed or certified health care professionals who complete a self-care class along with an advanced professional training program through the Arvigo Institute.
Contact: www.arvigotherapy.com

Biodynamic Massage

Biodynamic Massage is part of the theory and practice of Biodynamic Psychology, which was established by Norwegian clinical psychologist Gerda Boyesen. It is based on her observations that the brain and gut are intricately connected and affect each other, a fact confirmed in recent neuroscientific discoveries that the gut has literally thousands of neurotransmitters that connect directly to the brain. Biodynamic Massage is based on understanding what Boyesen called the "great secret of vegetative release," the discovery that there is a healing mechanism in the gut which dissolves muscle tension and resolves psychological conflict on the organic and unconscious level. She called this dual mechanism in the gut "psycho-peristalsis" to refer to the "tummy rumblings," which are the language of the body that indicates the psychological aspect of digestion and elimination in the organism. In Biodynamic Massage, a loudspeaker stethoscope is used to listen to and monitor tummy rumblings arising from the client during treatments in response to the specialized touch of the practitioner.

The massage works on the spontaneous movement of energy through the body, mind, emotions, and spirit. It focuses on how the vital life-force energy affects all body organs and what happens if this supply is interrupted, withdrawn, or frozen. Gerda Boyesen became interested in the effects of massage on people suffering from mental illness when she worked as a clinical psychologist in a Norwegian hospital during the 1960s.

Boyesen had undergone Reichian Psychoanalysis with Ola Raknes, who was trained by Wilhelm Reich. She built on Reich's focus on muscle and body armor (the subconscious defensive response to trauma) by combining talking methods and psychotherapy (where indicated) with specialized body techniques, for example, systematic and supportive holding of muscles until a full breath brought blood and oxygen to the muscle, used for people who were weak. If muscles were full or over tense, the relief techniques included pressing and squeezing to allow a build-up of charge to the "zone of firing" and supportive safe discharge and release, including deep-draining.

She also expanded on Reich's work by focusing more intensively on the effects of trauma or incomplete cycles in the viscera and by discerning different qualities in the connective tissue found through palpations. Boyesen believed that the effects of stress and unexpressed emotions are literally held in the alimentary canal by tension in the muscles of the walls of the canal. Nervous reactions like shivering, yawning, crying, and sweating, as well as stomach noises, especially during and occasionally some hours after treatment, indicate discharge and relief from tension and stress due to unresolved or unexpressed emotions. Therefore, the therapy places great emphasis on understanding and alleviating emotional or psychological issues held through tension identifiable in this area of the body. Combining massage and holistic psychotherapy into a process that relies on the body-mind connection, she created techniques that are directed toward a gradual softening of viscera, tissues, and muscle armor in order to free up the vital energy and release any repressed elements from the connective tissue so they can emerge and be assimilated or processed by the client. Underlying the work is the theory that energy moves through cycles that correspond to the four basic movements of the autonomic nervous system: contraction, expression, winding down, and relaxation. The aim of Biodynamic Massage is to reestablish the natural cycles of energy in the body by physical work on the viscera that pays very close attention to the intelligent biofeedback from the gut—now called in neuroscience the "second brain."

The bodywork session includes a wide spectrum of modalities such as deep draining work with muscles and breath to unravel the armor, connective tissue work, light energetic touch, and work on the biofield. The emphasis is on the client's psychological understanding of the body and the emotional holding-back that is the reason for physical distress. The massage is designed to soften the armor, release suppressed feelings, and free old fixed patterns in the body. Verbal therapy during the hands-on work is used as necessary to help the client recognize bodily sensations created by the massage and develop a better understanding of the reasons for any physical distress. Psycho-peristaltic responses and variations in a person's condition are listened to and monitored by using the electronic stethoscope placed on the abdomen of the client. By applying techniques that increase those organic sounds that indicate release, the practitioner can improve the client's emotional and psychological integration, restore normal digestion, and clear biochemical and hormonal components of armor from the tissues, thereby enabling better energy flow.

Various techniques, including orgonomy (gentle exercises to link the cosmic energy and the transpersonal aspects of human experience) and bio-release are also used to liberate and distribute the life force energy throughout the body. Physical techniques such as lifting, packing, holding, deep draining, stretching, basic touch, and connective tissue work help release tension, reduce stress, and calm or ground the client. In addition to using massage to provide deep and peaceful relaxation, reduce suffering caused by stress, and alleviate a variety of symptoms, the massage helps resolve the conflict between the involuntary muscle system and the involuntary emotional system. Specialized techniques use the breath to liberate trapped "vegetative" or nervous reactions such as the frozen fight-or-flight response arising from shock or trauma. As an aid to restoring normal sensations and responses along with homeostasis and health, the massage therapy is intended as a journey of affirmation and self-discovery where the body is encouraged to digest and release stress and come back to a feeling of well-being, optimism, and balance.

Contact: Gerda Boyesen International Institute of
	Biodynamic Psychology and Psychotherapy –
	www.biodynamic.org

Chi Nei Tsang (CNT)

Chi Nei Tsang, also referred to as an internal-organ chi-energy massage, is a holistic form of abdominal bodywork practiced in monasteries in ancient China and Thailand. Taoist monks needed to generate a high level of energy when performing their spiritual practices, so Chi Nei Tsang was created to support them in this endeavor. It wasn't until 1979 that Master Mantak Chia, the creator of the Healing Tao System, brought this practice to the West. He trained in the Shaolin Method of Internal Power, is well versed in the practices of Kundalini Yoga, Bone Marrow Nei Kung, Taoist Yoga, and Buddhism, and has taught and written many books about various methods of Eastern healing.

Chi Nei Tsang is based on findings of the Taoist sages of ancient China, who recognized that energy blockages were often caused by negative emotions, stress, injuries, drugs, poor food, toxins, or bad posture. These blockages could then manifest as knots and tangles in the internal organs of the abdomen, which would very likely lead to organ dysfunction and other physical ailments. Chi Nei Tsang, which might be considered a form of applied qi gong, was developed to deal directly with these types of dysfunction. By focusing on the status of the navel area (the lower dantien), where the chi energy has been centered since a person was conceived, CNT works to transform the energy of the internal organs, thus integrating the physical, mental, emotional, and spiritual aspects of the recipient's being.

The practices fused together in Chi Nei Tsang are intended to energize, strengthen, and detoxify the internal systems of the body; to clear blocked or stagnant energy; to help free up emotions; and to increase or guide the flow of healing life energy to specific organs and the five major systems of the body (the cardiovascular, lymphatic, nervous, muscular, and meridian systems). Abdominal manipulations also help improve elimination, correct postural problems, strengthen the immune system, assist in processing undigested emotions, and restore vitality. Practitioners of this form of bodywork incorporate many elements in their preparation, training, and practice: spiritual healing meditations; the practice of qi gong; the development of the ability to see with the intuition as well as the eyes; a strong recognition and sense of the five elements (wood, fire, earth, metal, water); a deep connection to the universal energy source and the pathways of chi in the body; and the appreciation of loving intention.

Proper observation of every detail of a client's condition is an important part of the preparation for treatment. The practitioner first assesses a client's condition by scanning the structures and organs of the body. Readings of the belly, face, skin, eyes, mouth, and tongue are combined with reading the pulse on the wrist. Depending on these diagnostic findings, different therapeutic techniques may be brought into play.

As the treatment proceeds, various manual manipulations with mostly firm but gentle and deep hand pressure are used on the wind gate points on the abdomen to open up blockages that limit the flow of vital energy. Sweeping and flushing hand movements can be combined with a number of Acupressure thumb techniques to further help remove any energy blockages. These detoxifying hand techniques include spiraling, scooping, rocking, kneading, shaking, patting, and elbow pressing. A variety of other techniques that relax the diaphragm and assist in better breathing are used to tone the organs, and gentle, shallow massage of specific organ holding points (areas where the energy of the organs can be accessed and balanced) are used to release emotional blockages. Additional manipulations detoxify the organs and lymphatic system; some of these begin at the navel and work outward in tight spirals in a clockwise direction. Each organ is handled in a precise way that caters to its specific condition. For example, some of the specific touch techniques used on the intestines are the figure five, double-finger cupping, the mouse, scooping, patting, and the clockwise wave. Additional manual techniques are also used for centering, balancing, and flushing the abdomen and the pulse. Recipients may be instructed in using six healing tonal sounds to give support and promote awareness through the visual, auditory, and kinesthetic senses. The methods used in Chi Nei Tsang can also be applied to other parts of the body to treat a large variety of complaints not necessarily located in the abdomen.

Depending on the extent of the problem, a number of sessions may be required to complete the therapy. Chi Nei Tsang not only teaches recipients self-awareness, but also guides them to become more responsible for their own health by improving breathing, diet, and other matters necessary for maintaining a healthy lifestyle. Contact: www.taoisthealingenergetics.org

Colon Hydrotherapy / Colonic Irrigation

This internal cleansing therapy, also referred to as colonic irrigation or colonic hydrotherapy, is a gentle process of cleansing and flushing impurities that can affect the health of the whole body from the colon and large intestines. This type of therapy has been traced to ancient Egypt, where certain devices were used to perform cleansing enemas. Over the last few hundred years, colon cleansing was popular in both France and Russia. During the early 1900s, Dr. John Kellogg of American cereal fame was instrumental in promoting abdominal therapy designed to prevent toxins from being absorbed into the body from fecal matter in the colon. At his sanitarium, he provided a variety of colonic irrigation techniques to treat patients with gastrointestinal problems. Today, the complete cleansing process is similar to an enema but more extensive. An enema can be done at home, but it bathes only the lower portion of the colon, whereas colonic irrigation applied by a trained practitioner cleanses significantly more of the colon. The process has also been shown to aid in the removal of parasites, which can be easily recognized in the collected waste material.

Although a gentle gravity-flow system is still in use, most therapists employ a pressurized water system in which a gentle infusion of warm, purified water at a controlled temperature and pressure softens and loosens waste and trapped impurities and removes them from the body, thus preventing the absorption of toxins and bacteria into the bloodstream. Certain herbs, oxygen, enzymes, and other purifying substances may be added to the water. A small, soft, narrow, sterile disposable rectal tube, known as a speculum, is inserted a few inches into the rectum while the client lies on her back or side. This can be uncomfortable but not painful. The cleansing water is gently pumped in for periods ranging from thirty seconds to a few minutes, allowed to circulate, and equally gently vacuumed out, carrying the impurities with it into a wastewater system so there is no mess or foul odor. This cycle is repeated a number of times during a session lasting about forty-five minutes. At some point, usually in the middle of the process, cold water is introduced to increase peristalsis, which helps the colon contract and release fecal matter. The therapist may also use Reflexology, aromatherapy, and gentle abdominal massage to help release impacted fecal material from the intestinal walls. Oral intake of a restorative electrolyte solution is sometimes incorporated at the end of a session. In most cases, recipients report feeling lighter and more energized after a treatment, though multiple sessions may be necessary for those with severe waste build-up, bloating, irregular bowel movement,

or constipation. As part of the ongoing support for a healthy colon, the therapist may provide information about the benefits of a proper high-fiber diet (including the use of flaxseed oil) to replace excessive intake of red meat. Castor oil packs placed on the abdomen may also be helpful in drawing out mucus and toxins. Colon-cleansing pills that stir things up are considered useful after a treatment, but only for those who have a relatively clean colon.

Contraindications include such things as blood in the stool, severe hemorrhoids, abdominal hernias, intestinal tumors, ulcerative colitis, certain forms of dysentery, Crohn's disease, colon cancer, and the later phases of pregnancy. It is best to discuss any troubling issues with a health care provider before a session. Contact: www.coloncleanse.net

Hara Bodywork

Visceral manipulation is a common practice in both Japan and China, where it has long been recognized that the lower abdomen, called the hara in Japan, is more than just a physical center. In fact, the hara is considered the energetic center in which the vital chi is stored. In China, this area just below the navel is known as the lower dantien and is recognized as the key to metabolism and the production of the chi energy that flows along the meridians. These meridian pathways run through the fascial tissue that holds and interconnects all of the internal organs and deliver the chi energy that promotes proper functioning of each organ and of the body as a whole. It is also believed that treatment of the hara helps remove energy blockages caused by emotional holding, thus allowing the free flow of chi. Diagnosing and treating this region is a central practice in Asian medicine. Hara Bodywork primarily integrates gentle techniques of organ-specific fascial mobilization with abdominal diagnosis, and treatments often incorporate techniques of Acupressure and Acupuncture. Shiatsu is also commonly employed; when performing Shiatsu on the abdomen, the tips of the fingers apply pressure perpendicularly at consecutively deeper levels so that the recipient remains relaxed. Both the yin-yang theory and the five-element theory play a role in Hara Bodywork.

In Hara Bodywork, each organ is seen as being connected to a different emotional trait or type of personality. The emotions each have both a positive and negative component. For example, the liver is related to depression and anger as well as confidence and intuition. The heart is associated with sadness and with love and peace. The condition of the spleen reflects worry or the feeling of being supported. The lungs relate to grief or to the sense of freedom found when letting go. The kidneys are connected with fear or with bountiful energy and a strong will. If an organ is in good condition, that often is evidence of a positive emotional quality, whereas a negative emotional condition may be confirmed by a weak associated organ. Therefore, when the recipient suffers from a particular form of emotional stress, the practitioner will focus the work on the related organ.

During the 1950s in Japan, Isai Misono was instrumental in the spread of Hara Therapy by introducing and expanding upon certain palpations used in earlier Chinese medicine practices. More recently, Japanese acupuncturist Kiiko Matsumoto brought hara diagnostics and therapy to the United States, where he teaches a style that bases acupressure point selection on the effect of applying pressure to points distant from the abdomen until the pain caused there by emotional and physical issues dissipates. This therapy is often complaint-centered with a focus on specific injuries or dysfunctional conditions.

As with most forms of abdominal therapy it is important for the patient to have an empty bladder and stomach while lying flat, face up to receive the treatment. Contact: www.shiatsuman.com/the_hara

Shatkarma

When it comes to internal cleansing and purification, the Ayurvedic system of health care has developed a number of therapies and practices, many of which can be self-administered once learned through working with an expert practitioner. One of these ancient practices, Shatkarma, employs a variety of internal yogic cleansing and purification techniques in and around the abdominal region; there are similar techniques for other areas of the body.

A number of methods are found under the umbrella of Shatkarma, with a specific form of treatment for each organ of the body. Nauli is an organ-cleansing process that "washes" the intestines by contracting the abdominal and rectal muscles in a standing position, thereby removing mucus, bile and gas and invigorating and stimulating the abdomen and gastrointestinal system. This exercise is done in conjunction with breathwork and requires training or guidance by a teacher. There are also advanced variations of this yogic practice that include abdominal movement exercises known as kriyas that help release stomach gas. Another internal cleansing technique called Dhauti focuses on cleaning the stomach. Basti is a colon-cleansing process that might be called a yogic enema, though it is more involved and considered very effective in dealing with digestive issues. In it, a liquid concoction of oils and herbs is gently introduced into the rectum. Other forms of treatment include Varisara and Agnisar Kriya intestinal washes, and Kapalabhati lung cleansing. Dough dams are also used to help with the functioning of the glands and in forms of cleansing such as Kati Basti, in which a dough dam is placed over the lower spinal area, and Uro Basti for the heart.

In addition, Raktamoksha includes methods for purifying and cleansing the blood; this was traditionally done by bloodletting, but can also be accomplished with herbs, gems, and colored-water therapy. Virechana is a therapy in which mild laxatives are ingested to flush and purge the intestines. A unique cleansing therapy is Vamana, an emesis therapy in which oral medications are administered to induce vomiting in order to help eliminate excess mucus from the body. There are many other Ayurvedic methods of internal purification, some of which can be done by individuals on their own and are not really practitioner-applied therapies. (See more under Ayurvedic Therapy in the Energy-Based Therapies section of this chapter.)
Contact: www.jkhealthworld.com/english/shatkarma

Shinden Jutsu

Shinden Jutsu, originally known as Ampuku, is an ancient form of visceral massage that is a primary part of Japanese Amatsu Therapy. When a constriction exists in, for example, the small intestines, this form of therapy recognizes that these restrictions could lead to illness, especially if the immune system is weakened with stress. Though direct abdominal massage is only part of the treatment, Shinden Jutsu's aim is to release restrictions from old strains or injuries that have become bound in the body by balancing and mobilizing the organ energies. This is accomplished in two ways. First, by using gentle movements and palpations, the practitioner's hands work directly with the ligaments to offer support to the joints. Second, by manipulating the fascia that surround and support all the internal organs, the body is gently coaxed to self-correct. The intention of both actions is to free tensions and imbalances that have become locked into the body structure. This is often accomplished by finding a pivot point or fulcrum that helps activate the release. Once balance is returned, the proper flow of energy resumes. During a treatment, the practitioner also uses deep pressure on the lower abdomen (hara), as well as on acupressure points there and on the back and shoulders, all designed to free up restrictions in the hara.

Contact: www.amatsugold.co.uk/more-about-amatsu.
html

Visceral Manipulation (VM)

Visceral Manipulation addresses the interrelationship of function and structure among the internal organs and the musculoskeletal system. This gentle form of hands-on therapy was developed by craniosacral therapist Dr. John Upledger in collaboration with French osteopath and physical therapist Dr. Jean-Pierre Barral, after, among other things, Barral studied the rather rough manipulations used by European folk healers known as bonesetters. The therapy the two created during the 1980s is closely related to Osteopathy and Rolfing Structural Integration and recognizes that the continuous connective tissue of the body (the fascial network) supports both the visceral core and the internal organs Visceral Manipulation also considers that organ mobility, rather than position, is the key to proper functioning. To perform optimally, both the fascia surrounding the organs and the organs themselves must be able to glide smoothly past and around each other while the body is in motion. Visceral Manipulation, also known as an organ-specific fascial mobilization technique, is a gentle method of normalizing visceral mobility, tone, and function by removing an assortment of adhesions (areas where membranes have become stuck together because of previous trauma, surgery, infection, pregnancy, poor posture, sedentary lifestyle, or injury). These adhesions can create constrictions, compensations, or areas of tension that can lead to constipation, neural disorders, structural imbalances, and an assortment of organ mobility issues. Since, in addition to surrounding all the organs, the fascial network runs throughout the whole body, VM also helps provide a balance between the body surface and the core while also strengthening the support of each internal organ.

During a treatment, the practitioner initially makes a thorough, three-dimensional assessment of areas where tension exists and how the organs are oriented within the visceral cavity. It has been recognized that the thickening of tissues (adhesions) in the body creates areas of greater mechanical tension that will pull on surrounding tissue and that the relationship between the viscera and the spine is a very close one because of their fascial interconnection. When abdominal adhesions occur, the result can be compensations that can twist and pull on the surrounding tissues, affecting spinal balance. A restriction in the bladder can cause a problem in the joints of the hip, and vice versa. A lesion in the lungs can lead to neck pain, and an adhesion in the gallbladder or groin can result in a painful restriction in the shoulder.

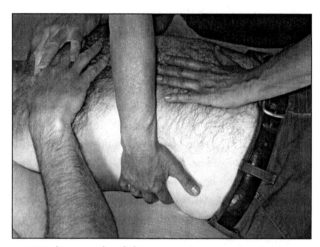

Working on the abdomen requires great sensitivity.

When treating the abdomen, the practitioner applies progressively deeper pressure with the fingers to this area while the client is lying face up, so it is important that the recipient has not recently eaten, has an empty bladder, and is relaxed during the session. A session incorporates specific, gentle, rhythmic techniques for engaging and releasing tension in the body. Light hand pressure flows into the lines of tension, instead of against them, to locate and release any adhesions. Most often, the more intense the client's sensations, the greater the relief will be, although tenderness also suggests the existence of more extensive adhesions that are in need of treatment. As part of the process, organs may be repositioned within the visceral cavity. VM also acts to stimulate the self-correcting tissue response in the body through specific manipulations of the ligaments, viscera, and particularly the fascia between and around the organs to create a harmoniously balanced state in which each organ can work compatibly with the others.

This form of bodywork is appropriate for treating a variety of digestive disorders such as ulcers, urinary tract infections, bladder problems, certain hernias, colon spasms, impotency, and constipation. Abdominal work can actually affect the lungs, heart, spleen, stomach, intestines, and kidneys not only physically but emotionally, since each of these organs is closely identified with certain emotional traits. Since emotional trauma can cause a tightening or constriction in the organs, a significant psychological release can often result from the manipulations. VM is well suited to be integrated with other types of massage therapy.

More recently, Jean-Pierre Barral joined with French osteopath Alain Croibier to develop the modality called **Neural Manipulation**, which is based on the results of their collective clinical research. Neural Manipulation concentrates on the relationship between the cranium and spine and their neural components. Since local nerve restrictions can have an effect on the rest of the body, especially in terms of ease of movement and pathological changes, manipulations using precisely applied pressure identify and release these restriction, which may have been caused by a broad spectrum of disturbances and trauma. Additionally, stimulation of the nerves has been shown to have a significant effect on the corresponding visceral organs.

In addition, Barral and Croibier developed the **Manual Articular Approach (MAA)**, formerly known as the Global Joint Treatment, which is a comprehensive approach to the treatment of joints, especially the major joints of the spine and pelvis. MAA integrates all components of joint function and movement, as well as the connection of the joints to the viscera and the emotions. It examines the nerves of each joint along with the ligaments, arteries, bones, meniscuses, and attachments, and also looks at all of the relationships between the bones of the body. The treatment involves the mobilization of soft tissues associated with bones and joints.

German Rolfer Dr. Peter Schwind, who also worked with Jean-Pierre Barral, combined elements of Rolfing Structural Integration, Craniosacral Therapy, Visceral Manipulation, osteopathic mobilization, and other manual methods to create a way of treating connective tissue known as the **Fascial and Membrane Technique (FMT)**. The focus of FMT is on the modification of the structure of the body by using a combination of form-stabilizing techniques, precise and gentle mobilization that includes special visceral techniques similar to those used in Myofascial Release, and craniosacral work emphasizing adjustments to the upper jaw. The treatment process directly and simultaneously affects the bridges between the fascia that surround the visceral, cranial, and musculoskeletal systems and thus may act on many interrelated systems at the same time. Emphasis is also placed on the diagnosis and treatment of breathing patterns as manifested in the myofascial structure. This is another example of how modalities are created by integrating unique combinations of existing therapeutic approaches to healing.

Contact: Upledger Institute – www.acsta.com or
Barral Institute – www.barralinstitute.com

VII. Trauma-Centered Therapies

As human beings, we constantly interact with the world around us, and that world and the people in it can sometimes deliver blows whose consequences we live with for many years. The word *trauma* comes from a Greek root that means "wound" or "damage," an apt description of the effect on the body, mind, and spirit. The cells of the body store the pain of injury, abuse, or surgery. The mind sets up defenses against feelings of fear and helplessness. The spirit no longer experiences the joy of living. The repercussions from shock and terror can plunge a person into the hell of post-traumatic stress disorder (PTSD), a frightening set of abnormal reactions suffered by returned war veterans and survivors of disasters, among others. Even more disheartening, the effects of traumatic experience can be cumulative. The more frightened we feel, the more likely we are to respond with fear, no matter the situation; the angrier we are, the more often we will lash out. We are not always conscious of these reactions, and so we stumble along under their burden, stuck in the habitual patterns of thoughts, feelings, and actions they have created.

Trauma is generally caused by stress of some sort, whether it's pressure to conform to cultural standards or live up to the expectations of our parents; an unpleasant situation that activates the body's fight-or-flight release of stress hormones and creates memories in the affected neural circuits; or environmental influences such as electromagnetic interference, radioactivity, and atmospheric pollution. People are also born into inherently stressful situations—poverty, war zones, dysfunctional families—that can have a profound effect on their ability to react to difficult conditions in healthy ways. Even changes in the weather or the seasons can trigger physical and emotional stress, not to mention the consequences of natural disasters such as tornadoes and hurricanes. If, indeed, all beings and all natural phenomena are interconnected, then the stresses that we put on our environment will affect all. As Mother Earth goes, so goes humankind.

In human beings, the by-products of trauma can invade the internal environment as well. Unconscious patterns of thought and action produced in response to traumatic situations can influence core beliefs, thoughts,

emotions, and energy flow. This is particularly true if an unresolved emotional experience occurred early in life or if stress continues over time. Fear—fear of pain, fear of death, fear of failure, fear of an abuser—can cause any of us to repress the experience and the expression of our true feelings. Held in the body, these stuck emotions and limiting patterns can result in structural distortion, pain, and disease; chronic conditions frequently follow. How each of us reacts to a particular traumatic moment can determine our psychological and physical health for years to come.

Ecstasy resides with our agony.

Examples of potentially harrowing situations are easily found during voyages on the high seas. New crew members often become apprehensive when a storm is approaching, and that fear can get in the way of seeing obvious solutions to problems that arise. As part of my captain's job, I had to find ways to turn what could be traumatic experiences into an opportunities for growth. My advice: rather than thinking too much and worrying about what might happen, the keys to weathering the storm are relaxation, self-control, and awareness of the boat's every movement and sound as it confronts the seas. In other words, pay attention to what is actually happening. With this knowledge, reactions are matched to reality, and the ship and the crew are joined together as a cohesive whole, responding to the changing conditions. Mother Nature is very strong; it is wiser to be one with every wave that pounds against the hull than to fight the situation. Once the storm is over, the realization dawns that spirit has overcome fear and can do so in the future.

The storm does not have to be one you encounter at sea; it can be some turmoil in your heart or the uncertainty of a significant health problem. When the emotions are overwhelming, a common reaction is to disconnect and feign ignorance. But this head-under-the-covers response will send the feelings underground as a vague sense of hopelessness and sorrow, negative emotions that hinder us from making healthful choices. To really resolve issues, we must come to understand the true causes of our problems and learn how to react in more positive ways. This kind of understanding is not something intellectual; it requires listening to the wisdom of the body and allowing intuition a starring role.

Certain circumstances may require that natural instincts take over. Years ago, when I was sailing along peacefully into the sunset on my small boat off the southern coast of Puerto Rico, my young crew member and I noticed a powerboat rapidly approaching us from the shore. As it came closer, we saw that there were two armed policemen on board. The boat maneuvered directly alongside us, and as it bumped against the hull, one officer jumped onto our boat, yelling and pointing his gun at us. He was literally up in arms and proceeded to say things in broken English that made no sense. My crew member started to react with anger, but I told him to just cool it, and we let the officer carry on talking in this strange and agitated manner. Probably because I was already in a peaceful, mellow mood, not inclined to react aggressively, I found myself instinctively responding calmly and pleasantly while answering some questions and empathizing with him as best I could. The cause of his disturbance never became clear, but the officer asked me at one point if I knew him. I just said no, refusing to let his belligerence goad me into becoming his problem. He became more relaxed, since our friendly responses didn't fuel his desire to use his power or his gun. Within a few moments he settled down, told us not to go ashore anywhere nearby, and zoomed off in another direction, possibly in pursuit of more action than he was getting from us. Listening to my instincts rather than emotions provoked by the stress of the situation helped keep the encounter from escalating into physical trauma.

The severity of the consequences of physical or emotional upheaval correlates with how sudden or violent the impact is, and time to prepare can influence the outcome. If there's no warning, the way we react afterward—perhaps using some kind of physical activity to help shake it off—can prevent the shock from causing lasting damage. And if the traumatic event goes on and on, we may be able to come to terms with it, though this is not always possible, especially when abuse is involved. Stress, anxiety, and depression are subtle forms of trauma, and when they accumulate over a long period of time, they may create constricted habitual patterns of behavior that can be difficult to resolve.

When my first mate and I were sailing through the Indian Ocean, we ran into a very powerful lightning storm that lasted eight hours. There was no way around it, so after taking all possible safety precautions, we simply faced our fears and took the most direct route possible to our intended destination, a small island still more than a hundred miles away. Things started gradually, but once we were in the thick of it, huge bolts of lightning exploded all around us every few seconds (or so it seemed). After intense strikes that seemed only a handshake's distance away, I would squint up to see if the mast was still there. Although our bodies would tighten up with each bolt of lightning, we chose to accept the possibility of a direct hit rather than allow our emotions to increase the stress and its effects. Funny thing. After the first three hours, we got a bit silly and started rating the intensities of each strike on a scale of one to ten. I think we even threw in some elevens and twelves. By the time eight hours had passed, we were quite weary and physically numb, but we had passed Neptune's test without lasting injury. Now we could shake off the stress and get some sleep.

Maintaining an attitude that does not give in to stress and negative emotions is not always possible in the throes of a difficult psychological situation. When there is no chance to release or integrate tension and stress, the body can become the vessel that holds on to the effects of trauma in its systems, in its organs, in its cells, or in its spirit. Physical symptoms of pain or inflexibility caused by emotional baggage can lead to dysfunction and can worsen if some event triggers an awakening of the original trauma. Physical symptoms are also signposts that alert us to the need to release the fear, pain, or anger that are blocking healthy functioning. Research on complementary and alternative approaches has shown that bodywork, especially when combined with body-centered psychotherapy, can lead to physical and emotional release of the aftereffects of trauma. Bodywork can also revitalize the subtle energy body, freeing up blockages that have restricted the free flow of energy that nourishes and supports all organs and all systems of the physical body. With the right help, it is possible look into the face of fear and transform it.

The bodywork modalities discussed in this section focus primarily on alleviating anxiety, emotional stress, anger, grief, shame, guilt, depression, fear, low self-esteem, phobias, blocked sexual energy, irritable bowel syndrome, post-traumatic stress disorder, panic attacks, unrealistic core beliefs, chronic or acute pain, or physical suffering caused by musculoskeletal or nerve pain. Each of these can be traced to the impact of past trauma—shock, surgery, physical or emotional abuse, chronic illness, injury, disease—held unconsciously in certain areas of the body. These holding patterns can actually change the shape of the body and create areas of tension that cause structural imbalances. Dysfunctions and imbalances are uprooted by a variety of means, most often some form of body-centered psychotherapy, emotional-release techniques, osteopathy, clinical methods of stress removal, neuroenergetic-release techniques, movement exercises, breathwork, supportive dialogue, restructuring therapies, core-issue therapies, and a variety of hands-on bodywork techniques. Many therapies also work to provide the personal transformation and spiritual awakening that come through the release of somatic tension. Most often the intention is to help an individual address specific conditions through a process of recognition, release, and assimilation; a client's feelings and emotional wounds are not problems to be solved, but rather reactions to be understood, often by meeting them head-on with forgiveness and acceptance. Nurturing support is essential in helping clients go beyond simply managing stress to allowing themselves to acknowledge and truly resolve a significant emotional issue and then to integrate the fresh and free paradigm shift of living fully and joyfully. Life has more meaning if we can thrive instead of just survive.

Advanced Integrative Therapy® (AIT)

This energy-based form of body-centered psychotherapy, formerly known as Seemorg Matrix Work, combines transpersonal psychology and spiritual healing to treat serious psychological and spiritual disorders by clearing a person's underlying traumatic emotions, core traumatic patterns, and core beliefs. The word *seemorg* refers to a bird in Persian mythology that symbolizes divine transformation. Asha Clinton, a psychotherapist, spiritual guide, and healer, developed AIT after working with Oneness Therapy, EMDR (Eye Movement Desensitization Reprocessing), Thought Field Therapy, and Core Belief Psychotherapy, all of which helped her clients but seemed to fall short of fully resolving inner traumas. AIT is a synthesis of her previous experience, chakra work, muscle testing, neurobiology, quantum physics, and a variety of energy-based psychotherapies. Understanding the client's history, building trust, and bringing about a connection to the deeper parts of the psyche are essential to the therapy.

Treatments employ visualization, meditation, creative expression, a form of muscle testing called pause lock, chakra clearing, and energy-transforming protocols carried out on thirteen specific points on the body to remove wounded energy and transform the negative effects of any traumatic occurrences. Instead of the acupressure points employed with Thought Field Therapy, the chakras are used to access a deep level of energy. The practitioner first engages the client by tapping downward through the chakra energy centers to remove negative energy and the interconnected core beliefs. A specialized protocol is used to lessen the client's resistance to healing. Energy-based techniques are applied to clear traumatic emotions and transform negative core beliefs and their related issues, desires, and fantasies into positive ones. These new core beliefs are fixed in the consciousness by the client, who holds each chakra, starting at the base of the spine and moving upward, while repeating positive core-belief statements at each point. Clients are taught the importance of meditation and are instructed in these practices. The therapeutic process caters specifically to the individual's needs and issues and can also be used to heal limitations that prevent someone from forming or improving relationships. Contact: Southeast Institute – www.seinstitute.com or www.aitherapy.org

Alchemical Bodywork

Alchemical Bodywork, developed by Kamala Renner, the founder of Kriya Massage, is used in combination with hypnosis to address the emotional source of chronic tension and pain in the body by loosening the stuck emotions, memories, and feelings that have been stored there. As the bodily distortions caused by these imbalances are released, resulting in a balanced posture, equilibrium is restored to the subconscious mind.

In the first stage of a session, the practitioner uses a hypnotic trance-induction technique to help the client relax deeply, enter into tense or blocked parts of the body, and engage with the emotional holding. The practitioner supports the process by placing her hands gently on either side of the body part, thus creating an energetic presence. The intensified energy allows the feelings held there to arise naturally and releases any holding by the subconscious. At the critical moment of release, the practitioner's hands will go deeper into the area to assist in removing the pain and to free up defenses the recipient no longer needs. In the final stage, the bodyworker gently moves this part of the body through its natural range of motion in a Trager-like fashion or with soft joint-release work, helping the client integrate and anchor the new feelings with the now unrestricted, loose, and balanced posture provided by the improved range of motion. The intention is to allow the client to be a whole person, fully integrated in body, mind and spirit.

Renner also developed another closely related therapy, though not really a form of hands-on bodywork, known as **Alchemical Synergy**. The process involves changing individual energy patterns by using a guided inner journey that focuses on achieving transformation by using the four universal forces: centripetal, centrifugal, gravitational and electromagnetic. The training places every experience in a category related to the force from which it originates. The intent of this program is for the synergist, as the practitioner is called, to help the client reclaim all fragments of consciousness in order to discover the whole person inside and to release the creativity that expresses inner passion. It blends ancient and modern techniques such as breathwork, emotional release work, etheric and alchemical bodywork, elements of yoga, and guided imagery in order to provide a way to clear emotions, empower the inner child, and achieve a transformation that modifies behavior patterns and allows a person to evolve to a higher understanding of the self.
Contact: www.alchemyinstitute.com/bodywork

Amanae Transformational Bodywork

A multidimensional spiritual healing process, Amanae Transformational Bodywork uses hands-on therapy to activate and release emotions and remove trauma that has been held in the body. It was developed by Australian Christine Day as a way to allow people to safely reexperience deeply held fear, anger, and trauma by receiving the inner light that reminds them who they really are. The underlying principle is that people are already spiritual beings and just need to remember and embody this. The process works to open a person up to receiving higher frequencies of light energy that activate new areas of the brain, repattern DNA, remove barriers on a cellular level, and allow a direct experience of her true nature. Once the inner light is activated, further healing can take place. The therapy is designed to open the heart, and a strong emotional release of the inner child is its aim. The experience can be very profound and cathartic, and the client may scream and cry as emotions come to the surface and are released.

A session uses four different hands-on techniques in which work is done at energy doorways on or just above the physical body so that pure frequencies of light energy can enter the body and help release what is stored in the tissues. In addition to this laying-on of hands, treatments also use deep-tissue massage techniques to transform and release bottled-up negative energies or defensive body armor. Breathwork is part of the process; the client is directed to breathe into the area of the body that is holding tension or trauma while the practitioner uses hands, breath, voice, and energy to meet the client in this area so that whatever comes up can be felt, expressed, and released. After the process of clearing out physical obstructions with the aid of light-energy frequencies, the client is filled with new spiritual light energies. However, for the process to work, the client must have a strong commitment and a willingness to change, especially if intensely traumatic emotions are involved.
Contact: www.frequenciesofbrilliance.com or
www.amanae-europe.net

Be Set Free Fast™ (BSFF)

BSFF was developed and refined during the 1990s by clinical psychologist Larry Nims, who had previously trained in the Callahan Technique, commonly known as Thought Field Therapy. Nims modified Dr. Callahan's more involved techniques into a simpler process that focuses more on the energy of thoughts than on the life-force energy. He theorized that the subconscious is the primary cause of emotional and physical problems, but also the solution. Therefore, it is necessary to engage the subconscious as an ally in the process of healing emotional dysfunctions. BSFF is intended to work at a deep level by using the intention of the client to access the power of the subconscious in order to rapidly eliminate the roots of unresolved, subconsciously embedded negative emotions and self-limiting beliefs that determine behavior and can lead to various everyday problems. Through BSFF, people can be freed from low self-esteem, blame, shame, fear, anger, sadness, and many other negative emotions; they can then react to life's challenges from a healthy emotional state that enables them to make better choices about their feelings, thoughts, and behaviors. This gentle and simple therapy uses the power of forgiveness to address emotional issues and recognizes the body's energy systems as a link to healthy behavior. BSFF reportedly requires only one simple treatment step to eliminate all identified problems. *Be Set Free Fast* is actually an acronym that stands for Behavioral and Emotional Symptom Elimination Training for Resolving Excess Emotion: Fear, Anger, Sadness, and Trauma. The process also addresses the mental and physical pain that accompanies grief.

At the beginning of a session, the therapist uses muscle testing to discover the emotional issues standing in the way; the client is thus empowered by becoming consciously aware of the issues that must be resolved. Then the client compiles a list of everything preventing him from reaching his goals. Next the client chooses a cue word for each issue as a trigger to signal an intention to the subconscious; it is used as an affirmation during the emotional-clearing sequence of tapping specific points on a meridian. The tapping and affirmation continue until there is a feeling of comfort and peace in relation to the issue. There is also a technique that is used to prevent the client from subconsciously sabotaging a positive shift. The session ends with a closing sequence to completely clear and eliminate the problem.
Contact: www.besetfreefast.com

Body Alignment Technique

The Body Alignment Technique, also referred to as Vortex Alignment, is a vibrational healing method that was developed during the late 1980s by Dr. Jeff Levin, an energy-medicine practitioner who once struggled with his own ill health. This method recognizes that the human body is a vibrating mass of energy particles and that unbalanced change in the frequencies of the subtle energy bodies can affect the denser physical body in a way that can manifest as disease. These vibrational imbalances can be caused by negative emotional experiences that have become locked into subconscious memory pathways and into the body at the cellular level, and the aim of this therapy is to clear away any problems in the tissues quickly and directly. When illness strikes, there is no such thing as a localized disease, since every cell in the body is affected by the vibrations of all the other cells.

Treatments are designed to identify imbalances or blockages and then release them by using access points on the body to balance the vibrational energy associated with each organ, gland, and system within the body. The therapy employs special vibrational cards that are placed on the energy access points on the body to activate the release of stress and emotional issues and to balance the physical structure, organs, glands, body systems, meridians, chakras, and subtle energy bodies.

A session begins by establishing the specific problems that are a priority for treatment. A pendulum or muscle testing is used to locate emotional blockages, and then vibrational techniques, including the vibrational cards, are used to clear the subconscious memory pathways and lift the body's vibrational frequency to its optimal level. As a problem or issue is cleared, another will often appear, requiring a different vibrational healing frequency. The process allows the client to view existing emotional quandaries from the perspective of new higher and healthier frequencies in the body, offering clarity and increased vitality. The healing can provide a transformational experience even for those who are not suffering from a particular disease.
Contact: www.body-alignment.com

Body Memory Recall (BMR)

Jonathan Tripodi, an ordained minister with degrees in Physical Therapy and Movement and Sport Sciences and a certification in therapeutic bodywork, has devoted many years to exploring body memory and its relationship to chronic pain, stress, illness, and behavior; he developed the Body Memory Recall approach in 1997. In his book, *Freedom from Body Memory*, he explains how the body can repress stressful memories as a survival mechanism and accumulate them over a lifetime.

This unconscious habit of repressing rather than expressing stress results in a phenomenon known as body memory, which can manifest as pain, fatigue, anxiety, and depression and can lead to destructive or negative patterns of thought, tension, and behavior. Contrary to traditional biological models that suggest that memory resides solely in the brain, Tripodi's expanded paradigm, supported by leading-edge scientists and medical pioneers, presents the compelling case that "the properties exist for information to be communicated and stored within the tissues, fluids, and cells of the body." In his book, he relates true life stories, history, and science that illustrate how repressed experiences lead to chronic physical, mental, and emotional imbalances that are often misdiagnosed or mistreated.

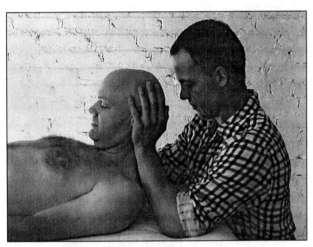

A Body Memory Recall session.
PHOTO COURTESY OF JONATHAN TRIPODI

Body Memory Recall is founded on the building blocks of therapeutic modalities dating back to the early 1900s that share the common philosophy that the body is innately designed to release suppressed stressful experiences in both body and mind and achieve increasing states of growth, health, function, and vitality. The purpose behind BMR speaks to the phenomenon that although release is a natural biological process, the release of body memory rarely occurs without support or therapeutic intervention because of unconscious habitual tendencies to suppress. BMR consists of specialized manual therapy, therapeutic dialogue, movement reeducation, and exercise training, all of which collectively support the complete recall, release, resolution, and transformation of body memory. As an international

speaker, Tripodi travels extensively to provide retreats and training in his BMR approach.

A typical BMR session consists of three steps. First there is an interview in which the practitioner asks the client for medical history dating back to birth, including previous health conditions, trauma, stress, and particularly challenging experiences (breech birth, accidents, abuse, injuries, surgery, or death of a relative). Current health conditions and goals for the treatment are also discussed. After the interview, the practitioner evaluates the client's posture, looking for tension that is pulling the body out of alignment and identifying epicenters of tension. These epicenters are located along the midline of the body and are where the protective freeze response is most active. (Imagine scrunching the center of a tablecloth; tension created at the center of the cloth extends to all four corners. Epicenter of tension have a similar effect on the human body.) Using the information gathered in the interview and postural evaluation, the practitioner places his hands on the body, relying on kinesthetic sensitivity to feel the location and gradually release protective tensions and body armor. Light, sensitive, and nurturing touch is used to create an energetic connection that deepens trust and encourages the client to initiate the release of tension. As the client relaxes, the release of tension and suppressed body memory allows the flow of energy to stimulate involuntary muscle movement in all directions; the therapist does not make this happen but simply supports its occurrence. The practitioner then uses an appropriate combination of multiple techniques to address specific systems of the body. Myofascial Release treats the muscular and connective tissue system; sustained pressure is applied to any myofascial tension and restrictions for the length of time necessary for the natural self-correcting release to occur. Gentle Craniosacral Therapy treats the central nervous system and restrictions around the spinal cord, sacrum, and head. Visceral Manipulation applied on the abdomen and diaphragm releases protective muscle guarding, stretches the organs, and improves breathing, digestion, elimination, and circulation. Unwinding treats the body as a whole, including the human energy field. When the session is over additional self-care and home exercises may also be provided to promote further body-memory transformation and integration.

Contact: www.freedomfrombodymemory.com

Emotional Freedom Technique™ (EFT)

An energy-based, vibrational therapy technique, EFT is used to resolve and release trapped negative emotions stored in the inner child or the nervous system. The basic theory behind this modality declares that all negative emotions are caused by disturbances in the meridian system and that healing these disruptions on an energetic level will lead to emotional healing. EFT is also described as a psychological acupressure technique that originated from Thought Field Therapy. Gary Craig, an engineer and student of Roger Callahan (the originator of Thought Field Therapy), created this technique during the 1990s after years of modifying and simplifying Callahan's techniques. EFT is intended to quickly relieve stress, anxiety, resentment, fears, post-traumatic stress disorder, depression, heartache, and grief, as well as unravel limiting beliefs.

The therapy proceeds in four basic steps and uses a simple technique of tapping on acupressure points at the ends of meridians, primarily on the head, the sternum, and the back of the hands, in order to resolve a variety of nagging issues. Points that are sore are often the ones that need the most attention, since the pain reflects imbalance and the lack of vital energy flow within that meridian and its associated body parts. Certain points along the meridians also have a close correlation with the functioning of particular glands and neurolymphatic reflexes. The client is guided by the practitioner about where to tap with the fingertips while focusing on the negative emotion and repeating a series of affirmative statements. The affirmations are intended to create a psychological reversal that enables the person to be more positive. Some breathwork and conscious self-acknowledgment techniques round out the process of creating a favorable change in emotional and physical health. The tapping sequence is constantly being modified, and many practitioners have created their own sequences to fit specific problems. Though it is hard to believe such a simple technique will have such a profound effect, clinically EFT has been shown to be effective in treating a wide variety of physical and mental problems; however, certain deep-rooted issues may require a number of treatments. The points and tapping sequence can eventually be learned and self-applied.

Contact: www.emofree.com or Awakenings Institute – www.awakeningsinstitute.org

Holographic Memory Release® (HMR) Technique

Holographic Memory Release is a healing technique that focuses on reframing and releasing hidden memories from the holographic mind-body communication network that have, on a subliminal level, acted as filters to a person's perception of reality and restricted the ability to self-heal. The term *holographic* is used to represent the three-dimensional living matrix in which all cause and effect reside. This subtle type of treatment was developed by acupuncturist, homeopath, and chiropractor Dr. Charles Daily after years of studying various therapeutic modalities. HMR Technique uses very light and specific digital contact and torque to generate waves of cellular resonance in the connective tissue matrix to instantaneously release and reframe memories stored in the body. The intention is to increase the recipient's somatic awareness and release tension patterns and self-limiting beliefs that have been stored in the body and mind. As these memories are reframed, the physical manifestations of those memories are released, and vitality is restored on a physical level and in the perception of self and others.

The healing process combines this hands-on energy work with dialogue, which helps enhance the client's self-awareness. While proceeding through a flow chart of actions, HMR practitioners assist the client in healing by accessing certain "touch points" on the body (primarily on the feet and Achilles tendon), which are part of the holographic mind-body communication network. Each of them is considered a microsystem that represents the entire body on one body part. When practitioners establish rapport with a touch point, they use "awareness tools" to gather all the information that they have learned from the body up to that point. With light touch and torque, the practitioner communicates this information directly into the client's holographic memory system. The client's body can then use this information to reframe a memory or complex of memories. HMR Technique also uses energetic healing techniques to enhance the psychotherapeutic process of releasing memories held within. The key part of HMR Technique is that the practitioner primarily acts as a silent observer who performs the process without judgment while gathering information that is communicated directly into the client's holographic memory system.

Contact: www.hmrtechnique.com

Holographic Memory Resolution® (HMR)

This body-mind centered therapeutic approach, developed by Brent Baum, who has done extensive work with trauma survivors, is founded on the principles of quantum physics and a deep understanding of the way trauma is induced and resolved. It acts in a noninvasive way to quickly release painful or traumatic experiences that have become embedded in the nervous system and energy fields of the body without the client having to relive traumatic events. The therapy recognizes that traumatic events signal the nervous system to go into survival mode and take actions to control physical or emotional pain, actions that freeze the memory in the physical body and the subtle energy body. HMR helps clients safely revisit that moment and reengage the nervous system in the process of releasing the body, mind, and energy without triggering any detrimental sensations.

The session begins with energy work to induce a meditative state that helps the client relax. Verbal techniques using exercises, guided visualizations, and meditations allow the client to view a negative experience in a more positive light and to send this new portrayal through the nervous system and energy fields to change the way that the event is fixed in the body's memory, thereby freeing up inhibited energy flow. A simple hands-on nervous-system support technique is also used to help the client get in touch with memories and to create a sense of safety that can be communicated throughout the body. The practitioner places one hand on an access point while the other hand rests over the point in the nervous system that holds the memory. This technique induces a relaxed, dreamlike but conscious alpha-theta brain-wave state, which enhances the client's ability to create a subconscious release. More energy work is done at the end to ensure that positive changes remain in the body, the subconscious, and the energy field. Holographic Memory Resolution draws on the self-healing power of the body to empower trauma survivors and allow them to quickly resolve emotional issues anchored in past experiences so that they can live more fully in the present.

Contact: www.healingdimensions.com

Neuro-emotional Technique (NET)

This method of finding and removing neurological abnormalities in the body was developed by chiropractor Dr. Scott Walker in the early 1980s. It is thought that these abnormalities are caused by negative emotional patterns that have manifested as imbalances in the spine, brain, muscles and energy meridians. The goal of this therapy is to remove harmful biochemical and bioelectrical information stored in the brain and the neurological dysfunctions it has created in order to restore balance in the body systems. NET uses a form of Applied Kinesiology's muscle testing, which is based on Chinese meridian therapies and recognizes the strong connection between energy, the nervous system, emotions, and health. However, Walker adapted the muscle-testing techniques to examine the strength of bioelectrical energy in a given muscle. Since emotions are a form of bioelectrical energy, their effect on the body can be tested with this technique. The practitioner's task is to help identify emotional baggage and unresolved negative associations that are stored in the body and then assist in their resolution.

In the standard muscle-testing procedure, the client holds a muscle group (usually the arm) straight out in a fixed position while the therapist pushes down on it to get an initial indication of the muscle's strength. Then the practitioner activates or sedates a specific point on the body to see if the muscle strength changes. If a change takes place, it may point to a dysfunction related to that point. The possibility of testing emotional energy is confirmed because if a muscle tests strong and the recipient then thinks of something distressing or upsetting, the previously strong muscle will become weak. In this type of muscle testing, practitioners of NET use acupressure points along the various energy meridians, because, based on the principles of Traditional Chinese Medicine, the twelve main meridians are associated with particular organs that correlate with particular emotions. For example, the liver meridian is associated with anger and resentment and the lung meridian relates to grief and sorrow. By using certain points on each meridian, the practitioner can discover emotional imbalances whether the client is aware of them or not and can then examine present feelings and problems to see if they lead back to an unresolved trauma or one that has been reactivated. When bioelectrical abnormalities found through muscle testing point to emotional imbalances related to a particular organ or meridian (commonly in the abdomen or spine), the negative emotions and the neurophysiological patterns and imbalances stuck in the body can be removed by work on the appropriate meridians. Conscious awareness of the connection facilitates the cleansing process. The overall goal of NET is to remove burdens such as the heaviness in the chest caused by sadness or the tightness in the tummy caused by anger or anxiety and to restore balance and well-being. Contact: www.netmindbody.com

Reichian Release Therapy

This form of bodywork was developed by Dr. Wilhelm Reich as part of his Orgonomic Therapy, which is a method that allows a person to recognize his essential identity by removing body armor—defense mechanisms that are trapped in the body. These defenses develop early in life when, rather than dealing with uncomfortable feelings, a person instead creates coping strategies as a shield. This defense becomes habitual and inhibits joyful living and a person's innate healing potential. Reichian Release Therapy is the bodywork portion of Orgonomic Therapy; it incorporates various ways to release the armor and the tension. This approach to dissolving the body armor includes character analysis through observation, therapeutic verbal dialogue between the client and practitioner, body movement, deep massage to release muscular tension, and breathing-enhancement techniques. The complete somatic process facilitates the expression and release of deep feelings.

The goal of the bodywork part of the therapy is to engage the body as a partner in emotional release, working toward expanding the recipient's capacity for wholeness. A treatment often starts with the therapist focusing on the eyes and the respiration. The eyes are considered crucial for communication, and when there is a restriction in the body, it will be evident there. Since the breath is essential to sustaining energy levels that will push emotions to the surface, it is considered important to dissolve blocks in respiration. Throughout a session, the therapist's intention is to locate painful constrictions and to loosen restrictions and unnecessary protective holding with deep massage from the head down to the pelvis, thus facilitating the expansion of the client's energetic potential as the practitioner peels back layers of embedded attitudes that hide emotions. The therapy is also appropriate for couples and groups in which individuals can discover habitual dysfunctional patterns and learn different ways of behaving through confrontation and support from others. Reichian Therapy has become the classical foundation for further holistic developments in somatic psychotherapy and bodywork. Contact: www.orgonomictherapy.com or Reichian Institute – www.reichianinstitute.com

SHEN® Therapy

Developed in the 1970s by Richard Pavek, SHEN offers both physical and emotional release. SHEN is an acronym for Specific Human Energy Nexus and comes from Pavek's insights into the functioning of an emotional matrix in the biofield, an energy field that surrounds each person. It is based on the premise that the biofield holds repressed painful emotions caused by stress or trauma that can trigger an auto-contractile pain response (ACPR), causing the part of the body affected by the emotion to contract, thus trapping the emotional pain in the body. This contraction can continue, sometimes for many years, until the emotion is released. When developing this therapy, Pavek recognized that the energy within the biofield tends to flow in certain patterns in most people, running up the right-hand side of the body and down the left. In addition, energy flows out of the right hand and into the left. SHEN Therapy works with this flow of energy by allowing the practitioner's biofield to merge with that of the recipient, opening this field so that the unwanted emotions can dissipate and be released.

The SHEN therapist first questions the client in a loving way about her current emotional state and how her body feels. The therapist then uses body scanning to determine the physical location of somatically held emotions so she can design and execute the appropriate release plan; changes in temperature and other subtle differences may indicate problems areas. Most emotions are held in four centers: the heart, the solar plexus, the navel area, and the perineum or root. The circular flow of energy in the biofield that runs through and connects these centers has a certain directionality, which the practitioner engages by gently placing paired hands above and below the client's body in specific polarized positions on these flow lines, matching the flow of the recipient's energy. One hand is considered the giver and the other, the taker, and they sandwich the body between them, directing energy through it. In this way, the practitioner boosts the energy flow through the emotional centers to loosen contractions and free the emotions. The hands are often repositioned at specific locations, similar to some of the chakras, to help lift a particular emotion to the surface of the body so that it can dissipate. The process is repeated until there is a positive emotional shift and a more balanced emotional base is established in the person's core. The therapist often directs the client to breathe in certain ways during this process, and she may apply gentle pressure or rocking to accelerate the release process.

Although it can be useful for providing anyone with more personal insight, SHEN Therapy is particularly helpful in dealing with chronic pain that cannot be traced to physical causes, as well as emotional blockages created by psychological stress or significant past trauma. This gentle, supportive form of therapy requires a series of sessions, especially for clients with deep-seated physical and emotional disorders.

Contact: SHEN Therapy Institute –
www.shentherapy.info

Somato Emotional Release (SER)

A therapeutic procedure that incorporates aspects of Craniosacral Therapy, Somato Emotional Release is based on the physiological response that occurs naturally when there is a release of trauma that has been held in the body's tissues. The basic premise is that the body often retains memories of traumatic events in the physical tissue as areas of congestion called energy cysts, which disrupt normal body functions and drain away energy. When a client can identify and expel the negative energy that has become embedded in the cyst by reexperiencing and resolving the unpleasant incidents, the mind and body will be released from any residual effects. It was during the late 1970s that clinical researchers Dr. John Upledger and Dr. Zvi Karni recognized the way in which the body retains physical evidence of any challenging life experience, no matter how benign or extreme. SER emerged as a way to deal with these

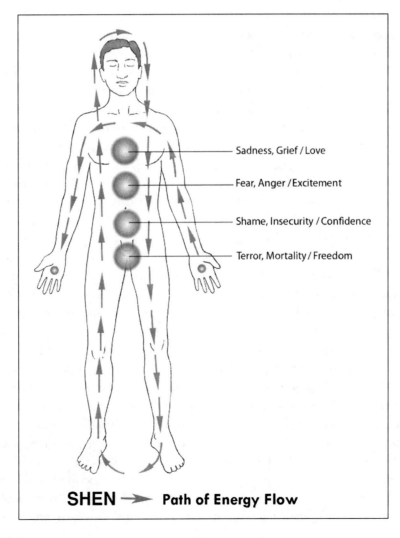

Sadness, Grief / Love

Fear, Anger / Excitement

Shame, Insecurity / Confidence

Terror, Mortality / Freedom

SHEN → Path of Energy Flow

emotional feelings held in the body tissues, which can manifest both physically and emotionally as pain, tension, anger, fear, or sadness. By unwinding and expelling these traumatic effects from the body, SER can free up long-held patterns of dysfunction.

The therapeutic treatment uses light palpations and elements of Craniosacral Therapy to release tissue memories and the contractions in both tissues and muscle that act as a protective reminder of painful experiences. By monitoring the craniosacral rhythm, the therapist can tell when and where a patient is consciously or unconsciously dealing with a significant issue. The therapist makes contact with the muscles in a way that awakens the area and evokes the memory associated with the initial trauma so that the client can become more aware of it and deal with it appropriately, and then gives the tissues time to release. Once the release is triggered, the muscle will begin to heal. As this happens, the client may make different sounds and start moving into various positions as the body-held trauma unwinds. The actual amount of release from the therapy will depend upon the person and the particular extent of the issues. The complete process of healing cannot be forced and may require a series of sessions. SER has been shown to be especially useful for veterans suffering from post-traumatic stress disorder. Contact: Upledger Institute – www.upledger.com or www.acsta.com

Somatic Experiencing® (SE)

After observing that wild animals are better able to shake off traumatic situations and restore themselves to equilibrium than humans, Dr. Peter Levine developed Somatic Experiencing during the late 1960s and 70s as a way to deal with human shock or trauma. It is based on the idea that people, unlike animals, hold in their bodies for long periods of time the intense energy mobilized for survival during shocks or trauma. Events such as a car accident, invasive surgery, an abusive relationship, acts of terrorism, or the death of a friend give rise to symptoms of bewilderment, anguish, fear, and torment when the energy remains trapped in the nervous system, where it can wreak havoc on the body and mind. The fight-or-flight response becomes fixated, and a person is no longer able to respond in an appropriate manner to the here-and-now environment.

SE considers that trauma is often the cause of physiological issues and works to slowly release this trapped energy without the psychological approach of reliving painful memories through long hours of therapy. Although SE can activate intense responses, the emotional release occurs in a way that avoids retraumatization, because it releases this intense survival energy a little at a time in cycles, with plenty of time in between for the client to return to a settled state before continuing. By acknowledging the mind-body connection, the therapy is designed to engage the body's innate healing wisdom through working with the direct experience of the body's felt sense. With increasing awareness of bodily sensations, clients can discover and adopt more appropriate responses without eliciting a massive cathartic discharge that may provide some initial relief but doesn't always lead to true integration.

A session employs a variety of strategies that gradually allow the recipient to come into close contact with a traumatic experience without forcing anything. Direct touch, guided imagery, movement patterns, hypnotism, bodily awareness techniques, visualization, and gentle manipulation of the joints, muscles and viscera all support the client's ability to be comfortable in exploring body sensations. By listening to and focusing on these inner sensations and noticing how they might manifest as subtle shifts in posture, trembling, vibrations, or pulsing, the recipient can ease into a state of observing from a place of conscious presence. When feelings surface, the practitioner and client can share observations that provoke new responses, enabling the client to assimilate and transform the pain. The process also offers a way to help trauma survivors develop the natural ability to eliminate the no-longer-useful energy caused by overwhelming events and by releasing this energy, to heal. SE has been used by those suffering from combat fatigue, rape, genocide, auto accidents, surgical trauma, and a variety of other conditions. A Somatic Experiencing Trauma Institute has been established for further training, education, and research into the prevention of trauma worldwide. Contact: Somatic Experiencing Trauma Institute – www.traumahealing.com

Somatosynthesis

The act of bringing awareness to a stressed or painful area of the body combined with touch therapy and dialogue make up Somatosynthesis, whose goal is releasing emotional blockages. This form of therapeutic healing was developed by Dr. Clyde Ford, a chiropractor who was trained in a psychiatric approach known as Psychosynthesis. Ford expanded upon what he had learned to create a more body-oriented method for stimulating personal insight in order to resolve emotional issues. By focusing on painful areas of the body, this approach, known as Somatosynthesis, is designed to evoke a spontaneous response whose energy will reveal and release unhealthy life patterns or experiences and the psychological or spiritual issues that underlie difficulties, pain, or illness. Rather than being called a client or patient, the recipient of this therapy is considered a traveler who is taking an exploratory journey with the aid of a guide, the practitioner.

During a session, the guide first analyzes restrictions in the body, which are the physical and energetic manifestation of emotional issues or the emotional expression of physical issues. The traveler is led into a state of profound relaxation and deep listening as the guide applies a variety of hands-on techniques with special attention placed on the breath. Dialogue, guided imagery, and gentle body movement are used to focus attention on the problem area and spark the release of any past emotional trauma. In effect, the traveler is guided by touch and by the enhanced internal awareness of energy to release emotional issues and unhealthy life patterns and experiences; this is promoted by the heightened flow of vital fluids, and stimulated nerve function. The overall goal is to renew the body, mind, and spirit and find a peaceful sense of well-being by reversing the negative effects of stressful emotional issues.
Contact: Somatosynthesis Training and Research –
www.clydeford.com

Spiral Release® Bodywork (SRB)

After years of living with a severe back injury and being told he would be in pain for the rest of his life, Tim Custis had a spiritual awakening during the late 1980s that led him to create Spiral Release Bodywork. In addition to incorporating elements of Ashtanga Yoga, SRB uses deep-tissue massage and a form of neuromuscular massage in combination with the recipient's active, conscious participation to address chronic conditions and release physical, emotional, and spiritual pain throughout the body at a deep functional level. The increase in body awareness provided by SRB helps clients feel, understand, accept, and work with the information that the body conveys. As the recipient becomes

more at ease with painful areas of the body that need to be released, he can relax and let go of negative energetic patterns, emotions, and trauma that affect all areas of life. Special attention is paid to the abdominal cavity, in which emotional trauma is often held on a cellular level. Once tensions in this cavity are freed, the organs can function more efficiently and emotional issues that restrict performance can be alleviated.

During a session, the client is moved into a variety of special positions related to those found in Ashtanga Yoga, using therapy balls and an adjustable bodywork table that enables the practitioner to gain access to parts of the body that would not be available on a flat table. The recipient's body tissues are released with a three-phase movement, which entails penetrating, lengthening, and releasing the connective tissue with spiral movements. The practitioner uses various parts of his body, including the forearms and elbows, for leverage and to stretch the client's body. The practitioner's intuition and touch along with the client's active intention and use of conscious energy-release techniques work to release holding patterns and stimulate the client's innate healing abilities. The whole process becomes a simple, fluid movement that may last for two or three hours as the client and practitioner work as a team to integrate physical movement, breathwork, and healing thoughts. With SRB, pain and fear are considered valid tools that can provide an opportunity to resolve issues, grow, heal, and transform positive intentions into reality.
Contact: www.spiralrelease.com

TARA Approach

A holistic, clinically tested system for resolving the psychological, spiritual, physical, and emotional effects of shock and trauma, the TARA Approach offers a new model for balancing the nervous system and restoring healthy energy flow to address the root cause of illness and disease. This approach was developed in Boulder, Colorado, by Dr. Stephanie Mines in 1994 after many years of research and clinical practice. It combines the ancient Japanese healing art of Jin Shin (a form of energy medicine), therapeutic touch, and dialogue with the intention of empowering the patient to be at the center of the healing process. Its aim is to open new neurological pathways by combining verbal guidance with visualization, gentle touch, intention, empowering action, and subtle energy medicine in a gentle, noninvasive, creative, and meditative way that relies on the will of the client. The TARA Approach works with the extraordinary meridians of the body, sometimes referred to as the Rivers of Splendor, and the etheric field, as well as the intelligence of the individual.

When shock (especially prenatal shock) stored in the body is activated, many other unresolved shocks can unconsciously and erratically rise to the surface, making it more difficult to solve the initial problem. The TARA Approach encourages people to be proactive in resolving both shock and trauma by making an internal shift that restores the essence of the soul, which is an integral element of their innate healing ability. Self-care practices are strongly encouraged.

During a session, the practitioner reads energy imbalances through pulses and then uses dialogue and subtle touch on specific areas of the body to awaken vitality, creativity, awareness, and joy. The practitioner recognizes that words have energies of their own and, when appropriately used, can have a healing power that transforms. Compassionate verbal assistance and gentle hands-on bodywork are therefore combined to empower the recipient. The energy medicine (called Jin Shin TARA) works to clear shock and trauma from the places where they are stored and stimulates a shift from within that allows obstructed energy to move and restore balance. Catharsis is avoided. Clinical trials have successfully tested the TARA Approach for the treatment of autism, stroke, aphasia, and traumatic brain injury. The TARA Approach is a recognized rehabilitative therapy. The system is fully explained in Dr. Mines book, *We Are All in Shock: How Overwhelming Experience Shatters Joy and What You Can Do About It.*
Contact: www.tara-approach.org

Thought Field® Therapy (TFT)

Previously known as the Callahan Technique®, this therapy combines traditional Chinese medical knowledge of meridians and body-centered psychology into a treatment that is designed to be a fast and easy way to address psychoemotional problems. It was developed from a combination of the use of meridian systems and Applied Kinesiology (AK) during the 1980s by Dr. Roger Callahan, an American psychologist specializing in anxiety disorders. He had worked with Dr. George Goodheart, who developed AK, and John Diamond, who used sound to address the emotions. Callahan used

tapping to address the emotions and meridians and reshaped it into his own complete healing system. TFT is based on the premise that a person's thoughts and energy are interconnected and that energy blockages and information in the form of trapped energy can cause psychological and emotional problems. Certain acupuncture points act as energy transducers and are connected to certain emotions and core issues, which can be released by tapping these points. If these points are addressed in a specific order or code, disturbances in the thought field that are causing the problems are cleared and rebalanced without the client needing to relive the trauma-inducing situation. Through using AK, Callahan discovered a way to elicit the necessary code for rapid resolution.

During a treatment, the client is first directed to tune in to the problems, traumas, or fearful events being treated and rate them on a scale of one to ten. Then the practitioner guides the client through a specific sequence of body tapping, called algorithms, at different acupuncture points on the body. The tapping is done with two fingers in a firm yet gentle way, providing an external source of energy that stimulates the circulation of energy through that meridian and cleanses any negative emotional charge. This is followed by a series of nine activities, which involves eye movements and humming that are accomplished while the client taps a spot on the back of the hand called the gamut spot. This balances the brain relative to the issues being addressed. At several stages of the treatment, the client is asked to rate the problem on a scale of one to ten. It is intended that by the end of the treatment, a person will be able to feel neutral and unaffected whenever the previous negative emotion comes up in the consciousness; all elements of the treatment continue until that neutral place is reached. If the problem has not been cleared, a special sequence is used to eliminate any psychological reversal that may be blocking the treatment. It is said that one session can be enough to treat or cure a phobia or other negative emotions. Once learned, TFT can also be used as a form of self-treatment for many conditions. The Emotional Freedom Technique and Be Set Free Fast were developed out of TFT. (See more on both of these modalities in this section.)
Contact: TFT Foundation – www.TFTFoundation.org,
     Callahan Techniques, Ltd. –
     www.RogerCallahan.com, or
     www.TFTPractitioners.net

Touch and Breathe (TAB)

Touch and Breathe is a variation on the Emotional Freedom Technique in which acupressure points are held rather than tapped while the breath and reminder phrases, similar to affirmations and related to particular fears, are used to help balance the client's energy system. Developed by psychologist Dr. John Diepold and others, the idea was to create a gentle, mindful alternative to the Applied Kinesiology method of point tapping, which can sometimes agitate or trigger people, especially if there is a history of the body being beaten or if they are experiencing extreme anxiety. The TAB process adds one complete, natural, unstrained respiration while the recipient holds a meridian point with two fingers. Consistent with Chinese thinking about the flow of chi energy, this breath brings vital chi energy into the body and facilitates the flow of chi to where it is needed. As acupressure points are touched in conjunction with the breath and reminder phrases, the flow of vital chi energy within the body is amplified. In addition, the physical motion and sound of the breathing process has a powerful calming influence. The therapeutic process follows either a generic sequence similar to the Emotional Freedom Technique or the sequence of points on the client's body that the practitioner determines will be most helpful for alleviating the distress. Variations in breathing techniques and the occasional use of both hands on certain points may also be employed during a session. Clients are also taught how to do follow-up TAB self-care at home. *The Energy of Belief*, a book written for the general public using the TAB method, contains additional elements of intentions and focused releasing affirmations.

Contact: The Center for Healing and Transformation –
www.MarySise.com/methods

Trauma Touch Therapy™ (TTT)

Trauma Touch Therapy was developed in the early 1990s by massage therapist Chris Smith after she recovered from her own experience of abuse and received training in the Hakomi Method. The TTT approach to providing release from trauma held in the tissues on a cellular level without retraumatizing the client integrates various self-awareness exercises with bodywork. Traumatic events need not be intense, one-time occurrences, but can be subtle and develop over time, such as when people experience a period of neglect or abandonment during certain stages of childhood. Rather than focusing on traumatic events, Trauma Touch Therapy works to help clients get in touch and be more present with the bodily sensations that reflect emotional wounds without becoming overwhelmed or further dissociated. The healing comes from being present in the body and being reintegrated with parts of the self that have dissociated or numbed out because of trauma. The goal of the therapy is to experience life in the body free from the constraining cycles of any trauma.

Therapy sessions, which take place in a safe, nurturing environment, combine breathing exercises, various body movements, client-directed touch, visualizations of body sensations, and creative forms of play to allow the client to be more present with the feelings in the body. The practitioner guides the client through an inquiry into his needs by supporting the ability to recognize the qualities of sensations in the body, letting them guide the healing process. The work is done with the client fully clothed on a massage table, in a chair, or in any comfortable position. The transformative process of lightening the load by identifying and releasing trauma held in the body and integrating a new, empowered, holistic sense of self is designed to be done in ten sessions, though people can take another ten if needed. Further empowerment continues as the client takes what is learned into daily life.

Contact: www.csha.net

VIII. Energy-Based Therapies

Energy is not a tangible thing, not an object that can be seen or touched. Sometimes we can experience it directly and unambiguously: through combustion, the energy stored in fossil fuels causes the parts in a car's engine to mesh together and its wheels to turn. A sailboat captures the energy of the wind to glide across the sea, and turbines use the power of moving water to make them revolve. Energy also manifests as a force that has observable physical effects; gravity and electromagnetism hold solar systems together but push galaxies apart. Sometimes we experience energy as that which allows everything to move and to change. In fact, cycles of change are a constant part of the rhythm of life—changes in the seasons, day and night, hot and cold, wet and dry, storms and calms, birth and death. Sometimes the changes appear in our moods and emotions: our days have ups and downs, sorrow and happiness, balance and imbalance, love and hate.

But energy is more than just a physical force. Cultures both ancient and modern recognize that there is a universal life-force energy that sustains all beings and, indeed, all of nature. It has many names in many traditions: chi, ki, gi, prana, lung, mana. It connects the physical with a spiritual realm full of wisdom, a wisdom of the mind and body that can motivate all of our actions and reactions. The human body is a miraculous combination of these realms, and they depend on each other to create good health and vitality. Just as the blood flows through the arteries and veins and the nerves send signals to the brain, so too the vital life force flows through a system of energy channels, nourishing the organs and cells of the body. Both are subject to the same kinds of problems: blockages, deficiencies, excesses, disruptions, and imbalances. When the life-force energy cannot flow freely, all manner of dysfunction can appear in our bodies and emotions. When the system is balanced and energy is flowing freely, we are open and eager to embrace all possibilities, floating on the waters of the inner ocean. From this may come physical action, a burst of creativity, a compassionate response to another, and if danger threatens, an almost superhuman ability can suddenly kick in.

Sometimes we surprise ourselves with what we can accomplish or endure. One time, my first mate and I were crossing from the South Pacific to the North Pacific Ocean, a voyage that would normally take about ten days. However, what became known as the "crossing from hell" ended up taking eighteen days because of a number of factors beyond our control. Again and again we were hit with squalls, monsoon rains, doldrums with no wind, variable sea conditions, and even a newly formed cyclone. As captain and the most experienced in handling these adverse conditions, I was often called upon to take action at a moment's notice, any time day or night. For most of the trip, I got very little sleep, but learned that a fifteen-minute catnap was enough to give me the energy to handle what needed doing. At anchor in our island destination, I slept for a day and a half, but awoke knowing that what I was physically, emotionally, and mentally capable of accomplishing under duress was much greater than I would have guessed. My inner potential had risen to the challenge, nourished by something beyond the physical.

Being on the water has always seemed to recharge my battery, even in situations that could have the potential to drain me. For that matter, a beautiful natural environment does the same thing. Each of us have experiences that seem to give us energy, that lend us inner strength in difficult situations, that allow us to face life—and death—with joy rather than fear. But we must take the responsibility for choosing a path that honors and strengthens this life-force energy. Energy can be bound up by limiting patterns in the body, mind, emotions, and spirit, but energy can also be called upon to liberate us from these patterns and return us to our true nature, a boundless store of love and compassion that we can share with all beings.

When life experiences create imbalances in the vital energy, an assortment of physical and emotional problems and illnesses can develop. Just as pollution interferes with a plant's ability to grow and wounded animals become so weak they can't search for life-giving food, when the flow of energy through the human body becomes restricted, our innate potential for wholeness and perfect functioning is obscured. If the restriction becomes pronounced enough to get our attention, it is surely time to find some therapeutic assistance. Energy medicine, or energy-based bodywork, has been recognized through the ages by many ancient cultures and is now rightfully gaining acknowledgment in the modern Western world. Through this work, it is becoming more evident that knowing how to activate and cultivate the vital life-force energy within is essential to our well-being.

Many of the forms of bodywork discussed in this section originated in ancient Asian cultures and other indigenous societies, though some are more contemporary developments in healing. Most of these types of bodywork therapy focus their efforts on the innate life-force energy that manifests in each of our physical bodies. This energy system has its own anatomy—internal pathways, known as energy channels, nadis, or meridians; energy centers called chakras or dantiens; and specific points, such as acupoints, marma points, tsubo, or pressure points—that allow a practitioner to work with the energy itself. Subtle as these seem, there are still more subtle aspects to the energy body: energy fields and biofields. Modalities that can transform them are discussed in the next section.

The primary intention of these energy-based therapies is to promote the balance and free flow of this vital life force. Energy can be influenced by our minds, attitudes, emotions, and beliefs; restrictions or blockages in energy's flow caused by the accumulation of life disturbances or traumas can prevent people from realizing their full human potential and experiencing the life they really deserve. These treatments most often assist the recipient in awakening, cultivating, restoring, revitalizing, and balancing the energy flow, with the practitioner acting primarily as a catalyst, often a powerful one, for the recipient's innate abilities to arise and an energetic healing to take place. Energy healing is an ancient, intuitive art with many continually evolving forms, suitable not only for preventing or healing an assortment of limiting conditions of disharmony or disease, but also as a means for enhancing overall well-being and providing spiritual transformation.

Each modality employs a variety of techniques to accomplish the desired result of removing disturbances, restrictions, or blockages within the energy system of the body. The methods can include various forms of diagnostics, affirmations, attunements, bioenergetic and bioelectric techniques, divine interventions, transmission of vital energy, loving touch, point activation and balancing, meridian massage, pattern clearing, pressure-point or reflex holding, psychic energy work,

quantum techniques, resonance repatterning, tantric energy work, tonification, breathwork, vibrational sound work, vital point manipulations, and numerous yogic practices. Often the practitioner's goal is to trigger the recipient's own healing response.

In addition, some modalities include techniques to balance, tune, and align the seven major chakras or energy centers, which are like spinning energy vortices, each associated with a particular gland, organ, emotion, mental tendency, element, color, and spiritual aspect of a person. Most chakra balancing awakens the universal life-force energies with specific, and sometimes unusual, prolonged sounding (overtones, chants, mantras, sacred vowel sounds, rainbow songs, and harmonics), the breath, colors, light, precious stones and crystals, meditation, invocations, energy awakening techniques, chelation, and prayer. The vibrations of each may be complemented by energy transmitted from the healer's hands. Although some may include work with the aura and the biofields, the emphasis of most of these modalities is on cultivating energy within the body, clearing away unhealthy energy blocks, charging depleted areas, repairing distorted patterns, and providing more inner balance and harmony. The amount of actual touch, hands-on manipulation, and pressure work used with each of these energy-based modalities may vary from minimal to extensive. But even the lightest touch can have great effect if applied skillfully in the right location and direction.

In most of these methods, it is essential for the recipient to be relaxed while the practitioner, directed by divine guidance, intuitive awareness, or higher sense perception, focuses on the different areas of the body to recognize and help alleviate any blockage in the energy pathways. This profound process often offers the recipient enhanced perceptions and insights that can help to free up energy and heal the body, mind, and spirit.

The following wide range of practitioner-applied modalities is just a sample of what is now available world-wide for energetic healing. Any potential precautions or contraindications associated with these therapies are covered within the discussion of each modality. (Further descriptions of related self-care aspects of these modalities can be found in Chapters 9 and 11.)

Abhyanga
Part of the East Indian Ayurvedic Panchakarma system of detoxification treatments, this full-body

oil massage is often the initial phase of a complete Ayurvedic healing session. Abhyanga treatments are very sensuous and are meant to nourish and cleanse the skin, relax muscles and tendons, remove toxins, purify the system, and balance body energies, thus promoting emotional and psychological well-being. It is common for two practitioners to work simultaneously on the recipient.

Each session follows a specific sequence of techniques on the client's body. The practitioner's hands move in a deep, firm, rhythmic, and synchronized manner during a complete head-to-toe massage, contacting both muscles and the marma energy points found at specific locations along the nadis (energy channels). Just as with the Chinese system of acupressure points along meridians, these points are worked on to remove blockages and stimulate the flow of vital energy. As with most Ayurvedic bodywork, liberal amounts of herb-infused oil are used.

There are many variations on this time-honored type of bodywork. The full-body Kayabhyanga massage is meant to pacify the symptoms of specific diseases by cleansing and rejuvenating the body. A complete session usually includes an oil massage combined with energy-point work and is often followed by a head massage and a hot-steam treatment known as Swedana. An ancient form of Abhyanga known as Vishesh massage uses much oil and deep, firm, rhythmic pressing and squeezing on the body tissues and muscles to relieve physical tension. It is intended to move out deeper-seated impurities and is also often combined with Swedana steam therapy. Udvartina massage is similar to this except that an oily herbal paste that penetrates deeply is scrubbed all over the body to exfoliate the skin and draw stagnant toxins out of the lymphatic system. A Garshana massage uses a dry herbal powder instead of oil to create friction that will remove dead cells from the skin, making it more receptive to any herbs and oils that may later be applied. One or two practitioners use raw silk gloves to rub and brush the body with light, brisk, and vigorous strokes that create friction and static on the surface of the skin. This action also helps increase circulation. There are also special types of Abhyanga massage directed to specific parts of the body that are designed for pregnant women, infants, and children, and certain forms concentrate on particular areas of the body, such as the head, feet, and spine. Any of these forms of treatment can be combined

with Swedana steam therapy. (See more under Ayurvedic Therapy later in this section.)
Contact: www.chopra.com or
www.diamondwayayurveda.com

Acupressure

Acupressure is one of the oldest forms of energetic healing, and individual elements of this method have been used around the world for a very long time. The traditional practice of Acupressure is a significant part of the ancient system of healing known today as Traditional Chinese Medicine, though its techniques are also seen in methods well established in Japan, Tibet, Thailand, and Korea. References to its use are also found in ancient Egypt. Today, it is rapidly taking on new incarnations and finding more recognition in the West.

Rooted in the practice of Acupuncture, Acupressure is likewise based on the principles of yin and yang, the five element theory, and the establishment of a balanced flow of vital energy (chi) along the twelve regular meridian pathways throughout the body. All organs and parts of the body are connected with these meridians and depend on this flow of energy. If the flow becomes obstructed, the associated organs become depleted of energy and the chance of illness occurring becomes more likely. Therefore, activating and maintaining this flow is the point of this type of therapy. The system of meridians is easier to understand if you visualize water flowing through a pipe. If the pipe is damaged or blocked, the water cannot flow. By working with these meridians, Acupressure can stimulate and release blockages, address dysfunctions, increase energy in the body, improve organ function, invigorate the nervous system, enhance circulation, and stimulate the body's natural healing abilities. This is accomplished by hands-on work on acupressure points (also called acupoints), which are locations along the meridians that are close to the surface and thus easily accessed by the hands of a practitioner. There are hundreds of these points all over the body; however, many are not used on a regular basis. (For more information about the meridians and points, see Chapter 9.)

As with most Asian healing therapies, it is understood that the root cause of disease is not necessarily indicated by the symptoms and that only by treating this root cause will its manifestations be alleviated. The root cause of an issue could be poor digestion, bad circulation, a weak organ, depression, or hormones, each of which will show up energetically in the meridian system, often in a location "downstream" from the problem area. The actual sequence of point work is based on the root cause. If, for example, it is determined that the root cause is poor circulation, points on the related meridian are treated first. Attention is then given to other meridians to influence organs associated with the circulation meridian. If done accurately in one or more sessions, Acupressure can address a number of issues, including asthma and diabetes.

Depending on the particular practitioner and the country in which it is practiced, Acupressure uses a range of techniques in which primarily the hands, fingers, or thumbs perform a combination of press-and-stroke or lift-and-press motions. The practitioner may press a single point once or several times in a certain direction and often works on a series of points in a specific order. The force of the pressure and the length of time for which it is applied varies among the individual points, and, although this pressure is key to the process, it must be adjusted to the client's tolerance level. Practitioners may also use techniques such as rolling, rubbing, squeezing, kneading, grasping, pushing, stretching, digging, dragging, plucking, tweaking, hammering, vibrating, knocking, and treading.

Other adjunct therapies, such as the subtle arts of pulse reading, face reading, moxibustion, ear-point work, cupping, and tapping, may often accompany Acupressure. Pulse reading in particular is an important part of the diagnosis in this therapy. By reading pulses at specific locations, primarily on the wrist, practitioners can diagnose issues with the organs and in the body as a whole and can determine the flow of energy in a meridian.

Many forms of Acupressure have evolved over the years, and the following are a sampling of those available today. Some have been used for centuries, whereas others represent recent developments in the field of energy medicine.
Contact: Acupressure Institute – www.acupressure.com

Mardana is the Ayurvedic equivalent of Acupressure that uses pressure on marma points to release blockages and encourage the flow of prana in the nadi energy channels. Deep pressure is applied with the fingers, thumbs, or fists to the specific points

that will address a client's problematic conditions. When points are pressed, they are often held and kneaded for a period of time determined by the particular constitution of the client. Much of this work is done on the back and feet, where the nerve endings are more accessible. Deep-tissue massage is also used to stimulate and loosen ligaments and muscles where they meet a marma point. Treatments are often combined with an aromatic herbal oil and paste massage.
Contact: www.ayurvedaclinics.in/panchakarma

Energy of Life® (EOL) includes Acupressure as part of a system intended to release emotional problems, alleviate chronic fatigue, relieve endocrine dysfunction, and enhance the immune system. EOL was created by medical intuitives Sue Singleton and Aaron Singleton as a method that transcends the boundaries of other existing systems by targeting the energy frequencies of the physical and psychological tension patterns in the body that cause trauma and illness. EOL is not based solely on meridian flows; its practitioners also use dialogue and qi gong energy work to activate the universal energies in order to create a deeper and more rapid release.

Treatments follow a specific sequence to amplify energy at each of about sixty different, highly effective acupoints on the body. The healing process also involves aromatherapy, chakra work, crystals, and ionic vibrational healing tools. Clients are encouraged to be active participants in regaining their own health. The Singletons have also created a Visionary Acupressure System as another way to help balance an individual's energies.
Contact: www.thewaytobalance.com

Magnetic Acupressure uses magnetic or polarized tools whose north and south poles provide specific effects on the acupressure points of the body to stimulate nerves and blood flow and help organs and glands function better. In ancient times, this Asian therapy used the mineral magnetite, which was applied to the skin in a poultice. Today, it employs steady or pulsed magnetic fields from either electromagnets or less powerful permanent magnets taped to the body for a certain period of time. The

use of small magnets taped to specific problem areas to enhance the healing process can complement many forms of bodywork.
Contact: www.magnecare.co.uk

Nambudripad Allergy Elimination Technique (NAET) is designed to put an end to allergies by performing Acupressure or Acupuncture on special acupoints on the body. It was developed by Dr. Devi Nambudripad in 1983, primarily as the result of her search for remedies for her own multiple illnesses. The basic aim of NAET is to reprogram the client's nervous system so it will not create energetic blockages in reaction to allergens. Particular allergies are first detected using Applied Kinesiology, in which the muscle strength in a client's arm is tested while he is holding a suspected allergenic substance. An allergy is confirmed when the muscle's resistance to applied pressure is weak.

Treatment is accomplished by exposing the patient to the allergen while the practitioner applies light Acupressure or Acupuncture along both sides of the spinal column in locations known as gate acupoints, places where the energy flow within a meridian intersects with a nerve root. This action is intended to release blockages associated with the allergy and thereby put an end to the body's negative response to the substance. This approach is considered to be a safe, natural way to detect and eliminate all types of allergies. Although there has been controversy about its usefulness, NAET has been shown by some researchers to be effective in treating a variety of allergies and disorders.
Contact: www.naet.com

Process Acupressure (PA) is a holistic form of Acupressure that combines ancient East Indian and Chinese health practices with contemporary psychological and spiritual understanding to open and balance energy pathways, strengthen the surrounding energy fields, and enhance psychological and spiritual growth. PA specializes in working with the multidimensional aspects of human energy systems and uses both psychospiritual processing skills involving dialogue and bodywork such as Acupressure and Zero Balancing to influence the body's mental, emotional, and spiritual state. It was

developed Dr. Aminah Raheem, a transpersonal psychologist, bodyworker, and teacher who also established Clinical Acupressure. These two practices are now taught as **Soul Lightening® Acupressure** by Soul Lightening International.

Process Acupressure is based on the principles of Process Oriented Psychology, developed by Arnold Mindell. Instead of trying to fix a particular symptom, condition, or attitude and impose some predetermined state of being, the practitioner follows what naturally arises in the recipient and guides her to the deepest possible level of self-awareness, the place where she can find her own healing wisdom. The treatment works through several phases to provide relaxation, enhanced self-awareness, the integration of a more spiritual state of being, and a soul-centered awakening.

A typical session first involves opening body energies with dialogue and a specific hands-on, twelve-step procedure to relax and deepen awareness of the body areas in need of attention. Gentle to deep finger pressure is used on certain interface acupoints to stimulate and open the flow of energy in the meridians and chakra energy centers. Rather than holding these points, the practitioner applies fulcrums to them in a manner similar to that used in Zero Balancing. When the energy starts to flow in a balanced way, all the body's systems will naturally come into harmony on their own. As that happens and the blocked feelings, body tension, and unhealed trauma are released, the practitioner gives further support by assisting the recipient in processing the experience. At the end of a session, the practitioner energetically smooths out and balances the chakras so the client can fully integrate the experience. Even if there is no apparent deep and soulful transformation, the treatments are useful for relaxation and the release of body tension, as well as for stress-related conditions such as post-traumatic stress disorder.

It became evident that the bodywork method alone, without verbal processing, was also effective in clinical settings, especially when the opportunity for dialogue was unlikely or inappropriate. Nurses, physical therapists, and other health care providers began requesting training to learn this method for use in their practices. **Clinical Acupressure (CA)** addresses the vital energy of the body without the psychospiritual aspects of Process Acupressure and is beneficial for people with a wide spectrum of physical symptoms and conditions. Acupressure formulas are given for common health issues such as headache, insomnia, cold and flu, digestion, and others, as well as powerful balancing formulas for addressing chronic conditions and stress-related issues. Though not intended to replace medical care for serious conditions, Clinical Acupressure is a natural treatment choice for those who do not have access to or are unable to receive Acupuncture and is often used to complement other forms of therapy. There are no harsh side effects.

Clients can also be instructed in the use of the simple Seva Stress Release practice, which can be used for further self-care at home. This workshop is also offered as part of Soul Lightening International's eight-module Acupressure for Anyone® curriculum, which is designed for laypeople who wish to learn to use Acupressure to balance and support health for themselves and their families.
Contact: www.soullightening.org

Su Jok combines both Acupressure and Acupuncture into a therapy developed around 1974 by South Korean scientist Professor Jae Woo Park after he completed a study of the principles of yin and yang, the five element theory, the six ki theory of pulse palpation, the eight origin methods of treatment, and the phenomenon known as correspondence. Correspondence describes how certain points on the hands and feet relate to the root cause of a disease or health problem. Su Jok is a highly condensed and time-saving version of earlier Acupressure therapies; it involves the simultaneous stimulation of points on both the hands and feet that are associated with the issues in need of attention. This simplified method is carried out with the aid of a constitution chart and an acupoint map of the locations of points on the extremities that correspond to internal organs of the body. A treatment can be accomplished in only a few minutes.

The six ki pulse palpation method, also known as chun in ji, is first used to ascertain the client's condition. After the diagnostics, light Acupressure is used to find the sensitive points, and deeper finger pressure is used to release any dysfunction or restriction. Acupuncture with needles is used only if necessary to treat more severe problems. Treatments may also use moxibustion, magnets, seeds, and metallic bells and stars, as well as colors or infrared lasers for those who are more sensitive, such as children. Some meridian muscle therapy and treatment of the chakras is also included. Su Jok is now taught at an international center in Mumbai, India, and it can also be used by clients as an effective self-care treatment for common ailments.
Contact: www.sujoktherapy.com or www.sujok.com

Tapas Acupressure Technique® (TAT) is a psychoenergetic therapy developed around 1993 by Tapas Fleming as a gentle and stimulating way of addressing and quickly alleviating complex problems and emotional trauma. This form of Acupressure uses a limited number of important acupressure points on the skull, the face, and near the eyes in protocols that address different emotional problems. While one hand lightly touches these points, the other hand holds the base of the skull. The practitioner performs finger tapping on these points as the client holds a pose, directs attention to the stressful problem that needs to be resolved, and speaks eight separate positive-affirmation statements until an energy shift occurs. Continuing this tapping and verbal-affirmation technique, the healing process continues in stages as the practitioner focuses on the energetic location of a problem and directs energy to heal the root cause. By employing acts of forgiveness and other verbally supportive ways of overcoming resistance and by working on any remnants of an issue, it then becomes possible for the recipient to choose a positive alternative outcome and integrate the healing into both body and mind. TAT has also been used for helping groups of people who have experienced a natural disaster or traumatic event.
Contact: www.tatlife.net

Tibetan Point Holding Acupressure is an ancient somatic practice that was further developed in 1989 by Karen Peterson and John Walsh. This form of Acupressure is distinguished by the prolonged holding of acupressure points to stimulate an energetic emotional release within the meridians and to help

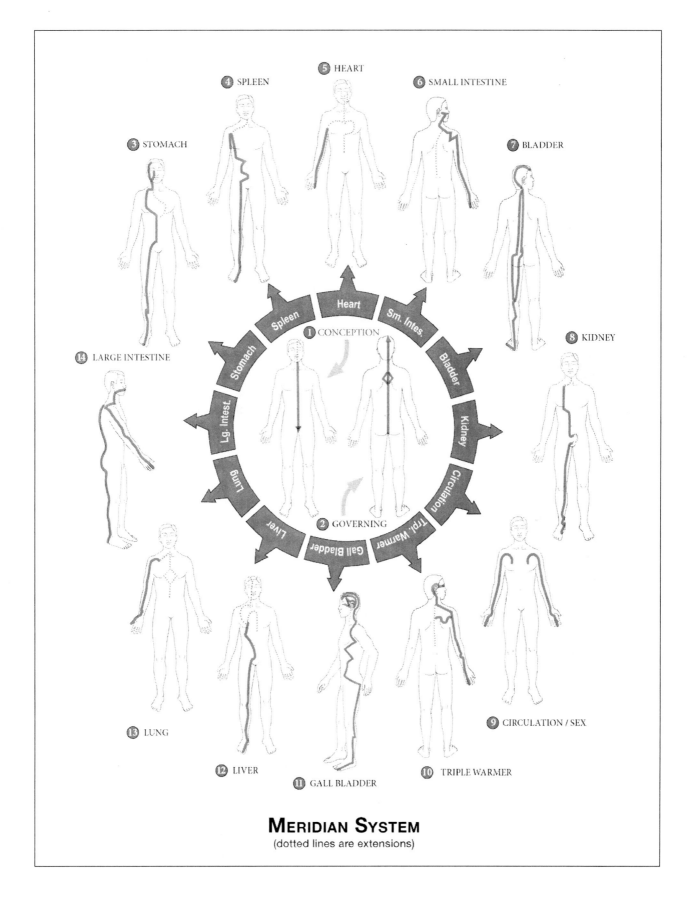

④ SPLEEN
⑤ HEART
⑥ SMALL INTESTINE
③ STOMACH
⑦ BLADDER
⑧ KIDNEY
⑭ LARGE INTESTINE
① CONCEPTION
② GOVERNING
⑨ CIRCULATION / SEX
⑬ LUNG
⑫ LIVER
⑪ GALL BLADDER
⑩ TRIPLE WARMER

MERIDIAN SYSTEM
(dotted lines are extensions)

resolve an assortment of issues within the body's muscular system. The lengthy holding allows the client more time to address internal thoughts and feelings as they arise. As many as five practitioners simultaneously hold specific pressure points on the recipient to promote relaxation, balance the flow of energy, and provide emotional release.

At the beginning of a session, the particular needs of the recipient are assessed through Iridology (analysis of the eye), Applied Kinesiology (muscle testing), and pulse analysis. This enables the practitioner to determine which meridians to work on. Next, the prolonged pressing and holding of meridian points is done in a fairly firm manner to provide the desired release. The session typically lasts for about two hours and is considered complementary to other forms of therapy.

Contact: www.ezinearticles.com/?history-of-
tibetan-point-holding&id=6449224

Acupuncture

Like Acupressure, this 5,000-year-old Chinese therapy, at one time known as Zhenjiu, is based on the theory that dysfunction or illness is a result of obstructions in the network of meridian pathways that extend throughout the body, causing imbalances in the flow of the vital chi energy. Health is maintained when the opposite forces of yin and yang are in balance and chi flows without interruption. Although some research suggests otherwise, these channels of energy do not exist in a physical form like a blood vessel, but are present in a more subtle, vibrational way. A total of twelve regular meridians, eight extraordinary channels, which include the two central channels, and an assortment of other channels of energy, most of which are divided into yin and yang pairs, are spread throughout the body along specific pathways at varying depths both near and deep below the surface of the body. Each meridian is associated and interconnected with the different body systems and organs, and when a particular meridian has a balanced flow of chi, the corresponding organs and body systems will have a better chance of functioning optimally. To cultivate and balance this flow, acupuncture points (acupoints) along each of the meridians are activated in order to dissipate any obstructions by inserting fine needles into them or by applying other forms of stimulation. In contrast to Acupressure, in which the hands and fingers are used, needles are more precise, tend to go deeper, and have a more profound effect. (For more information about the meridians and points, see Chapter 9.)

Acupuncture is one of the fundamental techniques found in Traditional Chinese Medicine and has been around since before the time of the Yellow Emperor, a time when shamanic healing was much more prevalent. The first tools used for this therapy were actually sharp-edged stones that have been dated to 3000 BCE. Over the centuries, the instruments used by the Chinese have evolved from bones to bamboo and, around 300 BCE, to metal needles. Today, stainless-steel needles in various sizes are the most common instruments used, although modern adaptations of the practice now employ heat, laser beams, electronic stimulus, and sound waves to stimulate acupoints. Acupoints can also be treated with moxibustion, press balls, magnets, and ion-pumping cords. Injection of sterile water, vitamins, herbs, or homeopathic solutions through the inserted needle is a special treatment that is done only occasionally. Although working on specific points in the body was practiced in ancient Tibet, India, Egypt, Arabia, and other parts of the world, what developed in China represents the most complete system of treatment. (For more information about Traditional Chinese Medicine, please refer to that section in this chapter.)

The Chinese practice of Acupuncture has evolved into many different forms, particularly in Japan and Korea. In 702 CE, the emperor of Japan established the Imperial Medical College, with Acupuncture and pulse reading each holding a prominent position in its course of instruction. As time passed, different schools of practice, such as Rampo, KoHo, Kampo, and Gosei, developed their own approaches to Acupuncture and meridian therapy. Some forms, such as that of the Rampo school, used needling on locations related to nerve function rather than on particular meridians. By the late 1700s, these various forms of meridian therapy were well established. Over the years, a large percentage of Japanese acupuncturists have been blind people whose highly developed extrasensory perception produced very effective practitioners. It was one of these practitioners who developed the insertion tube that allowed the use of finer and thinner goshin needles, which became the standard in Japan. Japanese methods are typically gentler than the Chinese, since they employ shallower insertions and use shorter needles. They are applied separately or simultaneously to work on core energetic and structural imbalances or for local symptomatic relief of a client's complaints. Other characteristics that define Japanese Acupuncture include variations from the Chinese point locations, an emphasis on feeling the qualities of specific points, different needle insertion techniques, and limitations on the number of points that are used. In certain forms, the focus is on the meridians as a whole rather than on the points. Diagnosis and manipulations of the hara (the abdominal energy center called the lower dantien in TCM) also developed into a significant practice of its own. In spite of the diversity of schools and technical approaches that employ different strategies with point work, there are still many similarities between Japanese and Chinese Acupuncture, especially with regard to the science of meridians and the diagnostic techniques that use pulse readings and other types of analysis.

Today, the Japanese Sawada style of Acupuncture, which emphasizes the stimulation of certain active acupoints regardless of the specific complaint, is the one most often taught in the United States and Canada. The Japanese style also teaches that since points are living phenomena and change in quality and location, their exact location is best detected intuitively through the experience and sensitivity of the fingers rather than by referring to a map. However, the Chinese approach of working with points specifically related to a complaint is considered appropriate when a disease or disorder is well defined and firmly established in the body. Although they often use thicker and longer needles than the Japanese, Chinese practitioners do use noninsertion needles, such as the blunt-pointed, pencil-size enshin needles or spring-loaded, pressure-controlled teishin needles. Both of these are simply pressed or rubbed on the points of more sensitive patients such as children. A wide variety of both Japanese and Chinese practices are now in use worldwide, and new forms (some consider them styles) are still being developed.

Korean practitioners have introduced their own versions of Acupuncture with distinct techniques and applications that often use only certain specific acupoints. In contrast to the Chinese practice, the Indian Ayurvedic health system employs a form of Acupuncture that works to stimulate and balance the pranic life-force energy in the body through a network of marma points that are unique to their view of energy pathways. Both ancient Egypt and Rome also had an understanding of pressure points, but neither established a significant system of Acupuncture. Interestingly enough, the Amazon Indians of South America used needle-like blowgun darts dipped in herbs to puncture various points in order to cure disease. This perhaps points to the wisdom of the body surfacing simultaneously in widely separated cultures to teach similar effective ways of promoting healing. In any case, today the usefulness of Acupuncture has been well documented, scientifically analyzed, and is rapidly becoming accepted in the Western medical world. Some insurance companies in the West now even include coverage for this kind of therapy.

As with most forms of Chinese medicine (and other Eastern practices for that matter), proper diagnosis is the initial and often the most important phase of any therapy, and, in some ways, diagnosis alone is considered healing. Although specific diagnostic methods vary with each practitioner, it is usually considered necessary before any treatment is undertaken. A diagnosis is developed through the five methods of looking, listening, smelling, asking, and feeling in order to gather as much information as possible about any preexisting patterns of disharmony. Looking at the client's body alignment can reveal numerous subtle signs about overall condition. A considerable amount of information about the state of the whole body can be determined by reading the face and tongue, as well as the feet, hands, ears, or eyes. Listening to the breath, voice, and qualities of a cough and smelling the various odors that emanate from a person also contribute to the analysis. Asking relates to inquiring about the various aspects of a person's daily life, sleep, and medical history. Feeling involves palpating the body to detect the temperature, moisture, and texture of the skin as well as to sense the flow of chi energy. Diagnosis may also include abdominal and urine analysis, which reveals much about the status of the vital internal organs. However, a pulse reading at the wrist is by far the most significant, respected, and common part of an analysis and is a prerequisite to treating all kinds of conditions, especially when the practitioner intends to prescribe the use of certain herbs. Diagnosis through pulse reading has proven very useful for many years and has played a vital role in the medical practices of China, Japan, Korea, Tibet, India, and other Asian countries. (For more details on pulse reading, see that heading in this chapter.)

Acupuncture treatments are primarily intended to release blockages, treat existing pain, address imbalances that have resulted in disease, and prevent illness from occurring by stimulating a balanced flow of chi. When a client requests a treatment, he must first indicate whether he wants to be treated just for a specific issue or would instead like to follow the more holistic approach of starting with a complete analysis of all aspects of his being. In this case, the first session will involve an initial interview in which the practitioner gathers detailed information about the client's medical history and present condition and then performs a diagnostic analysis including pulse reading. The remaining time, as well as any following sessions, primarily consists of the actual application of the needles.

During a session, the client is first made comfortable and encouraged to relax, most often lying on his back on a massage table. Fine sterilized needles are then painlessly inserted into the skin at specific points along one or several meridians considered most suitable for alleviating his condition. A trained practitioner may use points near a symptom, adjacent to it, on a meridian on the opposite side, at a place where meridians intersect, or at some other distant point on the meridian. Special Acupuncture treatments can also be done on the face, tongue, and ears to affect other parts of the body. The needles are intended to modulate, stimulate, disperse, tonify, sedate, or balance the flow of energy, depending on whether the existing energetic imbalance is caused by a deficiency, an irregularity, or an excess of chi.

Although an exact count of the points located throughout the body varies among experts, it is generally agreed that, of the more than 2,000 established acupoints found in the body, the most often used are about 365 regular acupoints, numerous special "extra" points, and painful ashi points. However, the actual number of points used during a session may be twenty or fewer, depending on what needs to be accomplished and the particular tradition in which a practitioner is trained. In Japan, practitioners of Acupuncture often use a large number of needles, whereas Chinese and many modern Western practitioners try to use as few as possible.

After inserting the needles, the practitioner usually leaves the room while the client rests, returning about twenty minutes later to remove the needles. The session then concludes with some discussion about what was revealed through the treatment. Depending on the extent of the problem or issue and the effects of previous sessions, a number of sessions accomplished over time may be necessary for resolution.

The process of being treated with needles is not really painful; however, when needles are applied to more sensitive points in the extremities of the hands and feet, there may be some tenderness or discomfort. These points are like small pools, unlike those in the trunk of the body which are relatively larger and more like lakes or seas in which any discomfort dissipates more easily. Some sensitive clients and children may prefer using one of the less invasive forms of Acupuncture (often with blunt contact needles or without needles) that have been developed over the years around the world. These alternative approaches can be used on their own or as an adjunct to a regular Acupuncture treatment.

There are also a few practices that, though not distinct modalities, are often used either to affect the acupuncture points directly or to complement an Acupuncture treatment. **Cupping,** in which heated glass, clay, plastic, rubber, or bamboo cups are applied to certain acupoints on the body, is a common adjunct to Acupuncture. Clear cups have the advantage of allowing better observation of the level of congestion or inflammation on the skin surface during a treatment. As the heated air inside the cup contracts during cooling, it creates a vacuum that helps pull out toxins from the area; sometimes a sliding motion is used to cover a broader area. The process creates strong suction on the skin, which causes small blood blisters to appear near its surface. This suction also causes tissue layers to separate, enabling increased blood flow to bring water and nutrients to the area. Because it draws impurities from the body, cupping is considered beneficial for the treatment of tension, pain, and the common cold, and when done on the back, it helps remove stagnant energy from the lungs. Today, the process of Medi Cupping, which uses a machine instead of applying cups by hand, has become common.

Moxibustion is a therapeutic practice often used by acupuncturists that can be applied to either specific points or particular locations on the body for a purifying effect. It basically entails the use of heat as a healing medium and involves burning certain herbs on or near the skin to increase the circulation of chi and blood in that area of the body. (More information on this is provided under its own heading in this section.)

Other related procedures sometimes used in conjunction with Acupuncture include **Gaomo**, in which healing liniments are applied to particular areas of the body. A **Gua Sha** treatment is an ancient method of scraping toxins from the surface of the skin with a flat, smooth instrument to promote blood and lymph circulation while removing impurities, toxic heat, and dead skin cells from the body (see more in the section on Substance- and Implement-Assisted Therapies in this chapter). Some therapists also incorporate the spinal therapy known as Zero Balancing in their practice (see more in the section on Spinal Therapies in this chapter). The use of these additional procedures depends on the particular orientation and training of individual practitioners.
Contact: American Association of Acupuncture and
Oriental Medicine – www.aaaomonline.org,
www.japaneseacupuncture.ca, or
www.acupuncture.com

Auricular Acupuncture uses acupuncture points on the outer ear. Therapists view the ear as an upside-down embryo in which specific points correlate to each part of the body. Working the points on the ear is effective in a way similar to Reflexology; sometimes seeds or press-spheres are taped to points to stimulate them in certain ways for longer periods. During the 1950s, French physician and neurologist Dr. Paul Nogier was one of those instrumental in the development of this process of diagnosis and treatment. In some cases, Auricular Acupuncture can be used to help a client kick bad habits such as smoking. It is also appropriate for infants. After years of studying traditional Chinese Acupuncture, Nogier also developed the pulse technique now called **Vascular Autonomic Signal (VAS)**, which is based on the way the arterial system displays a specific physical reaction when objects such as food, herbs, and medicine are placed nearby in the surrounding energy fields. Orthopedic surgeon Dr. Joseph Navach also completed studies that recognized compounds in acupoints and related distal points that resonate when electromagnetically stimulated. Dr. John Ackerman has continued the work of Nogier and Navach with research on the overall relationship between human biology and the energy fields.

In addition, Dr. Miki Shima from California made extensive contributions to auricular meridian therapy, developing his own technique called **Somato-Auricular Therapy (SAT)**, in which points on the ear are combined with secondary channel points. SAT focuses on chronic organ problems and other pain issues. He also promoted the Japanese **Akabane Method** of diagnosing and rectifying energy imbalances in the meridians by using the timing of the body's reaction to the heat produced by moxibustion applied to certain points. This method also uses short, shallowly inserted hinaishin intradermal needles that are taped in place for up to a week.
Contact: www.auriculotherapy.info,
www.acupuncturejournal.com, or
www.iaam.ni

Bee Venom Acupuncture (BVA) is a practice that stimulates acupoints to provide pain relief and to prevent or clear inflammation; it has promise for the treatment of arthritis. Using a technique called aqua-acupuncture, which was developed in the 1950s, bioactive compounds isolated from bee venom or herbal extracts are injected into acupoints with a hypodermic needle. BVA is especially popular in Korea, where it has been used in one form or another for more than 2,000 years.
Contact: www.bee-venom.net

Eight Constitution Acupuncture, now simply referred to as **Constitution Acupuncture**, was developed in Korea by Chinese Dr. Dowon Kwon in 1965, building on the work of herbalist Dr. Jema Lee, who first established the eight-constitution system in the early 1900s. Constitution Acupuncture works with meridians to categorize each person into a particular constitution that determines which areas of the person's body and which organs are strong or weak. The practitioner tailors the treatment to the individual primarily by treating the weakest link in fourteen different meridians with Acupuncture, herbs, and diet. The actual number of constitutional categories (based on the phases of yin and yang) has been increased over the ensuing years through the work of Dr. Tae Hwan Yom and Dr. Moon to a total of 264. Though Dr. Yom first determined each individual's constitution through a system of pulse reading, Dr. Moon now uses applied meridian kinesiology, which is a combination of muscle testing and Acupuncture.

During a treatment, needles are inserted superficially and removed quickly to promote the arrival of chi into the area and to balance the energy flow. The needles may also be inserted on a slant to tonify or purge the chi. The whole procedure is repeated a certain number of times on appropriate points along the meridian. The correct herbs are chosen through muscle testing for positive or negative reactions as the practitioner holds a particular herb up to the client's nose and then tests a specific muscle, whose strength or weakness indicates whether a substance will help or harm the client when ingested. The combination of prescribed herbs and meridian therapy produces a direct method of dealing with a number of issues.
Contact: www.ecmed.org or www.sedonaranch.org/8-body-type-acupuncture.html

Electro-Acutherapy or **Electro-Acupuncture Diagnostics**, a modern method developed by Dr. Richard Voll in Germany, is an integration of ancient Chinese medicine and new bioresonance research that uses different electrical current impulses and wave forms instead of needles to affect acupoints. Recent scientific studies have proven the existence of a vibrational exchange between cells, and the therapy recognizes that electrovibrational currents have a strong effect on the flow of energy within parts of the body. Treatments use electrical currents at specific frequencies to isolate and treat energetic imbalances. Different effects are achieved by changing the impulse to specific frequencies, since certain electrical frequencies are known to sedate or disperse electrical activity in the tissues or organs, whereas others will tonify or stimulate, each in a way similar to the use of needles. Adjustments in polarity are also used in a very precise way. The advantages of this relatively pain-free method are that extra stimulus can be applied for a longer period of time and that the intensity can be adjusted. The Germans, French, and Chinese have been treating acupuncture points this way for a number of years with good results, though the Chinese method actually delivers the electrical impulses through needles. Recent studies have shown that acupoints also respond to light, color, sound, and lasers.
Contact: www.biontologyarizona.com/electro-acupuncture/

Endo-Nasal Therapy is a form of Acupuncture that is performed on the nose. As with the ear in Auricular Acupuncture, points on and in the nose have an energetic connection to other parts of the body, and it is these points that are used in this method of treatment. This therapy is often done as an adjunct to other meridian work.
Contact: www.nasalspecific.com

Esogetic Colorpuncture™ or **Acu-Light Color Therapy** was developed by German naturopath and acupuncturist Dr. Peter Mandel. He began exploring this noninvasive technique in the 1970s, after working with Kirlian photography. Mandel coined the term *esogetics* to describe this holistic healing process, which is a synthesis of ancient esoteric doctrines, Chinese medicine, and modern energetic scientific developments. It is based on studies that show that human cells, and particularly acupoints and meridians, are able to absorb and transmit light; the flow of information along the meridians is a key part of the physics of cellular communication. Mandel developed a systematic set of treatments in which different-colored light (different frequencies of visible light) is applied to the points on the meridians where needles are traditionally used to create a healing effect; these points act as doorways to allow light to enter the body. Between seven and fourteen colors, each associated with a particular wavelength and photon intensity that have a specific effect on the body, are used to add or subtract energy from the meridian system. It was found that warm colors stimulate and cold colors sedate. This form of Acupuncture can be used as an alternative for children or adults who are uncomfortable with needles.

Treatments use a hand-held acu-light wand or a pen into which colored glass tips can be inserted, either of which can be set to a specific frequency. Mandel also uses light signals to stimulate the lymphatic system and detoxify the body, along with other pain-reduction techniques that involve infrared and colored light. His most recent work involves the use of tools to regulate brain waves and the application of tiny crystals to acupoints to perpetuate the harmonizing healing effect after a treatment.

Contact: www.wenwellness.com

Five Element Acupuncture is a practice that concentrates on correcting root imbalances in the body. This form of meridian therapy is based on the classical Nanjing system of Acupuncture and was originally introduced to the West by Englishman J. R. Worsley in the 1950s. One of Worsley's senior students, Professor Neil Gumenick, later established The Institute of Classical Five Element Acupuncture, Inc. in California. Rather than concentrating on addressing symptoms of ill health themselves, Five Element Acupuncture is used for restorative purposes through balancing the five natural elements (water, wood, fire, earth, and metal) foundational to Chinese medicine. Every individual is born with, or develops in the formative years of life, a primary imbalance in one of these elements. Each element relates to a particular organ/function and its meridian. Wood relates to the gallbladder and liver; fire to the heart, small intestines, pericardium, and triple heater; water to the bladder and kidneys; earth to the stomach and spleen; and metal to the lungs and colon.

Five Element Acupuncture emphasizes identifying the primary imbalanced element, called the "causative factor," diagnosed by assessing the patient's predominant odor, color, sound, and emotion. The causative factor element and its related organs are the source of symptoms manifesting anywhere, and at any level—body, mind, and spirit. Having first identified and removed any of seven energetic blocks that may be present, the thrust of the treatment is to balance and harmonize the causative factor, which will, in turn, restore balance to all the rest, thereby resolving symptoms wherever they may be. Readings of the radial pulse are considered in determining the appropriate points that will be selected to bring balance and harmony, as well as the spiritual connotations indicated by each point's name, translated from the Chinese characters. Through skillful questioning and rapport, the true needs of the patient are revealed. Each point is a response to those needs. Once the basic patterns of deficiencies, excesses, and mental or spiritual needs are determined, imbalances are corrected using the fewest number of needles and moxibustion to tonify, sedate, and control patterns of disharmony in a person. The practitioner also transmits an abundance of his or her own healing chi during a treatment.

Contact: Worsley Institute –
   www.worsleyinstitute.com,
   The Institute of Five
   Element Acupuncture Inc. –
   www.5elements.com,
   or www.feacom.com

Iridology, though sometimes conducted on its own, is an evaluation process that is often part of a complete Acupuncture treatment. It is a diagnostic science based on the fact that the iris, the colored part of the eye, is a microcosm of every part of the body. Therefore, noninvasive study of the appearance of the iris reveals conditions and dysfunctions in the corresponding organs. Based on the findings, a practitioner can counsel and recommend appropriate preventive measures, such as changes in diet or lifestyle. No needles are inserted. Though this is primarily an evaluative process, skilled practitioners recognize that a person's health and consciousness can be affected as the eye is stimulated by color and light.

Contact: www.iridology.webs.com or
   www.iridologyassn.org

Korean Hand Acupuncture (KHA) is a Korean form of Acupuncture that does not necessarily use traditional needles. Based on the principles of yin and yang and the five element theory of Traditional Chinese Medicine, KHA is a significant part of Su Jok Therapy, also known as Su Jok Chim. (In Korean, *su* means "hand" and *jok* means "foot".) In Su Jok Therapy, Acupuncture is applied to both, whereas in KHA the focus is primarily on points on the hand. It was founded by Korean Dr. Tae Woo Yoo around 1973 after he recognized not only that points affecting all parts of the body, including organs and feelings, can be mapped out on the hands at locations that correspond to fourteen meridians, but that the hand is one place where the polarity of the twelve primary meridians changes from yin to yang, as one meridian ends and another begins. He also introduced the concept that the kidney constitution is important to an individual's energetic health. A session incorporates the precise and important ancient method known as yin-yang pulse diagnosis and offers different levels of treatment that work to sedate or tonify a meridian as deemed appropriate by the diagnosis. The goal is to reduce the patient's pain, strengthen the flow of chi energy, and establish harmony between the yin and yang pulses.

Treatments are usually performed on both sides of both hands, and the points are stimulated by Su Jok Chim micro-needles, mini-pellets, moxibustion, magnets, lasers, or an electro-acupuncture method that applies electrical microcurrents. Special organ therapy, massage of acupoints, and other point work may also be used. With all the options available, this form of Acupuncture is appropriate for children and sensitive people who are afraid of needles. Heated mini-pellets may be taped to the skin to provide ongoing balancing while the patient is away from therapy. Treatment of chronic diseases naturally takes more time for resolution.

A simple form of this treatment, developed by the South Korean scientist Jae Woo Park, a student of Dr. Yoo, has many protocols and focuses on stimulating points on the hands and feet that correspond to the distressed parts of the body either with special small needles or most often simply by using finger Acupressure techniques (see the Su Jok entry under Acupressure in this section).
Contact: www.handakupunktur.nu

Manaka Yin Yang Channel Balancing Therapy is a Japanese Acupuncture meridian treatment process that proceeds systematically through five phases and relies primarily on pulse reading and abdominal (hara) palpations for diagnosis. It uses moxibustion, advanced subtle point needling techniques, ion-pumping cords that move excessive heat to normal areas of the body, press tacks or spheres, magnet therapy, the practice of cupping, the Shonishin technique, Sotai Ho Therapy, and many other

techniques to control symptoms and treat their root causes. There are also special treatments for the abdomen and back that use both subtle and strong stimulation techniques. This therapy was developed by Dr. Yoshio Manaka, a respected Japanese healer, researcher, and practitioner. Manaka's therapy also works on the eight extraordinary channels, which represent a network of meridians that are not related to specific organs but are pivotal in revitalizing the network of regular meridians in the body. Manaka has also promoted the use of tiny, short hinaishin intradermal needles and Sotai exercises for structural alignment.
Contact: www.nwhealth.edu/acupuncture or
www.meridians.japaneseacupuncture.info

Marmapuncture is the Ayurvedic form of Acupuncture that has been used for thousands of years in India. Its exact origin is unknown, and there is debate about whether it was influenced by Chinese practices. In the twelfth century, when Muslim influence became dominant in India, the practice of Marmapuncture therapy declined and became relegated to remote areas in northern and southern India. The Ayurvedic system employs marma points that reside on the nadis (energy channels); their locations, sizes, and numbers are different from those found in Chinese medicine. Though the intention of balancing the internal energies, organs, and body systems is the same, the Ayurvedic system works with balancing not only the basic five elements but also all levels of the physical and emotional being through methods that increase the digestive fire, or agni. It also recognizes the three basic qualities of an individual—vata (cool, dry, and flowing), pitta (hot, light, and moist), and kapha (heavy, slow, and solid)—called doshas, and the actual treatment is based on the diagnosis of these qualities. (For more information on Ayurveda, see later in this chapter.)

During a treatment, the number of fine needles used depends on the particular constitution of the patient, though it is usually no more than about fifteen. Marmapuncture emphasizes mild manipulations of needles on the marma points to gently stimulate the flow of energy through the nadi. The needles are applied sequentially in the direction of the flow of prana within these channels

and are sometimes medicated by being dipped into an herbal liquid before insertion. The insertion of the needles is carried out gently, in concert with the breath of the client, to avoid aggravating the cold, dry conditions of vata. The practitioner follows principles of synergistic cooperation, gentleness, and continuity so that the treatment will produce an effect not just on the physical body, but on many levels of the person's being, which helps provide a release both mentally and emotionally. There is also a different form of marma acupuncture known as Suchikarma that is considered to be more spiritual, since it works with a person's karmic energies through the etheric balancing of the subtle levels within the akashic field.
Contact: www.marmapuncture.com.au

Penman Laser Technique uses a cold laser beam that is applied to specific energy points on the hands, ears, nose, wrists, knees, and feet. This therapy was developed in 1992 by Englishwoman Anne Penman and is intended to stimulate the release of endorphins, which encourages the reduction of cravings or stress. Among other things, it can be useful for those wanting to lose weight or stop smoking.
Contact: www.annepenmanlaser.com

Saam is a Korean form of Acupuncture, formulated during the 1600s by a Buddhist monk named Saam, that is different from traditional forms in that it uses only sixty points—though some say only eight—below the elbows and knees. As with other forms of Eastern medicine, the main principle behind this form of Acupuncture states that any organ deficiency should be tonified and any excess purged or sedated, but Saam is based on a simpler curative mechanism that posits that only certain points are really effective for treating specific conditions. It does not require memorizing all 360-plus regular points and their curative effects as required in most traditional forms of Acupuncture. Besides having a strong recognition of how the five elements apply to healing, a practitioner must understand the five transport points known as su points on the extremities of the four limbs. It is reported that this therapy is also done with the recipient immersed in warm water.
Contact: www.koreanmedicine.net

Shonishin is an ancient and specialized Chinese style of **Pediatric Acupuncture** that has been used in Japan since the seventeenth century. It is intended primarily for infants, although it is very appropriate for children up to age twelve. This very gentle form of point work is only slightly different from a regular pediatric massage. Diagnosis is made through light touch, and techniques include rhythmic rubbing, tapping, scratching, and contact needle work without insertion, along with energy balancing. After age five, occasionally a few needles may be lightly inserted. Shonishin is considered effective in treating various diseases (especially digestive problems) in both infants and young children. Treatments are often done quickly, since a child's energy tends to move rapidly. Parents also have the option of Pediatric Remedial Massage for children who are too young for Acupuncture. This method uses the Acupressure technique of pointing and pressing on the body surface with the practitioner's hand.
Contact: www.jcm.co.uk, www.pedacu.com, or www.acupuncturepediatrics.com

Sonopuncture, a form of Acutonics, is a modern synthesis of Chinese medicine, acupoint therapy, and the harmonic properties of sound frequencies. Rather than needles, this therapy applies sound vibrations to acupoints with either an electrical device that directs a beam of high-frequency sound or with a tuning fork placed on the point. This alternative approach is most appropriate in pediatrics. It presently is not widely available, since it requires a practitioner who is well versed in the principles of both Traditional Chinese Medicine and sound therapy. (See more on Acutonics under Sound Therapy in the section on Special Therapies in this chapter.)
Contact: www.sonopuncture.org

Taegeuk is the form of Acupuncture found within the Korean Sasang Healing System, which emphasizes the acupoints of the heart meridian. These points are stimulated to alleviate basic imbalances among the energies of the major organs. If additional tonification and purgation are needed, the practitioner can treat any excess by purging the strong organ and correct deficiencies by tonifying

the weak organ. Sasang uses the same acupuncture points as Traditional Chinese Medicine and employs the same medical herbs used in Japanese herbal therapy (Kampo). Sasang also employs a personality typology that uses a person's biopsychological traits to explain individual differences in behavioral patterns, physical characteristics, and susceptibility to certain diseases. People are divided into four types based on these traits, and the nature of each type is exemplified by the four emotions of sorrow, anger, gladness, and enjoyment. The treatment of these traits stimulates the health of specific related organs and vice versa.
Contact: www.koreanmedicine.net

Toyohari Meridian Therapy, a very popular form of Japanese Acupuncture, is a noninvasive method of addressing the imbalance of chi energy primarily by using a technique called contact needling, in which a special needle or probe is held over the skin without piercing it. Needles may be made of different metals, such as silver, gold, copper, and zinc. Practitioner training emphasizes the development of sensitivity to chi energy, which is a requirement for accurate abdominal analysis, pulse reading, and needle placement. This therapy was developed within the tradition of meridian therapy in Japan during the 1930s by blind acupuncturist Kodo Fukushima, who founded the Toyohari Association, which is open only to blind practitioners. Many techniques have been refined over the years by research groups in the Toyohari Association, and the therapy is used to both maintain health and treat a wide range of illnesses.

During a treatment, the therapist takes a case history, gently palpates the abdomen, and feels the pulse at the wrist to make a full diagnosis of a client's condition. The therapy is not painful, since it uses either very shallow needling with an insertion tube or methods that don't involve insertion. Contact needling over selected points is accomplished by stroking and pressing the skin with a rounded blunt silver instrument called an enshin. Treatments are appropriate for sensitive patients including children. Moxibustion may also be used to stimulate certain points.
Contact: www.toyohari.org

Amatsu Therapy

Amatsu Therapy, a Japanese practice based on ancient Chinese practices that came over to Japan around 550 CE, was once part of the secret Budo School of breathwork, which included physical and energetic martial-arts practices. Over time, the therapy has become a fusion of more modern modalities that use massage, mobilization techniques, repatterning procedures, cranial balancing, energy balancing, and the stimulation of acupressure points. Amatsu Therapy works with the body's primary components of physical structure, mental processes, the nervous system's electrical energy, chemical processing (food and digestion), and environmental influences to create better health and harmony. Since it is a holistic approach, Amatsu recognizes that none of these components exist in isolation, for they are all linked together and should be treated as such. Therefore, it is not always necessary to treat a problem directly; the underlying problem may be resolved by attending to other areas of the body. This concept of interconnectedness is the foundation of Amatsu Therapy. Until recently, the knowledge and skills of this traditional healing art resided in only a few to whom it had been passed down through the generations. Japanese practitioner and Grand Master Dr. Masaaki Hatsumi is the present-day head of this traditional therapy in Japan. He was instrumental in teaching the handful of students who then brought the practice to the West.

Amatsu is somewhat unique in its energetic approach to healing because it balances the whole body and its energy systems by working on the soft tissues of the muscles, ligaments, tendons, and organs as well as the meridians. During an Amatsu treatment, the layers of pain or illness are peeled away like an onion in order to reach and alleviate the core problem, which may be hidden because of years of adaptive movements and changes as the body copes with the original problem or circumstance. Treatments use a blend of modalities that depends on the needs of the recipient, and the actual protocol is developed after an evaluation in which the recipient is observed, muscle-tested, palpated, and touched. Sessions focus on and specialize in treating nerve pain sites, acupoints (tsubo in Japanese), meridians, and joints of the body. Techniques for stretching and unwinding the neuromuscular system are also employed.

When performing Amatsu Therapy, the practitioner uses healing techniques that transmit his own chi through his hands and fingers to the recipient. Practitioners use the Chinese practice of Nei Gong to enhance their own capacities and improve the effectiveness of Amatsu Therapy. Nei Gong is the internal energy-generating method used for revitalizing depleted body systems and requires a considerable amount of training. It is considered an "internal" method, because it works with the circulation of energy through the pathways of the Microcosmic Orbit.

There are four forms of Amatsu Therapy. The first, which became known as Amma, is a Japanese style of massage treatment that fuses together Chinese Anma and Japanese Sotai Ho. Although Amma incorporates many massage techniques, it concentrates on the state of a person's inner energy and on restoring the flow of life energy in the body by affecting the meridians (see more under Amma in this section). Seitai is the Amatsu approach to physiotherapy that improves body structure and balances the energy, strength, and function of the organs primarily through craniosacral work and attention to the meridian circuits. Its focus is on the head, neck, spine, pelvis and feet (see more under Spinal Therapies in this chapter). Shinden Jutsu is considered the heart of all Amatsu practices because it incorporates the ancient art of Ampuku, which evaluates and releases restrictions around the organs or visceral system through the use of pressure, gentle movements, and manipulations that correct ligament imbalances (see more under Abdominal Therapies in this chapter) The fourth part of Amatsu, known as Kenku Jutsu, refers to craniosacral work done on the head and spine to provide craniosacral balancing, which improves spinal movement and hence reduces discomfort in the rest of the body while also charging the immune and nervous system (see more under Spinal Therapies in this chapter.)
Contact: www.amatsu.info or
www.amatsu-medicine.com

Amma Therapy

This ancient, rhythmic form of massage, which is rooted in Chinese Anma Massage, can be considered the precursor to Shiatsu. It originally became a significant part of Japanese bodywork therapy around 530 CE; there was once a school for blind masseurs who performed this healing work. These practitioners were honored with certain rights and privileges and were able to form their own guild. Its popularity faded for a time

after 1868, when Western medicine first came to Japan and became favored by the emperor, but it returned in a new form that combines both Eastern and Western principles. During the early 1900s, Dr. DoAnn Kaneko and a number of other practitioners were instrumental in the further development of Amma as well as in transforming many of its principles and elements into what became known as Shiatsu. As in the equivalent Chinese therapy of Anma, the Japanese practice of Amma primarily uses hands-on techniques to restore balance and harmony to the body through deep-tissue massage and pressure work.

Amma bodywork comprises a number of massage techniques such as pushing, pulling, squeezing, kneading, effleurage, and percussive manipulations done with the thumbs, fingers, arms, elbows, and knees. Specialized stretching, rolling, stroking, and unwinding, along with postural ergonomics, alignment methods, and neuromuscular techniques are used to soften and melt away muscular tension. A key element of the practice is the application of pressure on points along the meridians with additional friction and touch to stimulate and balance the flow of chi through 140 specific acupoints (called tsubo in Japanese) along the twelve regular energy meridians and two central channels. Treatments also involve manipulations that focus on the lesser-known tendon-muscle channels. The overall prescribed sequence, called a kata, is designed to relax and rejuvenate the body. Practitioners are also trained in the principles of holistic nutrition, herbal supplements and proper diet.

Amma Therapy also found its way to Korea primarily from Japan, and it was then synthesized with Western manipulation practices and principles. Dr. Robert and Tina Sohn were instrumental in the development and promotion of Amma in Korea, and they added some of their own energetic points. Later, during the 1970s, they brought it to the United States.
Contact: www.ammatherapy.net or
www.shendaoacupuncture.net

Anma Massage

Anma is the traditional form of Chinese massage that comes from one of the oldest forms of bodywork known to the world. Anma was originally known as Anmo, which was the first written character for massage found in ancient texts that told about the mythic figure of Chinese healing known as the Yellow Emperor. Its name means "to push and pull." The essence of Anma is based on the five element theory, the principles of yin and yang, the three major forms and phenomena of chi energy (heaven, earth, and human), and the study of various types of acupoints as they relate to positions on the meridians, all of which are employed within the methods of diagnosis. When introduced in Japan, Anma came to be known as Amma, and it was through this Japanese form that Shiatsu was developed. Today, the difference between traditional Anma and present-day Shiatsu is subtle. Likewise, since Chinese Anma Massage and the practice of Amma found in Japanese Amatsu Therapy are so historically closely related, many similarities can be found in their applications. Yet as time passed and each modality evolved into different forms of bodywork in different parts of the world, changes in focus and application took place.

Traditionally, Anma emphasizes the importance of rhythm, precision, and form in massage and promotes the use of deep, long breaths to help release energetic blockages. It is a form of physical and energetic therapy that uses pressing, light stroking, squeezing, stretching, rolling, kneading, and various percussion and vibrating techniques performed with the thumbs, fingers, elbows, knuckles, knees and feet on specific acupressure points along the major energy meridians, as well as on muscles, ligaments and joints. According to the principles of Traditional Chinese Medicine (TCM), gentler massage such as some forms of Anma tonify the human energy system, whereas the stronger, more vigorous hand work used in what developed as Tuina sedates it. Attention is also given to structural deviations, muscle spasms, and skin temperature changes. As in most forms of TCM, analysis of the pulse and tongue along with palpations of the body are used to assess and diagnose problems. Treatments do not use any oils and can be carried out with the client clothed while seated or lying down. The most common contraindications cited are fever, recent surgery, skin infections, the use of pain medications, and the existence of any contagious illness.
Contact: www.yotsumedojo.com/yotsume%20anma% 20dojo/anma.htm

Applied Physiology (AP)

Applied Physiology is a system of stress-management procedures that was developed in Arizona during the 1980s by Richard Utt as an outgrowth of innovations in energy kinesiology and his effort to find healing for his own life-threatening illness. Belying its name, Applied Physiology is actually part of the field of energy kinesiology. Utt's therapy expands upon the Chinese five element theory (earth, fire, water, metal, wood) by adding air and ether to create a three-dimensional, holographic seven element theory, which allows for additional ways of gaining information about the meridians as well as possibilities for moving the energies in different directions. Stress is considered to be something that a person can dispel through active conscious action, and disease is considered a messenger that signals an individual to take action to rectify a dysfunctional condition. The aim of AP is to create a balance in the energetic functioning of the body's musculature by removing contractions that cause fatigue and injury. This system of healing allows practitioners to pinpoint specific stresses that impede function at the deepest level of cellular activity and guide the client's energy system to heal itself. The therapy also targets particular parts of the brain.

The bodywork uses a muscle-testing and monitoring technique in which muscles are put through their normal range of motion and monitored to determine where stresses reside. This allows for direct evaluation of stress in various parts of the nervous system, especially the limbic system of the brain. Acupoints are also evaluated to find specific stresses. The stress states throughout the body are charted to see how they affect a person's performance. Then a multitude of techniques that include the use of acupuncture points, sound healing with tuning forks, special chi keys, and crystals are employed to balance the chakra energy centers in the body. AP provides the means to address a multitude of complex health issues, and this energetic system of healing is often used in conjunction with other forms of massage therapy. Practitioners of Applied Physiology are often involved in developing and employing mathematical models and clinical devices for physiological control and feedback.
Contact: www.appliedphysiology.com

Ayurvedic Therapy

One of the world's oldest holistic forms of health care, the Ayurvedic system of healing from India contains a very sophisticated and comprehensive compilation of traditional therapies, disciplines, and practices that provide numerous methods of detoxification, purification, and rejuvenation. All of these methods are directed toward the creation of harmony and conscious self-awareness through the process of energetically balancing all aspects of the human body, mind, emotions, spirit, and soul. They not only act to address the root cause of dysfunction or disease and prevent illness from developing but also strive to awaken the ultimate potential and spiritual capabilities of the individual.

Ayurveda is based on teachings contained in the Sanskrit verses of the Vedas, sacred texts that originated in India between approximately 2500 and 1200 BCE. After the original *Rig-Veda* came the *Sama-Veda*, *Yajur-Veda*, and *Atharva-Veda*. The Vedas include the theory of creation and the basic philosophies and principles of the development of life in which human existence is seen as a trinity of body, mind, and soul consciousness. Sometime around 400–200 BCE, a great sage and physician published the *Charaka Samhita*, which revised some of the ancient texts and helped further spread the knowledge of Ayurveda. These sutras contain knowledge and teachings about rituals and internal and external healing practices along with a healing lifestyle regimen, all of which eventually evolved into two distinct schools, with one for physicians and the other for surgeons. Other major treatises on Ayurveda were also compiled between that time and 500 CE, when the *Charaka Samhita* was revised. When the Maurya-dynasty emperor Ashoka the Great conquered all of the Indian kings and unified the country in the third century BCE, he encouraged the development of Ayurvedic medicine along with the spread of Buddhism. In the second century CE, Buddhist philosopher and Ayurvedic physician Nagarjuna greatly influenced the establishment of both Ayurveda and Buddhism throughout all of India. The various practices of yoga, established in the early centuries CE, have evolved over the centuries and contributed much to the sacred and spiritual aspects of Ayurveda.

Evidence shows that Ayurvedic therapy has influenced many healing systems around the world. As Buddhism spread to both Tibet and China, Ayurveda came with it. Through sea trade with India, the Egyptians learned about it even before the invasion of Alexander the Great in the fourth century BCE. Greeks and Romans came to know about Ayurveda soon after. The Arab and Persian Unani form of traditional medicine also incorporated elements of Ayurveda. Islamic physicians, who were well versed in the principles of Ayurveda, even helped formulate some of the European medical traditions. More recently in the twentieth century, the awareness and use of Ayurveda took on a new dimension worldwide, thanks in part to the work of Deepak Chopra and Dr. Vasant Lad. As more medical doctors, homeopaths, and naturopaths practicing outside of India use Ayurvedic therapy, this form of health care, which recognizes the deep interconnection of the body, mind, and soul, has gained more acceptance among practitioners of Western allopathic medicine, and many of its traditional purification practices are now an integral part of spa therapy.

Ayurveda means "life knowledge" in Sanskrit, and it is based on both the vital energetic life force called prana, which flows through all beings, and the relationships among the five elements of ether, air, fire, water and earth. Each of these elements is associated with conditions, qualities, and functions of all parts of the body and represents different manifestations of consciousness. Earth refers to form, substance, and solidity and reflects the crystallization of consciousness. Water represents the flowing motion that gives life cohesiveness; it demonstrates the liquidity of consciousness. Fire denotes light and heat and governs all transformation in the body, including the process of comprehension. Air signifies the movement that enables the breath and bodily functions and relates to the activation of expression in all of creation. Ether represents the space that contains all the other elements and allows communication between all parts of the body; it expresses the ultimate openness and totality of all consciousness. A particular blend of all these elements is contained not only within the human body but also in all life, all natural substances, and the entire universe. The intention of Ayurveda is to help maintain a balance of these elements to prevent dysfunction and promote a being's ultimate potential.

This system of healing teaches that there are three bioenergetic constitutions known as humors or doshas (called vata, pitta, and kapha) and that every person's makeup is a unique combination of these doshas and the five elements. Vata relates to the quality of movement as exemplified through digestion and circulation. Pitta governs transformation, since it represents the energy and heat involved in metabolism. Kapha concerns the substance that makes up the bulk of the body's structure and regulates nourishment and growth. In each individual's constitution, one or more doshas may predominate, giving that person a propensity to feel, act, and live with certain habitual physical, emotional, and mental qualities or tendencies. Knowing the client's constitutional type helps a practitioner determine the most appropriate treatment plan. It is believed that doshas have a strong influence on the flow of prana, so keeping the individual doshas in balance is critical to good health and the prevention of illness.

Ayurveda is a powerful way to address the root cause of imbalances or disease because it treats the body, mind, and spirit through a wide assortment of practices, diagnostics, and therapies that include pulse diagnosis, diet, nutrition, naturopathy, herbal medicine (Unani/Rasayana), essential oils, aromatherapy, minerals, crystals, color and gemstones (applied to specific marma points), regular Acupuncture with needles, Marmapuncture with needles dipped in liquid herbal medicine, moxibustion, massage, internal cleansing programs, energetic disciplines, yoga (Hatha, Kriya, Asana, and others), breathwork (pranayama), sound healing (mantras), counseling (Sattvavajaya), etheric/akashic field bodywork (Prana Chikitsa), and a variety of meditations. Individual treatments can employ many combinations of these therapies. The primary healing art and practice of Ayurvedic bodywork is known as Panchakarma.

Panchakarma is considered to be the science of longevity and involves many interconnected healing programs applied internally or externally to cleanse, purify, and rejuvenate the body, mind, and soul while enhancing consciousness and uplifting the spirit. Most internal Panchakarma work is intended to clear the mind and purify the digestive system by removing by-products of incomplete digestion that accumulate and affect the balance and functioning of the internal organs. It involves systematic treatment to dislodge toxins from the cells and flush them out of the body through the sweat glands, blood vessels, urinary tract, and intestines. Clients follow a special diet and take specific herbs to aid the process. External bodywork treatments vary in their approach, technique, and intensity, but mostly use soft but firm touch and rubbing while essential oils are liberally applied. There are special practices within the scope of Panchakrama used only on particular areas of the body such as the head. Many forms of energetic massage work can be done with either the hands or feet to balance the chakras and stimulate the flow of prana energy

within the 107 marma points located along the network of 700 nadis (energy pathways). Work is also done on the surrounding energy fields. (This energy anatomy of Ayurveda is similar to, but different from, the meridian system used by the Chinese.) Besides the focus on energy, many of the therapies specific to Panchakarma work on various parts of the physical body such as the muscles, myofascial tissue, bones, nervous system, skeletal system, lymphatic system, and circulatory system.

A number of closely related forms of bodywork are part of Panchakarma and can be used in various combinations, depending on the client's needs. Most are discussed in different sections of this chapter. The primary full-body therapies include basic Abhyanga massage and its variations, Marma Massage, Mardana acupressure massage, Marmapuncture bodywork, and Swedana hot-steam therapy. In addition, there are special forms of massage that work on specific, localized areas of the body, such as the Shatkarma abdominal treatment, the Merudanda spinal treatment, and variations of Shirobhyanga done only on the head and upper body. Shatkarma also contains internal therapies such as Shodhana purification treatments. There are other specialized forms of bodywork or massage that are either unique in their particular method of application, in that they use the practitioner's feet, or in their focus on special populations. Spiritually oriented therapies such as Prana Chikitsa work on the akashic dimension in the surrounding energy field. Panchakarma practices also vary between the more ancient ways and the more recent Kerala approach from that province in southern India.

When it comes to healing in India, there seems to be a constant love affair with fragrances and lubricants. Aromatherapy and essential oils can be used with almost any form of treatment, including skin therapies, baths, enemas, inhalation therapies, drug therapy, and cleansing methods that induce vomiting, or they may be simply spritzed in the air. Some forms of Ayurvedic bodywork also employ colors and gemstones.

An **Abhyanga** body massage is used to treat a wide variety of physical and psychological ailments. This is a very soothing and relaxing type of bodywork that incorporates light, rhythmic, circular strokes performed in a prescribed pattern on different segments of the body from head to toe. Liberal amounts of herbal oil specific to the recipient's particular constitution are generally used, and hot stones may be placed on the body to enhance the therapy and elicit a deep relaxation response in the nervous system. Gentle pressure work on marma points is often done during a session to remove stagnant energy and move the vital pranic life-force energy. There are a number of traditional types of Abhyanga treatments. (See more under its own heading in this section.)

Marma Massage is a type of bodywork that focuses on applying pressure and hand movements on and around the marma energy points of the body. Though there are 107 of these points, not all are used in a single massage. The goal of the treatment is to identify blockages, release them, and balance the energy in a way similar to Chinese Acupressure. However, unlike the Chinese system, the points are larger in size and fewer in number. Basically, treatments follow a specific sequence of lightly holding points without extensive manipulations. It is primarily a body, mind, and spirit massage that is intended to work on a deeper level so that true healing will occur. (See more under its own heading in this section.)

A **Mardana** treatment is a form of marma-point acupressure massage that works to release blockages of energy in the nadi channels. Pressure is applied to specific marma points that relate to previously diagnosed symptoms. The intent is to balance not just the function of the organs, but all systems within the body that have a connection to a particular problem. (See more under its own heading in this section.)

Marmapuncture is the Indian equivalent of the Chinese practice of Acupuncture. However, the needles, which are often dipped into an herbal liquid, are applied to marma points instead of the acupoints used in the meridian system of China. A particular variation, known as Suchi Karma, is often referred to as a form of karmic Acupuncture. (See more on Marmapuncture under Acupuncture in this section.)

Swedana hot-steam massage is also known as the "sweating therapy." The recipient's body is placed in a steam box or casket that encloses all but the head and contains special herbs that aid the cleansing process. Swedana often follows an Abhyanga massage; the massage gets the circulation moving and then the herbalized steam helps soften the tissues and permits toxins to be released in the sweat. (See more in the Aquatic Therapies section of this chapter.)

A number of treatments are applied only to particular areas of the body such as the head, face, spine,

abdomen, and feet. Treatments done on the spine are known as **Merudanda**, and they are designed to deliver deep relaxation, stress reduction, and nourishment for the nerve roots along the spine. It is a stimulating though subtle and gentle massage that is followed by sponging with hot or warm herbal oil to cleanse and hydrate the cells. (See more in the Spinal Therapies section of this chapter.)

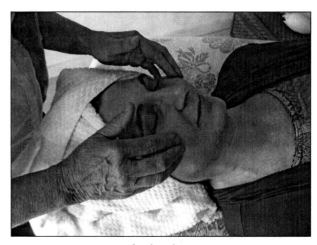

Ayurvedic facial treatment.

Localized treatments done on the head are among the most notable. The bodywork known as **Shirodhara**, which is a part of the upper-body massage known as **Shirobhyanga**, refers to an energetic head massage that uses large quantities of heated natural oils. In a Shirodhara treatment, heated herbal oil is gently poured in a narrow stream over the forehead for nourishment and improved blood circulation. Another type of special head massage is **Bindu**, which combines exfoliation, herbal treatment, and light massage on the forehead. There is also the **Champissage** treatment, which is a traditional form of head massage that has expanded to include more of the upper body along with chakra energy healing. Various kinds of facials can include wraps, masks, and the inhalation of aromatic steam, often used in conjunction with full-body baths. (See more on these methods under their own headings in this section or in the Special Therapies section in this chapter.)

Shatkarma cleansing therapies receive a great deal of attention in India and include both external and internal applications. Abdominal cleansing massage is very important in Ayurvedic medicine, for it places emphasis on the condition of the internal organs. A particular sequence of hand movements is used during treatments in this area of the body, and much emotional, as well as physical, release is common during an abdominal treatment (see more in the section on Abdominal Therapies in this chapter)

The internal Shatkarma practices referred to as **Shodhana** are yogic cleansing therapies (also used in Kriya Yoga) that do not include massage, but instead focus on purifying and cleansing the internal organs, viscera, and various body parts through an assortment of active external processes. There are a number of Nasya methods for cleansing the nasal cavities that include nose drops. Besides the practice of inhaling aromatic steam and herbal oils, there is the practice of Neti, in which a fine thread is passed through the nasal cavities to alleviate sinus congestion and thereby enhance the capacity for better breathing. Shatkriya cleansings for other areas of the face include the Netra Tarpana eye bath and Karma Dhauti ear cleansing. The tongue and anus can also be treated. The practice of ingesting butter or oil known as Sneehana has also been used to relieve certain internal imbalances. For an effective treatment of the internal organs, the Basti colon-cleansing process is often used (see more in the section on Abdominal Therapies in this chapter). There is actually a specific form of treatment for each organ of the body and even a Nabhi Basti for the emotions. The practice of Trataka is a meditative technique of eye gazing that purifies the mind by focusing the gaze and attention on one specific spot. Each of these methods of Shodhana are intended to prevent illness by creating balance and harmony within all the systems of the body; once learned, some can be done at home.

Other parts of Panchakarma therapy involve primordial sounds, mantras, meditation, pulse diagnosis, aromatherapy, and bliss techniques. There is also the practice of Prakritik Chikitsa, which is the naturopathic art of self-healing. Sattavavajaya is another special Ayurvedic therapy that incorporates yoga and counseling in its approach to mental disorders.

In addition, akashic or etheric energy-field work represents one of the most spiritually oriented therapies within Panchakarma. The akashic field is the all-inclusive energy field that exists within the all-pervasive void of the universe where all matter originates. This kind of work balances the energies and brings health to all levels of the self; it can be done as a self-help

practice or as a form of therapeutic bodywork. Known as Prana Chikitsa, the method deals with the various energy fields around the body and the energy centers or chakras within the body. The basic intent is to enhance or balance the free flow of pranic energy to stimulate a person's innate healing ability. Better health comes with more energy, and there will be less chance of illness or disease. There are many approaches to this type of therapy, and much importance is placed on the emotional body, though the primary work may first be on the outer causal energy field. Prana Chikitsa involves a high degree of attention, intention, sensitivity, and intuition, but the results of this work on the astral planes can be very rewarding.

Ayurvedic practitioners can call on a number of different substances and techniques as adjuncts to their internal and external treatments. These include hot footbaths, hot stones, moxibustion heat therapy, poultices, liniments, medicinal or cosmetic plasters, muds, salts, rice, herb fibers, herbal oil sponging, a Hauschka compress, a milk and herb paste, vegetable protein, or sandalwood. Herbs such as turmeric, gotu kola, and triphala along with other spices are often used to detoxify and soften the skin and are helpful when taken internally. When a mask of herbal paste has been applied and dried, the skin can be dry brushed to stimulate it as the mask is removed. This practice is commonly followed by a shower, after which essential aromatic oils are applied by hand with light soothing motions. Additional therapy can be done with the application of gems and colors. There are also other forms of cleansing, such as myofascial massage, that work on layers beneath the skin. The possibilities seem to be endless.

Ayurvedic practitioners are not limited to either solo or hands-only treatment methods. In the special form of bodywork called Padabhyanga, the feet are used to massage the recipient's body. In northern India, this is known as Chavutti Thirumal Massage or Indian Rope Massage. In southern India, it is called Keralite Massage. (See more under Special Therapies in this chapter.) An older Ayurvedic rejuvenating bodywork treatment known as Rasayana employs either the feet or hands along with plenty of oil. In the "royal" treatment known as Pizhichil, two practitioners use large quantities of warm herbal oil and work in unison on the recipient in a special, gentle, rhythmic way, often applying pressure on the nerves for long periods of time, sometimes over a number of days. Particular applications of bodywork are also used for infants and pregnant women, to enhance personal beauty, or to reduce the effects of aging.

A number of different energetic bodywork modalities have developed out of Ayurvedic healing over the years. They include such therapies as Agni Dhatu, Bhakti Massage, Kriya Bodywork, Kundalini Massage, Neurotherapy (Mehta Face Massage), Pranassage, Pranic Healing, Pryanta, and Omega Pattern Clearing. These are all discussed in other sections of this chapter. Contact: Ayurvedic Institute – www.ayurveda.com or National Ayurvedic Medical Association – www.ayurvedanama.org

Bagua Bodywork or Yin Style Bagua (YSB)

Part of the ancient Chinese system of Taoist martial arts, health and chi cultivation, and internal medicine, this form of energetic bodywork originated from the practices found at the Imperial Court in Beijing during the Qing dynasty. This therapy, originally known as Bagua Zhang, was developed in the mid-1800s by the legendary Chinese martial artist Dong Haichuan and is based on the philosophy presented in the *I Ching,* also known as the *Book of Changes.* He passed the knowledge of Bagua chi cultivation on to Yin Fu, who taught martial arts at the Imperial Palace and worked as a bodyguard for the wealthy. Later, Men Baozhen learned Bagua from him and then modified the Bagua defense and movement meditations into a form of healing massage. Men Baozhen then taught the entire system to the Beijing medical practitioner Dr. Xie Peigi. Sadly enough, the first person to whom Xie Peigi taught the complete system died soon after learning it, so when he met with some interested Western students, Xie Peigi decided to break with the tradition of teaching it secretly to only one student and open it to the world.

The primary principle of Bagua is to heal without medicine or drugs. The applied bodywork aspect of this energetic practice combines elements of Acupressure, Tuina, and Anma; it is similar to other forms of Chinese healing in that it emphasizes the practitioner's need to acquire sufficient vital chi energy before performing any healing work. Just as with its martial arts counterpart, YSB requires a high level of sensitivity and chi development on the part of the practitioner, who must practice extensively through a series of chi-cultivating exercises to gain and maintain personal strength. Although

practitioners commonly train in qi gong exercises such as Daoyin in order to be more effective bodyworkers, these practices are appropriate for anyone.

Bagua Bodywork involves eight development and sensitivity exercises that help store chi and twenty-four hands-on techniques that will then be necessary for increasing body energy and providing a complete bodywork treatment on a recipient. These hand techniques include patting, pushing, grasping, pressing, vibrating, and combing. Most of the time, both touch and manipulations are quite light, yet they can generate powerful sensations in the patient. During a treatment, point striking and grasping is used at different locations, and with the application of Tuina, chi energy is directed to various acupoints on the recipient's body. There is also an octagonal Bagua diagram with symbols that represents the fundamental principles of reality within the Taioist cosmology and is used as a guide to understanding what methods of treatment are most appropriate for an individual. As a complete form of therapy, Bagua is a useful tool that supports individual healing in the same way that Feng Shui is applied to the environment. (See information on the self-care Bagua Exercise Program in Chapter 11.) Contact: www.academychinesearts.org or www.baguamastery.com

BEST (Bio Energetic Synchronization Technique)

BEST is a gentle, hands-on, energy-balancing procedure created by Dr. Ted Morter that is used to reestablish the full healing potential of the body. It acknowledges the concept of unconscious interference by which people often create mental and emotional conditions and patterns that can lead to imbalances in the nervous system and exhaustion in the organ systems and interfere with the capacity to heal. The therapy recognizes the body's need for the proper balance of acid and alkaline foods, bone strength, and structural alignment. BEST includes a releasing process that uses exercises, such as special stretching techniques applied with conscious thought, and emotional memory components that use kinesiology to test body reactions to emotional thought and memory patterns. The intent is help balance muscular activity and allow the body to function better, while identifying emotional patterns based on current situations rather than on past experiences.

The physical treatment addresses imbalances by using light-pressure contact on the body surface to modify

patterns of stress and discomfort while the client lies on a floor mat. The actual bodywork includes a leg check, palpations on the spinal muscles, and the subsequent holding of pressure points along the spine, sacrum, and skull. A power-march technique that employs cross-crawling and stretching is used to rebalance the muscles. BEST also uses methods developed to modify the expression of detrimental mental and emotional interference in the physical body that can be taught to individuals. Procedures are used to help identify and override emotional patterns such as worry, fear, and anger that are based on past experiences. When limiting conscious thought patterns and emotions are removed, the true expression of the body's healing capacity is restored. pH testing of the saliva and urine is used to establish proper adjustments in nutrition.
Contact: www.morter.com

Bhakti™ Massage

This heart-centered, intuitive energy modality heals primarily by increasing personal consciousness. Bhakti Massage is a spiritual healing therapy that came out of the practice of the Bhakti Yoga of adoration, devotion, and divinity. The healing process of Bhakti Massage relies on devotion to a person's own healing process.

This gentle yet deeply effective style of relaxation massage flows slowly and continuously all over the body from one part to another. The treatment serves to calm the nervous system and awaken a meditative healing state while balancing the flow of energy through the body. The practitioner sends energy into the recipient to provide a harmonious balance through which the life force can move freely through the body. The massage uses deep, long, slow, flowing strokes and incorporates elements of Neuromuscular Therapy, Myofascial Release, and Reiki energy work to draw out tension and induce a deep state of relaxation. A session ends with a technique for balancing the chakras with chants and prayer.
Contact: www.bhaktihealing.com

Bioenergetics (Bioenergetic Analysis)

A form of Neo-Reichian Therapy, Bioenergetics represents a way of understanding the personality in terms of the whole body and its energetic properties. The therapy was created by Dr. Alexander Lowen as an outgrowth of his studies during the 1940s with Dr. Wilhelm Reich, who was famous for delineating orgone energy, body armor, and the connection between the mind and the body. Lowen, a psychiatrist, shifted the healing approach to focus on helping individuals learn how their emotions affect physical tension in their bodies. His therapy is based on the premise that all body cells record emotional and energetic reactions; its aim is to release chronic stresses and muscular tension by freeing up energy blocks caused by an illness or past psychological and emotional problems. The therapy may also include aspects of biofeedback, Chinese medicine, herbs, and homeopathy. Group sessions are also used for healings.

A complete treatment often involves psychotherapy, deep breathing, stretching, strenuous yoga posture work, relaxation techniques, verbal acknowledgment, pressure-point work, and gentle touch to relieve muscle tension, starting with the pelvis and moving upward. The idea is to help a client attain a stronger and more vibrant sense of self through increasing body awareness and the ability to express feelings honestly. The psychotherapy component includes exercises to help patients release emotions through crying, screaming, kicking or other suitable expression. Sometimes a client is stretched backward over a special breathing stool to open up the chest and spine and release any breathing restrictions. Practitioners work to read various aspects of the patient's demeanor to ascertain problems so they can eliminate problems and balance energy disturbances within them, after which the inner child can heal itself.

Another form of Neo-Reichian Therapy that evolved out of the pioneering psychoanalytic bodywork of Dr. Wilhelm Reich is known as **Gentle Bio-Energetics**. Dr. Eva Reich, Reich's daughter and closest assistant, spent many years paying close attention to her father's gentle touch with infants and children. While working with premature babies at a New York hospital in the 1950s, she created her own form of delicate touch therapy known as **Butterfly Touch Massage**. She later found that the bodywork was appropriate for people of all ages, and her work followed her father's basic strategy of melting the body armor that had been created by repressing past traumatic events. Eva Reich taught workshops worldwide, and since her retirement in 1992, her work has been carried on by one of her protégés, Richard Overly. In 1997, what eventually was to become the Gentle Bio-Energetics Institute was established to help people of all ages deal with all forms of trauma.

This gentle yet profound, noninvasive form of energetic release begins with the client learning how armor stops the free flow of energy. The work that follows involves the melting away of the armor through touch, the gentle experience of honoring the surfacing emotions, and the healing and integration of the body-held memories in a way that restores the natural flow of energy and provides the recipient with a more complete sense of being present with life experiences. As well as alleviating the effects of trauma that has been held on a cellular level in the body for years, Gentle Bio-Energetics can prevent the development of future repression and its consequences.

Contact: www.bioenergetics-society.com or
www.gentlebio-energetics.com

Body Talk™

Body Talk was developed in 1995 by Dr. John Veltheim, an Australian chiropractor, Reiki teacher, martial artist, and acupuncturist who had been a lifelong student of self-realization. This form of bioenergetic therapy combines elements of Applied Kinesiology, Hatha Yoga, Acupuncture, psychology, physics, energy medicine, and Western medicine into a method that helps the body engage any blockages, synchronize and balance its parts, and facilitate the flow of vital energy. Treatments integrate subtle muscle testing, finger-tapping techniques, guided focusing methods, and breathing practices. An integral part of the treatment is light tapping with the fingertips on specific acupuncture points, the sternum, chakras, and other energy centers in order to move and balance energy so that the body can initiate its own self-healing. Head tapping is also used to increase brain activity.

Tapping techniques, which are also employed in other modalities, involve tapping on points along meridians to help balance them and disperse any associated issues. There are many levels of tapping, ranging from a simple, relaxing routine that assists with massage work to a more advanced process that constitutes the primary aspect of a healing treatment. A number of different modalities, such as Thought Field Therapy, the Emotional Freedom Technique, Emotrance, and the Bowen Technique, use tapping techniques for addressing a variety of dysfunctions. These techniques have been around for centuries, but gained a resurgence in the 1980s; they are used in hospitals and clinics around the world.

During a Body Talk session, dialogue and the simultaneous tapping of body points are used to determine what issues need to be addressed. When testing the energy system, the practitioner refers to a protocol flow chart as a reference tool for muscle testing while asking a specific series of questions. This is done to test for interruptions that determine where lines of communication have been broken and to assess where problems or imbalances reside. The practitioner places one hand on a particular location such as the client's belly while the other hand conducts the muscle testing. She then moves her hands to other locations around the body while testing for weaknesses. The client is often asked to breathe in a certain manner and simultaneously hold areas that are associated with the links in order to help the healing process. When a weak area is discovered, the practitioner places her hands there and then taps the client's head to let the brain know what is needed or taps the client's heart to activate the flow of information carried to the rest of the body. The intention is to get the body to engage any blockages, which will facilitate the free flow of vital energy.

Contact: www.bodytalksystem.com

Breema Bodywork®

Breema Bodywork's name comes from the village in the Kurdish mountains where the therapy originated. The practice has been passed down through the generations by local masters and is now found not only in Iran and Afghanistan but also in the West. Malicheck Mooshan learned this form of healing from his grandfather and then brought it to the United States, where he developed a teaching center during the 1980s. Breema Bodywork teaches people to be present with the experience of their bodies in motion. Working with its nine principles of harmony creates balance and cooperation between the mind, body, and feelings and awakens and revitalizes every cell of both the practitioner and the recipient. Like other Eastern forms of bodywork, Breema Bodywork recognizes that the act of cultivating the life-force energy, known to Kurds as del-aka, is an essential part of healing.

The applied bodywork, done on a fully clothed client lying on a padded floor, uses a variety of techniques ranging from the simple holding of points on the body to movements that enhance flexibility and dexterity. From the traditional point of view, Breema Bodywork should balance all the energy systems as a part of daily life, so the delicate or vigorous sequences of body movements used in activities such as forming bread dough or doing farm work are also employed. The bodywork is similar to Thai Massage in the way the body is rhythmically flexed by the practitioner's forearms, feet, knees and hands, but differs in the types of brushes, bends, rhythmic stretches, and holds that are used. Breathwork is also incorporated with stretches during the treatment. As with most energetic modalities, the work is intended to activate the body's own self-healing forces.

This comprehensive system of healing includes additional self-help Breema Exercises that are safe, nurturing, and energizing and taught to clients for their personal use. These employ natural rhythmic movements that depend on the relaxed weight of the body rather than external force. (See details in Chapter 11.)
Contact: Breema Center – www.breema.com

Chikwando

Chikwando is a Japanese method (with Chinese roots) of using chi energy for healing that was developed by Dr. Masato Nakagawa of Japan. Although it incorporates elements of Tai Chi and other martial arts, it is primarily a form of bodywork and integrates elements of macrobiotics, Tibetan medicine, yoga, and the Japanese Zen healing practices of Oki Do Shiatsu, Oki Do yoga, and meditative Shinkiko bodywork. During the therapy, chi that has been gathered by the practitioner from the heavens is transferred to the body of the client. It is similar in part to the practice of Medical Qi Gong, in which the transfer of this vital energy enables the client's own energy channels to open and become more energetically balanced. However, Chikwando focuses more on using the light of divine energy.
Contact: www.shinkiko.com

Hoshino Therapy

Hoshino, also known as Hoshino Amma, is a form of bodywork that combines Amma Therapy and Acupuncture. This form of pressure-point therapy was developed during the middle of the twentieth century by Japanese professor Tomezo Hoshino. Hoshino's method evolved slowly over a period of time while he was living in Argentina and dealing with an assortment of personal physiological disorders. When Acupuncture alone failed to relieve his condition, Hoshino created this new form of therapy using his own hands to heal himself. In 1952,

the Argentine government officially recognized his new method, and it became part of the regular program for physical therapists and kinesiologists. Both curative and preventive, Hoshino Therapy is a nonintrusive approach that deals primarily with conditions of poor posture, inhibited body movement, and muscle disorders.

Through the use of the heat of the hands, finger pressure, and cross-fiber friction on 250 acupoints on the body, Hoshino energetically treats musculoskeletal pain caused by the hardening of muscles, ligaments, or tendons due to injuries. When the tissues become soft, more elastic, and resilient, waste products are able to exit the cells and the circulation of blood and energy increases. Unlike the way the fingers are used in Shiatsu, Hoshino relies on strong pressure produced with the first joint of the thumb and full-hand contact. The pressure and friction caused by this can be painful, but it is very stimulating and helps to loosen the muscles. The overall effect can be very stimulating, relaxing, and invigorating. Clients are also taught daily exercises that complement the bodywork.
Contact: www.hoshinotherapy.org

Insight Bodywork™ (IB)

This playful yet sacred energetic therapy, developed by Barry Kapke (who is also known as Kondanna) is based on both the meridian system of Chinese medicine and the chakra and nadi framework of Indian Ayurveda. This intuitive form of energy work integrates massage, movement, and meditation to increase the flow of the vital life-force energy. Insight Bodywork addresses the energetic body in a complete way by incorporating the practices of mindfulness (sati) and loving kindness (metta) to reveal the causes of suffering and bring a harmonious flow of chi energy to all parts of the body. At the same time, it is a gentle but vigorous physical approach that uses elements of Shiatsu, Acupressure, Thai Yoga Bodywork, and Breema Bodywork. IB emphasizes mutual support between the practitioner and the recipient so they can journey together into the sensory experience of the recipient's body. Rather than intervening to correct specific problems, IB's aim is to help the client mindfully engage the body's own innate wisdom to remove any obstructions and acquire a more balanced, integrated sense of self.

The therapy mobilizes almost every joint in the body while working on energy channels, marma points, and acupoints through stretches and pressure applied with the hands, elbows, forearms, knees or feet. Pressure can be applied to multiple points at the same time as the practitioner leans in, using her relaxed weight. The therapist works without any agenda and enters into a state of intuitive stillness that allows deep listening to the client's needs. Her hands carry out seamlessly fluid and creative applications of Acupressure and myofascial techniques that are intended to touch the physical, mental, and emotional body in a deep and profound way while balancing the flow of energy. A variety of unpredictable and deeply penetrating percussions are used to stimulate the release of stuck energy. Nurturing physical and emotional support is given to the whole body while mobilizing the joints, moving the body into deep stretches that are integrated with soothing rhythmic brushes, holds, cradling actions, and when appropriate, energizing motions that include shaking, rocking, swinging, or dropping. IB is a gentle, safe, intimate, and spontaneous somatic approach to bodywork that promotes awareness of an embodied experience while facilitating an energetic balance and flow within the body. Contact: Bodhiwork Institute – www.bodhiwork.org

Jin Shin Do® (JSD®)

Jin Shin Do® Acupressure is a transformational process that integrates Eastern and Western modalities. It was developed, beginning in the early 1970s, by psychotherapist Iona Marsaa Teeguarden. Besides taking classes in Jin Shin Jyutsu with Mary Burmeister, Iona studied East Asian health arts with Michio Kushi, Jacques de Langre, Shui Wan Wu and Kok Yuen Leung, Sung Jin Park, Johng Kyu Lee, Se Han Kim, and Jean-Claude Thomas. In 1976, she spent three months in Japan, which included studies with Dr. Haruki Kato, a student of Jiro Murai, the originator of Jin Shin Jyutsu. Iona Marsaa Teeguarden, M.A., L.M.F.T., AOBTA® CI, Dipl. ABT (NCCAOM®) eventually integrated aspects from a number of traditional practices to create a transformational process she called Jin Shin Do® Bodymind Acupressure®.

Jin Shin Do means "The Way of the Compassionate Spirit." It recognizes that the inner spirit that resides in the heart—called Shin in Japanese and Shen in Chinese—has a strong influence on both the body and the emotions, and that verbal interaction and emotional processing can help release physical and emotional tension.

Jin Shin Do® Bodymind Acupressure® uses gentle yet deep finger pressure on specific acupoints and verbal Body Focusing techniques to help release "armoring" or chronic tension, balance the qi (chi) or energy, and improve vitality. This clothes-on method helps relieve stress- and trauma-related problems. A unique synthesis of a traditional Japanese Acupressure technique, classic Chinese Acupuncture and Acupressure theory, Taoist philosophy, qi gong (breathing and exercise techniques), Reichian segmental theory, and principles of Ericksonian psychotherapy, it is recognized as a major form of Asian Bodywork Therapy by NCCAOM® (National Certification Commission for Acupuncture and Oriental Medicine) and AOBTA® (American Organization for Bodywork Therapies of Asia) among others.

The form of Acupressure used in Jin Shin Do is unique in that focuses on both the twelve primary meridians and the eight energy channels (four yin and yang pairs) called strange flows or extraordinary meridians. These extraordinary vessels include a pair of regulating channels, a pair of bridge channels, a belt channel and a penetrating channel, and the governing and conception vessels. The energy in these strange flow channels is a reservoir that the regular meridians can call on when uneven energy distribution needs balancing.

Initial assessment of the meridians includes pulse reading, questioning and listening to the client, and assessing the tension by palpating (slowly feeling) important points in the neck, shoulders, chest, abdomen, and back. Iona's "Emotional Kaleidoscope" diagram maps the relationship of about a hundred emotions and feelings with the Chinese five elements and organ meridians, and so assists the practitioner in locating tense points that need release and meridians that need to be balanced. For the "Emotional Kaleidoscope" diagram plus explanations and case stories, see Iona's second book on Acupressure: *The Joy of Feeling: Bodymind Accupressure®* (1987). Iona Marsaa Teeguarden is also the author of *Acupressure Way of Health* (1978) and *A Complete Guide to Acupressure* (1996, revised in 2003).

Using mostly the fingertips and thumbs, and relying on precise point location and firm, direct pressure delivered at specific angles, Jin Shin Do aims to release tense and armored points and facilitate the flow of the released energy along the strange flow channels so that they can better balance and harmonize the twelve primary meridians. JSD also offers bodymind awareness techniques such as qi gong breathing meditations and methods of engaging cognitive resources that enable the client to actively participate in the release process, as well as methods of disengaging the smart brain so as to get in touch with the bodymind. Jin Shin Do® Acupressure promotes a pleasurable, trancelike state during which the recipient can get in touch with feelings or emotions that may be related to physical conditions.

After objectives are discussed, a treatment session most often begins with work on the neck and shoulders to help the client relax and to open up avenues of awareness and communication. Throughout the session, the client is gently encouraged to focus on the breath, and on tense points and places of comfort, in order to be more aware of the shifting conditions within the bodymind. The client may feel the change in energy flow as a pleasant pulsing stream or tingle.

The practitioner applies gentle but firm pressure to combinations of acupoints by using one hand to hold the blocked point on a meridian and the other hand to hold one or more distal points that help its release because they are functionally related, often because they are on the same meridian or vessel. Pressure is applied slowly, and tense points are held for a few minutes to allow the deep release of tension. As the treatment progresses, pressure can be increased for deeper penetration as permitted by the recipient's tolerance for pressure or by the release process. The simultaneous holding of two points provides a more effective release at the blocked point and a general balancing effect, caused in part by the creation of an oscillating current between the two points. The gentle yet deep finger pressure softens tissue without forcing muscles and relieves blockage and tension without causing pain. The acupoints and meridians are located in interfascial spaces—spaces within the connective tissue, or fascia, that envelop all the organs and muscles. Because of this interconnection, the benefits are easily transmitted throughout the whole body.

At the end of the session, it is particularly important to hold a series of vital points in the shoulder and neck. Then important points on the central channel are held, and the feet are massaged for grounding.

Jin Shin Do® Acupressure can also be self-applied, and it is effective even at a basic level. An International Directory of Registered Jin Shin Do® Acupressurists and Authorized Jin Shin Do® Teachers and information on

booklets, charts, CDs and DVDS, and the user-friendly Jin Shin Do® teaching method are available.
Contact: Jin Shin Do® Foundation for Bodymind Acupressure® – www.jinshindo.org

Jin Shin Jyutsu® (JSJ)

As part of the compassionate Japanese physio-philosophy of life, the aim of Jin Shin Jyutsu is to balance and harmonize the flow of energy throughout the body while promoting self-awareness. This art of realigning the recipient's energy and awakening self-awareness was established in the early 1900s by Master Jiro Murai, through his own experiences and research on Asian healing arts, including those revealed in early Japanese texts. He went on to teach others what he had learned about influencing the flow of energy by simply placing the hands on the body. One of his students, Mary Burmeister, brought the practice to the United States in the 1950s.

All the various forms of Asian bodywork are based on the concept that energy circulates throughout the universe and within each person and that healing energy is always present and just needs to be drawn on. This energy manifests in both the physical and nonphysical forms in different layers or levels known as depths. Jin Shin Jyutsu recognizes that, in addition to the twelve major channels, there are three primary pathways referred to as the trinity flows that help integrate and unify all parts of the body. They include a main central channel, in which the revitalizing flow goes from the top of the head down the front to the pubic bone and back up to the top of the head in a continuous oval, and a left and right "supervisor" channel on each side of the body in which energy can also rise. In addition, there are diagonal mediator channels that run from side to side; their energy flow circulates and harmonizes the three trinity flows. Jin Shin Jyutsu understands that the root cause of illness is a restriction in the flow of energy, and the breath is considered the ultimate tool for enhancing the flow. What makes JSJ unique is the way the treatment is accomplished.

After the fully clothed client is made comfortable on a padded table, the energetic pulse in both wrists is used to determine which specific safety energy lock (SEL) points along a meridian need to be cleared to restore the flow of energy. There are twenty-six of these points, which can be thought of as circuit breakers,

where blockages often manifest as dams in the flow of energy along the twelve major channels and the trinity flows. Although the actual blockages occur in the safety energy lock points, pain or dysfunction may appear in distant parts of the body. Both hands are used during the treatment process; Each hand is placed on an SEL point on the particular flow pathway, one hand on one SEL, the other hand on another. The hands essentially act as jumper cables that restart the flow of energy through the pathway. This releases the blockage that would otherwise restrict the flow of energy to the place where it is needed and inhibit the body's ability to heal itself. Once the energy is flowing smoothly, the distant problematic condition will disappear. The body is simply touched or cradled during the process without any manipulation or massage. Treatments use only light pressure holds for a few minutes with palms, thumbs, fingers, or the backs of the hands both to feel the pulse of energy flow and to release blockages or congestion. Then the practitioner's hands move to different holding positions up the back and down the front along the twelve major channels or the trinity flows. In addition to this sequence of energy work, Jin Shin Jyutsu incorporates some breathing exercises along with hand mudras and exercises that the client can also do at home to release tension and help to revitalize organs. Since most energy pathways terminate and originate at the fingers, each part of the fingers on both hands has been mapped out according to the related emotion and organ associated with these meridians. Therefore work on the fingers can have a particular healing effect.
Contact: www.jsjinc.net

Johrei Massage

Described as more a way of life than just a therapy, this form of bodywork originated in the 1920s through the work of Mara Rocha of Brazil for the purpose of removing toxins from the body by working primarily on the lymphatic system. Although it contains some elements of Reiki and the Japanese practice of channeling healing energy with either gentle pressure or no physical contact at all, the bodywork uses a special form of lymphatic drainage and involves the transfer of subtle spiritual energies to free the body and mind from negativity and toxic substances. Practitioners focus on directing universal energy into a person to cleanse, detoxify, and accelerate healing.

After an initial inquiry about the client's physical and mental health, the practitioner carries out the treatment by holding the hands over the recipient's body in order to channel healing energy. Gentle pressure is used to find areas with toxic buildup. The toxins are then channeled to the kidneys so they can be flushed out of the body. These actions also help boost the immune system and improve the flow of lymph. The principles of gratitude, purification, and spiritual affinity are integral to the process, and a series of treatments may be necessary, depending on the client's condition. Clients are encouraged to help perpetuate the healing process by devoting more of their lives to the study of Johrei and its use on others.
Contact: www.johreicenternorthfort.com

Ka-Lei Therapy

Previously known as Zarlen Therapy, this hands-on healing method comprises basic as well as intermediate and advanced techniques. Dr. Jonathan Sherwood, an Australian, first created Zarlen in the 1980s with information he received from a spirit guide who was also a past-life existence. The therapy is intended to help repair and elevate recipients' brain function.

Initially, the therapist accesses his own healing energy, tunes in to the frequency at which the client's brain operates, and then uses techniques called hand exercises to initiate the healing process. An energy-enhancement exercise gives the client's brain a boost of energy, and a point-repair technique activates points on the head that stimulate the flow of vital energetic information, which promotes correct functioning of the nervous system. This technique starts with the practitioner scanning for damaged points with a specific finger that is sensitive to energy emissions on the skull; a full body-point chart was created to guide the process. Once points are located, another finger inputs energy to repair patterns created by stress, thus eliminating the problems they create. This same technique is applied to the seated client's neck and back. The occasional use of fine quartz crystals helps focus the energy more precisely. Advanced techniques involve creating a direct telepathic link between the therapist and the recipient, sometimes through the use of visualizations, while the therapist applies the fingers in a certain sequence to points across the skull. As yet, there is no known correlation between these points and acupuncture points.
Contact: www.rajon.com/clinic

Kiatsu Ryoho

Kiatsu Ryoho is a Japanese method of sending the vital energy of the universe (chi or ki in Japanese) into the damaged parts of a person's body. It is based on the theory that when a practitioner's highly concentrated mind sends the energy of the universe into a body, the recipient's own life-force power will be stimulated, and as the free flow of energy nourishes the cells, the vigorous metabolism required for good health will be enhanced and sustained. Kiatsu was developed by Japanese Aikido master Koichi Tohei in the 1940s. It is similar to, but different from, Acupressure, Acupuncture and Shiatsu, and Kiatsu is often considered a secondary practice that can also be self-administered. What really makes it unique is that Tohei worked with his own set of meridian lines rather than the usual fourteen major meridians (twelve regular and two central). Kiatsu also doesn't focus on acupoints, but rather on energy lines, and it makes more extensive use of the thumbs as well as the fingertips to transfer chi energy.

Kiatsu embraces five basic principles. The first is that a practitioner must learn how to extend chi from the abdomen. The second is knowing how to prevent putting tension into another body when applying chi. The third is to always press perpendicularly toward the center of a body while applying chi. The fourth aspect is that when the practitioner has developed the strong, meditative power to concentrate the chi into the thumbs and fingertips, the results will be vastly improved. The final principle is that knowing how best to extend the vital chi into another is more important than knowing where the channels or energy lines are.

During a session, the practitioner affects the cross-flow meridian channels by pressing the thumbs and fingertips on energy pathways instead of points, because the acupoints can move as a body changes position while the meridian lines remain the same; the work can be done with the client resting in different poses. The healing process initially focuses on the part or organ of the body that is most depleted or in need of attention. After this, secondary areas are attended to. Another part of Kiatsu Therapy consists of clients learning methods to strengthen resistance to disease through individual exercises for developing vital chi energy.

Another form of Kiatsu also developed by Tohei is **Shinki Ryoho**. The primary difference is that improvements were made to create a more tangible form of feedback that enables the practitioner to feel more direct contact with the receiver's chi. A related form of treatment known as **Kiai** is used to revive someone in shock by "hitting" them with blows of chi or sound waves. Contact: www.aikido-health-center.com.uk

Korean Massage / Korean Martial Therapy™ (KMT)

Korean Massage, often referred to as Korean Martial Therapy, began in Korea more than 400 years ago as a self-help therapy that was beneficial for keeping warriors in top condition and enabling them to recover quickly from battle injuries. It recognized that the movements and energy pressure-point work that could disable others could also be used to heal and provide balance. (Chi is called gi in Korean.) The therapy consisted of pressure-point work, self-initiated or assisted stretches, and exercises to establish balance, enhance the flow of energy, and reduce stress. Over the years, new techniques were added, and today this healing therapy includes elements of Hapkido martial arts and traditional Korean energy medicine. Jae "Johnny" Kwon Yun was instrumental in introducing this modality to the United States.

The bodywork uses a form of deep-tissue work that includes massage strokes, pressure-point therapy, stretches, assisted body movement, Korean energy healing, and elements of yin-yang therapy. The various techniques, accomplished without stress on the practitioner, can be used selectively or in any combination. During a session, the recipient can be placed in many positions on a table, the floor, or in a chair; the application of oils is considered optional.

Another form of Korean bodywork known as **Chun Do Sun Bup (CDSP)** is rooted in the ancient Chinese Taoist system of energetic healing. *Chun Do Sun Bup* means "heavenly way to recover body, mind, and spirit," and it is considered an art of inner alchemy for self-mastery, self-healing, and self-realization. This 6,000-year-old form of martial-arts training was passed down secretly through the generations until South Koreans Dr. Haeng-Yong Mo and his wife, Gui-Dai Park, revitalized and opened its teachings to the modern era. A form of energy training, CDSP recognizes that everyone is born with healing powers and that all illness is essentially created by energy blocks. The primary aim is to teach people how to develop their innate healing abilities and help them reconnect to nature by balancing and harmonizing their energy. CDSP is a complete healing system that includes energy training as well as practices of energy healing. The self-help and applied-bodywork methods all provide ways to remove toxins and negative emotions and to restore physical and emotional balance while realigning the body and mind with the principles of harmony.

The hands-on massage portion of CDSP is known as Chunsoo, "heavenly hands," and the practitioner essentially transmits cosmic energy through Acupressure, vibrational energy techniques, and hand work, all with the intention of locating and releasing blockages that create knots or illness anywhere in the body. The practitioner also makes loud vocal sounds of certain frequencies to help the energy flow and release any negative energies in the recipient. The bodywork combines chanting, breathwork, meditation, and movements in a way that is synchronized with the rhythms of nature.
Contact: Korean Martial Therapy Association –
    www.urban4est.com,
    Chun Do Sun Bup Institute –
    www.manta.com, or Korean Physical
    Therapy Association – www.kpta.co.kr

Kriya Yoga Bodywork and Kriya Massage

Kriya Yoga Bodywork is a style of energetic therapy that was developed by Kamala Renner, the creator of Alchemical Bodywork, in 1970. The massage therapy combines yoga, energy work, and classical methods of massage to allow the recipient to experience spontaneous energy movement. The therapist seeks to become synchronized intuitively with the rejuvenating flow of energies between herself and the client, with the emphasis on honoring and caring for the client's body by respecting all its needs on all levels. The primary purpose is to create a shift in the client's subconscious that will provide the space for emotional and mental healing.

During a treatment performed on a floor mat, the therapist gently leads the client into yoga postures in order to release restrictions in the muscular system, using changes in the client's breathing as a guide. The passive yoga body positioning is combined with Swedish Massage, Neuromuscular Massage, Acupressure, soft-tissue manipulation, energy work, or forms of somatic emotional release work, all done in a smoothly flowing, rhythmic pattern. The recipient may or may not be fully clothed during a session. Besides increasing flexibility, reducing stress, improving posture, and increasing body

awareness, the therapy is aimed at providing mental, emotional, and spiritual healing. A simpler form of this therapy, referred to as Kriya Massage, works less with yoga postures. It instead emphasizes providing a nice, flowing massage delivered on a bodywork table.
Contact: www.carlagoldenwellness.com

Kundalini Massage

Kundalini bodywork is based on ancient energy practices found in the spiritual and medical healing systems of Tibet and India. It is a rejuvenating and potentially ecstatic yogic therapy that recognizes the innate human potential for energetic healing. The body is considered a sacred temple that is directly connected with the vital life force of the universe, and the practice of kundalini healing actually encompasses a wide range of practices designed to tap into the unused energies of the nervous and glandular systems and help people perform with more balance and harmony in life. Although in the past, the various practices of kundalini were restricted to members of secret cults, the teachings and healing techniques have recently spread and are now more accessible to the Western world. Among others, East Indian Yogi Bhajan has been instrumental in bringing awareness of these energetic healing practices to the West.

Kundalini is the powerful life-force energy that lies coiled up like a dormant serpent at the base of the spine, and kundalini bodywork is intended to awaken this energy so that it can rise through the chakras and release restrictions throughout the whole body. When the energy permeates the body, heart, and mind, a significant physiological, psychological, and spiritual transformation can take place. The releasing and rising of kundalini energy can also be triggered spontaneously by such phenomena as extraordinary sexual experiences, profound states of altered consciousness, near-death experiences, extreme physical trauma, or during particular spiritual practices. If they don't know how to really understand and integrate these experiences, individuals can become extremely anguished or disoriented and find themselves facing some kind of spiritual emergency or psychosis. Kundalini Massage alleviates this concern by providing a supportive environment and an experienced practitioner who can guide this energetic awakening into a safer transformative experience.

The energetic anatomy of kundalini includes three primary channels in the spinal area. The sushumma is the primary central channel through which the powerful kundalini energy rises and circulates. The pingala, referred to as Shiva, is the male energy channel to one side of the sushumma, and the female ida channel, referred to as Shakti, is on the other side. Opening and balancing the flow within the right and left channels is considered critical to enabling the flow within the central channel. The chakras also contain vital energy, but it may be locked in because of old fears and attachments. Treatments also focus on tapping into this source of energy as well as releasing pairs of sun and moon points with opposing polarities. The continual manipulation of the chakras and the energy fields that are a connection to cosmic energy by light physical touch is intended not only to awaken the previously restricted flow of vital pranic energy but also to increase spiritual awareness.

In preparation for a treatment, the practitioner enters a clear, neutral state, free of bias or disruption, in order to become a strong instrument for healing that will allow the recipient to openly release. The complete bodywork process involves a combination of manual pressure work, massage techniques, meditations, extensive breathing techniques, mantras, hand mudras, and sometimes ecstatic tantric sexual practices, depending on the particular form of kundalini bodywork employed by the practitioner. Massage of the neck and shoulders is considered essential to releasing the tension caused by everyday life burdens. Firm pressure is usually applied to certain points to open gateways and meridians in the body; the pressure is adjusted to the tolerance level of the recipient, although the practitioner strives for the maximum possible pressure to attain the greatest effect. The intention is that applying steady, rhythmic pressure for a short time at each point will evoke a rejuvenating restructuring of energy from the body memory. This technique is used to activate, change, balance, and stabilize the distribution of kundalini energy, and the strategy of smoothly switching from one set of points to another helps release old holding patterns. The awakening process often involves methods of physically connecting the sacrum to the area below the back of the skull in order to invite kundalini to arise. When the practitioner simultaneously places one hand on the sacrum and another where the neck joins the head, she can get a read on how the energy is flowing as it rises. In addition, various unique spinal massage techniques and the act of blowing warm air up the client's spine can also

be employed. Once the energy is balanced, vibrational sounding (such as "om" and "aah") is used by either the practitioner or the recipient to further integrate and sustain the balanced energy. Some ancient tantric practices regularly stimulated the kunda gland under the sacrum through massage (often a vigorous chopping pressure) to awaken the kundalini energy. Hundreds of other techniques for preparing and awakening the flow of kundalini, including those found in Ro Hun Therapy, have been employed over the years.
Contact: www.yogibhajan.org

Kunye Massage Therapy

Kunye Massage is an ancient Tibetan method of massage therapy that addresses both internal energetic imbalances and a variety of physiological problems. *Kunye* basically means "to give a massage" in Tibetan, but the practice is also referred to as the inner massage, because of its understanding of both the relative and ultimate aspects of an individual. A significant part of Tibetan medicine, it was thought to have developed as a tantric yoga practice to help monks balance their life-force energy. Besides keeping the energy channels open and free of stagnation that can lead to disorders and illness, its goal was to support both physical flexibility in yogic positions and the ability to seek enlightenment through meditation. In terms of origins, it should be recognized that Tibetan medicine is not only a synthesis of Ayurvedic, Chinese, and Unani healing practices, but has elements that are purely Tibetan, often with roots in the shamanic Bön tradition. Although Kunye was mentioned in the *Bumshi*, a Bön medical text, around 2000 BCE, more recent tantric literature also speaks about its use within Tibetan medicine. Kunye Massage has been passed down through the ages by trained practitioners and laypeople living in communities.

This form of bodywork therapy was not well known until Tibetans, exiled by the Chinese occupation of their country, brought this practice with them. Since then, Lama Tarthang Tulku has helped to propagate the spread of Tibetan medicine, and Chogyal Namkhai Norbu and Menpa Phuntsog Wangmo have been particularly instrumental in bringing Kunye therapy and Tibetan medicine to the United States, where in the 1990s the Shang Shung Institute was established to provide training in traditional Tibetan medicine, using the same curriculum as schools established in Italy, India, and other parts of the world. More recently, because of some relaxation of restrictions by the Chinese, new schools of Tibetan medicine are being reestablished in Tibet.

Kunye Massage Therapy primarily works with disturbances of the wind element, known as lung in Tibetan, and can simply reduce stress and relax tension or be used to treat specific disorders. The mindful presence of both practitioner and recipient leads to awareness that can be used to explore the thoughts, feelings, and sensations that manifest in the recipient's physical form and spirit. This open, curious attitude can allow direct, nonverbal communication between the two individuals, a state in which experience rather than thought is the guide, a state of non-doing that can lead to true transformation. The bodywork brings the awareness to both the breath and the touch in order to release attachments or holding patterns and revitalize the energetic pathways, thus supporting true transformation.

Kunye is considered a gentle internal form of massage used to melt tension by physical means that also have a significant psychological effect and help the recipient integrate feelings in the body. A variety of strokes and movements are used to open energy channels and increase the flow of energy and vitality. Although there are many types of Kunye treatments, the bodywork often employs a variety of massage techniques that include pressure-point therapy, joint mobilization, deep-tissue massage, assisted stretching, essential oils, compresses, gemstones, moxibustion, and hot and cold stones therapy. Besides deep structural adjustments, additional release work can be done on the cranium, head, neck, and spine. Moving or kneading joints as well as rubbing and tapping to loosen muscles and tendons may also be incorporated. If there is a specific problem in the body, then acupoints are pressed, rotated, and tapped with the fingers or a stick tool. Treatments can be applied to the whole body and are performed on either a massage table or chair. Some methods are taught to the recipient to be done as a form of self-massage.

There is also a related Tibetan self-care practice called Kum Nye Yoga that combines very slow-moving yogic and Tai Chi stretching exercises, breathing exercises, and meditations. (See details under Tibetan Yoga in Chapter 11.)
Contact: Shang Shung Institute of America –
www.shangshung.org

Mago Energy Healing

It was through the work of Dahn Yoga teacher Ilchi Lee and healer, herbalist, and doctor of Oriental Medicine Banya Lin that Mago Energy Healing, which comes from the same ancient Korean practice as Dahn Yoga, became established in the United States. The complete therapy includes a number of hands-on energy-based practices that work on a cellular level to deal with the root of a problem. The goal is to balance energies of the physical, mental, and spiritual bodies to produce a happy, balanced, and healthy life.

Woonki Acupuncture is a practice that Banya Lin created to open the circulation of energy within the channels of the body by combining her own form of Acupuncture with gentle, rhythmic brain-wave vibration exercises and imagery in order to release stagnant energy and relieve many disorders. A single needle is placed on one acupoint on the very top of the head to affect the brain and stimulate all parts of the body. A variation known as Spiritual Acupuncture works to release blockages in the meridian channels by tapping into the energy field to discover the root cause of a blockage. This is accomplished through a combination of spiritual reading, energy healing, and Acupuncture. Sessions can be done in person or through distance healing.

In addition to the hands-on bodywork, Mago Energy Healing also applies Asian healing principles in a set of exercises known as **Position Therapy**, designed not only to prevent disease but also to promote optimal health. In this practice, the therapist formulates a combination of exercises based on an analysis of the client's energy body; they may include chakra exercises, posture corrections, meridian stretches, breathing corrections, intestinal detoxification exercises, energy healing, meditations, and Acupressure. Aura reading, the practice of Dahn Yoga, Oriental herbal therapy, moxibustion, and life coaching round out the practices included in Mago Energy Healing.
Contact: Mago Healing Center –
www.magohealing.com or
www.ilchi-lee.com

Marma Massage

One of the most important elements of Ayurvedic Panchakarma therapy, Marma Massage, also known as Marma Chikitsa, is concerned with treating the seven energetic chakra centers and the marma points that influence prana, the vital life-force energy. This ancient Eastern form of therapy was introduced to the West only during the twentieth century. One of the guiding principles of Ayurveda is that disease can be prevented by harmonizing the human body with the rhythms of nature, and Marma Massage is one of the ways that this is accomplished. Like other rejuvenating forms of Panchakarma Therapy that emphasis the relaxing, cleansing, and purification of the body, Marma Massage can improve circulation, respiration, digestion, and the body's ability to function to its highest potential. In common with other forms of Ayurvedic bodywork, aromatherapy and the prolific use of natural oils are also employed in the treatment.

Marma Massage is designed to heal the body, mind, and spirit by balancing them all at a deep level. Energetically active locations on the body, known as marma points, which are considered junction points between mind and matter, are used for this purpose. The Ayurvedic system postulates that there are 107 of these invisible but palpable and vital marma points along fourteen key pathways or channels, known as nadis, that extend throughout the body. Like acupressure points, marma points correlate with specific energy channels, body regions, and internal organs; they also connect with chakras and influence the flow of pranic life-force energy. They are classified not only according to location

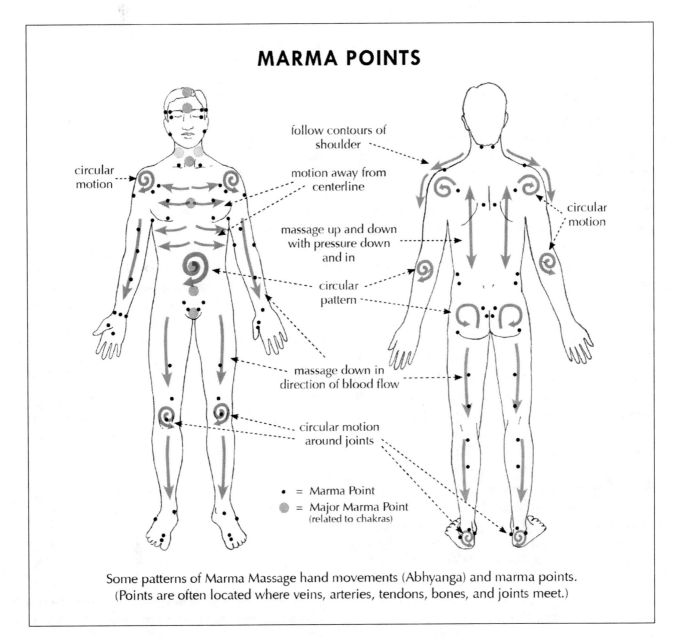

MARMA POINTS

follow contours of shoulder

circular motion

motion away from centerline

massage up and down with pressure down and in

circular pattern

circular motion

massage down in direction of blood flow

circular motion around joints

• = Marma Point

⬤ = Major Marma Point
(related to chakras)

Some patterns of Marma Massage hand movements (Abhyanga) and marma points.
(Points are often located where veins, arteries, tendons, bones, and joints meet.)

but also by their effect on the body's condition. These marma points are often located where muscles, veins, arteries, tendons, ligaments, bones, and joints meet and are often at the intersections of important nerves where the flow of the vital life force is most apparent. The locations of certain major points correspond to particular chakras, and all these sensitive marma points hold great importance for connecting the body, mind, and spirit.

Marma Massage is performed in a precise sequence and direction on marma points and the three major energy centers at the head, chest, and abdomen, primarily for the purpose of balancing energy. Working with marma points, the practitioner can gain access to repair damage caused by stress and bad habits, remove blockages, encourage the free flow of prana, boost resistance to disease and environmental threats, and promote good health and longevity. Since these points are often sensitive to touch, gentle pressure is used, primarily with the thumb though also with the fingers, to open the flow of energy in the area. Marma points may be lightly massaged with a circular motion done clockwise to stimulate, tonify, and strengthen the internal energy, organs, and tissues, or counterclockwise to sedate excesses, reduce and disperse energy, and help detoxify the body. The practitioner may hold these points lightly in order to sense the balance of the three doshas (qualities associated with the elements of air, fire, and water) that make up the recipient's constitution and then release blocked energy by arousing or calming the doshas as necessary. When they are balanced, energy will flow freely and the person can function harmoniously. The sensitive process of moving energy may require the simultaneous holding of different points. Although oils may be rubbed up and down either side of the spine at the end of a treatment and various forms of manipulation such as stroking, tapping, kneading, rubbing (with or without oil), and squeezing may be used, the focus of Marma Massage is on stimulating points rather than massaging the body. However, methods of massaging the musculature are often included to support the process of releasing physical tension. There are also some self-applied marma massage techniques that are taught to clients. All Ayurvedic therapies work on prana energy in some way, but Marma therapy is one of the most direct ways to influence it.
Contact: www.reconnectmassage.net or
www.ayurjyoti.com

Moxibustion Therapy

Moxibustion, also known as Moxa or Zhenjiu (its old Chinese name), is an ancient Chinese form of heat therapy. A number of methods are used, but most often a cone of smoldering mugwort leaves (sometimes mixed with ginger, salt, or garlic) is placed on specific acupuncture points on the body to warm them and promote the circulation of chi energy and blood. The hot cone may be quickly moved to different points in order to stimulate energy in the whole area. Moxibustion is often used to treat patients diagnosed with cold or stagnant constitutions, but not for those diagnosed with too much heat. Moxa also invigorates the immune system and is often used to treat chronic diseases. Although it has been used in conjunction with Acupuncture for many years, some Chinese practitioners prefer to use Moxa rather than Acupuncture because of the effectiveness of heat as a healing agent. Even though it does cause a certain amount of irritation, it is not particularly painful. However, some practitioners employ a more indirect method that uses a moxa stick roughly the size of a small cigar, holding it close to the area being treated for a few minutes. In some instances, a heated acupuncture needle or a less irritating smokeless moxa stick can be used to provide the same effect. In all cases, when the intensity of the heat rises close to the painful level, the practitioner quickly removes its source.

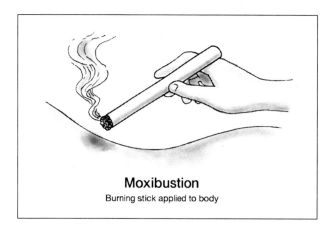

Moxibustion
Burning stick applied to body

A similar therapy called Metsa has also been used since ancient times in Tibet to help energy circulate, reduce pain, and treat a variety of disorders. In Tibet, the burning cone can be applied in several ways: for extended periods for specific problems, directly or indirectly on the appropriate meridian points for general

disorders, or lightly as a warming heat treatment for children.
Contact: www.acupuncturemoxibustion.com

Neuroenergetic Release™ (NER)

Neuroenergetic Release is a holistic system of body-work that uses touch to correct core distortion patterns such as imbalances, irregularities, and patterns of compensation that are held in the whole body from head to toe. These patterns of distortion often develop because of traumatic life experiences, injuries, or even during birth. They can be held physically, emotionally, and energetically. Over time, minor imbalances can develop into significant problems. These core distortions also create contracted or weak spots that not only make the body susceptible to injury but also can surface as a variety of physiological symptoms.

NER was developed by manual therapist Donald W. Kipp after his own physical challenges with a back injury propelled him to examine a variety of bodywork techniques, some of which he used to heal his own condition. NER draws from the ideas and theories of many therapies, such as Neuromuscular Therapy, Trigger Point Therapy, Therapeutic Massage, Chiropractic Therapy, Myofascial Release, Craniosacral Therapy, Osteopathic Manipulation Therapy, and Polarity Therapy, as well as its own principles, to create a comprehensive, powerful healing system. Working with unique neuroenergetic points, the therapy balances the neurological, energetic, and muscular systems of the whole body. Holding patterns, structural imbalances, and emotional blockages are released. By giving the nervous system new information, bones, muscles, and soft tissue release in seconds without force. This improves posture and provides a more natural alignment of the skeletal system, which can be seen and measured with the naked eye, in as little as one minute. The strategy is to gently and naturally facilitate the body's self-correcting response rather than forcing a change. Core distortion patterns are released by working globally rather than just where pain or dysfunction is located.

The treatment begins with the practitioner analyzing the client's physical structure to locate any postural or structural distortions. This points to useful neuroenergetic points associated with the observed distortion. The practitioner then proceeds to apply slight pressure on two corresponding neuroenergetic points at a time,

moving across the client's body and down its length, quickly releasing the abnormal tension and distortion in the muscles and tissues that are holding the body in a faulty position. The client is instructed to take a shallow breath simultaneously with each touch. Structural charting serves as an objective measurement for gauging the client's progress during the course of a treatment. The therapy is appropriate for an assortment of musculoskeletal problems, rehabilitation, pain relief, injury prevention, and maximizing physical performance and health.
Contact: Body Awareness® Institute –
www.body-awareness.com

Neuro Energetic Repatterning (NER)

Neuro Energetic Repatterning was developed by chiropractic physician and psychotherapist Dr. Lynn Bamberger for the purpose of releasing conditioned reflexes and limiting programmed patterns and reestablishing the natural flow of vital life-force energy through the nerves, meridians, and brain. NER is based on the belief that disruptions in the flow of energy are caused by mental and emotional disturbances resulting from unresolved or buried traumatic life experiences. It recognizes that it is necessary to deal with the attitudes, beliefs, judgments, and emotions, rather than just the traumatic memories themselves, since the way a person deals with what happens is more important than what actually happens in terms of causing disease or dysfunction. Once hidden dysfunctional patterns and unresolved emotions are released, a more positive response to events can occur, bringing greater health and happiness. This transformative process works through a combination of bodywork and holistic psychotherapy to put the client in charge of reducing or eliminating a habitual negative response to life challenges.

The healing process first focuses on releasing dysfunctional patterns of behavior by evaluating the body's ability to function from a variety of perspectives. The initial assessment includes muscle testing to identify the overall vitality of all cells, tissues, organs, and glands of the body. In addition, the energy pathways and the electromagnetic fields are analyzed to determine where restrictions exist and what method of treatment is most suitable. Disruptive emotions, beliefs, and traumatic memories may be linked together as stress loops, and in order to heal an illness or behavioral pattern, it is considered necessary to uproot and clear the entire stress loop.

The actual release of disruptions in the flow of energy is accomplished through hands-contact with various neuroenergetic centers of the body and a combination of gentle spinal and cranial Chiropractic work, Acupressure, and Acupuncture. The repatterning portion of the therapy is a form of coaching that strives to empower patients to assume greater responsibility for their own care by accessing the wisdom in their bodies. As the disruptions are being released, the client is directed to use transformational affirmations to redirect the flow of vital energy in a positive way; various other methods are used to create healthy mental and emotional behavioral patterns. Patients are instructed in methods based on the four pillars of love, support, acceptance, and appreciation, which they can use to empower themselves to restore and maintain optimal health.

Contact: Bamberger Health & Wellness Clinic –
www.bambergerhealth.com

Ohashiatsu®

Wataru Ohashi was born near Hiroshima, Japan, and became a sickly child after the atom bomb was dropped near the end of World War II. After his health was eventually restored by Eastern healing techniques, he decided to dedicate his life to the practice and teaching of the Japanese pressure-point therapy of Shiatsu. The practices of Zen Shiatsu, established by Shizuto Masunaga, were the basis for Ohashi's modified Ohashiatsu, which came to fruition after his arrival in the United States in 1970.

Ohashi actually means "big bridge," and his method links the practitioner and the client through the balance and harmony produced by their natural presence in the moment and the quality of movement in the practice. Trust, sensitivity, and respect are essential. Unlike many forms of bodywork, the well-being of the practitioner is emphasized, because when the giver is comfortable, natural, joyful, curious, and childlike, he can be more sensitive to the client's needs and more open to change, rather than working to a set agenda. The bodywork itself energizes and rejuvenates the practitioner's energy as he moves in a relaxed, meditative way, ready for anything but not wasting energy by exerting himself. This attitude communicates itself to the receiver, who will be more relaxed and more likely to reveal what needs attention. In this practice, the receiver is considered the teacher, since listening to his needs is what guides the giver.

Ohashiatsu puts great emphasis on training practitioners to feel the flow of the life-force energy (ki in Japanese) in the body. Being able to sense ki requires a deep understanding of the qualities of energy called kyo and jitsu. Kyo is considered more yin and represents a lack of energy, whereas jitsu is more yang and signals an abundance of energy. When the practitioner finds that a location or point on a meridian is low in energy, he may need to tonify it. If there is too much energy, then some dispersing or sedating is likely necessary. However, to accomplish the proper redistribution or balancing of an individual's ki requires a profound understanding of the quantum and spiritual levels of energy, in which qualities, waves, vibrations, resonance, and the universal energy field are distinguished. Paradoxically, the actual laws governing energy change as the interactive resonance between the giver, receiver, and the universal energy field takes on a deeper dimension in which conscious awareness takes the lead rather than a particular technique. When considering the nature of energy, there is always more to experience.

Ohashiatsu treats the whole body rather than just symptoms and uses elements of Shiatsu that can have a psychological and spiritual effect on the recipient. Essential elements include smooth and effortless continuity of touch and movement, the use of two hands, respectively known as the mother and messenger hand, and the techniques of cross-patterning movement. Continuity means that there is constant contact with the receiver's body without any disruptions that cause the client to feel disconnected. First, the practitioner positions his relaxed body so that his hara (the lower abdominal energy center and the center of gravity) is close to the receiver's hara, while leaning into the client's body and supporting it. As the practitioner gradually changes positions, this contact is maintained. The bodywork's two-handed techniques and its seamless flow of gentle movement and stretches become an energizing dance that gives comfort to the client as his awareness expands. The mother hand is usually the one that provides a constant, stationary connection to energy and communicates with the receiver, while the messenger hand roams to various locations and applies pressure to meridians under the direction of the mother hand. All pressure is applied in a sequence that follows the direction of ki flow within the meridians. There is a constant, deep, subtle level of communication between the hands throughout the session. Rather than working on specific tsubo (pressure points), the emphasis is on affecting the overall energy flow throughout the body to create balance while relieving stress, tension, and fatigue. As the practitioner moves to work on different parts of the receiver's body, he uses a crawling movement pattern called cross-patterning that requires less effort and prevents fatigue.

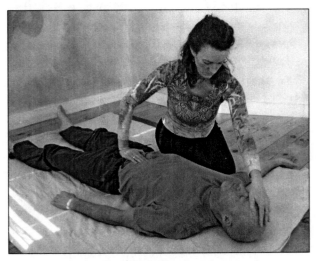

An Ohashiatsu session.

A session starts with a complete form of diagnosis in which the practitioner uses observation (a broad and full way of seeing), touch (energetic contact with the client's core), questioning (open discussion), and deep listening (using the entire body, not just the ears) to understand the recipient's whole body. The state of the client's hara is examined to see which meridians need work and if there are any excesses or deficiencies of energy that need to be sedated or enlivened. Since every part of the body tells a story about a person's condition, the diagnostic process can also incorporate reading the lines on the face; the appearance of the eyes, mouth, tongue, nose, and ears; and the condition of the skin and feet. These readings will give information about the person's strengths and weaknesses; the identification of strengths can give a client a sense of hope for either improvement or recovery. It is also considered important to realize that even the most extreme condition or problem can offer an opportunity to achieve its opposite by turning it into an advantage. A complete diagnosis is not meant to give the client a pile of issues to worry about, but rather to uplift and inspire him through awareness of the unity of his body, mind, and spirit.

The bodywork is begun with the client lying face-up on a floor mat. Although there is no fixed routine, since the sequence of work is determined by the specific needs of a client, a session often progresses from the hara to the lower body and then to the upper body. The practitioner gently and smoothly moves the receiver's body into positions in which he is sitting, lying face-down, or lying on his side so that there is better access to different areas of the body. Great respect is given to the neck, as that is considered a very sensitive area. Pressure is often applied to the Ohashi point on the back center of the neck. Hands are often placed on acupoints or meridians as the client exhales, and hand pressure during a session can be gentle or as deep as needed, but without causing the pain that is commonly associated with traditional forms of Shiatsu. Even though the hands, thumbs, fingers, and elbows are used (and sometimes even the knees), the contact should be felt as a solid, relaxed, energy-based presence. As the practitioner gradually moves, without abrupt changes, to work on different areas, the client's body parts are stretched in various ways that help free up the flow of energy within particular meridians. The client is also assisted with the stretching exercises, called meridian stretches, before and after the treatment. Contact: Ohashi Institute – www.ohashiatsu.org

Okazaki Restoration Massage (ORM)

A form of bodywork closely aligned with the ancient Japanese holistic bodywork healing art of Seifukujitsu, Okazaki Restoration Massage is often referred to as a long-life massage because its intention is to promote longevity. Professor Seishiro "Henry" Okazaki, the founder of the martial art of Danzan Ryu Jujitsu, continued to develop his form of restoration therapy by integrating it with other modalities during the 1920s in Honolulu, Hawaii, where he formed the Nikkon Sanatorium of Restoration Massage. To the basic attributes of self-control, concentration, and the ability to project life-force energy found in the practice of Jujitsu, he added elements of Amma Therapy, Shiatsu, Acupressure, Lomi Lomi, Deep Tissue Massage, Swedish Massage, Reflexology, Chinese methods of healing, and the use of herbs to create ORM. Okazaki was intent on developing ORM as a way to conquer adverse health conditions. He once used this form of bodywork to treat President Franklin Roosevelt and worked with a number of other celebrities and politicians. Its primary goal is to balance and restore the flow of vital energy within the body and heal injured soft-tissue areas.

The bodywork basically focuses on treating musculoskeletal ailments and nerve problems. The practitioner works to remove toxins and help obtain proper realignment of the body by applying pressure with the fingers, forearms, and particularly the elbows. It is also considered a circulation massage because it influences the body's vital fluids. The treatment is known for a technique that uses the forearm and elbow as a steamroller on the body. This deep form of bodywork can be useful in alleviating physical injuries even years after they were acquired.

Contact: www.elbowmagic.com/ort.html

Pranassage®

Originally known as Yogassage, this restorative form of energy bodywork is a synthesis of yoga poses, massage, and assisted stretching. It was created in 1987 by Amba and Don Stapleton, the founders of the Nosara Yoga Institute in Costa Rica. Pranassage is based on the idea that healing changes can be brought about through a combination of touch, movement, traction, and proper stretching. It incorporates both Western and Eastern massage techniques to create an option for those who want to deepen the effects of yoga and expand their capacities to function well by experiencing the feeling of pranic energy in the body. Through touch, applied pressure, deep breathing, and assisted postures, a deep sense of relaxation that helps her feel and activate prana is induced in the receiver, thus creating the optimal condition for learning new patterns of movement. In addition, the opening of the joints helps increase the flow of life-force energy. The whole process is intended to bring a new sense of well-being, flexibility, energy, and openness.

During a treatment, practitioners act as partners in the healing process as their hands assist the client in moving through a series of yoga positions that resembles a smooth dance while synchronized, conscious deep breathing activates prana energy to open up blockages and heal the body. The physical support provided by the practitioner allows the client to concentrate on feeling what it's like to enter and maintain the posture and to experience forgotten possibilities for these actions. Massage applied with both the hands and feet to the lightly clothed client, who is holding an extended pose on a floor mat, provides deep relaxation, flexibility, mobility, improved circulation, muscle strengthening or lengthening, and the energetic removal of stress. Thai Massage is frequently used, as are Acupressure, neuromuscular techniques, Swedish Massage, and other forms of bodywork. Sessions are always tailored to fit the particular client's fitness. Different levels of therapy are used, and the work includes assisted yoga postures in conjunction with Acupressure, and extensive feedback from the client to help melt holding patterns that inhibit the flow of prana in the body. Body leverage is considered an integral part of all the twists, turns, and pulls that are employed. A session is concluded with clients resting in the corpse pose, referred to in yoga as Savasana, and entering a meditative state in which they can absorb and integrate the energetic changes acquired through the session on a deeper level.

Contact: Nosara Yoga Institute – www.nosarayoga.com

Qi Gong Medical Massage

Within the Chinese system of health care is a branch of self-healing through energy work called qi gong. It is written that the original forms of qi gong were developed from the shamanic breathing practices of the Tang Yao tribes on the Yellow River before the time of the Yellow Emperor Huang Ti (around 2700 BCE). From these distant roots, it has developed over many years in close association with Daoyin, Tuina, and Taoist bodywork practices, which are a principal part of the ancient Chinese science of natural healing methods. Like many of the other practices found in Traditional Chinese Medicine, qi gong is based on the principles of chi energy, the yin-yang theory, Taoism, Acupressure, and the balancing of meridians. Essential to any qi gong practice are methods of cultivating energy: breathwork, gentle flowing movements, meditation, visualizations, and conscious intention. The practices can be carried out both through exercises a person performs at home and through bodywork carried out by a trained practitioner. In either case, preventive care is always considered superior; it involves exercises and massage treatments that aid in accumulating, developing, nourishing, circulating, and regulating the internal energies to ensure better health.

Qi Gong Medical Massage evolved from Anmo, which in Chinese means "to press and rub" or "have skill with life energy." In all its forms, it advises that practitioners must continually recharge their own chi if they are to be able to transmit this vital life-force energy to a client. Qi Gong Medical Massage is performed in a specific sequence, following the pathways of chi, zones, and gates of energy. This can be accomplished in two basic ways.

The first method (exemplified by Qi An Mo, described below) is done with very little light contact. The practitioner enters into a meditative state and performs an energy-cultivating practice before tuning in to the needs of the client, who simply rests on a bodywork table. The therapist then energetically transmits his personal chi into areas of the client's body that need attention. Using subtle awareness and deep perception, the practitioner can recognize areas of blockages and effect the distribution of vital energy by either sedating or stimulating energy, depending on the recipient's needs. The practitioner's hands move in a specific way over and above the client's body to manipulate and move the energy. A prescribed sequence that nevertheless allows for flexibility in dealing with particular issues is employed to bring the recipient into an energetically balanced and flowing state of being.

The second method involves more contact—with both hands on the body—using circular motions and a variety of surface manipulations, such as pushing, grabbing, pressing, piercing, pointing, rubbing, caressing, point striking or knocking, vibrating, holding, raising or lifting, pulling, kneading, supporting, shaking, slapping, flicking, swinging, dividing, combining, folding, rolling, chopping, carrying, transporting, striking, shifting, slipping, squeezing, bending, waving, scraping, connecting, cascading, pecking, swaying, rotating, combing, reeling, wiping, brushing, and cupping. All of these hand techniques are systematically employed to stimulate the meridians and points along these energy pathways to access, loosen, and move the healing chi energy. Although not always done in a prescribed sequence, the hands often move outward from the centerline of the recipient's body, covering all areas from the head to the feet. The massage can be mildly painful, since no oil is used. This work can be done in conjunction with herbal remedies to help improve health.

Three of the four different types of Anmo massage treatment found in the field of Qi Gong Medical Massage use the second method, the exception being Qi An Mo. The first is a general type known as Pu Tong An Mo, which involves lots of pressing on certain concentrated chi spots all over the body. The next, known as Tui Na

An Mo, depends on a push-and-grab technique, along with hand movements called piercing and pointing applied to locations with restrictions. It is useful for treating injuries and illness because it spreads out stagnant chi. The form currently used is often referred to as Tuina. The third is Dian Xue An Mo, which includes pointing, cavity pressing, and work on energy channels for the purpose of adjusting the chi and the organs. This type is considered the root of Japanese Shiatsu. The last type, called Qi An Mo, is distinct from the other three in that it works specifically with the gates of chi energy without much physical contact. There is no pressing and rubbing involved with this type of energy work. Although the hands can make light contact, the practitioner primarily relies on his mind to direct the chi to where it is needed. This form of Qi Gong Medical Massage uses a guided meridian meditation in which, having already cultivated personal chi, the practitioner stands in a relaxed position above the client and focuses intuitively on the transference and replenishment of chi energy for healing; this is different from the methods of building chi found in the qi gong exercises a person might perform himself.

Many variations on Qi Gong Medical Massage have been developed since its inception. **Ashi Acupoint Meridian Qi Gong** is one type of treatment, developed by Dr. Xu Hongtao, that combines Acupressure and meridian massage bodywork with qi gong energy therapy. It is designed to open up all the energy channels and allow the chi to flow freely throughout the body. Another related form of therapy also incorporates hot-stone massage and Acupressure along with aromatherapy, in which essential oils are applied to the meridian acupuncture points. An ancient therapeutic technique for rejuvenating the blood and bones, called the Bone Marrow Nei Kung Method, is primarily a self-help practice that was employed by martial artists to cultivate power by absorbing cosmic energy into the bones.

Contact: International Institute of Medical Qi Gong –
www.medicalqigong.org,
www.ashitherapy.com, or
www.healingtaousa.com

Reflexology

This therapeutic method, also known as Zone Therapy, is believed to have originated in ancient Egypt around 3000 BCE, although variations were also practiced in ancient Africa, Russia, India, and China. Some of the earliest known records of this form of bodywork have been found in the ancient Egyptian tomb of Ankhmahor. Reflexology is basically a manipulative technique in which pressure applied to points on the feet, hands or ears creates a reflex response in distant organs, systems, and other areas of the body that helps release blocked energy. During the early twentieth century, Dr. Erdal of Norway made use of Zone Therapy and assisted in its reemergence. Around 1914, Dr. William Fitzgerald, often considered the father of modern-day Reflexology, introduced it to the United States after he studied earlier zone work, including that of Sir Henry Head of London. However, it wasn't until the 1930s that Eunice Ingham, a physiotherapist, mapped all the pressure points, or reflex points, on the feet. Later, French Dr. Paul Nogier made a complete reflex map of the outer ear. Since then, reflex points have also been mapped on the tongue, nose, hands, and ears.

The map of the foot shows the correspondence between the reflex points and the organs as ten zones that run from the top of the head to the toes, with five zones on each side of the body. When working on a specific point within a zone, a practitioner can affect the energy in any other part of the same zone. Although there are some similarities to Asian meridian therapy, most of the reflex points are not the same as acupressure points. The feet are most often used, because they are easily accessible and because work there is effective since the nerve endings are close to the skin surface and the greatest amount of toxins accumulates there.

A treatment often starts out with a variety of soft, relaxing strokes to loosen the feet and prepare them for deeper work. Tender areas suggest that more work is necessary in those spots, because the tenderness points to problems or congestion in the organ or gland associated with that reflex point. The effect of the pressing can be

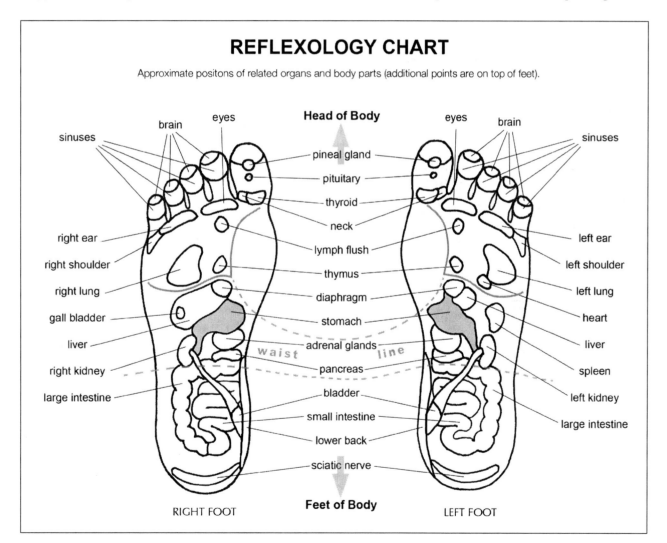

REFLEXOLOGY CHART

Approximate positons of related organs and body parts (additional points are on top of feet).

exhilarating or painful when there is local inflammation or adhesions. If there is an accompanying sensation in a related organ, that signals a potential problem with that organ, in which case a variety of manipulations are focused on the related reflex point. Much of the success of the treatment depends on the diagnostic skill and sensitivity of the practitioner and the presence of a specific complaint. As the treatment progresses, the practitioner often works on the points on the foot by using medium to deep pressure with the thumbs to break up crystal uric acid deposits that can form there and to increase the flow of energy. However, some practitioners believe that very gentle touch can have equal or even better results. In any case, the practitioner and even the recipient can get an idea of an organ's condition through the sensations precipitated by the process while the work is being done. This therapy can be beneficial for clearing up deep-seated metabolic irregularities or malfunctions in the body.

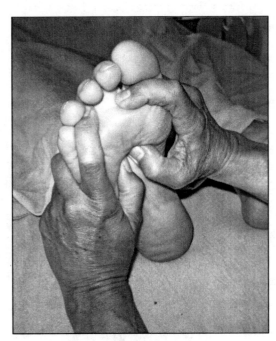

Oh, it feels so good!

Other forms of reflex therapy focus on different areas of the body or use the application of different substances to create a reflex response. The following is a sampling.
Contact: International Institute of Reflexology –
    www.reflexology-usa.net or
    Reflexology Association of America –
    www.reflexology-usa.org

Grigorian Organic Spa Reflexology is a special type of Reflexology, developed by Dr. Gabrielle Grigore, in which nutrients, fruits, and vegetables are applied to reflex zones on the hands, feet, and face; they can also be placed on the neck, shoulders, and arms and are held in place with a comforting towel wrap. As the healthful nutrients are absorbed into the skin, the body's natural healing capacity is stimulated. This is followed with an invigorating foot and lower-leg massage.
Contact: www.neiwh.com

Integrative Reflexology, a modern method of Reflexology developed in the 1990s by Claire Marie Miller, is considered an energy-based, full-spectrum massage therapy, since it goes beyond work on just the feet and hands. Using techniques that aren't as hard on the practitioner's hands, its focus is on unifying the whole body by working with the meridians and the lymphatic system. Instead of using just the fingers and thumb, the manipulations are done with the whole hand, using the knuckles, fists, sides of the hands, and thumbs for support. This lessens the intensity of the sensation for the client. The treatments are more creative and do not adhere to the strict regimen found in more traditional Reflexology. The treatment uses simple detoxifying techniques that work all over the body with focus on the meridians and lymphatic system.
Contact: www.clairemariemiller.com

Korean Hand Massage (KHM) is a form of Reflexology that employs a variety of both Korean and Western massage techniques primarily on specific areas of the recipient's hands and the reflex points there in order to treat an assortment of ailments. It was developed in 1971 by acupuncturist Dr. Tae Woo Yoo and is closely related to his Korean Hand Acupuncture. KHM, which is based on the belief that every joint in the hand corresponds to a joint elsewhere in the body, focuses on treating musculoskeletal problems by massaging these joints. This work also recognizes the meridian system of Acupuncture in which points on the hand are the endpoints of meridians that influence other areas and organs of the body. If a person has a pain somewhere in the body, then there will be a corresponding tender point in the hand, and treatment of this spot will send a soothing message to the related part of the body. Clients can also be taught this method for self-application. (See discussion on Korean Hand Acupuncture under Acupuncture in this section.) Contact: College of Chinese Medicine – www.ccmlondon.com

Resonance Repatterning® (RR) / Holographic Repatterning

Making quantum changes in people's lives requires that they really examine whether they are resonating with something enhancing or something inhibiting. Resonance Repatterning, originally referred to as Holographic Repatterning, is a method of healing that is intended to identify and release restricting patterns that have been a recurring part of an individual's life. It is based on the ideas that all matter consists of pulsing frequencies of energy; that all beings are part of a unified energetic ocean of vibrating frequencies; that quality of life depends on a person being able to resonate with frequencies that elevate the spirit; and that people always have the choice of resonating with life-enhancing frequencies. It is understood that everyone and everything has a vibration or resonance and that what a person resonates with will dictate what he attracts in his experiences. The aim of this therapy is to help clear the beliefs, behaviors, negative emotions, and subconscious patterns that create limitations by identifying and transforming those energetic frequencies that cause a person to opt for life-depleting rather than life-enhancing patterns and by generating the resonance of quantum change. When the recipient reestablishes a balanced alignment of energies through the application of resonant vibrations, the empowering and self-healing truth beneath every problem is revealed.

During the 1990s, after years of study in Polarity Therapy, the five element system of Acupuncture, sound healing, and Edu-Kinesiology, Chloe Wordsworth took elements from these and from the principles of physics, kinesiology, psychology, neurobiology, and the healing wisdom of India and China to form Resonance Repatterning. This energy-based system of healing revolves around nine key interrelated elements that are represented in a mandala of geometric patterns that aids the practitioner in meditation and healing. The nine keys can be summarized as follows: everything is energy; changing your resonance will change your life; we are kinesthetically wired for coherence; we should orient ourselves in the direction that nurtures the soul; every problem has an empowering truth; all great outcomes begin with intention; repatterning can bring what is hidden to light; modalities can balance and harmonize the flow of energy; and every coherent action leads to more coherence. These key elements also describe activities that are required for real quantum change. Essential to the healing process is the awareness of body responses and feelings known as the felt sense. When accessed, this innate kinesthetic sense can help the person realize how he really feels inside about almost anything.

Resonance Repatterning is based on the concept of holographic representation, in which the human body is a microcosm of the universe, and each part of the body is an expression of this unity. Therefore, it is possible to affect the whole when working on one part of the body, such as the muscles. Muscle checking, which is Wordsworth's preferred term for muscle testing, is the primary tool used for identifying both patterns with negative frequencies that a person habitually resonates with, which can manifest as physical pain or emotional dysfunction, and the positive-frequency patterns needed for change. This change allows the client to choose more coherent action, which can help develop new neural pathways. Two kinds of muscle checking that elicit a reflex response to information from the nervous system are used at the beginning of the repatterning process. First, a resonance muscle check identifies existing negative frequencies and noncoherent unconscious patterns. This is followed by a coherence muscle check that determines which soothing or energizing modality or technique will bring a positive resonance that provides greater coherence and a shift in attitude. Besides being diagnostic, this process connects the recipient to his body-mind field so he can recognize options for positive change that identify those modalities or healing techniques that are most appropriate for helping the client.

Once information is obtained through the muscle-checking process, energy blockages and the patterns of the energy underlying the problem or pain are cleared by the practitioner, who is guided by inner wisdom and a connection with the recipient that allows greater awareness of the underlying patterns. The therapist has more than seventy-five repatterning protocols available in training manuals, including the use of light and color, listening touch, acupoint work, vocal and tonal

sounding, affirming statements, laughing, breathing techniques, body movement, fragrances, qi gong, meditation, self-massage, and other forms of energy centering and balancing. These help reestablish a coherent alignment within the client's body-mind system by repatterning the underlying energies of the recipient, thus bringing the recipient closer to being fully receptive to spirit. At the end of a session, muscle checking is used again to identify how well blockages have been removed and what action is necessary for the client to sustain positive resonance after the treatment. Each session is intended to bring the recipient to some point of resolution so he is not left at an incomplete stage of healing. Individuals can also learn a number of self-healing techniques that can be used along with self-performed muscle checking. Contact: Resonance Repatterning Institute –
www.resonancerepatterning.net

Samvahan Vibrational Massage

The origin of this form of bodywork goes back more than 4,000 years to the Indian Vedic scriptures. After being practiced for centuries, it fell into obscurity during the time of foreign invasions and the period of the British rule of India. Indian chiropractor Dr. Ram Bhosle revitalized this ancient and powerful technique during the 1930s. After spending years with yoga masters in the Himalayas, Bhosle cared for Mahatma Gandhi, Winston Churchill, and other leaders from around the world. Since 1995, Michael Trembath, an apprentice of Dr. Bhosle, has been instrumental in teaching this therapy across the globe. Samvahan recognizes that everything in the universe is vibrating at specific unique frequencies and that the rhythms and harmonics in the human body are the same as those found in our natural environment on and off the planet. Quantum physics supports this with a principle known as wave-particle duality, which says that every physical particle is also a form of energy vibration called a wave function. Each part of the body sends or receives vibrations at a certain frequency, and illness is caused by vibrations that are out of balance. The hands-on bodywork in this healing process uses natural energy vibrations transmitted through the practitioner's hands to harmonize and balance the internal rhythms and vibrations of a client's body. In a sense, the therapist "tunes" the client's body as if it were a musical instrument. Healing music acts as both an accompaniment

and guide with vibrations that penetrate and soothe a recipient's body in many beneficial ways.

Samvahan Vibrational Massage brings harmony and balance to regions of disharmony or dysfunction by introducing a pure, balanced vibration into a body part through entrainment, in which the client's dysfunctional vibrations migrate naturally toward the more harmonic frequencies offered by the hands of the practitioner. Working with the physical body's subtle energies and the surrounding energy fields, the therapist will vary the frequencies of the vibrations to address, move, and entrain the subtle energies of the recipient, which will in turn affect physical condition and thereby prevent disease. This requires letting the body in need hear the tune of its own wellness and vitality.

Initially, the practitioner produces gentle vibrations by allowing energy, whose frequency is connected with the earth's daily rotation, to arise from the root chakra energy center at the floor of her pelvis. The vibrations are directed up the central channel in the spine and out through her hands, which transmit the frequency to the recipient; the vibrations of Samvahan can also be offered with tuning forks and singing bowls. Generally, much of the focus is on the nervous system, and most of the hands-on bodywork is done on the spine, because that area is considered to best express the energy imbalances pertinent to the client's overall condition; however, hands can be moved to any areas of dysfunction or disharmony that call for attention. The treatment also focuses vibrational frequencies on certain marma points or chakras to balance energies and induce more healthy functioning. Movements and vibrations can be either slow and heavy or soft and pervasive, depending upon the part of the body being treated and the desired effect, and the vibrational frequency may be varied to balance specific areas of the body. The vibrations provided by this therapy create a unique sensation that frees up constrictions and enables a subtle energetic shift that provides a healthy balance at the recipient's physical, emotional, mental, and spiritual levels.

Music, vocal chants, and harmonic sounds are an important accompaniment to guide the healing session. Most often tuning forks set at certain frequencies are used, but Tibetan singing bowls, CDs, or toning sounds (specific notes made with the voice) can provide the appropriate vibrations. A number of these tonal sounds, which come spontaneously through the practitioner, are not only unique to the particular resonant nature of the client but also deliver the most useful healing vibrations. On certain occasions, special smooth, wooden healing sticks, electronic massagers, needles, and some hydrotherapy treatments are used to provide stronger or more subtle vibrations during the bodywork. The bodywork and music become a series of intermingled vibrations that penetrate the body, playing a tune of wellness and vitality for the body to hear. The effects of Samvahan are said to be cumulative, and at times, repeated treatments may be required for long-term change, especially for those with chronic problems. At present, there are only two certified practitioners doing advanced forms of Samvahan in the West.

Contact: www.samvahan.com/point-of-change

Seiki Soho Therapy

This method was developed by Akinobu Kishi, who studied Shiatsu under Tokujiro Namakoshi and Shizutu Masunaga and taught its practice around the world. However, after a serious illness, he created Seiki Soho to engage the body's own wisdom in the healing process. Seiki Soho can be characterized as a meditative massage with no set regimen of techniques. It recognizes that all of the natural expressions of the body, whether health or illness, are reflections of the state of the vital life-force energy, or ki. Ki has a self-balancing nature, but stagnant energy can disrupt this innate ability. Seiki Soto is designed to help release the stagnant energy that causes dysfunction and support self-correction. The practitioner doesn't heal the client, but simply reminds the body's intelligence of its power. However, some practitioners say that the therapist actually transfers universal healing energy through the recipient's crown.

Seiki Soto uses a simple method of diagnosis in which the energetic state of the client is sensed through light touch. As the treatment begins, the practitioner's first aim is to enter into resonance with the recipient so that the two begin to act as one. This begins as the practitioner closely observes the recipient's breath and begins to resonate with the energetic vibrations within it. He may also lightly touch the recipient in order to deepen the connection between them. Once resonance is established between the two, the therapist makes contact with an area of the recipient's body that attract his attention. Very light touch either on or just off the body draws the recipient's consciousness to those areas; this

touch is not physically based but instead is ki making contact. The practitioner is simply allowing the ki the freedom to do what it naturally wants to do. Attention is held on the area until a change in the client's breathing signals that the body's innate self-healing ability has awakened. These actions continue as the practitioner is spontaneously drawn to other areas of the body that may be blocking the body's innate healing ability. In the end, the recipient comes into a natural state of equilibrium and harmony.

At certain times during a treatment, the client may feel spontaneous movements or reactions such as crying or laughing. In the practice of katsugen, concentrated inner awareness is focused on these natural expressions, and they are allowed to become stronger and stronger until a release occurs. The effects of Seiki Soto are also enhanced by the practice of gyo-ki, in which a person is connected with the cosmic energy of the universe. This involves either sitting seiza (the Japanese style of kneeling on the ground) or standing in a relaxed manner and breathing consciously with the focus on the hara in the lower abdomen. This allows a direct connection with personal ki and with the higher vibrations of the universal energy.

Contact: www.healththroughhealinghands.com/
what-is-seiki-soho-therapy/

Shiatsu

Although it is derived from traditional Chinese Anma techniques and the principles of Acupressure, Shiatsu, which means "finger pressure," is a system of healing that originated in Japan. It essentially treats physical and psychological problems through the stimulation of pressure points to release blocked energies. When the Chinese Buddhist monk Gan Jin Osho brought Chinese medicine to Japan around 600 CE, Anma was adapted into the Japanese Amma therapy, which, when combined with meridian therapy, evolved into what eventually became Shiatsu. However, Shiatsu really became established as a separate therapy in 1915, when Tamai Tempaku published a book called *Shiatsu Ryoho* ("finger pressure way of healing"), followed by another in 1919 called *Shiatsu Ho* ("finger pressure method"). His work combined Anma, Ampuku (an ancient form of abdominal massage for infants and pregnant women), and Do-In exercises with Western anatomy and physiology. Soon after, Tokujiro

Namikoshi, a student of Tempaku, became instrumental in expanding and popularizing Shiatsu. As a youth, Namikoshi had developed a pressing technique that helped heal his mother's rheumatoid arthritis. After later founding the first Shiatsu clinic, he established the Nippon Shiatsu Institute in Tokyo and taught a form of Shiatsu that combined elements of Western physiology. Since then, partly because of the influence of Western medicine, a number of different styles have developed, with therapies such as Amma and Amatsu retaining a close association with Shiatsu. At certain times, European influences caused the practice of Shiatsu to go underground, and after World War II, General Douglas MacArthur outlawed all forms of Japanese medicine. It wasn't until Helen Keller persuaded President Harry Truman to legalize these modalities again that the restrictions were dropped. However, the Japanese government fully recognized the therapy only after Mr. Namikoshi treated a number of notable individuals, including Marilyn Monroe in the 1960s. It was during the late 1950s that Toshiko Phipps became the first qualified therapist to bring the practice of Shiatsu, in a form known as Integrative Eclectic Shiatsu, to the United States. Soon after that, others brought more forms (often considered styles) of Shiatsu to the West.

Shiatsu therapy concentrates on unblocking and balancing the flow of the subtle vital energy called ki in Japanese by pressing specific points along the meridian lines in the body. These blockages may be caused by or lead to stress, infection, trauma, disease, or dysfunction. Its primary intention is to promote self-healing, relieve acute physical problems, and prevent disease from developing. Each of the primary meridians is associated with specific organs and body functions, and although Shiatsu emphasizes treating the whole meridian, it sometimes concentrates on the specific points that are most effective in stimulating and balancing the flow of vital chi energy along these pathways. The process also helps regulate the opposing forces of negative yin energy and positive yang energy.

Traditionally, during a treatment the client lies fully clothed on a floor mat, but today massage tables are often used. Treatments begin with the practitioner assessing the strength or weakness of energy in the organs and meridians by taking pulse readings on the wrist, feeling the muscles, listening to the breath, sensing the energy, palpating near the spine, and questioning the client about her medical history. This may be followed by evaluations that focus on the quality of energy in the abdomen, or hara, which is an important vital energy storage area. Once a strategy is determined, the practitioner moves on to apply rotating pressure (without any rubbing) to acupoints along the meridians. The pressure is most often applied with the fingers, thumb, and palm, although some styles of Shiatsu use the elbows, knuckles, or feet. The amount of pressure applied can vary from slight to deep, and the pressure can be applied in ways that are sustained, interrupted, fluid, concentrated, vibrational, or stimulating, or that providing suction, depending on what is most appropriate. Shiatsu can work on specific surface zones above and along meridian lines or on fixed acupressure points, known in Japanese as tsubos, which provide direct access to the internal energy system of the body. Even though there are hundreds of these points, most pressure work is done on only a few to tonify (increase energy flow) or to sedate (minimize the flow of too-abundant energy). Shiatsu often focuses primarily on the abdomen and back, but the whole body can be treated. Other techniques include gentle rotations and stretches to release tension and improve mobility. Shiatsu therapy can incorporate some soft-tissue manipulation, work on the feet, active and assisted exercises and stretches, rebalancing techniques, the use of healthful medicinal foods, and breathwork. However, massage oil is not used.

One important aspect of the treatment is that when the practitioner has one hand working to strengthen weak or depleted energy areas while the other hand is in contact with an area where excess energy is backed up, the excess energy will automatically release and disperse to where it is needed, balancing the energy between two meridians or between two locations along a pathway.

Over recent years many different forms (styles) of Shiatsu have evolved through different lineages. Although their approach and techniques vary, they all essentially work with the same objective of promoting and balancing the flow of chi through the meridians, thereby enhancing the ability of the body's organs and systems to function at an optimal level. Besides the forms described below, there are also other styles of Shiatsu bodywork that are discussed separately under their own headings in this section and elsewhere in Chapter 6. They include Ohashiatsu (earlier in this section), Seita Shiatsu (in Spinal Therapies), Ashiatsu (in Special

Therapies), Tantsu (later in this section), and Watsu (in Aquatic Therapies.)

Contact: www.topshiatsumassage.com or
www.holisticonline.com/shiatsu

Integrative Eclectic Shiatsu was one of the first forms of Shiatsu to be brought to the United States in the 1950s by Toshiko Phipps. The therapy incorporates elements of Eastern and Western medicine in an approach that is now practiced worldwide. Practitioners of this form use the traditional Japanese/Chinese medical therapies of Ampuku abdominal massage, Acupressure, and Anma therapy along with Western methods of physical therapy, soft-tissue manipulation, and myofascial bodywork. Dietary and herbal practices are also included to create a more comprehensive, integrated method of treatment.

Contact: www.acupuncturestlouis.com

Macrobiotic Shiatsu is based on George Ohsawa's philosophy that each individual is an integral part of nature, and it points out the need for a natural lifestyle. It was founded by Shizuko Yamamoto in Japan. Assessments are made visually, verbally, and with touch and pulse readings. Treatments use noninvasive touch techniques, pressure work using both the hands and bare feet, and meridian stretching to facilitate the flow of chi and strengthen the body and mind. Dietary counseling, medicinal plant remedies, breathing techniques, corrective exercises, postural rebalancing, Shiatsu self-massage, and qi gong exercises are also part of the therapy.

Contact: www.imssmacrobiotic.net

Namikoshi Shiatsu is a form commonly found in Japan that was developed during the 1920s by Tokujiro Namikoshi and his son Toru Namikoshi. Because of the dominant influence of Western medicine, the senior Namikoshi did not elaborate on the aspects of meridian therapy, but instead put the emphasis on working with neuromuscular points. Namikoshi's son Toru spent years teaching and spreading this form of Shiatsu in the West. This system of bodywork, known as the Nippon style, is based on the principles of modern Western anatomy, physiology and pathology and is the most widely known form of Shiatsu used today. The

pressure-point therapy aims to prevent and cure illness by stimulating the body's natural powers of recuperation through work on all the tissue and fascia to affect the neuromuscular, musculoskeletal, circulatory, lymphatic, respiratory, digestive, eliminative, and craniosacral systems. Rather than working solely on meridians, a practitioner often uses vigorous pressure on the cells to move stagnant toxins; digital compression on soft tissue to relax muscles, improve body function, and strengthen the immune system; and manipulations on the connective tissue to loosen and rebalance the myofascial structures that extend throughout the body. Namikoshi Shiatsu also uses a precise sequence of repetitive press-and-release movements to raise the energy levels within the tissue. All components of this form of Shiatsu are intended to create a cascade of rejuvenating effects.

Contact: www.namikoshi-shiatsu.com.au

Okido Shiatsu is an integrated form of Shiatsu therapy developed by Japanese yoga master Dr. Masahiro Oki that uses a combination of elements from Indian yoga, Chinese and Tibetan medicine, Chinese Chikwando, Tai Chi, Zen meditation, macrobiotics, and laughter. A significant part of this self-healing therapy is a variety of flowing exercises and natural movements similar to yoga asanas that are designed to mobilize, purify, strengthen, and balance an individual through the cultivation of harmony in the body, mind, and heart. Besides the application of Shiatsu bodywork, the overall practice includes the use of Zen exercises, meridian stretches, sound healing, and meditations, with the primary emphasis on developing core strength. The whole program is considered more a complete self-actuated exercise process than a specific type of applied bodywork therapy.

Contact: www.okido.us

Shiatsu Anma, developed by Dr. DoAnn Kaneko, is a style based on traditional Chinese medicine that combines the hands-on, soothing bodywork of Anma Massage with the more focused pressure work of Shiatsu to influence the flow of chi in the body. Besides the use of pressure to stimulate key tsubo (acupressure) points, this practice employs

kneading, light stroking, percussion, stretching, tapping, and vibrational techniques, as well as Ampuku abdominal massage. By combining massage with energy work, this form of therapy helps relax the muscles in a way that allows the blood and energy to flow more freely through the organs to release toxins in the body.
Contact: www.shiatsu-anma.com

Shinso Shiatsu is a style developed by Tetsuro Saito, a student of Shizuto Masunaga, during the 1960s. Saito is warmly recognized as the father of Shiatsu in Canada. Shinso Shiatsu puts greater emphasis on the traditional Oriental principles of meridian pathways than other forms of Shiatsu and is considered a natural extension of Zen-style Shiatsu. Saito's research has led to a more in-depth view of how energy really flows in the body and of the nature of the meridian system. His work with the extraordinary meridians is particularly interesting.

Beginning with the twelve regular meridians (those recognized as the most important in the practice of Acupuncture), Saito has identified three levels or degrees of imbalance and has carefully charted how each meridian will shift its position and flow along a slightly different pathway depending on the degree of that imbalance. When the regular meridians are incapable of handling a more persistent condition or serious disease, the extraordinary meridians become involved. Eventually, the divergent meridians and oceans of energy within the cosmic (tai kyoku) energy system may be called into action.

Shinso Shiatsu proposes that by balancing energy at its deepest level in one meridian system, the other meridians/systems will also become balanced, even without direct treatment. The success of this form of healing depends on practitioners' abilities to develop their own levels of chi. The practice relies heavily on a technique called the Finger Test Method, that enables practitioners to sense, precisely trace, and diagnose each meridian so they can locate both structural and energetic imbalances in the body. After these imbalances have been mapped out, the most suitable of several treatment protocols is selected. Besides using finger pressure on selected points, a Shinso Shiatsu treatment may incorporate

diodes, ion-pumping cords, yaki hari, and moxibustion. These serve to enhance Shiatsu's effectiveness in relieving the patient's symptoms (hyoji-ho) and to further its powerful capacity for revitalizing energy (honji-ho). The Finger Test Method is also used to identify sources of electromagnetic disturbance in rooms, test foods and supplements, and monitor meridian systems on a daily basis. Shinso Shiatsu is considered suitable for integration into any style of Shiatsu, Acupuncture, and other form of therapy.
Contact: Shinso Shiatsu International –
www.shinso-shiatsu.com

Taikyo Shiatsu was developed in the 1970s by Asian-American Ping Lee after he completed extensive training and studies in Zen and Namikoshi Shiatsu, Tuina, Tai Chi, qi gong, and forms of martial arts. Working with the principles of Tai Chi, qi gong, and the teachings of the Taoist yin-yang theory, Lee created an integrated style of Shiatsu bodywork in which the practitioner performs an energetic meditative practice such as qi gong or Tai Chi while carrying out the treatment. The practice of Taikyo, the name of which is actually taken from the Japanese word for Tai Chi, emphasizes the philosophy and essentials of Traditional Chinese Medicine. Using Taoist principles and the practice of Tai Chi with its beneficial breathing techniques enables the therapist to gain efficiency in posture and movement. The Taikyo essentials of maintaining an energetic spirit, a strong intention (but an empty mind), calmness, a properly centered posture, good balance, a sense of presence and readiness, intuitive insight, and simplicity are considered necessary to achieve optimum effectiveness in the transmission and distribution of energy for the purpose of healing. Qi gong breathing from the lower dantien, or hara, which is the energy storage center in the lower abdomen near the navel, is one of the key requirements for generating powerful energy output; energy is gathered into the lower dantien on the inhalation and on the exhalation is extended to the client.

During the treatment, the focus is on stretching along the paths of the meridians with the palms rather than working on particular acupoints; the gentle stretching of the meridians is similar to that found in Zen Shiatsu. This work helps eliminate

blockages, induce the discharge of stagnated energies, and enhance the circulation of oxygenated blood to the organs. A distinct part of the treatment is a unique wave technique that reflects the action of an ocean wave forming, cresting, and falling. This is employed to support the recipient's perception of the growing energetic potential as energy expands and reaches a peak, falls, and then spreads throughout the body. To create this wave, both hands are placed on the body, with one hand providing balanced support (yin) while the other hand (or arm and elbow) does the active (yang) work of promoting the open flow of energy. While working a wave, the circular-motion technique called "reeling the silk" is used to provide further manipulations by gripping with a wrist motion that produces pressure without using the fingers. The length, size, and duration of the wave vary with the part of the body being treated. Painful areas of the body caused by stagnant energy often require repetitive wave movements. Other techniques combined with the wave enable efficient massage of the eighteen key joints of the body; primarily smooth and subtle rhythmic pressure is applied to varying degrees. Taikyo Shiatsu considers any bodywork that creates pain to be counterproductive because it can cause the client to tighten up; therefore no sudden, abrupt, or percussive movements are used. Although traditionally performed on a floor mat, Taikyo Shiatsu can also be carried out on a table or chair. This energy-transforming bodywork is useful not only for rehabilitation but for anyone desiring a revitalized sense of being.
Contact: www.bodycontinuum.com/taikyo

Tao Shiatsu, developed by Ryokyu Endo, is a form of Shiatsu based on the studies of Shizuto Masunaga and is intended to better meet the needs of today's Westerners, who are often deficient in energy and therefore suffer more from chronic conditions. This condition is attributed to a fast-paced, stressful lifestyle, which has the tendency to drain the vital life force from individuals, thereby creating conditions of empty (kyo) energy. Tao Shiatsu adds new elements such as Ki Training, the Ki Method, the principle of the basic twenty-four meridians, and improved systematic methods of diagnosis and treatment to existing forms of Shiatsu with the intention of providing a more comprehensive and flexible system of treatment. The basic Shiatsu technique of pressure and movement accomplished with the fingers, hands, elbows, and knees is retained.
Contact: www.taoshiatsu.com

Tsubo Therapy, like other forms of Shiatsu, influences the body's energy by work on tsubo (acupressure points), but in addition to applying finger pressure to these points, Acupuncture, moxibustion, massage, and electrical stimulation of the skin are also employed. Tsubo Therapy was created by Katsusuke Serizawa, a medical doctor from Japan who was born visually impaired. As has been the custom in Japan since ancient times, blind people are often trained in Acupuncture, Anma Massage, and various forms of energy medicine. After his training was complete, he conducted extensive research into the electrical properties of the skin and the signatures that are evident at traditional acupuncture points. His work focused on discovering which vital points were most useful for alleviating a variety of ailments, and by the 1970s, he had developed specific Shiatsu treatments for specific illnesses. This practice is not only directed at relieving common issues related to stress and fatigue, musculoskeletal dysfunction, and skin disorders, but also addresses problems caused by invasive Western medical procedures.
Contact: www.balanceflow.com

Zen Body Therapy® (sometimes referred to as Zen Shiatsu), rooted in Buddhist meditation practices, was created by Shizuto Masunaga with the intention of returning the practice of Shiatsu to its Eastern origins. In addition to refining existing methods of diagnostics, Masunaga used his own extraordinary sensitivity to energy to formulate a system that modified and extended the traditional location of meridians described in the classical Chinese system. His work culminated in the publication of a meridian chart that depicted the twelve regular meridians along with abdominal zones useful for the diagnostic assessment of each meridian; this chart helps the practitioner determine which meridians have blockages and need to be stimulated. In 1977, he published the book *Zen Shiatsu*, which is one of the primary general texts on Shiatsu, regardless of style. His therapy uses techniques that integrate Zen training in Buddhist meditation with Eastern teachings on the five element theory and the circulation of vital energy through the meridians. All practitioners are required to practice meditation in order to have better awareness of the flow of vital energy. This style does not adhere to a fixed sequence or set of methods, but rather adapts treatments to the needs of each individual, based on the initial diagnosis of the condition of the hara (the energy storage center in the lower abdomen). Zen Shiatsu focuses on meridian lines rather than specific points and uses a more strenuous form of Acupressure, as well as deep-tissue work that includes stretching exercises to open the meridians.

The success of Zen Shiatsu depends on the meditative state of the practitioner as pressure is applied along the Masunaga meridians. Zen Shiatsu's distinct features include a technique of abdominal palpation for diagnosing energy within the twelve meridians that pass through that area; the particularly graceful and connected way the practitioner moves while working on all areas of the recipient's body; and deep, perpendicular, stationary pressure directed inward rather than pressure applied by pushing at an angle. Pressure is applied with the palm, thumbs, or fist in a rhythmic fashion along the meridians rather than on specific points. The elbows, knees, and feet can also be used while the client is in different positions. The goal is to establish a normal pattern of energy flow by working with the concept of kyo jitsu, which relates to maintaining the redistribution and balance between the absence of ki (kyo) and excess ki (jitsu). The practitioner works repeatedly on deep-tissue layers to remove aberrations that have built up over years of stress and strain.

Unlike other forms of Shiatsu in which the fingers of only one hand are used, Zen Shiatsu includes two techniques that employ both hands. In the first, the hands rather than just the fingers contact the recipient's body in a rhythmic pattern that traces all portions of the meridians. The second is a two-handed technique in which one hand stays still, holding and listening and providing support while the other is actively palpating, penetrating,

and directing the flow of energy. Zen Shiatsu also includes special self-care exercises known as Makko Ho that are designed to help individuals correct imbalances in the flow of chi energy through their meridians. The basic goals of Zen Shiatsu are to integrate the body, mind, and spirit by balancing yin and yang, to eliminate disharmonies between internal organs, and to remove blockages that inhibit the circulation of chi, which is called ki in Japanese.

Contact: www.shiatsu-masunaga.ni

Tantric Dakini Approach

A dakini is a female Tibetan wisdom being who has unique spiritual healing powers, and tantric bodywork draws on Buddhist energy practices, often of a sacred sexual nature, that can be used for many levels of inner transformation. This method of bodywork opens the heart and brings out kundalini energy with the intention of honoring all parts of the body, releasing tension, stimulating the flow of energy, and heightening awareness of physical sensations.

The bodywork is sensual, with the recipient held in a gentle, swaying motion and massaged with calm flowing strokes that not only relax the body but get under the skin to interconnect and activate vital energy. Though sensual or even erotic techniques may be part of a treatment, the goal is not the performance of any sexual acts, but rather the experiencing of feelings of trust and joyful intimacy. Some practitioners have violated this form of sacred touch by not respecting personal boundaries; therefore, those considering one of these sessions would be wise to get references and make their intentions clear beforehand. The affectionate holding, nurturing, rhythmic stretching, tender touch, and soft pampering can be combined with many other styles of bodywork, including Swedish Massage, Shiatsu, Lomi Lomi, and deep or light tissue work. Pranayana breathwork, music, aromatherapy, and the application of herbal oils often accompany the bodywork session. The bodywork is particularly useful for people with sexual dysfunctions and emotional wounds that limit their level of comfort with intimate contact.

Variations within the spectrum of tantric bodywork also incorporate other energy-based modalities, and there are a variety of self-actuated tantric energy exercises in which meditation, concentration exercises, yoga, mantras, and energetically balanced sexual acts are used to enhance cosmic energy, unity, and vitality. Contact: www.dakinisophie.com or www.tantraschool.co.za

Tantsu Tantric Shiatsu

This intimate, energy-transforming bodywork modality was developed by Harold Dull, who also created an aquatic version of tantric Shiatsu known as Watsu. Tantsu nurtures the recipient during manipulations and point work as the recipient is cradled by the practitioner's whole body and embraced by this loving physical contact. The main focus of the treatment is on connecting the chakras and freeing the natural movement of vital chi energy along the spine.

During a session, the practitioner uses a process called co-centering. By leaning in close with the whole body, the practitioner allows his hara (abdominal energy center) to touch or be close to the hara of the recipient, creating a deep nurturing connection between the therapist and the client. Shiatsu point work is employed along the meridians and on the chakra energy centers along with powerful stretches to release the life-force energy. The bodywork is done in a dance-like pattern, with each movement flowing into the next. When appropriate and consented to by the client, more intimate methods that include a prostate massage and other sensual forms of touch can be used free up and transform dormant sexual energy. Contact: Harbin Hot Springs – www.harbin.org

Thai Yoga Bodywork

Far from being the beachfront massage offered by young women to tourists in Thailand, Thai Yoga Bodywork, often simply referred to as Thai Massage, is really an ancient method of bodywork that was traditionally known as Nuad bo Rarn, which literally means "ancient massage." Nuad Thai is the name of an early branch of traditional Thai health care that may have originated from Vajrayana Yoga practices found in Tibet, though it is also believed to be based on an Indian Ayurvedic and Buddhist spiritual practice that combines yoga with a form of Acupressure. Some believe that it was developed by an Indian doctor who was the personal physician of the Buddha and the king of Siam, whereas others say it came in ancient times from the Yellow Emperor of China. Whatever its origins, it was often employed by the monks in Buddhist monasteries to help relieve the pain caused by sitting for long periods of time in meditation, and in Thailand, it was used by the king and his family for healing purposes rather than pleasure. Traditionally, pulse analysis was used to determine those elements that were out of balance so that the practitioner could better direct attention to resolve dysfunctions, and the complete therapy included diet, herbs, and prayer. These elements are generally not part of the modern form of Thai Yoga Bodywork.

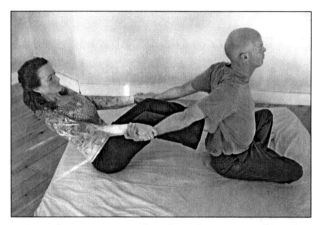

One of many positions found in Thai Yoga Bodywork.

Traditional Thai bodywork (also known as Sombat Tapanya) has two styles, the Northern and the Southern. The primary difference between the two is that the Southern style is more invasive and more painful than the gentler Northern Thai style. However, there is often overlap between the two styles, and many practitioners employ variations of the traditional forms. Another form of Thai massage, known as Piradara, includes the use of hot herbal compresses with or without oil. Burmese Massage is similar to Thai, but involves variations in body positioning, flexing, and twisting and in the use of different parts of the practitioner's body for leverage. The bodywork can be painful when sensitive areas are being treated, but, for the most part it is very exhilarating and helpful for providing adjustments and realignments that bring the body back into balance. All of these approaches can be carried out by two practitioners working simultaneously.

Today's Thai Yoga Bodywork is usually performed on a mat on the floor with the recipient dressed in loose, comfortable clothing. It acknowledges the body-mind connection, and the practitioner tries to work in a state of mindfulness in which every breath is connected to each moment. The massage focuses on ten major energy conduits or pathways, known as sen lines, and acts as an external stimulus to produce specific internal effects, opening and creating space within the body to allow it to move harmoniously. Rather than using points as in Acupressure or Shiatsu, a practitioner applies slow, deep, rhythmic compression and pressure to release blockages and balance the energy along the sen lines by using the fingers, thumbs, palms, hands, elbows, forearms, knees, and feet. Myofascial stretching techniques, soft-tissue manipulations, and energy balancing can also be part of the treatment. Simultaneously with the hands-on bodywork, the practitioner stretches the client into a wide range of yoga-like poses while the recipient is sitting, lying down on the stomach or back, or inverted, and sometimes gently and rhythmically rocks the client, often aligning the movements with the client's breath. Thai Yoga Bodywork is like a passive, assisted form of yoga in which the recipient doesn't have to work at holding active Hatha Yoga postures.

Though emphasis may be placed on the abdominal area during the treatment, the arms and legs are the body parts most frequently moved, often in ways that twist and stretch the spine, hips, and joints. Tractioning of limbs is also used for dealing with issues of sciatica, spinal compression, and bursitis caused by tightness in a joint. The role of conscious breathing is an important part of Thai Yoga Bodywork, and the client is often instructed to synchronize the breath with the practitioner's movements and to breathe into areas of resistance. Quite often, the releasing process will spontaneously cause shifts in the recipient's breathing patterns. The Ayurvedic concept that the wind element is important in supporting body function is also incorporated into the therapy, since the pressing and deep compression promote the correct movement of wind in the body, thus freeing stagnant energies. Today, some clinical forms have adopted minor modifications, but Thai Yoga Bodywork is still concerned with the balance of energy and the creation of a powerful meditative healing experience that promotes wholeness of mind, body, and spirit.

Contact: Institute of Thai Massage –
> www.thai-massage.org,
> www.healthtraditions.com.au, or
> www.holisticmanchester.co.uk

Swe-Thai is a recent variation of Thai bodywork, developed by Margie Meshew, that fuses two different forms of treatment: the traditional, energy-centered Eastern methods of Acupressure and Thai Yoga Bodywork and the more biomechanical Western methods of Neuromuscular Massage and the soft-tissue techniques found in Swedish Massage. Swe-Thai essentially combines yogic stretches and energy point work with the muscle-relaxing effleurage and petrissage movements of Swedish Massage. Trigger-point practices may also be used. One technique found in this combination of modalities is rolling the forearm on specific muscles during sustained assisted yoga stretches. Swe-Thai is most often done on a massage table rather than on the floor.

Contact: www.utimassage.com

Tibetan Medicine

Just like Traditional Chinese Medicine and the Ayurvedic system of health care from India, Tibetan medicine has a long, rich history of development that has resulted in a vast array of intricate therapies. The earliest traces of this holistic system of health care are found in the indigenous traditions first seen in the Kingdom of Tazig in western Tibet (in the area of Mount Kailash) more than 15,000 years ago, when medicine men carried out shamanic protection and healing rituals. A close connection with nature and a tradition of healing both the body and the spirit were retained when the legendary Bön master Tonpa Shenrab Miwoche established and taught the Bön religion, whose doctrines and practices (including healing practices) were carried by his disciples to the kingdom of Shang Shung, traditionally believed to be located in western and northwestern Tibet. What had been ways to protect against natural calamities and disorders caused by malevolent spirits evolved into a system of healing that contained more advanced and involved healing practices and numerous methods of divination. A long line of spiritual masters, including the legendary naked "Buddha-like" Bön master Tapihritsa, became well established, along with their illuminating teachings of ways to attain enlightenment. In 127 BCE, King Nyatri Tsenpo became the first of a long line of rulers of Tibet, bringing the Bön religion and culture with him.

As the centuries passed, Tibetan culture, religion, and its system of healing integrated core principles and knowledge of spiritual practices and medical systems from India, China, and Persia through trade along the

Silk Road. The Persian Galenic tradition may have been the first to arrive, but around 100 CE, Indian Ayurvedic philosophy and concepts began to exert their influence. The healing practices of Tibet before the arrival of Ayurveda seem to have included pulse reading, moxibustion, hot-stone therapy, essential oils, special herbal pills, bloodletting, hot and cold fomentation, some forms of bodywork, healing rituals, and astrology. Meditative practices already existed, but after the Ayurvedic teachings arrived, more involved yogic and meditative forms of spiritual practice were eventually adopted. Though there are signs of an early exchange of ideas from China, the Vedic teachings seem to have had the strongest influences on Tibetan thinking. When Buddhism came to Tibet from India between 500 and 600 CE, the teachings contained in its four medical tantras quickly began to affect the definition of health and how to achieve it. Throughout its history, the form of health care that evolved in Tibet as Bön and Buddhism became intertwined definitely had more of a spiritual element than in most countries of the world. Tibet's geographic isolation helped retain these traditions for centuries. Even when there was a threat from foreign invaders, the mystic impression of Tibet as a land of enchantment would often hold the destructive forces at bay.

Tapihritsa sits absent of any ornaments.

Tibetan medical practices were not usually institutionalized, but instead were passed on directly from healer to student. The rough terrain and high-altitude environment of the Tibetan plateau and Himalaya mountains hindered the development of a unified approach, but allowed unique beliefs about the nature of healing to be preserved. During the seventh-century

reign of King Songtsen Gampo and in the golden era of cultural expansion in the eighth century when the country was ruled by King Trisong Detsen, Tibet was unified into one nation with a written language and Buddhism as the state religion. Prominent Indian Buddhist masters and experts in a variety of disciplines came to Tibet from all directions. The king's personal physician, Yuthog Yonten Gonpo the Senior, considered to be the father of present-day Tibetan medicine, traveled afar to India, Persia, and China to study various systems of healing and promote the Tibetan medical system; the first international medical conference was held during this time in central Tibet. Gonpo translated and composed numerous books on medicine, which may have included a very significant text on indigenous Asian medicine known as the *Gyushi* manual. He also wrote about spiritual practices until his passing at the age of 125 years. However, the origin of the *Gyushi* text is debated, and some say that it had been transmitted earlier to the Buddha Vairocana by a Kashmir pandit (wise man), whereas others say it is based on the *Bumshi*, a Bön medical text.

Between the ninth and eleventh century, Buddhism and healing practices based on Buddhist principles experienced a period of decline after the forty-second king of Tibet attempted to stamp out Buddhism and revive the Bön religion. In fact, in 833, the tantric teacher Padmasambhava, who eventually cleared the path for Buddhism by pacifying local spirits, hid certain medical texts, which were not revealed until the eleventh century. However, by the twelfth century, Yuthog Yonten Gonpo the Younger, who was considered by some to be an emanation of the Medicine Buddha, in addition to his spiritual writings also made a major contribution to Tibetan medicine by adding revisions to the *Gyushi* manual, which became one of the primary reference texts on healing for years to come; this manual had 156 chapters and information about more than 3,000 healing ingredients.

Over the centuries, more translations of teachings came from both China and India; however, it was the yogic practices from India, which arrived during the eleventh century, that had a particularly strong influence on the spirituality of Tibetans. Meditative Vajrayana and Tantric yoga practices found a strong following in Tibet, including the Six Yogas of Naropa that the Tibetan master Marpa the Translator learned in

India just before Moslem armies invaded that country in 1172 and quashed the Vedic practices in their homeland. Marpa helped establish the yogic tradition and meditation practice in Tibet, and from his teachings, a great number of schools of yoga developed in Tibet. Although the Buddhist teachings and practices waned in India under Moslem rule, Buddhism flourished in Tibet during the following centuries. In the seventeenth century, the regent Sangye Gyatso spent twenty years revising the *Gyushi* medical manual and bringing Tibetan medicine to its classical maturity, and in 1696, the fifth Dali Lama founded the Chagpori School of Medicine and Tibetan Astrology near his winter palace at Ice Mountain. Over the centuries that followed, a number of other medical schools were established, and Buddhism and Tibetan medicine continued to thrive up until the Chinese invasion in 1949.

It is an ironic twist of fate that it was the Chinese government's invasion of Tibet in 1949 that liberated the knowledge and wisdom of Tibet and Tibetan Buddhism from its mountain fortress and allowed it to spread throughout the world. This is definitely an example of the gift within a seemingly negative action. Since then, a number of Tibetan teachers and healers, led by His Holiness the Dalai Lama, have made the wisdom of Buddhist and Tibetan medicine practices available to many Westerners. It's impossible to list the hundreds of enlightened masters and healers who have taken part in this effort, but some of the earliest who spoke particularly about healing practices, often intertwined with spiritual practices, include Chogyal Namkhai Norbu, Yantra Yoga practitioner Lama Lobsang Palden, and two masters of the Bön tradition, Lungtok Tenpai Nyima, and Yongdzin Tenzin Namdak. Though its motivation is unknown, the Chinese government has recently supported the creation of a new institute and museum for the promotion of Tibetan medicine in Tibet. It may be that their consciences got the better of them, but it might more likely be the political act of the government trying to tell the world that it is supporting Tibetan culture.

Although the Tibetan system of medicine incorporated many elements of healing from Persia, China and India, what eventually developed was unique to Buddhist Tibet. In a culture that differentiates between the relative and ultimate natures of an individual, the primary goal of Tibetan medicine is to transform the negative emotions caused by attachment, aversion, and ignorance that lead to suffering and disease and to allow the innate kindness and healing power of each being's true nature to emerge. Through the centuries, the direct experience of awakened practitioners gave rise to a treasury of specialized instructions and spiritual wisdom, which underlie all of the Tibetan healing practices and therapies and can be called on to address internal imbalances and eliminate the energetic causes of dysfunction and disease. Meditation to dissolve clinging to a sense of self and to liberate inborn compassion, as well as yogic practices, became an integral part of most healing practices.

Tibetan medicine has developed its own way of describing the makeup of the human body. It includes the five elements (earth, water, fire, wind, and space), consciousness, the three humors or constitutions (wind, bile, and phlegm), and the three energetic components of life. Tibetan healing seeks to bring all these components into harmony. The humors of wind, bile, and phlegm each represent the characteristic positive and negative aspects of a person's character and relate to the ability to process life's occurrences, both physical and emotional. Wind pertains to the air that is breathed and the movement of energy in the body. Bile pertains to the fire responsible for all body heat. Phlegm pertains to water and all bodily fluids. They correspond to the constitutional types of Vata (air), Pitta (fire,) and Kapha (water) in Ayurvedic medicine. The five gross elements, which are similar to those found in other Eastern therapies, define different qualities contained within the body and mind of a living being and, in fact, in everything. Within all the Tibetan methods of healing and inner transformation, the element of space is considered the most important, since none of the other elements could exist without it.

Rather than relating the mind simply with the brain as in the West, Tibetans believe that the mind has several locations, and in fact, when asked to position it in a part of the body, they call it the heart-mind. The gross mind located in the head contains all sensory consciousness and is the active director of bodily functions as it sends and receives to and from other parts of the body. The subtle mind is found in the heart and allows people to hold all memories and feel emotions, both positive and negative. The less-active very subtle mind, well protected in the central channel below the navel in the lower abdomen, receives and carries the memory of all experiences throughout time. These three levels of consciousness are constantly communicating among themselves and with the physical body, and healing the negative emotions and afflictions of the mind is considered necessary for healing the body.

The energy components of the subtle body consist of tsa (the energy channels and the five chakras), lung (psychic wind energy), and tigle (essence drops). Each of these contributes in its own way to the flow of energy. Lung is especially important, since it is the force that moves energy in five principal ways through the body. It can be affected in a positive way through the practice of Tibetan yoga, for example, the meditative breathing practice of Tsa Lung, which harmonizes the flow of this wind energy through the energy channels and chakras in the body. The practice called tummo uses psychic heat to ignite the fire in the energy center below the navel; it has been used by monks meditating in mountain caves to keep warm and to burn up ignorance. Tigle or essence drops are the energy of the earth and water elements that come from the digestive transformation of food that fuels the body.

Tibetan pulse reading is most often the primary method used to discover the nature of a disease or dysfunction. The radial artery on the wrist is like a messenger that carries information, which is communicated through the characteristics of the pulse. Readings give indications of the balance of the humors, organ energy, and the psychic pulse within the blood. In effect, the practitioner translates the language of the organs and the heartbeat into specific information about the condition of the body and the existence of disease. Pulse readings can fluctuate over a short period of time according to factors such as type of diet, amount of sleep, and exercise, and these factors can easily influence the client's body in a way that skews the diagnostic process. Therefore, in order for a Tibetan medical doctor to make a valid pulse reading and true assessment of the nature of a client's disease, the client must make certain preparations at least one day before the treatment.

The overall aim of Tibetan medicine is to rejuvenate the body, bring back harmony, and restore equanimity and balance to the mental, emotional, and spiritual aspects of a person by working directly with the body, speech, and mind. Extensive questioning and diagnostic evaluation of the client's pulse, tongue, and urine are considered essential to discovering the person's particular constitution, energy status, dysfunction, and disease. The treatment of any imbalances found is accomplished holistically with medicinal plants and mineral remedies (including specially made jewel pills), preventive tonics, special diets, hands-on bodywork, behavioral lifestyle practices, meditation, yoga, and spiritual healing practices. Creating herbal jewel pills could take several months, and they are given spiritual power by a meditative blessing ritual performed under the full moon. Today, it is becoming possible to procure some of these herbal remedies in the West. These natural medicines are often prescribed in conjunction with various forms of bodywork, mostly commonly the hands-on massage therapy known as Kunye. Other modalities that draw on the principles of Tibetan medicine, including Tibetan Cranial, Tibetan Point Holding, Tibetan Pulsing Healing, Tibetan Universal Massage, Tibetan Vita Flex, and Yantra Yoga Massage, are now available on a limited basis. In addition some forms of Reiki and tantric modalities of bodywork are also available. (Each of these modalities are discussed under their own headings in this chapter.)

Because they have been available outside their home countries for many years, both Chinese medicine and Ayurveda are more well known than Tibetan medicine, so it might be worthwhile to look at the differences, which are often subtle. Tibetan medicine and Ayurveda are somewhat similar in their views about an individual's constitutional makeup. Tibet's nepas and India's doshas both describe three humors, but they have slightly different qualities. Tibetan medicine does not use marma points or the nadi energy channels, but, like Ayurveda, recognizes three central energy channels within the spinal area. When considering yogic practices, Tibetan medicine considers that the body has five chakras rather than Ayurveda's seven. The five elements used in Tibet are slightly different from those used in India; space is used instead of ether and wind is used instead of air. In comparison with Chinese medicine, in Tibet air and space replace wood and metal. The Chinese medicine system includes the theory of meridians and its energetic connection with organs and the principles of yin and yang, but point work and Acupressure are only occasionally practiced in Tibet. The methods of pulse reading are also somewhat different, and Tibetans consider that analysis of the urine as well as the pulse is essential before prescribing a remedy. Tibetan medicine does not share the Chinese medicine emphasis on promoting longevity, for, as in the Ayurvedic system, the human body is seen as temporal, to be left behind after death. The healing practices in Tibet put more emphasis on mental attitude as an agent of transformation, and special meditations invoking the power of the Medicine Buddha are also unique and may be carried out as an everyday personal practice. In any case, all three systems share a holistic and energy-based approach to healing.

Over the years, Tibetan bodywork has been reestablished or developed in the West and is presently available to a limited extent. Access to Tibetan diagnostics, medical practices, and herbal remedies is slowly improving as some of the same obstacles to acceptance that Chinese medicine experienced are overcome. Some of the more widely recognized forms of treatment, including the traditional Kunye Massage, are discussed separately under their own headings. Other Tibetan spiritual practices, which can have a profound influence on physical health, are found in the chapters covering breath, meditation, and yoga.
Contact: www.shangshung.org or
www.tibetanmedicine-edu.org

Tibetan Pulsing Healing

This adaptation of an ancient ritual healing practice found within the monasteries of Tibet involves an energy-healing process in which a practitioner communicates with the inner workings of the various organs of the body. Over recent decades, the American James Murley, who became known as Shantam Dheeraj, has been instrumental in further developing this method as he learned how to talk directly to a person's particular organs and energy circuits and heal through touch. After working on stressed-out Hollywood actors, Murley constructed maps of the inner workings of the nervous system. He also created the Osho Institute in India for the support of this and other healing practices.

The healing process recognizes that illness starts when energy is not flowing properly in a particular circuit. The therapy is based on an understanding of personality and the set of psychological or emotional feelings and physical characteristics associated with each organ (such as bladder problems equating to stress). This method balances the emotions, relaxes the mind, and renews the physical body. It represents a system

for understanding energy and human consciousness that requires the practitioner to intuitively sense the many different subtle qualities which each organ of the body manifests and how positive energy flow can be enhanced.

In Tibetan medicine, and for that matter, Tibetan Pulsing, disorders are recognized by analyzing the characteristics of the three humors (wind, bile, and phlegm). Although visual diagnostic methods such as urine analysis, tongue diagnosis, and readings of the ears and veins can also be done to get an indication of particular pathologies, the primary initial diagnostic tool used in Tibetan Pulsing is reading the eye. The eye is considered to be a map of the condition of all the internal organs, and the brightness and clarity of the eye reflect the overall health of the body. All of these methods are used to determine which organ of the body requires attention.

Pressure-point work that engages with the pulse of energy through selected points is the central component of Tibetan Pulsing work. At the start of the session, while the client relaxes, music that specifically resonates with the organ being treated is played. The practitioner then holds certain energy points related to the affected organ or body part to release the energy held in patterns of suffering caused by shock or even perhaps by past-life trauma (remember that Tibetan Buddhists believe in reincarnation). A positive flow of energy is directed into negatively charged areas to help the release. Releasing pain and shock from the body also cuts through the hold that negative thoughts in the mind have on the client's ability to function. During a treatment session, two or more people can join hands and tune to the cadence of the recipient's pulse to access the heart and the bioelectric energy. Gentle pressure pulsating in rhythm with the heartbeat is applied to these energy points to bring loving energies to areas needing healing. Besides providing physical and emotional relaxation, this method of healing brings increased awareness and understanding of the inherent patterns of behavior in the recipient.
Contact: www.tibetanpulsingworld.com

Tibetan Universal Massage

This ancient form of Tibetan massage has been handed down through generations and was recently reintroduced in India by Dr. Dhondup. It is intended to alleviate an assortment of conditions from muscle soreness to breathing problems and uses a wide variety of methods and techniques to treat the root cause of any symptom and increase the recipient's vitality.

The bodywork incorporates a fluid, flowing massage technique that, unlike Acupressure, works primarily on the wind energy (lung) of the body that carries the essence drops of energy (tigle) to all parts of the body through the energy channels called tsa. The therapy starts with a complete diagnosis that includes an assortment of traditional methods along with postural assessments and then proceeds to open the flow of energy in the recipient by using a combination of rolling massage techniques, physical therapy, Reflexology, manipulations with petrissage and kneading on areas such as the kidneys, bone marrow techniques, energy work, and chakra balancing work.

Contact: www.tibetanmassage.com

Tibetan Vita Flex Therapy

A twentieth-century redevelopment of an ancient Tibetan form of bodywork similar to Acupressure, Tibetan Vita Flex uses the complex network of reflex points in the hands, feet, and other parts of the body to stimulate and revitalize all the body's internal functions, organs, and systems by accessing and awakening the body's natural healing energies. Vita Flex, which means "vitality through the reflexes," was perfected during the 1920s by Stanley Burroughs.

The therapy is a specialized form of pressure-point massage that uses vita flex points to release many kinds of tension, congestion, and energetic imbalances. The activation of these points sends a minute electrical impulse along the meridians to balance the energy in a specific area of the body. Rather than applying the steady stimulation found in Reflexology, the practitioner uses rapid movements to apply light to medium pressure in a rolling and releasing action with all four fingertips on the reflex points. This technique is repeated a few times on each vita flex point in an area before moving on to the next area relating to the system of the body being treated. A few drops of essential oils are applied to certain related contact points on the feet to deliver the healing benefits throughout the body. This combination of hands-on point stimulation and essential oils works to bring the body into structural and electrical alignment.

Contact: www.rehabilitationmassage.com/en/vita-flex-
technique.html

Tom Tam Healing System and Tong Ren Healing

The Tom Tam Healing System is a modern version of an older Chinese method of Acupuncture called Huatuojiaji. Like most forms of Chinese medicine, the therapy is based on the premise that disease is caused by energy blockages. As a result of his experience and a desire for knowledge, in 1982 Tom Tam, a Tai Chi master and Acupuncture practitioner, began formulating his healing principles, which are based on a combination of both Eastern medicine and Western anatomy and physiology and place a strong emphasis on the central nervous system. After many years of practice and study, in 1992 he added Tong Ren energy therapy to the healing system. Tom Tam's practice and philosophy is based on the form of Acupuncture taught by the famous Dr. Hua Tuo, who lived in China 2,000 years ago during the Warring Kingdom period in the first century CE. Because of the politics of the time, Dr. Hua Tuo was killed at the age of almost 100 by a paranoid ruler who suspected the doctor of plotting his assassination.

The theory of the collective unconscious was a cornerstone of Carl Jung's work in the field of psychology and is also the basis of the energetic source used in healing with Tong Ren therapy. Tong Ren uses universal energy (chi) to open bioelectrical blockages, which are considered the root cause of any problem. Using qi gong techniques to generate energy, the practitioner directs the collective group energy into the patient's blockage points to affect the healing process in a fashion similar to entrainment. By using the focused attention on the universal energy already established in the subconscious mind of the practitioner, Tong Ren can affect brain impulses and help bring healthy bioelectrical signals to diseased organs and cells of the body. There are other techniques that utilize these healing principles, with most requiring no touching or physical contact; Tong Ren can also be performed as distance healing. In some cases, physically stimulating and loosening the muscles along the spine can release physical blockages that inhibit the natural bioelectrical circulation of the body.

The primary goal of the Tom Tam Healing System is to remove blockages that will cause physical or emotional illness by treating both the sympathetic and parasympathetic nervous system with a combination of therapies that will support the free flow and balance of energy, thereby reducing the fight-or-flight response and promoting rest and digestion. Qi gong, Tai Chi, diet, and Tong Ren can all be called on. Most Chinese diagnostics detect energy blockages by analysis of the pulse and tongue; however, Tom Tam believes this is a limiting and inaccurate measure of illness. He recognizes and uses three energy loops (in the brain, nervous system, and organs) and four types of points (chi points, blockage points, cranial points, and painful "ouch" points). Special attention is paid to key nerve blockage in the hua tuo points, which are the points along the spine called jia or ji points depending on which side of the spinal column they are located. These spinal points, each connected to specific organs, are the ones most often treated. They extend from the cervical spine down across the sacrum and are a thumb's distance apart on either side of center. Any form of pressure works well on these jia and ji points, and they are easy to use and locate. Tom Tam also developed a cranial chart with brain acupoints.

The pressure-point work can be done with Acupuncture, a Wartenberg pinwheel, a tuning fork, a Gua Sha percussion instrument, a teishin needle that does not penetrate the skin, laser, or just firm Acupressure with the fingers. Concentrated attention with the hands can fill up a deficiency of chi or draw out the excess chi. Electrical and hot and cold stimulation may also be used. The Tuina practice of pressing and rubbing to remove blockages, especially in the area of the neck, is another integral part of the healing process. The length of time a blockage or acupuncture point is stimulated will vary depending on the particular conditions of the recipient, as will the number of sessions required. For short or long distance healing, rhythmic tapping of a magnetic reflex hammer on an acupuncture figurine (doll) helps focus the practitioner's attention and create a link between his subconscious mind and the blockage point in the patient's body.

Tom Tam has also created small portable ultrawave healing devices that send signals of prerecorded, specifically calibrated, low frequency vibrations and brain waves to specific points on the body. It emits these signals through a probe or low-intensity laser light to entrain the brain and nervous system in order to remove energetic blockages and improve cellular functioning. This unit has been shown to provide relief for an assortment of disabilities and diseases, including cancer. The Tom Tam system is now also being used by some chiropractors for the treatment of pinched nerves. Free

group Tong Ren healing classes are offered at various locations.

Contact: www.tomtam.com

Touch for Health® (TFH)

Touch for Health was developed by chiropractor Dr. John Thie (along with Bruce Dewe), who studied with Dr. Goodheart, the developer of the original form of Applied Kinesiology. The therapy reflects the principles of Traditional Chinese Medicine and the five element theory and uses point work along with chiropractic techniques and the muscle-testing diagnostics of Applied Kinesiology. Many types of muscle testing are used in Touch for Health to assess imbalances, inhibitions, or blockages in the musculature and meridian system of the body; each meridian system has a unique set of key test points. Touch for Health is used to relieve tension, emotional stress, and physical dysfunction while improving posture and increasing the flow and balance of energy throughout the body.

The treatment session focuses on energy circuits (meridians) and the five elements and incorporates point holding, emotional balancing, pulse work, and tapping painful areas and points. Before a client starts a session, certain preliminary balancing exercises are carried out through hand motions on the body and point work on the ears. This gives an energetic lift, clears away any scrambled energy that might confuse the results of muscle testing, helps resolve general energy blocks, and balances the energy points in the body's meridian system. After the initial use of muscle testing to locate what needs attention, the practitioner employs seven different types of touch to create a reflex that helps facilitate and balance muscle function, influences postural alignment, and generates energy flow. Neurovascular points on the head are also gently stimulated to soothe the energy, release emotional stress, and improve the functioning of the forebrain; this emotional stress-release technique is considered essential to releasing behavior patterns that no longer serve the recipient. Certain neurolymphatic points throughout the body that can amplify the healing potential of other acupoints are stimulated as a general energizer for the muscles and energy circuits. Other points used include energy alarm points that express painful areas, luo points, and energy lock points. Firm pressure is generally applied to all of these points. Both color and sound techniques help balance the five basic

elements (fire, wood, water, metal, and earth) and relieve mental, emotional, and physical tension. Touch for Health also offers simple self-help techniques for clients to use to release stuck energy on their own.
Contact: www.touchforhealth.us or
www.touch4health.com

Traditional Chinese Medicine (TCM)

Traditional Chinese Medicine (TCM) is an ancient internal-medicine system that is based on the five element theory, the opposite but complementary forces of yin and yang, the vital life force of chi energy, and the philosophy of Taoism. At the core of its approach to healing are methods of cultivating a balanced, harmonious flow of energy within the human body. TCM uses not only energetic practices such as meridian work, Acupuncture, moxibustion, herbalism, and pulse reading but also offers a holistic system for improving and prolonging a person's life. This system of healing includes a wide range of therapies and practices such as massage, meditation, meditative movement, breathwork, tantric energy work, and Taoist sexual yoga. Central to most practices is the use of extensive diagnostics and the treatment of underlying imbalances rather than specific symptoms. The various modalities of massage and energy transformation that come from different lineages have changed and evolved over thousands of years into separate and distinct types of bodywork.

Though it's impossible to know for sure, as in many parts of the world, most of the earliest forms of healing in China were probably performed by the spiritual doctors known today as shamans. Very little of this knowledge was written down, since it was primarily passed on verbally through the generations. However, the earliest records of Chinese medicine do reveal shamanic practices using the three forms of energy called the "three treasures," and Tang Yao, a dancing form similar to qi gong that was performed by the Tao Tang tribes to treat health problems. In addition, records from the oracle bones show that herbal remedies and stone needles played a part in healing practices.

The most significant period in the early history of Chinese medicine was around 2700 BCE, when the legendary Yellow Emperor, Huang Ti, wrote and taught about the internal-medicine therapies of Nei Ching and qi gong. Huang Ti was one of three mythical emperors who supposedly recognized healing as an art; the other two were Fu Hsi and Shen Nung. Much of what we know about the Yellow Emperor is contained in a publication known as *The Yellow Emperor's Classic of Internal Medicine* (in Chinese, *Huang Ti Nei Ching Su Wen*), which was actually first published many centuries later, in 200 BCE, and whose origins are still debated. This classic text is written in the form of a dialogue in which the emperor seeks information on the art of healing from his health minister Dr. Chi Po (or Chi Pai). When the emperor inquires about the origins of the healing wisdom and the creation of the location of acupuncture points that Dr. Chi Po has conveyed to him, the minister remarks that it was obtained from those living in ancient times who lived in complete harmony and rhythm with all the laws of nature, the elements, and the heavenly astrological cycles. Chi Po also reports that people living in this way were able to keep their bodies and souls united and resist disease, thus living long lives without needing Acupuncture or other forms of healing therapy. They were the healers of their time and knew exactly how each herbal remedy would affect their internal organs, as if they had glass abdomens through which they could see inside their bodies.

By the time of the Yellow Emperor, these internal-medicine practices recognized five elements (wood, fire, earth, metal, and water) that each corresponded to a particular sound, season, organ, flavor, emotion, color, direction, and weather condition. Reference is also made to the involved yin-yang theory of opposites along with practices such as Acupuncture, meridian channel work, moxibustion (zhenjiu), and pulse reading. These might be combined with massage, meditation, breathwork, and even a form of tantric yoga. There were many exchanges of ideas and culture throughout the different parts of Asia at that time, and historians disagree about where some of these oral traditions and practices really originated. However, we know they were present in China at this early developmental stage of Chinese medicine.

Early teachings about qi gong, the practice of linking energy work with the breath, appear around 2000 BCE. Sometime around 1000 BCE, bodywork became well recognized as a part of Chinese healing therapy. And it was about this time that the legendary Peng Tzu instituted the practice of Daoyin, in which chi is moved through abdominal breathing and physical exercise. Early writings on the philosophy that would come to fruition as the *I Ching* also appeared at this time. Around 600 BCE, the "father of the pulse," Dr. Pien Ch'ueh, wrote a book about disease and was the first to provide written information about making a diagnosis by feeling the pulse.

It was during the period of the Warring States, around 500 BCE, at a time of intellectual creativity and the promulgation of Confucianism, that Lao Tzu came on the scene. He developed his own system of gymnastics and massage, known as Laozi, which was a synthesis of Indian healing practices, qi gong, Daoyin massage, and Anmo (one of the first forms of massage to be described in writing). Within a few hundred years, Anmo was renamed Gaomo and seemed to be the most dominant modality of the day, though Tuina and qi gong were also flourishing. It is also known that Gaomo made liberal use of external liniments during a treatment. In addition, information about the use of minerals and herbs such as the "golden pill" was written down. During this period of cultural renaissance, significant medical books on Acupuncture, moxibustion, respiration, and massage were also published. Rather than being part of a spiritual quest, much of Chinese medicine revolved around the idea of strengthening the energy of the body in order to live a long life and carry this vital force into the afterlife.

Around 200 BCE, historian Suma Chien contributed significant writings on internal medicine, among which may have been the previously mentioned classic about the Yellow Emperor (though the true author and the date of this text is still debated). Others, such as An Qiao and Wei Po-Yang, wrote about Taoist alchemy, breathwork, magic potions, and different aspects of internal medicine. It was around this time that the Silk Road was becoming well established as a trading route throughout Asia. This allowed a significant and open exchange of information with India, Tibet, and areas in the Near East. In 26 CE, Li Chu Kuo made an important contribution by compiling a collection of established medical writings from previous centuries, one of which was a rewrite of *The Yellow Emperor's Classic of Internal Medicine*. This version remains one of the most significant records of early Chinese healing methods to this day.

Around 300 CE, more important contributions were made by Dr. Wang Shu He, who wrote about pulse reading and published another commentary on the legendary Yellow Emperor. Around 527 CE, the Buddhist monk and warrior Ta Mo (also referred to as Bodhidharma) arrived from India. Besides bringing Chan Buddhism to China, Ta Mo is credited with starting the practice of martial arts at the Shaolin Temple after he meditated in a cave for nine years; some amazing stories of his life have been recorded. Ta Mo was also instrumental in bringing many Indian Vedic therapies to China, including pranayama breathwork, the divine Brahman massage (the old name for yogic massage), and other yogic practices. All were assimilated into the existing practices of Chinese medicine and massage. At the time, qi gong was known to have more than 260 distinct therapies, all with wide applications. Developments of Yi Ren Gong, celestial studies, and the Complete Reality Taoism of Lu Tung-Pin were significant events of this period. Gaomo therapy regained its original name of Anmo and became the official state bodywork therapy. Soon after this time, Tuina replaced Anmo as the primary bodywork therapy taught at the Imperial Medical College.

During the ensuing 500 years, there was an upsurge of Taoist exercises and therapeutic qi gong practices. Most of the Chinese medical practices as we know them today had become established, as had Taoism, and Buddhism flourished. Bone-marrow cleansing became a well-recognized part of qi gong. Bagua continued to develop, along with Daoyin. The practice of Tai Chi was conceptualized and spread by Chang San Feng, and Tuina and Anmo gained more prominence. Bone-setting massage methods became an important practice, since surgery was not a viable option, primarily because there was nothing available to prevent infection. Around 600 CE, after years of traveling, studying herbs and alchemy, and meditating for long periods in caves, Sun Szu-Miao wrote a noteworthy book on the art of healing known as *A Thousand Ducat Prescription*. For a period of time, he was known as "the king of medicine" and lived to the age of 101. Practicing medicine in China had become a highly respected profession, but doctors were paid for services only if their treatments were successful in restoring a client's health. Physicians to the emperor's court were under great pressure, for if their efforts failed, they could be executed. However, many had good relationships with their rulers and were allowed to carry out much experimentation and research; with many energy-based practices readily at hand, they had a large mix of healing modalities and techniques at their fingertips.

Soon after 600 CE, Chinese medical practices and a number of modalities based on meridian therapy began to spread to other countries such as Japan, Korea, the Philippines, and Thailand, where further modifications and developments brought about the creation of other modalities such as Amatsu, Shiatsu, Sotai Ho, Thai Massage, Korean Hand Massage, and Jin Shin Jyutsu. Since that time, there have been many contributions to Chinese medicine, notably that of Lio Wan So, who in 1150 classified diseases into basic types. Many methods of bodywork used to treat both injuries and illness emphasized the importance of manipulations, and the treatment of infant illnesses and child massage became well established. In 1749, a group of massage therapists wrote a highly regarded book, whose title is translated as *The Golden Mirror of the Art of Healing*. This classic was the last significant publication of its type. Other modalities that stem directly from Traditional Chinese Medicine, such the Yuen Method and the Tom Tam Healing System, have been created during more recent centuries.

The history of medicine in China is complex and was often affected by the politics of each dynasty and the evolving philosophies of its time. During the earlier dynasties, medical practices reflected the interests of the emperor and the wealthy. Several times over the centuries, official doctrines limited the use of classical healing methods, whereupon unofficial "folk medicine" doctors would carry on the traditional practices in secret. Under the rule of Mao Zedong after World War II, much of what was considered spiritual in healing was again rejected and forced underground. Luckily enough of this knowledge has been retained for present use partly because certain Chinese practitioners came to the West and brought ancient traditional practices with them.

Many forms of contemporary massage have their roots in ancient Chinese medicine, but the relationship between these modalities and TCM is often hard to untangle, since the same modality may have come through different lineages and may have changed over time and evolved into separate but related types of bodywork. Additionally, Western forms of bodywork, for example, Polarity Therapy, have combined TCM with other traditions, such as Ayurveda, and a number of modalities that have been created in recent decades have incorporated elements of modern science into both Acupressure and Acupuncture. Some of these recently developed modalities often portray their therapy in terminology that glosses over the fact that concepts and aspects central to their practice come from ideas about energy flow and transformational methods contained for millennia in Traditional Chinese Medicine.

It is primarily just the history of TCM that has been discussed here, but further details about the essence, nature, and practice of all the above-mentioned modalities of Traditional Chinese Medicine and any others that stem from this tradition are discussed individually under their own headings in this and other sections of this chapter.

Contact: www.acchs.edu, www.acos.org, or
www.tcmworld.org

Tuina

One of the oldest forms of Chinese bodywork, which dates back to the Shang dynasty around 1700 BCE, Tuina, originally a form known as Yi Zhi Chan Tuina, came into prominence when chi energy work was becoming an important part of the traditional Taoist medical practices of Anmo, or Gaomo. By around 650 CE, Tuina had developed into a separate, distinct course of study at the Imperial Medical College. It was during that time that Tuina replaced Anmo as the primary form of bodywork practiced within China. It was often the case that blind people with their heightened sense of touch were practitioners of this therapy. Today, Tuina practices flourish in China and are spreading worldwide.

The therapeutic practice facilitates the healing of specific health problems by regulating and harmonizing the circulation of chi energy and blood throughout the body. With a proper flow of energy, the body is able to function properly, resist disease, and heal itself. The primary focus of the therapy is on acupressure points and energy meridians, although soft-tissue work is used to realign joints and improve the musculoskeletal relationship. *Tuina* actually means "to push, lift, and grasp," yet a great variety of techniques are used during a treatment, ranging from light, soothing sedating strokes to deep, invigorating tissue work. These manipulations can be applied in different directions, either with or against the flow of energy or spiraling inward or outward in different directions from an energy center. Each method has different effects. Rolling methods are used directly on sprains and areas with structural problems to loosen the muscles and open the channels. For example, in Gun

Fa, physical injuries or sprains are treated as the back of the hand is rotated rapidly back and forth over the skin, acting like a rolling pin. In Chan Fa, the fingers apply pressure by pushing on specific acupressure points. Formerly used for the rapid revival of people injured in martial-arts combat, Chan Fa now addresses a number of internal dysfunctions.

Practitioners of Tuina approach a treatment with awareness of the breath and of the action of the chi energy contained in their hands. The local, nearby, and distant points on the various energy channels stimulated in a treatment are the same as those used in Acupuncture. The controlled use of very deep, moving pressure is one of the key points of Tuina massage. Quite often a practitioner will use slow, deep, circular pressure that zeros in on a particular point for a moment before moving to repeat this same action at another location. The direction of the circular movement is opposite for men and women. A specific pattern of hand movements is used when manipulating the meridians and points on the recipient's body, and the effects of the work are meant to continue down through the different layers of tissue to the internal organs. The full-body treatment applies yang techniques to expel stagnant chi and activate the flow, whereas yin techniques calm and relax. Various techniques, similar to those used in present-day Shiatsu, may be employed to help loosen the muscles.

After firm but gentle kneading to open up the flow of chi, Tuina treatments incorporate vigorous rhythmic manipulations of the body using finger pressure to stimulate the chi energy by pushing and pulling. In addition, rolling, rocking, kneading, twisting, lifting, beating, patting, shaking, vibrating, pounding, scrubbing, squeezing, pressing, rotating, rubbing, waving, dragging, and grasping techniques are used to stimulate acupressure points and disperse and smooth out obstructions. Various manipulation techniques such as rolling soft tissue, one-finger pushing, and Acupressure are used for treating internal disorders. Through its numerous manipulations, Tuina establishes a more harmonic flow of chi in the whole body by balancing yin and yang; restoring deficient chi or removing excess chi; regulating, smoothing and promoting the flow of chi and blood; and improving organ functioning. Certain lubricants such as talcum powder, sesame oil, holly leaf oil, and other herbal emulsions may also be applied, especially if excessive friction from rubbing and stroking may occur. External herbal poultices, compresses, liniments, and salves may also be used during a session to enhance the healing effect.

An ancient subspecialty of Tuina known as Bone Setting realigns musculoskeletal and ligament relationship by using soft-tissue massage with the arms and hands, stimulation of acupressure points, and other manipulations. It is used primarily for injury management in cases of broken bones, dislocations, or nerve pain.

Today, Tuina clinics are found in all Chinese hospitals. Of all the different schools of Tuina that have developed over the years, the Yi Zhi Chan form is most prevalent today. It concentrates on the twelve regular meridians and the two meridians in the great central channel, the points along them, ashi pain points, and nonfixed channel points. The complete therapy may include self-massage, dietary plans, detoxifying herbs, and exercise, and special forms of Tuina can be used to treat both infant and adult digestive problems. Tuina is a highly refined system of medical massage designed to treat specific dysfunctions, particularly chronic disorders or sites of pain, and is not intended for those seeking a mild, relaxing massage.
Contact: www.tcm.health-info.org/tuina

Yantra Yoga Massage

Yantra Yoga Massage is part of the ancient Tibetan Buddhist yogic system of healing. The bodywork is an offshoot of the Yantra Yoga practice, which has similarities to Hatha Yoga and Asian chi work. The healing practices were originally attributed to the teachings of the Buddha Vairocana in the eighth century. After the Chinese invaded Tibet in 1959, the practices went underground, and in the 1960s, it was brought to the West by Lama Lobsang Palden. Rather than a set of postures, the yoga practice is a series of 108 flowing exercises in which the body moves into various positions in concert with mantras, meditations, and pranayama breathing techniques, combined in a way that circulates and revitalizes the body energies. Certain props can also be used to facilitate the holding of poses without strain. Yantra Yoga Massage brings all these elements into a form of applied bodywork.

The massage work is often used on students who have difficulty performing Yantra Yoga movements because of blocked energy channels, but can be helpful for anyone. This form of bodywork not only helps stretch and loosen muscles, but can simultaneously relax and energize the recipient. Healing sessions use gentle vibration and energy work on the chakras and energy channels, integrated into a gracefully flowing sequence. During the treatments, Acupressure, hot rocks, mantras, chants, and sacred sounds are used to move vital energy, purify the body, and open the energy channels with an increased flow of energy while balancing the mind, body, and spirit. It can be a deeply spiritual experience in which the participant simply relaxes while receiving the healing energies. At present, there are a limited number of practitioners performing this form of bodywork in the West.

Contact: www.lamalobsang.com

Yuen Method™

The Yuen Method, also known as full-spectrum healing or Chinese Energetics, is a blend of the ancient energy-transforming practices originally found in the Chinese Shaolin Temple and modern Western therapies that incorporate knowledge about anatomy, physiology, structural analysis, and quantum physics. The therapy was developed by Shaolin grand master of martial arts Dr. Kam Yuen, who was a master practitioner of Kung Fu, Tai Chi, and qi gong and became a chiropractor and homeopathic doctor as well. Besides being influenced by his grandfather, who was well known for his Acupuncture and herbal treatments, Dr. Kam Yuen was able to study a variety of traditional therapies under the guidance of Chinese-medicine master Junyu Wu. Dr. Kam Yuen abandoned a successful competitive career in martial arts when he realized that his innate understanding of energy could be used to heal others. After years of additional research in both Eastern and Western therapies, he developed his own system of full-spectrum healing to treat a myriad of manifestations of disease at a deeper, quantum level as well as to promote the art of better living. Though touch is not used in the treatment, the healing process is not considered to be a psychic practice; therapists must be rigorously trained in meditation and the principles of nonresistance and in the healing techniques once used by the Shaolin priests.

The Yuen Method eventually became a synthesis of Acupuncture, Tuina, Chiropractic Therapy, Feng Shui, qi gong, anatomy, physiology, structural analysis, herbal medicine, quantum physics, chi energy cultivation techniques, and the spiritual practice of Shen Gong. The premise of the therapy is that humans are multifaceted beings with multiple levels of consciousness and that pain is a sign that something is wrong with the flow of energy in the body. When dealing with this energy flow, the Yuen Method suggests that people have two responses to everything in life. Pain or a dysfunction indicates the flow of energy is weak, as if it has been switched off. If the flow is strong, the flow has been switched on and the body functions well.

During a treatment, muscle testing is used on the client's outstretched arm to determine where imbalances exist, based on the client's strong or weak response. Once an imbalance is located, the practitioner places attention and the intention to heal on that area and strengthens it with a variety of energy-transforming techniques that make corrections rapidly. If a client tests weak around the vertical midline of the body, the practitioner focuses attention at a weak spot on the spine to help switch the energy back on. The process continues by monitoring other weak spots along the spine and performing additional muscle tests to check whether the problems have been resolved. The Yuen Method tests for many levels of influence—emotional, physical, psychological, and spiritual—so that the client's intuition and conscious awareness can be enhanced as energy is strengthened. Even if a patient experiences the recurrence of a symptom, each session builds upon the previous one until the person is free of dysfunction. The Yuen Method is designed for those who want quick results in treating dysfunctions and hard-to-cure diseases by making energy corrections rapidly. It is often used as an adjunct therapy with other modalities and sessions can also be done remotely by phone.

Contact: www.yuenmethod.com

IX. Energy Field and Spiritual Therapies

All heavenly bodies—our earth, its sun, planets, stars—are surrounded by an invisible force field that spreads out into the space between them. Likewise, the human body (and indeed all life) is blessed with its own energy field which is not only interwoven with the physical but also interconnected with unseen realms beyond. Just as the sun's rays can affect the earth's magnetic field, vibrations from other dimensions can create fluctuations in the individual human biofield and energy anatomy. Conversely, the current condition of the inner core within the physical, whether it's the earth or the human body, can affect the surrounding field of energy. It is as though we are all heavenly bodies powerfully interconnected through the space within and around us.

Quantum physics has demonstrated that the boundless space within our universe (we call it outer space) is not empty, but full of an unnameable energetic essence that underlies and pervades all life. Since energy and matter are interchangeable on the quantum level, the inner ocean within our bodies contains the timeless and formless energy that affects all the elements of life, but like the outer oceans on our planet, there is much that is unseen and unknown. The spiritual and scientific exploration of inner space has only just started to recognize that this realm is a great repository of awareness and wisdom. The true potential of our innate healing ability will most likely lie within dimensions of reality that we have just barely touched upon. Like an iceberg, the big picture of what is ultimately possible for human beings can only be seen below the surface.

This section discusses bodywork therapies that go beyond the energetic anatomy within the body to include the etheric realms and the invisible, luminous energy field that permeates and surrounds the physical body. This energy field actually contains a progression of layers of fields that are connected to the internal energy centers and extending out from the physical body to the infinite reaches of the cosmos to the divine. Depending on the context—biological, scientific, quantum, or spiritual—it is referred to as the subtle energy body, the etheric field, the unified field, the biofield, the aura, the electromagnetic field, the bioplasmic field, the bioelectric field, the bioenergy field, the noetic field, the morphogenetic field, or the divine energy field. Each of these names is used interchangeably in the text, but mean the same thing. This multidimensional area can be considered an overlapping and interlocking dynamic matrix of subtle energies that holds the blueprint to all that we manifest, whether in the past, present, or future. It can also be described in terms of vibratory frequencies and as the domain of the more expansive higher self that exists on the soul level or in the realm of the divine. It is essential to realize that these realms, though difficult to visualize, do not pertain just to some distant heavenly place, but to the infinite possibilities within each of us. I sometimes liken energy fields to the unknown weather beyond the horizon, which is governed by the vast and ever-changing planetary atmosphere and can potentially have a direct effect on my well-being.

Although much of the following discussion about the many aspects of energy fields includes things that are hard for the pragmatic or skeptical mind to fathom, recent scientific studies have revealed and validated the presence of these ambient fields and have shown that they not only contain light, sound, and electromagnetic waves but also subtle energy and information, all of which have a significant effect on a person's health. Recent advances in electronic scanning have revealed that all living creatures have both electrical and magnetic properties that show up in the surrounding energy fields, and research has shown that these fields are constantly changing as an individual's physical, mental, and emotional health change. It has also been confirmed that defects in the energy fields can have a specific effect on the physiological functioning of the body. Some studies of the bioelectric energy fields of psychics and experienced meditators have demonstrated how strongly the mind and energy fields are connected. If you are skeptical about the existence of energy fields and the workings of vibrational energy medicine, you might want to check out the publications of James Oschman and Dr. Richard Gerber, both of whom have compiled numerous records of scientific research that verifies the fields' existence and their effect on the human body.

Treatments carried out on energy fields operate outside the familiar framework of our known reality, so it is difficult for most of us to comprehend how they work, what the effects could be, or how subtle changes that are beyond words actually occur during the healing process. This is definitely the case with some of the empathic, vibrational "miracle healers," psychics who speak with

angels or intuitives who work in and beyond the three-dimensional earthly realm of reality. The transference that happens when the healer invokes, connects, and harmonizes with the divine universal energies and uses them to enhance the energy and well-being of the

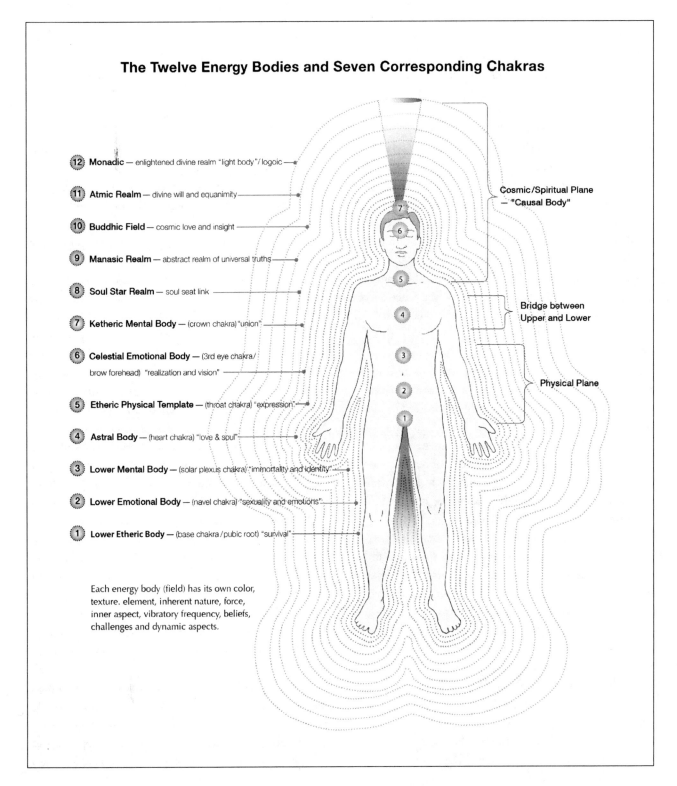

The Twelve Energy Bodies and Seven Corresponding Chakras

12 **Monadic** — enlightened divine realm "light body" / logoic

11 **Atmic Realm** — divine will and equanimity

10 **Buddhic Field** — cosmic love and insight

9 **Manasic Realm** — abstract realm of universal truths

8 **Soul Star Realm** — soul seat link

7 **Ketheric Mental Body** — (crown chakra) "union"

6 **Celestial Emotional Body** — (3rd eye chakra / brow forehead) "realization and vision"

5 **Etheric Physical Template** — (throat chakra) "expression"

4 **Astral Body** — (heart chakra) "love & soul"

3 **Lower Mental Body** — (solar plexus chakra) "immortality and identity"

2 **Lower Emotional Body** — (navel chakra) "sexuality and emotions"

1 **Lower Etheric Body** — (base chakra / pubic root) "survival"

Cosmic/Spiritual Plane — "Causal Body"

Bridge between Upper and Lower

Physical Plane

Each energy body (field) has its own color, texture. element, inherent nature, force, inner aspect, vibratory frequency, beliefs, challenges and dynamic aspects.

recipient is a subtle, felt experience shared by the two. Life teaches us that something can be recognized as real, even if it isn't fully understood. When investigating these modalities, it is best to be open-minded and take it all in. If what you find doesn't resonate with you, forget about it and don't worry, for someday it might, especially when your life experiences allow it.

The interrelationship of the energy fields and the bioelectrochemical activity in the body and in the pathways of the nervous system that determines the condition of the whole body has been recognized by adepts, yogis, and spiritual leaders in ancient Eastern cultures for thousands of years. Contemporary researchers have now begun to grasp the extent of the interrelationship of the human body, mind, and spirit and how it can offer a more holistic approach to health and healing. The time is ripe for complementary medicine's perceptive healers and therapists, those with the ability to intuitively see, sense, and feel the more subtle realms, to be welcomed with more open minds and eyes. We can hope that the influence of energy fields will soon be recognized as part of our own natural and innate ability to create a more enlightened and healthy way of life, full of vitality and love.

The therapies included in this section treat blockages, dysfunctions, and deficiencies in the energy fields primarily by enhancing and balancing the flow of energy in and around the body. Although the multidimensional fields of energy extend far beyond a person's body, most of the therapies work on the auric field, the portion of these fields that can be seen by those with extrasensory ability. According to specialists in this discipline, there are seven layers of energy fields surrounding the body, although twelve have been recognized by other enlightened souls. It is generally agreed that the seven biofields (or energy bodies) extend out from the physical body into the universe in this order: lower etheric body, lower emotional body, lower mental body, astral body, etheric physical template, celestial emotional body, and finally ketheric mental body. Although each is essentially contained within all others, these fields stretch out in layers of varying thicknesses—from a few inches to several feet beyond the physical. Each field correlates with certain human qualities and the seven chakras found within the physical body. The energy bodies close to the physical body can be seen as an aura of different colors by those with this intuitive gift; these colors reflect the condition

of each of the fields. Beyond these seven, there are an additional five energy fields that connect the physical body to the soul and to the divine infinite realm of the universe. These higher fields are also considered causal bodies in that they have the energetic capacity to influence our lives, and each has a particular deep connection to our ultimate state of existence here on earth. Expanding outward in every dimension, these higher-self fields are referred to as the soul star realm, manasic realm, buddhic field, atmic realm, and the monadic realm, though other names have also been used. There are only a few modalities in which intuitive practitioners work with these subtle realms, but since we are each innately connected with these fields, it is possible for us to learn how to make contact with them.

Many of the therapies that work with energy fields believe that a problem in the physical body is caused by imbalances in the biofields, since this is where the physical body's blueprint exists; therefore, working on these fields will have a direct effect on the health of the physical body. However, some of these modalities do use the body's internal energy pathways to influence the fields around the body. In most cases, there is very little actual physical contact made during the treatment session. Energy healers will instead use highly refined intuition, sensory perception, energy-based disciplines, or altered meditative states of loving consciousness to enable them to effectively scan, feel, or see mental and emotional blocks in the energy field. Once intuitive healers have identified weaknesses or disease in the physical body by observing variations in the colorful spiral vortices of energy in the aura, they can proceed to use subtle methods to alleviate any imbalances and restore equilibrium.

Practitioners of energy field therapies may use a number of techniques to help an individual recognize and clear problems that arise either within the surrounding energy fields or in the body's energetic anatomy. Each healer has particular personal abilities and may use a combination of healing methods, including akashic-record sensing and reading, alpha and beta process work, ascension process work, attunements, auric massage techniques, awareness release techniques, bioenergetic analysis, body scanning, breathwork, chakra balancing, channeling the assistance of spirit guides, clairvoyance (seeing), clairaudience (hearing), core star healing, crystal healing, distance healing, DNA processing, dowsing or chakra dowsing with a pendulum or aura meter, Egyptian emotional clearing, electromagnetic therapy, energetic chelation, esoteric healing techniques, etheric pulse restructuring, etheric source point activation, extracellular matrix modification, field restructuring, gemstone healing, geometric or vibrational repatterning, hara cleansing, harmonic sound healing, hypnosis, hologram grid work, holographic resonance repatterning, illuminations, incantations, karmic cleansing release work, love-light frequency restoration, magnetic radiatory healing, magnified healing, meditation, multi-incarnational methods, mystical union methods, paramatmic healing, past-life regression work, pattern clearing, pranic energy work, prayers, psychospiritual integration, quantum techniques, rebirthing techniques, reflective healing, sacred healing methods, shamanics, soul-focused healing, spinal cleaning, techniques for running energy, thought field intervention, transference, vibrational energy intervention, and visualizations. (Whew!)

Many of these transformative forms of healing have elements that have been applied in similar ways within and around the human body for hundreds of years, and many may use similar methods to activate the healing process. There is often a fine line between the differences in each of these modalities, since their essences are closely related. Each in its own way uses the practitioner as a catalyst in awakening the innate healing ability of the recipient. The healing process may be a dynamic dance of energetic relationships in which the practitioner and recipient's biofields join together. Some of these therapies are also integrated with basic energy work and other types of treatment that have more physical contact.

Practitioners of energy field therapies often incorporate reflective healing, which involves the use of guided imagery and energetic manipulations done without physical contact. Guided imagery is an interactive process of visualization and relaxation that uses the imagination and verbal directives to influence a person's mental state and emotional health. Imagery works with the natural language of the unconscious mind and has a powerful influence on stimulating all vital functions of the human body.

In most types of auric or energy field healing, the practitioner, who has already entered a meditative state, begins by accessing the recipient's inner core and tuning in to the invisible energy field. The process of scanning

for disturbances, recognizing and evaluating imbalances, removing energy blocks, restructuring broken parts of the etheric field, balancing the flow of interlocking fields with the internal energy pathways, and replenishing the client's energy system requires the practitioner's full attention, loving compassion, heightened perception, and focused intention. Through entrainment with the healer's energies (including any divine energies passing through), the recipient can experience a shift in perception that can open the doorway to deep inner awareness. This change in consciousness can awaken innate healing abilities and lead to powerful release and transformation. Because energy is capable of connecting and resonating at a deep soul level beyond space and time, these practices can also be carried out for distance healing. The number of treatments necessary will depend not only on the severity of a person's particular dysfunction but also on the intensity of the wish to heal and the depth of spiritual awakening desired.

You may notice that there are several methods of purely spiritual healing in this section that do not really fall into the category of biofield therapies. Spiritual healing goes beyond most recognized forms of bodywork, but since energy field work reaches into the infinite realms where our spiritual essence is found, this section seemed an appropriate place to include these modalities. From a spiritual standpoint, it is wise to recognize that in every moment of our existence, the physical body is sustained by the spirit and the energy it contains.

Although, as with any form of bodywork, you may need to consider personal issues that might be contraindications to this kind of therapy, in general it is difficult to misuse the energy that we receive since it often simply goes where it is needed, even if we don't recognize this need. Certain people may have psychological issues for which other forms of therapy are more suitable. But since many of these methods of laying-on of hands do not involve direct contact with the skin or manipulations of the body, they are suitable for those individuals who are don't like to be touched, are overly sensitive to touch, or have particular injuries or conditions that would make contact ill advised.

Most significant changes happen only when we are ready for them, and they are often the culmination of a number of small changes. The primary ingredient that allows any transformation to happen is the loving intention to resolve issues, patterns, and habits that no longer serve us well. If we listen, our heart and soul will tell us which modalities fill them with longing.

Advanced Energy Healing

This intuitive, spiritually guided, and loving approach to healing, formerly known as the Awareness Release Technique (ART), was developed by Dr. Robert Jaffe as an active way to release blocked energy and clear all negative patterns that cause suffering within both the body and the matrix of the energy fields. It involves a journey into higher realms to invoke the spirit and connect clients with their divine higher selves so their subtle electromagnetic energies can resonate with the universal creative force. Its goal is to remove dysfunctional patterns, to integrate gratitude with increased self-awareness, and to create a state in which consciousness is aligned with the soul.

The therapy uses aura analysis and clairvoyant diagnosis to evaluate the recipient's energy fields for core wounds and energy leaks. The practitioner uses his intuitive skills to scan for disturbances in the energy field and then carries out soul merging and third-eye awakening along with a process known as magnetic radiatory healing, which is a heart-centered technique that uses higher soul frequencies to help release and remove energetic disharmony. A treatment session employs chakra work, pranic energy work, breathwork, and methods of restructuring the energy fields. The therapy is considered complementary to other forms of medical treatment.

Over the years, Dr. Jaffe has expanded this advanced form of energy healing into a full-spectrum modality that is called the Heart Energy Awareness Release Technique (HEART). This healing process works to clear all energetic and emotional patterns that cause suffering by opening up the potential for unconditional self-love within the heart. HEART focuses on releasing emotional trauma or restrictive belief systems that create blockages that drain physical vitality, sabotage personal happiness, and limit the ability to feel, receive, and express more love. The process works on reconnecting specific areas in the body with newly directed self-love from the heart.
Contact: www.drjaffemd.com

Amanohuna

Amanohuna, which means "the abundance of the right way of life" in Hawaiian, is a very high frequency feminine energy that is complementary to and comparable with Reiki energy. Part of an ancient healing system that was rediscovered by massage therapist, clinical psychologist, and Reiki master Arthur Cataldo when he received a channeled teaching in Hawaii in 1984, Amanohuna uses tonal sound and symbols to activate healing energies. Energy is acquired through an attunement ceremony in which channeling, chanting, and toning bring in sacred healing frequencies. These sounds can help a person feel relaxed, stay energetically connected, and maintain a state of enhanced wellness. Amanohuna has ten degrees of activation that retune all twelve chakras, the solar plexus, and the energy fields with progressively higher frequencies. This enables an individual to balance the physical, emotional, mental, causal, and spiritual energy bodies and become more grounded and powerful. After working on the lower chakras, the attunements of degrees six through ten assist in gaining access into the higher dimensions by working with the five transpersonal spiritual chakras above the crown chakra on the head that are related to the cosmic energy fields. This process can help turn on unexpressed genes in DNA, connect a person to the soul body, and unite the recipient with the energy fields of the earth, the solar system, the galaxy, and the universe. When all twelve chakras are activated and retuned, individuals can ultimately grow into their true natures as cosmic beings and become one with all that is.
Contact: www.metaphys.com/practitioners/bford.html

ARCH™ (Ancient Rainbow Conscious Healing)

Reiki master Laurie Grant instituted this form of healing after a spontaneous visionary healing experience through kahunas (priests) in Hawaii. ARCH essentially uses ancient shamanic healing techniques to help people remember their true selves. This divine vibrational and energetic healing method is said to be able to tap into the very high frequency energy of the creator, which can be transmitted through the hands directly to a person or at a distance and heals instantaneously. This approach can be seen as a healing process in which all the frequencies of the multicolored rays of life-force energy are received.

ARCH uses ritual, images, and the full spectrum of colors in rainbow light to promote a conscious healing that goes to the root of the problem and removes the energy blockages that are responsible for any dysfunction.

The healing is also considered to be a bridge to oneness with the divine source located in the cosmic realms. This spiritual healing method is considered to be a quantum leap beyond Reiki therapy because it deals with a higher divine source of energy. ARCH places emphasis on honoring the body and removing energetic blockages so the recipient can wake up to his own divine true nature.
Contact: www.archhealing.com

Attunement Therapy

Attunement is a sacred healing therapy that originated during the 1930s after Lloyd Arthur Meeker experienced a spiritual awakening in which he was able to acknowledge the presence of his divine self. In the 1940s, he developed a spiritual ministry and an intentional community to further enhance and share the principles of self-awareness. Under the pen name Uranda, he wrote, spoke, and developed Attunement Therapy, a spiritual practice of clarifying, deepening, and aligning the capacities for personal expression with one's true identity through the sharing of the radiant energy of being (love). Attunement works directly with the energy of being/self. This sacred therapy focuses and balances the seven levels of radiant energy contained in a person's being as expressed through and differentiated by the seven endocrine glands. Attunement healing work uses stillness, listening, and energetic bodywork to release any nonresonating vibrations and to encourage a balanced expression of love, light, forgiveness, and gratitude in living. In Attunement Therapy, emphasis is placed on releasing the client's radiant presence. Health and healing come from the individual.

An Attunement Therapy session will balance the flow of a being's energy through the endocrine glands and other body systems that regulate growth, metabolic processes, and the various activities of the organs. Each endocrine gland is said to be a portal of radiant light energy, a unique focus of a level of spiritual self-expression whereby a greater expression of one's presence can be made manifest. Many other holistic forms of energy healing are used to complement the attunement process. Attunement Therapy includes nontouch, light touch, and long-distance work and can be used to balance energy fields to assist individuals before and after surgery or any other invasive treatment. Practitioners may integrate energetic work on the chakras and the nervous system (the other complementary energy system in the

human body) with other healing and energetic balancing techniques such as sound, color, sacred geometry, prayer, and toning.
Contact: International Association of
Attunement Practitioners –
www.attunementpractitioners.org or
Heartland Attunement –
www.heartattune.com

Auric Healing

Auric healing is a process that involves special subtle-energy harmonizing work on the auric biofields, the energy fields that surround the denser physical body. The aura can be described as a network of layers of interrelated energy fields that vibrate at a higher frequency than the physical body and relate not only to a person's emotional, mental and spiritual states but also reflect the state of the physical body. The intuitive healer can see or sense the color and condition of the aura around the whole body and around the individual chakras. The various colors of the aura in and around the body portray particular known qualities and are often used as a clue about where a restrictive or positive condition exists. These colors can change with changes in a person's condition. After this evaluation is made, the healer moves the energy around in such a way as to open up blockages and release patterns that are unhealthy. This involves subtle methods of opening and moving energies for the purpose of cleansing and balancing, and is often done without physical contact. The various colors of the aura can also be seen with special types of photography, which is sometimes used to educate the client.
Contact: www.aurichealing.co.nz or
www.aurichealingonline.com

Bi-Aura®

In the 1990s, after years of studying complementary energy medicine, Maire Dennhofer established this form of therapy to help clear unhealthy congestion in the aura and chakras. In 2000, she established the Bi-Aura Foundation in England to further the teachings and development of this bioenergy healing therapy. The intention of Bi-Aura is to remove overwhelming stress and trauma and enhance the free flow of healing energy. The therapy focuses on two major energy centers: the root chakra at the base of the spine, which draws in earth energy, and the crown chakra at the top of the head, which takes in cosmic energy from the universe. Practitioners are trained to tune in to blockages and then to manipulate the biofield with very little physical contact. The aim is not to heal, but to restore the energy that can allow the client's body to do its own healing. When all seven chakras in the body spin correctly and in balance, the energy flows freely and nourishes the body and its organs.

A session begins with the practitioner's hands scanning the fully clothed client's energy field from the bottom of the spine to top of the head to identify and release any possible blockages, often without touching the body. The hands are considered to be magnets that pull congested energy out of the client's field and release it out to the universe. Once this detoxification of the energy centers is complete, the practitioner transmits fresh cosmic energy into the client. After the client's energy field has been cleared and energized, a second scan may be performed to determine if further treatment is needed. The complete process is usually done with the client standing, and gentle music and aromatherapy can complement a session. Treatments generally require a minimum of four sessions to be most effective.
Contact: www.bi-aura.com

Bioenergy Therapy

Bioenergy Therapy is a modality that works with the currents of vital life-force energy within both the body and a person's external electromagnetic energy field. Although this healing therapy is used mostly in Europe, its roots are found in the ancient energetic healing practices of India, China, and Tibet. It was established as a distinct therapy in the 1980s by Polish-born healer Mietek Wirkus, who had shown special healing abilities as a boy. In 1982, Bioenergy was officially approved in Poland to supplement the work of medical professionals. The therapy embraces the importance of maintaining a balanced flow of energy between energy points in the body and within the energy field. This healing method uses Tibetan breathing, meditation exercises, and Therapeutic Touch, and it focuses on the chakras, which serve as distribution centers for the life-force energy that emanates from the energy fields that surround the body.

During a session, the therapist uses light physical touch that combines the manipulations used in various forms of bodywork with an energetic process of repatterning the higher energy bodies and chakras. The

healer acts as a channel, allowing positive energy to flow through one hand while the other hand extracts negative energy from the recipient. The goal is to stimulate relaxation by reducing stress and releasing the root causes of physical symptoms associated with dysfunction or disease. This approach to healing recognizes the body-mind connection and endeavors to trigger a physiological change by enhancing the flow of energy within the chakras and energy fields.
Contact: www.mietekwirkus.com

Brazilian Light Energization™

This energizing process was developed by Brazilian healer Mauricio Panisset. It is said that people saw flashes of light soaring out of his body when he performed a healing. His widow, Kimberly Panisset-Curcio, continues his work by training other healers in the process at the Delphi University, which was founded by Patricia Hayes in 1974.

Brazilian Light Energization is a systematic energy initiation that invokes higher spiritual frequency pulsations of love and light from the cosmic realms to align with and modulate a person's biofields and psychic awareness. This sacred process is accomplished by changing the pitch of the electromagnetic currents in the recipient's energy field, invoking the divine blueprint of her DNA with the help of spirit guides, and expanding and balancing the major chakras of her body. The idea is that by opening up blockages in the chakras, a person's capacity to receive universal energy is increased. Awakening the kundalini energy and bringing it up through the chakras enables those intent on spiritual awakening to have a mystical experience that connects them with their inner spirit.
Contact: Delphi University & Spiritual Center –
www.delphiuniversity.us

Brennan Healing Science® (BHS)

Brennan Healing Science is a complete energy-healing experience developed by Barbara Brennan, an intuitive, author of *Hands of Light, Light Emerging,* and other books, and founder of the Barbara Brennan School of Healing®, which is dedicated to the evolution of the human spirit and offers teachings at various locations around the world. Brennan Healing Science combines hands-on healing techniques that work through the human energy field with spiritual and psychological processes touching every aspect of life. Based on the dynamics of the human energy-consciousness system and its relationship to the greater world of which all are a part, this method is intended to transform a person's life into the balanced, enlightened experience of mystery that was always desired.

The luminous human energy field, also known as the aura, with its infinite number of higher frequency levels, is recognized as the deep, quantum level of personality in which psychological processes and psychosomatic reactions take place. Since the physical body arises out of the energy field, any imbalances or distortions in this field will eventually cause disease in the physical body; therefore, it is essential to heal these distortions so the body can heal. The system acknowledges the psychological aspects of the chakras and their related energy field and how these energetic elements create and affect a person's reality in terms of relative health and illness. Brennan Healing Science propels this wisdom of the ancients into several new, sophisticated dimensions in which behavioral patterns, personal issues, and past histories are addressed. An extensive curriculum with a choice of programs is available for those who wish to study at the school. Intention, integrity, and professional responsibility are the cornerstones of the method.

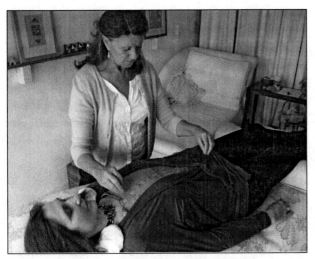

Practitioner balancing the chakras.

Practitioners are well trained in higher sense perception, acute self-awareness, and integrative care and have learned how to read the energy field and discern why it is damaged or distorted. They call on a vast array of healing techniques, including hands-on methods, to bring physical, emotional, mental, and spiritual health into being in a compassionate and transformative way. Personal transformation that brings about a greater understanding of the body is a major component. Healings may also incorporate a practice known as the Hands of Light® as a way to establish a deeper connection with the heart's true longings, strengthen intentions, reinstate healthy core beliefs, and increase awareness of energy dynamics.

Since no set of rules can fully anticipate or regulate the variety of situations that a practitioner may face, in any given session, BHS practitioners may employ varied techniques and incorporate elements of multiple modalities depending on the unique circumstances and needs of each client and the level of the practitioner's training. The bodywork can be spiritually transformative for clients, especially when removing various types of dysfunctions and blockages that restrict the flow of vital energy through the client's body. Practitioners are trained to use auditory and visual sensing to directly access and interpret the conditions of the auric energy fields. Then the practitioner's hands bring in the healing light that will gently release and cleanse the energy fields and the energetic anatomy of the body. A variety of noninvasive techniques of laying-on of hands are employed, with or without direct touch, that assist energy transference and healing in different dimensions in and around the client's body. Other elements, all of which help the recipient unite with the spark of divinity and the higher self within, include restructuring all seven layers of the auric field, balancing the corresponding chakras and the channels through which energy flows, and stimulating the vertical power current, or energy hose, that interconnects the chakras and energy bodies. This healing process is often used for people with emotional issues or imbalances, yet it is effective for anyone wishing to live life fully.

Sessions may include breathwork, color therapy, sound healing, geometric repatterning, chelation energy charging, running energy through the body, spinal cleansing, hara (abdominal organ) cleansing, etheric template healing, restructuring of the auric grid, Reiki work, core star healing, pendulum dowsing, the use of time capsules, guided imagery, rebirthing techniques, centering meditations, and channeling with the use of spirit guides. At the close of a session, the restructured energy is sealed with a protective energy shield. The goal of this deep energy-healing process is to empower the recipient's own healing potential on all levels—emotional, physical, mental and spiritual. As with many forms of healing, the degree of success depends on a recipient's active desire to receive and the strength of his commitment to be open.

Contact: Barbara Brennan School of Healing –
www.barbarabrennan.com

Chelation Therapy /
Bruyere Energy Medicine

This form of energy medicine was developed by Rev. Rosalyn Bruyere, a pioneer intuitive energy practitioner who established the Healing Light Center Church, which sponsors workshops worldwide that focus on energy healing, the chakras, auras, and the body's energy systems. Her methods are influenced by her ability to see energy, her own scientific studies on the electromagnetic field, and her involvement with sacred geometry, ancient mystery schools, Egyptian temple symbology, Tibetan Bön practices, and Native American healing. Bruyere has collaborated with physicians and scientists to study the effects of energy medicine and teaches energy-based techniques in clinical settings. A significant part of her hands-on energy work, known as Chelation Therapy (not to be confused with the chelation treatment that works to remove heavy metals from the body), is used to clear restrictions in the flow of vital energy from the inner energetic pathways and energy fields. Although more of a technique then a complete modality, Chelation Therapy can still be the primary part of a body-work session. The intention of this healing process is to remove stagnant or blocked energy by lifting it from the client and then filling and balancing the aura with fresh healing energy, allowing the recipient to experience inner peace, renewed lightness, and the absence of pain.

The therapy works first on the lower physical vibrations in the lower chakras before moving into the more subtle energetic vibrations found in the higher chakras. The practitioner acts as a conduit of universal energy and begins the process by gradually drawing energy up from the earth and into the soles of the recipient's feet, then guiding it through the lower chakras and slowly upward in stages through the other chakras to the crown of the head. This process cleans, repairs, and charges the chakra energy centers while opening the pathways. Actually touching the body is considered to have more of an effect than if the hands are held away from the body, so the therapist places both hands on different areas of

the body and holds them there for a certain period of time in order to invite the energy to flow upward. Special attention is given to skeletal joints (the location of numerous secondary chakras) in which energy is often trapped. This stagnant energy can be scooped or pulled out, and then fresh energy is pumped in and directed to where it is most needed. When the chakras are in balance, their spins return to a natural clockwise rotation, which enables the healthy functioning of the energy system. Chelation Therapy can be performed on its own, but is more often part of healing modalities that work to activate the vital life force.

Contact: Healing Light Center Church –
www.rosalynbruyere.org

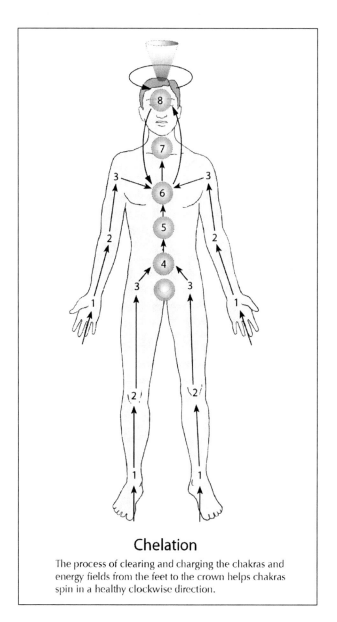

Chelation

The process of clearing and charging the chakras and energy fields from the feet to the crown helps chakras spin in a healthy clockwise direction.

Christopher Method

The Christopher Method is a form of energy therapy that utilizes sound waves. It originated with Christopher Benham in 1995 and works without physical touch on the multiple energy fields of the body in order to restore psychological, physiological, and emotional balance.

During the treatment, the high-frequency vibrations of light and sound within the cosmic realm are passed through the practitioner's aura to the recipient's aura to clear blocked energy, restore and reinforce natural polarity, and align and strengthen proper energy flow. These vibrational frequencies continually run through the healer's hands throughout the session and can be stored in the recipient for a long period of time, during which they are subtly working through various blockages of energy. The overall intent of this method is not only relaxation and healing but also to create a resonance through which a feeling of oneness and well-being can be established and further imbalances that might also cause illness prevented.
Contact: www.massage-christopherbenham.co.uk

Divine Clairvoyant Channeling

Channeling is not so much a form of hands-on bodywork, but rather the process by which a psychic, medium, or clairvoyant makes contact energetically with spirits in other realms. It generally involves communicating in an altered state of consciousness with other dimensions and supernatural beings, such as guardian spirits, deities, ascended masters, guardian angels, extraterrestrials, spirits of the dead, or the higher self. Channeling may be spontaneous or arrive through a trance induced by meditation, prayer, self-hypnosis, fasting, dancing, chanting, breathing techniques, or hallucinogenic drugs. Most often, the channeler is partially or totally aware of the process, but channelers can also enter an altered state in which their personalities are displaced when another entity takes temporary possession and speaks with a different voice and gestures, often producing some physical or psychokinetic manifestations. In this case, they are often completely unaware of what is being said during a session and have no memory of it when they come out of the trance. Other practitioners can receive information through dreams. The channeling process may also increase the healer's spiritual awareness of another person's auric field. The messages conveyed through the process itself and through the practitioner's intuitive questioning can give the recipient new insights, answer questions, and provide comfort, all of which may enable healing.

Communicating with other dimensions was an integral part of early shamanism, and conversing with gods while in a trance was a highly developed practice among the priestly classes of many ancient cultures. Divinations and healings were also performed by wizards, witches, and some prophets. In more recent times, the channeling of higher entities was accomplished by masters such as Barbara Brennan (Heyoan), Jach Pursel (Lazaris), Jane Roberts (Seth), J. Knight (Ramtha), Pat Rodegast (Emmanuel), Elizabeth Prophet (Saint Germain), and the clairvoyant spiritual teacher Alton Kamadon. Each practitioner uses different methods to spontaneously or intentionally receive these messages, whether it's in a reading requested by a client or a communication dictated by a divine entity. Besides those who created modalities found in this chapter, numerous channelers practice at Spiritualist churches and can also be found within the Theosophical Society.
Contact: www.spiritualclairvoyencechanneling.com,
www.theosophical.org, or www.nsac.org

Dynamic Energetic Healing® (DEH)

This energy-based psychospiritual therapy blends Process Oriented Psychology, core shamanic practices, ancient Eastern therapies, and a number of contemporary body-oriented energy therapies to intervene in a way that identifies, releases, and eliminates the energetic origins of restrictive emotional, mental, and spiritual conditions. It is also intended as an alternative to the overuse of antidepressants and hours of talk therapy for individuals suffering from post-traumatic stress disorder, depression, addictions, anxiety disorders, and even the effects of unconscious painful past-life memories held within the energy fields. DEH was created in the late 1990s through the collaboration of a group of professional therapists that included Howard Brockman, Mary Hammond, and Nancy Gordon. The principal aim is to remove mind-body-spirit restrictions that continue to interfere with the client's stated therapeutic goals, such as eliminating anxiety or having a mutually respectful and loving adult relationship.

The shamanic techniques of journeying, soul retrieval, and drumming are employed to help determine the root cause of a psychological dysfunction or illness, and practitioner training leads to developing the skills of a psychopomp. Soul retrieval involves the process of journeying to find fragments of a person's soul that have split off during a traumatic event. Psychopomps are guides who assist the passage to the next world for souls of the dead that are unable or unwilling to move on; this method of intervention is used when a deceased person's spirit is attached to or intruding into a client's energy field in a way that creates mental or emotional problems. When the unwanted and often disoriented spirit is freed and sent away from the client's energy field, guided by one of the facilitator's helping spirits, the client will be able to function in a healthier way, no longer emotionally compromised. In addition to these shamanic techniques, DEH employs body-oriented therapies (many originating within the Energy Psychology discipline), such as Applied Kinesiology (muscle testing), Thought Field Therapy, the Emotional Freedom Technique, the Tapas Acupressure Technique, and Neuro Linguistic Programming, to further help individuals become empowered, achieve their goals, find their soul's purpose, and live their passions.

Treatments are conducted in a co-created sacred space. The practitioner begins by muscle testing the client to identify the issues that need healing and the way in which they should be treated. The treatment that follows is not regimented, but remains flexible so that issues can be dealt with as they arise. Trained practitioners learn how to follow the client's process with increasingly heightened awareness, and as the treatment progresses, muscle testing is repeated to gain feedback on how the client is responding to the treatment. The client sits or stands during the muscle testing as traumatic residue is methodically mapped out; this includes the client's negative thoughts and traumatic life patterns. Drumming or auditory frequencies provided by chimes, Tibetan bowls, or rattles are frequently used during a treatment. As needed, the client can be aided and empowered by somatic emotional therapies, regression techniques, energetic boundaries therapy, and past-life work. DEH also works to clear the biofield with simple energetic strategies such as tapping meridian points and balancing the chakras. This helps the client access the soul's purpose, deepen intuition, and embrace a spiritual outlook on life. This multifaceted approach also gives the client simple, concrete, and practical self-administered techniques that can be used after the session to further deepen the healing that has occurred during the session. Contact: www.dynamicenergetichealing.com

Eden Energy Medicine (EEM)

Eden Energy Medicine is a health and wellness modality based on the methods taught by Donna Eden, a healer, teacher, and author of *Energy Medicine* and *Energy Medicine for Women*. The aim of this comprehensive therapy, rooted in traditional Chinese medicine, Applied Kinesiology, and other systems of energy healing, is to cultivate and balance the energies within the body and the surrounding energy fields in noninvasive ways and to enhance physical, emotional, and spiritual health. EEM empowers the energy anatomy through a set of holistic healing techniques that empower people's innate healing abilities and assist in their evolution in adapting to modern stresses. EEM uses energy as the medicine and holds the belief that energy is the prime mover behind all we see and feel.

Eden Energy Medicine recognizes nine different energy systems in and around the body—the meridians, the chakras, the aura, the Celtic weave, the basic grid, the five rhythms, the triple warmer, the radiant circuits, and the electrics. The meridians and chakras are part of the human internal energy system, and the aura contains the energy fields surrounding the body. The Celtic weave is an ever-changing web of bright, woven, crisscrossing energies that form different patterns of various sizes through and around the body; this pattern is often a spiraling figure eight. The basic grid is the foundational field of energy underlying the rest of the energetic anatomy; working with the grid is a very advanced process. The five rhythms are considered the building blocks of the universe that direct the tone and mood of all the energy systems of the body. The triple warmer refers to one of the twelve regular meridians, which functions specifically to mobilize energy for the immune system during any time of trauma. The radiant circuits are the extraordinary meridians that act as a back-up system to deliver energy to the other meridians when they are deficient in energy. Electrics pertains to the subtle cellular and electromagnetic energy system that interconnects with all the other energy systems. Energy testing, similar to kinesthetic muscle testing, is used in EEM to evaluate the energy systems as well as assess the progress of the work being done.

Eden Energy Medicine is both a practitioner-applied and a self-care modality of energy work. Underlying the effectiveness of this therapy is the ability of the practitioner to perceive the subtle energies within and around the body. An integral part of the therapy is teaching clients how to maintain health and stimulate the flow of energy throughout their own body as part of a daily self-care.

During a session, shared exercises, the application of pressure to specific points on the body, and work in the subtle energy field around the body may be used to balance energy systems. These subtle healing techniques can stimulate or sedate energies in the meridians, boost vitality and stamina, strengthen the immune system, relieve physical and emotional pain, sharpen the mind and memory, and balance hormones. Many of the energetic techniques are also intended to reduce energy drain, make connections for better flow of energy to where it is needed, unscramble the biofield, and increase metabolism.

With her husband, David Feinstein, Eden has written several widely available books about her practices and established Innersource to offer workshops and resources for EEM. Eden Energy Medicine practitioners are certified through an intensive multi-year training program administered by Innersource in Ashland, Oregon.
Contact: www.innersource.net

EMF Balancing Technique®

The EMF (Electromagnetic Field) Balancing Technique®, developed by Peggy Dubro, is a thirteen-phase series of energy-balancing techniques, which is based on scientifically proven research that acknowledges that human energy fields are made up of electromagnetic energy. These fields store energy from past events, which can create repetitive patterns that prevent people from reaching their fullest potential. EMF works to release or transform this energy without the recipient's having to relive any past emotional traumas. The therapy is designed to clear and balance the energy fields and strengthen the central channel through which a person receives and holds energy from the universe. The balancing process works with the Universal Calibration Lattice® (UCL), which is a twelve-chakra system in the human energy anatomy that connects each person to the cosmic energy lattice of the universe. The goal of EMF is to clear and amplify the flow in all the energy centers of the body and throughout the Universal Calibration Lattice with a technique that aligns and balances the electromagnetic field.

The first four phases of the technique are arranged in a series, with each session using a precise sequence of graceful movements combined with words of spoken intent to facilitate a powerful realignment and awakening of more supportive energy patterns. The first phase works to release stress and establish a new pattern of freedom by balancing the energies of the head and heart and clearing the way for more harmony and wisdom. The next phase focuses on providing self-direction and support by working with the energy of stored emotional issues. In the third phase, the movements of the practitioner facilitate activating, intensifying, and radiating core energy within the chakras that can enhance the possibility of being more centered and dealing better with stress. The fourth phase focuses on empowering the client to joyfully create the awakened inner ability

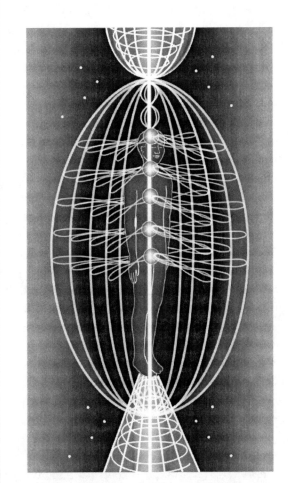

Electric Magnetic Field and Universal Calibration Lattice

to determine her own reality and accomplish things beyond what previous limitations allowed. Upon completion of the four phases, an individual can choose to repeat any that seem appropriate for her needs or continue with another of the thirteen phases.

Before a session, the practitioner familiarizes the recipient with the basic principles of EMF and the UCL. As the client lies comfortably on a therapy table, the practitioner uses a series of graceful, Tai Chi–like movements with the hands passing around and through the recipient's UCL energy field to guide and facilitate the flow of the universal energy into her energetic anatomy. During the clearing process, some gentle touching of the chakras is employed to stretch the fibers of energy and to facilitate the flow of energy. This is followed by a balancing process in which the practitioner's hands are placed on or above the chakras. The practitioner always follows the precise movements of the technique and is a clear channel for the flow of energy from the cosmic lattice to the UCL. This attitude allows the results of the session to always be determined by the inner wisdom of the recipient without any judgment by or perceptions of the practitioner. Depending on the intention of the client, results can simply reduce stress or be life transforming.

Contact: EMF Worldwide –
www.emfbalancingtechnique.com

The **Tulsi Biofeedback Imaging System** is a closely related form of energy field therapy, which was developed by clinical psychologist Dr. Tulsi Milliken, who trained with Peggy Dubro. This energy-healing therapy focuses on the root cause of a number of human dysfunctions and incorporates elements of EMF in conjunction with Reiki healing, aura analysis, spiritual counseling, life coaching, color therapy, plant therapy, elements of Matrix Energetics, and other forms of energy work found in Chinese medicine. During a session, subconscious core beliefs are accessed and released to provide greater mental and emotional freedom. Counseling assists clients in learning how to effectively use the law of attraction by changing their thoughts and feelings. The therapy also incorporates an advanced biofeedback imaging system to better assess and treat any form of dysfunction within the client.

Contact: www.inphase.com

Energy Interference Patterning (EIP)

Energy Interference Patterning, developed by Margaret Ruby, is based on the concept that certain thoughts and beliefs that are part of an individual's character have been passed down through his genetic history and are stored within his DNA. These subconscious core beliefs often contain low-frequency vibrations of emotions that distort the DNA and create limiting patterns that can have a significant effect on the way he creates his reality and that can cause unhealthy reactions to life events. This form of therapy is intended to provide an immediate transformative shift in habitual response patterns that will free a person from physical and emotional limitations or dysfunctions.

During a session, EIP works on a deep cellular level to establish better communication between all the systems of the body by eliminating restrictive patterns. After the practitioner identifies the negative core beliefs through a diagnostic process in which the client relaxes and answers some simple questions, a series of brief guided meditations are used to clear the beliefs from the DNA and imprint new, positive affirmations in their place. Limiting patterns are cleared out of the client's spine, organs, chakras, and psyche with energetic methods that work with strong intention and unconditional love on a karmic and soul level. Old behaviors no longer automatically occur, and with the improved intuition provided by this therapy, a person can be free to make better choices in life.

Contact: www.eipdna.com or www.possibilitiesdna.com

Energy Medicine (EM) / TYLEM™

TYLEM stands for Transform Your Life through Energy Medicine. It was developed in 1996 by Dr. Mary Jo Bulbrook, a clinical specialist in psychiatric mental health nursing, spiritual and medical intuitive, and academic. The methods of TYLEM come from her worldwide lectures, training, and practice using her holistic nursing theory, Healing From Within and Without, which was first presented in the 1980s at the International Nursing Diagnosis Conference in Calgary, AB, Canada.

Since then, the focus of TYLEM has been to promote body, mind, emotional, and spiritual health and healing using a variety of original, innovative, energy-based interventions to cleanse the body of any blocks or dysfunction and to balance and repair the energy flow.

Dr. Bulbrook founded the Energy Medicine Partnership to spread TYLEM throughout the world, making it more accessible to all people. Energy Medicine Partnership programs are linked to Akamai University, an accredited, distant education university headquartered in Hawaii, where a person can receive college credit for TYLEM training at the diploma, master, and doctoral level. TYLEM was influenced by Dr. Bulbrook's collaborative work with Therapeutic Touch, Touch for Health, and Healing Touch. All three of these modalities helped shape TYLEM. The philosophical underpinnings contributed by Virginia Satir, the friend and colleague who was the founder of family therapy, added a family-based, transcultural, psychospiritual flavor to the work.

Treatment with TYLEM is a co-creative process using subtle energy assessment, energetic diagnosis, energetic interventions, and evaluation to address all forms of physical, emotional, mental, and spiritual dysfunction by treating simple and complex energy patterns. A combination of the following energetic aspects serves as the foundational work in TYLEM: energy centers (chakras), energy fields, the aura, energy tracts (meridians), central power current (hara), light expansion (core star), interfering energies, and fragmented energies that can block functioning. TYLEM helps remove any blockages in energy flow and reinstate a proper, balanced flow of energy throughout the person.

During a session, an in-depth energetic assessment and intake is used to identify the recipient's needs, problems, and issues. This is followed with a meditative process to ensure the highest level plan of action guided by spirit. It can include drawings, the use of inspirational cards, and, based on the energetic assessment, the choice of the specific interventions that will reset or repair the person's energy system. This interactive, integrative, preventative, and complementary form of holistic therapy honors the healing of the body, emotions, mind, and spirit. Training in self-care is available as well as training to become an Energy Medicine Practitioner or Energy Medicine Specialist.
Contact: www.energymedicinepartnerships.com

Esoteric Healing

Esoteric Healing is a system of healing that originated with the energy field work done during the 1940s by Alice Bailey and physical therapist Bernadette Bloom. The word *esoteric* refers to things that are hidden deep within. The goal is to restore good health to the whole body by clearing and balancing disrupted energy pathways in and around it. The internal energy vortices of the chakras and the energy field that flows through and around the body are treated primarily by bringing down healing energies that emanate from the highest divine sources and anchoring them in the body. The process uses the support of spirit guides to connect a person with the divine universal energy of love and light by working at the level of the causal energy field.

During a session, the therapist relies on the sensitivity of his hands to energy and his inner perception to scan for weak, imbalanced, or congested areas in the energy fields. Then he uses his hands to cause alterations that will allow the person's subtle energies to flow more freely. Much of the work is done by placing the hands lightly on or above specific points on the client's body and projecting energy to the recipient from the healer's connection to the divine; the recipient simply sits or lies down in a relaxed and receptive state of being. Through meditation, the healer calls on the etheric energy surrounding the chakras and endocrine glands to release blockages that restrict the flow of soul-level energy. Since the energy fields have a strong influence on the mind and emotions, it is common for a release of memories and feelings to surface as the energy flow is altered. This can happen any time during a session or for days after the treatment. If the recipient keeps an open mind with the intention to heal without resistance, an empowering release is more likely to happen, bringing the body and consciousness into a deeper state of health and vitality. There is now an international network of esoteric healers who teach this method of healing.
Contact: International Network of Esoteric Healing –
www.ineh.org

Etheric Pulse Therapy (EPT)

Etheric Pulse Therapy was developed by Neva Howell and is based on the belief that the physical matter in the body is shaped by and anchored to the energy matrix within the surrounding etheric universal field of energy. This matrix acts as a blueprint or template for all that is manifested. The aim of Etheric Pulse Therapy is to open the recipient to the universal life force present in the divine celestial energy fields to gain greater awareness of the soul's purpose, enhance the understanding of how blockages were created, establish the energy balance necessary for optimal health, and obtain a profound sense of spiritual peace. The therapy primarily transforms the etheric, emotional, mental, astral, and celestial levels of the energy field in a way that translates into physical healing.

During a treatment, the practitioner works on the energetic rhythms found within both the physical and subtle energy bodies of the recipient. A gentle hands-on method is used to evaluate and enhance the functioning of the craniosacral system. This is accomplished by feeling the pulsations of the cerebrospinal fluid and making adjustments to balance its flow. The energy pulse in the etheric physical template associated with the physical cranial rhythm is sensed, supported, expanded, and balanced. Sacred symbols and tones of certain frequencies are used to affect this etheric level, and energy points are activated throughout the course of the session. Simultaneous adjustments are made on other levels of the surrounding energy field until optimum balance is achieved. As with many modalities, the results depend heavily on the skill of the particular practitioner.
Contact: www.theamt.com/etheric_pulse_therapy_
an_ancient_healing_modality.html

Harmonyum®

Rooted in the mystical Universal Kabbalah, Harmonyum is a transcendental healing system that identifies the cause of physical problems as dysfunction in the spiritual realms. It works to purify the astral body (the energy field relating to the heart chakra that lies midway between the ketheric mental body and lower etheric body) by raising its vibratory frequency and cleansing all layers of the aura to eliminate karmic blocks from the past. As a result, the body, mind, and spirit are energized with pranic light coming from the divine, and the innate self-healing powers of the body are empowered to attend to the root causes of any dysfunctions. The Kabbalistic Tree of Life is used as a metaphor of the process in that the tree represents the astral body, whose seed is the mental body with the fruit in the physical body. The astral body is considered the easiest field to work on to bring about healing in other areas because it acts as a bridge between the upper and lower energy fields. Harmonyum also focuses on nurturing and giving unconditional love to the recipient to counteract the effects of disease, which tend to separate a person from the energetic flow of love. This subtle form of healing was founded by Dr. Joseph Levry, a yogi and Kabbalah

master also known as Gurunam. He is also the creator of Naam Yoga, which is a synthesis of the Kabbalah and yoga.

A Harmonyum healing session is calming, gentle, and noninvasive. During a treatment, spiritual force is transmitted to awaken the energy of the divine that lies deep within the core of the recipient. When this energy is activated, information can flow freely within the body, heart, and soul, thus enhancing self-awareness, melting away negative energies and physical tension, and replacing these destructive elements with positive divine energies. The nervous system, the information pathway between the mind and the physical body, receives special attention during a treatment. Several sessions can raise a person's vibrational frequency to such an extent that all human faculties are enhanced. The therapy, which can be eventually used as a method for self-healing, is a powerful way of reinvigorating the primal essence that is the birthright of all beings.
Contact: www.naamyoga.com/harmonyum-healing-
naam-yoga-la.html

Healing Touch (HT) Program™

Healing Touch is a holistic and caring form of bodywork primarily carried out by nurses to restore harmony to patients through hands-on techniques that clear, energize, balance, and align the human energetic anatomy and energy field. HT was developed during the 1980s by Janet Mentgen and Dr. Mary Jo Bulbrook (who is also a medical intuitive) as a comprehensive way to identify and correct disruptions in the flow of energy within and around a patient's body. HT is a spiritual practice done from the heart, grounded in the conviction that unconditional love and caring support are the key motivating factors for healing. All forms of touch are believed to be useful in encouraging the body's defense and healing mechanisms, and when a person feels love and a sense of peace, the immune system will naturally be enhanced. The quality and impact of the healing is largely influenced by the relationship between the giver and the receiver, who is treated more like a partner then a patient. The therapy continues to develop, but presently there are over thirty healing techniques, ranging from simple to complex, that can reduce stress, release acute pain, address specific disease states, and restore harmony and balance. All the methods are designed to help the patient's body learn to heal itself, and during a treatment, the patient is encouraged to consciously understand this potential source of healing.

Treatments use both light touch on the body and techniques in which the hands are held a few inches away from the body; these practices cleanse, repair, and repattern damage done to the etheric energy fields. Work on the energy fields includes magnetic clearing and methods for unruffling and sealing wounds from past traumas. The practitioner may use techniques that focus energy beams to break up painful blockages; methods that assist in the removal of blockages from the joints, spine, neck and back; effective ways of draining and relieving severe pain; and techniques that work to strengthen the lymphatic system. Also employed are Color and Sound Therapy, Chelation Therapy, Laser Therapy, ultrasound, meditation, and techniques for clearing the mind and connecting the chakras. Depending on a patient's condition, the interventions can be executed in either a vigorous and animated or a slow-moving and steady fashion.

Advanced practices include spiritual surgery and a process known as reflective healing. In spiritual surgery, the practitioner taps in to the energies of specific higher-dimensional beings and uses this to repair the spiritual template and repattern the etheric body to a healthier vibrational state. Reflective healing replaces the life-limiting stored beliefs and vibrational pattern of a diseased organ or tissue, which are held in the etheric body, with a healthier pattern that alleviates any form of dysfunction. This is accomplished by placing a hand directly over the disturbed area to seal the wound or leak in the energy field. Then a healthier vibrational pattern is introduced to help the ailing organ realign itself with a healthier blueprint. In this way, the body itself provides the healing with the guidance of the practitioner.

Healing Touch Therapy is endorsed by the American Holistic Nurses Association and the Canadian Holistic Nurses Association. A complete training program is now available, and many hospitals are now offering this therapy to their patients.
Contact: Healing Touch Program –
         www.HTPprofessionalassociation.com or
         Healing Touch International –
         www.healingtouchinternational.org

Heart & Soul Healing™

The intention of Heart & Soul Healing is to help people discover their inner truth by removing or releasing patterns of behavior, fears, or interpersonal conflicts that no longer serve and by integrating the whole being—body, mind, emotions, and spirit—with the higher self. This method of deep healing, developed by Ken Page and his wife, Nancy Nester, uses energetic clearing and releasing techniques to balance the recipient's energy and promote positive vibrational changes within the energy bodies that will break down and release old energy patterns at the cellular level and in the nervous system. Once these inhibiting subconscious patterns (from this life or a previous one), self-made mental or emotional barriers, and inner conflicts are set free, the client can become empowered by facing the fears that may turn out instead to be strengths. The healing works to help the recipient regain pieces of the soul that became separated from the body at an early age. A foundational principle of Heart & Soul Healing is that each person needs to develop and trust unconditional love for both the self and others. From this space of compassion, the world and all the beings in it can be healed.

While the client rests on a massage table, the treatment begins with an interview to evaluate the issues. This is followed by a guided meditation during which the practitioner scans the client's personal energy field. The session continues with the practitioner implementing the specific selection of energetic protocols most appropriate for the client. Techniques are available to discover the influence of the past, to release past traumas, subconscious conflicts, or psychic burdens, and to spin, balance, and clear the chakras and open the flow of energy within the meridians. Also at the practitioner's disposal are field-clearing methods, creation techniques, rebirthing processes, methods of balancing the nervous system and spinal cord, clear light arts, a living-light breathwork method, soul retrieval, techniques for removing energetic attachments or dark energy, and practices that integrate the heart and soul. At the end of the session, the client is given time alone to integrate all that has happened. Additional suggestions are given to help the client stay balanced and integrated in the days after the session.
Contact: Institute of Multidimensional Cellular
         Healing – www.kenpage.com

Inner Focus

This spiritual method of healing, developed by Dr. Alix-Sandra Parness, is referred to as a soul-directed energy healing. Parness is an ordained minister and doctor of divinity who was trained in many energetic healing modalities and has channeled enlightened information from the realms of higher healing energy. She opened the Mystery School for Divine Mastery in order to train other potential healers in meditation and the other processes used in her method. The primary goal of Inner Focus is to help individuals get to the core of any problems and return to wholeness by aligning themselves with the higher frequencies of the soul realm that can clear energetic blockages that cause disease and by using conscious awareness to connect with the wisdom of the body that will guide the healing process. One of the soul's objectives is to help solve problematic and conflicting life patterns and help people live in an unconditional state of light and love; therefore, awakening the heart chakra is essential to the healing process.

Tapping in to the power of the soul requires both absolute presence and willingness on the part of both the client and the healer. Once a client has agreed to let go of old ways of thinking and is willing to explore a new state of consciousness, the session begins with the practitioner's energy field forming a deep healing relationship with the energy field of the client. With strong intention, the healer allows energy from her heart chakra to flow through her hands to the client. While the client relaxes, often in an altered state, loving energies begin to build. The client is held with care in awareness and love as the healer performs various techniques to aid the healing process. These techniques include such things as the ascension process of harnessing the power of the soul, awareness release techniques, dynamic magnetic sound healing, work with the central hara line, the dance of light and shadow, energetic cord-cutting of unwanted attachments, divine visionary skills, and numerous other energetic methods, including those developed by Barbara Brennan. As the mystery and true essence within the recipient is revealed, she is naturally empowered by the light. It is then possible for her to accept and love herself exactly as she is.
Contact: www.innerfocus.org

Integrated Energy Therapy® (IET)

Work on clearing and balancing the energy fields can take place in many dimensions, and Integrated Energy Therapy works on the soul level with the energy of angels. This form of energy field therapy, created during the 1980s by Reiki master Stevan Thayer, uses what are known as the divine, high-frequency, violet, angelic energy rays, which are received from healing angels within the divine dimension of the energy fields. The therapy involves a number of energy attunements that work directly on a cellular level to bring the DNA's twelve strands (rather than the two posited by modern science) into alignment with their full power by clearing any suppressed and worthless physical or emotional energy blockages from the cellular memory and by channeling angelic energy to form an empowering imprint that replaces the cleared blockages. Though it was once believed that a person's DNA was fixed, thereby genetically determining his capacities, recent scientific research has validated what some ancient healing arts already knew: it is possible to alter DNA through specific transformative actions.

Rather than being a modality that diagnoses or treats disease, IET is designed to evaluate the flow of energy in the body and to support the client's own innate self-healing on the physical, emotional, mental, and spiritual levels. It is considered a safe and gentle process that works to transform pain into joy. Practitioners learn through four intensive levels of attunement how to feel, interpret, and identify various levels of energy blockages and to develop a step-by-step treatment process that begins by clearing a client's pain and ultimately advances to finding his soul's mission in life and and helping him live it.

The process of clearing and balancing the client's energy field is only done in person, not remotely. After completing an initial discussion about the focus of the therapy, the practitioner proceeds to systematically direct energy into specific areas and points on the body to trigger the release of blockages that cause restrictions. While doing this, the practitioner stays connected with both the angel Ariel and the client's own angel. Specific IET techniques and gentle therapeutic touch are employed, often accompanied by soothing music and special power symbols. This process energizes the recipient by channeling angelic energy through the energy fields and integrating this energy by working with specific acupressure points known as integration points. As a result, any karmic energy imprints are cleared from the human energy field, thereby removing pain and limitations from the past. Advanced therapeutic techniques include working on the genetic soul profile and activating a state of spiritual surrender so the soul will align with the divine. This genetic soul profile is recognized as a person's highest potential and resides within the area of the energy field above his head. The aim is to open that space so he can awaken the soul's memory of this potential. IET is considered a complementary therapy to other holistic energy field bodywork techniques such as Reiki and Therapeutic Touch, as well as certain forms of massage.

Contact: www.integratedenergytherapy.net

Intuitive Energy Healing

Intuitive Energy Healing refers to healings done by those with special capabilities rather than to a specific modality. Although practitioners of many modalities of bodywork, especially those involved with subtle-energy therapies, can be somewhat intuitive, practitioners of Intuitive Energy Healing have a special ability to recognize the cause of a particular health problem and discern the best remedy. Intuitives are healers who are either trained in or naturally gifted with the power to see beyond the obvious physical or emotional distress that a person is experiencing. Most intuitives have psychic abilities, which can include empathy (the ability to understand another person's feelings), clairvoyance (the ability to see things not normally perceived by the senses), clairaudience (the ability to hear beyond the normal range of perception), or clairsentience (the ability to feel things not normally felt by most people). Many are able to channel divine energy from the sacred universal source and transmit that energy into a client. Although this work can be done remotely, a hands-on session done in a safe, loving, and supportive environment is often preferred.

During a treatment, many intuitives are able to clear and balance chakras, release emotional blockages, and give the client greater mental discernment, insight, and perception by replacing stagnant energy with new, healthier energies that resonate harmoniously within a person's core. Initially, the client sets her intention, after which the intuitive healer "feels" or "sees" the areas of discomfort and analyzes the flow of energy in the client's systems. Channeled energy from the universal source is often directed to the areas where blockages exist. Angels, spirit guides, or other beings of light may also be of assistance by providing spiritually healing vibrations. Each intuitive healer may have particular methods or techniques in her repertoire. They can include methods of turning the underlying key that unlocks the pain of seemingly unrelated issues, ways of restructuring the body into alignment by removing the root of energetic disharmony, or the Spiritual Response Technique (SRT), which dives deep into the akashic records (the aksashic realm is the storehouse of universal information) to touch the soul and clear the inner child of life trauma or past-life energies that may be causing problems. Some practitioners, known as environmental intuitives, work with ailments caused by various detrimental aspects or imbalances found in the client's surroundings. They then assist the client by prescribing natural remedies, as is done in Medical Intuitive Therapy.

Carolyn Myss, a well-known medical intuitive healer who has a natural ability to see energy, developed her own system of healing that is now being taught worldwide. Myss can read a person's invisible energy anatomy—the surrounding etheric field, or aura, and the meridians and chakra energy centers within the body—to ascertain specifics about the client's physical, emotional, or mental condition. Each chakra also reflects a particular emotional and mental ability that may or may not be fully activated and balanced. Myss also has the ability to recognize which part or organ of the body is not functioning well or is diseased and why that is so. Myss's therapy is based on emotional release, forgiveness, and the wise distribution of energy within the body. It also recognizes that the energy which comes in from the universe through the crown of the head is often lost or leaks out of the body because of regrets, desires, attitudes, and unhealthy thoughts that a person has kept alive over the years. The healer can help the client become conscious of where energy is being lost so that she can make the necessary changes that will enable her to become energized and healthy. This is accomplished by the practitioner's making corrections in the flow of energy within the aura or chakras in order to enhance the client's innate ability to improve overall health and live fully. By learning to live mindfully in the present moment and forgiving themselves for things that are rooted in the past, even those who are unconsciously afraid to heal can acquire the ability to honor themselves in a way that is loving and truthful. Myss has shifted her personal priority from doing scannings and healings to teaching others the subtle insights and techniques that will increase their awareness of this transcendent process for providing better health and happiness.

Contact: www.myss.com

Intuitive Energy Medicine (IEM)

Energy medicine is a general term used to describe the wide and ever-changing field of energy healing practices. But Intuitive Energy Medicine is a complete healing package developed by Suzanne Louise that works on the core imbalances held on a cellular level in a person's energy system. IEM healing is accomplished by creating a sacred space and then applying a dynamic process that releases all tensions and brings the energy fields back into balance. The process addresses all aspects of a person's condition, whether it is physical, emotional, mental, or spiritual, by enhancing the flow of energy and providing a shift in consciousness.

The treatment begins with an evaluation of the client's issues using intuitive muscle testing to tap into the client's innate wisdom and identify the root causes of any imbalances in the body. With focused intention, the practitioner employs various techniques—guided meditation, heartfelt inquiry that requests the body to heal, specific harmonic frequencies, color and light therapy, the massage of neurolymphatic points, meridian balancing, DNA reprogramming, and personal harmonic numbers—to relieve pain, remove blockages, correct the energy flow, and bring in healing light. Except in certain extreme circumstances, only one treatment of IEM is required to release toxins and bring the body into balance. There are also a number of daily exercises with different types of breathwork that are taught to clients to help them learn how to ask their bodies to heal, to boost the immune system, to release chemical toxins, and to balance energy. Other closely related forms of energy medicine, each with their own particular emphasis and process, have been developed by a number of other intuitive healers.
Contact: www.dhamiboo.com/healing.html

King Solomon Healing

In ancient times, healing therapies were part of daily rituals and special spiritual ceremonies. Some of these rituals and ceremonies are now coming back to life. King Solomon Healing uses a combination of primarily ancient modalities for the purpose of helping people embrace the full light of their spiritual essence. This form of ceremonial therapy involves a series of eight sacred healing sessions that include washings, anointing, energy evaluations, special prayers, and invocations to prepare a client to receive high levels of spiritual light and energy. Additional healing ceremonies, including a powerful DNA activation, are carried out to balance, enhance, integrate, empower, and harmonize all aspects of the individual. It is said that the therapy was developed by King Solomon (the son of King David) after he studied for years in Tibet and returned home to assemble an assortment of world healers, shamans, and oracles at his newly established temple for the purpose of shared study and the continued empowering of high priests and priestesses. Certain mystery-school traditions have maintained and used these methods and other alchemical arts throughout the ages to enhance personal transformations.

Each of the ceremonial healing sessions includes a variety of practices and processes that are intended for those who wish to manifest their highest potential. Initially, a Tree of Life healing uses Tibetan bells to awaken, activate, illuminate, and balance the blueprint that gives access to the ten archetypal aspects of human existence that are manifested in all creation. A Seal of Solomon healing employs sacred stones, healing symbols, and potent energy to balance, align, and re-create the body in accordance with the seven directions and the original divine DNA blueprint. In a stone healing ceremony, stones with the highest vibrations open, heal, and harmonize the chakra system so a person can experience the spiritual being within the physical body. An aura healing is carried out by first scanning the auric field for unresolved black areas with holes that leak vital energy and then filling these holes with healing light to clear past traumas and give renewed vitality. A purification by light uses waves of divine light to remove foreign negative energies and awaken the seven principles of life in order to bless and seal the sacred self. An etheric body healing relies on the power of sacred spoken words and mantras to invoke powerful energies that heal the seven energy bodies and help a person reclaim the true essence of his spiritual nature. The last healing session involves a mental body healing and uses thirteen sacred aromatic oils to awaken and increase brain function for enhanced peace of mind. Each healing session is a unique ceremony and is concluded with a 22-strand DNA activation tune-up and a cord-cutting process to assist in integrating the new energy level established during the ceremony. It is preferred that a client commit to doing the entire series of sessions at certain intervals so that a full powerful shift can take place.
Contact: Living Light Foundation –
www.thelivinglightfoundation.com

LaHo-Chi^{SM}

A multidimensional energetic healing system, La-Ho-Chi removes imbalances and activates the subtle energy fields by focusing on the divine love-light frequency and the movement of the vital life-force energy. In 1991 in Santa Monica, CA, the instructions for this healing process were channeled through a spiritual teacher named Satchamar by the divine masters who serve the light and love of the universe. He instructed a group of thirty students to build a matrix of this energy, which they did, meeting twice a day for an entire year. Also that year, three months prior to the birth of LaHo-Chi, Satchamar brought forth the Angel Light Healing frequencies to the same group during twice-daily Light Sessions with him. Since that time, the matrix has grown exponentially and the frequencies have become more refined, giving the practices greater force in providing an internal shift in consciousness and higher sense perception. In 1993, Dan and Rio Watson, two of the original co-founders from this group, became directors of the LaHo-Chi Institute of Energy Healing and spread the teachings and training across the United States and in Europe. In 2012, the directorship of the institute was passed on to Beloved Heartsong of Mt. Shasta, CA.

A simple hands-on healing process, LaHo-Chi uses high frequencies of healing light, including Angel Light Healing, to move energy to the places where it is needed. The divine memory is first placed in the outer layer of the energy field, and the process transmits this energy to the body, mind, and spirit, increasing the meditative state of the recipient and accelerating the awakening and development of her innate healing powers. At the same time, the brain is activated and aligned with the higher spiritual chakras (eight through twelve) above the head, thereby making a connection to the heart and mind of the divine, which can then be fully anchored in the self. The multidimensional grid system that acts as a blueprint for physical and energetic integrity is also realigned. The healing process involves light hands-on contact, transformative meditation, and a form of point work done in the etheric energy field that balances the cranial fluid and pulse while at the same time repairing leaks in the energy field caused by inhibiting life experiences. The process also brings in the healing energies and vibrations of color, harmonic overtones, and vocal toning in order to cleanse and open the flow of energy in the organs, meridians, chakras, and subtle energy field bodies. This process can also be done remotely or with a group.

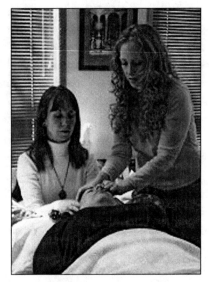

LaHo-Chi training session.
PHOTO COURTESY OF SHELOR DUFFEE

During a session, the LaHo-Chi energy creates a seal of protection around the recipient and the practitioner to guard against vibrational interference and to protect both people from negative energy that could impede the healing. Depending on the client's situation, initial contact is generally made with the hands on the head in order to clear her mind of mental and emotional blocks such as fear that may impede the flow of healing energies. This simple act of hands-on contact in a state of meditation begins to activate the transfer of universal life-source healing energies. Proceeding from a meditative space filled with stillness, love, and compassion, the practitioner becomes a vehicle of subtle, luminous healing energy as she gently rests her hands on certain areas of the recipient's body. There is no physical manipulation of the client's body, and the only movement occurs when the practitioner changes position. She simply holds a space in which the refined light energy can cleanse and clear away blockages and activate an awakening of the super-consciousness. Periodic vocal toning may be used by the practitioner to enhance the process. LaHo-Chi offers a means for personal development in which the depths of pain in life can be transformed into a more enlightened state of self-awareness.

Contact: Laho-Chi Institute of Energy Healing – www.lahochi.org

Lenair Healing Technique / SHE (Self(s) Healing Experience)

This form of healing was developed by medical intuitive Rhonda Lenair, who demonstrated the ability to discern and work with subtle energies at an early age. She eventually created her own special way of manipulating the electromagnetic energy field that surrounds all living organisms in a way that honors the uniqueness of each individual. This delicate hands-on process simultaneously detects and corrects frequencies within that field. The goal of the work is to bring all psychological and physical imbalances into harmony by eliminating the elements that contribute to or exacerbate any dysfunctional problems. Lenair's energetic process brings the bioelectrical systems of a client into a state of equilibrium by transferring healthy energetic currents to weak or damaged parts of a person's energy field. The therapy focuses primarily on relieving addictions, compulsions, fears, phobias, and stress-related problems. Unlike many other therapies, a personal medical history and total willingness on the part of the client are not required for achieving a successful outcome.

Treatment entails a process in which the practitioner's own energy is used to affect, alter, and correct the client's own basic energy anatomy, bringing about rapid change within the recipient's physical, emotional, and mental being. The practitioner either has or has developed a powerful intuitive ability to see a problem, whether or not the client is conscious of it. The healer deliberately clears her own mind to better sense and decipher the network of frequencies within the energy field of the recipient and then uses gentle touch to become aware of and connect with the subtle vibrations within the client. The practitioner continually adjusts her own frequencies to perfectly match those of the client so that her subconscious can absorb information. By becoming an energetic mirror image, the practitioner can feel what the client feels. Then the healer's own frequencies can be used to recalibrate the client's energetic and physical infrastructure, reconnect body-mind systems, and thereby eliminate problems, often within a short period of time. The treatment is not considered a psychic experience, but rather a process of transference and repair of the electromagnetic frequencies, which begins when physical contact is made. Once the best protocol for eliminating the problem or addiction is recognized, recommendations on the use of herbs, supplements, diet, exercise, and changes of lifestyle may also be made.

In 1999, the Lenair Healing Foundation was established to make available rehabilitation programs and workshops that increase public awareness of this particular type of energy medicine. The foundation has since developed a program known as the Self(s) Healing Experience (SHE) to help people who cannot control behaviors such as addictions regain their highest power and attain peace of mind without pain, withdrawal symptoms, or troubling side effects.

Contact: Lenair Healing Center – www.lenair.com

Light Body Activation

Light Body Activation's purpose is one of advancing people into a state of complete physical, mental, emotional, and spiritual wholeness by clearing and releasing the deepest layers of their core issues and activating their potential as perfected beings of light. This process was in part brought to life by the female being Tashira Tachi-Ren, a soul from a higher realm that came into another's body to complete that body's karmic work. This is different than channeling, because it involves an actual takeover of a living body by a divine soul that comes with the purpose to teach a more evolved consciousness.

Light Body Activation involves a twelve-step process of ascension to the upper dimensions, where more energy and light is held, in order to attune the cells to a specific resonance and reestablish a stronger connection with the creative light body of the god within each being. This light body, known as the Merkabah, is seen as a gridwork of sacred geometry containing encoded information. It is imaged as a spinning field of light energy at the center point of a person's being and is considered to be the blueprint of the DNA that forms the physical and subtle bodies and through which the life journey and the soul's purpose are made manifest. The activation process increases dimensional light and wisdom in the recipient's life as spirit descends from the upper dimensions, where true identity lies, and merges the higher self and the physical body. By removing ongoing cycles of limitation that are based on the illusion of separation from the higher dimensions, an individual can then embody greater wisdom.

The stages of the process of Light Body Activation are nonlinear, and the transformation can be immediate or take years, depending on the will of the spirit; once a person trusts the process, angelic assistance is available for those who ask for it. The practitioner acts as a conduit for delivering the light and higher energy frequencies of the Merkabah on a deep cellular level. During each session, tonal sounds and color are employed, and light energy and geometric patterns are transmitted through the practitioner's hands, which are placed on or above the recipient's body. How much is offered depends on what best serves the recipient at that particular moment. Progressing through each of the twelve levels of transformation, a series of shifts, often with periods of disorientation, will occur as new states are integrated and a new vision of life is unveiled. Once a person is merged with true divine potential, this transformative healing process provides deeper levels of opening in the heart center. Although Tachi-Ren taught some individuals the process, it has never been fully formulated into a distinct bodywork modality that people can easily train in or experience on their own.

Contact: www.celestialwellspring.com/lightbody

Lovestream® Touch

Lovestream Touch is a form of etheric healing that is intended to enhance the flow of energy to all areas of the body and provide a spiritual awakening. The therapy is based on ancient healing traditions that purify the chakras, meridians, and energy fields and harmonize and balance the flow of vital energy in the body. This form of energy healing was developed by Sol Ta Triane, founder of the Lotus Organization, after he received secret teachings from spiritual masters in the Far East. The cosmic energy force delivered by seven rays gives the client a life-changing spiritual experience. Each of these rays has a different vibrational frequency and color that has a particular healing effect on the recipient. The aim of the process is to help people make the adjustments necessary for them to live more connected and abundant lives. Practitioners are trained by receiving spiritual empowerments so that they can quickly purify and balance their own energy channels and thereby allow them to better help others.

A personal treatment provides a hands-on energy healing with a spiritual blessing in the form of an attunement that helps recipients awaken to their true nature. This revitalizing, intuitive form of bodywork is considered very subtle, soothing, loving, and empowering.

The session harmonizes the flow of vital energy in the entire body in a manner similar to Acupuncture without any manipulation or invasive action. Practitioners can incorporate this profound form of gentle energetic touch with other healing modalities. Participants can also learn through an empowerment how to perform this energetic awakening on themselves.

Contact: Lotus Organization – www.thelotus.org

Luminous Energy Field Healing

Luminous Energy Field Healing is an ancient practice developed by Inca shamans in Peru to heal a variety of physical ailments, anxieties, emotional traumas, and soul wounds. It was even used as a death rite to assist the spirit in passing into the afterlife. This healing practice was handed down in secret through the generations until medical anthropologist Dr. Alberto Villoldo was given instructions by Inca shaman Don Manuel Quispe. Villoldo has since become one of the better-known shamans in the modern world, and in 1984, he established the Four Winds Society as a way to perpetuate this ancient indigenous knowledge. This form of energy medicine works through the human energy field, or light body, and heals through spirit and light. The practice often deals with soul wounds, and as healers with wounds of their own learn to transform the pain, grief, anger, and shame that they have lived with into sources of strength and compassion, they can become more enlightened and of greater help in healing others.

The practice focuses on extracting and clearing negative imprints from the luminous energy fields that surrounds every person's body and acts as both a blueprint that controls what she draws in to her life and a template that determines how she lives, heals, and perhaps even dies. Intrusive energies that don't belong to the individual become dense and hardened and need to be removed. As part of an illumination healing process, shamanic energy extraction is used to eradicate unwanted negative energies that have penetrated a person's field of energy. This process helps prevent any disconnection, dysfunction, or illness from expressing itself physically.

A therapeutic treatment accelerates the healing of old emotional wounds and enhances the immune system by targeting the deeply held issues that are causing problems. The recipient performs conscious breathing exercises, visualizations, meditations, and a process known as movement sounding in which sounds are made while moving the body. Meanwhile, the therapist helps the recipient focus on body sensations and any pertinent information stored in the muscles or cellular memory. Further shamanic work is done to clear the energy loops, cellular memory, emotional and mental blockages, and the chakras. The hands-on bodywork, applied on or above the body, is accomplished in a free-style manner and has no set sequence. The particulars involved in a session will vary with each individual shamanic practitioner and the specific needs of the client. These healers often call on such tools as drums, rattles, chimes, feathers, and Tibetan singing bowls. Herbs are used for clearing the energy field by smudging; for example, a wand of burning sage is waved over and around the client. The goal of the therapy is to help the recipient gain awareness of the innate wisdom of the body, become more connected with nature, experience balance in the body and soul, and attain greater peace of mind. Contact: Four Winds Society – www.thefourwinds.com

Magnified Healing®

This ancient vibrational healing process was channeled to two American intuitives between 1983 and 1992 from the Chinese Buddhist goddess of mercy and compassion, known as Kuan Yin. It is reported that this healing was previously used only in the higher realms for divine purposes by ascended masters, those who once walked upon the earth. But Kuan Yin responded to the need for the spiritual advancement of humanity by directly transmitting the information to Gisele King, a clairvoyant counselor and healer, and Kathryn Anderson, an ordained minister and shaman. Although they were initially reluctant to take on this new responsibility, the continual guidance of Kuan Yin and other ascended masters helped them carry out the work and also teach others how to arouse and magnify their own healing abilities and establish a constant flow of energy between the heart and their own divine sources. Although the healing process can ease the suffering of the body, mind, and soul, it is really targeted at the etheric light body to activate the DNA strands so that recipients can experience a powerful spiritual healing and a heightened ability to become one with their light bodies. As more individuals become healed, a more complete healing of the earth will be possible through a cosmic energy paradigm shift.

The vibrational healing process primarily focuses on the heart, but integrates breathing techniques, empowering meditations, chakra alignment and balancing techniques, methods of sensitizing and awakening the nervous system, techniques for clearing the light channel and enhancing the light body within, specific hand movements based on the principles of sacred geometry, and inspirational affirmations spoken out loud. During a session, the practitioner and recipient work together to bring in the divine energy, which is passed through the client's body and releases imbalances. A single drop of an undiluted divine essence can also be applied to support greater receptivity and openness in the client. The actual healing session does not take long, and the entire process is considered to be rejuvenating, energetic, powerful, and softly feminine. It can be carried out individually or with a large group of people who have shared a traumatic experience.

Magnified Healing is considered to be different from Reiki, Pranic Healing, and most other forms of vibrational healing primarily because the highly intuitive practitioner essentially becomes one with the divine energy while bringing this energy from the heavenly dimension. This energy is considered to be high vibrations of pure love and light, and this process of bringing it to the earth epitomizes the cosmic energy shift that is now helping bring the original creation consciousness to humankind.
Contact: www.magnifiedhealing.com

Matrix Energetics®

Matrix Energetics® is a cutting-edge consciousness technology, developed by Dr. Richard Bartlett, that provides for instantaneous and lifelong transformation at the physical, mental, emotional, spiritual, relational, and social levels. It merges the sciences of subtle energy and quantum physics with the power of active imagination and focused intention to create new ways of perceiving and experiencing reality. Based upon the widely known principles of Quantum Physics and the lesser known principles of Torsion Field Physics, Matrix Energetics taps into the morphic field of infinite potential and provides easy access to unlimited possibilities. Life and reality is a very malleable illusion through which people are constantly creating and uncreating. Matrix Energetics® is intended to help participants wake up and experience transformation, empowerment, and infinite potential, shifting patterns (often long-standing) in their reality in an easy, playful way. By moving into the field of the heart, individuals can learn to access this field of potential, known as the Zero Point Field, from which intuitive awareness and all the tools of Matrix Energetics are accessible.

Skill sets include a two-point method (in which one hand is placed on the recipient's body and another on a nearby source point in the surrounding energy field), time travel techniques, parallel universe theory, and heart-centered awareness; all are combined with play-fulness to create real-time changes. Intuitive capabilities are enhanced through use of Archetypes, Spatial Clair-voyance, and Remote Accessing; opening up whole-brain awareness; and interacting with the morphic fields of information contained within the Unified Field of Consciousness. Rather than running energy through pathways or meridians, Matrix Energetics works on sustaining a state of potential from which anything is possible and the perfect outcome can freely manifest.

Matrix Energetics® seminars from Fundamentals to Mastery are delivered by Dr. Bartlett and his co-in-structor Melissa Joy, teaching participants how to use this life-changing consciousness technology in a creative way for the benefit of themselves and others. Particular emphasis is placed on helping students get out of their own way as well as quickly letting go of any limiting patterns of behavior and conditions. Matrix Energetics® Certified Practitioners are listed in the web site.
Contact: Matrix Energetics International –
www.matrixenergetics.com

Medical Intuitive Therapy

Medical intuitives may seem to have magical pow-ers, but they are really just individuals who have a well-developed and often innate ability to see the body, mind, and spirit as a whole, full of deeply related aspects. Medical Intuitive Therapy is performed by an intuitive counselor or therapist who, through a strong sense of knowing, can recognize where, why, and how a person is losing energy from the body and discover the underlying physical, mental, emotional, and spiritual factors that contribute to acute or chronic dysfunction caused by this energy loss. Some intuitives are born with the gift of this strong sense of knowing, but it can be developed through practice.

Rather than making a diagnosis based simply on physical symptoms, intuitive therapists find the true cause of blockages or imbalances by scanning energy

centers, chakras, and energy fields to energetically read the organs, glands, and other parts of the body. (It is rec-ognized that life lessons that have not yet been learned are captured at a cellular level in the body and are re-flected in specific chakras.) These therapists also un-derstand that toxic food substances and environmental poisons can have a significant effect on individual func-tioning and strongly influence energetic imbalances. Kinesthetic practices, including various forms of muscle testing, can complement the diagnostic process.

The actual healing process and the recommenda-tions made for the client can vary depending on the particular perspective of the therapist. Medical intu-itives' concentration on the physiological implications and the biochemical aspects of the client's condition is subtly different from the focus of Intuitive Energy Ther-apy practitioners. However, both can use heart-centered techniques that bring in the higher soul frequencies of energy that will help clients release their troubling issues. Medical intuitives may also use an assortment of methods such as magnetic healing, affirmations, guided imagery, meditation, methods of etheric restructuring, and techniques for stress management during a heal-ing session. Although special dietary solutions to the recognized imbalances are often recommended for the client, changes in lifestyle and environment may also be required.

Some of the many notable medical intuitives in-clude Carolyn Myss, Edgar Cayce, Louise Hay, and Phineas Quimby. Carolyn Myss has the innate ability to see directly into a person's energy anatomy and de-termine the emotional or mental issue that is causing an energetic imbalance or physical issue. Edgar Cayce, known as the sleeping prophet, could diagnose patients from a dream state and treat patients who were not even in his physical presence. Louise Hay has an inner knowing that allows her hands to move to exactly where they are really needed to energetically heal a client's problems. Dr. Phineas Quimby had a clairvoyant ability to place his mind, which was in an altered divine state, upon another person's being in a way that allowed him to read problems clearly. There is definitely a large vari-ety of unique and specialized abilities employed by all intuitives when doing their healings. Medical Intuitive Therapy cannot really be seen as a specific modality with specific techniques, but is rather a form of healing that includes a large range of special abilities employed by

healers with enhanced insight into the underlying interrelated energetic mechanics that effect overall health.
Contact: International Association of Medical
Intuitives – www.medical-intuitives.net

Melchizedek Method

A form of light-body activation, the Melchizedek Method of clairvoyant healing was channeled in 1997 from ascended master Thoth to spiritual teacher Alton Kamadon. It is said that Melchizedek serves as a benevolent teacher from his place in the realm of the spirit world. What Kamadon received through this transmission and messages from other ascended masters and angelic realms is essentially considered a holographic representation of the refined energy vibrations of cosmic consciousness as displayed through the sacred geometry of the Merkabah.

The Melchizedek Method seeks to enhance a person's healing abilities, awaken her heart, and open her to the hologram of unconditional love. This hologram serves as the basis for the treatment, which is considered a voyage into oneness with the higher realms and involves work that is centered around the Merkabah. The process incorporates guided meditations, initiations, and various healing techniques that work on the chakras, meridians, and energy fields in order to address and heal whatever issue the client presents by channeling in the energy of the divine light body.

During a session, the practitioner activates a hologram of love around both herself and the client to provide a welcoming space for the transmission of high-frequency healing energy. The practitioner's channeling of the divine light body may be spontaneous or induced by meditation, prayer, self-hypnosis, fasting, dancing, chanting, breathing techniques, or hallucinogenic drugs. The messages and healing information conveyed through the channeling help increase the healer's spiritual awareness of the recipient's auric field, as well as raising the client's vibrational state of being and reinstating the original divine blueprint, thus revitalizing her self-healing abilities.
Contact: United States Melchizedek Center –
www.melchizedekusa.com

Multi-Incarnational Recall

Multi-Incarnational Recall is a form of intuitive energy healing developed by Chris Griscom, the founder of the Light Institute of Galisteo, that involves a series of sessions that work to provide a new sense of a harmonious and balanced self. It is based on the idea that within the realm of human health, there are many inexplicable and seemingly chronic conditions that have built up slowly into a crisis not just within this life but over several lifetimes. These conditions, which have a significant effect on quality of life, often result from unwise or unnatural habits, incomplete transitions, and the holding of seemingly innocent assumptions and attachments, all of which may be unconscious to the client. They can manifest as limited patterns of living and modes of thinking that can become hardwired into the makeup of the physical body. This therapy is intended to resolve these habitual patterns and facilitate the dawning of a wiser state of being.

A series of sessions address the different causes of dysfunction, which may have arisen over any of the times the recipient has been on earth. The initial session focuses on contacting the client's higher self and bringing the emotional body into balance. Three more sessions assist with recognizing and releasing energetic residue and repetitive themes in a person's life and with awakening a direct dialogue with innate divine qualities. Other protocols explore dissolving projections from significant relationships, such as those with parents, and there are practices that work with sexuality, inherited genetic imprints, and cosmic genetic encoding.

Advanced sessions concentrate on the balance of inner male and female energies, the transformation of the soul, and the connection to cosmic energies. One advanced technique uses gentle touch and cranial balancing methods on the acupressure points known as Windows to the Sky to remove blockages and awaken kundalini energy. There are also multidimensional spiritual healing methods that rely on the presence of spirits and other intangible energy forces to enable a person to recall other incarnations or past lives. Other work deals primarily with this lifetime and explores the emotional body by connecting the recipient to her inner child and the wisdom it holds. This may be followed by a soul-centering practice in which the mind is directed to look inward at the higher self. There are also protocols that provide assistance for clearing issues in children and teenagers.
Contact: Light Institute of Galisteo –
www.lightinstitute.com

Noetic Balancing / Noetic Field Therapy (NFT)

Noetic Field Therapy, now referred to as Noetic Balancing, is a psychoenergetic therapy that works on a spiritual level to remove imbalances and blockages in the aura, the energy field that permeates and surrounds the human body. *Noetic* is a Greek word that means "spiritual mind," and it refers to everything not only within the human body but also in every subtle realm beyond it. (This therapy should not be confused with the work of the Institute of Noetic Science in California, which does research on energy medicine.) Noetic Field Balancing was developed by a group of people who took inspiration from the therapy methods of the transcendentalist Phineas Quimby, who did spiritual work with the "inner Christ" during the 1800s. During the 1960s, Dr. Neva Hunter blended Quimby's work with that of others to form a new energetic approach that was called Aura Balancing. The central feature of this therapy was the use of a pendulum and self-forgiveness to correct auric imbalances and distortions created by previous life experiences. Dr. Hunter and Ellavivian Power founded the Quimby Center, where they provided balancings to groups of participants for hours at a time. Later, Dr. Robert Waterman founded Southwestern College and modified the work into what became known as Noetic Field Therapy. This name reflects the idea that the spiritual energetic mind or higher intelligence resides in the noetic field, or aura. Waterman combined the principles of noetic balancing with other practices to develop his own soul-centered therapy that eventually evolved into a mystery-school approach. The original Quimby Center closed with the death of Neva Hunter around 1980. In 1997, counselor Rebecca Skeele was drawn to Waterman's teachings, and when another shift occurred in 2002 with the development of Waterman's mystery school and with the passing of Ellavivian Power, the mantle for continuing the spread of this work of aura balancing was passed on to a group of Dr. Waterman's advanced students. The name morphed into Noetic Balancing, and Skeele became a teacher of Noetic Balancing training in 2008.

Each of these approaches to noetic field work recognizes that the energy field has seven major interactive layers that extend outward from the body. According to Waterman, these layers are the physical, etheric, emotional, imaginary, archetypal, spiritual, and mental. The aura carries scars developed through a lifetime of

adversity, and since any blockages in the aura affect an individual's physical condition and interfere with the agenda of the soul, it is imperative that these issues be made into allies so that their transformation can diminish limitations and allow a person to experience more understanding, strength and awareness.

Noetic Balancing focuses first on the energy fields before attending to the physical body and its psychological aspects. It acknowledges that at the core of any destructive pattern is a spiritual essence striving to be actualized and fulfilled and that trapped energy signifies an incomplete expression of true potential. The therapy uses an increased vibrational frequency in the noetic field to clear away issues so that recipients can experience the greater reality of who they are. Finding blockages in the field is done primarily by using a pendulum and through prayer, as well as with inner seeing, spiritual vision, and scanning with the hands. The healing continues by deconstructing the psychological and spiritual wounds and any blocking beliefs while concentrating on the flow of spiritual energy. Subtle techniques, such as the releasing, reframing, and healing of memories and the stimulation of self-forgiveness, help balance and boost the energy. Verbal questioning is used to make clients aware of their blockages and to invite them to listen to what their souls really need. The practitioner holds the space that allows clients the experience of opening up to their fullest potential.

A series of three sessions, with each providing a foundation for the next, is often employed, depending on the recipient's individual circumstances and condition. Each session sequentially focuses on the physical, emotional, and mental-spiritual aspects of that individual. After an initial orientation to relax the client, the practitioner begins with a prayer to align both of them with the spiritual forces and to invoke an altered, open state of consciousness in the recipient. This is followed by using a crystal pendulum to open the aura just above the solar plexus and unlock any imbalances in the aura. Next, the practitioner scans the aura with her hands to sense and see blockages, which are then engaged with the pendulum to balance any distortions. This process of opening and balancing continues to the other chakras and different areas of the auric field with the circular rotation of the pendulum transforming the energy. Except for some guiding words of encouragement, questions that awaken self-forgiveness, and suggestions for deep

breathing, the process is carried out in silence. When the practitioner senses the need for something to be cleared, she may request that the client touch an area of the body and frame an appropriate self-forgiveness statement to help clear and balance the energy field. The practitioner acts as an energy transformer, increasing the energy available as the healing progresses, and she simply stands as a witness rather than imposing any attitudes or beliefs. As the healing proceeds, the recipient identifies and lets go of the self-inflicted judgments, beliefs and patterns that imbalance the aura, all of which are dissolved throughout the session. Near the end, the aura is filled with radiant energy, closing the connection between the client and the practitioner and sealing the changes. A closing blessing of spiritual light and love completes the session. Healthy habits free of disruptive influences are then recommended for the recipient during days following a session, which is considered a time when the client experiences a new sense of what is normal. With the aura now balanced, the resulting peaceful and spiritual sense of being reflects the awakened state of the soul, rich with power and free from limiting mental constructs.
Contact: www.quimbyamenti.com or
www.mystery-school.com

One Light Healing Touch® (OLHT)

One Light Healing Touch is a grounded and heart-centered method intended for personal transformation and the healing of others. It focuses on clearing blockages and rebalancing the human energy field by using both spiritual and energetic hands-on healing practices and techniques. OLHT was developed by Ron Lavin, who is an innately gifted psychic and spiritual healer with a strong background in shamanics and other esoteric spiritual healing modalities; he has participated in a number of landmark healing studies with the National Institutes of Health. His work draws on a blend of ancient spiritual teachings, including the healing knowledge of Sufis, Tibetans, Rosicrucians, and Native Americans. The goal of OLHT is to help individuals access their own healing potential.

The healing process may use any combination of over thirty-three sacred and effective healing techniques that include scanning, aura work, chakra and energy balancing work, chelation, time line therapy, color therapy, white light healing, breathwork, meditation, visualization, sound work, movement, magnetic healing,

sacred initiations, and past life therapy. In addition, radiant healing techniques are used to open and embody various vibrational levels of the life-force energy. The aim of the process is to facilitate and increase a person's energetic vibrations and awareness by strengthening the immune system and opening the recipient to the god within or the higher self. This evolutionary healing journey is an energy-moving process of activating better ultimate health as the practitioner opens up the recipient to a higher vibratory light so the body will heal itself.

The healer is trained to develop special gifts of intuition and clairvoyance, which enable him to see energy and blockages within the body. He can also perceive the trauma that caused an illness and provide a space that light energy can come into and heal. To be most effective, practitioners are trained in a variety of energetic self-healing and strengthening practices such as the Nine Point Protocol, the six position movements, grounding tools, clearing the field, energy running practices, meditation, breathwork, visualization, alchemy, auric cleaning, sacred ceremony, akashic records, archangel initiation, distance healing, and methods of eliminating blockages and strengthening a client's connection to the core of his being. The preparation and energetic cleansing of the practitioner is strongly emphasized. Lavin also maintains the importance of listening from the heart and acting upon the truths that flow from the source into awareness.

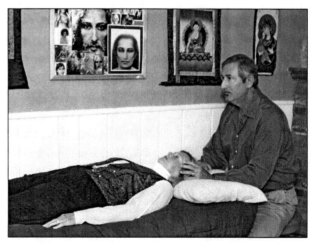

Ron Lavin carries out One Light Healing Touch.
PHOTO COURTESY OF RON LAVIN

The primary parts of the treatment involve applying healing light energy from the universe. This is done by using the hands as the loving instruments of the heart. Actual physical contact is optional and done only with the consent of the client; any contact is noninvasive and nonmanipulative. The basic principle is that when vibratory rates and levels are raised, a person can take in and maintain more clear light energy. The recipient is assisted in remaining grounded as light energy is sent through the body, chakras, and auric field. OLHT recognizes that the condition of the lower chakras is expressed in the auric layer closest to the body, and the higher chakras leading up to the crown are expressed in the outer layers of the auric field.

During a treatment, the healer runs energy from his hands in stages by first gathering it from the energy field, then increasing it, and finally sending it to where it is needed. Through the compassionate intention of both the practitioner and the client, the energy is raised and circulated. When the hands are applied to a chakra, the goal is to open it by rotating and holding it, thus allowing the energy to flow. Each chakra is worked in stages in a meditative open-minded manner that allows the universal energy to flow out through the practitioner into the recipient. When working on the crown chakra, energy is released down the spine to the tailbone so it can then flow freely into every organ of the body. When the energy in the hands is applied to a calcified or painful spot and the energy is turned on, any pain will then naturally dissipate out of the body. Many aspects of a treatment work on a soul level to release restrictions and shift old patterns of behavior into a state of being that is more energetically connected. Old adopted belief systems that constrict and no longer serve are dismantled, removed, and released from the body. Clients are also given holistic healing tools to help facilitate their healing between sessions and empower them to be more actively involved.

Since the original school was founded in 1996, Lavin and his wife, Penny have established sixteen schools with workshops teaching OLHT and additional exercises to many who want to either become intuitive healers or simply live with their heart more open on a daily basis. Contact: www.onelighthealingtouch.com

Oneness Blessing®

Oneness Blessing, originally referred to as Oneness Deeksha when it was created in India, is a consciousness-awakening process in which spiritual energy is transferred from one person to the neocortex in the brain of another through a combination of touch and intention. The aim is to create a shift in perception in which heightened awareness allows the recipient's consciousness to unite with the wisdom of the universe, thus providing inner peace. The founders of Oneness Blessing, Sri Amma and Sri Bhagavan, created the process as a quicker way to gain the experience of awakening than is provided by methods of study, meditation, and prayer. The blessing is said to set in motion a series of neurobiological shifts within the brain of the recipient by which previously dormant functions of the frontal lobes are activated; this eventually results in a new enlightened perception of reality.

During a session, the healer applying the Oneness Blessing places her hands over the top of the head of the receiver and transfers energy to that area for a short period of time. The practice essentially puts the recipient into an alpha brain-wave state that is very favorable for healing many aspects of the body, mind, and spirit. Strong intention is employed to create a balanced energy system as the practitioner uses her hands to remove blockages from the energy biofields and chakras. This subtle releasing process is carried out quietly with unconditional love. The blessing can also be given without touching simply through the power of intention, and it can also be conferred collectively on a large number of people.
Contact: www.onenessuniversity.org

Ortho-Bionomy®

Martial arts instructor and osteopath Dr. Arthur Pauls developed Ortho-Bionomy in England during the 1970s. By combining elements of Osteopathy with Japanese martial arts and Homeopathy, he created a gentle, noninvasive method of working with movement and alignment patterns in the physical body to enhance energetic and emotional well-being. The therapy is based on the principle that structure governs function, and it gives attention to the way energy moves in and around the body. It works with the body's natural ability to self-regulate and shift toward balance by using a profound method of spontaneously releasing both simple and complex patterns of neuromuscular stress. To do this, the practitioner allows the client's body to guide him as he moves it into a comfortable position in which it can spontaneously self-correct.

Treatments work through the path of least resistance in order to create a long-lasting, balanced state in the recipient. Movement and compression around the joints produce important reflex actions that activate the nervous system and rebalance the muscle tone, which in turn releases chronic holding patterns caused by previous physical trauma. Instead of using force or painful manipulations, the muscles are gently moved into positions that encourage this reflex action. Tension points are first located, and then slack is created by moving the body to a specific angle while applying slight compression. The compression helps the nervous system signal the muscles to let go of unnecessary holding, and tight, knotted area can become loose. After waiting for a short period—up to a few minutes—to monitor the release, the practitioner may apply neck cradling while gently rocking the client's body to help integrate the muscle release, especially around the joints. Palpations of certain points of tension with the muscles in the fully extended position helps to soften, to ease tension, and to expand range of motion. The therapy also uses movement education, dialogue, energy field work, emotional freeing therapy, and energetic work on the client's aura. Ortho-Bionomy can be incorporated with other modalities and is ideal for those who can't tolerate deep bodywork.

Contact: Society of Ortho-Bionomy International –
www.ortho-bionomy.org

Osho Illumination Therapy

Osho Illumination Therapy is a systematic approach to spiritual healing that uses transomatic dialogue (an element of Gestalt Therapy), the chanting of "Om," the application of colored light, light hypnotic trance, illuminations, and meditations to access, perceive, and dissolve any dissociated memories that can manifest as life-limiting issues or physical ailments. The therapy was developed by dentist Dr. Charles Newman, spiritually known as Swami Devageet, after he received teachings and insight from the enlightened master and mystic Osho in India and trained in Peter Mandel's Esogetic Colorpuncture Therapy. The healing process is based on the concept that each part of the physical body is a memory bank that contains remembrances of a person's evolutionary roots. It is believed that each of these memories are color-coded in the mind and may be manifested as emotional cysts that limit potential and

cause disease. The therapy recognizes that many current illnesses are rooted in long-forgotten events and their associated emotions and that by consciously accessing and clearing specific repressed emotional memories, a person can actualize rapid and profound healing of any physical, emotional, and psychological dysfunction or disease. Increasing self-awareness is seen as the route to higher consciousness and real spiritual development and can enable self-realization and authentic personal transformation.

The complete therapy comprises a series of sessions that work progressively to dissolve a person's barriers to self-awareness and permit the recall of core memories. To accomplish this, it is considered essential that the recipient's mind and body are deeply relaxed; this is accomplished by creating a trance state. The therapist induces a hypnotic transomatic trance that enables the recipient's own voice and awareness to express and communicate with the contents of the core memories. During a treatment, colors of light are applied to certain acupuncture points on the body to affect metabolic activity and stimulate the recall of memories from events that happened early in life. A verbalization process known as elucidation helps the client recall detailed memories as they are released from the unconscious mind. Further physical and psychological healing is accomplished as the process stimulates the natural, simple tendency to heal that is liberated once people are truly in touch with their essence and inner core.

Contact: www.omweb.com/osho/devageet

Physiohelanics™

Physiohelanics is a method of natural healing that was developed during the 1980s by somatic therapist and doctor of behavioral science C. Diane Ealy as a way to provide personal spiritual growth and integrate a person's physical, emotional, intellectual, and spiritual aspects. A method of chakra and energy field healing, Physiohelanics uses the body's own energy system to address the needs of the whole person by taking directions from the individual's higher self. Rather than focusing on a specific symptom or fighting disease, the aim is to enhance individual strengths, since a person's strengths will always bring about optimal functioning. As in many energetic therapies, the healer aligns himself with the divine universal earth energy so that he can better connect with this healing energy and channel it to where it is needed. This is accomplished by using a technique known as Psychosynthesis in which the practitioner sets up a triangle of energy between his higher self, the client's higher self, and the universal energy source in order to enhance the movement of energy between the three. The healer may use pendulums, crystals, stones, and toning sounds and may invite communication with spirit guides and totems (animal spirit guides) while working on a client. Through Physiohelanics, the client's body and awareness are reminded how it feels to have physical and spiritual energy flow naturally in abundance. When the physical body is integrated with an increased level of energetic vibration, it becomes a very uncomfortable place for viruses, bacteria, and any form of dysfunction.

A treatment begins with cleansing, balancing, recharging, and repairing the first three layers in the etheric energy field that surrounds the body. This is accomplished without any direct physical contact. When this activity is complete, the practitioner shifts his focus to the physical body and concentrates on connecting the major and minor energy chakra in the body, thus clearing the way for the natural flow of energy within. As the client lies face down on a massage table, the practitioner gently runs energy down his back from the shoulders to the hips in order to release blockages. This process includes some very light touch, though no massage or manipulation, and is usually targeted at specific areas that require cleansing and clearing. Afterward, the client turns over onto his back, and the practitioner runs energy between the minor chakras in the joints, feet, and hands and the eight major chakras of the body that form a line up the center of the body from the base of the spine to the top of the head. Finally, all of the energy is connected, cleared and balanced at the heart. After the treatment, the practitioner discusses the issues he found and instructs the client on basic energy-channeling techniques that can be used to maintain the newly balanced energy state for as long as possible. Ealy acknowledges that Physiohelanics is a flexible modality that is constantly evolving as it taps into finer vibrational states and dimensions. She now also employs the process of Soul Memory Discovery in her work. (See description in Chapter 7.)
Contact: www.cdianeealy.com

Polarity Therapy

Polarity Therapy, one of the more well-known contemporary holistic healing methods, integrates Western skills and knowledge with Eastern healing methods. Dr. Randolph Stone, a naturopath, osteopath, and chiropractor, developed this modality in Austria during the mid-1920s after many years of studying healing methods from both the West and the East. The primary insights about this modality came to him through traditional Ayurvedic and Chinese Taoist health practices and the concepts of the vital life-force energy, the five elements, yin and yang, and energy flow. He combined these ideas with contemporary knowledge about electromagnetic currents and the complex system of interfacing energy fields, added his own belief that health is based on a person's awareness of her own deeper truth, and created a method that focuses on restoring the balance of the energetic fields and the currents of the energy anatomy. This transpersonal therapy works primarily with the human energy field, energy centers, and flow lines to release physical, mental, and emotional energy blocks and restore rhythmic balance to the currents of energy that flow through and around the body. When he retired, Dr. Stone appointed Pierre Pannetier to carry on his work, and soon after Dr. Stone's passing, a core group of practitioners founded the American Polarity Therapy Association.

Polarity Therapy is based on the universal principles of energy attraction, repulsion, and neutrality and the view that all energy moves through an evolutionary cycle of expansion and contraction from a neutral source to a positive field, then through a negative phase, and back to its source. Positive and negative poles, some of which correspond to chakras, are located at different points on the body, and their opposing polarities cause energetic currents to flow between them; each cell also has a positive and a negative pole. Three types of energy currents are worked with: long lines that flow north and south, transverse currents that run east and west, and spiral currents that begin at the navel and flow outward. All of these currents move in pulsating waves with interrelated harmonic patterns. Obstructions are described as areas of stagnation or holding patterns that interfere with the flow of energy and can lead to disease.

The human energetic anatomy is considered to be a manifestation of the less dense cosmic realms of existence. In Polarity Therapy, the soul is seen as a divine force that emanates from the nucleus of the higher energy fields and steps down into the physical field of the body, which has its own consciousness and is sustained in every moment by the spirit. By understanding various aspects of the elements in the body, the energy fields, the chakra energy centers, and the energy pathways, a healing practice can release many restrictions that limit someone's full potential. Real health not just the absence of pain and symptoms, but a way of living in energetic balance and harmony with a person's inner being grounded in the conscious realization of her true nature. In this sense, Polarity Therapy is really more a method for improving overall lifestyle than simply a form of therapeutic bodywork.

Polarity Therapy is an integrated, multipart system that combines pressure-point bodywork with yoga, exercise, nutritional counseling, breathwork, and work with the universal energy. The therapist acts as a stimulus for healing by finding imbalances and patterns that have become fixed in the recipient's body by negative thoughts and attitudes and then reflecting them back to the client to enhance her ability to heal herself. The hands-on bodywork focuses mostly on the feet, pelvis, sacrum, diaphragm, heart, joints, spine, and body core, and the actual protocol of the assorted hand positions will vary depending on the practitioner and her

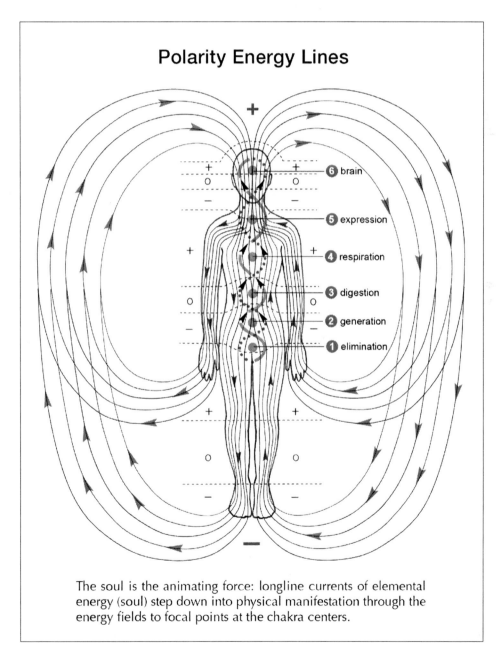

Polarity Energy Lines

6 brain
5 expression
4 respiration
3 digestion
2 generation
1 elimination

The soul is the animating force: longline currents of elemental energy (soul) step down into physical manifestation through the energy fields to focal points at the chakra centers.

particular interpretation of the vast collection of information left behind by Dr. Stone. Some practitioners are very intuitive and work closely with the client by using their hands as loving conductors of energy, since love is an essential element of this healing method.

After initial questioning to determine any problems, the recipient relaxes and breathes deeply as the therapist carries out an assessment of the cranial pulse and rhythm in order to determine the extent of any energy blockage in the body. This is followed by a series of gentle to vigorous manipulations with probing, rotating, holding, rocking, and shaking movements that are performed along with the application of light to deep pressure at various places on the body. These actions help connect, amplify, balance, and free up the energy. Three types of touch with the fingers, which originated in Ayurvedic bodywork, are used: the firm but gentle and subtle sattvic touch to balance and stabilize energy; a variable and vibrating rajasic touch to stimulate the flow of energy in an ascending direction; and the deep, firm, dispersing tamasic touch which disperses energy blockages and stimulates flow in a descending direction. Touch is also used to magnetically balance and harmonize the positive and negative charges of energy in the body. Gentle rocking of the body may be done with the hands resting on specific points. After completing a treatment, certain rhythmic yogic stretching exercises, breathwork, and sounding may be recommended. The therapist may also offer support to enhance positive thinking and provide some counseling with regard to a cleansing diet that will help the client maintain good health.

Contact: American Polarity Therapy Association –
www.polaritytherapy.org

Pranic Healing®

Pranic Healing is a synthesis of Tibetan, Chinese, Indian and Filipino healing methods that uses prana (the vital life-force energy) to correct the energetic imbalances that underlie most ailments. This bioenergetic healing treatment with a focus on the bioplasmic auric energy body was developed by Master Choa Kok Sui, a Chinese-born resident of the Philippines. A chemical engineer who became a yogi at a young age, he tested and verified the techniques of pranic healing and eventually created a fusion of technology and the inner conscious workings of the heart and soul. According to Master Choa, one does not need to be a clairvoyant to practice pranic healing. Through a very pragmatic approach, several techniques of healing and self-development have evolved to treat a wide spectrum of physical, mental, or emotional ailments, at the same time empowering an individual to become more responsible for his own health and well-being.

Techniques of scanning and energy realignment are used to cleanse, balance, and revitalize the energetic health of the body's electromagnetic field by increasing the flow of prana so that the disruptions that are causing disease in the physical body will be dissolved. It is a simple yet powerful noncontact method of energy healing that supports the body's innate healing ability by balancing, transforming, and harmonizing the bioenergies. Besides working with the different dimensions of the biofield, Pranic Healing also concentrates on the two central channels which run through all the major chakras—the conception channel, which runs from the top of the head down the front of the body to the base of the spine, and the governing channel, which runs up the back of the body from the base of the spine to the top of the head. Pranic Healing recognizes that prana comes from three principle sources: the air, earth, and sun, and that all three can be drawn into the body through the chakras.

A healing session begins with pranic breathing techniques guided by the practitioner, after which he scans and feels the aura with specific manual techniques to establish the problem that needs to be healed. While constantly scanning the biofield to ascertain its condition, the practitioner proceeds with various hand motions to first sweep or clean congested energy and seal any energy holes and cracks. The sweeping technique helps remove devitalized, congested, diseased, or stagnant energy, thereby freeing the biofield and energy centers of any blockages. Finally, an energizing water-pump technique is used to replenish any deficiencies in the cleansed aura and energy centers with fresh prana. This invigorated flow of energy will enable the body to remove the cause of the ailment and heal itself. Advanced practitioners deliver healing even down to the cellular level. Throughout the treatment, the practitioner monitors the condition of the recipient through meditation and yogic breathing practices. Other aspects of the healing process include decontamination techniques; the systematic application of energy to the chakras; advanced pranic healing with intention, color and visualization; a psychotherapeutic method to heal emotions that provides a quick release of crippling energy patterns; and a guided meditation on the twin hearts of the individual and Mother Earth. Pranic distance healing can be used for those who can not physically get to the practitioner.

Master Choa has also developed a multilevel course called Arhatic Yoga, which is a synthesis of different yogic practices and meditation techniques that are used to activate and align the chakras and safely awaken the sacred fires of kundalini energy. (See description in section on Yoga in Chapter 11.)
Contact: www.pranichealing.com or
www.pranichealingcenter.com

Primus Activation Healing Technique™ (PAHT)

This approach to vibrational energy medicine was developed in 2003 by Naisha Ahsian and uses techniques based on recent neurocardiology research combined with the evolving model of human energetics and the physical laws of resonance to synchronize the recipient's brain and heart using a powerful energetic field that is transferred through the electromagnetic field of the healer. PAHT leads the recipient to an energetic and emotional state that has a discernible impact on the biochemistry of the body and the surrounding electromagnetic energy field, enabling the person to shift into an optimal state for healing. This state, known as the primus state, is the first and most important part of the healing process. Besides providing relief from pain, emotional discomfort, and physical ailments, PAHT allows the body and mind to experience personal growth and a state of powerful spiritual expansion.

During this noninvasive, hands-on healing treatment, the practitioner activates and clears different energy centers along the recipient's body by transferring her own enhanced and powerful energy field to the recipient through the physical laws of resonance. This provides an identifiable impact on the biochemistry of the body and assists the recipient in recognizing her own inner joy and divine perfection. Certain breathing techniques, a progression of hands-on healing positions, and chi exercises are used to stimulate the flow of energy. In addition, the recipient is trained in specific meditation techniques to sustain primus states of energy and emotion that lessen the damaging effects of stress and improve creativity. In the course of a session, the healing

process is empowering for both the practitioner and the recipient.

Naisha Ahsian has also developed the modality known as Crystal Resonance Therapy (CRT), which uses the natural energies of the earth and the electromagnetic frequencies of crystals, stones, minerals, and other natural sources of energy combined with specific self-exploration journeys to achieve a harmonious balance between body, mind, and spirit. This noninvasive energy treatment helps the recipient explore, identify, and treat all the imbalances within her being.
Contact: Crystalis Institute –
www.crystalisinstitute.com

Pryanta

Pamela Schlade and Raven Tompkins developed this deep energy work as a way to assist others in creating a fluid balance of the mental, emotional, and physical energy bodies in order to facilitate the emergence of the higher self. Its name—pryanta—is the sound that gives voice to the continuum of awakened consciousness that transcends all duality. The techniques used in this method release energy that has become fixed or controlled by habitual thought or choice through a multilayered process customized to each individual's particular needs. It may include removing detrimental cords of energy attachment or energetic debris, clearing inhibiting dreamscapes, retrieving missing parts of the self through the process of soul retrieval, balancing chakras, restructuring the chakras and the hara line, releasing cellular memories and restrictive patterns, repairing and restructuring the energy field, breaking up inhibiting curses, and extracting unusual dark energies and spirit attachments. Although the unveiling of the hidden parts of the self can be uncomfortable, the practitioner provides nurturing support for the continual exploration of any issues that may arise. All of the work is designed to remove life wounds and place a client in a fluid state in which energy can move freely, allowing for profound life changes.

During an initial interview, done either face-to-face or over the phone, personal information is obtained, the energy field is read, and the results of that reading are discussed. The practitioner may consult the akashic records and spirit guides to determine what energies are affecting the client. Once a healing plan is created, a number of healers work as a team as the client lies fully

clothed on a massage table. After an opening invocation in which spirit guides are called upon for assistance, the bodywork is done with hands either on or off the recipient's body to facilitate the release of blocked energies and to connect and balance the energy fields and chakras. A variety of healing stones may also be used to assist the healing process. The work penetrates deep into the recipient's consciousness, and the removal of any blocked energy can allow the profound release of buried issues. The client's willingness to take personal responsibility is critical, since choosing to ignore what arises can restrict growth and diminish the benefits of the session. Core issues of unworthiness, isolation, abandonment, betrayal or separation often surface during a session, and all such wounds are treated in a compassionate way to enable resolution. Each recipient's healing process is unique and proceeds at its own speed. After the long initial session, shorter follow-up sessions may be recommended depending on the client's situation. Practitioners may also recommend other forms of therapy or self-care as a way to promote ongoing healing.
Contact: www.pryanta.com

Quantum Energetics™ (QE)

A form of energy medicine developed by Jo Dunning, Quantum Energetics uses the subtle life-force energies to trigger the body's own natural healing process. Dunning created these techniques after she experienced a major life trauma that resulted in a spiritual awakening. Traumatic life events held in cellular memory create disruptions in the energy grid, which is connected with all cellular memory; these disturbances reduce the flow of energy in the body. QE assists in restoring the energy flow by working on this energy grid. Rather than focusing on symptoms, which often mask the root of the problem, this systematic therapy follows a non-invasive, holistic approach that works with the foundational cause of a problem. It focuses on early detection and prevention of health problems by strengthening the immune system and repairing any injured or diseased tissue. This is accomplished with a variety of techniques that include muscle testing, directing energy through the fingers with intentional touch, cranial work, and methods to align the energy fields. It also uses numerical codes whose vibrational frequencies correspond with specific conditions present on the energetic level. These codes are combined with muscle testing to get a yes or

no answer from the client that indicates a disruption in the flow of energy to and through a certain area, organ, or muscle in the body.

All corrective measures are meant to expand divine awareness and deal with energy disruptions caused by stresses, injuries, and life traumas that tend to get locked up in the body and become preserved in cellular memory. When the practitioner performs the correct procedure in conjunction with the client's breathing for a specified period of time, the result is an increase in energy flow. The basic healing process involves directing energy from the practitioner's hands to the specific location where the root cause of the problem exists, which is often distant from the area of dysfunction suggested by the symptoms. A variety of methods are also employed to stimulate the client's healing energies by clearing and balancing the chakras and restoring the surrounding energy field. A Quick Pulse Technique is used to rapidly rebalance aspects of the body, mind, and emotions and quickly resolve any life issues that an individual is struggling with. A unique form of cranial work that provides a series of energetic connections is also performed. A series of initiations is used to activate the pineal gland and the endocrine system, as well as to activate and restructure the DNA and return it to its original divine structure and blueprint. A number of transformative energetic disciplines can also be taught to individuals.
Contact: www.jodunning.com

Quantum-Touch® Therapy

A vibrational energy modality founded by Richard Gordon, Quantum-Touch Therapy depends on the power of resonance to activate a healing response in a recipient's energy field and energy flow. Though based on concepts similar to those of Polarity Therapy and Reiki, Quantum-Touch has its own distinct approach. The basic premise is that everyone has the innate ability and body intelligence to heal and, with training, can practice this healing method on themselves or others. The training involves learning a series of meditations to tap into higher sources of energy so that high energetic vibrations are present in the hands. Two concepts are crucial to the therapy: the practitioner must be fully present and the essence of healing is love.

A practitioner works on a client by first increasing the energy in the hands and then running the energy into the recipient's body. The principles of resonance and

entrainment ensure that the recipient's energy vibrations will rise to meet the higher vibrations made available by the practitioner; this helps accelerate the healing process on a subatomic or quantum level. The hands can also be sandwiched on either side of a problem area to accelerate the inflow of healing energy. Key elements in the therapy are the client's guiding the placement of the practitioner's hands, perhaps to a painful area, and the therapist's sensing the quality of the energetic interaction between the hands and the recipient's body. The therapist must abandon any expectations and simply hold a highly resonant field of vibrations; the energy will go where it is needed. Sounding and breathing techniques may be used by the practitioner to increase the energy available, and advanced techniques include harmonic toning and chakra spinning. The intention of Quantum-Touch is to decrease pain and enable the spontaneous adjustment of misaligned body parts. Although the overall process is simple, the benefits can go beyond the physical realm and hasten healing on many levels that alter a person's consciousness.
Contact: www.quantumtouch.com

Rapa Yad™ Bioenergy Healing Technique

The Rapa Yad Bioenergy Healing Technique was developed by London-born practitioner and triathlete Michael Cohen, whose years of studying transformative healing practices led to a method that allowed him to overcome years of suffering from his own disorders. This treatment process has evolved over time, and it now employs a wide range of techniques that focus on the bioelectromagnetic energy fields, connective energy pathways, chakras, and neurological circuits of the body. Cohen and his wife have their own research foundation and clinic in London.

The process is intended to clear and release memory patterns on a cellular level, enhance cellular regeneration, treat chronic conditions, mitigate learning disabilities or developmental disorders, and allow people to move beyond past limitations and restrictions so that they can achieve enhanced levels of functioning. By releasing blockages and memory patterns on a cellular level, the client's natural healing abilities can also be activated. Rather than attempting to interpret symptoms, the technique works on a purely energetic level to determine what needs to be cleared and then proceeds at the right pace to deal with those priority concerns.

A session starts with the practitioner using the eyes and hands to scan all of the client's bioelectrical circuits to pinpoint the root cause of any physical, emotional, physiological, or psychological blockages that need attention; scanning continues throughout the session. This is followed by a hands-on or hands-off technique in which the index finger is applied to blockage points that are related to this primary cause. Energetic manipulation of blockage points is considered helpful in sending a message to the brain to activate a neurological healing response. Light touch with the hands or the fingers on or near the body is then used to release emotional blockages, and an energy stretching technique that leads the client's energy outward can remove memory patterns and clear any existing blockages from the body. A practitioner can feel imbalances through the sensations in the hands and often uses one hand to extract negative energy while the other hand acts as a pathway to allow positive energy to flow into the client. Feedback about the sensations the client is feeling is also requested; this helps recipients become more conscious of the body. Sometimes two practitioners work on a client at the same time. Most clients receive a series of sessions depending on their particular needs, and additional elements for self-maintenance, including nutrition, fluid intake, physical exercise, and breathwork, are often proposed as part of a complete healing program. Distance healing can also be accomplished with this technique.
Contact: Bioenergy Treatment Research Foundation – www.bioenergytreatment.co.uk

Reconnective Healing®

Although Dr. Eric Pearl never considered himself a psychic, while practicing as a chiropractor, he found that some kind of force was bringing a new gift of healing to him. After experiences with insistent spirit beings in which he received channeled phrases about how he could heal others energetically, he became adept at seemingly miraculous healings by calling on an extradimensional source of energy, a source beyond the dimensions of space and time that are usually regarded as physical reality. He gave up his chiropractic work and devoted his life to this new-found power that came naturally through him. By 1993, his method had become known as Reconnective Healing, a process that recognizes that past shock or trauma frozen in a person's body may have caused a detachment from the universal field of energy, leading to disease and dysfunction. By harnessing the natural frequencies and vibrations of the universe, this link between the client and this energy can be reestablished.

This form of healing uses the hands of the practitioner to focus a flow of high-level, fifth-dimensional light and energy into the auric field of the recipient, awakening dormant strands of DNA and reconnecting the meridians of the body to the grid lines that encircle the planet and connect humans to the universe. Pearl believes humans have the potential for twelve strands of DNA rather than just two. All DNA strands are considered to be subtle forms of energy that vibrate in resonance with the universal field of intelligence and energy at specific frequencies that can pass through the smallest particles of matter and can heal all with that resonance. Through entrainment, the reconnection process brings in and activates new lines of vibratory frequencies from a dimension outside ordinary reality, which allows the exchange of light and information and the reconnection of missing or dormant DNA strands.

Healing occurs as a result of the reestablishment of communication between the client's energy field and the universal energy field through the resonant support of the practitioner. The therapist acts as a catalyst in the transference by providing the frequencies that the client's body wants or needs. In Reconnective Healing, there is no manipulation of energy such as is found in Reiki or Pranic Healing. The energy simply travels through the practitioner into the recipient's body. There are no specific techniques, since the healing occurs spontaneously when the practitioner is in a transcended and open state in which he can simply recognize any existing issues and allow the reconnective energies to enhance healing. Reconnective Healing requires that the practitioner get his own agenda out of the way, let go of expectations, be silent, observe, listen deeply, and develop the ability to strongly sense whatever arises from within the client's field of energy. He must be grounded, relaxed, and able to take on the responsibility of simply allowing the healing rather trying too hard to make it happen.

After an initial inquiry about the intentions of the client while making him comfortable lying fully clothed face up on a massage table, the treatment starts with the healing practitioner holding a loving and expansive space that promotes the receiving of information from the client's energy field. Once this is in place, it is possible for the therapist to open channels of energy from the universal field that allow the client to reconnect with his fullest potential. The recipient need only to close his eyes, relax, be available, and direct his attention inward, at the same time letting go of expectations and mental chatter as best he can. There is no set sequence to the process, since it is adapted to each individual's uniqueness, and the healer focuses on those areas of the client's energy field that require the most attention. The practitioner's hands move around the body, usually without any physical contact; sometimes this work focuses on meridians. By determining which body parts want to be reconnected and then bringing in and activating new lines of vibratory frequencies, he establishes a link to the gridlines within the universal field of intelligence so that the client's body can entrain with the needed energy. When the recipient's energy starts to flow, all preexisting conditions and limitations melt away. As each area is treated, the practitioner pauses and allows for some integration on the part of the client before moving on to another area. Sensations such as tingling, throbbing, shaking, and other more subtle energetic vibrations are often felt by both the practitioner and the recipient. Various responses, such as spontaneous movements, tears, laughter, and verbal expression, can arise from the recipient, and the practitioner uses this feedback to monitor the client's condition. Sessions are often concluded with a period of open discussion about what has transpired. The practitioner also conveys information about what was revealed to him energetically through the session. Contact: www.thereconnection.com

Reiki

Reiki is a simple yet profound form of energetic healing whose origin is Japanese, although some of its primary elements can be traced back through China to ancient Tibet and India. Many of the principles of Reiki—especially the idea that disease shows up when the body is energetically out of balance—were present in advanced self-healing methods of qi gong and in sacred practices derived from esoteric rituals of Buddhist monks in Tibet. The ancient form of Reiki involved summoning a deity consciousness or divine being from beyond the self that could guide the practitioner, and this other-dimensional assistance is part of some styles practiced today. Although currently, especially in the West, Reiki is usually seen as a way of healing others, it originally was intended for self-realization and personal spiritual growth through work with the universal life energy. The ability to heal others was simply a beneficial side effect.

Reiki symbol.

Reiki is a lineage-based system that is generally transferred from master to student through attunements, after which different frequencies of pure life-force energy can be directly activated and cultivated within any individual. Attunements help trainees develop sensitivity to powerful life energies through meditation, chanting, toning, prayer, mindfulness, and special energetic opening and cleansing work with the ultimate goal of establishing perfectly balanced energy. The hands can then be used for healing others. Disciples of many Reiki teachers added elements to what they had learned, and several schools of practice exist today.

The most widely known modern form of Reiki was introduced in 1922 by Dr. Mikao Usui, a Tendai Buddhist practitioner who, while fasting and meditating on Mount Kumara in Japan, was shown a vision of hands-on energetic healing methods called teate in Japanese and secret, sacred symbols that could be used for spiritual transformation. Usui's findings and his experiences with using this powerful energy for healing were passed down to others as the original system of Usui Reiki Ryoho, which is the primary practice still used in Japan today. Dr. Chujiro Hayashi, a student of Usui, opened a Reiki healing center in 1925 and made some modifications in the system, placing more importance on the symbols and attunements. Besides passing these practices on to Toshihiro Eguchi, Kaiji Tomita, and others in Japan, he taught Japanese-Hawaiian Mrs. Hawayo Takata, who brought it to the West in the late

1930s with a greater emphasis on the clinical healing of others rather than its original spiritual approach. Mrs. Takata initiated twenty-two masters before her death in 1980. After her passing, new, nontraditional forms, different from those of the Usui lineage as taught in Japan, were created. Although it allowed many options for seekers, this development caused much discourse and controversy over the ensuing years. Even though the Reiki Alliance was formed to standardize practices, debate over the true Reiki system continued.

The perplexing, though appealing, side of the evolution of Reiki is the number of choices created by all the forms that now exist. Developers of some nontraditional forms claim to have received channeled information from ascended masters from Tibet, India, or even Egypt, who walked the earth many years before Usui Reiki Ryoho was formulated by Mikao Usui. Some of these newer forms have incorporated elements of other healing practices, such as kundalini energy work, Tibetan tantric healing methods, point work, chakra clearing, and even Western therapies. Others have returned to the emphasis on personal spiritual transformation that was retained in Japan. Practitioners of nontraditional forms may use crystals, stones, plants, colors, visualizations, affirmations, energy manipulation, massage, chanting, singing, and psychic work. Symbols may be traditional or nontraditional symbols, and attunements to open the energetic pathways and activate the innate healing potential may or may not be used. In addition, practitioners may have different methods for connecting and transmitting the universal life-force energy. There is literally something for every body. Although the constructs of each form of Reiki may differ in energy frequencies, attunements, sacred symbols, sacred sounds, breathwork, and levels of empowerments, each form, no matter how it was conceived, works with the finer frequencies of the universal life-force energy in essentially similar ways.

Reiki addresses the condition of the biomagnetic (auric) energy field in a process also referred to as physiospiritual etheric body healing. Whether performed on the self or others, these practices clear, align, and balance energy pathways weakened or disrupted by negative thoughts or emotions, which may cause physical symptoms and illness. When the higher frequencies of divine universal energy are absorbed and integrated into a person's body and energy field, personal energy is enhanced and the pathways that promote healing are opened and revitalized, creating a new spiritual alliance between the body, mind, emotions, and spirit. Since the basic elements of Reiki can be quickly learned, many individuals are tempted to jump prematurely into helping others before working with the practice to heal themselves. But it can take a lifetime to master all of its profound subtleties, and proper training is necessary if real healing is to be accomplished. Reiki has become very popular worldwide and is now being used in many health care facilities and hospitals in the West.

Mastery of Reiki is usually developed through three or four levels of ritual attunements or empowerments that initiate practitioners into the meaning and use of sacred healing symbols; align them with the vast realm of higher energetic frequencies; teach proficiency in detecting and tapping in to the life-force energy; and help impart the ability to transmit this energy to a recipient or at least deepen the recipient's connection to it. The sacred symbols used during an attunement or healing session are like keys that open the doors to higher frequencies of energy. These symbols, passed on through a master teacher, in dreams, or by channeling, are believed to hold specific knowledge that is transmitted and activated through their use. Each resonates with a certain area of the human energy system; they may open and clear the inner central-light column, stimulate the physical and subtle etheric bodies, or enliven the heart chakra. Advanced Reiki training can include the use of Reiki crystal grids, important ancient healing and meditation symbols, and special breathing techniques. Sometimes, specific guides—spirits or ascended masters—work with individual practitioners to assist the healing process. As a student progresses through the various levels, or grades, to advanced forms of practice, an enlightened master's natural tendency is to teach that true spiritual transformation is synonymous with compassion for others and the desire to heal them through energetic transformation.

During a treatment, energy is scanned, beamed, or sent through a set series of hand positions on specific parts of the body; the areas contacted correspond to vital locations, including those of the chakras and organs. Although the client, seated or lying on a massage table, need not do anything but relax and absorb the vibrations, the extent of the healing often depends on her willingness to receive and use the energy. The practitioner's hands may gently contact or be held just above the recipient's body as the she passes on the universal energy that has entered through her crown chakra, all the while keeping in mind the ancient meditation symbols that will direct the cosmic energy to where it is needed. This is done slowly, holding one position for a few minutes before moving on to another area. The work is usually accomplished by starting on the head and then moving down over the glands and chakras to the feet. When the front of the body has been attended to, the client rolls over, and the process is repeated on the back side. After the series of hand positions is completed, the client may request that the practitioner return to a particular area that needs more attention. A Reiki session is very gentle and relaxing, and a variety of subtle sensations may be experienced by the recipient. A series of sessions may be necessary for those with significant issues, and up to six practitioners can work on the recipient at one time. Each session works in stages to bring awareness to imbalances, clear any disruptions, and then integrate a new, harmonious state of being.

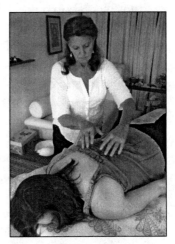

Reiki session.

A complete listing of all the various forms of Reiki would be overwhelming, but some of the many well-recognized forms are included below. For those who wonder what else might be out there, here are a few more: Ascension Reiki by Jayson Suttkus, Jikiden by Mrs. Chiyoko Yamaguchi, Jinlap (Tibetan) Reiki by Jin Lap Maitri, Non-Traditional Usui Reiki by Diane Stein, Osho Neo Reiki by Himani, Re Hu Tek by Allen Burns, Reiki Plus by David Jarrel, Saku Reiki by Eric Bott, Satya Reiki by Shingo Sakuma, Tibetan Reiki by Ralph

White, Tomita Ryu Hands Healing by Kaiji Tomita, and the Vortex School by Takichi Tsukida,
Contact: International Association of Reiki
        Professionals – www.iarp.org or Reiki
        Alliance – www.reikialliance.com

Alchemia Reiki is a form of channeled healing that involves activating the universal fifth-dimension energy. It evolved out of Magnified Healing and was created by Kamala Renner, the founder of the DoveStar School of Holistic Technology. This form of Reiki uses different geometric shapes as keys to trigger states of consciousness that allow healing and vibrational attunements to occur. The bodywork incorporates techniques that release both etheric and subconscious energy blockages and trauma that are stored on a cellular level. In addition, heart-focused Alchemia Reiki uses Shamballa energy work, touch therapy, and breathwork to transform karma, free suppressed energy, and achieve a state in which the recipients can receive and give unconditional love. To become a master requires three levels, or degrees, of training.
Contact: www.reiki-healing-touch.com

Gendai Reiki is a modern formulation of ancient methods of Reiki practiced in Japan. It was established in the 1990s by Hiroshi Doi, who was a member of the Usui Reiki Ryoho Gakkai society that Mikao Usui founded in Japan. Although Gendai Reiki practice is based on the energetic form of Usui Reiki taught to him by Mieko Mitsu, who was trained in the Radiance Technique, Doi combined modern therapeutic healing methods with traditional techniques including hands-on teate healing, nishino breathing, crystal healing, and elements of Johrei Reiki. In time, Doi was able to bring more of the original spiritual aspects of the practice out of Japan to the West, and he also created his own form of meditation and energy work. There are four levels of empowerment teachings, known as Shoden (introductory level of self-healing), Okuden (expanded deeper techniques), Shinpide (self-purifying teacher level) and Gokuikaiden (highest level that focuses on both physical and spiritual healing).
Contact: www.gendaireiki.com

Jin Kei Do Reiki, referred to as the way of compassion and wisdom, represents a completely different Reiki school of healing with roots in Tibet. It evolved from the teachings of Dr. Chujiro Hayashi, a principle student of Mikao Usui, which were transmitted to Seiji Takamori, a monk who then embarked on a twenty-year search for the origins of Reiki, which took him to India, Nepal, and Tibet. In Tibet, he found a sect whose members practiced the Buddho system of healing, an ancient meditation and healing system that evolved out of early Buddhist practices. After years of studying with them, he returned to teach and pass on the healing system to his student, Ranga Premaratna, who in 1997 renamed it Jin Kei Do Reiki, which means "integrating compassion and wisdom into daily life." The teachings give more detailed attention to the attunements, which can be performed one-on-one or in small groups. It is unique in combining qi gong practices with mindfulness and meditation. Jin Kei Do Reiki is primarily a meditative form of daily spiritual heart opening, but students are gradually introduced to methods of hands-on healing.
Contact: www.reikijinkeido.com

Johrei / Vajra® Reiki evolved from Raku Kei Reiki, an early system that came primarily from Tibet. Johrei Reiki was created by Mokichi Okada, a contemporary of Michao Usui, and in Japan, it was considered both a healing method and a religion. It incorporated various spiritual healing practices including the use of a highly focused, "hotter" energy activated through a Raku Kei breathwork practice known as the Breath of the Fire Dragon. While in India during the 1970s, Wade Ryan revised the Johrei system into what he called Vajra Reiki by combining greater use of mantras and meditations with the fiery energy that is said to be more effective in dealing with the powerful bacteria and viruses now on the planet. For practitioners, there are three levels of attainment, and the Buddhist Vajrayana Om-Ah-Hum mantra and the practice of meditation are integral to maintaining the integrity of their subtle-body energy systems. Various specific hand positions and both traditional and nontraditional symbols are used. It is said that as they cover the entire body, the hand positions can reverse the

polarity of the recipient. An energetic bodywork modality found in Brazil, known as Johrei Massage, evolved out of Johrei Reiki.
Contact: www.vajra-reiki.tripod.com

Karuna® Reiki is a form developed in 1995 by William Rand from Usui/Tibetan Reiki, which he previously formulated with Diane Stein. Karuna Reiki enables the practitioner to invoke the assistance and healing energies of the higher self, angels, and ascended enlightened beings (spiritual guides) and thus develop an energetic frequency that is said to provide more powerful sensations than that used with Usui Reiki. Karuna Reiki is considered a method of compassionate action that uses some of the same symbols as other systems of Reiki, but works with a different attunement process. During an attunement or treatment, the practitioner chants and intones the names of eight additional symbols to create a profound shift in the vibrational frequency that helps the healing energies penetrate deeper into the cells and tissues of the client's body. The practice of awakening kundalini energy through the contraction of the hui yin point in the perineum in conjunction with the Violet Breath visualization practice is fundamental to the healing process. The overall aim of the method is to teach people how to be more open to receiving guidance from ascended spiritual beings and taking action that diminishes the suffering of others.
Contact: www.reiki.org

Karuna Ki Reiki, developed by Karuna Reiki practitioner Vincent Amador, relies on compassionate heart energy and shares common symbols with both Karuna and Tera Mai Reiki, but adds different attunements (two with four levels), meditations, mudras, and other techniques along with chanting, toning, and the use of the Tibetan Violet Breath practice. This meditative breathing practice involves visualizing the Tibetan master symbol and circulating white light within the conception and governing channels in the body in synchronicity with the breath. Karuna Ki is a more flexible form of Reiki that is not trademarked to allow the teachings to change and develop however teachers see fit.
Contact: www.reikiblessings.com

Komyo Reiki Kai, a simple form that represents Reiki as it was practiced in Japan before the 1940s, reflects the original understanding of Reiki as a system for personal spiritual growth and development rather than as a way to heal others. Komyo Reiki is a blend of transformative practices that was developed by Pure Land Buddhist monk Inamoto Hyakuten after receiving his primary teachings from Chiyoko Yamaguchi, a student of Chujiro Hayashi. He eventually added to these lineage practices by bringing in elements from William Rand's Western Karuna Reiki lineage and Buddhist practices of mudras and meditations on the breath; he also made some changes in symbols to create a practice that has spiritual transformation as its goal. Four levels of initiation involve empowerments and attunements that represent specific purposes in relation to the understanding of the flow of the universal energy within. The first two levels focus on self-healing and on training a practitioner in applied therapy, and the last two deal with spiritual development. Komyo Reiki Kai strongly emphasizes healing the self before working on healing others.
Contact: www.komyoreiki.com

Kundalini Reiki is a simple healing technique that does not require intense study or complex procedures. It was introduced by Ole Gabrielsen after it was channeled to him by ascended masters (enlightened spiritual beings who once lived on earth). Kundalini Reiki focuses on opening the root chakra and allowing a complete cleansing by assisting in the flow of energy through the body up to the crown chakra at the top of the head. Three levels of attunement are used along with crystals and meditation to permit the full rising of kundalini energy.
Contact: www.kundalinireiki.com

Lightarian™ Reiki was developed in the United States through the efforts of Jeannine Jelm and Christopher Jelm, a spiritual counselor and conscious channeler of the angelic realms and ascended masters. The Jelms also founded the Lightarian Institute for Global Human Transformation. This method incorporates four levels of attunements that aim to support spiritual transformation and awaken humanity to six higher vibrational bands of Reiki

energies without using symbols. It also involves two meditations to introduce energies of ascended master Buddha, one for self-healing and one to connect to divine vibrational healing energies.
Contact: www.lightarian.com

Magnified Healing — See separate listing in this section

Mariel Reiki, known as Beloved of God Therapy, was developed by Ethel Lombardi and is used to both balance the overall body energy and assist in spiritual transformation. A typical treatment session incorporates interactive dialogue with gentle laying-on of hands to release negative emotional or physical blockages held as memories in the cells of the body that often lead to pain and stress. The emphasis is on transforming repressed emotional energy on a cellular level into positive energy that will foster personal growth.
Contact: www.universityofreiki.com

The Radiance Technique® preserves the authentic practice of Usui Reiki as transmitted to Dr. Barbara Weber Ray, a clairvoyant astrologer who was one of the twenty-two masters taught by Mrs. Hawayo Takata. The therapy focuses on accessing and using the natural universal energy and involves energy balancing, meditation, and prayer. The Radiance Technique stresses that love will be of great assistance in resolving life's problems. A session is non-manipulative and involves light hands-on or hands-off techniques to balance and align the body's vital energetic anatomy and energy field. There are seven levels of training involved. Ray is a successor to the direct line of Usui Shiki Ryoho, and The Radiance Technique was passed on to Mieko Mitsu, who later taught Hiroshi Doi, the creator of Gendai Reiki.
Contact: www.trtia.org

Rainbow Reiki is a blend of numerous healing modalities and traditional forms of Reiki that was developed by Walter Lubeck. This spiritual form of Reiki is focused on healing the self and combines Usui Reiki with the practices of Feng Shui, meditation, shamanism, holistic communication sciences, and human psychotherapy. In addition to many

symbols and mantras, Rainbow Reiki uses techniques such as karma clearing, astral travel, and crystal healing, as well as Neuro Linguistic Programming and therapies that work with the inner child. The three key elements of Rainbow Reiki are love, self-responsibility, and consciousness.
Contact: www.rainbowreikiusa.com

Raku Kei Reiki, also referred to as the way of the fire dragon, was revitalized and modified by Arthur Robertson. Iris Ishikuro, who was one of Hawayo Takata's students, also made contributions. This form incorporates the Tibetan practice of the Breath of the Fire Dragon, also called the Violet Breath, which is an energetic activation exercise done by contracting the hui yin point in the perineum. Raku Kei Reiki also uses the white-light symbol from the Japanese Johrei religion, spirit guides, the Tibetan master symbol and other Tibetan practices, the fire serpent symbol, mudras, frequency generator plates, the sui ching water ritual, and kundalini breathwork. In this form of Reiki, *raku* refers to the vertical flow of energy in the body, and *kai* represents its horizontal flow; both are activated through special breathwork practices. This form of Reiki has four levels, or degrees, and has influenced other types of Reiki. For instance, Mokichi Okada, a contemporary of Mikao Usui, later developed Johrei Reiki partly from elements of Raku Kei Reiki. Raku Kei Reiki can only be transmitted to those who are already Usui Reiki masters
Contact: www.spiritsofnativelight.org/raku_kei_reiki.asp

Seichim Reiki is a complete healing system that uses a different vibrational frequency than most forms of Reiki; it is referred to as the living light energy. This method involves the transmission of a very high vibrational energy that works on the soul level to enable deep growth and healing. It is believed to have originated with high priests in ancient Egyptian temples, although of the four distinct versions that have evolved, two have elements that have a closer resemblance to Tibetan Reiki and Japanese Usui Reiki. The system was rediscovered in 1979 by Patrick Zeigler and has since evolved into subtly different forms of energy healing. (The modality of Seichim is covered in detail in this section.)

Shamballa Reiki, developed by John Armitage, is considered not only a form of healing but also a way of accelerating spiritual development. It is said to have originated from ascended master Saint Germain, who lived in Atlantis and journeyed to Tibet after Atlantis was destroyed. It currently employs forty-three of Reiki's 352 recognized symbols, including those used for DNA activation, in the Mahatma (divine self) initiation and the large number of initiations that work with all of the twelve chakras. A total of four attunements are used to bring a student to the level of a master practitioner. Shamballa is recognized as the energy of unconditional love which comes through the heart chakra to help heal self and others, and when Shamballa is combined with Reiki, a very loving healing modality is created.

The primary purpose of the initiations, or activations, is self-empowerment. The Mahatma initiation activates the divine higher vibrational energy so a person can live in love and light with the natural world. Mahatma is considered the living consciousness of the creator, which is present in everything and can reconnect all to their higher spiritual aspects through the higher chakras that extend outside, above, and beyond the physical body within the divine energy fields. In this system, the five higher chakras are called the soul chakra, Christ consciousness, the archangelic kingdom, the source council of twelve, and the I AM consciousness of God. When the union with the consciousness of the creator in the Mahatma initiation is complete, the individual soul will awaken to complete spiritual transformation. A Shambhalla healing is multidimensional and involves the transmission and concentration of high-frequency loving energy into a person's body for healing and personal transformation.
Contact: www.shamballareikitraining.co.uk

Tera-Mai™ Reiki combines elements of Usui Reiki, Raku Kei Reiki, and the Egyptian energy-based healing system of Seichem and uses its own special attunements and additional channeled symbols. This form of Reiki work, developed in 1995 by Kathleen Milner, bestows an attunement on the feet to open the body to electromagnetic healing from the earth. Both Karuna Reiki and Tera Mai Reiki were previously known as Sai Baba Reiki, although the history is a bit unclear. It has three degrees of initiation that include the Violet Flame attunement, the Yod attunement, and the Order of Melchizadek initiation.
Contact: www.kathleenmilner.com

Transformational Reiki is part of the Reiki Mystery School found within the original Usui and Shiki Ryoho Reiki methods. It has been perpetuated and taught by Karyn and Dr. Steve Mitchell. This form of Reiki works with the chakra system and the interdimensional energy fields by using an assortment of meditations, some of which involve meeting an interdimensional guide, and the higher healing vibrations in the divine Unisonium field. The practitioner and the recipient use a powerful invocation practice to call on this very intense energy, which is a link to the grand soul of the interdimensional reality in the divine realm. It is this connection that brings the recipient's soul purpose to life.
Contact: www.drmitchellnd.com

Tummo Reiki makes use of both the universal life-force energy and kundalini energy in attunements and techniques that are designed to provide effective Reiki healing and a safe, immediate, blissful and purifying kundalini awakening. The spiritual practice of tummo came to Tibet from India, and in fact, *tummo* is a Tibetan word that means "inner fire." In 1998, Irmansyah Effendi brought the practice of developing tummo into Reiki and started teaching Tummo Reiki in Indonesia.

This meditative practice, which is similar to that found in Kundalini Yoga, can generate and distribute vital energy, slow down the metabolism, cleanse and balance the chakras, free the mind, and increase the vibrations in the surrounding energy bodies. As the main energy channel is fully opened, allowing a great release of dormant prana, the root chakra and crown chakra are opened as well. This makes it possible to connect with both the earth energy and the divine universal Reiki energy. The

union of the activities of kundalini and universal Reiki energy allow this practice to provide healing on a very deep spiritual level.
Contact: www.reikitummo-la.com

Usui/Tibetan Reiki combines the original Usui Ryoho Reiki and Raku Kei Reiki with advanced Tibetan Reiki training and practices. It was developed by William Rand and Diane Stein, who were instrumental in popularizing Reiki through written publications. Rand was also influenced by both Seichim Reiki and Tera Mai Reiki in the creation of this system, which consists of a number of extra levels of training and a variety of additional techniques that use crystal grids, spirit guides, healing attunements, psychic surgery, meditations, visualizations, and several additional Tibetan symbols, especially the Dumo, the Tibetan master symbol. The Dumo represents the fire of kundalini and is used in an awakening process that incorporates the hui yin point on the perineum and the Violet Breath practice to ignite the sacred fire and open the chakras to higher frequencies of healing energy, which can remove negative energy and disease from the body and mind.
Contact: www.reikirays.com/375/usui-tibetan-
reiki-master-teacher/

Violet Flame Reiki is a form dedicated to Lady Kuan Yin, the goddess of compassion and mercy in East Asian Buddhist traditions. Reiki practitioner Ivy Moore developed this form when she channeled various symbols from ascended master Lady Kuan Yin. This feminine, nurturing method focuses on clearing away mental control, purifying the energy fields, and healing with a pure heart though the use of colored energies. The violet-flame energies lead to transformation, transmutation, purification, and divine alchemy. The lavender flame element used in this form of Reiki is a more gentle and nurturing version of violet energy that soothes away negative energies by slowly purifying the energy fields to bring back energetic balance and harmony.
Contact: www.violetflamereiki.com

Wei Chi Healing™ Reiki was channeled to Kevin Emery and Thomas Hensel by a Tibetan monk who gave his name as Wei Chi. He is considered by some to be the original creator of what we now call Reiki. This method is considered more actively therapeutic than other passive forms of Reiki, because it concentrates on transmitting healing to others. Wei Chi Reiki focuses on the immune system and the undifferentiated energy field that manifests in and around all life. The method is considered a particularly powerful way for healing imbalances caused by emotional issues, as well as providing a defense against harmful environmental pathogens. During a treatment, the practitioner uses intuitive intention to absorb information from the recipient; this is then verbally shared in order to help empower the recipient to heal more deeply. The practitioner incorporates a skin-brushing technique in which the hands are moved in no particular sequence to wherever they are drawn. Powerful visualizations facilitate a release during more intensive treatments. Recipients need to be willing to be responsible for their own healing and to continue that process after the treatment. A series of three or five treatments is considered normal for a complete therapy.
Contact: www.essential-reiki.com/wei-chi-tibetan-
reiki.html

Ro Hun™ Therapy

Ro Hun is considered a spiritual purification therapy that blends psychotherapy, hypnotherapy, regression therapy, and energy field manipulation. It was developed by intuitive medium and visionary healer Patricia Hayes during the 1980s as a way to clear the energy field and rapidly awaken the healer within each person. Ro Hun is a spiritual entity that Hayes channeled during a long series of meditations. She then transformed the information given into this system of healing. The process relies on the identification, understanding, and release of faulty thoughts and negative emotions that combine to produce destructive, self-sabotaging behavior. Beyond that, Ro Hun connects the client to her spiritual nature, the source of all healing. As the client gains spiritual strength, she is more able to address her faulty thoughts and negative feelings. Ro Hun recognizes that unhealthy thoughts, images, and feelings exist as energies within the chakras and various levels of the surrounding auric energy field. These create energy blocks, which can have a strong impact on the functioning of the physical body and can separate a person from the life she wants to live. This transformational method is intended to interact with and release these negative emotional and mental energy patterns and the personal traumas associated with them. Instructions are also given to help increase the recipient's sensitivity to the energy fields and her own spiritual nature. The approach is structured yet flexible. Through creative interaction with the energy field of the therapist, the client is systematically guided in locating, identifying, understanding, and releasing negativities and faulty thought patterns. The dramatic shift in belief patterns and increased self-awareness help arouse the inner healing potential of the recipient.

During a treatment the client and therapist, working as a team, identify negative thought patterns and emotional traumas stored in the client's consciousness. The client, with the assistance of the therapist, establishes a new set of healthy thoughts and feelings. This purification process takes place in a series of three three-hour sessions and is repeated for each of the seven chakras. Along with noninvasive energetic manipulation, special cards and a series of chakra scannings may be used. Practices often include an initial cleansing; a purifying Ro Hun skim process to release subconscious issues; a shadow purification to heal deep core issues; a soul-and-ego origin process to gain insight into the causes of issues; a seven-visions process to expand the client's potential; an androgynous balancing process; and a final, deep psychotherapeutic deconstruction of previously created limitations. Ro Hun also incorporates hypnotherapy techniques to guide the client to look at issues in the subconscious and replace them with more holistic positive beliefs. Advanced sessions provide the client with an expanded view of the self as a spiritual being. These deal with the inner child through the heart chakra, original archetypal patterns, deeper chakra work, a divine mother process, and the further balancing of the male and female energies. The end result of this work is not only the release of negativity, but the discovery of wisdom, confidence, and strength as an ongoing part of life.
Contact: RoHun Delphi University
of Spiritual Studies – www.delphiu.com

RYSE®
RYSE stands for to Realize Your Sublime Energies and represents a system of energy field therapy that was developed by Nancy Risley, the founder of the Polarity Realization Institute. It is based on the ideas that every problematic condition exhibits a combination of energetic patterns that can affect the whole person and that any corresponding energetic dysfunctions can be corrected with the tools that make up the healing system. The goal of RYSE is to clear energetic blockages from the chakras and energy fields and to restore the individual to a more integrated level of functioning. The healing process addresses energy patterns from the past or from current issues that are still held in the body's memory and may be those of the inner child. Besides activating and releasing limiting energy patterns, RYSE also teaches clients how to remain in a state of self-alignment by learning how to manage their own subtle energies.

The treatment employs intuitive methods of sensing or seeing a person's energy fields and chakras, followed by therapeutic methods that bring about a more energetically balanced state. Practitioners may use a number of healing modalities, such as Polarity Therapy, massage, chakra balancing, and vibrational energy channel work. As an energy-awareness therapy, RYSE can easily complement other forms of holistic medicine.
Contact: www.ryse.com

Seichim, Seichem, Sekhem, SKHM and SSR
Though the origins of Seichim are somewhat unclear, it is generally believed to be an ancient Egyptian form of high-frequency energetic healing. Seichim is similar to Reiki in that it creates a connection between the recipient and the universal source of vital loving energy in the surrounding energy field in order to stimulate personal growth and heal the physical, mental, emotional, and spiritual bodies. But it is different from most forms of Reiki, because Seichim uses a very high vibrational energy that resonates on the soul level. The three distinct forms of Seichim actually include elements of Reiki and Tibetan and Egyptian healing.

During the 1980s, this form of spiritual healing was introduced to the United States by Patrick Zeigler, who received it through what he called a spontaneous initiation after spending the night in the king's chamber of the Great Pyramid in Egypt, as well as through an empowerment from a Sufi master. Zeigler never tried to organize the information into a particular system, and although he initially used Reiki-style techniques and attunements to develop Seichim, he eventually left it behind to teach the all-love practice of SKHM. Two earlier practitioners and teachers, Tom Seaman and Phoenix Summerfield, developed their own amplifications and variations of this system of healing. In the mid-1980s, Summerfield created a high-vibrational, seven-facet Seichim system that incorporates some additional symbols. Summerfield and the Australian Helen Belot later developed Seichim into a slightly different form known as Sekhem, and after Summerfield's death in 1998, Belot continued the work. Although each of these forms of energy healing has unique differences, all use the same energy stream emanating from the source of all love.

The aim of Seichim, the foundation of the other forms, is to connect the recipient to the energetic source and the higher vibratory frequencies of living light love and to then use this energy and conscious intention to promote healing on all levels. The original form of Seichim uses sounds, symbols, attunements, meditations, and reflections to access this energy, though later forms use flowing meditation more often than attunements. The intention of Seichim is to balance the energy fields and cleanse the aura so that healing can take place on physical, emotional, and mental levels. During a session, the practitioner acts as a conduit and transfers vibrational energy with the hands placed on or above the recipient, allowing and guiding the flow of energy. While tailoring the vibrational resonance to the recipient's present needs, a column of light with new frequencies is brought into the higher chakras to resolve any dysfunctions and free up any stuck patterns of behavior. Any physical contact consists of holding and pressing the body in a warm, firm manner.

From Seichim, Patrick Ziegler developed the approach of SKHM (now called All Love) for soul realization; it safely accelerates spiritual growth by identifying and clearing emotional blockages. With sound healing and flowing meditation, reflections rather than attunements are used to access love energy and to connect the universal and earth energies together in the heart. Instead of attempting to alter the energy field, SKHM uses initiations that bring the recipient into closer alignment with the light energies. This is done through an internal process of allowing and guiding the activation and flow of energy. Expansion of consciousness is supported by visualizations, source healing, various meditations, symbols, and mantras. There is also a special SKHM Infinity Dance with body movement, breathwork, and toning

that has been incorporated into group healing sessions and can be used by individuals for a spontaneous initiation experience. The living light energy activation in SKHM differs from Reiki because the hands are moved in a figure eight instead of a spiral. Most of Zeigler's work and teachings now revolve around the experience of group meditations, which explore an expanded understanding of the nature of SKHM energy streams and related healing systems.

After she met Patrick Zeigler in 1997 and experienced her own spontaneous awakening along with the initiation aspects of the SKHM energy stream, Reiki and Seichim Master Diane Shewmaker (a student of John Harvey Gray, one of the twenty-two original Reiki Masters taught by Hawayo Takata) joined Reiki and Seichem with new channeled information and symbols to create a updated, full-spectrum healing system she named **Sekhem-Seichim-Reiki (SSR)**. This variation on Zeigler's original Seichim and Summerfield's Sekhem incorporates an expansion and amplification of the energy that uses a light-body activation process to connect the soul body with divine insight and help lift trauma out of cellular memory, thus repairing old soul memories. This shift can allow issues to unfold and old patterns to connect with the higher divine self, where they can be repaired. SSR acts as a bridge to the soul level, and clients may need a series of sessions to integrate the adjustment so that they can be in balance and harmony.

During an SSR session, the practitioner acts as a channel for healing and incorporates a number of elements in a certain sequence. The elements include an initial prayer to set the healing intentions and trigger a heartfelt opening; the use of divine light helpers; sacred symbols; body scans; crystal bowl and tuning forks; a process for opening the central light column with the breath; the use of certain hand positions in which the body is held firmly or energetically without contact; an angelic light-weaving technique; and methods for sealing auric leaks and releasing unwanted patterns of behavior. In addition, Shewmaker may sing healing soul songs that arise from the recipient's being. A special energetic closing spiral helps the client integrate all that has transpired. The whole process is carried out lovingly and lightly so that rather than shutting down, the receiver is able to open up to a transformative shift.
Contact: www.celestialwellspring.com

Soul Focused Healing™ (SFH)

During the 1990s, Deborah Mills, a healer, minister, spiritual guide, and teacher of advanced energy healing, developed Soul Focused Healing as a form of preventive health care. It works to improve people's relationships with themselves and their environment by clearing restrictions and patterns that limit the potential of the mind, body, heart, or soul. SFH combines elements of ancient healing arts with modern scientific systems of energy healing to clear and balance the aura. Practitioners use the art of sensory perception to enable them to better understand and work with the client's complete physical and energetic anatomy, which includes the chakra system and its interconnected reflection in the biofield. The aim is to prevent illness from developing by awakening the remembrance of the soul's potential through treating—preferably at the early stages of dysfunction—the root cause of any symptoms that are held in the energy field. The heightened self-awareness that results can awaken the remembrance of the soul's alignment with the divine.

During a session, the client is encouraged to take the responsibility of being an equal partner with the practitioner in eradicating any problem or disease. Although recipients can definitely relax during a treatment, they should maintain strong intention and pay attention to the healing process. The practitioner proceeds with the art of palpable sensing (intuitive touch) to release blockages, rewire broken circuits, restore the natural design of the client's energy field, and allow the light of the soul to flow through from the source of all being. When the biomagnetic energy field is clear and balanced, the recipient's innate intelligence and the divine wisdom of the soul can express itself freely through the personality and physical body. Clients are then capable of living with more vitality, fully aligned with their true purpose of their lives.

Contact: www.soulfocusedhealing.com

SourcePoint® Therapy

SourcePoint Therapy, developed by Bob Schrei and Donna Thomson, arose from years from study and experience across many fields, including the healing arts and energy medicine. The work took shape over nearly twenty years based on their work in his Rolfing Structural Integration practice and her channeling and meditation. It is a noninvasive approach to healing with the intention of helping individuals reconnect with the energetic template. This universal blueprint of health is recognized as the matrix of healing energy that contains all of the information about order, balance, harmony, and flow that is necessary to create and sustain life. SourcePoint Therapy works primarily with the points close to the body in the energy field that connects directly to the universal blueprint. It is based on the fundamental principle that the body has the ability to heal by downloading and using the flow of information from this blueprint of health. By working to repair disruptions in the energetic structures and facilitate a healthy flow of energy, it is then possible to bring the structures back into alignment with the flow of information contained in the blueprint.

During a session, the practitioner first uses a body scanning technique on the information from the universal blueprint. A number of treatment strategies may be used, including the holding of geometrical patterns of points around the body, such as the Diamond Points, the Golden Rectangle, and the Navel Point. These are held without physical contact and energetically activated to facilitate the flow of healing information from the universal blueprint within the energy field. Other points on the body, such as the guardian points, may be used to engage the body's own systems of clearing and balancing. Different geometric shapes may also be used to facilitate the body's processing of the information it has received about how to achieve better health. More advanced SourcePoint Therapy practitioners may also use the Navel Point to work with blockages in the physical, emotional, trauma, karmic, or symptomatic layers.

The practitioner can work anywhere in the body, bringing to it the wisdom of the blueprint to improve order, balance, harmony, and flow, and people come to SourcePoint Therapy for all kinds of physical, emotional, and spiritual reasons. As well as being a standalone practice, SourcePoint Therapy blends well with other healing methods. SourcePoint therapists can be acupuncturists, Rolfers, craniosacral therapists, meditators, and mothers. The work is taught in short workshops interspersed with individual practice.

Contact: www.sourcepointtherapy.com

Spiritual Healing Massage

This somewhat generic title represents a broad range of divinely inspired bodywork therapies that are directly involved with freeing the highest potential of the body, mind, and soul. Many types of spiritual massage are used by medical intuitives, psychic healers, and spiritually enlightened masters. Some are born with this healing ability, and others go through extensive training in different systems of healing. The soothing bodywork is carried out to release blockages in the energetic channels, energy centers, biofield, and the body-mind-soul connection to the divine realm. A spiritual massage has qualities similar to other energy field therapies as well as recent DNA therapies, Sufi healing practices, and theta healing practices, which work through altered states of consciousness.

The treatment options for Spiritual Healing Massage are actually as numerous as the collection of applied spiritual and energetic practices found within this book. Each practitioner carries out the work in a distinctive way, and treatments will vary from one client to the next. A complete session may use massage, movement therapy, advanced breathing techniques, special movements derived from the laying-on of hands, chakra balancing, energy medicine, energy field work, spirit alignment, and a light but vigorous tuning massage with or without crystals. Loving pressure and touch is applied in a way that goes beyond normal bodywork. Some of the more spiritual elements may include the initial use of devotional prayer to purify the intentions of both the client and the therapist, followed by deep affirmations of the soul spoken by the recipient to increase inner awareness; meditations to awaken the true nature of the mind; visualizations of aspects of the divine universe; and a head massage to enhance the recipient's innate capacity for higher consciousness. The goal of all these practices is to revitalize recipients in body, mind, and soul while increasing self-awareness, connecting them to the harmony and balance of the soul's true life purpose, and discovering the divine, compassionate nature that connects them to all living souls.

Contact: www.spiritualhealingmassage.com

Spiritual Response Therapy (SRT)

This form of metaphysical healing, which operates on the soul level, was developed during the 1980s by minister and spiritual counselor Robert Detzler after working with Dr. Clark Cameron's original Response Therapy, which was based in part on clinical hypnotherapy. Detzler expanded upon Cameron's work to create a more spiritual system for searching the subconscious mind and the soul records to quickly find and release disharmonious and limiting ideas and replace them with loving, supportive ideas and beliefs. Detzler believed that each person has one or more souls within the realm of the higher self, which is beyond normal conscious awareness. The higher self can be thought of as a more awakened and complete self that is free from limitations and constrictions. SRT therapy was established as a way to gain access to relevant information through guidance from the spiritual souls and to provide a precise and painless way of allowing people to live more freely. It uses the guidance of the higher self to find restricted energies, subconscious blocks, and negative soul programming, all of which may come from this life or a previous one. Once these blocks and negative energies are identified, they are cleared from the akashic soul records contained deep within the subconscious. The healing works on all levels, freeing the soul and offering more enlightened peace of mind.

The therapy uses the muscle-response reflex to bypass the controlling conscious mind and any existing negative programming and allow a connection with the subconscious and the innate wisdom and guidance that is found within. A special set of fan-shaped charts are employed to identify soul patterns, and then a pendulum is used to pick out a number of healing symbols from these charts. While communicating with the awakening higher self, the recipient's hand is placed over these symbols to receive the healing vibrations that will clear negative energies and blockages. Statements of release and affirmations may be used to heighten awareness of the wisdom contained within the higher self. Through this process, a person may experience decreased anxiety, positive energy, inner peace, and spiritual growth on a cellular level. An SRT clearing session also enhances the effects of other healing modalities.

Once SRT has been used to clear blockages, **Spiritual Restructuring (SpR)** can be applied to energetically provide physical and vibrational balancing by reprogramming the structure of the body. The techniques used can include emotional healing, hands-on methods for aligning the body's muscles, organs, and glands, kinesiology, dowsing, and methods of vibrational energy healing. SpR with purely spiritual intent can also be done remotely at any distance.

Contact: Spiritual Response Association –
www.spiritualresponse.com

Therapeutic Touch® (TT)

Therapeutic Touch® is a holistic, evidence-based therapy that incorporates the intentional and compassionate use of universal energy to promote balance and well-being. Like other methods that work within the human biofield, this practice aims to restore health by releasing energy, imbalances, and blockages that cause anxiety and illness. This method of healing, done primarily without physical contact, was developed in the early 1970s by Dr. Dolores Krieger and her colleague, Dora Van Gelder Kunz, a medical clairvoyant. TT is a blend of contemporary methods and ancient healing practices intended to clear, rebalance, and repattern the energy field and mobilize a recipient's own inner healing capabilities. Rather than starting with the diagnosis of a disease, the practitioner works by perceiving any disturbances or interruptions in the energy field and how these have manifested within the whole physical body. It is recognized that disruptions in the biofield indicate problems in the physical body and that to effectively direct universal healing energy requires the practitioner's disciplined, compassionate belief in the client's natural healing potential. The therapist primarily acts as an energy support system for the recipient by modulating the energy in the biofield that surrounds and interconnects with the physical body. By tapping in to and directing this universal energy to the client, the practitioner facilitates the mobilization of the recipient's own inner healing capabilities without depleting her own energy.

A session involves four phases. First, the healer centers herself by entering a state of stillness that allows her own inner wisdom to connect with that of the recipient. From this space, she assesses the client's energy field and then intervenes with techniques to balance, soothe and clear the energy, ending with an integrative closing.

At the start of a treatment, the hands, which are the most sensitive tool of the healer, scan the client by slowly and rhythmically sweeping over the body to detect vibrations, areas of pressure, temperature differences, and any other subtle sensations that indicate the nature of the person's energy pattern. Then, by using strong focus, positive intention, and visualizations, the practitioner's intuitive mind encourages the proper amount of universal energy to move through her to the imbalances in the client's biofield. Next, the hands are held a few inches away from the surface of the body and moved outward from the centerline of the body, to smooth out, clear,

and balance any wrinkles in the energy field. Once the field has been cleared, the practitioner directs universal energy to the recipient by modulating the flow to areas that feel empty or cold, relying on the interconnection of the body's energetic network to soothe pain that may be caused by but distant from the site of the energy deficiency. The hands may make light physical contact on those places in the body most in need of healing, but there is no soft-tissue manipulation. The client's needs are constantly reassessed throughout the session. This process of energetic rebalancing can be incorporated into other types of therapeutic treatments, and since Therapeutic Touch has been taught to many nurses, it is now widely available in hospitals.

Contact: www.therapeutic-touch.org or
www.councilforhealing.org/tt

Theta Healing® and DNA Activation

Theta Healing is a highly sensitive form of therapy that was developed by intuitive therapist Vianna Stibal. After being diagnosed with cancer, she was able to heal herself through a meditative process that is believed to use a theta brain-wave state. The theta state describes a certain vibrational frequency of brain-wave activity in which the mind is in a deeply relaxed and meditative state. By contrast, the beta state denotes normal brain activity when a person is fully awake and alert; the gamma state represents periods of higher mental activity; the alpha state, also known as a calm state, occurs when a person is relaxed and daydreaming; and the delta state is present during deep sleep.

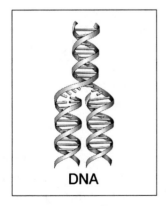

DNA

Theta Healing primarily strives to transform the recipient's mind and involves the use of belief work, downloads, and special readings. It primarily deals with resolving any mental issues or unhealthy core beliefs that can block an individual's path to living at his fullest potential. The practitioner accomplishes this healing from within a meditative theta brain-wave state that connects him with a higher god-source power. The healing is done on the seventh plane of existence in which the pure energy of creation can be used to clear past traumas and quickly awaken consciousness. The practitioner must stay constantly aware in order to witness the subtle changes that take place in the client; immediate feedback from the recipient is also essential to the healing process.

The initial intuitive readings accomplished by scanning both the physical body and chakra energy centers allow the recognition of any existing dysfunctional core beliefs, psychic hooks or cords, and energetically attached entities. It is theorized that old core beliefs that are no longer helpful may be held in several ways: as genetic records in the DNA, as beliefs instilled from childhood in the subconscious mind, as historical beliefs held in deep genetic memories or past lives, or as conditions that exist on a soul level. Reprogramming done from the theta brain-wave state will resolve or cancel out these beliefs and replace them with those that may assist the client in a more positive way. The session is concluded with a co-creating process with the individual's higher source of self and the creative energy of all that is. Many beliefs can be cleared in one session, depending on the client's readiness and intention as well as the extent of any limiting factors.

Contact: Theta Healing Institute of Knowledge –
    www.thetahealinginstituteofknowledge.com
    or www.thetahealing.com

Unified Field Therapy™ (UFT) / Quantum Vortex Technology™

Quantum physics reveals that all matter is supported by an dynamic force field of energy and that spirit appears as matter in our physical universe. Rather than focusing on a particular problem in the body, this transformational healing process strengthens self-awareness and self-love through interaction with this unified field of energy, which contains an extensive matrix that forms a sacred vortex field within which all conscious life is connected. Unified Field Therapy posits that a human being's body, energy anatomy, patterns, and potentials are determined by this matrix through the swirling strands of DNA that convey the blueprint of genetic information contained in this force field. Because this unified field can have far-reaching effects on human consciousness and bring enormous transformation, conscious access to it can bring about a significant and healthy shift in body and mind and spirit. A deep energetic interaction with this field of energy can stimulate a bioenergetics transformation and alleviate the disconnection from the soul's true purpose that often leads to disease.

Intuitive healer and channeler Meg Benedicte developed Unified Field Therapy as a way to observe and release blocked energy, clear past traumas, and awaken consciousness by transforming the molecular patterning underlying the thoughts, choices, and desires that create the human experience. According to quantum physics, time and space are nonlinear, so this change can happen instantaneously as the therapist leads the client into a deep meditative state that penetrates the vortex of spinning light. Since developing UFT, Benedicte has expanded on its principles and formulated the meditative activation process known as Quantum Vortex Technology™, which deals with the physics of the Zero Point Field and the activation of portals to self-realization. She also created the Quantum Healing Center, where people can learn how to enhance the ascension into higher dimensions, open up to their higher soul-self, and accelerate awakened consciousness, bringing them closer to spiritual enlightenment.

At the beginning of a UFT session, the practitioner takes the client into a deep, expansive, meditative, sacred space within the spinning vortex of light in which divine guidance can be obtained. By reading the energetic soul blueprint or akashic record within the unified field, the practitioner can locate and assess the source of existing limiting patterns of dysfunction. She then palpates and integrates the energetic fields of consciousness within the unified field that surrounds and permeates the recipient to make the corrections that can transform the molecular patterns in the physical body. This not only allows the release of stress and energy blocks but also clears away negative behavior and provides a shift in perspective in which old assumptions, intentions, and beliefs are replaced by choices that heal on a quantum level and bring a stronger connection with the divine. The treatment can be carried out with the hands on or off the body and can also be done remotely. Since a therapist will not try to verbalize the results of the therapy, it is up to the recipient to define for herself how her consciousness integrates and changes as a result of this work. A session can be experienced individually or as part of a group, and meditation CDs are also available. Contact: www.unifiedfieldtherapy.org

Vortex-Healing® / Divine Energy Healing

Vortex-Healing is a spiritually oriented healing system that is based on the premise that disease is the result of imbalances in the energy system. These imbalances are usually the result of deep emotional issues, which at their root are created from a sense of separation from the divine. Hence, healing becomes a process of not simply "fixing" but of creating greater wholeness on many levels. The ancient origins of this form of healing are reported to have begun over 5,600 years ago with an avatar—a divine incarnation—named Mehindra. After his death, he brought seven higher-dimensional beings together to form a special healing realm. He then merged his own divine energy and consciousness with the basic life force of the universe, forming an interdimensional Vortex that linked this special healing realm with the physical universe, enabling it to be used here for healing. It is from this Vortex that Vortex-Healing derives its name.

Around 750 BCE, Mehindra, introducing himself as Merlin, transmitted this Vortex to a spiritually evolved man in England. The Merlin lineage thus began on earth, along with its healing practices—Vortex-Healing. It is said that the lineage died out in the twelfth century, when the last lineage holder was unable to find a qualified student who could carry the energy of the lineage. However, in the 1990s, Ric Weinman had a divine visionary experience of and resurrected this method of healing. He began imparting it to others, both for healing and to deepen their spiritual awareness.

Rather than a conceptual technique taught by a teacher to a student, Vortex-Healing is learned through a form of direct divine-light and consciousness transmission. Once the healer receives the transmission, he is able to channel the divine energy or light, as well as divine consciousness. Divine energy is not considered the same as vital energy, personal chi, or pranic energy, which are manifested energies of creation. Divine energy is the source of these vital energies and exists at a higher vibrational frequency.

There are forty-nine different forms of divine Vortex energy, each with a different function. For instance, one is used for grounding, one for burning out infections, another to energize and clear blockages, another carries the energy of divine love, and so on. Until recently, the Vortex healer also channeled the consciousness of a higher-dimensional healing realm, but with the evolution of the lineage, the healer is now taught to bring in something deeper: divine consciousness itself.

Sessions can be done in person or at a distance. If done in person, the practitioner typically places his hands on the receiver's head and then starts to bridge divine energy and consciousness into the receiver's body. The healer does not need to be a psychic or have a special attunement to energy, for the divine intelligence that is the source of the Vortex-Healing lineage is present within the energy being channeled, and guides it. Vortex Healing not only works on the physical and emotional level, but is intended to release deeply held karmic issues, as well as to ripen the receiver spiritually. Vortex-Healing is both a healing art and a path to awakening. Contact: www.vortexhealing.org

WISE™ Method

The WISE Method is a integrated form of intuitive energy medicine that was developed in the late 1980s by psychotherapist Dorothy Martin-Neville after her research into a variety of energetic healing modalities. The therapy is an eclectic approach taking elements from Acupressure, Reflexology, Reiki, Brennan Healing Science, Jin Shin Do, Consegrity, hypnotherapy, and breathwork combined with the wisdom of psychotherapy. In supporting the body's energetic balance and healing, this integrative approach works to release constricting energies that repress the human potential and soul connection, thus inhibiting personal development on all levels. The WISE Method works with any physical, mental, or emotional problem no matter what level of conscious awareness the recipient may possess. The basic belief is that by providing a grounded, loving, and nonjudgmental environment while moving energies within the body and releasing energetic blocks, it is possible to enable true healing to occur. This healing brings a deeper understanding of belief systems, enhances self-awareness, and provides balance for the body, mind, and emotions.

During a session, the therapist works intuitively to recognize what imbalances exist in the client's body and then performs various energetic techniques that focus on clearing and revitalizing the flow of the vital life force within the body. This is accomplished by working on the body's acupressure points, meridians, energy centers (chakras), and energy fields with a unique combination of the modalities listed above.

Contact: www.energyhealing.abmp.com

Zenith Omega Healing™

Zenith Omega Healing, formerly known as Zenith, uses the vibrational energy frequencies of etheric light, color, and sound to empower a person's energy bodies (the physical, mental, emotional, and spiritual energy fields). These energy bodies can then recall restrictive memories and patterns stored within them and can clear these energy blockages, thereby restoring the individual to a higher state of being that manifests the potential for a more effective and balanced way of living. The development of Zenith Omega Healing began during the 1980s as a result of the unusual life of Minister William Whiltshire and his wife, Annie. The impetus came when Whiltshire had a heart transplant and a near-death experience on the operating table. At this time, he encountered three beings who enabled him to channel information from a higher realm and also channel this healing system, which is The Language of Light. Each of these spirit beings channeled the Zenith system to bring back this part of the Language of Light to the planet.

Zenith Omega Healing is designed to open the self to its source by using all of the seven interconnected and interactive energy bodies, or electromagnetic fields, that make up a human being's unified energy field. Human emotions are recognized as an important electromagnetic and energetic part of the energy fields, and they have a significant effect on overall physiological well-being. Over time, these fields accumulate past memories, perceptions, response patterns, and influences that can limit a person's potential. Each of the seven energetic levels contained within the unified field vibrates at its own frequency, and negative information stored there can trigger a reaction that is felt in the physical body as disorders or pain. The aim of the therapy is to support the release and clearing of these negative influences and thought patterns held and stored on a cellular level within the body and in the unified field and to restore the recipient to a higher state that will lead to a deeper experience of love, happiness, and enhanced self-healing.

During a treatment, the client is lovingly assisted in opening and balancing the flow of energy in all the meridians, chakras, and energy fields. Zenith Omega works in all planes, all time periods, and all dimensions. Through utilizing pure, high-frequency light, sound, and color along with focused intention and sacred geometry or guides, the therapy helps a person's body release the energy that is held captive by thought patterns and emotions in both the cells of the body and the surrounding energy fields. The process works on all energy bodies, even those from other lifetimes, to clear and balance challenges that the recipient has blocked so she can heal interferences in her life and encourage her soul's recognition of its true potential, thus awakening to her higher purpose. This spiritually transformative therapy can be used as a form of distance healing.

Contact: www.zenithexperience.net,
www.anneangelheart.com, or
www.twelveuniversallaws.com

X. Special Therapies

Life can confront us with unique problems, and the best possible remedy might be found where we least expect it. When I returned home after cruising the world, people often asked about my favorite place or pirates or the worst storms I experienced. Rarely did they ask about unusual situations that required special solutions, even though at sea there are many times when unexpected events require adaptation and innovation. I recall the time on Easter Island when we were anchored in a small basin rafted up to a group of other boats. This would normally not be a problem, but on an otherwise-beautiful day, the storm surge from a gale hundreds of miles away caused twenty-foot waves to break across the entrance to the basin. As tons of water surged in and out of this confined area, chaos reigned. For hours on end, the boats were tossed about, and we all invented new ways to secure and protect lines and prevent as much damage as we could. Though the local Polynesian men were a big help, swimming out with huge mooring lines scavenged from their backyards and positioning old tires on the wharf to prevent chafing, I truly believe it was the heart-centered action of the local women, who sat nearby on the shore all night and prayed for the seas to calm down, that we could thank for our survival. In each of our lives, there are many times when a different or unusual approach can help resolve a situation.

This section focuses on modalities of bodywork, often innovative ones, that just don't fit in the other nine categories that make up this chapter. Some are special because they focus on parts of the body that aren't highlighted in the broader established categories. These include modalities that are limited to, for example, work on the head, the breasts, or a single body system. Some are here because it is the method of delivering the bodywork that is unusual. Where else would you put a massage performed without using the hands or while hanging from a rope or a bar? Some focus on particular population groups, such as animals, infants, children, the elderly, cancer patients, or pregnant women. There are those that act in the sacred realms, gathering information from spirit guides or directly connecting the recipient with the divine, and those that place recipients in an altered state of consciousness so they can access the healing power that lies within. Some could be equally at home in more than one category; Applied Kinesiology uses the physical body as the vehicle for testing energy, and the various forms of sound healing affect both the physical and energy bodies. Certain modalities may be scientific or sacred in nature, while others employ indigenous or shamanic methods of healing. I invite you to explore and wonder at these special approaches to healing and to try out those that speak to you from these pages.

AcroSage

AcroSage is a special type of bodywork in which the recipient is literally suspended upside down in a variety of inverted positions while supported on the hands and feet of the therapist. It was developed by former circus clown and acrobat Benjamin Marantz in 1992 after he sustained a back injury. With newly acquired skills in massage, he began experimenting with his partners in an acrobatic troupe. Marantz eventually created a form of therapy that combines massage, acupoint work, yoga positions, and acrobatics to restore graceful ease and encourage the exploration of a deeper sense of trust and joyful surrender. However, it may be a challenge—though possibly a learning experience—for those who cannot trust another for support in these inverted positions.

One of the many positions found in AcroSage.

During treatments, the practitioner uses the legs and hands to support the recipient in a variety of inverted yoga postures. This upside-down position relieves any pressure on the neck or spine. In certain positions, the practitioner's arms and hands are free to massage the upper body of the client. In addition, as the recipient relaxes in an inverted position, the spinal column can naturally readjust itself. Inversions improve circulation, increase blood flow to the brain, and allow the organs to relax in a position free from the usual restraints of gravity. AcroSage can even help a person view her identity from a different perspective, revealing a deeper purpose with more possibilities.
Contact: www.acrosage.org

Agni Dhatu Therapy

A peaceful, fluid, and spiritual form of hands-on bodywork based on Ayurvedic Samadhi Yoga, Agni Dhatu assists a recipient in cultivating the inner metabolic fire, referred to as the energy of bliss, by working with the psychic energy channels of his divine nature, the secret flame deep within the heart that witnesses all states of consciousness and their daily manifestations. In Sanskrit, *agni* is the fire that acts as a catalyst for healing by stimulating the flow of vital prana energy through the body, and *dhatus* are the seven foundational elements making up the body. Ayurvedic health care considers that when the seven dhatus (blood, plasma, muscles, fat, bone, bone marrow, and reproductive fluids) are in proper equilibrium within the body, a person can function in harmony with his divine nature. However, when disturbances arise, disease can occur. Agni Dhatu therapy helps enable the recipient experience super-consciousness by healing the subconscious and alleviating any resistance or blocks that interfere with a sense of oneness with his divine nature and soul purpose in life.

The massage involves manipulations of the soft tissue and muscles along with a technique known as air pumping, which has a strong effect on pranic energies and helps the recipient connect to the deepest layers of the psychic channels. The therapy includes a purification process, known as Zenith Omega Pattern Clearing, that works on the surrounding energy fields. (See more under that heading in the section on Energy Field and Spiritual Therapies in this chapter.) Nutritional supplements also play an important part in Agni Dhatu therapy.
Contact: www.ayurbalance.weebly.com/dhatu.html or
www.nzhealth.net.nz/ayurveda/dhatus.shtml

**Akashic Record Analysis /
Akashic Field Therapy™ (AFT)**

It is believed by certain insightful individuals that information about everything that has transpired on every level of reality since the beginning of time is contained within a subtle dimension known as the akashic realm or akashic field. This realm is considered to be a virtual sea of energy beyond time and space that is the storehouse of holographically embedded records of all the events, thoughts, words, and actions of the universe. This realm of cosmic collective consciousness is beyond the normal perception of reality; it is similar to the universal mind that exists at a quantum level within each being. The akashic records are seen as a divine, soul-level spiritual resource full of impressions that can impart beneficial wisdom. Direct communication with all other beings is made possible in the akashic realm, and the wisdom revealed is useful in healing dysfunctions and providing spiritual transformation.

For most people, direct communication with the akashic field is not possible, because it can only be accessed at a deep level within. But yogis, psychics, clairvoyants, parapsychologist, and others with special abilities have been able to "read" these records while in an altered state of consciousness. American mystic Edgar Cayce carried out his readings in a trance sleep state; some yogis accomplish it through deep meditation. Individuals who have undergone extreme life events, such as near-death experiences, have sometimes gained access to this dimension of perception. However, it is considered possible for almost any individual, given the correct guidance, to enter a transcendent state of mind in which expanded sensory perception provides direct access to this information.

Once pertinent information and counsel from the akashic records is acquired and integrated, it is then possible to resolve any personal problems or traumatic memories that limit a person's potential. Most people will need to find a clairvoyant, mystic, or adept who is capable of accessing and analyzing the records and verbally relaying these insights. Some adepts have claimed to be able to guide the novice in channeling the information, but how this is accomplished is not totally clear, although it seems to be a process of mutual meditation in which the guide facilitates an initial opening into the akashic realm. Using a process similar to entrainment, the recipient is then brought into a highly resonant altered state of awareness. This profound form of spiritual activity is not considered to be a modality or therapy in the usual sense, and it definitely requires the participant to have strong commitment and the willingness to enter a deep state of consciousness.

In recent times, two individuals who have been instrumental in the study of akashic records and in training people to access this information are C.J. Martes and Linda Howe. Each has founded a center to further this work.
Contact: www.akashicfieldtherapy.com/
cjmartes_akashicfieldtherapy.asp or
www.lindahowe.com

Animal Bodywork or Pet Massage

Although it is based on the same principles and uses methods similar to those applied to humans, this form of bodywork is obviously for animals, although I personally have a cat that applies the Paw Pressure Technique to those she loves. There are professional massage therapists who work on animals, but a number of different forms of pet therapy can be offered to favorite animal friends by anyone with some basic, simple training. Treatments can be carried out on cats, dogs,

Receiving a paw-pressure treatment.

horses, and even elephants (in Malaysia), and generally use some form of Swedish massage, though other modalities, such as Reiki or Reflexology, are also helpful in restoring healthy functioning to an animal. The bodywork is also useful for creating a human-to-animal bond and helps with an animal's dysfunctions in the same way it does for humans. In many cases, simply gently holding the traumatized area of an animal's body is sufficient, though in other instances, this may not be possible if the animal is too unsettled. The ability to give a complete (though often short) treatment depends largely on

familiarity and friendship with the animal. Animals will often move away when they have had enough of a treatment. This is quite noticeable to those who pat their cats.
Contact: International Alliance for Animal
Therapy & Healing – www.iaath.com or
www.animalmassageguide.com

Komitor Healing, also known as **Healing Touch for Animals**®, was developed by veterinary technician Carol Komitor during the 1990s. Her mission was to develop a deeper connection between animals and humans during treatment of an animal's injury, illness, wound, or behavioral pattern. The techniques concentrate on the animal's energy centers and energy fields. Komitor acknowledges that animals are very receptive to healing energies and that the actual techniques will vary with the particular needs of the species. Some animals are very amenable to hands-on treatments, but wild animals must often be treated from a distance.
Contact: www.healingtouchforanimals.com

Tellington TTouch® is a gentle method of animal bodywork that was developed by Linda Tellington-Jones to improve an animal's functioning on the cellular level. The method can also be used on humans. Since a typical session incorporates circular touch with light pressure on the skin, it is most appropriate for animals who have already had some human contact.
Contact: www.ttouch.com

Applied Kinesiology (AK)

Kinesiology can be described as the study of movement and muscle response, and Applied Kinesiology refers to a noninvasive method for diagnosis known as muscle testing, in which an elicited reflex response of muscles provides feedback. Modalities using Applied Kinesiology combine this muscle testing with bodywork to create physical, mental, and emotional integration, restore harmony, allow fluid movement, and alleviate dysfunction. Besides muscle testing, sometimes referred to as autonomic response testing, diagnosis of existing problems also includes a thorough analysis of lifestyle, habits, and posture. Bodywork such as joint mobilization, acupoint stimulation, craniosacral techniques, and soft tissue work can be part of the treatment, and nutrition and exercise are important in the overall therapy.

Applied Kinesiology uses the bioenergetic feedback from muscle testing to access the wisdom held in the body on an unconscious level to quickly determine the source of a problem and to suggest ways to remedy the situation. Various types of muscle testing have been developed over the years, but they all share a key concept: that the strength or weakness of a muscle in response to a specific stimulus can show the condition of the body system being tested and indicate where imbalances may exist. These imbalances indicate disruptions in the flow of energy to the muscles, and evaluating acupoints and their underlying meridians can also give information about the status of energy flow and the condition of the internal organs or the immune system. Since emotions have an electrical quality, muscle testing can be useful in determining a person's emotional relationship to various aspects of his life.

Muscle testing with the arm extended.

In practice, the basic testing is fairly simple. The practitioner asks the client to extend an arm (or another limb) and resist any attempt to move it. Then the practitioner "asks a question" with a stimulus, such as touching a certain point on the body in a specific way, and applies pressure to the outstretched arm in an attempt to move it. The strength or weakness of the arm in resisting this force answers the "question," thus revealing any imbalances in the energy flow. Muscle testing can be used to inquire about environmental stresses; the effect on the body of thoughts, emotions, memories, or specific places; and the body's response to sounds, movements,

smells, and tastes. By holding a specific substance near or against the body, reactions to allergens and the beneficial or harmful effects of foods or supplements can be determined. Testing can also be done through gauging the body's response to verbal questioning while touching problem areas. Once a problem area has been identified and treated with the appropriate form of bodywork or energy medicine, retesting can confirm the success of the treatment. Remote or surrogate muscle testing has also been used successfully.

Chiropractor Dr. George Goodheart first developed Applied Kinesiology techniques during the treatment of a patient in 1964; he primarily employed muscle testing as a way to help maintain spinal adjustments by testing the vertebrae. This method is now being used by many chiropractors to assist in structural corrections, among other things. In 1970, Dr. John Thie, an associate of Goodheart, went on to create a more holistic system called Touch For Health, which used muscle testing to identify the flow of energy through meridians. He was instrumental in spreading Applied Kinesiology around the world. Since that time, various forms of Applied Kinesiology have been created for therapeutic and educational purposes; the following listings are a sample of some of the specialized forms presently in use. Related modalities that use elements of Applied Kinesiology, such as Body Talk, Dynamic Energetic Healing, the Emotional Freedom Technique, the Jaffe-Mellor Technique, NeuroPhysical Reprogramming, Resonance Repatterning, and the Yuen Method, are discussed individually in other sections.

Contact: International College of Applied
Kinesiology – www.icakusa.com,
www.kinesiology.com, or
www.appliedkinesiology.com

Applied Resonance Therapy (ART) is a form of Applied Kinesiology that was developed by Lynn Abbott after her studies of the Chinese meridian system and the philosophy and teachings of the Seneca Indians. This form of therapy is intended to help educate the client about energies that are out of balance because of environmental influences. ART uses muscle testing to determine the energetic effects on the body of certain resonant indicator substances. Treatments are accomplished by holding the acupuncture points along the meridians in

specific ways to make corrections in the vibrations of the energies and to awaken the natural energetic healing wisdom held in the body.
Contact: www.lynnabbott.com

Behavioral Kinesiology is a prevention-oriented method based on the energetic principles that all disease is a result of stress, which causes imbalances in the body, and that thoughts and intention can be powerful tools for discovering the true cause of a problem. This psychotherapeutic form of Applied Kinesiology was developed by Dr. John Diamond as a way to defuse unwanted habits, emotional and mental patterns of behavior, and addictions. Rather than studying muscles and movement, this approach focuses on how and why people move through life and develop certain behavioral patterns. Since the muscles act as the circuit through which energetic information passes, it is possible to quickly get to the core cause of an issue by working with them. Muscle testing, typically done by checking resistance on the extended arm, is used to bypass the client's conscious mind and locate the negative energy around any limiting or restrictive patterns so that it can then be effectively released. Special focus is placed on the thymus gland, since it plays a key role in regulating a person's psychic energy. The therapy essentially works by evaluating and defusing any stressful stimuli and rebalancing the energy by connecting it with the wisdom held in the circuitry of the body.
Contact: www.drjohndiamond.com

Bio-Kinesiology (BK) was developed by John Barton during the 1970s as one of the first modalities to research in detail the hundreds of tissues in the body, their related emotions and meridians, and the possible corrections that can be employed. An atlas of over 800 tissues has been compiled. This practice analyzes the effects of the emotions on the body and investigates what might be appropriate nutritional supplements by using a variety of muscle testing methods. In conjunction with biokinetic exercises and massage, it provide a holistic way of balancing all the parts and systems of the body. Since its inception, the therapy has grown into a research program, known as Bio Data, that uses various methods for

screening sensitivities to numerous foods, supplements, enzymes, minerals, chemicals, and nutrients. The complete program now includes various forms of massage and recommendations regarding posture, diet, clean living, and emotional healing.
Contact: www.biokinesiology.com

Body Management is a system developed by Al Berry that uses coordinated muscle testing to assess the physical, structural, emotional, mental, and spiritual harmony of a client. This intricate yet simple system focuses on the structural alignment of bones and organs to release blocked nerves and the flow of vital energy. The energy centers and meridians are activated and balanced, while body scans are used to defuse and release emotional and mental stress. It employs a specific protocol of assessment and corrective techniques for the realignment and release of restrictions in the musculoskeletal system, internal organs, lymphatic system, and joints. A method of cold-laser cranial realignment is used in conjunction with Acupressure and nutritional and environmental support.
Contact: www.kineticamovements.ca/
　　　specialized-kinesiology

Contact Reflex Analysis® (CRA) is a simple form of what is now known as Applied Kinesiology that was developed during the 1920s by chiropractor Dr. Richard Versendaal and a number of other professionals as a natural way to analyze the body's structural, physical, and nutritional needs. This method of analysis uses seventy-five known reflex areas and points on the skin to reveal the energetic root causes of a client's health problem. These diagnostic locations are derived from the Chinese system of and relate to various organs, glands, and bone structure. CRA is based on the idea that when a part of the body becomes dysfunctional, the neurological pathway that carried the energy between that part and the reflex is interrupted. When standard muscle testing on an extended arm is carried out while holding different parts of the body with the other hand, the weak point in the energetic circuit that has been interrupted can be detected by the response of the muscle. It is then possible for the related deficiency to be properly treated with the most

appropriate structural and nutritional techniques. Rather then trying to simply treat disease, the aim is to help enhance the body's own ability to correct health problems through the use of a personally designed clinical nutrition program. The therapy also recognizes that physical deficiencies can be caused by a variety of detrimental environmental factors, such as viruses, bacteria, and chemicals, which can inhibit the necessary flow of energy and nutrition to a specific organ, muscle, or gland.
Contact: www.crawellness.com/

Educational Kinesiology® (Edu-K) or **Brain Gym®** is a system designed to help anyone improve learning skills and developmental processes. A synthesis of Touch for Health, some neurological techniques, and optometric vision training, Edu-K teaches that physical movement is the key to activating the brain. After extensive research on ways to enhance learning abilities, Edu-K was created by Dr. Paul and Gail Dennison as a physical activity program that focuses on improving the functioning of the nervous system by developing the brain's neural pathways through natural movements. Twenty-six targeted repatterning movement techniques are taught to help reconnect the right and left sides of the brain so that they function simultaneously and enable the recipient to learn, communicate, and move properly with less stress. The therapy includes stimulating neurovascular holding points and trauma points on the body, massaging the ears, rubbing certain points on the top and back of the head, holding the navel while rubbing the sides of the sternum, whole body breathing, spooning the bottom of the feet, and a cross-crawl exercise that activates both hemispheres of the brain. All of the movements are intended to help activate internal energy and integrate different areas of the body and brain. A seven-minute tune-up involving breathwork, touch, and some simple physical exercises is also taught to clients. The consistent use of these practices and drinking plenty of water are highly recommended for improving personal health.
Contact: www.braingym.org

Health Kinesiology™ (HK) is a system of body-mind energy work developed by Canadian scientist Dr. Jimmy Scott. It is based on the principles of Acupuncture, Applied Kinesiology, and Touch for Health, but has been expanded to employ unique elements of psychophysiology and electromagnetics. This therapy is a specific form of bioenergetic kinesiology that uses muscle testing on the outstretched arm as a means of monitoring responses and gathering energetic information that identifies the stresses presently interfering with the client's well-being. This helps determine the most appropriate order of energy balancing that needs to be done. The practitioner then uses only light touch on specific acupoints and other energy reflex points to correct imbalances. HK also employs a variety of bioenergetic balancing methods to help the client alleviate stress, trauma, or phobias and thereby make significant life changes. Tapping techniques for clearing intolerances can be used, sometimes in conjunction with the placement of crystals, magnets, and homeopathic remedies at certain locations on the body.
Contact: www.healthkinesiology.co.nz

Muscle Resistance Testing (MRT) is a form of muscle testing used specifically together with the Jaffe Mellor Technique developed by Dr. Carolyn Jaffe. MRT is used primarily for testing the body's response to a specific substance, which could be a pathogen, a potential allergen, or even a medication, that is held in the client's hand to test whether it is dangerous or beneficial. The subconscious identifies the substance's energetic signature, which travels along the meridians via the nervous system to the brain to create a reaction that can be simply interpreted by the response of the target muscle when it is gently stressed. As with other forms of muscle testing, the process relies on the client's body to access the memory held within. MRT is used in conjunction with a number of bodywork modalities. (See the Jaffe-Mellor Technique in this section.)
Contact: www.jmttechnique.com

Neural Systems Kinesiology is a testing method that addresses the autonomic nervous system as it relates to neurological, structural, biochemical, or psychological issues. It was developed by Hugo Tobar and recognizes the importance of the survival systems of the body controlled by the brain and the autonomic nervous system, which is the primary regulator of normal and abnormal body functions and includes the sensory and motor nerves and their associated organs, tissues, and cells. The therapy, which has evolved into a practice known as **Neuroenergetic Kinesiology**, consists not only of multiple neurological tests that assess the most common forms of dysfunction in the nervous system and relieve stress, but has expanded to include testing and techniques for treating memory issues, learning disorders, and behavioral problems. Muscle testing is done with one hand touching the patient's normally strong indicator muscle while the other hand touches the skin above another area of the body. If there is a problem in that area, the indicator muscle will test weak. The testing can be done in a variety of ways on different limbs of the body, although the straight arm technique is most common. Protocols can then be applied to correct any dysfunctions in these survival systems. The complete therapy includes additional techniques that work on the neuroemotional pathways and imbalances in the chakras. A technique called "formatting," which uses acupoints to improve neuroenergetic processing, is also employed.

Contact: www.kinstitute.com or
www.healthandgoodness.com/article/
what-is-neural-system-kinesiology.html

Nutritional Response Testing (NRT) is a structured form of biofeedback that was initially developed by Dr. Dietrich Klinghardt and Dr. Louisa Williams as part of Klinghardt's Autonomic Response Testing (ART) method. The process uses standard muscle testing while holding selected acupressure points to discover the root cause of disturbances by analyzing the energetic response of the autonomic nervous system, which reflects the functioning of organs, tissues, and cells, and to evaluate the nutritional remedies that will be most beneficial in correcting a problem. The testing evaluates not only specific supplements needed to correct the underlying deficiency or imbalance, but determines the most appropriate dosage. The dietary supplements are then provided in highly concentrated formulations available in tablets, capsules, or powdered form. These special formulas contain whole organic foods concentrated in a cold-press vacuum system that preserves all of their active enzymes and vital components. Dietary changes may also be required depending on the client's condition. When nutritional or neurological imbalances are properly corrected through this detoxification process, any previous symptoms caused by improper diet, fungus, bacteria, parasites, or chemical toxins will disappear.

Contact: www.thenutritionalhealingcenter.com/
services/nutrition-response-testing/

One Brain System™, also known as the Three-in-One Concept, was created in 1995 after years of research and development by Gordon Stokes and Daniel Whiteside. It is designed to improve learning abilities and eliminate the emotional stress or trauma that limits an individual's potential This method works with the negative emotional charge that has been created rather than with the symptoms of a dysfunction. The goal is to release the emotions that interfere with the balance of the mind, body, and spirit in a way that does not cause additional stress. This system uses a unique behavioral barometer as a tool to help clients, who often have learning disabilities, identify why and how they have come to be in certain situations and what better choices can be made to enhance their health. In addition, a specific form of biofeedback called clear circuit muscle testing is used to obtain an understanding of a person's emotional issues and identify any subconscious stress that affects the body and mind. By defusing emotional stress, the client can then see new, positive options for resolving personal issues. Specific eye-movement exercises are also used to balance positive and negative emotions. The One Brain System offers training sessions, client-centered programs, and special-interest workshops, all aimed at providing new choices where none seemed to previously exist.

Contact: www.danielwhiteside.com

Total Body Modification (TBM) is a restorative therapy developed, by Dr. Victor Frank and Dr. C. Harold Havlic, that uses a sophisticated form of muscle testing to enable a practitioner to energetically evaluate, unblock, reset, and restore balance to the vital life force and the nervous system and to rebalance internal organs and other body functions. TBM essentially takes chiropractic techniques and combines and modifies them with new techniques, which together first correct how the body works before dealing with the influences on its structure.

TBM primarily focuses on the spine and nervous system and uses standard muscle testing on the arm and work with reflex test points to find and remedy the problems. Muscle testing is done by the practitioner holding a place on the body with one hand, and contacting a specific reflex point related to a particular organ or gland with the other hand. Over one hundred reflex points can be used as indicators of a client's condition; although there are many such points located all over the body, most are located on the torso and along the spine. The practitioner essentially reads the response by "listening" to the reflex as pressure is applied to it. The strength of the response helps the practitioner ascertain the condition of the related organ, and the actual adjustment or restorative correction used depends on upon these findings.

When intervention is needed, a subtle method of stimulating reflex points along the spine is used to galvanize the neurons of the brain into regaining control of the body and thereby enabling the nervous system to function properly and communicate healing to the organs. Further interventions that remove restrictions and restore balance and alignment are also accomplished by means of spinal adjustments, soft-tissue corrections, or joint manipulations. At certain times, the client is encouraged to breathe deeply while point work is being carried out. The practitioner works progressively with what attracts her attention most strongly and keeps the client informed about the condition of each organ as it is revealed throughout the session. Blood glucose metabolism is considered critical to proper organ functioning, so additional guidance and information about maintaining a diet with the proper sugar level is provided. TBM also helps a practitioner fine-tune parts of the immune system by identifying and attacking specific pathogens responsible for infection in the body. TBM is compatible with Polarity Therapy, and clients

not only come for a series of sessions to relieve specific issues but on a regular basis for preventative wellness care that helps them physiologically self-regenerate their inherent healing abilities.
Contact: www.tbmseminars.com

Transformational Kinesiology™ (TK) is a holistic educational and therapeutic process developed by Grethe Fremming and Rolf Havsboel for identifying and relieving limitations and blockages in a person's energy. Its aim is to improve quality of life by alleviating stress, enhancing learning skills, improving performance, eliminating dysfunctions, providing emotional balance, and transforming limiting beliefs. This integrative modality is grounded in the science of subtle energies and employs elements of energy clearing, transpersonal psychology, holistic counseling, esoteric healing, visualization, meditation, and Acupressure to facilitate personal and spiritual growth.

During a treatment session, in which the client is seated fully clothed in a chair, the arm-extension method of muscle testing is first used to check aspects and qualities of an individual's energy. These include such things as the level of energy, polarity, weaknesses in the energy field, dehydration, and lack of presence or centeredness. After a goal based on the client's wishes is identified for the session, the therapy continues with the use of Acupressure, structured dialogue, visualizations, movement, sound, color, fragrant oils, meditation, and a combination of the vibrational techniques deemed most suitable for energetically balancing the individual. Muscle testing is used throughout the session as an indicator of how the client is responding to the treatment. After all the balancing is complete, all the previous blockages are rechecked to confirm their release. In closing, old limiting beliefs are reprogrammed so that a person can make consciously healthy choices.
Contact: www.tk-usa.com

ARC (A Return to Consciousness)

ARC, or ARC-Work, combines bodywork with a form of therapeutic dialogue called BodySpeak. Pietro Abela, an energetic bodywork practitioner and visionary, studied energetic healing with Barbara Brennan,

Rosalyn Bruyere, and Daskalos in Cyprus. By his second year of professional practice in 1991, Pietro was enjoying a full practice with a lengthy waiting list. Working with a significant number of people allowed him to see how physical pain and discomfort often correspond to stress, past unresolved emotional issues, and insufficient emotional representation and expression. Through his familiarity with rhythm from his years as a musician and a six-year reign as a child ballroom dance champion of Northern England, he began to discern an innate rhythm in his clients' sentences—selected words stood out for him more than others. He experimented by creating questions around the words that stood out rhythmically. Later he discovered that when this line of questioning was timed around changes in body language, the client experienced significant personal changes. Pietro called this line of questioning BodySpeak. Throughout the next three years, as the BodySpeak technique was developed, seven additional therapeutic forms of communication, or BodySpeak Steps, were added to complete the technique.

BodySpeak asks questions that draw upon the body's own wisdom, helping the body remember in a safe and gentle way. Facilitators of BodySpeak quickly discovered how to form questions based on both the story that is presented and the unconscious language clients provide. This process provides a window into what lies beneath a person's surface behavior, opening the door to providing for needs that often go unrealized and unheard. An ARC practitioner, who is fully versed in the BodySpeak technique, is a professional who may choose to converse therapeutically with a client for the entire session using the BodySpeak technique while also carrying out a hands-on bodywork method. The prime focus for the practitioner in an ARC session is to create a level of safety that allows clients to share the deepest aspects of themselves, be authentic as people, and live a conscious lifestyle. ARC Bodywork has proved to be successful working with any physical, emotional, or spiritual concern or issue. A practitioner may use ARC's proven techniques in traditional settings, such as sitting face-to-face with the client, or while using energy work or another hands-on relaxation technique with the client lying down. Some ARC practitioners provide long-distance phone or skype sessions. Pietro has recently completed his first book, *A Return to Consciousness*.
Contact: ARC Institute – www.thearcinstitute.com

Ashiatsu Oriental Bar Therapy®

Ashiatsu Oriental Bar Therapy is a form of Asian massage with roots in the Philippines and India, that—as the word *ashiatsu*, which means "foot pressure," indicates—is primarily carried out with bare feet instead of the hands. American Ruthie Hardee has made adapations to this ancient form of massage and has established her own training program, which includes a new design of portable bars. The bodywork is performed by applying pressure to specific parts of the body, incorporating elements of traditional Japanese barefoot Shiatsu, Traditional Chinese Medicine, Thai Massage, Indian Keralite foot massage, and forms of Western bodywork such as Deep Tissue Massage and Swedish Massage. The bar refers to bars attached to the ceiling, which the practitioner holds on to for support and balance while standing on the recipient. This allows the practitioners to take advantage of the force of gravity, distribute her weight in a balanced way, and apply varying amounts of pressure in a gentle but effective manner that minimizes any discomfort for the client. The practitioner can also work harder and longer without becoming tired.

Traditionally, the recipient would lie on a floor mat, but these days a massage table is sometimes used. During a session, the practitioner stands on the back side of the client and performs leg strokes and rolls over an extensive area of the body to alleviate any blockages or stress. She uses her body weight, gliding foot compression, and toe action on strategic points along the muscles, as well as using her feet to create a push-pull pumping action that elongates the disc space between the vertebrae on the recipient's spine. Although this may sound like a rough form of bodywork, an expert practitioner can provide deep relaxation and relief from pain in the back and other areas of the body in a gentle way.
Contact: www.deepfeet.com

BioGeometry®

BioGeometry is an emerging science that deals with the energy of shape, and it uses shapes, colors, motion, orientation, and sound to produce a vibrational quality that balances energy fields. BioGeometrical shapes are two- or three-dimensional shapes specially designed to interact with the earth's energy fields to produce multilevel balancing effects on biological systems. Founded after years of research by Egyptian scientist Dr. Ibrahim Karim, this method contains a practical application of ancient secret temple sciences. It is based on the concept of the resonant relationships among the multiple levels of energy fields with the harmonizing quality of an amplified form of the energy found in sacred power spots (BG3). One branch of the science, known as BioSignatures, uses precisely constructed linear diagrams that resonate with the energy patterns of the body organs and correct the energy flow and qualitative balance of the organ.

This science recognizes the interconnection of the internal energy systems of the body, including the chakras and meridians, and the energy fields that surround and permeate the body. The states of the external energy fields have a direct effect on the flow of energy through the meridians and thereby influence the condition of the body and its organs. As well as being locations where energy can be blocked, acupressure points along the meridians are considered receptors of information from the external environment. By placing certain open-ended linear patterns within the external energy fields, resonance with subtle energy patterns within the organs can be established, which will amplify and correct the energy flowing to the corresponding organ, thereby bringing it into energetic balance. Dr. Karim has compiled over seven hundred specific BioSignature patterns that can be used in the process. Futhermore, BioGeometry has been proven to help protect against the harmful effects of various environmental stress factors, such as electromagnetic fields and geopathic stress, as seen in the BioGeometry large-scale town solutions for the towns of Hemberg and Hirschberg in Switzerland. BioGeometry was successful in eliminating ailments caused by electrosensitivity, among a number of other health conditions that it remedied, as well as positively impacting the overall ecology of the area. BioGeometry solutions have also been successfully used in the fields of transportation, agriculture, and architecture, and interior design.

A consultation begins with an interview in which an assessment of the environment a client lives in determines the areas that need improvement in the quality of their subtle energy. BioGeometry-licensed home energy balancing practitioners qualitatively balance the client's home environments, including electrical systems, building materials, and grid crossings underneath the bed. This solution alone can be effective in relieving environmental stress on the physical, emotional, and mental levels. For

personal solutions, clients can also wear the BioSignatures pendant or ring, which contains a vast number of general BioSignatures to balance the body qualitatively. BioGeometry also offers a home kit that will harmonize the negative effects of electromagnetic fields as well as earth radiation and radioactivity from building materials in the home. These products are simplified versions of full-scale BioGeometry solutions implemented by Dr. Karim in research and commercial projects.
Contact: www.biogeometry.com

Brainwave Optimization® (BWO)

Brainwave Optimization is a holistic, science-based, noninvasive method of achieving greater brain balance and harmony. It was established in 2001 by Lee Gerdes, a computer engineer and quantum physicist, who used this background to develop a technique that would lessen symptoms of post-traumatic stress disorder that he suffered after being physically attacked on the street. Improved bilateral symmetry (balance) and the site-specific proportionality of brain frequencies (harmony) have been shown to have a beneficial effect on numerous pathologies including physical health and well-being, focus, memory, anxiety, stress, pain, sleeplessness, addictive dependencies, weight loss, learning challenges, and more. Traumas—both physical and emotional—can cause an imbalance in the bilateral symmetry of the brain. The resulting imbalance is often exacerbated by physiological and psychological ailments and disorders. Brainwave Optimization is an effective, drug-free methodology that allows the brain to auto-calibrate its own functioning and return to a state of harmony. Benefits include marked changes in the ability to think, focus, and communicate. The scientific term for Brainwave Optimization is HIRREM® (High-resolution, Relational, Resonance-based Electroencephalic Mirroring).

Brainwave Optimization is an individually tailored, real-time methodology for monitoring, analyzing, and reflecting brainwave activity using sophisticated software algorithms to translate brainwaves into musical tones. During an optimization session, participants relax in a "gravity-free" chair and actually listen to their brain. In response, the brain recognizes any imbalance and auto-corrects itself. Unlike the pain recognition response of the body, the brain has no internal feedback loop that will allow it to rebalance or heal itself. By being exposed to its own activity patterns through

the medium of sound frequencies, the brain identifies any imbalance or disproportionality and responds by recalibrating its patterns of hemispheric symmetry and spectral power. The process is similar to fine-tuning appearance by looking into a mirror. BWO is not driven by symptoms or achieving a "cure," instead allowing the balanced state to auto-regulate any pathologies.
Contact: www.brainstatetech.com,
             www.islandbrainworks.com, or
             www.brainawakening.ca

Breast Massage

As the name suggests, this special form of massage is used to improve the health of breast tissue and functions as a preventative measure to reduce the risk of cancer. It is not sexual in any way. The technique entails specific kneading, rubbing, and squeezing strokes applied to the soft tissue to increase lymph and blood flow and clear the build-up of toxins in the ribs under and alongside the breast. This massage can be helpful for recovery from breast surgery.
Contact: www.massageden.com/breast-massage.shtml

Cayce/Reilly Massage® Therapy

This form of massage therapy, developed by medical clairvoyant Dr. Edgar Cayce and physiotherapist Dr. Harold Reilly during the 1940s, can employ an assortment of modalities, but primarily relies on an advanced style of Swedish Massage. The treatment is accomplished after an assessment of any protective body armor that a client may have developed over time because of difficult or traumatic experiences. The massage is designed to balance the sympathetic nervous system with each of the other systems in the body to stimulate blood and lymph circulation while balancing spinal nerves and providing increased range of motion in the joints.

The bodywork incorporates vigorous rhythmic pressure with continuity of contact as well as compression in a relatively intensive method of treatment involving the manipulation of tissue and joints. Warm, moist castor oil or glycothymaline packs may be used, and treatments may incorporate energy-balancing work. A research foundation and school of healing therapies has been established in honor of the developers, who had a significant influence on establishing new insight into the psychological and physiological aspects of bodywork.
Contact: www.edgarcayce.org/massageschool/

Chair Massage

Rather than being a modality itself, Chair Massage describes a brief type of treatment given to clients who simply sit fully clothed in a chair. The chair could be located in the work place, the office, or on the side of a street that people use on their way to or from work. A number of therapeutically designed portable massage chairs are now available to practitioners, although they can use whatever is available. This form of treatment often uses either Swedish Massage or Shiatsu, but other modalities could be carried out as well. Sessions are generally quite short and simple, typically focusing on the back, shoulders and neck. The aim is to provide a soothing and relaxing experience that will alleviate any stress held in the body, reduce muscle constrictions, and improve circulation. Chair Massage is becoming popular for those with busy lifestyles and only time for a short break.

Champissage™ / Mehta Face Massage

Champissage is the modern-day form of an ancient Ayurvedic head massage called Champi, traditionally performed within the family by women to help their hair and scalps stay healthy. Champissage was brought to England in 1981 by blind osteopath Mehta Narendra, at which time it became known as Mehta Face Massage. Narendra modified and expanded the traditional form to include work on the face, neck, upper arms, and shoulders, which are areas of the body where everyday stress and tension accumulates. The practice now also includes more subtle forms of energy work on the energy centers, or chakras, to bring the energy of the entire body back into balance.

A Mehta Face Massage treatment is gentle, firm, and rhythmic, and during the massage, the client is encouraged to relax and breathe deeply so that more oxygen is supplied to the tissues. A session often begins with deep kneading and probing of the neck and shoulder muscles to relieve the stress often held there. Work on the head includes rubbing, squeezing, tapping, and prodding, and the hair is tugged and then combed with the finger tips. Acupoints on the face can be pressed to relieve sinus pressure. Besides stimulating the scalp, the goal of the treatment is to relax the head muscles, stretch and mobilize the tissues, tonify and ease muscle tension in the upper body, disperse toxins, nourish the skin, stimulate the movement of lymph, and increase

---

blood circulation. Since no oils or special equipment are necessary and the client remains fully clothed, this treatment can really be done anywhere.
Contact: www.indianchampissage.com

Chavutti Thirumal Massage

Chavutti Thirumal Massage is a traditional Ayurvedic treatment, also known as Keralite Massage or Indian Rope Massage, in which the practitioner uses the feet instead of the hands to massage another's body. It was originally developed in Kerala, a province in southern India, to provide practitioners with an alternative way to heal and promote suppleness and flexibility in a client. In this type of whole-body massage, the practitioner stands on the recipient while holding on to ropes hung from the ceiling for support.

During a treatment, the bare feet manipulate the energy pathways (nadis) on the back and front of the recipient's body while also addressing muscle and bone alignment. Long, controlled foot strokes are used in a deep, continuous movement, one foot after another, and well-trained feet can stretch, probe, knead, and soothe every muscle and ligament. The rope support allows the practitioner's feet to travel the full length of the body in one sweeping motion and prevents putting too much weight on the client. Balanced in a standing position, the therapist can, if necessary, use much greater pressure to remove deep-seated tensions in the recipient's body. Using liberal amounts of oil and body weight, the practitioner can call on all parts of the feet, including the instep, toes, and heels, to complete the work with great precision and accuracy in a deep yet subtle way. The recipient is encouraged to use deep breathing to help relax during the treatment. Back problems are among a number of issues reported to respond well to this type of treatment.
Contact: www.dhanurvedam.com/treatments.html

Couples Massage

This is not so much a form of bodywork as a way in which bodywork can be carried out. In Couples Massage, two people in the same room are massaged simultaneously by two different therapists. This service is often offered by spas in a special suite as a way for partners or friends to have a shared experience that may enhance their relationship. It can also be a wise way to introduce a shy partner to his or her first bodywork

experience. Sessions may include aromatherapy, ecstatic music, steam showers, and lounging beds. Although conversation between partners is possible during a treatment, it can also be distracting for some participants; it would be best for the recipients to agree about verbal communication before the treatment session begins.

Four-Hands Massage

As the name implies, this form of massage is applied by two practitioners. The actual bodywork may not be unique, but when two therapists work on a recipient simultaneously, his senses can be so overwhelmed that the mind disengages and allows him to surrender fully to the soothing experience. Four-hands massage is most often used simply simply for relaxation, but certain modalities call on more than one pair of hands to treat injuries or dysfunctions. Some energetic modalities of bodywork, such as Reiki, can be carried out with even more than four hands by employing a number of practitioners; however, in the example of Reiki, the actual physical contact is limited, since the work is focused on the surrounding energy fields.
Contact: www.dimasmassage.com

Geriatric Massage

Geriatric Massage is often found in a long-term-care facility or hospice, where many elderly or seriously ill patients reside. Although treatments are often short and use mostly soft-tissue manipulations and gentle strokes to improve circulation, relieve pain, and increase range of motion, they can be tailored to suit the specific health conditions and concerns of the senior client. Though individual sessions frequently use elements from Infant Massage or basic Swedish Massage, many other techniques of massage therapy can be incorporated. Appropriate care is necessary for those who suffer from age-related diseases, such as arthritis or heart conditions, and may require practitioners with specialized knowledge. Since a variety of contraindications must be recognized and considered, therapists need to be familiar with each client's medical history and problems that might arise as a result.
Contact: www.daybreak-massage.com

Healing Touch Spiritual Ministry (HTSM)

The Healing Touch Spiritual Ministry developed by Linda Smith works to perpetuate the legacy of healing touch displayed when Jesus performed hands-on healing for people suffering from all kinds of disorders. Besides hands-on therapy, HTSM provides educational programs about the spiritual and scriptural aspects of healing touch for faith communities and caregivers worldwide. This healing work, a heart-focused process that enhances the light of God, strives to bring brilliant hues of light to those in need through a process that includes the use of prayer, creative visualization, hands-on energy healing, and anointing with essential oils. The aim is to raise the body's energetic vibrations through entrainment, moving them toward a dynamic state of equilibrium and balance. This can correct any underlying electromagnetic imbalances that cause disease or dysfunction. Like energy healing itself, therapeutic-grade essential oils contain energetic frequencies that naturally support a body's health and heal through harmonic vibrational resonance. In each session, the practitioner strives to find the right combination of aromatherapy, prayer, and hands-on work that will help the client move toward a state of harmony and balance. Educational courses in the application of hands-on energy healing and the use of essential oils discussed in the Bible are provided for groups of students.

Contact: Institute of Spiritual

Healing & Aromatherapy –

www.htspiritualministry.com

Hikmat Healing
(Unani Tibb Medicine Therapy)

Hikmat Healing, also known as Unani Tibb Medicine Therapy, is based on healing wisdom from ancient Egypt and Mesopotamia that was later influenced by the Greek physician Hippocrates. This Islamic healing system was formalized by Arab and Persian physicians and was propagated by Hakim (doctor) Ibn Sina (also known as Avicenna) in his *Canon of Medicine*, written during the Middle Ages. The philosophy and methods eventually arrived in India and are now practiced throughout the Near East. Because of the far-flung trade routes of the ancient Persian Empire, certain elements of Unani can be recognized as both coming from and influencing ancient Tibetan medicine. Hikmat affected the development of homeopathy, and in India, branches of Hikmat medicine cover the disciplines of internal medicine, gynecology, obstetrics, pediatrics, toxicology, psychiatry, rejuvenation therapy, sexology, diet therapy, and hydrotherapy.

Hikmat Healing is rooted in the body-mind connection and the belief that spiritual peace is essential for good health. Each individual's constitution is seen as composed of four elements (air, fire, earth, and water), four humors or body fluids (blood, yellow bile, black bile, and phlegm), and four qualities (hot, wet, cold, and dry). Treatment involves balancing these components. A person's environment (especially the air), food, physical movement, rest, sleep, wakefulness, and emotional or mental states are major factors that affect the ability to maintain good health and may need to be corrected. Herbal remedies are integral to the healing process, and a wide variety are available today. The practice of Unani Tibb Medicine Therapy remains a strong healing force for millions of people in many parts of the world.

Bodywork is only one part of the Hikmat Healing system, and it is generally a mix of other modalities with a variety of techniques. However, today it does seem to primarily include Reflexology, Ayurvedic methods, and elements of some Western modalities, such as Osteopathic Manipulation. Two unique components sometimes incorporated for infections, injuries, and illness are bloodletting, carried out by puncturing certain reflex points, and the use of cold and hot suction cups. Although these practices are now most likely done just in Asian countries, they were still in use in the West up until the late 1800s, after which allopathic medical approaches became dominant.

Contact: www.unani.com

Holoenergetic Healing®

Developed during the 1980s by physician and holistic energy practitioner Dr. Leonard Laskow, this integrative form of healing focuses on both the energy of unconditional love and the energy wasted by maintaining the misperception that the mind and body are separate entities and that we are each separate from all other beings. It recognizes that love and compassion can produce transformational changes that can be measured scientifically, a concept supported by his research into their effects on tumor cells, molecules of water, and the structure of DNA. Holoenergetics goes beyond the simple relief of symptoms to determine and resolve the fundamental source of distress and illness. It is designed to energetically empower a person to transform and heal himself through breathwork and techniques that invoke love, intuitive awareness, forgiveness, and conscious choice. Love has the power to dissolve the recipient's sense of separation and open him up to his true nature, which is the foundation of healing into wholeness.

In summary, Holoenergetic Healing is a method of healing that "traces" illness, suffering, and distress back to their experiential roots and releases these separative energies, perceptions, and beliefs at their core, bringing a person back to wholeness with himself and his spiritual essence.

Contact: www.laskow.net

Hypnotherapy / Hypnotrance

Although not a form of hands-on bodywork, this type of therapy has the same goal as many: to return the recipient to a state of maximum well-being. However, its methods are quite different. States of deep relaxation and awareness induced by guided imagery and the powerful suggestions made by a therapist allow the recipient to access the subconscious. The therapist guides the client to access memories, conflicts or trauma buried in the subconscious and bring them up safely to the conscious level to be recognized, understood, and released. Hypnosis is often misunderstood to be a form of mind control; however, the therapist is totally dependent on the client's willingness to be receptive to positive suggestions and cannot act against her will. By reprogramming the subconscious mind, old habits can be broken up and replaced by new, healthier ones. The shift in the subconscious will then be reflected in the recipient's conscious activity.

Hypnotherapy can be used for many purposes, such as behavior changes, weight loss, smoking cessation, hypnobirthing, and as a way to help a woman give birth without pain. In hypnobirthing, a client is taken back to the time of birth to help alleviate issues that were caused by that event. Regressive therapy is a particular type of hypnotherapy in which a client's awareness is directed back in time to recall, understand, and heal a repressed experience. The process can be carried out with people of all ages and can be quite transformational. Hypnotherapy has been used for medical problems and as part of psychotherapy.

The origins of hypnotherapy have been accredited to Jean-Martin Charcot, who was the first to identify various hypnotic levels back in the 1870s. Since that time, other forms have been developed. The Ericksonian Method of hypnosis, developed by psychiatrist Dr.

Milton Erickson, is one of the most widely respected methods; it uses a combination of relaxation, fixation, and suggestion. In this form of hypnotherapy, various techniques can be used to induce an altered state of mind, including the progressive relaxation technique in which the client is made so comfortable that thoughts and images can be directed deep into the subconscious to address any problematic issues and create beneficial changes. Today, the Ericksonian method represents a standard for the practice of hypnosis, which has been incorporated into a variety of other bodywork modalities.
Contact: American Society of Clinical Hypnosis – www.asch.net or The Milton Foundation Inc. – www.erickson-foundation.org

Infant / Child / Pediatric Massage

Bodywork performed on an infant or child has had an important place in many cultures. It is common in Asia and the Pacific Islands, where midwives may use massage to correct skull deformities caused by the birth process. In China, the massage therapy known as Tuina includes a form of infant massage. Shonishin, a Japanese form of Acupuncture performed without needles, is appropriate for children of any age. In recent years, infant massage has gained popularity in the West, although education continues to be needed to overcome the negative association of touch with the horrors of child abuse. Scientific research has revealed that touch can enable infants to attain better balance, posture, coordination, and behavioral patterns. Some cross-cultural studies show that babies who are held, carried, rocked, breast-fed, and massaged grow up to be adults who are more good natured, compassionate, and cooperative. Parents can learn to lovingly massage their babies as a simple way to encourage a child's growth and digestion, alleviate any birth trauma, demonstrate a relaxed and nurturing family environment, and create a healthy bond between child and parents. Massage has been shown to be particularly beneficial for premature babies.

Parents can easily massage their babies while sitting with the infant resting in the lap. The techniques most often used are those found in Swedish Massage, but the touching is softer and simpler. The firmness of touch depends on the individual infant, and the hand movements are usually smaller, often circular, and carried out with a wavelike motion. Stroking the torso is considered good for the digestion. The length of a session is generally brief, because infants are often restless. The use of oils is discouraged, since they may get into the child's mouth, although vegetable oil can be applied if necessary.

Who is massaging whom?

Many infants or young children are easily bored or quickly become fidgety, but a way to avoid this is to make hands-on contact more playful or even humorous by presenting it as a story told by the fingers. This can be accomplished while using the fingers to represent animals, little creatures, or people going on some sort of adventure or exploration on the terrain of a child's body, covering the back, legs, and head. The ears make a great cave for hiding, and the hair can be a dense jungle. It is particularly enjoyable for children ages four to 10 and, with the right story, is a great way to calm them down and put them to sleep. A gentle, relaxing form of pediatric massage, known as BART (Bonding and Relaxation Techniques) Therapy, was developed by Virnala McClure. It incorporates a complete program for nourishing the bond between parent and child.
Contact: International Association of
Infant Massage – www.iaim.net,
www.infantmassagefoundation.com, or
www.ahn.mnsu.edu/fcs/infant_massage.pdf

Integrated Awareness® Therapy
Integrated Awareness Therapy was developed by Lansing Gresham as he explored how energetic touch relates to emotions and personal transformation. It is well known that feelings and thought patterns can create blockages in the physical body. By combining elements from a number of modalities that use energetic touch, self-guided movement, and conscious awareness,

Integrated Awareness is designed to induce a state of consciousness in which blockages that limit a person's fullest potential can self-release. Changes in the client's experience can impact her mental, emotional, physical, and energetic states of well-being. This form of therapy, which can be customized for each individual, can not only eliminate dysfunction and improve a person's energy level but also promote personal healing through a transformation in consciousness.

During a session, elements of holistic modalities such as Craniosacral Therapy, the Feldenkrais Method of Somatic Awareness, Shiatsu, Visceral Manipulation, Zero Balancing, and other somatic techniques are used to help release blockages caused by pain from past traumatic experiences that have been held in the body. However, Integrated Awareness Therapy expands upon these modalities by physically contacting multiple sites either simultaneously or in succession. This allows the recipient to experience an awareness of different behaviors, feeling states, and thought patterns and the way in which they connect to the body's tissues, fluids, and organs. With this awareness, the body recognizes new choices and shifts into a natural restorative state and a higher level of functioning. By working with both the body and the psyche, all levels of perception are enhanced, and the recipient may have a sense of expansion and clarity at the end of the session. Individuals may choose single or multiple sessions, depending on the nature of their issues, and after the initial session, a dual session with two practitioners working at the same time can be scheduled. Each treatment plan is unique, honoring choice as the individual moves through her own transformation.
Contact: Center for Integrated Awareness –
www.inawareness.com

Integrated Kabbalistic Healing™ (IKH)
This compassionate system of healing, developed by Buddhist teacher and Kabbalist Jason Shulman, combines the traditional Judaic metaphysical path with Eastern mysticism, the Western notion of healing touch, and the broader understanding of a person recognized in holistic forms of psychotherapy. Shulman is also the founder of The Society of Souls, a meeting place of the heart and a school offering training in this method of soul-centered healing. IKH uses the profound divine insights of the Kabbalah to access a person's innate healing

power by revealing how divinity penetrates all spheres of reality as displayed in the Tree of Life, the Etz Chaim. The subtle methods used are intended to empower a return to the true self and open the way to a deeper truth than has been realized before. A sophisticated process works to rectify the recipient's distortions, imbalances, and disconnections at the deepest level possible at that time so the individual can get beyond any overwhelming spiritual crisis and enter a world of expanded perception.

A typical treatment session consists of an initial exploratory discussion followed by hands-on healing methods that are determined based on the results of this dialogue. As the treatment continues, the work spirals deeper toward existing core issues and their corresponding divine states of being. Treatments are not based on energy systems, but instead explore the potential magnitude of consciousness; physical or emotional issues that a person brings to a session are considered to be the actual doorways leading inward to these deeper truths. The goal is to undergo personal transformation by removing psychic wounds and changing patterns that inhibit awakening. The effects are unique to each recipient and will vary, but should include change at some level of consciousness.

Contact: A Society of Souls – www.societyofsouls.com

Jaffe-Mellor Technique™ (JMT)

The Jaffe-Mellor Technique is an energy-based healing method for treating allergies, chronic and complex health disorders, and the emotional disparity which often accompanies ill health. It was created by Dr. Carolyn Jaffe, DOM, ND, a naturopathic physician and doctor of Oriental medicine, and Judith Mellor, RN, C.Hrb., a holistic nurse and certified medical herbalist. With their backgrounds in Western medicine and vast knowledge of energy medicine, they created this healing process that successfully resolves 75-100% of symptoms related to arthritis, autoimmune disorders, and many other chronic illnesses that more than two decades of their clinical research have led them to believe are caused by an overgrowth of specific bacteria and/or invasion of specific virus strains. JMT recognizes that diseases caused by pathogenic microorganisms are far more prevalent than commonly believed.

To understand how the body can become so ill, it is important to understand that humans are made up of cells and bacteria that adapt continually to defend,

support, and maintain good health. Stress in any form can all have a serious effect on the body and ultimately create a breakdown in the delicate balance between the internal bacteria and cells in the body. Stress can be created by the emotions or by poor diet and exposure to a wide range of stress-producing substances: pollutants and other toxic materials; foods adulterated with antibiotics and hormones; recreational, prescription, and over-the-counter drugs, including fluoride; radon in basements; lead in drinking water and exhaust from cars; chemicals released from landfills, household cleansers, gasoline, alcohol, pesticides, fuel oil, or cosmetics; or GMO foods, plants and animals whose organisms have been genetically modified with DNA from bacteria, viruses, or other plants and animals. As the delicate balance between the bacteria and the body's cells breaks down, the internal bacteria begin to colonize at an astounding rate for the sake of their own survival, and the immune system's natural wisdom is compromised. It is provoked into a frenzied state of hyper-defensiveness, wildly attacking its own tissue in search of what it believes is a threat to the cells. This race for survival between bacteria and cells is further compromised as the pathogens defend themselves with the release of cytotoxic enzymes and waste material that create an even more toxic environment, resulting in symptoms for the host (the human body) that can even be deadly if not brought under control.

In JMT, working with the immune system is considered key. The aim is to neutralize the effects of pathogens while reinforcing the immune defenses so that the specialized cells can identify, isolate, tag, mark, destroy, and ultimately eliminate these aggressive microorganisms, returning the body back to a state of harmony between the friendly bacteria and the cells of the body. The technique includes a very sophisticated and focused form of Muscle Resistance Testing, a process of desensitization and intervention, and Acupuncture. More advanced cases may require the addition of injection therapy with specific herbs or homeopathic remedies to reinforce the immune system and detoxify the body.

Muscle Resistance Testing (see under Applied Kinesiology in this section) enables the practitioner to determine the underlying cause of the patient's condition. The test is done using vials containing the energetic signature of specific pathogens. As with a homeopathic remedy, even though the pathogens are no longer alive, the energy of the microorganisms is still resonating, so it is safe for the patient to hold the vial for testing without any harm. The sensitive tactile receptors (sense of touch) send information to the brain, which responds by creating a weakness in the testing muscle, indicating the immune system had been compromised by the substance in the vial. It is often necessary to test many possible vials until the brain isolates the exact microorganism resulting in the weakened testing arm.

Asian medicine proposes that there are meridians running bilaterally throughout the body with each set of meridians linked to a specific organ and or organ system. The bladder meridian runs parallel to each side of the spinal cord, which of course is protected by the cage of spinal bones. The JMT practitioner percusses specific points along the bladder meridian, which agitates the neurotransmitters, just like shaking up a snow globe. These chemical messengers carry, boost, and modulate signals between neurons and other cells in the body. The recognized pathogen in the vial being held by the patient together with the purposed action of the signals to the brain start to create a positive change throughout the body, initiating a more deliberate and focused immune response. Verbal commands from the practitioner that act on the patient's sense of hearing serve to further enhance the JMT treatment.

Next, a protocol called Essential Energy Treatment (EET) is carried out. The patient relaxes while continuing to hold the suspected vial(s), and acupuncture needles are inserted at specific points that influence the affected body systems. The needles are left in place for about fifteen minutes to deactivate or neutralize the detrimental effects of the pathogen(s). Once the immune system is working at full potential, the therapist focuses on deactivating the bacterial strain that had been causing chronic stress on the immune system. The principal goal with a JMT treatment is to interrupt the patterned immune response so that it will not flair up again. Besides Acupuncture and Acupressure, practitioners also use energy-adjusting techniques to complement the healing process. Homeopathic remedies may be prescribed, as well as a series of follow-up treatments. With each treatment, there should be a marked decrease in the client's symptoms.

Contact: Jaffe-Mellor Associates –
    www.jmttechnique.com

Kayakalpa Therapy

This full-body rejuvenation therapy, whose name can be translated as "body transformation," is part of the ancient East Indian Ayurvedic system of healing. Brought to the West by Dr. Raam Pandeya, this yogic therapy, sometimes referred to as the alchemy of enlightenment, is dedicated to promoting longevity. It uses Panchakama detoxification techniques, breathing exercises, nerve toning, herbal and mineral preparations, dietary guidelines, purifying bodywork, and exercises done to regulate the endocrine system, as well as some customized practitioner-applied bodywork. Kayakalpa Therapy is designed to release physical and emotional toxins and energetic blockages and to nurture and purify the senses, the physical body, and the mind.

Each therapy session is customized to the particular needs of the individual and can take up to four hours. After the initial consultation, known as a constitution analysis, a series of techniques is chosen by the practitioner. A typical detoxification regime begins with Nasya, in which specially prepared oils are placed in the nose, which is considered the gateway to the brain and nervous system. This is followed with Anjana eye therapy, which uses various herbal-mineral drops to purify and nurture the eyes. A herbal paste, known as Alepa, is then applied to the various vital energy points, nerves, and energy channels on the body to enliven the skin, help eliminate impurities, and nourish the cells of the body. When the paste is dry, it is removed, and a Sneha mix of rich herbal oils is applied to the whole body to nourish the cells of the skin. This is followed by a herbal steam bath, known as Swedana, that allows the oils to penetrate deeper, further purifies the skin, and releases deep-seated toxins that can be eliminated through the digestive tract. The session is concluded with Dhara Kalpa in which herbal oils are poured on the forehead as the recipient is guided in specific breathing techniques designed to stimulate the psychoneuroimmune system. Then the recipient rests in deep meditation. This revitalizing form of therapy, whose goal is to awaken the dormant life-force energy, is often accomplished through a series of sessions; the results are cumulative and most beneficial when done within a specific time frame. The main office is in Punjab, India, but workshops and training programs are available worldwide.

This bodywork therapy constitutes only part of a complete Kayakalpa retreat experience, in which instructions are given on a number of self-care therapies, such as yoga, energetic movement exercises, breathing practices, and dietary guidelines that help transform inner intelligence and enhance the awareness of the divine within. (See more under Kayakalpa Yoga in the section on Yoga in Chapter 11.)

Contact: www.kaya-kalpa.org or www.skysociety.org

Kodo Massage Therapy

Kodo Massage Therapy is a form of hands-on bodywork, formerly part of the therapeutic practices of the Australian Aboriginal people. These indigenous people honor the beliefs of the sacred Dreamtime, which acknowledge the deep connection between humans and the natural elements of the earth and emphasize the importance of truth and living in harmony with the present moment. Everything in life is linked to a sacred seed power, and their healing techniques offer a person a glimpse of his true connection to the earth. Bodywork and herbal remedies are considered a natural part of their traditional healing practices.

Kodo Massage Therapy is a rhythmic massage intended to tone and align the energy flow within the receiver. It incorporates smooth, continuously flowing circular movements, a skin-rolling technique, and soothing strokes, all intended to relax and restore tired muscles. A form of pressure-point therapy is also used in conjunction with herbal treatments. Over time, certain practitioners have incorporated various forms of skin care and aquatic therapy into this healing treatment.

Another unique form of Australian massage known as a **Kiradjee Massage**, which originated with several gifted Aboriginal spiritual healers, combines a number of different healing methods. It starts with a relaxing sequence of "dreamtime" movements on the face, neck, scalp, and upper back that move energy up through the shoulders to the neck and head, where it is cleared through a specialized cranial massage. This encourages the client to fall into a very relaxed state conducive to healing. The Lowanna facial part of the massage uses a hot face towel dipped in blue cypress essential oil. This sets the stage for further massage work that blends Acupressure, joint and limb mobilization, trigger-point work, body balancing, deep-tissue work, and Swedish methods, all in one holistic treatment. The practitioner works to energize the body, promote better breathing, and generally seduce the muscles into surrendering their

knots of trapped memories in a pain-free manner. This form of massage is also called "floating" bodywork, and today, this Aboriginal form bodywork is often combined with a footbath, foot massage, color therapy, aromatherapy, and other Western therapies to create a unique spa experience.

Contact: www.healinglifestyles.com/index.php/
jan2005-spaandbeuaty-spaalacarteaboriginal
or www.vital-life.com.au/massage.asp

Kolden Techniques

This gentle method of bodywork, developed by Sandra Skildum, uses a combination of techniques to release pain and open energies within the body. The treatment includes—but is not limited to—Craniosacral Therapy, Neuromuscular Therapy, Swedish Massage, Myofascial Release, Trigger Point Therapy, cross-fiber muscle work, and some energy work.

Practitioners first listen to the patient's body, muscles, tissues, and energy to determine where congestion or blockages that can cause pain, distress, or disease are located. As the treatment progresses, a series of manipulations are applied to specific muscles or at precise points to create a release and enhance the flow of energy by creating a vibration that sends waves of energy to other areas in the body that need balance and harmony. This is followed by techniques that work on a specific painful spot or area of congestion in a way that will help encourage the body to heal itself. The bodywork is done with light touch that is effective even when the client's body is clothed, and there are pauses between moves that give the client's body time to assimilate the changes in energy and vibrations. The number of consecutive moves is limited during a session so that the body doesn't get overloaded. This full-body treatment is meant to be a relaxing experience with a combined focus on energy and muscle work. This healing technique, or rather combination of techniques, can be used with many other forms of therapy.

Contact: www.massageregister.com/bodywork/
kolden-technique

Lomi Lomi Massage (Hawaiian Bodywork) and Huna Therapy

Hawaiian bodywork is part of the sacred system of healing used by the Hawaiian priests called kahunas ("experts") in their ancient ritual practices and ceremonies. Like many other holistic therapies past and present, its aim is to restore balance and harmony on the physical, emotional, and spiritual levels by using the sacred energy of mana (the universal life force). It works with three levels of the self: the unconscious, conscious, and higher self. In its purest form, this ancient healing technique enables a person to connect to her highest wisdom by utilizing seven sacred healing principles. They represent an ethical code of behavior and deeds that can turn inner knowledge and wisdom into outer success in life. Although they can be expressed in many ways, these principles essentially advance the ideas that an individual will be healthy when she is aware of illusion; will be free when able to accomplish and give without limits; will be prosperous when focused, since energy flows where attention goes; will be successful when fully present in the moment; will be happy and self confident when she has the ability to love; will be powerful by focusing the attention within; and will be positive by realizing that the power of belief is most effective when a person is aware of the truth. Real healing is viewed as an ongoing life process that requires living by these concepts and their associated behavior.

Kahi Loa Ho'okhi (Mana Healing) represents a traditional form of healing that was used by the Hawaiian masters. *Kahi Loa* means "long glide," and *Ho'okhi* means "oneness," and the healing is accomplished by stimulating the flow of sacred mana to harmonize the mind and body with nature. Passed down by oral tradition through many generations, this practice was part of a sacred healing ceremony and was firmly established in family life. The kahunas saw that all life springs from the same elemental force, and, through their ceremonies, they called upon the vital energies with breathing rituals, blessings, and chanting. The healing powers of plants, herbs, and stones were also used, as well as the well-known healing power of touch. The primary form of bodywork used by the kahunas was known as Huna Kane Temple Massage. It was a considered a sacred process that focused on the god within and the enhancement of innate psychic abilities. *Huna* is Hawaiian for "secret," and that name began to be used when Western missionaries drove the practices underground during the 1820s. But even after it was outlawed, the elders and lapa'au ("special healers") continued the practices in secret. In the early 1900s, Max Long devoted his life to uncovering the methods and teachings of what he called

Huna Therapy. He founded the Huna Fellowship and was instrumental in spreading awareness of the practices.

Bearing a significant part of the Huna philosophy, Hawaiian Lomi Lomi Massage evolved out of the temple massage originally performed by medical kahunas. This method of bodywork was first introduced to the United States in the 1880s by Douglas Graham, but it wasn't until the 1970s, when Auntie Margaret Machado brought Lomi Lomi to the general public, that the practice resurfaced as an accepted form of therapy and was spread throughout the world by her students. many styles were passed down orally in all levels of society, the temple style known as Ke Ala Hoku and Machado's Big Island Kahu style are the ones most commonly found today. Although the term *Lomi Lomi* is now widely used, in Hawaii the people performing the bodywork are called *Kanaka Lomi*, which means "massage person."

This spiritually based form of massage, sometimes called loving hands therapy, represents the best of the traditional spirit of aloha combined with modern wisdom. The invocation of the power of mana, breathing techniques, visualization, chanting, and prayers asking for the free flow of energy through the recipient are blended with a variety of long, flowing massage strokes. This work is primarily about touch that embodies the principles of caring, support, and nurturing—giving love through skilled touch. The practitioner holds a space of giving and receiving so that a healing change of mind, body, and spirit can take place in the recipient. The practitioner also connects with a higher power while identifying the client's problems and applying the therapy. The primary goal of Lomi Lomi is to help recipients remove all sorts of blockages, become more aware of their inner and outer environments, and create a more harmonious appreciation of themselves and the world around them. These are often feelings that come from the gut rather than from the mind. Today, the essence of the practice remains the same, though it has mostly lost the ceremonial aspects. However, depending on their particular lineage or training, some practitioners still retain some of the ritual. The most frequently used adjunct practices are Ho'oponopono (the restoring of harmony and healing of relationships with reconciliation and forgiveness), colonics, cleansing steam baths, and the use of cleansing teas.

A full-body treatment, Lomi Lomi uses the power of loving intention and prayer to stimulate the flow of mana while the practitioner's palms, elbows, forearms, and sometimes feet apply both gentle pressure and vigorous rubbing, stroking, and kneading. The intention is to relax the muscles, increase circulation, and break down adhesions. This work focuses on the skin, which is the largest organ of elimination in the body, as well as particular body points known as kaomi. Massaging the skin with light finger pressure or stroking movements is intended to release toxins back into the bloodstream for later excretion. The whole body from head to toe may be treated by raking, pinching, and sweeping the hands over its surface as the practitioner "listens" with the hands. The progressively deeper, rhythmic strokes flow directly from one area to the next over the whole body. The continuous, fluid strokes, very broad hand movements, rotations of recipient's body, and deep, rhythmic vibrational rocking are similar to Swedish Massage, but they are more often done with the palm, elbow, and forearm and include figure-eight patterns. The major joints are stretched and rotated for further deep-tissue relief. Acupressure point work and Hot Stone Massage may also be used. Special forms of this treatment have been developed for women before and after giving birth.

Since access to the body surface is important, Lomi Lomi is usually performed in a warm setting on a unclothed client who is draped with a cloth or sheet. There is ample use of coconut or kukui-nut oil, except when applying cross-fiber friction techniques, and herbs, ti leaves, and smooth, hot volcanic stones are sometimes placed on certain spots to soften and warm the body while the hand work continues.

Many other Polynesian islands spread across the Pacific Ocean use forms of massage therapy similar to that found in Hawaii. Generally speaking, the traditional Polynesian massage found among these island groups shows some variations in technique, but for the most part uses similar stretching, body flexing, and rubbing movements with only moderate pressure, often in conjunction with the soothing use of aromatic oils and hot stones.
Contact: www.hhacdirect.com or www.lomilomi.

Pohaku Welawela Lomi Lomi
(Hawaiian Hot Stone Massage)

Throughout the ages, people have felt better after lying on sun-warmed beaches or riverbed stones. Heated stones have also warmed their beds or kept their extremities warm, safe, and cozy. On islands in the Pacific, healers had secret uses for small, colored stones in diagnosis and treatment; larger stones were used by some for rubbing and compression. Hawaiians would heat stones in a shallow outdoor oven, wrap them in medicinal leaves (ti, 'awa, or castor) or cover them with sand and leaves, and then lie on the warm stones to heat and relax their backs. The heat could last for a long time.

Today, Wesley Sen, Dane Silva, and others have trained Lomi Lomi body therapists to carry out Pohaku Welawela Lomi Lomi or to use hot stones as massage tools, since both the heat and smooth pressure of these stones can enhance the massage work. Pohaku Welawela is a traditional, prayerful, focused massage that uses coconut oil applied like melted butter, followed by massaging the body with smooth hot stones in gliding compression strokes from toe to head and down again on both the front and back sides of the body. These smooth heated stones press deeply into the tissues to release spasms, scar tissue, and stagnant life energies. Today in spas, Pohaku Welawela Lomi Lomi with scented oil is considered a luxury treatment that restores harmonic balance to stressed locals or visitors. It may be combined with a salt rub, which was also part of the Hawaiian method of healing and cleansing.
Contact: www.islandmassagebycharlo.org/Massage-Services.html

Lympho-Fascia Release (LFR)

Lympho-Fascia Release is a form of bodywork that combines the benefits of gentle Manual Lymphatic Drainage with the more physical manipulations of Myofascial Release. After years of training in Western medicine and traditional Eastern practices, French physician Bruno Chikly developed this form as a efficient way to promote powerful healing with the least amount of force. The hands initially use the lightest touch possible and then increase the pressure as the body dictates, taking the soft touch of lymphatic drainage just a little deeper to engage the fascia, thus combining the benefits of both methods in a single stroke. As the lymphatic system and fascia work together, tension is released, and the body's healing response is maximized. The result of releasing stagnation, inflammation, and adhesions can be immediately felt as a deep wave of release throughout all the systems of the body. Creation of this wave is not forced, but only assisted by the practitioner. As with many modalities, the key to success lies in the practitioner's ability to listen deeply to the recipient's body to find specific restrictions.

Contact: Chikly Health Institute –
      www.chiklyinstitute.org/learn-chi/ldt/
      manually-identify-lympho-fascia

Manual Lymphatic Drainage (MLD)

The lymphatic system is an important circulatory network that serves the body by removing foreign matter, proteins, and metabolic waste products from tissues. The fluid lymph transports these substances to the blood vessels to be eliminated from the body. Hundreds of lymph nodes throughout the body act as reservoirs or filtering stations along this network, and they contain the infection-fighting white blood cells that are an integral part of the immune system. Lymph nodes may swell as they fill with additional immune-system cells created in response to disease. When the lymphatic system is damaged or blocked by disease or surgery, lymph cannot flow properly, and fluid may build up in the tissues, resulting in lymphedema (excessive accumulation of fluid). Massaging the lymphatic passageways can help return proper flow to the system. Many forms of hands-on bodywork can have a positive effect on the lymphatic system, but Manual Lymphatic Drainage, developed in the late 1930s, by Danish bodyworker Dr. Emil Vodder and his naturopath wife, Estrid Vodder, works directly on the lymph vessels to stimulate the flow of lymph. and strengthen the immune system. This treatment has been found to have a positive effect on many chronic conditions and is especially useful before

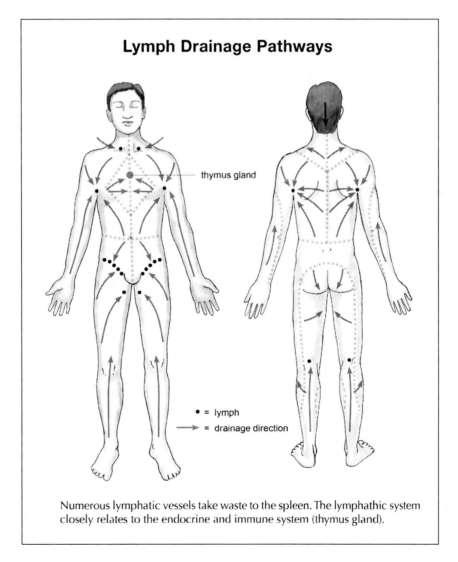

Lymph Drainage Pathways

thymus gland

• = lymph
⟶ = drainage direction

Numerous lymphatic vessels take waste to the spleen. The lymphathic system closely relates to the endocrine and immune system (thymus gland).

and after surgery and for individuals with weakened immune systems or bad circulation.

Rather than soft-tissue manipulation, MLD uses a specific sequence of precise, gentle skin massage along the lymphatic pathways with subtle on-and-off pulses of pressure to pump the lymph and drain cellular waste from the lymph nodes. This very light, rhythmical form of massage is applied in the same direction as the natural flow of lymph and uses slow, repetitive strokes that carefully stretch and twist the lymph channels, stimulate the circulation of lymphatic fluid, and relax the nervous system. Because many of the lymph vessels are found just below the surface of the skin, a thin layer of lymph can actually be seen when the flow is stimulated; some experienced practitioners are able to precisely map the flow to find alternative pathways for drainage. Treatments also incorporate techniques such as stationary circling, thumb circling, fork action, pumping, fan strokes, and scooping or rotary movements that accelerate lymph flow and drain the lymph nodes. Specialized techniques have been developed for addressing the lymphedema that is often a consequence of surgical treatment for breast cancer. In specific cases, deeper manipulations of muscles and soft tissue are incorporated to relax and relieve tension. Other methods of lymphatic drainage are found around the globe, and laser therapy has even been utilized to enhance lymphatic drainage.
Contact: North America Vodder Association of
Lymphatic Therapy – www.navalt.org

Metamorphic Technique (MT)

This transformational form of Reflexology, also known as Metamorphosis and originally as **Prenatal Therapy**, was developed during the 1950s in England by naturopath Robert St. John to treat unconscious genetic patterns and traumas originating in the womb. It is based on the understanding that stress or negative patterns formed during gestation and held inside are often related to behavioral problems or illness. Metamorphic Technique relies on a psychological map that can be superimposed on the body's reflex points. It pinpoints patterns of behavior relating to factors such as the mother's emotional state that influenced a person from conception to birth. The goal of the therapy is to change mental attitudes and resolve limiting patterns of behavior by allowing the effect of the gestation period to be witnessed on a cellular level, The treatment is

intended not only to release emotional stress but also to awaken the vital life force and set healing energy in motion by connecting the recipient with his spirit and inner intelligence. MT is also used by pregnant women and midwives for easier pregnancy and birth.

Practitioners do not speak during a treatment and practice a form of active detachment that allows the client total freedom of response. Metamorphic Technique involves a subtle process of triggering the spinal reflex areas of the feet, hands, and head with gentle touch. While working on the spinal reflexes, the practitioner's fingers stimulate healing energy that allows a physical release of undesirable patterns that were created before birth. Since no mental processing is required, the release happens without the client reliving any trauma. This reflex work is different from standard Reflexology because rather than focusing on the source of pain, it works on points that stimulate energy. It is not uncommon for the practitioner to make unusual reflexive noises (like burps or grunts) as blockages are released from the client's body and pass through the healer's hands to disappear into the air. It is considered a very relaxing treatment, and recipients may even fall asleep. A slight variation on this therapy is found in a method practiced by Jeffery Gail, which involves primarily touching the spinal reflex points on the feet.
Contact: www.metamorphictechnique.org

Mongolian Cluster Massage

Mongolian Cluster Massage, rooted in ancient tantric practices performed in the tribal areas of Mongolia, is one of those forms of bodywork that are difficult to find. In the West, its use seems to be limited to certain alternative-lifestyle groups located in California. The bodywork takes place within a ritual that explores the power of sensual play. The process is a group massage in which a person positioned in the center becomes a percussion instrument, and the individuals surrounding her become drummers, using their hands to create repetitive, evocative rhythms on her body. The drummers use various forms of massage and tantric breathing techniques while rocking in time with the music. Each participant gets a turn in the center of this shared cluster massage and is encouraged to take part with energy and joy. The rhythmic bodywork session is followed by a period of group dancing The process blends energetic vibrations, rhythmic sounds, and conscious mirroring movements with sensual, warming, and stimulating bodywork techniques.

Contact: www.tribe.net/recommendation/Mongolian-cluster-massage

Mongolian Koyashai Massage™

Mongolian Koyashai Massage is one form of bodywork from remote areas that has been revived and expanded in the last few decades. It originated from traditional Mongolian shamanic practices and was influenced by Tibetan healing methods. In Mongolia, massage (known as bana zasal) was an important part of folk medicine in family life, and children were often taught to massage their elders. Each nomadic family had its own way of performing this massage. *Koyashai* literally translated means "sun and moon," and although it focuses primarily on soothing and relaxing muscles on the feet and upper face, it is often part of a full-body massage. It is said that the main aim of this treatment is to cool the bile in the eyes and warm and liberate the stale wind in the feet. Besides being useful for improving eyesight and alleviating foot pain, it brings harmony and balance to the body, mind, and spirit.

Koyashai treatments use various manipulation techniques, essential oils, moxibustion, pulse reading, and Acupressure. It also incorporates many components that can be practiced separately. The process is slow, very relaxing, and meditative. The bodywork session is usually performed with the client lying fully clothed on a massage table, but can be adapted for the kind of recliner used in Reflexology. In recent years, this ancient form of treatment has been reestablished and developed further by Terri McLean and Gaye Sturrock. They also created a special treatment called the **Mongolian Milk Back Massage** that uses warm milk and chick pea powder to massage the back.

Contact: www.ayushiholistic.com or
www.lotusbodhi.co.uk/therapies

Myomassology

This form of bodywork was developed by Irene Gauthier as an alternative to Swedish Massage at a time when that method was one of the few forms recognized in the West. *Myomassology* means "the practice of muscle massage," but it actually combines a number of other modalities. It is an integration of ancient and new methods including basic Swedish Massage, Reflexology, Acupressure, Shiatsu, Reiki, Iridology, Herbology, Craniosacral Therapy, aromatherapy, chakra energy balancing and ear candling. Clients are also instructed in Tai Chi, qi gong, meditation, yoga, and nutrition. The therapy is designed to provide the body with a deep sense of well-being, relieve pain, and reduce tension through a program that uses deep-tissue work and other holistic approaches. As with many other approaches, the therapist recognizes that each person is unique, so all treatments are tailored to specific needs.

Contact: www.irenes.edu

Native American Healing

Indigenous peoples, including Native Americans, have used hands-on healing throughout the ages. These cultures recognized that the health of one person benefited the community as a whole. The medicine man's knowledge of healing, shamanic rituals, and energy practices was extensive, and cleansing and purifying techniques were handed down through the generations. However, much of this knowledge has been lost over the centuries, especially practices from the Aztecs, Mayans and Incas. Fortunately, some of these practices were kept alive in secret, and a few of the old healing methods can still be found in use today. Offering healing touch to sweep away negative energy and activate its positive opposite seems to be universal, but a complete picture of the healing methods and practices used by Native Americans is hard to piece together, though certain aspects have been handed down to present-day healers.

In North America, each tribe—many of them nomadic—adopted its own methods of healing, sometimes influenced by or influencing those developed in Central and South America. Hands-on healing was only one part of their medicine, but a very integral part. Some Native American bodyworkers recognized the concept of holding the front and back sides of an infected area to activate a healing flow. Many healers warmed their hands over hot coals before touching someone's body. The Zuni people of North America used high-velocity adjustments to the neck and spine, and bonesetting was practiced by the Navajo people. The Hopi people developed a form of bodywork that is the basis of Hakomi Massage and includes the application of hot and cold stones. Most of these ancient cultures were strongly connected to the earth and nature in a way that gave insight into the principles of balance and harmony. The existence of a Great Spirit was recognized by many, and the practice of going on a vision quest for guidance is found in numerous tribal groups.

Native American totem of a wild woman on a vision quest.

The Cherokee people had a long-established system of medical and spiritual knowledge. A medicine man's job was to dispel intrusive spirits or negative energy from the body with ceremonial practices and healings that involved the use of physical medicine, herbal remedies, hot stones, crystals, dream work, prayers, and the conjuring of spirits, all applied according to the laws of nature. A unique form of Cherokee bodywork, known as **Hisko-liya Massage**, employed a combination of persimmon wood implements, heating the skin, breathwork, and hands-on work that incorporated deep pressure and gentle rocking. They also had a form of point therapy using thorns or porcupine quills to stimulate reflex points.

Of the many healing practices of the Lakota people, the most well known is the cleansing sweat lodge; a group shared in a ceremony to dispel illness or negative energy and cleanse the spirit with steam created by hot sacred rocks and ritual prayer and song. Here, the individual's paramount intention was to work in union with spirit helpers to help those in need of healing. The giving of the heart to another in need was, and still is, considered to have the power to heal the giver.

The healing that comes with Native American methods is not done by thinking about a problem, but through personal experience, often of a spiritual nature. Practices such as smudging with herbs, ear candling, calling on animal totems, and sweeping to dispel negative energy are found in a number of tribes; one unique practice included bleeding with leeches to pull out disease. Herbal remedies were an important part of Native American medicine, and each shaman had his own medicine bag. The ingesting of natural mind-altering plant medicine, used only in a sacred manner to enable a connection with spirit, has been employed not only by Native Americans, but many traditional indigenous cultures worldwide. This was also accomplished by ceremonial tests of endurance, such as the Sundance. Although some of these practices are no longer used or are no longer considered beneficial to personal health, others are still carried out, and elements of Native American healing have been incorporated into present-day forms of bodywork.

Contact: www.nativetimes.com or www.health-for-wellness.com/native-american

NeuroPhysical Reprogramming© (NPR)

As a outcome of using natural methods to heal herself of a tumor caused by exposure to radiation, naturopath Dr. Theresa Dale created NeuroPhysical Reprogramming in 1991 as a noninvasive yet deep way of discovering and releasing the core issues that can be the main cause of mental and physical illness. Dale's research indicates that there is a holographic blueprint of all of a person's experiences, identities, and beliefs stored in each cell. Through contact with the cellular intelligence, it is possible to transform this blueprint and reestablish healthy cellular communication. NPR is intended to accurately pinpoint the causal energy pattern of any life condition, determine its location in the body, and empower individuals to permanently release it. A reproducible, hands-on protocol that bypasses the conscious mind is used to locate and release emotions, belief systems, and identities that are creating abnormal energy flow and disease. Its techniques can also free up genetic predispositions, alter DNA memory, affect the immune system, and change the way the recipient thinks and feels. Distinct to this healing protocol is the use of exclusive high-potency neuro-emotional homeopathic remedies that eliminate emotional issues anchored by identities. In addition to locating and releasing energy patterns that create illness and depression or sabotage the healing process, NPR assists in the reengineering of the psyche and the rejuvenation of the physical body. It embraces spiritual psychology and mind-body healing and encompasses noninvasive methods that are directed to the core of any illness on all levels of consciousness.

NPR's five-element protocol provides accurate testing and therapy localization that incorporates various techniques to access the body's chemical, structural, and electromagnetic systems. Among its methods are the testing of reflex points, dental health, and the immune system, along with techniques to identify scar tissue blockage, genetic predispositions, immune dysfunctions, and the compatibility of nutritional supplements. A significant part of the protocol is the use of the Meta Point (an acupuncture reflex point on the governing vessel) located in the center of the occipital lobe of the brain, an area which stores foundational belief systems and identities that can make a disease difficult to heal. As the healing process begins, the practitioner makes verbal statements on a variety of controversial life topics to the recipient, and her body's responses are tested. Then the NPR protocol and Neuro-Emotional Remedies (high-potency homeopathic remedies with drainage properties that release core issues) are administered, and the testing process is repeated. However, this time the patient herself verbalizes the identical statements out loud, giving greater accuracy in this form of kinesiological testing. Further testing and questioning may be used to verify the release of limiting energy patterns. Analysis of the test results will reveal the neurological changes that signal the release of the inhibiting core issues and restrictive energetic behavior patterns. In every part of the work, the expression and honoring of the client's feelings and emotions is considered key to the healing process of NPR. Dale now offers health providers training programs in NPR and other forms of complementary health care.

Contact: www.naturalhealingpro.com or
www.traditionalnaturopathy.com

Neurotherapy (NT)

Neurotherapy, in which the feet rather than the hands carry out the bodywork, is a precise, traditional form based on the Ayurvedic system of healing known as Ladara or Kerali. During the 1970s, after intensive studies of anatomy and physiology, Dr. Lajpatrai Mehra adopted this method to treat various types of disease by addressing biochemical imbalances within the body. Balance is restored by returning normal functioning to the organs and glands so that they produce the optimal amount of biochemicals and hormones. Maintenance of the nadis (energy channels), nerves, and the body's acid-based balance is considered very important in maintaining good health.

Carrying out Neurotherapy with the feet.

After verbal and visual analysis of the patient and palpations of any tender spots, the practitioner proceeds by using the feet to slowly apply rhythmic massage and skillfully controlled pressure on the energy channels, organs, and glands (especially the pituitary and thymus glands) of the recipient, who is lying on the floor. The practitioner balances by supporting the arms on objects placed at either side of the patient. Pressure is first applied with the feet and occasionally the hands for six to forty seconds to stop the flow of blood to a specific area of the body. When the pressure is released, the force of the ensuing blood flow can activate or deactivate associated nerves, glands, and organs. A gentle rocking motion is also used at times. The practitioner repeats this process on specific locations all over the front and back of the body. The pressure is often light and gentle, but can be hard and heavy when attempting to reach points deeper in the body; however, it is adjusted according to the age, sex, and tolerance of the patient. Traditionally, there is a special focus on the abdomen, so the therapy is considered beneficial not only for intestinal nerves, but also for digestive disorders. Dietary recommendations may also be included as part of the treatment. Generally, people with hernias, surgical issues, or hip injuries should avoid this practice. At present, there are only a few practitioners of Neurotherapy outside India, but this may change as more individuals are trained.

Contact: www.neurotherapyhealthcare.com

No Hands® Massage

Though not typical within the practice of most forms of bodywork, after years of clinical research, British therapist Gerry Pyves developed techniques for providing a deep, releasing, rejuvenating, and nourishing massage without using the hands. Instead, the practitioner works with the forearms and elbows, which results in a treatment that provides deeper manipulations than a conventional hand massage. There is no stress on the joints of the practitioner's hands, and improved posture results in less strain and fewer injuries. A variety of no-hands strokes have been developed and can be used in a modalities that treat the whole body or any of its parts. These techniques are taught to massage therapists so they can incorporate them into their own practices. Contact: www.nohandsmassage.com

Oncology Massage

Now recognized as a specialized form of body-mind therapy, Oncology Massage employs many different modalities to soothe and strengthen those suffering from cancer. It is becoming a significant part of hospice care and requires therapists to have a special sensitivity to the issues that trouble patients who are being treated for cancer, since in addition to physical factors, emotional and psychological aspects add to the complexity of the care. To provide the right amount and quality of touch, all practitioners need to have a great awareness of the dehumanizing experiences that cancer patients go through. Although the practice was originally frowned upon by professionals who thought it might spread cancer cells, this possibility has been disproven. Practitioners need to be emotionally strong enough to be present with the cancer patient's suffering and be prepared for possible encounters with death and the emotional aspects of this experience.

Although many methods of bodywork are used, nurturing energy-based treatments that work with trauma and the immune system are most appropriate, though a simple, soothing massage can at least make the patient feel more human, calm, and relaxed. Gentle Swedish bodywork and movement therapy are offered for this purpose. However, subtle-energy techniques such as Reiki, Polarity Therapy, Jin Shin Jyutsu, Acupressure, and warm stone applications are also noninvasive and provide energetic balancing as well as relaxation and comfort. Reflexology has also been found to be appropriate, since work can be done on a distant point relating to the compromised area of the body. Treatments that work with lymphatic drainage are particularly beneficial for the immune system. Controversy still surrounds direct work on tumors, so it is best to refrain from deeper massage therapies, such as Neuromuscular Massage and Myofascial Release, on those areas until the patient is in the recovery phase, at which point the goal is to soften any scar tissue and help the patient get some strength back.

Certain precautions are certainly necessary for patients undergoing radiation, chemotherapy, and surgery; however, the idea that massage can spread cancer cells is no longer a real concern. Still, certain contraindications may be present, and bodywork with hands-on contact is not advisable in areas affected by radiation, since the skin may be damaged.
Contact: S4OM Society for Oncology Massage – www.s4om.org

Pregnancy or Prenatal Massage

Massage for pregnant women has been used for centuries by indigenous cultures as part of midwifery practices. Various caring and nurturing methods are used before, during, and after childbirth. Before birth, a women's body systems are working hard to support the new life that is coming into being, and bodywork can be very supportive and prepare the body for labor. A gentle, rejuvenating, and stimulating massage carefully carried out can reduce stress, combat fatigue, promote well-being, tone and strengthen the muscles, increase blood circulation and lymphatic flow, and reduce swelling. Postpartum massage is also important for relieving the fatigue and tension incurred during labor and delivery and to help the new mother tone and strengthen muscles.

The bodywork often employs Myofascial Release, Acupressure, muscle energy techniques, reflex techniques, and assisted resistance stretching, all of which can alleviate back pain and postural stress on the joints. Treatments commonly focus on the lower back and abdomen and may be done in positions other than horizontal; certain practitioners have special massage tables with a hole in the middle so the recipient can lie on her stomach. Specific treatments may also aid in shortening labor time. Supportive Doula Therapy accomplished during pregnancy, labor, and delivery may also be used in conjunction with bodywork.

Contact: American Pregnancy
    Association – www.americanpregnancy.org
    or www.pregnancymassage.com

Pulse Reading

Just as the force of the wind as it blows is never steady, the rhythms of energy flowing in the human body are constantly changing. This flow creates waves of energy whose rhythm reflects the power of the energy flowing within, just as the waves on the ocean demonstrate the strength of the wind that is driving them. The heart and lungs play a vital role in the circulation of both blood and the personal energy called chi; where chi goes, the blood will follow and vice versa. Therefore, it is possible to examine chi by analyzing the flow of blood.

Pulse reading connects the practitioner directly with the behavior of the energetic wind and its influence on the vibrations of the vital life-force energy. The pulse acts as an energetic messenger carrying information about the whole body, and the goal of pulse reading is to identify the nuances that reveal the true condition of a patient. Successfully reading the pulse involves sensing, feeling, touching, observing, and experiencing all of its distinctive aspects and qualities to gain deeper insight into the patient's condition. Pulse reading is not a stand-alone modality, but it contributes in-depth diagnosis to any healing process and is an integral part of many Asian healing practices, especially when choosing the proper placement of acupuncture needles or prescribing the mix and dosage of herbal remedies.

This energy-based diagnostic method has been used in Eastern systems of health care for thousands of years and has now been incorporated into a variety of modern healing modalities. In China, the father of pulse reading is considered by some to be Dr. Pien Ch'ueh, who wrote about this form of diagnostics around 450 BCE. Another book on this topic was also written in China around 100 CE by Dr. Wang Shu He. However, the true origins of this practice likely go back before the written word to the time when herbal remedies were prescribed based on its findings, and its usage was not limited to China. Pulse reading is also used in the Tibetan and Ayurvedic systems of healing, but there is more emphasis on imbalances in the patient's constitution.

The pulse is most often taken on the inside of either wrist over the radial artery. Although readings can be

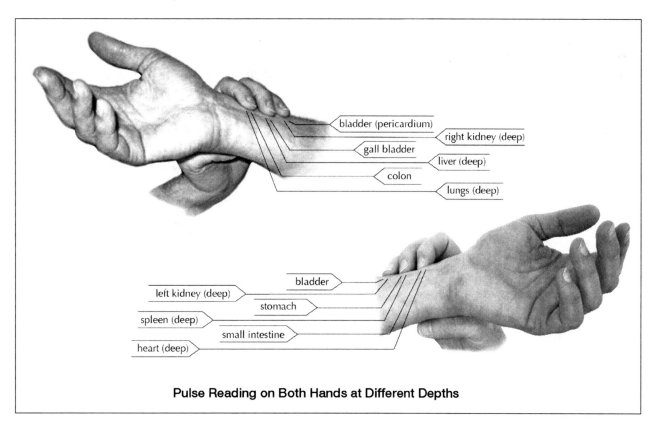

Pulse Reading on Both Hands at Different Depths

taken at a number of other locations for specific purposes, the pulse in the wrist is very accessible and is far enough away from the heart, whose noisy beating might interfere with a correct reading of the pulse's subtle qualities. One practitioner likened taking the pulse at the wrong location to working near a waterfall: the extraneous noise would overwhelm the subtleties of the pulse.

During a reading, the practitioner places the index, middle, and ring fingers on three points on the client's wrist and changes the amount of pressure to read the pulse at different depths. These three locations and three depths—superficial, medium, and deep—on each wrist total nine combinations that provide much valuable information. Organs in different areas and at different depths in the body are examined in the superficial and deep readings. The condition of the body and its systems, the state of specific organs, the flow of chi energy through the meridians, the constitution of the recipient, and any imbalance or disease can be determined by collecting information from the pulse. Needless to say, the practitioner must undertake arduous study and training to develop the intuitive ability to sense the different complex ways that health and disease can manifest in the pulse.

When a practitioner palpates the pulse, it is possible for him to recognize seven basic physical traits that relate to the physiological and energetic states of the organs—movement, rate, rhythm, force (pressure), amplitude (volume), temperature, and condition of the vessel wall. The amplitude and rate of pulse are often considered the most revealing. The strength of the pulse and the depth at which it is located also provide important information about the severity of a patient's condition.

The sensitive fingers of the practitioner also explore the energetic qualities of the pulse; it is said there are twenty-eight different qualities, although some experts have claimed they can recognize up to fifty. Common qualities include healthy and stable (the ideal), unstable, fast, slow, full, empty, slippery, smooth, rough, twisted, loose, wiry, taut, rolling, and even missing. Individuals with "hot" diseases, such as fever, inflammation, or infection, can exhibit qualities that are overflowing, furious, tight and rolling; people with "cold" diseases, whose energy flow is deficient, show a pulse that is weak, sunken, slow, loose, or empty. Each quality tells a different story about the condition of the patient. Blind practitioners excel at this primarily because they have

fewer distractions and can therefore focus better on the tactile sensations of the pulse.

Pulse reading can be successfully accomplished in a number of physical locations other than the wrists to provide different kinds of information. Readings on the wrist mainly examine the client's energy systems and can suggest imbalances caused by some restriction or dysfunction within the organs of the body. In certain Tibetan modalities, pulse readings are carried out at specific locations on the cranium and at certain points along the spine. For children under the age of about eight, the ears can be used. Other practices rely on readings on the side of on the foot, the back of the neck, the spine, and the abdomen to assess the physical conditions of the client. Readings on the abdomen have a stronger relationship with physiological conditions than those on the wrist. (If a healthy person eats a big dinner and all his energy goes into digestion, a reading on the wrist might show low energy, but a reading on the abdomen may show that the organs are in fine condition.) There are specialized pulse readings that can be done on the ulnar artery in the forearm to assess the life pulse, and the artery in the foot can be used to tell if a person is in a near-death condition. In Tibetan practices, the "seven wondrous" pulse readings can determine the sex of an unborn baby, the effects of solar and lunar influences, or even the extent of harm done by an enemy or evil spirit; success in these readings require years of deep meditation on part of the practitioner. These are just a few examples.

Because pulse readings are very subtle and can fluctuate over a short period of time because of factors such as diet, stress, emotional and mental state, and the amount of sleep and exercise, for a pulse reading to be valid, the client must adhere to a moderate diet and pattern of behavior at least during the day before the reading. It is important to refrain from excessive consumption of certain foods or stressful activities and to be in a relaxed state before a reading. The most accurate readings are accomplished during the early morning hours when the body is in its most stable, neutral, and rested condition and imbalances caused by certain activities are at a minimum. If there is some existing abnormality, it will be most evident and detectable at that time. Of course, these days, especially in the West, it is not often possible have a pulse reading at this time. In this case, the actual analysis becomes less than the ideal, and the findings may not be as complete.

Visual diagnostic methods—analysis of the urine, the tongue (its texture, coating, and color), fecal material, vomit, and blood, as well as readings of the ears, eyes, and veins—can be performed in conjunction with pulse reading to home in on a particular physical pathology. Urine analysis holds a prominent position, because whatever the digestive system cannot fully process will ultimately show up there and reflect interior imbalances, disorders, and diseases. Just as with pulse analysis, a proper reading of the qualities in the urine depends on the client's adhering to certain precautions and refraining from excess physical exertion, exposure to sun, electrical interference, and certain foods or alcohol. The best samples are collected in the early morning and tested immediately when the urine is fresh; if the urine can not be tested when it is fresh, clean glass or metal containers should be used for its transport to the doctor. A complete analysis is made by observing the qualities and position of sediment, the color and cloudiness, the vapor (steam that arises), the sounds made, the condition and size of the bubbles (when properly stirred), the secretions found within, and the clarity of the sample.

Considering how useful and simple expert pulse reading is for assessing a person's condition, it could be a cost-effective part of preventive medicine. Besides being affordable, pulse readings are very safe, easily accomplished, fast, comfortable, reliable, accurate, portable, and very handy for someone with little time for visits to a clinic. In an ideal world, there could be a fleet of expert pulse readers roaming the countryside and periodically visiting patients at their homes in the early hours to provide this service. How convenient and suitable would that be!

Contact: www.yinyanghouse.com/theory/chinese/
pulse_diagnosis, www.acupuncture.com/
newsletters/m_mar06/main2.htm, or www.
ayurvedacollege.com/articles/students/pulse

Rapid Eye Technology (RET)

Through research starting in the 1960s, psychoenergetic studies of REM (the rapid eye movement that occurs during dreaming) have scientifically recognized that stress and harmful emotions are released from the mind while a person is in this state. After working with eye-movement exercises to help her autistic son, Dr. Ranae Johnson integrated elements of complementary energy medicine with findings on the REM state to develop Rapid Eye Technology as a way to alleviate stress by releasing energy-based memories stored in the body on the cellular level. This process uses blinking, eye movements, breathwork, imagery, and stress-reducing energy work to help relieve physiological problems, reframe traumatic memories, release emotional holding, and process pain.

After an initial review of the client's medical history, the practitioner (known as a technician in this therapy) leads the recipient through some relaxing breathwork and energy techniques to relieve stress. Then the technician helps the client slip into a mental state similar to REM sleep by moving a hand-held wand in front of the client's eyes while he blinks rapidly. The technician simultaneously communicates with the client in a way that connects his conscious mind with his subconscious. The energy accessed through the blinking is thus released from holding stressful memories on a deep cellular level. In the second half of the treatment, stressful memories are reframed by changing thought patterns, altering perceptions into a more positive viewpoint, improving the ability to make better choices, gaining an understanding of cause and effect, using gratitude to create a sense of abundance, and developing a new sense of connection, happiness, and harmony. Sessions usually last between one and two hours.

Contact: The Rapid Eye Institute –
www.rapideyetechnology.com

Rubenfeld Synergy Method® (RSM)

As a result of her rigorous practice as a musician and orchestra conductor, Ilana Rubenfeld developed painful back spasms that required medical intervention. Seeking relief, she went to a teacher of the Alexander Technique. When gently touched by her teacher, Ilana experienced a softening of her back muscles accompanied by a welling of tears. Untrained in the emotional realm, the Alexander teacher referred Ilana to a psychotherapist. With the absence of touch in her therapy sessions, her emotions felt distant and inaccessible. The combination of these two very different experiences led her to understand there was a connection between the body and emotions.

Intrigued by this connection, Ilana became an Alexander Technique teacher. She then sought a more all-encompassing solution by studying Gestalt Therapy and the Feldenkrais Method of Somatic Awareness. In the 1960s, her studies led her to formulate the Ruben-feld Synergy Method, a hands-on approach combining education, touch, kinesthetic awareness, imagery, and verbal expression. Like many other body-mind thera-pies, it is based on the principle that the body, mind, emotions, and spirit are highly interrelated and that a therapist must address all aspects of the self to be effective. The therapy focuses on managing stress and is meant to engage the recipient both physically and emotionally. The goal is to explore the root cause of a physical problem through a synthesis of what Ilana coined "listening touch" and verbal dialogue, as well as a method in which the practitioner guides the client into creating an inner dialogue so that emotions caused by previously unresolved issues are given expression. The aim is to help the client access feelings and release stored emotions and blockages, for to simply remove the physical symptom is not enough.

The typical treatment session uses very gentle, car-ing touch; verbal processing encouraging the expres-sion of emotions; and physical movements that allow the recipient to sense areas or patterns of emotional holding, tension, or pulsations that block the flow of movement in the body. All is done gradually in a non-forceful manner to create a safe environment in which the client has the opportunity to assimilate feelings and the time to recognize other ways of responding to the original incident that caused the patterns to emerge. The practitioner, called a Synergist, also addresses the client's breathing patterns and postural habits by using kinesthetic-awareness methods to increase the client's sensitivity to the ways in which stressful feelings are held in the body. In addition, visualizations, work with the imagination, sound work, breathwork, intuition, and humor are used to guide the client to break these holding patterns and access more self-awareness. The Synergist focuses on treating the psychophysical causes of the problems people carry, rather than treating ill-nesses or other manifestations. The Rubenfeld Synergy Method is used to assist people with a wide variety of issues.
Contact: International Association of Rubenfeld
    Synergists – www.rubenfeldsynergy.com

Shamanic Healing Methods
Though bearing different titles in their ancient in-digenous cultures, spiritual healers or medicine men following the old ways—presently referred to as sha-mans—carry out their healing work for both individ-uals and the community as a whole. Recognizing that removing the detrimental spiritual components of an illness can clear the pathway to healing physical and emotional symptoms, their methods embrace ritualistic practices for sensing and removing pain, illness, or spiri-tual disharmony. Central to these activities are rhythmic drumming, chanting, dancing and organic psychoactive plant medicine, which all lead the shaman into an altered state of mind. This paves the way for a shamanic journey in which he can gain insight from other dimensions and receive guidance from spirit helpers or power animals (also referred to as totems) for healing the recipient. The shamanic spirit passage or journey, which crosses the dimensional barrier between time and space, is one of the primary processes used in shamanic therapy.

Vision quests to connect with spirit guides are also an important element of shamanic healing, since it is believed that a stronger connection to power animals and spirit helpers will strengthen and empower a per-son, and new spirit helpers may reveal themselves in difficult situations. A vision quest begins with receiving spiritual advice from a shamanic guide, and the seeker then maintains a fast while journeying alone into the wilds of nature to learn life lessons. He can receive subtle insights, visions, or a significant emotional release as a result of this powerful unraveling process.

Healers, sometimes in the company of a client, can journey to the realms of the lower world for soul re-trieval. In this way, the healer discovers the source of a person's wounds and retrieves fragmented or disowned parts of his soul. Once the missing soul pieces have been gathered, a ceremony is conducted in which the recipient is reconnected with his soul, thus restoring his vital essence. Extraction methods may be used to remove unneeded patterns of energy that contribute to an illness. Sound toning helps increase a recipient's energy vibrations and restores spiritual light. Some sha-manic therapy aims for karmic or spiritual release for the so-called inner child. In the Native American tradition, much of the shamanic healing is based on the medicine wheel and the act of reestablishing a connection with nature. Today the healing process is more conservative, tame, and noninvasive than in the past, although seem-ingly weird and bizarre ceremonies can still be found in remote tribal cultures.

Any bodywork that may be involved in shamanic healing is only a small part of a complex process, but at any stage of the experience, gentle touch will be comforting and will help the client become more embodied. Although today there is nothing typical in a shamanic healing session, the recipient is often lying on a massage table. Initially, he may be asked to choose a rock that resonates with him from an assortment provided by the practitioner. He is next asked to focus on the existing problem or yearning he has brought with him and feel where it is held in the body. Then he places the rock on that spot. While the recipient focuses on his issue, the practitioner scans the body to confirm its location and works on the individual's energy field and chakras to open up and move the energy. Although the patient is instructed to relax, he may find it beneficial to remain attentive to the matter in question and to the feelings emitted by the body as the practitioner scans for and extracts any energetic intrusions, wounds, or restricting beliefs. Like peeling the layers of an onion, the shaman works to open up deeper closed-off areas of the subconscious. At certain times, the shaman may make suggestions relating to the recipient's breathing or a perceived shift in his consciousness. After some final energy sweeping and clearing of blockages, the shaman finishes with an energy-replenishing technique to strengthen the wounded area and seal any holes in the patient's energy field. The patient is then given tips on self-care and ways to deal with any paradigm shifts that may occur in the days or weeks to come after the session.

In recent years, there has been a resurgence of shamanic practices as some of the few remaining elderly indigenous shamans have agreed to passed on their traditional knowledge to a select few. Dr. Alberto Villoldo and psychotherapist Sandra Ingerman are just two of the healers who have received such teachings; they have both created schools where further training can take place. In the late 1980s, Villoldo created the Healing the Light Body School, and Ingerman founded the Foundation for Shamanic Studies. Today, many feel disconnected from life and are stuck in the wounds and patterns of the past. The shaman knows that most illness is a symptom of these kinds of imbalances or the displacement of the live-giving spiritual essence. Though its value is not appreciated by many in the modern Western world, shamanic practice ministers to the realm of the inner spirit, which can heal these imbalances if it's called on for help.
Contact: www.thefourwinds.com,
www.sandraingerman.com, or
www.questforvision.com

Shirodhara

A nice head massage can be a wonderful thing. Shirodhara is a special, localized form of Ayurvedic Panchakarma in which a steady, thin stream of heated, herb-infused sesame oil is poured onto the forehead to nourish the sixth chakra and balance pranic energy in the brain. Soft, loving touch accompanies the process. Besides reducing stress, this method calms and relaxes the central nervous system and can enhance the circulation of blood to the brain and promote overall well-being. It is often given after an energetic Abhyanga (Sirobhyanga) massage of the head and upper body that works on the nerve roots and may be performed before a full-body Swedana steam bath treatment.

A variation of this head massage is the **Shirodhara Nasya**, an upper body massage followed by deep inhalation of aromatic steam and a stream of warm, herbal sesame oil dripped on the forehead. Champissage, discussed earlier in this section, is another gentle type of Ayurvedic herbal massage done primarily on the head and upper body.
Contact: www.ayurveda-foryou.com/panchakarma/
shirodhara

Sotai Ho Massage Therapy

A system of structural integration combined with a form of Japanese physical therapy and elements of Shiatsu, Sotai Ho uses both active and assisted passive exercises to remove physical distortions, provide better balance, and establish musculoskeletal alignment. The therapy was developed in the 1930s by Dr. Keizo Hashimoto and is based on the premise that healthful living requires certain elements such as proper breathing, nutrition, movement, thoughts, and environment. Sotai Ho works on problems by asking the recipient to move slowly and consciously into the feelings in the body rather than by analyzing them with the mind.

The massage treatments use noninvasive methods of manipulation and adjustments that realign the body without using extreme chiropractic techniques that might cause pain. A session includes a type of neuromuscular reeducation that focuses on bone structure and the alignment of the spinal column, which protects the various nerves associated with the internal organs. Sotai Ho emphasizes awareness of subtle sensations, along with energetic pressure-point work, breathing techniques, and special movements to unwind holding patterns in the muscles. It also focuses on sensitive points on the liver meridian to channel vital energy. This simple system can be applied quickly and is an effective complement to Acupuncture and other forms of bodywork.

The simple Sotai Exercises integral to therapy are a system for releasing muscular tension developed by Japanese Dr. Yoshio Manaka, who worked with Hashimoto. They can also be used as a self-care practice. The exercises are designed to reeducate muscles and nerves through comfortable movement rather than moving into the pain. Sotai Exercises are based on studies that have revealed how painful motions affect the body. A simple breathing pattern is followed as the recipient moves in in pain-free directions. The movement is executed as the client exhales, and only a moderate amount of force is applied by the practitioner to counter the movement.

Contact: Sotai Professional Organization –
www.sotai.net

Sound Healing

It has long been recognized that music and certain sounds can be both pleasurable and healing. The vibrations that create sound are picked up by the whole body, not just the ears, and they deliver a kind of subtle massage; just think of those times when music made your skin tingle. This form of vibrational therapy has been used since ancient times to facilitate healing. It recognizes that the universe itself is constantly vibrating and that harmonic resonance with these vibrations can affect a person's inner and outer awareness. New forms are constantly being developed, and a variety of instruments, including the human voice, can be used to create the sounds. Sound healing is often carried out during bodywork, but it can also be self-administered to cleanse and uplift the emotions, the heart, the mind, the spirit, and the soul.

Healing with sound uses harmonic vibrations, music, and inspirational prayers or songs to aid in restoring the body's natural resonance. By working with pitch,

resonance, rhythm, melody, harmony, timbre, and toning, practitioners can focus particular vibrational frequencies on the chakra energy centers or meridian pathways; other techniques direct specific vibrations at specific imbalances within the body. Vocalizing, hearing, and internalizing certain sacred sounds can create meditative states of deep relaxation and shifts in consciousness, both of which help the body assimilate healing vibrations.

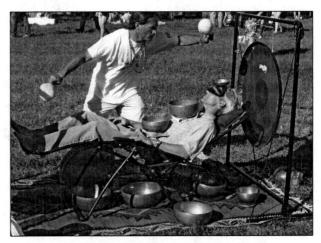

One form of vibrational sound healing.

Resonance is the basic element in almost every form of sound therapy, and it is believed that every organ, bone, and tissue of the body has its own resonant frequency. Disease or injury can cause a part of the body to vibrate out of resonance with the rest of the body; therefore, a person's body, like a musical instrument, may need regular tuning to restore harmony. Harmonic vibrations can act as a powerful bridge between the physical, mental, and emotional aspects of an individual. The different brain waves, each of which has a characteristic vibrational frequency, are correlated with specific states of consciousness, and many sound therapies use entrainment with harmonic resonance to affect a client's inner and outer awareness. It has been shown that certain resonant frequencies are beneficial for reducing pain, fostering relaxation, activating tissues, increasing circulation, enhancing the functioning of the brain and nervous system, and accelerating the healing of damaged body parts. Science has also shown that strong vibrations at certain frequencies can even cause cells to restructure themselves. Harmonic vibrations can produce a mind-body shift towards spiritual awakening, and vibrational sound therapy can rectify physical problems by balancing the resonant frequencies of the surrounding energy field, or astral body, whose existing dysfunctions may be reflected in the physical body.

The way sounds are produced and how they are directed varies with the different methods of sound healing, and the energy the practitioner puts into producing the sound will affect its power. Practitioners may project a specific harmonic sound into an area of imbalance and allow entrainment to move that area into a more balanced state. Toning, the process of sounding a note with the voice and holding that note for a long period of time, is frequently used in sound healing, especially to balance the chakras. The practitioner may change the tone to higher frequencies as she moves up the body from the feet to the head. In some instances, chanting is used to remove blockages, while sacred vowel sounds resonate with and align each of the individual chakras. Some frequency-based healing modalities utilize the harmonics of the Lambdoma frequencies, which come from an ancient musical mathematic theory that relates music to ratios. Many forms of vibrational therapy incorporate breathing techniques to increase body awareness. The following is an overview of a few of the more well-known forms of sound healing, some of which incorporate electronic instruments into their therapies.
Contact: Sound Healers Association –
www.soundhealersassociation.org

Acoustic Touch System (ATS) is a form of vibrational sound healing that transmits the vibrations produced by music to the body through a variety of objects placed either around or in contact with it. The aim is to create a deep sense of meditative relaxation, which can help ease pain, relieve stress, and balance the whole body. In some instances, the vibrations are transmitted through a specially designed massage table directly to the recipient's body. Precisely calibrated tuning forks can be placed on various acupuncture points, sections of the spine, or other locations, and at other times, Tibetan bowls, crystal bowls, rattles, and other sound-making instruments are placed near the body. While the recipient is resting or experiencing a massage, these instruments are sounded to create a specific effect. ATS was created by Dustin Fox, who also

developed the Vibrational Attunement Massage discussed below.
Contact: www.massageprofessionals.com/profile/ dustinfox

Acutonics® System, a methodology for the therapeutic use and application of tuning forks, is an energy-based approach to wellness that is rooted in Asian medicine and the concept that most disease arises from a core blockage in a person's energy system. This accessible, noninvasive modality is an adjunct therapy that can be easily integrated into the practice of Asian medicine, massage and bodywork, nursing, psychology, physical therapy, and many other health care disciplines. This system of sound healing was co-developed by visionary acupuncturist Donna Carey and has evolved over the past seventeen years through the combined efforts of Donna, Ellen Franklin, and more than fifty Acutonics instructors who teach this work around the globe. Basic techniques for self-care can be taught to reduce stress, lower blood pressure, ease the symptoms of depression, help achieve physiological homeostasis, and balance the body, mind, and spirit. Ellen has been conducting additional research exploring self-care intervention using Acutonics to ameliorate symptoms of severe stress in nurses. Carefully documented case studies that speak to the efficacy of this modality have been collected and published.

In this form of vibrational healing, precision-calibrated tuning forks are applied to specific acupoints to access the body's meridian and chakra energy systems. These tuning forks represent a natural harmonic series based on the orbital properties of the earth, moon, sun, and planets. The vibrating sound waves of the forks travel deep into the body along energy pathways that have been proven to impact both the body and the mind. Their rich resonance and vibration connects with and supports the body's natural frequencies, stimulates and balances the body's physical and subtle energy fields, and promotes wellness, deep inner harmony, and a sense of well-being, attunement, and homeostasis.

Acupressure points provide noninvasive access into the core energetic systems within the body. The frequencies of the planets represented in the tuning forks provide musical intervals, archetypes, and correspondences that help practitioners fine-tune the therapeutic frequencies that are applied to the body. These frequencies are based on the actual planetary velocity originally calculated by Johannes Kepler in the early 1600s. Since then, further research into the development of additional precise frequencies that are used in the calibration of the tuning forks has been accomplished, providing more highly specific treatment protocols that have a significant impact on human physiology.

The Kairos Institute of Sound Healing, creators of the Acutonics System, has a number of related publications and provides continuing education offering a full in-depth certification program for aspiring practitioners working in an assortment of modalities.

Contact: Kairos Institute of Sound Healing –
www.acutonics.com

Biosonic Repatterning™ is based on the sound waves present in nature and uses sacred sounds to align the body, mind, and spirit with more harmonic patterns. Sound is one of the purest forms of energy, and tuning forks, healing mantras, and toning create a sympathetic resonance with these sacred sounds deep within the recipient, helping activate energetic qualities in the body. This method was developed by John Beaulieu to reduce stress, provide relaxation, improve circulation, and restore the optimal natural vibrations of the body. Tuning forks are calibrated at specific frequencies to provide healing to different areas of the body; as the nervous system attunes to the pitch, the sound creates a resonance that repatterns the whole body on the cellular level, thus releasing constrictions around the organs and giving dysfunctional or imbalanced organs or tissue an energetic boost. The spiritual effects of Biosonic Repatterning can produce higher levels of consciousness and deeper personal insight.

Contact: www.biosonics.com

Bio-Tuning® provides customized Sonic Induction for an individual. It is a holistic, pleasant, noninvasive approach to a health challenge or the desire to personally grow and excel. The process balances the brain and nervous system by using precisely

tuned frequencies customized for the individual. All are formatted to bypass the rational mind, which frequently blocks healing and true growth, and to access the energetic blocks causing the health challenge(s). Bio-Tuning® was developed by Dr. Jeffrey Thompson, a physician, musician, researcher, scientist, and composer, and he uses it extensively in his clinical practice.

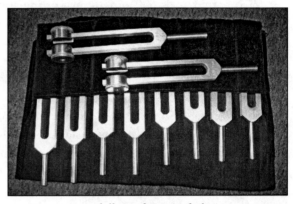

A full set of tuning forks.

To accommodate the physiological body and its functioning, Dr. Thompson uses his specially designed Vibroacoustic table or chair, which gently and effectively resonates every cell of the body. He also uses Full Frequency Headphones and Light Glasses; the glasses were also designed by him to work in concert with his mind-body harmonizing system. Feeling what you are hearing, hearing what you are seeing, and seeing what you are feeling not only provides kinesthetic, audio, and visual stimulation but also deep healing and a pleasurable experience for each recipient.

Bio-Tuning promotes physical, emotional, and mental healing, removes energetic blocks to true meditation, and opens doors and possibilities for personal growth, which is frequently transformative. The person's own clarified voice is used to customize the session, which includes personalized brain-wave entrainment with resonant frequencies that enhance the specific desired state of consciousness needed to accomplish the goal at hand. Entrainment occurs easily as a participant simply relaxes, listens to the musical soundscape, and enjoys the experience. Each participant is given the sound program heard during a session to take home. This

gentle but powerful form of healing is suitable for anyone, regardless of the cause, age, gender, or race.
Contact: Center for Neuroacoustic Research –
www.neuroacoustic.com

Bone Toning is a form of vibrational and harmonic sound healing developed by chiropractor Dr. June Leslie Wieder after she completed extensive research on the relationship between sound, movement, and form as they relate to health and healing. The therapy is based on the concepts that sound can move and reshape matter and that the human body responds to harmonic vibrations. Everything that vibrates has its own natural resonant frequency; when a similar frequency is applied, spontaneous vibration will occur in response to the external stimulation. The bones of the spine each exhibit their own frequencies, and applying specific vibrational frequencies directly to the vertebrae generates a sympathetic response, activating embedded harmonics that support healing. Rather than relying on tuning forks, Dr. Wieder developed a hand-held device called the BoneToner™ that delivers the correct frequency to each vertebra in turn and can also be used to generate brain-wave frequencies. Muscle testing verifies the effectiveness of this retuning process by evaluating how the body reacts to stimuli applied to the spine and the nervous system.
Contact: www.songofthespine.com

Cymatic Therapy is a form of bioenergetic sound therapy, developed in the 1960s by osteopathic doctor Sir Peter Manners of England, that is based on studies of wave-form phenomena. *Cymatics* refers to the effect sound waves have in moving and reshaping matter. The underlying theory is that life is permeated by sound and that every part of the body vibrates at a certain frequency. Illness occurs when the rhythms of the heart, brain, and other organs are not vibrating harmoniously with each other. Cymatic Therapy creates a healing environment for the cells of the body by neutralizing the vibrations of any intruding disease and reinforcing the harmonious frequency patterns of the organs. The therapy uses a method in which a portable, computerized sound generator directs beneficial sound-wave vibrations through the skin to acupressure points. The audible

frequencies selected are related to those normally emitted by that part of the body when it is healthy, and the sound waves can be directed toward the diseased organ or transmitted along the meridians. These generated sound signals are intended to establish healthy resonance in unhealthy tissue. In some of the newer cymatic devices, an oscillating magnetic field has been added to the sound waves.
Contact: www.jilaensherwood.com/cymatics.html
or www.quantumchanges.wordpress.
com/cymatics/

Holographic Sound Therapy uses multidimensional sound vibrations to uncover limiting life patterns and create a balanced, healthy, and integrated state of being. The therapy incorporates spiritually inspired techniques, specific intentions, vocal toning, crystal singing bowls, physical and emotional energy movement techniques, and counseling to provide personal transformation. Paul Hubbert developed this form of therapy to help provide individuals with a renewed sense of physical, mental, and emotional well-being and spiritual peace. It is considered complementary to the Melchizedek method of healing.
Contact: Institute for Holographic Sound –
www.holographicsound.com

Infratonic Sound Therapy calls on low-frequency sounds below the auditory threshold of the human ear to tune every cell and molecule of the body. Scientific research in China and Russia has shown that the resonant frequencies of these tones are effective for healing. A special instrument, known as a biomagnesonic transducer, transmits both tones and pulsed electromagnetic fields directly to the body, in a manner similar to a massage. By this action, the healing force can be aroused, organs stimulated, and accumulated toxins expelled from the body. The process is an on-going entrainment exercise in which the repeated administration of the tones helps teach organs to vibrate at their optimal potential, thus creating normal biological functioning. Since the equipment is portable, the therapy may appeal to clients who want a method of sound healing they can use at home on a daily basis.
Contact: www.soundvitality.com

Vibrational Attunement Massage (VAM), developed by Dustin Fox, combines the vibrations contained in music with massage to heal on a soulful level. Evocative or melodic music has a direct impact on a person's emotional state and is often played in the background during bodywork because it helps the recipient relax. However, VAM takes it a step further by allowing the recipient to actually feel the vibrations of music during the massage. This is accomplished with the previously mentioned Acoustic Touch System (ATS), which transmits vibrations directly to the client's body through the massage table or chair. The practitioner synchronizes the massage with the vibrations created by the music, blending the two together into a symphony of healing.
Contact: www.massageprofessionals.com/profile/dustinfox

Vibro Acoustic Therapy (VAT) marries the vibrations of relaxing music with those of pulsed, low-frequency tones. It was developed in the 1980s by Norwegian therapist, teacher, musician, and inventor Olav Skille, who first explored its use for stimulating healing in severely disabled children. Skille discovered that the physical vibrations of sound could not only provide relaxation but also help eliminate stress and pain without the detrimental side effects of chemical intervention. He also found a correlation between specific frequencies and the reduction or elimination of pain or stress in different body parts. Extensive experimentation revealed that low-frequency sounds reduce tension, music without sudden changes in tempo aids relaxation, nonrhythmic music can pacify the body, and rhythmic music can invigorate it. Certain vibrations can enhance or reduce voluntary movement and range of motion in spastic clients, and low-frequency sounds cause more perceptible physical vibrations than higher frequencies. Seven basic frequencies were identified as those most helpful in relieving chronic disease symptoms. Therefore the proper selection of musical sounds or tones is essential and should be what the client enjoys.

During a VAT session, sound is sent into the client's body through speakers embedded in the acoustic sound bed or chair in which the recipient is resting. The sounds are pulsed, low-frequency, pure harmonic tones that are intended to relax and sooth the body. Quiet instrumental music can also be played in conjunction with these low-frequency sound. The physical vibrations provided by the music and low frequency tones are received by the client as an internal massage. The therapy became known as Physioacoustic Therapy in Finland and has been used for years in Scandinavian countries. Specialists in other countries have since developed similar practices that treat clients with special needs or those with postoperative surgical conditions, and VAT is now used by various medical institutions around the world.
Contact: www.vibroacoustictherapy.com

Syntropy Insight Bodywork
A synthesis of neuromuscular repatterning techniques, qi gong, somatic self-inquiry, Taoist techniques, Buddhist meditation, and Polarity Therapy, this form of touch therapy was created by Shari Sunshine and her son, Tobin Rangdrol. It is designed to work with places in the body and mind that are already open, free, vital, and capable of providing healing guidance. Rather than confronting problem areas, the aim is to access and empower the recipient's innate healing ability and natural body intelligence by focusing on what is already functioning well and then encouraging and enhancing it through touch and movement. This therapy uses deep sensing, touch, and movement to assist the client in determining her real needs and then invoking her inherent ability to meet those needs in a meaningful way.

A treatment uses supportive, gentle touch in conjunction with an assortment of modalities of movement, meditation, and energy work to release negative thought patterns and emotional wounds by acting directly on the nervous system to dissolve chronic patterns of tension or pain. The work is carried out in three phases. First, there is the gentle phase of getting the body accustomed to a sense of ease. Next comes the disintegration phase in which a moving meditation uses neuromuscular release repatterning to awaken the body's natural healing ability. The final phase involves reintegration and often incorporates more rapid movements, gentle shaking, and finally standing and walking. Syntropy Insight Bodywork is a noninvasive therapy that can be used on its own or as an adjunct to other therapies.
Contact: Syntropy International – www.syntropy.net

Unergi Therapy

A holistic experiential learning process developed by Ute Arnold, Unergi Therapy aspires to provide a recipient with increased energy and a sense of wholeness by increasing personal awareness. It combines elements of the Alexander Technique, the Feldenkrais Method of Somatic Awareness, Gestalt Therapy, and the Rubenfeld Synergy Method with listening, nurturing touch, creative expression, the healing forces of nature, chakra tuning work, dream therapy, and spiritually based techniques. Guided visualization and meditation lead the awareness away from the head to the heart and body in a way that helps a client release habitual physical and emotional patterns and realize his true creative potential. The therapist essentially invites the body to speak its truth and be heard, reassured that all that transpires will be honored.

During a session, the therapist uses intentional listening, touch, and movement to encourage a dialogue between the client's mind and body. This allows the recipient to feel his own physical and emotional responses and to access memories, feelings, and limiting patterns that need to be clarified, released, and consciously resolved. Specific psychophysical movement sequences stimulate the neuromuscular memory, which enables the discovery of new connections in the body and mind that provide an opportunity to make new, healthy choices. Besides lengthening and energizing the physical structure of the body, the therapist stimulates creative mental expression through supportive verbal assistance, psychotherapy, and visual aids. The healing process helps the client learn to activate and appreciate the inner intuition that lies beyond the realm of the intellect. The ultimate aim is to encourage the recipient to really feel the full range of emotions that can lead to more empathy and compassion for himself and everyone else.

Contact: Unergi Center – www.unergi.com

Vibrational Healing Massage Therapy® (VHMT)

Vibrational Healing Massage Therapy, Levels 1–4, was developed over thirty-three years by Patricia Cramer in her personal quest to heal the deep-seated imprints of her embryological trauma. It is composed of both energy work and deep structural bodywork and produces consistent and permanent deep healing in both practitioner and client. Blending elements of age-old Eastern and newer Western healing therapies into a process, VHMT contains transformational tools that assist people in completely changing the way they think about and carry their bodies and in accessing prenatal imprints. The therapy not only restores energy flowing through the body but also enhances flexibility, decreases chronic pain, relieves stress, and increases the ability of the recipient to feel the body as alive and vibrant. At its finest, VHMT restores a person to the fluidity of their embryonic development, awakens cellular memory, and aligns the dimensional frequency sequences of the soul and source to all other systems throughout the body. As new energetic vibrations move within the body, the circulation of basic metabolic fluids flows more strongly to once-rigid areas.

VHMT includes new concepts that stimulate awareness in thinking, speaking, walking, standing, sitting, and breathing, which creates a fully connected and communicative body. These concepts are: The Fluid Body Model® —a collection of knowledge through which people experience being in their bodies in a whole new way, acknowledging and honoring the fluidly evolving processes that they are; Disease as a Strategy® —a self-responsible way of thinking that allows better access to self-healing and growth; The Language of Healing® —a way of speaking responsibly about the body and life, so that when people speak, they are accessing healing and transformation and causing it to happen; and Fluid Body Breathing® —a practice that restores the ribs and spine to their natural curves and mobility.

As practitioners feel and listen to the recipient's body rhythms and frequencies, by using VHMT's clear, intuitive distinctions, they facilitate a clothes-on massage therapy that is sensitive, rhythmic, and fun, yet deeply healing and long lasting. The bodywork galvanizes the release of built-up tensions and restores a balanced flow of energy to the body's circulatory, lymphatic, and nervous systems with more than twenty bodywork techniques that align, loosen, and connect the body's energy systems so that tension can be released and vital energy can flow. This simple yet powerful therapy can be experienced as a short treatment for stress relief, as a longer session that will have a more extensive effect on the whole body, or as an adjunct to other forms of bodywork. Sessions can take place anywhere, with the recipient seated in a chair, lying on the floor, or in any other comfortable position.

Patricia also established another therapy, known as Structural Foot Balancing®, which is a transformational approach to whole-body structural balance accomplished through various techniques that interact with the feet. Participants are also trained in an easy-to-learn self-help method, known as Foot Freedom®, which uses self-massage.

Contact: World School of Massage
and Holistic Healing Arts –
http://www.worldschoolmassage.com/
vibrational-healing-massage-therapy/

Vunkuwa® Massage

The Bantu and Bushman peoples of southern Africa have been practicing the healing arts since the dawn of humanity. Living close to nature, they learned to use plants and herbs for healing, and various techniques for massaging the body were passed down from generation to generation. One such practice, used by the women of the Sotho tribe, is the Vunkuwa Massage, which is designed to activate the flow of energy through the body and rejuvenate the mind and spirit. As a descendent of these people, Carol Mathebula has been instrumental in perpetuating the spread of this vigorous form of

bodywork in Belgium. The treatment uses a combination of deep-tissue work, manipulations of the bones and spinal cord, and pressure-point work for energy balancing. Great emphasis is placed on the bones and the power that they generate, and great respect is given to listening to the inner rhythms and voice of the body's fluids. The application of massage oils and creams made from medicinal native plants is an essential part of the bodywork.

In the Zululand region of South Africa, a similar approach to bodywork is used. However, here it is common to encounter more forceful body manipulations, with two practitioners work simultaneously on a recipient. Many parts of their bodies, including the feet, give a vigorous massage to the joints, muscles, and bones. The one time I experienced this method, I found it quite intense, and although I was initially a bit sore, the treatment definitely made my body looser and more limber. Through the grapevine, I have heard that this Zulu practice has spread beyond the confines of Africa.

Contact: www.vunkuwa.com or www.eurothermen.at

Some Final Thoughts About These Modalities

Only a half century ago, there were a relatively small number of bodywork modalities available in the West, and the concept of complementary medicine had yet to take root. However, as the Age of Aquarius commenced in the 1960s, followed by developments that led to today's age of instant communication, change happened quickly. People began to want to create healthy, loving, and inspired lifestyles, supported by more holistically based health care. The popularity of yoga expanded exponentially, and health food stores became more common. Nowadays, even the major chain groceries offer organic choices. An influx of ancient philosophies and spiritual practices inspired new ways of looking at the body, and many of the ever-growing number of complementary and alternative bodywork methods now rely on the wisdom in the body-mind connection to improve mental and physical health. Powerful new therapies reveal how work on the cellular level of the body can affect the mental, emotional, and spiritual aspects of our lives. When we count the number of modalities that have expanded into or grown out of the field of holistic health care, it is heartwarming to imagine what may come in the future.

Many of the bodywork modalities described in this book were created by people who experienced a dysfunctional condition that motivated them to pursue an alternative solution. This concept of creating opportunities out of seemingly negative events demonstrates the Buddhist conviction that the experience of suffering can lead to the wisdom and insight necessary for true, compassionate healing. Many present-day modalities reflect such ancient wisdom, which honors the metaphysical properties found not only in the natural world but also in our own true natures. Newer modalities, whose language, concepts and procedures are based on knowledge from modern research and quantum physics, care for human beings who have the very same basic qualities as those who lived far in the past. There does seem to be a tendency for the spiritual and scientific perspectives to eventually converge as their core realities are increasingly found to resemble each another. This merging of old and new may very well be the future of true healing.

When examining how various modalities approach holistic healing, it is apparent that there are essentially two avenues that can be taken to correct a problem. The first and most common strategy is to look at a health issue as something that needs to be fixed by discovering and treating the root cause of any apparent symptom. The other way is to bring about healing by focusing on a person's strengths, thereby awakening the natural ability to heal, and by relying on the power of love to embrace the problem. This approach to healing moves away from struggling to fix a problem toward a state that allows, supports, and amplifies the capacity to be well. There is an old story about a man who had multiple problems and looked as though he were at death's door. His wife was extremely worried and took him to a wise old Asian doctor recommended by a friend. During the initial interview, she pointed out her husband's various ailments. The doctor sat in silence and just looked at the man for a bit. To the woman's surprise, the doctor then remarked that her husband was really not that bad off, for he was still alive and must have something powerful within him that kept him from dying. So instead of trying to fix things, he proceeded to heal the husband by enhancing his existing strengths.

Both methods are valid ways of dealing with health problems and empowering individuals, and in many forms of therapy, elements of both approaches are used. The appropriate approach depends on a number of factors, including the individual, the particular issue and how extensive it is, the skill of the practitioner, and the ability and desire of the recipient to awaken inherent abilities. In the end, it is often simply the healing presence of love, whether felt through touch or in the vibrational energy all around us, that melts away our issues.

The difference between the ideal and real life may influence the success of a treatment. For instance, the best time of day for a pulse reading is considered to be early morning and only after the client has adhered to certain requirements regarding diet and level of strenuous activity. Here in the West, getting a treatment at this time of day is not always practical, and many individuals don't have the discipline to carry out the requirements. Therefore, it is likely that a pulse reading will not provide the most accurate assessment of a person's condition. In another example, people may be leading such busy lifestyles that after a session they don't take the time to relax and allow for integration, instead going right back to a stressful job. Either of these situations can detract from the effectiveness of a treatment. Ideally, a person would walk away from a bodywork treatment feeling like a million bucks, but there is a limit to how much can be done during a single session. Perhaps there is only time to treat part of the body or to just begin the release of an acute condition. With problems that have become fixed in the body or chronic conditions, it stands to reason that a series of sessions will be required for a successful outcome.

The importance of a complete diagnosis can't be underestimated, since without it, all of the good intentions and skillful techniques may not have the right effect. Taking the time for a proper diagnosis that examines the whole person should be a primary part of any healing session, and in Eastern practices, the action of diagnosis is recognized as having healing properties of its own. Independent practitioners who work outside the busy atmosphere of a clinical setting often can take the time to make a more complete and accurate analysis of a problem, and certain practitioners can intuitively ascertain the cause of a problem by simply observing the client, her patterns of behavior, and how she holds herself. Whether the practitioner is taking your medical history, visually analyzing your features, scanning your aura, or reading your pulse, these assessments are multifaceted, and the more analytical tools that are used, the more useful is the information acquired. The right treatment is only possible when the whole person is illuminated.

The correct interpretation of the cause of a problem and the determination of the most effective procedure for alleviating it is a complex process that can become confusing for the client, especially since every issue may not be traceable to a physical cause. Emotions, thoughts, and beliefs, as well as social and spiritual factors, can have a significant effect on health. Many practitioners, even within similar fields of healing, have their own perspectives on what a particular manifestation signifies and which procedure will be most useful as a remedy. One therapist may see a symptom as due to a particular cause, while another has an entirely different explanation for it. Although sometimes, especially for chronic conditions, it may be helpful to get the opinions of several therapists, but if no consensus is reached, the only course may be to trust your intuition about the correct course to follow.

If careful diagnosis doesn't reveal the root cause of a problem, the practitioner may choose to simply work on enhancing your innate healing ability. This will really do no harm, and chances are during this healing process, the surface issues that may have confused the diagnosis will dissipate for no apparent reason, and what remains may reveal the true cause. The practitioner can then proceed to deal specifically with that issue.

Many of the modalities covered here also have a self-care component (found in Chapter 11) that you can use to maintain or extend your own innate healing capacity. Although these self-care practices are powerful used on their own, they are especially beneficial in helping the recipient of bodywork perpetuate the healing work done by the bodywork practitioner. Likewise, these practices are a necessary requirement for any practitioner or healer who wants to be successful in caring for others.

Even though life will continue to throw situations at us that may cause suffering, any imbalances and dysfunction can be dealt with as they occur, making the journey through life more comfortable and enjoyable. Symptoms of ill health signal you to wake up and become attentive to the needs of the body. They alert you by directing your attention to the problems that need to be solved. Rather than seeing ill health as an obstacle to be controlled or eliminated, it is better to be grateful for this warning sign from the body's wisdom and to heed its request for change.

Specific Types of Contact Used in Bodywork

Within the broad assortment of healing modalities, there are a number of ways that a practitioner's hands can be applied to the recipient's body. The following list represents the many forms of manual intervention accomplished through touch, including manipulations and movements delivered by the palms, fingers, thumbs, knuckles, elbows, forearms, hips, knees, or feet of the practitioner during a bodywork session. Some involve subtle touch, for example, sensing or palpating the energy field, or don't contact the physical body at all. Energetic adjustments, manipulation, or cultivation used in energy medicine are excluded. You can find these in Chapter 9.

During a treatment, practitioners may use a variety of these noninvasive forms of contact at different degrees of intensity, in a certain rhythmic fashion, or in a certain sequence on either broad areas of the body or specific parts, such the fascia, muscles, joints, nerves, bones, and organs. Many can be used to effectively stimulate, repattern, balance, and trigger a healing response in the client. They are listed in the accompanying table. Try reading this list slowly and visualizing the unique effect each technique can have. It's amazing how the internal world of the body-mind complex responds and communicates as a result of these forms of contact.

All of these methods of making contact can influence the physical body, energy body, mind, emotions, and spirit on many levels. Each modality simply takes a different approach to deal with the diversity of needs or dysfunctional issues plaguing their clients.

Numerous practitioners, especially those working with modalities of energy medicine, have told me that upon completion of their training, the instructor suggested forgetting about technique and simply carrying out a treatment with an empty, open mind and no expectations. This will allow the wisdom of the recipient's body to direct the hands as they become instruments of true healing.

Types of Contact During Bodywork

aligning	dragging	hooking	pumping	squeezing
arching	draining	jiggling	pushing	stretching
balancing	effleuraging	J-stroking	raising	striking
beating	enveloping	kneading	raking	stripping
bending	extending	knocking	reeling	stroking
broadening	fanning	leveraging	reflexing	supporting
brushing	feeling	lifting	rocking	swaying
bouncing	filing	mobilizing	rolling	sweeping
caressing	filling	motioning	rotating	swinging
carrying	flexing	oily rubbing	rubbing	tapping
cascading	flicking	palpating	scanning	tractioning
chopping	floating	patterning	scooping	treading
clapping	folding	pecking	scraping	trembling
combing	framing	percussioning	scrubbing	tweaking
compressing	frictioning	petrissaging	sculpting	twisting
connecting	frottaging	picking	shaking	unwinding
contortioning	gliding	piercing	shifting	vibrating
contouring	grabbing	pinching	slapping	waving
cracking	grasping	plucking	sliding	wiping
cradling	guiding	pointing	slipping	wringing
cupping	hacking	pressing	smoothing	
damming	hammering	pulling	spiraling	
digging	holding	pummeling	spreading	

Optimum Health

Optimum health is more than just being free of disease. The human body, a collection of cells, tissues, organs, and circuitry, is a miraculous thing that conducts its business without our conscious intervention. The lungs take in oxygen that circulates oxygen through the blood to nourish all the systems. The bone marrow fabricates red blood, and the skin covers a wound with new cells. The digestive track breaks down food into the nutrients that help the body function. The network of nerves sends signals to activate the muscles to move. But beyond these everyday miracles, we are beings with a mind and a spirit. We have feelings, we have thoughts, we hope and dream. Optimum health requires integrating the physical, emotional, mental, and spiritual into a space of well-being from which to explore the unknown deep within. From this vantage point, we can transform the limitations caused by ignorance, accidents, or life experiences and expand our awareness of our interconnection with all beings.

The problems we have inherited with our DNA, have acquired from our families and our environment, or have created from our own experiences are tools that can be used for transforming dysfunction into optimum health. They are lessons in living that challenge us to change our perspective, beliefs, thinking, and habits. As we cultivate the capacity to reach our fullest potential, we learn that resistance creates blockages that require release that leads to the optimum health in which energy flows.

A common thread in bodywork is the commitment to awakening the recipient's innate healing ability. Until this natural capacity is aroused, bodywork treatments and self-care methods can lead us forward. With proper self-discipline and the wisdom gained through these transformative practices, we can develop the self-awareness and sensitivity that enables us to be a catalyst in healing ourselves and others. It could be said that healing yourself is the first step to healing the world. As more people take the responsibility for becoming truly healthy, the more they will be able to influence others to improve themselves. Maybe true health and happiness infused with compassion and wisdom is our soul's purpose.

CHAPTER 7

Progressive Body-Mind Psychotherapies

It wasn't long ago that the philosophy and methodologies of psychotherapy were somewhat limited from a holistic point of view. In the bad old days, anyone who acted abnormally was often labeled deranged or crazy. Not fit to be part of human society, they might be locked up in primitive facilities that offered little if anything that could be considered therapeutically beneficial. Public awareness about how to relieve the suffering of these individuals was limited, and families with a disruptive member in their midst might disown or otherwise reject that individual. In extreme cases, they might resort to locking people in cages and tending only to their basic needs. (This actually happened during the 1920s to a "wild man" in the small Maine town where I grew up.) Among professionals, there was little understanding about the interconnection between the brain and the emotions, and the knowledge that feelings can be held in the body was not widespread.

Humans have always attempted to answer questions about their consciousness, the workings of the mind, and its effect on behavior. In the early twentieth century, Sigmund Freud and Carl Jung developed psychoanalysis using techniques to uncover what may be buried in the unconscious. Early explorations in Gestalt psychology by Max Wertheimer and others influenced the work done by the less-well-known Elsa Gindler, a somatic therapist who influenced Wilhelm Reich, often thought of as the founder of body-centered psychotherapy. Other innovators such as Fritz and Laura Perls and Erich Fromm followed. These pioneers and many others provided a new platform from which fresh research and exploration would create better understanding by bringing more awareness to the role the body plays in mental and emotional health. What has transpired since then is the creation of a number of unique approaches to alleviate, heal, and transform the innumerable issues from which many of us (not just the "crazy" ones) suffer.

Psychotherapy and counseling have evolved enormously since those early days, treating individuals not just with talk therapy but with many other modalities as well. Although conventional clinical treatment of

neurosis and psychosis based on scientific knowledge about genetics, brain chemistry, and neurology can be necessary and helpful, alternative therapies have emerged as a response to recent findings about the nature of mental illness and human consciousness, research that has given rise to a new paradigm of awareness and a broader understanding of human nature. Not only has the idea of what constitutes mental illness changed, but the meaning of *appropriate treatment* has progressed to include many and varied pathways to real transformation. Today, a wide range of open-minded therapeutic methods approach healing in a more sensitive, considerate, honoring, loving, and less condescending way with an acknowledgment of the deep connections among the body, mind, emotions, and spirit. The acceptance and forgiveness intrinsic to these practices can provide more insight into a person's true nature and enable her innate healing abilities to surface.

It is now apparent that imbalances and illness can be caused not only by environmental factors such as electromagnetic interference, radioactivity, and various forms of chemical pollution but also by internal influences such as our core beliefs, thoughts, emotions, and the effects of trauma. Research has shown that the actual memory of trauma and its emotional repercussions are often stored on the cellular level, and when these memories become fixated in the body, they can take on toxic forms that have a detrimental effect on health and well-being. It is conceivable that all physiological illness has an emotional counterpart embedded in both the nervous system of the body and the surrounding energy fields. Not only can the repercussions create disturbances and dysfunctions, but as a person accumulates and holds more and more detrimental emotions within the body, energy itself is consumed. This diminished life-force energy dampens a person's potential vitality, and overall health and performance suffer.

We all grow up with the pressure to perform and live up to the standards of our parents and the demands of our peers. The continual strain, anxiety, and stress brought on by the social, religious, and political aspects of our culture add to our difficulties. We struggle to feel worthy, and fear the pain of failure, and the sensitivities these produce may prevent us from properly dealing with the inevitable difficult situations in life. As we grow older, our earthly ambitions may give way to a yearning to connect with the subtle, heart-centered aspects of our being, but as we look back on what we have and have not accomplished, that feeling of unworthiness may still be rearing its ugly head.

Although no one really wants to experience painful feelings, there comes a time when it is necessary to move beyond a limited and limiting comfort zone and find a way to confront what we normally tend to avoid. To really resolve things, we must come to a better understanding of the true causes of our problems and learn how to react to situations in a more positive way. This kind of understanding is not something intellectual, for it requires a deeper kind of insight that involves great empathy, love, and compassion for ourselves. Ignorance about what makes us tick will certainly create problems in our relationships with others. If we can't understand and love ourselves then how will we truly respect and love others?

Who is without a mask?

When we can't recognize and transform our negative feelings, we tend to become gluttons for punishment, conditioned to living with our dysfunctional limitations and our suffering. Like us, many others are in the same boat because of their own upbringing and life experiences, and those whose behavior appears to be the worst are probably suffering the most. All of us become addicted to certain patterns of behavior that prevent us from reacting to the difficult situations we

encounter in ways that are more positive. Most of us, even the "together" people, are stumped at one time or another by life's struggles and find ourselves anchored in a state of mind and emotions that binds us to the past. Some of us become disillusioned and apathetic and resist exposing ourselves to the truth that can set us free, fearing the pain of change more than the pain of living in our current state. But many of us take heart and courageously face the fear of becoming intimate with ourselves and vulnerable to any pain that may accompany transformation.

In this chapter of the book, we'll take a look at progressive and holistic forms of therapy that are guided by a facilitator rather than applied by a bodywork practitioner. These methods, which recognize the mind-body connection, approach healing from a psychological perspective, with the focus and emphasis placed on the mental and emotional health of the individual and the way in which it affects the condition of the body as a whole. These programs, which are designed to promote emotional, psychological, transpersonal, and spiritual well-being, advise and instruct recipients in methods that explore and resolve personal problems, increase self-awareness, heal emotional wounds, transform core beliefs, deal with learning disabilities, improve communication skills, change habitual patterns of behavior, fashion new ways of living, and help guide people further along a spiritual path.

A number of these holistic body-mind therapies, though useful by themselves, are beneficial complements to practitioner-applied bodywork. Bodyworkers may recommend psychotherapeutic counseling therapies, especially if there is an emotional or traumatic element that needs greater attention. Many of these therapies can help individuals retain vital energy and further activate and integrate healthy changes that have been prompted by a bodywork treatment. Some forms are particularly useful for those who do not readily entertain the idea of any form of touch therapy, though many do use physical touch and techniques that can help an individual become more embodied, thus allowing the more conscious perception of what is being held within. When the mind and the emotions are engaged with the body, it is possible to release restrictions that limit potential and to transform problems into life-enhancing opportunities.

Most of these psychotherapies are somatic in nature and share fundamental ideas about why and how individuals develop certain inhibitions, but their techniques may differ. Although the primary methods employed are usually not those of traditional bodywork, many recognize the need for embodiment and do incorporate some physical manipulation, noninvasive touch, muscle testing, body postures, physical movements, and energy-field work. These kinds of modalities often include dialogue with verbal exchanges, techniques that facilitate reprogramming and reeducating mental and emotional patterns of behavior, reflective therapy, hypnotic suggestion, transference, guided imagery, dream work, body awareness techniques, neurolinguistics, breathwork, techniques to enhance sensory perception, and techniques for cathartic release. Most require that the client be an active participant who is willing to listen, imagine, and act in a manner prescribed by the facilitator. For those who desire psychotherapeutic methods that include more physical bodywork, take a look at the modalities in the section on Trauma-Centered Therapies in Chapter 6.

Some of these therapies can be experienced by attending group seminars or training programs facilitated by health professionals, and others are accomplished in one-on-one private sessions. In many instances, once individual participants have been able to learn and integrate the instructions provided by a professional, they can incorporate them into a daily practice. There are many other counseling and coaching psychotherapies available today, and new forms of therapeutic treatment are constantly being created. The modalities in this chapter are just a sample of integrative mind-body centered psychotherapies and training programs, including those that have a transpersonal or spiritual emphasis.

When speaking of transpersonal psychology, it is helpful to keep in mind that it is essentially a study of human potential rather than the analysis of a problem. The practices open the doorway to what a person is really capable of accomplishing with a strong sense of presence and focused attention. Rather than seeing psychological issues as weakness or disease, anything that arises, no matter how intense or debilitating, is considered an opportunity for growth. Any life crisis can provide a psychospiritual awakening that will allow more freedom and happiness if the issues that come to the surface are embraced rather than pushed away. Fear and depression often emerge in response to major life transitions, but if we can fully honor these shadow sides

of our being and allow ourselves to recognize the innate wisdom contained within our struggles for wholeness, we can connect more deeply with our true nature.

Astrological Consultation

For many centuries, the relationship of the science of astrology to the human psyche and personality has been shown to be helpful in promoting self-awareness. Its origins are rooted in many ancient cultures around the world, and different spiritual traditions have their methods of interpreting the messages from the heavens to create an astrological analysis of individuals, places, and even countries. Kings, queens, and emperors used astrological guidance to help determine their next political moves. Some cultures have used it in combination with hand readings to help individuals become more deeply acquainted with themselves and find their true paths in life. Astrological counseling can help clients recognize areas of strengths and limitations in their personalities by highlighting individual character traits and tendencies as well as potential challenges. Astrological methods have also been used to predict the weather, sometimes with great accuracy. Although the belief in the usefulness of astrology has fluctuated over the millennia, today it is very easy to find a consultant to compile and interpret a natal horoscope chart and subsequent transits.

Autogenic Training (AT)

Autogenic Training is a method of relaxation and stress management that consists of a series of exercises designed to teach the body to switch off the fight-or-flight stress response to challenging situations. This straightforward method of maintaining inner balance was developed during the 1920s by Dr. Johannes Schultz of Germany. Later, Dr. Wolfgang Luthe expanded upon the process. The series of six simple body-mind relaxation exercises enables people to handle stressful situations in a calmer, more effective way. The method helps individuals gently focus attention on the body, which enhances the mind and body's natural ability to cope in the face of any physical and psychological disorders. People also gain awareness of how restrictions of their abilities to function caused by stress can leave them at increased risk of illness. At the same time, as with other meditative relaxation methods, it is likely that the work enhances the immune system and stimulates innate healing abilities.

A typical session begins with an interview to determine current health concerns. Emotional issues are then addressed by positioning the body comfortably to reduce the effects of any outside stimuli and subvocally repeating specific positive statements. Regular practice helps rebalance the natural self-regulating mind-body systems, which in turn enables a calmer approach to stress. The autogenic state is one of inner calm that helps people cope better with a wide variety of physical and psychological problems. The process relies on concentration, sensations within the body, and gentle breathing to help induce the relaxed, peaceful, and receptive state in which anxiety naturally subsides. A training session may stir up old emotions, and autogenic therapists are trained to safeguard their clients as they become aware of, understand, and learn to manage such challenging times. Both group and individual training are accomplished in a simple manner and taught in a series of sessions with six standard exercises adapted for affirming personal healing. A variety of intentional exercises are also offered to help a client deal with unresolved issues. Once learned, these exercises can be done anytime and anywhere. Those who are committed to maintaining a regular practice are most likely to obtain the most benefit. The training is also useful for healthy people who simply want to expand their ability to perform better physically and be more creative mentally and emotionally.

Contact: Autogenic Training Institute –
www.autogenictherapy.com.au or
British Autogenic Society –
www.autogenic-therapy.org.uk

Bodynamic Analysis[SM]

A form of somatic psychotherapy developed in Denmark by Lisbeth Marcher, Bodynamic Analysis recognizes the strong correlation between the way a person's body and psyche have developed, given that emotions held within the body's musculature can affect the condition of the muscles. This method combines physical therapy and psychotherapy to find existing blockages, release their hold, and help the individual reestablish a better connection with his emotions. Using a developmental body map and focused work on current psychological issues, Bodynamic Analysis strives to access unconscious psychological material and provide a client with the ability to make healthy choices and improve relationships.

A session begins with the therapist acquiring a detailed history of the client's relationships, past trauma, and any issues that are currently a problem. Next, a body map is created to show where different states of tension exist within the body. The client and therapist then make an agreement about the work that needs to be done. The session continues with a combination of verbal exchanges and gentle hands-on contact to energize certain muscles in a way that supports the emergence and release of psychological material that has been blocked or forgotten. The particular condition of a muscle—elastic, stiff, or over-extended—often indicates the psychological perspective of the client and his way of handling ongoing personal issues. Increasing elasticity allows defensive muscle patterns to relax, which helps alleviate any associated psychological aspects. Collapsed muscles, which reflect current issues, are usually treated first. The therapist continually tests the amount of contraction in various muscles to assess their condition, and then refers to the body map to ascertain what these findings represent in terms of existing psychological issues. While working with a muscle or group of muscles, the client gains information from the physical feelings and emotions that arise in each area, and the therapist then helps the client use this knowledge to integrate and reclaim his ability to function better. Long-term therapy may be required for clients whose issues are significant or complex.

Contact: Bodynamic Institute – www.bodynamicusa.
com/documents/35.html

Core Beliefs Psychotherapy[SM] **(CBP)**

Core beliefs represent both positive and negative ideas and concepts that a person has adopted especially during early childhood, often through the influence of parents and existing cultural standards. These beliefs have a strong and often unconscious effect on a person's attitudes, thinking, and ways of handling life experiences. Mistaken or limiting core beliefs can inhibit potential by creating conditions of low self-esteem, anger, depression, or anxiety. They can become core wounds that manifest as feelings of unworthiness, inadequacy, or emptiness, which, if not resolved, can lead to further disconnection from the true self. Over time, this disconnection can lead to a permanent state in which a person just tries as best she can to cope with, for example, the pain of a core sense of inadequacy. Many therapies are not as successful as they could be because they do not address these core beliefs.

Core Beliefs Psychotherapy, developed by therapist Alice Brown Gagnon, addresses the root cause of these issues by bringing awareness to the mistaken concepts in a way that allows a reversal of feelings and a change in the perception of reality, which results in more confidence, freedom, and personal power. CBP employs a highly specialized set of dialogue techniques and role-playing to bring to light and correct any mistaken core beliefs that the individual has not been fully aware of. Rather than probing into repressed memories, the therapy uses a process of mindful questioning and conscious affirmations to bypass the effects of mistaken core beliefs and to provide the insight that is revealed through a deeper exploration of the inner self. The intention is to provide a rapid intervention that helps the recipient take a closer look at what is really true in her life.

Contact: Core Healing Center –
    www.core-beliefs-psychotherapy.com

Core Energetics

Core Energetics was one of the first holistic, body-centered psychotherapies to join spirituality with psychology by working with emotional or energy blockages caused by past traumas and painful mental and emotional experiences that have been held deeply in the body, perhaps since childhood. These pent-up emotions are referred to as frozen history, and Core Energetics is designed to find those hidden defenses and free up the blocked energy. Although this psychoenergetic transformational healing process is built on the work of Sigmund Freud, Carl Jung, and Wilhelm Reich, it is based on a deeper understanding of the ways in which energy and consciousness work together in human development. This bioenergetic therapy was developed during the 1970s by Dr. John and Eva Pierrakos. After studying with Alexander Lowen in the 1950s, John Pierrakos created his own form of healing known as Core Energetics. Spiritual aspects were incorporated through the channeled transmissions of Eva Picrrakos. The therapy combines touch and physical movement with psychotherapy, breathwork, and spiritual work to activate a stronger flow of energy and to create a deep, conscious experience that helps a person willingly examine and release painful issues and identify himself with his core energy and feelings of joy.

Sessions take place in a nurturing environment, either alone or in a group. The practitioner uses verbal inquiry and visual analysis of the client's body language to gain an understanding of his frozen history, which shows up as constrictions in the client's potential. The inquiry also serves to stimulate the client's self-awareness about particular issues that he may then want to resolve. The work does not rely on talk therapy alone, but encourages the client to actually feel the feelings he's been protecting himself from by incorporating free expression of emotions, breathwork, and physical techniques for homing in on energy blocks. As part of the treatment, the client uses his own body in exaggerated actions that galvanize the muscles and allow energy to flow, such as kicking, punching, and holding specific positions. In addition to these exaggerated postures, making sounds or replicating facial expressions, as well as connecting statements to movements, are part of the process. These actions are often proposed by the practitioner as a way for the client to see which physical or verbal expression has the closest energetic relationship to the truth of an issue. When a client is confused, he may be directed to alternately make positive and negative statements out loud while hitting a padded object and then take a moment to discern which statement most correctly reflects how he feels. The release and discharge of trapped energy that occurs within the process can also come about through spontaneous involuntary movements and reactions, such as vibrations, muscle twitching, crying, laughing, or rage. No free or spontaneous cathartic expression of feelings is considered taboo. Although the active experience of body movement and verbal expression are the keys to the process, release can also be encouraged by soft, hands-on techniques working with the energy field. Core Energetics is also appropriate for those simply desiring personal transformation, and sessions are tailored to individuals, groups, couples, or families. Several sessions may be necessary to achieve the desired result.

Contact: Institute of Core Energetics –
    www.coreenergetics.org

Degriefing Therapy®/
Integrative Grief Therapy

Degriefing Therapy is a somatic form of psychotherapeutic healing whose essence is recognizing and supporting the relationship between the body and the emotions. It depends on the body-mind connection and is based on the premise that grief is the most available and untapped resource for personal transformation. As the body's natural response to any form of loss, grief plays an important role in triggering unresolved feelings that are held in the body, and since the mind and body are inextricably linked, grief can create a state of physical and mental disharmony. Therefore, it is necessary to understand grief's effect and to work to resolve any disharmony through nurturing care that addresses the root cause of emotional, mental, and physical symptoms. Although not part of this contemporary therapy, it is interesting to note that certain African cultures have traditionally used a similar approach for dealing with grief through the enactment of special ritual practices, such as those led by Sobonfu Somé.

Degriefing Therapy combines verbal counseling with individualized physical-care techniques in order to recognize the mental and physical pain that accompanies grief. This form of psychological counseling is designed to help recipients express rather than suppress or marginalize their grief and help them move through it in a constructive way by easing any associated emotional distress, unlocking blockages that have developed in the body, and healing emotional wounds. A variety of integrative therapies that are customized to the uniqueness of each individual are called on to reduce the strain on the body and immune system. Physical care can include massage, yoga, or meditation. Clients are also educated in the use of practical self-care techniques that can minimize the potential for developing serious chronic disorders. The therapist also provides referrals to other forms of treatment as appropriate. Degriefing Therapy can be accomplished on an individual basis or in a group with a team of supportive people. Medical professionals who are unable to deal with a client's emotional distress may suggest Degriefing Therapy as a way to help deal with grief and loss.
Contact: www.degriefing.com or www.sobonfu.com

EMDR Therapy™

EMDR stands for Eye Movement Desensitization Reprocessing, and it can be helpful for those who have suffered from years of anxiety, depression, phobias, or memories of trauma. Dr. Francine Shapiro developed this integrative psychotherapeutic approach, which uses an eight-phase process to address a wide range of dysfunctions caused by unresolved past experiences. It is safe, simple, and noninvasive, and uses no drugs or hypnosis. EMDR incorporates a blend of traditional and holistic psychotherapies that work with the body-mind connection to release unwanted patterns and unresolved blockages that inhibit personal well-being.

After the initial history-taking session in which a treatment plan is developed, the therapist makes sure the client is emotionally stable enough to handle the procedures and then works to help him recognize the issues. First the client identifies vivid visual images related to the memories and emotions of a distressing event or a negative belief; he is then instructed to name a positive belief as his goal. Next, while the client concentrates on the images, beliefs, and related emotions and body sensations, his eyes follow the therapist's hands as they move back and forth across his visual field for half a minute or more. The therapist may also include a dual stimulation procedure that uses auditory tones, the tapping of certain points, and other forms of tactile stimulation in conjunction with the eye movements; the duration is customized to the needs of the patient. After this intervention, the client is instructed to simply notice whatever happens in the body or comes to mind. The process may be repeated a number of times until the physical sensations become positive and the recipient's response indicates that he can better identify with the positive belief that was chosen at the beginning of the session. Then the therapist will proceed with the closing phase, which includes self-calming activities, and the client is given a period of time to reflect. He is then given a journal in which to document any related material that arises after the session. Some time later, a final reevaluation session ensures that any emotional stress related to the memory or anxiety-producing situation has been eliminated.
Contact: www.emdr-therapy.com

Emotrance

Emotrance is a noninvasive form of energy psychology that works with the human energy system at the emotional level. Silvia Hartmann, one of the early practitioners of meridian energy therapy, created Emotrance as a simple self-help technique that allows a person to release and transform the energy of emotions that are stuck in the body. Hartmann sees emotions as a way to receive direct feedback about the state of the body's subtle energy system. Emotions are considered to be energy in motion, and when trauma occurs, the flow of energy becomes blocked and creates a disturbance that leads to the manifestation of negative emotions and the possibility of health problems. This work primarily involves focusing thoughts on distressed parts of the body and treating these areas directly with the vital life-force energy. Important to the techniques used in Emotrance are paying attention to the physical sensations that accompany emotions, softening and releasing the internal pressure, and restoring the flow of new positive energy and emotions. Rather than just alleviating symptoms of emotional or mental pain, the goal is to move the recipient from a state of pain into a positive and uplifted state of joy and happiness by bringing back an even flow of energy to all the systems of the body. The client is considered an equal partner, actively engaged in the healing process. Since it includes some physical contact, Emotrance can be incorporated into many other healing methods, including forms of applied bodywork.

The healing process does not use any of the tapping or muscular testing found in other forms of energy therapy or any activation of points, symbols, or charts. Instead, Emotrance moves stuck energy by the power of vision and focused intention, physiological feedback, and the direct experience of perceiving exactly where the disturbance is in the energetic body. Once the client finds the disturbance, she is often instructed to breathe deeply while the therapist applies her healing hands to promote the flow of energy. The therapist has an in-depth understanding of energy medicine and brings a variety of energetic healing techniques into the process. They include various ways to resolve energetic stress, work with energy shields, methods for changing thought fields, work within the energy matrix, healing with crystals, a process of soul guidance, and an assortment of methods for feeling and working with the oceans of energy that exist in the deeper realms of human existence. The result is to bring the recipient into a place of alignment and harmony from which she can function with more self-awareness and grace.
Contact: www.emotrance.com

Energy Psychology (EP)

Energy Psychology is a progressive form of psychotherapy that uses an assortment of approaches to address the way energy is related to emotions, awareness,

behavior, and health. EP primarily focuses on shifting the bioelectrical energy in the brain and the body by stimulating specific energy points on the body as the client's mind focuses on a problem or negative emotional state. The energetic components of this therapy include the bioelectrical activity of the nervous system, heart, meridian energy channels, radiant circuits, biophotons, chakras, and biofields. Among many others, Dr. Fred Gallo was involved in the development of this holistic approach to healing, which goes beyond psychological analysis of thoughts and emotions to explore the energetic basis for any existing psychological issues. The actual bioenergetic process continues to evolve as ongoing clinical research into the emotional and cognitive dynamics of the energy fields and mind reveals new therapeutic insights.

At the start of a session, clients are fully assessed in order to determine the method of treatment that is most appropriate. An EP session works on the underlying energetic aspects of a psychological problem through muscle testing, visualizations, affirmations, expressed intentions or assertions, the assumption of specific body postures, and physical movements. Treatments usually incorporate a form of self-applied Acupressure to stimulate nerve endings by tapping or holding specific discrete points such as those under the eye and on the collarbone, along with focused thought and breathwork guided by the therapist. These techniques reduce or eliminate any irrational anxiety and fear, thereby enhancing a more integrated state of self-awareness. This therapy strives to rapidly accomplish measurable results without causing unnecessary emotional stress and is continually revealing itself to be helpful in treating a variety of dysfunctions. The term *Energy Psychology* can describe a wide range of therapies that have been developed over recent years.
Contact: www.noetic.org/noetic/issue-thirteen-august/ energy-psychology/ or www.energypsych.com

Formative Psychology

Based in part on the principles and therapeutic work of Wilhelm Reich and Alexander Lowen and formerly known as Somatic Emotional Psychotherapy, Formative Psychology, developed by Dr. Stanley Keleman, concentrates on the way in which life events, both physical and emotional, affect a person's physical form. Each kind of event has emotional and physical components, and together they organize a person's reality as he develops; when a person is challenged either mentally or physically and cannot tolerate the effects of the challenge, his shape can be distorted and the natural functioning and vitality of the body diminished. Rather than using cathartic methods for release, Formative Psychology relies on self-management and cultivation of the ability to simply not react to painful stimuli in order to release and prevent limiting patterns of behavior.

The first step in the process is to identify the somatic attitude or emotional stance as it exists within the body. The therapist instructs the client in identifying how he is compressing and contracting himself because of an emotion. The client then works to intensify the pattern of compression and then slowly reduces the amount of compression a little at a time. After repeating the cycle a number of times, the recipient simply waits and allows any associated feelings to arise. This pause between what has ended and what has not yet arrived enables the client to reflect with an attitude of openness on the experience and learn how to practice new ways of seeing and handling himself. The therapy demands discipline and is not considered a quick fix or a short-term solution.
Contact: Center for Energetic Studies –
www.centerpress.com

Gendlin Focusing

While working with psychologist Carl Rogers in the 1960s, philosopher Eugene Gendlin pointed psychotherapists to the practice of focusing. Gendlin developed a technique by which clients could easily discover, understand, and deal with the felt sense, a subtle and vague awareness of memories and unresolved feelings within the body. The vagueness is often caused by the fact that the body and mind can become disconnected because of problematic emotional issues, tension, depression, and anxiety, and the felt sense remains below the conscious level. For many, the felt sense is evasive and cannot easily be expressed in words. (Just think of the way people pause when trying to find the words to describe some subtle inner feeling.) *Focusing* refers to holding open, nonjudgmental attention on something that is experienced but is not fully comprehended or cannot be verbalized. The act of focusing is used to make clear what is really felt or wanted so that the felt sense is more tangible and easier to identify and work with. It is now frequently considered essential to successful psychotherapy.

Gendlin was able to devise a series of steps to teach the process of focusing on the felt sense; they are closely correlated with the act of deep listening. This approach also makes the client more aware of the meaning behind the words or images chosen to represent the felt sense. The therapist pays close attention to his own felt sense as a source of insight during the therapeutic process. The client can use a journal or sketchbook or may be assisted by a professional listener, who is trained in sensing undercurrents. The overall goal is to enhance the ability to trust the self, to get past repetitive thoughts and feelings that go nowhere, to feel more connected to and guided by feelings, to discover new choices, and to be able to make wiser decisions that provide a deeper connection with the self and others.
Contact: The Focusing Institute – www.focusing.org

Gestalt Therapy

Because it provides a secure environment without any problematic consequences, Gestalt Therapy may be a good choice for those who have difficulty expressing and releasing feelings freely. This form of psychotherapy was developed during the 1950s by Fritz and Laura Perls with the intention of finding the right balance between supporting and challenging a client who sought to resolve dysfunctional issues. The therapy recognizes that people have had to adapt to many difficult circumstances, often by hiding their sadness and anger. In time, these buried feelings can lead to heaviness and hopelessness that inhibits the potential to live fully in a positive way. The principle behind Gestalt Therapy is that the therapist is a participant in a trusting relationship rather than a detached observer. In this way, rather than deciding beforehand on a specific methodology, the practitioner works alongside recipients to discover the best way for each individual to express and release trapped emotions and feelings.

During a session, attention is given to encouraging the increased awareness of feelings through active listening while providing the client with a comfortable environment in which she can feel free to express herself in any way. The therapist observes how a person behaves while expressing herself, and then works to liberate any of the client's suppressed feelings by encouraging free cathartic expression through crying, swearing, shouting, moving the body in any way possible, or other dynamic forms of release. Throughout the process, the therapist provides an atmosphere of acceptance. As the therapist assists the release process by comforting the client's fears, listening to her anger, and acknowledging her sadness, the client can realize that it is possible to make new choices about what to do with these feelings and to create more healthful opportunities in life. Contact: www.gestalt.org

Grinberg Method®

The Grinberg Method was developed during the 1980s by Avi Grinberg, who had studied with many different traditional healers. After finding it frustrating trying to treat those who wanted to rely on the therapist for all the work, he gave up his practice and opened his own school in Israel so that he could teach others how to heal themselves. Grinberg's method is a form of somatic psychotherapy that uses body education to teach clients how to regain access to their own resources. This method is based on the idea that enhanced perception of bodily sensations can strengthen the natural human capacity to learn, grow, make good choices, and evolve. It offers a structured way of learning through the body that enables an individual to recognize and abandon repetitive and restrictive physical and behavioral ways of being. The basic principle is to make the fear, pain, and unwanted feelings that are usually perceived as obstacles into opportunities for healing by allowing them to surface so that they can be released more successfully. The keys to success are a willingness to change, development of the ability to perceive through the body, and the use of willpower.

The systematic process starts with the client learning to define pain and continues by teaching the recipient to recognize obstacles and develop the specific qualities needed for true resolution. The client continues to learn through the body how to become aware of the accumulation of past experiences, the way they are expressed in the present moment, and how they might influence the future. The method incorporates movement, breathing, touch techniques, and exercises to develop better attention and perception. The therapist helps the client learn how to actively deal with fears, thus allowing more space for pain to surface and for willpower to be exercised, enhancing the ability to let go of what really is no longer useful. Instead of learning through the mind, this method focuses on rediscovering that the body is capable of gathering its own resources for maintaining health and gaining personal fulfillment. Contact: www.grinbergmethod.com

Hakomi Method

Hakomi is an experiential body-centered method of psychotherapy that is also "mindfulness centered," integrating an active form of mindfulness into the therapy session. Hakomi was created in the 1970s by Ron Kurtz, a therapist who integrated aspects of Buddhism, Taoism, and other body-mind therapies. He wanted to create a noninvasive way of accessing core, unconscious psychological material, and developed a methodology that includes many somatic techniques. These help bring to consciousness the powerful unconscious forces, beliefs, and habits that shape a person's life outside conscious awareness. This process enhances self-knowledge and self-awareness. *Hakomi* is a Hopi Indian word translated as "Where do you stand in relation to the many realms?" or more simply "Who are you?" Hakomi operates from five fundamental core principles: mindfulness, unity, mind-body integration, nonviolence, and organicity (the idea that the psychological process will unfold organically when supported). In addition to being a guiding principle, mindfulness is a key element for allowing the process to unfold, and most of the therapy session is actually conducted in mindfulness.

Hakomi's somatic techniques include the client's heightened awareness of felt sensations, the therapist's observations of subtle body patterns and movements, and gentle support of chronic areas of tension in the body. These may become "access routes" to unconscious core material, which consists of memories, body impressions, emotional imprints, and habitual thoughts, beliefs, and attitudes that have been developing since infancy in response to challenging situations. These often show up as the armor of habitual muscle tension and energy restrictions that no longer contribute to well-being and also profoundly influence behavior, self-image, and relationships.

During a session, the loving presence of the practitioner creates limbic resonance with the client and establishes a safe space in which to explore core material and to bring previously unconscious attitudes and feelings to the surface. The therapist guides the recipient's attention toward present-moment experiences, including body awareness, thoughts, and feelings. Hakomi techniques used in mindfulness help the client uncover core material and access key formative memories safely, and these emerge in consciousness with a powerful felt sense for the client. Although many Hakomi therapists do not use touch, gentle touch may be used when appropriate, with the consent of the client, as a supportive gesture or to help access unconscious material in the body. Once core material becomes conscious, it is available for change and reintegration. Hakomi works gently and safely at this core level, often with the inner child providing the "missing experience" that allows the child to have a safer, more supportive experience of the world. These therapeutic experiences are then integrated for the conscious adult, so that he or she can transform limiting beliefs and behaviors, and move into new, more satisfying and supportive options in life. Although Hakomi does not include bodywork, there is "Hakomi for Bodyworkers" training for bodyworkers who wish to incorporate Hakomi into their practice.

Contact: Hakomi Institute – www.hakomiinstitute.com

Heart Math® Therapy

Could it possible that the heart has a brain of its own with an intelligence that can have a significant influence on human physiology? Recent scientific research on the heart has revealed new insights into its nature and has given rise to a number of techniques that focus on positive emotions to reduce stress, fatigue, and detrimental behaviors while fostering physiological wholeness, emotional well-being, and overall performance. Heart Math Therapy is a scientifically validated system of biofeedback that focuses on how the connection between the heart and the brain relates to a person's health. It was created through the research of Doc Childre with the goal of helping people engage their hearts to reduce stress and improve overall health. The Institute of Heart Math, a research institute cofounded by Dr. Rollin McCraty, has been instrumental in the study of the interactions between the heart, the energy fields, the nervous system, and the brain, with particular emphasis on the emotions. New evidence shows that the heart is a master organ with its own intelligence and nervous system (neurons) that regulate its beat and respond to certain conditions faster than the brain. The heart is able to emit all kinds of signals (energy, heat, light, and others) and when affected by positive feelings will radiate an optimal state of coherence to the rest of the body. The electromagnetic energy created by the heart's contractions every time it beats creates a pressure wave that is felt by the neurons of the brain. In fact, the heart has been found to have more of an effect (both energetically

and emotionally) on the brain than the brain does on the heart. Heart Math focuses on the significance of the variations in the heartbeat as well as on the energetic interactions with other parts of the body.

Heart Math Therapy works primarily by relaxing the heart and allowing it to beat with a balanced, coherent rhythm and then encouraging the brain to become entrained with this balance. This allows the brain and nervous system to enter a more harmonious state in which healing can take place by influencing patterns of activity in the nervous system that occur when strong emotions are experienced. The goal of the therapy is to intervene with positive, emotionally focused techniques that engage the heart, enhance its interaction with the brain, and alleviate emotionally stressful issues.

The actual therapy involves a particular kind of biofeedback that is initially accomplished with the aid of a computer. The process induces a very pleasant relaxation response, which can be called upon when a particular issue or problem is brought into conscious awareness. Specific techniques are employed to reduce the variations in heartbeat that occur as a response to nervous-system disorders. Music is also used to enhance the relaxation response by improving the client's mood and reducing irregular nervous energy. Heart Math teaches clients how to resolve conflicts and problematic issues by increasing their awareness of how quickly thoughts can affect physiology and provides them with the ability to make more rapid choices to resolve personal conflicts and to improve physical, mental, and emotional coherence and health. Once the client learns the techniques that prompt a relaxation response, they no longer need the feedback provided by the computer.

Contact: Institute of Heartmath – www.heartmath.org

Imago Relationship Therapy

Imago Relationship Therapy consists of programs that help couples and individuals understand the root causes of any deep emotional problems or issues. Rather than attempting to fix a person, it tries to provide a safe, supportive, and positive way to explore issues without blame or shame by providing an emotionally safe environment in which individuals can hear and be heard without judgment or criticism. This counseling therapy was pioneered during the 1980s by Dr. Harville Hendrix, Ph.D. and his wife Dr. Helen LaKelly Hunt, Ph.D. as a way to create rewarding relationships by turning conflict into personal growth through changing the way people handle the inevitable clashes between two different personalities. The word *imago* represents the emotional blueprint that comes from emotional wounding during childhood. This wounding includes all emotional scars, states of depression, the sense of alienation, and disappointments that have limited a person's full potential. Even in a healthy relationship, there are times when a partner can feel alone, unloved, and unsupported. The aim of this therapy is to give deeper insight, to provide a sense of connection, to empower each individual with the ability to do his or her own work, and to help integrate a new sense of personal awareness. In Imago, there is no right or wrong, and no one is trying to inject a preconceived solution. The challenge is to learn how to better communicate about things that really matter, and the counselor simply acts as a coach in the process.

Imago Relationship Therapy relies primarily on creative, sensitive dialogue to help precipitate healing. When couples are being counseled, the process often starts with a discussion about the positive aspects of the relationship. Since the therapy is often begun when a couple have already distanced themselves from each other, there can be a dramatic shift, leaving each person with a sense of finally being heard. In practice, the therapist has the two people face each other as they speak directly, taking turns listening without interruption. The counselor guides the Imago Dialogue process, making sure that the session is safe, positive, and effective. Sometimes the counselor will suggest part of a sentence to be completed, for example, "And when you did that I felt . . ." This can help the dialogue go deeper. The whole process supports each individual in learning skills that strengthen the relationship and creates a shift in perspective through which each takes ownership of the work that required for healing. The idea is to make it possible for rapid progress to occur with relatively few follow-up sessions. Information on training in Imago Relationship Therapy is available through the website. Contact: www.harvillehendrix.com or
www.imagorelationships.org

Integrative Body Psychotherapy (IBP)

Integrative Body Psychotherapy is a transformational form of body-centered psychotherapy that is designed to provide mental, physical, and emotional health and well-being. It essentially unifies the most effective elements of psychoanalysis, Gestalt Therapy, Reichian Therapy, Bioenergetics, the Feldenkrais Method of Somatic Education, transpersonal psychology, and much more. IBP was developed by Dr. Jack Lee Rosenberg and Dr. Beverly Kitaen Morse as a way of helping clients reconnect with their natural body intelligence with the therapist using minimal physical touch. The basic premise is that the body knows best and that every insight gained should be felt by and experienced in the body's core. The aim is to enable clients to directly access knowledge that goes beyond the mere conceptual level by giving them a new, somatically integrated experience of themselves so they can see life through a different lens.

IBP uses subtle methods of breathwork, physical movement, and self-release techniques to increase aliveness and authentic self-awareness. The process empowers a client to distinguish and release disruptive repetitive patterns held in the brain and throughout the body, thereby stabilizing the true core self. The therapist helps clients resolve any compelling emotional body-mind patterns that cause their worldview to become fragmented, distorted, or pervasively undermining. The practitioner guides clients to acknowledge faulty emotional patterns, beliefs, and defensive habits developed from childhood and teaches body-and-mind health skills for sustaining a sense of self, somatic constancy, well-being, and inner wisdom. The therapy is intended to be a quick-acting process for creating balance and inner stability, accessing the deeper wisdom of the body and engaging the body's capacity for change with growth and development. Contact: IBP Central Institute – www.ibponline.org

MAP (Medical Assistance Program) Therapy / Perelandra System

MAP stands for "Medical Assistance Program" and is one aspect of the Perelandra program, which is a complete system of healing that is employed at the Perelandra Center for Nature Research. This program partners with the intelligence of nature by focusing on the environment, personal health, and gardens, as well as other creative projects that do not grow in soil. The intent of the program, which was developed in 1976 by Machaelle Wrights, is to work with nature in ways that help get the information needed to create an inclusive environment based on nature's principles of balance and harmony. MAP uses a very involved and comprehensive program for humans that employs a special calibrated map of the body along

with muscle testing, verbal exploration, and the guidance of ascended masters or devas in a co-creative partnership with nature to address both physical and emotional health issues. The body map is provided in a book that acts as a medical assistant to provide insight into what is needed to promote healing. Various bodywork therapists have incorporated MAP Therapy in their work.
Contact: Perelandra Center for Nature Research – www.perelandra-ltd.com

Neo-Reichian Therapy

A number of different Neo-Reichian therapies have been developed since Dr. Wilhelm Reich, a contemporary of Sigmund Freud, first carried out his groundbreaking work on orgone energy. Reich's Orgonomic Therapy, also known as Orgone Therapy, was a method of character transformation that recognizes the essential identity of the mind and body. The therapy analyzes the patient's character as it presents itself in her behavior and then provides ways to enhance self-awareness, change habits, and free up more open expression. Key parts of this therapy are locating painful constrictions and facilitating the growth of an individual's innate healing capabilities.

This form of therapy combines dialogue, breathwork, physical manipulations, and movement to resolve suppressed emotional issues and physical tensions that are held in the body. These constrictions develop over time as a way of coping with difficult feelings or events, and eventually they become a habitual response, which the person is then trapped into defending. This leads to denial and avoidance that further limits true potential. Reich recognized that these suppressed traumas create protective physical layers he called "body armor." During therapy, various techniques are applied according to individual needs to release both physical and emotional tension by making a person conscious of self-distorting tendencies. Several forms of Neo-Reichian Therapy were developed in the 1960s by students of Wilhelm Reich. Since some of these body-mind therapies like Reichian Release Therapy and Bioenergetics do include actual hands-on bodywork, they are discussed in the section on Energy-Based Therapies in Chapter 6.
Contact: www.orgone.org

Neuro-Linguistic Programming™ (NLP)

Neuro-Linguistic Programming was developed during the 1970s by therapist Richard Bandler and Professor John Grinder after they studied why certain people succeed brilliantly in their endeavors and others fail. It is based on the assumptions that all behavior has its origin in the neurological processes of the nervous system and that how people communicate is based on the mental patterns through which they organize ideas and actions. However, these patterns can become neurologically fixated and require reprogramming. NLP looks at the way the whole brain works and at the memory codes and experiences present in a consistent, detectable pattern that may or may not be beneficial to well-being. The word *programming* in its name refers to how these patterns are recognized, understood, and acted upon by the brain. The therapy represents a self-help technique that is intended to quickly help an individual find what is unconsciously holding her back from success or change and to assist her in making better choices. The process involves an educational and counseling program that teaches how to increase potential by developing tools that will transform life's stresses into opportunities that enhance personal evolution. It emphasizes personal development, the communication between the conscious and unconscious mind, and ways in which people can help themselves achieve goals by transforming the way they communicate, influence, achieve, and choose what is best for them. The therapy recognizes the strong connection between body language and the thought process and that there are three modes through which people communicate: visual, auditory, and kinesthetic (through the body and its feelings).

The basic educational process uses techniques such as modeling and mirroring to give the client specific tools with which to raise actions and reactions to optimum levels. Clients are coached in methods that will allow them to get along better with others, remain in the best emotional state, set and achieve goals, think and act flexibly, and develop acute awareness. NLP has been found helpful for people suffering from post-traumatic stress disorder, depression, anxiety, addictions, difficulties in learning, and an assortment of emotional disorders.
Contact: www.richardbandler.com

Nonviolent Communication (NVC)

NVC is a model of communication, developed by Marshall Rosenberg, that uses a series of experiential exercises to demonstrate how people do not properly express their feelings and needs and to provide a frame-work for effective communication. This approach emphasizes empathy and compassion as the motivation for dialogue rather than fear, guilt, shame, blame, demands, coercion, and threat, thus preventing subtle forms of miscommunication that inhibit true understanding. NVC involves learning communication skills based on understanding what is truly necessary for individual well-being, taking into account interdependence with others. The goal is to work together to better meet the needs of all concerned. NVC skills assist both individuals and groups in dealing with major blocks to communication, and its principles have been introduced in troubled parts of the world, including the Middle East.

The process encourages the recognition of the effects of habitual patterns of miscommunication, which, rather than reflecting a person's own feelings, often include blame and judgments about the other. A better approach is to connect thoughts, feelings, and words to underlying basic human needs and the values of protection, support, and love. During the training, people learn to express themselves honestly without attacking, while also becoming skilled in making clear requests. Participants learn to recognize and meet their own deeper needs and those of others and to identify and clearly articulate what they are observing. When this is accomplished, they can relate more honestly with each other. These transformational teachings take place in group settings and have been used in the arenas of business and government.

Contact: Center for Nonviolent Communication –
www.cnvc.org

Primal Therapy

Primal Therapy is a trauma-based psychotherapy created in the early 1970s by Arthur Janov at a time when icons such as John Lennon were searching for a truly transformative experience. Although Lennon and others pursued these techniques for a time, the approach faded from popularity when it seemed to fail to produce effective results. Like other forms of psychotherapy, Primal Therapy posits that neuroses are often caused by the repressed pain of childhood trauma. Its intention was to bring this pain to conscious awareness and then to resolve the anguish by reexperiencing the incident and expressing the resulting pain or repressed emotions in a safe and secure therapeutic setting. It is intended to be

more effective than the talk therapies that were popular at the time, since it took the focus from the mind into the nervous system. The title of Janov's book, *The Primal Scream*, reflects the fact that clients would often experience a cathartic release that manifested itself in screams and other kinds of emotional outbursts. Although this provided some much needed momentary release, it did not always cause a significant long-term change in patterns of behavior. However, at the time, the idea of directly confronting trauma in order to resolve it was a novel idea, and Primal Therapy led to a new paradigm for psychotherapy.

The therapy often begins with an intensive three-week period with a number of open-ended sessions in which a therapist guides the individual into contacting any repressed feelings. After this, the patient joins group meetings to do further work on connecting feelings from the past to the present and bringing meaning to the emotions. The process lasts for an unspecified period of time, sometimes months. The principles on which Primal Therapy is based changed the course of psychotherapy as a whole, and certain of its elements have been refined in ways that are more effective in providing a truly integrative and transformative release of negative emotional issues.

Contact: The Janov Primal Center –
www.primaltherapy.com

Process Oriented Psychology (POP)

Process Oriented Psychology is a multidisciplinary approach that supports individuals, groups, and organizations in the quest to provide counseling, coaching, and conflict resolution by offering a method for increasing self-awareness. Although it was originally based on Taoism, physics, and Jungian psychology, the process work that Dr. Amy Mindell and Dr. Arnold Mindell began in Switzerland in the 1970s has since evolved into a form of consciousness-based therapy. Noticing sensations and signals arising from personal experiences, including comas, near-death episodes, the body, and the surrounding environment, as well as those arising in situations involving social action, diversity, and organizational management, are key in the process. The theory and practice of POP is based on the multidimensional view exemplified by the Tao in Chinese philosophy in which nature and the individual are seen as being one with the whole universe. All aspects of the process revolve around noticing and following what is happening now in a way that enhances a greater interconnection between the various parts of an issue and the being who is experiencing it.

POP uses methods of enhancing inner awareness to track and illuminate psychological and physical issues that create problems. Three levels of focus deal with the many possible facets of reality. First, individuals and groups use feelings and facts to describe conflicts, issues, or problems in order to reach a description of reality all can accept. Second, work is done on the level of the dreamlike perceptions of deep feelings, unspoken truths, unintentional body signals, and the role of ghosts in stories and myths. By entering this type of state, individuals can use inner awareness to gain a better understanding of what the critical, troubled, or dreaming mind is really trying to tell them. The third level of focus includes psychological work on subtle, nondualistic tendencies that are not easily expressed in words. Taking individuals to the edge of their comfort zone, the whole meditative process strives to help people look more closely at what they are doing and how their primary identity is involved; notice what annoys them and how they usually handle it; and recognize what is possible when the view of the experience changes. Art, music, and puppets are also used in the learning process. This training is facilitated by a network of centers around the world.

Contact: www.iapop.com or www.aamindell.net

Psychic and Spiritual Renewal Counseling

Today, many forms of spiritual counseling are available around the world. These practitioners may not have traditional psychotherapeutic training, but instead possess the extrasensory ability to feel, see, and connect with energy fields and subtle vibrational dimensions of the soul and the spirit world beyond the boundaries of normal reality. This heightened awareness is used to obtain and give spiritual guidance and insight to a client, who may be deeply troubled, grieving, or seeking personal growth or spiritual illumination. Some counselors act as a channel to deliver spirit messages that assist in creating transformations and resolving emotional or mental conflict by enabling clients to increase their own inner power.

The healer can employ a variety of methods to achieve the desired results. Many advanced spiritual counselors use past-life regression, soul retrieval, karmic cleansing, transformational therapy, quantum healing techniques, and energy medicine. Some healers are mediums, who, unlike psychics, usually focus on connecting with vibrations and messages from the spirit world and are capable of conveying messages from those other realms to a client by clairvoyant means. Mediums most often work with the spirits of loved ones who have recently passed away, usually for the purpose of helping the client find answers to questions that will provide closure and the resolution of grief. Psychics, on the other hand, in most cases seek to find and provide information that can be used for personal spiritual guidance and the integration of fractured parts of the self. Many psychics do readings that provide insight into the true nature of the client's mental and emotional condition or disclose answers about changes in a client's relationships, occupation, love life, or personal destiny. Of course, the findings provided by some of these psychics and mediums should be taken with a grain of salt since, unfortunately, some are charlatans, cashing in on desperation, and others may be able to pick up only bits and pieces that don't really represent the whole truth. However, sometimes the information provided can be quite remarkable. Those highly intuitive psychics who work primarily by accessing the client's higher self rather than some other entity are likely to be the most helpful. In any case, the client should be open to receiving whatever information these intuitives acquire, and even if all it does is stimulate inner reflection, it may be useful for providing valuable insight that can guide future life endeavors. However, a client's present or future actions should not be based solely on the findings or predictions of a psychic or spiritual counselor but should be directed by his own intuition or free will.

Psychosynthesis

Psychosynthesis, originally developed by Roberto Assagioli in the early 1900s, is an approach to psychology that addresses both the process of personal growth and transpersonal development. It was one of the first humanistic approaches to the kind of psychology being practiced while Freud and Jung were still formulating their theories. Assagioli recognized the idea of the collective unconscious and developed a diagram that comprised the various realms of the unconscious along with a linear progression of the stages of conscious self-awareness. Psychosynthesis incorporates methods of self-actualization based on the philosophies and spiritual traditions of both the East and West, and its primary principle is to respect the complexity and uniqueness of each person.

A variety of techniques are used to assist the client in broadening her perspective by providing her with greater recognition, acceptance, and validation of the whole range of human experience. The aim is to eliminate any conflicts or obstacles that block the harmonious development of the personality by using active techniques to stimulate the functioning of the psyche. Guided imagery, dialogue, dream work, art therapy, journaling, bodywork, behavioral techniques, and meditation, along with individual and group psychotherapy, are all incorporated to assist the individual in what is considered both a linear and nonlinear progression through the various stages of increased self-awareness. The first stage most frequently deals with the healing and transformation of past wounds, repetitive life patterns, self-destructive behaviors, and an assortment of other negative issues. This is followed by a deeper exploration into the subtleties of the individual personality. The next aspect works with personal meaning and purpose in life. The process continues with an inner dialogue about whatever is felt to be the ultimate truth in the client's life. The final stage involves discovering a person's higher calling.
Contact: The Institute of Psychosynthesis –
www.psychosynthesis.org

Radix®

Radix is an educational, body-centered, Neo-Reichian method that teaches people how to release emotions and tension held within the muscular structure of the body. The word *radix* is Latin for the root or source, referring to the vital force that underlies all life. Learning how to sense the pulse and flow of energy within is essential to discovering its effect on behavior. This holistic form of personal development psychotherapy, established by Dr. Charles Kelly, employs a very detailed investigation into the physical, emotional, and mental nature of the individual and emphasizes working out old traumas and moving into new, soul-connected experiences. Guided by the principles of comfort and trust, the somatic experience of Radix helps individuals become more engaged, connected, and conscious of themselves

so that they can find the inherent wisdom contained within their bodies and use it to make conscious life choices. This is considered to be most easily accomplished when there is a direct experience of integrating the mind and body with all the thoughts, feelings, and behaviors. How this is achieved for each client is taught over the course of the training program.

The therapist begins work with the client by carefully observing the pulsations or rhythms of his body and making sure he is fully grounded and centered. The therapist keeps track of changes in the recipient's condition and awareness throughout the process by carefully observing the client's eyes and respiration. The therapy uses vocal sounds, some noninvasive touch, body movement, and methods of transference, reflective therapy, and cathartic breathwork. Techniques are applied according to individual needs to help provide the release of any limiting issues. For example, a person who never cries and an individual who tends to have temper tantrums will receive two different processes. The whole process of this training program is very detailed, yet once appropriate elements are learned, they can easily be integrated at least periodically into the client's life.
Contact: Radix Institute – www.radix.org

Regression Therapy

Regression Therapy is based on the premise that everything an individual has ever experienced is recorded and retained somewhere in the mind. It recognizes that the mind has three levels of consciousness (the conscious, the subconscious, and the super-conscious soul or spirit element) and that emotional problems of which a person is not fully aware or that remain unresolved are connected to different physical, mental, or emotional disorders. The origin of an emotional issue can come from either a past-life experience or something traumatic that occurred during birth or early childhood. Using hypnosis techniques, Regression Therapy works to first identify the source of the trauma and then discover and isolate the associated disturbance. Once the origin of the emotion is determined, the individual is assisted in regressing to the point at which the emotion was stored and reliving the experience in a way that can help her recognize that she can choose how she relates to the experience. The awareness of the capacity for free choice can help dissolve any negative emotions so that she can heal. However, as is the case with many other therapies, it is essential that the individual have the desire and the sense of inquiry that will make the process effective. Although Regression Therapy was developed relatively recently through the work of a number of psychotherapists, it has similarities to ancient shamanic work in that it can be used to remove spiritual attachments (possessions by another spirit), retrieve fragmented and lost pieces of the soul, and release encumbering impressions from past lives.

The therapeutic process is accomplished by using hypnotic suggestion to stimulate the imagination into creating a different reality of the experience at the subconscious level. Changes at this level will in turn provide changes in perception on a conscious level that automatically have the additional effect of resolving physical, mental, and emotional issues. The process of reliving any strong emotional experience through hypnotic regression does not mean that the recipient will become burdened with more problems, since the hypnotic state does not allow the event to become overwhelming in a detrimental way. Instead, it simply allows for the simple recognition and observation that bring greater awareness. In its response to hypnotic regression, the mind may express knowledge that is not related to any experiences from the present lifetime; this does not require a belief in reincarnation or past lives, but simply suggests that many issues are deeply rooted in the subconscious. The important point is to be able to fully recognize any trauma without being bound by it. Regression Therapy keeps this point in mind as clients slowly come to realize the root cause of emotional issues and recognize that there are other options and ways of dealing with these issues that can free them up to live more fully. The solution to many physical and emotional problems can also be brought about with the aid of spirit entities that come into the process to give support. The result is the recognition that freedom of choice is always crucial in resolving the issues.

Contact: International Board for Regression Therapy – www.ibrt.org

Sensorimotor Psychotherapy® (SP)

This synthesis of somatic therapy and psychotherapy, formerly a temporary branch of Hakomi called Hakomi Integrative Somatics, was developed by Pat Ogden after she apprenticed with Ron Kurtz. It works on treating dysfunction in a gentle way similar to that of the Hakomi Method; however, the emphasis is on the psychological elements of unintegrated trauma and their devastating effects on the body and mind. Based on studies in neuroscience, psychotherapeutic principles, and attachment theories, the therapy has developed ways to understand the role of fixed sensorimotor patterns in trauma survivors and how they can be used in effective treatment. Simple body-oriented interventions identify, track, and work with disruptive somatic patterns, disturbed cognitive and emotional processing, and the fragmented sense of self experienced by so many traumatized individuals. A central institute has been created, and courses are taught worldwide by a group of certified trainers. Practitioners are well trained in distinguishing the relationship between interrelated and unresolved traumatic events and developmental issues that result from early attachment problems caused by such things as family dysfunction. Interventions are accomplished in a variety of ways that not only stabilize and reduce symptoms, but help the client tap into the wisdom of the body. The training is appropriate for professionals working in a broad range of therapies— psychiatry, social work, family therapy, and counseling.

During a session, the therapist uses a variety of observation skills and supportive psychosomatic approaches to alleviate the effects of trauma through interventions that speak directly to how these effects are driven by the body and the nervous system. The therapist constantly refers to body sensations to differentiate between the two kinds of personal wounding—physical and emotional. Techniques are adapted to individuals with special needs by adjusting the pace, working on different combinations of body parts, increasing the number of times techniques are repeated, and increasing the client's level of tolerance. A number of techniques are employed that may be suitable for clients suffering with complex symptoms and dysfunctional issues such as PTSD, chronic depression, bipolar disorders, personality disorders, and extreme anxiety.

Contact: Sensorimotor Psychotherapy Institute – www.sensorimotorpsychotherapy.org

Shadow Process Therapy

A transformational therapy created by Debbie Ford, the Shadow Process is a form of self-exploration that focuses on a person's dark side, the side that holds on to self-punishing patterns and sabotages any chance of success. These shadows often become so ingrained in people's lives that they are seen as normal, and fear arises with the thought of disturbing them. The idea of this therapy is that rather than viewing failings and insecurity as obstacles to moving forward in life, it is very possible to embrace these so-called defects as the powerful teachers that they really are. Making peace with the painful, rejected parts of the self can awaken the profound realization that what has been rejected is really the bearer of the greatest gifts.

Shadow Process Therapy guides recipients through self-exploration in a safe environment in which they can address any repressed and unresolved issues that keep them from experiencing the whole self in a free and open way. The process uses guided imagery, meditation, and enlightened conversation to integrate the shadow self and find the forgiveness and self-love that will help resolve any shame and allow clients to realize their great worth. The process requires a willingness to fully engage with issues that often reside on a subconscious cellular level. The therapist works to decrease resistance to the dark side by helping clients realize that knowing the shadow can promote awareness and by calling on their positive qualities. Once the benefits of expressing and coming to terms with the pain held in the body is realized, it becomes easier to release blocked emotions, embrace the authentic self, and find the light in the darkness.

Contact: The Ford Institute – www.thefordinstitute.com
or www.soulfulliving.com/the_shadow_
process.htm

Soul Memory Discovery

Social worker and psychotherapist Ellen Dosick had suffered for years from a degenerative auto-immune disorder, and doctors told her she would live for only a few more years. Desperate for some help and on the recommendation of a friend, she went to see a psychic who identified things in Dosick's past life as possible sources of her current illness. Although the session was intense, Dosick did not put much faith in it. However, a return trip to her doctor a few months later revealed that her condition was nearly normal. This became a powerful impetus for Dosick to continue with further studies of this healing process. What she learned eventually grew into her own form of therapy. Soul Memory Discovery is a form of spiritual healing that addresses memories held in both the

soul and the cells of the body. These memories sometimes create negative and limiting beliefs that can cause pain and distress that separate people from the happiness that is rightfully theirs. This simple practice works to access and identify the source of pain, release all limiting issues and memories, and replace them with new, more expansive beliefs that can manifest positively in a person's life.

The healing process involves a sacred ritual that uses the power of language and spirit guides to effect change with a combination of special sacred words that can open portals to higher realms. The discovery process begins with a quick polarity balancing to align the flow of the recipient's energy field with that of the earth and to gain access to clear information from the soul's memory bank. In addition to moving energies, answers are then obtained through logical yes-or-no questions that identify, release, and clear the origins of the problems. One or two sessions are used to clear any issues and provide a soulful transformation.

Contact: www.soulmemorydiscovery.com

Time Line Therapy® (TT)

Time Line Therapy, which developed out of Neuro Linguistic Programming, is a psychotherapeutic method for creating powerful, rapid change. It is based on the idea that a subconscious shift will give individuals a clear picture of what they truly believe is possible in their future. This therapy was developed in 1985 by Tad James as a new type of quantum healing to help a person in let go of unwanted thoughts, behaviors, and restrictive negative emotions that originated in past traumas or life situations and that prevent her from attaining the desired quality of life. The therapy utilizes the individual's own internal time line to work with the unconscious mind. This time line represents the way in which memories, some from the past and some as a projection of the future, are unconsciously stored. Since the therapy posits that real behavioral change cannot come about consciously, it employs techniques that work at the subconscious level to release the inappropriate programming that limits abilities.

Time Line Therapy uses three specific coaching techniques that allow clients to make a subconscious shift in order to gain emotional control over their lives. The first of these neurolinguistic techniques releases undesired negative emotions from the memories that hold them. The next leaves limiting decisions and beliefs

in the past where they belong, allowing the recipient to learn from experience and to create useful and empowering alternatives. The final technique works through the imagination to provide a way to create an inspiring future. When this is accomplished, there is a better chance of not overreacting to life's challenges and making choices that change behavior and increase personal happiness and professional performance.
Contact: www.timelinetherapy.com

WOW Processing

WOW Processing is energy psychology in the form of two guided meditations, "The WOW Process" and "WOW-in-Love Process," created by Rev. Louisa Dyer and Laura Cirolia for the purpose of fast, deep, and lasting healing of the mind, body, and spirit. WOW uses what Eckhart Tolle calls "building presence to heal the painbody" to address what Western medicine calls stress. It is designed to discover and clear the negative effects of stressful thoughts, feelings, situations or illness, whether held consciously or subconsciously. WOW Processing provides an unconditionally loving format for deep healing, and almost anyone can learn to facilitate WOW for another person, using the e-book *WOW, You Really Can Feel Better!* WOW recordings are used for self-healing, and are recommended after experiencing facilitated sessions.
Contact: www.thewowprocess.com

PART TWO

Self-Directed Healing Practices

There are many ways to explore our inner ocean and reap the rewards that will change our lives and the world around us. In contrast with the modalities of applied bodywork found in Part One in which recipients are passive though engaged, Part Two contains life-enhancing exercises and body-mind practices in which you become the practitioner, actively carrying out the transformational work. Most of them fall into the category of preventive medicine, and some perpetuate the benefits received from other kinds of bodywork. In the long run, they can save you money, because even though there may be some initial expense in learning a practice, prevention can go a long way toward averting costly medical care in the future. You'll often find that professional bodyworkers use these same kinds of practices, because they understand that healing the self is the first step in becoming a healing presence for others. Once these self-care skills are learned, they will always be available.

The first two chapters of Part Two discuss concepts that underlie many of the practices in this book. Chapter 8 focuses on the positive effect that conscious breathing and the accompanying breathwork practices have on our lives. In Chapter 9, we look at energy as medicine, what goes on within our energy anatomy, and how we can cultivate this vital life force. The topic of Chapter 10 is the shift in consciousness necessary for true healing, whether it comes spontaneously or through the practice of meditation. Like Chapter 6 in the first part of the book, Chapter 11 is a compilation of the many forms of self-directed practices, exercises, and movement therapies that can enhance our physical, emotional, mental, and spiritual capabilities. They include activities such as aquatic exercise, dance, stretching, self-massage, qi gong, yoga, sound healing methods, and an assortment of other enjoyable and playful activities. Chapter 12 is a collection of the thoughts that tickle my brain when I contemplate the heartwarming vision of our bodies and minds floating comfortably on the inner ocean. I'm convinced that then we can all live according to our true natures and reach a state of health and happiness beyond our wildest dreams—or maybe it will *be* our wildest dreams.

CHAPTER 8
Breath Is the Way

Everything in nature pulsates: the winds as they respond to atmospheric changes; the ocean as it comes ashore in waves and then recedes; the plants as light and moisture push and pull the sap that brings nutrients to their cells. So too, the natural rhythm of the breath—the expansion and contraction of the inbreath and the outbreath—brings in the oxygen necessary for life and carries away the carbon dioxide produced as the cells do their work. And the life-force energy that comes in with the breath connects us to the pulsations of the universe and sustains not only the body but also the mind and spirit.

Of course, people are born knowing how to breathe. It occurs automatically and naturally. However, we so often take the act of breathing for granted, unaware of how it affects us or if we are breathing efficiently. Unhealthy habits that unconsciously modify and restrict the breathing process may develop without our recognizing the change. Breathing may become too shallow and rapid because we are in a hurry, have failed to get enough exercise, or are stressed out. Traumatic events can produce restricted breathing patterns that replay an initial response to a disturbing situation. Incorrect posture that prevents the lungs from expanding fully can prevent the easy flow of the breath. Fatigue or muscle tension can cause the breath to become faster, shallower, and shorter, reducing the amount of oxygen available to the cells, and air pollution only adds to the problem. In addition, both overbreathing and underbreathing can reduce the efficiency of the lungs and adversely affect the nervous and immune systems, resulting in lower resistance to disease. All of these deviations from natural breathing patterns result in insufficient oxygenation, imperfect elimination of carbon dioxide, and the buildup of toxins in the body, leaving you with reduced vitality. You feel run-down and tired.

Fortunately, conscious breathing practices can reverse these tendencies. Conscious breathing is possible because breathing is the only autonomic body function that you can also perform voluntarily (though it could be argued that some adepts can control other autonomic functions as well). Most of us recognize there are many simple and beneficial ways we can use the breath to relieve tension and deal better with stressful situations in our daily lives, for example, taking a deep breath while stuck in traffic or before reacting to the angry words of another person. The old saying, "Count to ten..." could be rephrased as "Take ten deep breaths," and those breaths will have other benefits besides leaving a little space to contemplate the choice of actions. However, even in everyday life, proper breathing can be our ally. And when we are breathing more completely and feeling more alive, our vibrations are elevated, so we are more likely to resonate in a way that not only attracts good things but also enables others to become enlivened with our good vibes.

Since breath and emotions are also closely linked, changes in breathing can signal changes in our emotional states. For example, you set out to sea in a small boat on a peaceful day only to find that the weather changes as a storm approaches. You grow anxious, and your breathing becomes rapid. There might come a time when a romantic relationship turns sour, and your heartache gets in the way of the breath—"It hurts so much, I just can't take a breath." On the other hand, you may be running a marathon and enter an altered state in which your breathing pattern shifts in a way that carries you forward with renewed energy. Then there are those occurrences that are so exciting that your whole being vibrates. These occasions often precipitate wonderful moments that blossom into powerful peak experiences or "aha" moments, literally "taking your breath away" and filling you with energy. This may come through an awareness of natural beauty, the smile of a child, a moment of extreme physical exertion, a psychedelic experience, a powerful sexual encounter, an amazing dream, a powerful musical performance, or a momentary spark of realization brought on by the words of a wise teacher. These experiences create energy, and since the breath follows energy, we breathe in the winds of change that allow us to move forward in a new, positive direction.

Sometimes changes in the breathing pattern happen when we are startled or aroused, and they are felt very intensely. (Just remember the way your breath stopped when a loud sound startled you or the heart-pounding fear that made your breathing quick and shallow.) In other instances, they develop slowly and subtly over time because of habitual patterns of behavior and, since deeply embedded, are hardly recognized. When any strong feeling—everything from pleasure to pain—arises, breathing is affected, whether it becomes restricted and constrained or expanded and uplifted. Since any new patterns we adopt will influence how our body, mind, and emotions handle future situations, it is worth developing the ability to discern how these life events affect our capacity to breathe in a healthy way.

Breath can be a bridge between the body and mind and between the conscious and unconscious, sometimes calming and sometimes energizing. Almost all traditional spiritual practices, especially those from the Far East, have a multitude of time-tested meditations that use special breathing methods to bring harmony to the heart, mind, and spirit. Breathing techniques can soothe the mind, remove emotional blockages, and refresh our energetic state. Breathwork can also help control pain or fear, reduce the level of anxiety stored in the body, cultivate inner strength, and even alleviate symptoms of illness. It has been integrated into many meditative or therapeutic practices and exercises such as those found in various forms of yoga (Kundalini, Prana, Purna, Yantra, and Kriya), as well as into Buddhist and Hindu meditation, tantric bodywork, personal counseling therapies, rebirthing therapies, psychospiritual group therapies, integrative mind-body therapies, body-oriented psychotherapies, hypnotherapies, addiction therapies, shamanic soul retrieval, and other types of bodywork. Many advanced practices work with the image of breathing in cosmic energy and breathing out stale or spent energy. Others focus on entering into a meditative state of consciousness in which you are very relaxed, observant, and resting in that peaceful stillpoint where the breath and life-force energy flow freely. Some highly evolved methods even allow practitioners to control metabolism and consciousness itself. But any changes that improve the capacity to breathe better will increase embodied awareness and the ability to function physically, emotionally, and mentally in a more harmonious and energetic way.

Conscious breathing practices and exercises that have been developed over many years and even centuries all strive in some way to increase whole-body awareness and balance the vital energetic flow within by improving the strength, control, and flow of the breath. Most of them work to remove blockages that limit this flow. When the flow is strengthened and deepened, feelings of anxiety or tension will automatically dissipate, thus strengthening the immune system and improving innate self-healing abilities. In all healing work, whether practitioner-applied or self-administered, additional focus on the breath will enhance the total experience by clearing your mind, relaxing your body, improving your outlook on life, reducing agitation, releasing stress, and allowing you to be more fully present in the moment.

Some Basics About Conscious Breathing

During my time at sea, encounters with dolphins reminded me that the breath brings energy to all creatures. These conscious breathers would rise to the surface, open their blowholes, and spout loudly on the exhalation to clear the airway before inhaling strongly and plunging back into the depths of their deep-blue aquatic underworld. Hearing this wondrous occurrence in the light of day or especially in the dark of night always thrilled everyone on board, and that included the ship's cat.

Deep, full, conscious breathing is the primary technique used by many breathwork practices to enhance overall health and well-being. Breathing in this way helps engage the abdomen, increase oxygenation, maintain the proper balance of oxygen and carbon dioxide in the blood, improve digestion, nourish the nervous system, rejuvenate the glands, and expand the lungs, while massaging the heart and abdominal organs through more expansive movement of the diaphragm. The workload of the heart is also reduced, since deep breathing in a slow, rhythmic manner provides more oxygen and causes a reflex response that prompts the nervous system to relax the heart muscles, thereby reducing the heart rate. Additional oxygen results in more normalized brain activity and decreases the level of any existing anxiety.

Our breath is intimately linked to the energy flowing within. This vital life force actually dwells within the breath, and when we breathe in consciously, we can become more aware of bringing in revitalizing energy. Deep abdominal breathing also helps us absorb more vital chi energy, not just from the air or even from the space around us, but from the energies of heaven and earth. This not only helps the mind and body relax and become more unified, but also provides an energetic boost that helps increase self-esteem and generates more positive feelings, thoughts, and attitudes, as well as a general sense of wholeness. Conscious deep breathing goes hand in hand with awakening to a more complete and conscious state of being.

Breathing can be controlled through conscious movement of the diaphragm, and by strongly focusing your attention, you can guide the breath and shape its direction, rhythm, and speed. Full, deep breathing involves the belly, midchest, and upper chest. It usually involves first learning how to breathe more fully into the abdomen, since many people take shallow breaths in the upper chest that do not engage the abdominal muscles.

Before attempting breathwork practices, it will help to analyze how you are already breathing and its effect on you, proceeding in a gentle, accepting way with a sense of humor and not taking yourself too seriously. As you pay attention to your inhalations and exhalations, you will become more aware of how your body, chest cavity, diaphragm, and abdomen move and thus recognize your habits and limitations as they are here and now. Once you recognize your own particular ways of breathing, you can move on to learn practices that increase your ability to breathe in a more full and balanced way, and as your exploration of breathwork continues, you will heighten the awareness of how your body affects and interacts with the breath. Since how we breathe is closely connected to how we feel, breathing practices may reveal ways emotions are held in the body, and working with the breath may change how you react emotionally. You may find that your existing breathing patterns keep you bound to certain ways of acting or perceiving and may wish to investigate how working with the breathing process can help you make changes.

Before attempting any enhanced breathing practices or therapies, particularly any that are combined with physical exercise, there are a few basic points worth considering. Since these practices can help improve self-awareness, a quiet location without distractions will help you keep attention on the subtleties of the process. Even if you are practicing with a group, try to keep your focus inward, and don't worry about what others are doing. Although sitting erect in a relaxed yet balanced position is usually best, you can lie down on a mat or even practice standing up, depending on the established protocol. But try not to practice on a full stomach. Before you begin, make sure that your intentions are clear and that your consciousness is engaged with these aspirations. Prepare yourself by doing a few simple stretches to get the kinks out and loosen up the body. Start slowly, and proceed without straining or overexerting yourself. Always strive to be relaxed, peaceful, still, and comfortable. And, perhaps most important, embrace a sense of open inquiry and a willingness to explore without holding on to any particular expectations.

Aspiring practitioners may want to find a professional instructor leading a beginner's class in yoga or qi gong that is not too demanding and takes into account the uniqueness of each individual participant's abilities. If your goal is the release of psychological or physiological issues, the facilitators of many forms of breathwork therapy usually have the experience and intuition to guide and nurture you through any physical or cathartic release that may arise. Good instructors can be recognized by how well they present the practice and how sensitive they are to your particular abilities and needs.

Enhancing Breath Awareness

To really enhance, integrate, and retain significant changes in your breathing patterns and lung capacity, it is necessary to find a way to develop greater awareness of the breathing process and how it affects you. Just as in learning to ride a bike or sail a boat, you have to get out there and do it. There are five different ways you can approach this challenge:

1. Individual Self-Awareness Practices
2. Breathing During Applied Bodywork
3. Group Breathwork Therapy
4. Mindfulness and Meditative Practices
5. A Mix of the Above

All require the initial guidance of a teacher, practitioner, or health care provider. Each has its own particular approach, which may or may not be the most suitable for you at a certain time. Much depends on the type of person you are, your patterns of behavior, and which kind of practice you honestly believe will be most helpful. Perhaps you are dealing with some emotional issues and need a breathwork practice that is more psychoanalytical or therapeutic. It might be that a physiological problem needs addressing. On the other hand, maybe you just want to improve your breathing so you can dance longer or perform better at sports. It could be that you are interested in exploring natural ways of entering altered states of consciousness or are on a spiritual path and seeking enlightenment. All of these reasons and many more are good motivation for taking up a breathwork practice. The breathing process is always with us and can therefore play an important role in all that we are capable of doing or being.

Individual Self-Awareness Practices

Solo practices can eventually be done at home, but are usually learned from a skilled professional, who might be a facilitator of Pranayama Yoga, Tai Chi, qi gong, and other approaches that combine body movement with breathwork to influence both the physical and energy bodies of the practitioner. Somatic practices usually work in a slow, methodical, meditative way, allowing the breath to guide the physical movements and to increase awareness of the connection between it and the various parts of the body. Deep, slow, continuous breathing maximizes the experience and the beneficial effects of each movement. In Pranayama Yoga, some of the breathing techniques can be very involved and intensive, requiring a significant amount of practice and discipline to master, but as the vital life-force energy is strengthened, inspiration and insight can come at any time during the practice of breathwork.

There is a simple breath-awareness practice that will help you become more conscious of your present condition and perhaps create a spark of motivation. Sit or stand comfortably in a quiet location. Then begin by calming the mind and focusing the attention on the navel area. Just breathe naturally and slowly, but do it by breathing in through the nose and out through the mouth, a method that is preferred by many experts in the field. The nasal cavity filters impurities from the air and cleanses, humidifies, and warms it before it enters the lungs. Resistance in the nasal cavity helps slow the passage of air, which provides more time for the lungs to absorb oxygen and release carbon dioxide. The nose is also better at absorbing subtle energy from the air, and since it is close to the brain, inhaling through the nose can have a calming effect on the nervous system.

In addition, this style of breathing not only causes the jaw to relax but also signals the rest of the body to relax.

Gently place your attention on your navel (the energy storage center) for a few minutes. Slowly allow awareness to go deeper into the abdomen, and recognize the movement of the diaphragm in the space where the ribs meet the front of the body. Initially, just focus on recognizing how this area feels as you breathe, and then slowly emphasize the movement of the diaphragm and consciously take a deeper breath. Explore how it affects the movement of the diaphragm and the rib cage. Continue to breathe deeply until a gentle, strain-free rhythm is attained, and simply maintain that rhythm for a minute or two. If you feel the need to stretch your spine and drop your shoulders, let that also happen. Try to notice any subtle changes in your breathing pattern, but don't linger on this recognition. Now that you are breathing more deeply than in the initial stage of this practice, return your focus to the navel area and rest in the natural ease of deep, conscious breathing. When you are ready, move your attention to the toes, and then slowly shift your awareness to the different parts of your body, moving progressively upward to the head. As you come to each section of the body, pause and take a few slow, deep breaths, and notice how your body feels. When your attention reaches the head, let the breath slowly become very relaxed and quiet. After a few minutes, give up trying to influence the movement of the breath, and let yourself breathe in whatever way seems most natural. Continue tuning in to how you feel as you continue with your day's activities. The whole exercise can take anywhere from fifteen to thirty minutes and is a simple way to relieve stress and increase awareness of your internal state.

Breathing During Applied Bodywork

There are many ways that proper breathing can enhance applied bodywork. During a bodywork session, conscious breathing helps you relax, clear away stress, and awaken a state of healing that is supported by the body, mind, and emotions. In fact, the bodyworker may ask you to incorporate certain breathing techniques to increase the effectiveness of a treatment. Skilled practitioners listen for spontaneous changes your breath to gauge how you are responding to the treatment. When things are going well, you may respond with deep natural, breaths, especially when there has been an energetic shift or release of tension. Changes in breathing patterns may be distress signals when the practitioner works on a restricted or painful area of the body. Agonizing sensations can become intense just before pain or tension melts away, and breathing into the pain or any resistance not only helps you to relax but also to tolerate deeper contact. By itself, the breathing process helps release blockages or constrictions as the inhalation connects the recipient with the source of pain or tension and the exhalation releases it. When tension is released, healing energy will automatically flow more easily through that area.

Practitioners involved in energy-based or other spiritual modalities may spend the opening stages of a treatment by using their breath to enter into a meditative state. This allows them to hold a centered and balanced sacred space in which they can be fully aware and present. Many of these therapies depend on the process of entrainment, in which the vibrations of the recipient are drawn in by and become synchronized with those of the practitioner. When the practitioner and recipient are breathing as one, this creates a tendency for the client's energies to resonate with the healthier vibrations of the practitioner. It also helps develop a sense of trust that allows the practitioner to more directly lift away the client's pain.

Since the hand pressure and strokes of a bodyworker can be more effective when performed in concert with the recipient's breathing, the client can be more than a passive receiver. Breathing gently but deeply in and out with each stroke of the practitioner's hands will help keep your mind focused on what is happening in your body and on the healing process. You might want to imagine that the physical expansion during the in-breath creates a space in which healing can take place. When the practitioner is working on a painful area, it can be particularly helpful to consciously connect with the practitioner's hands and then use a visualization during the exhalation to release the blockage and allow the pain to melt away. (This process can be very subtle, so don't look for something big to happen.) It is also wise to allow yourself to pause in the stillness between breaths, a space in which you can rest calmly, free of any effort to control. This allows the mind to stay open and empty so that the breathwork can touch your soul and transform the energy, feelings, and emotions contained in the body. Each moment within this practice may not be always smooth, but by focusing on the breath, you can better ride the ups and downs as things are released along the way.

If you are interested in modalities of practitioner-applied bodywork that emphasize breathwork or use certain breathing techniques during a session, you could check out those listed in the accompanying table, all of which are discussed in Chapter 6.

Modalities that Emphasize Breathwork

Active Release Techniques	CORE Myofascial Therapy
Ai Chi	Craniosacral Therapy
Alchemical Bodywork	Emotional Freedom Technique
Amanae Transformational Bodywork	Etheric Pulse Therapy
Biodynamic Craniosacral Therapy	Hanna Somatic Education
Bioenergetics	Heart & Soul Healing
Bioenergy Therapy	Integrative Energy Therapy
Body Memory Recall	Jin Shin Do
Body Talk	Jin Shin Jutsu
Bowenwork	Kripalu Massage
Breema Bodywork	Kriya Massage
Brennan Healing Science	Kundalini Massage
Champissage	Luminous Energy Field Healing
Chi Nei Tsang	Lomi Lomi

Magnified Healing
Myofascial Release
Muscle Release Technique
Neuro-Structural Bodywork
Noetic Field Therapy
Ohashiatsu
One Light Healing Touch
Osteopathic Manipulation Therapy
Phoenix Rising Yoga Therapy
Polarity Therapy
Postural Integration
Pranassage
Pranic Healing
Qi Gong Medical Massage
Quantum Energetics
Quantum Touch Therapy
Raindrop Therapy
Reichian Release Therapy

Reposturing Dynamics
Rosen Method
Rubenfeld Synergy Method
Seiki Soho Therapy
SHEN Therapy
Sotai Ho Massage Therapy
Spiral Release Bodywork
Spiritual Healing Massage
Tantric Dakini Approach
Taikyo Shiatsu
Thai Body Work
Touch and Breath
Vibrational Healing Massage Therapy
Waterdance
Watsu
WISE Method
Yantra Yoga Massage
Zero Balancing

Group Breathwork Therapy

Group breathwork therapies use specific breathing techniques and the support of a group to bring about a psychological or transformational shift within the participants. Many group sessions work primarily with dysfunction and trauma that require a significant release of fear, phobias, or other limiting patterns of behavior, but these types of therapy can also be very useful for individuals who simply want to become more self-aware. The many variations of group therapy may combine breathwork with touch, sound, dialogue, movement, and mindfulness practices.

Participants in group breathwork therapies with a psychotherapeutic approach may experience the release of blockages in a cathartic fashion in which pent-up emotions are spontaneously discharged, often with loud sounds, crying, screaming, and yelling, along with agitated body movements or gyrations. This kind of work often involves a high-intensity exercise that induces a radically altered state of consciousness that precipitates a release. One of the techniques used involves breathing continuously in a rhythmic cycle in which inhalation and exhalation follow each other rapidly and without pause. This way of breathing melts away customary patterns of behavior, shifts your focus inward, allowing you

to come face-to-face with inner stirrings, and stimulates the self-healing energies that can cleanse and recharge your psychophysical being. Strong emotions can surface, but as you breathe through any resistance that arises from these negative emotions or patterns of habitual control, release can occur spontaneously. As the intensity of the process increases and you reach the point of transformation, your breathing will often change from intense to quiet, so that the experience ends with a feeling of peace. Continuous breathing techniques can vary, but are a standard part of many of these facilitated therapies, including Holotropic Breathwork, Integrative Breathwork, Rebirthing Breathwork, and Transformational Breath, which are discussed later in this chapter.

However, each person is unique and different, and an extreme experience is by no means required. Many find a release to be a subtle, gentle shift in self-awareness that happens in a simple, quiet, meditative way; sometimes changes are not recognized until days after a session. Cathartic release can be helpful for those who are resistant to facing their fears, but a significant amount of follow-up work may need to be done to integrate positive changes in self-awareness, and if a person is emotionally unstable, catharsis will need to be balanced with proper grounding.

Mindfulness and Meditative Practices

Mindfulness, meditation, and conscious breathing definitely complement each other. In a sense, the breath has the ability to take us beneath the disruptive waves on the surface of the mind to the deep ocean of awareness and possibility that resides within. The simple act of mindfully observing the breath can lead to profound psychological transformation as you stop trying to make things happen and simply surrender to gently allowing. Besides relieving tension, softening tightness, and calming the body, the stillness of the meditative state creates a sacred space in which it is possible to observe the breathing process more closely, and any emotional experiences that arise can be faced more compassionately. With sufficient training and many years of contemplation, there are those who can even use the breath not only to attain but also to maintain a nonordinary state of consciousness.

Mindful and meditative breathwork includes Pranayama Yoga and qi gong, forms of practice in which movement is primarily that of the subtle life-force energy, the earth energy, and divine cosmic energy. Many of these methods work with the flow and balance of the energy carried by the breath to allow fear and pain to naturally melt away and the compassion and wisdom of our true nature to flourish. When a release does happen, it is often occurs in a very smooth and subtle way. As the breath takes us into a deeper energetic level of awareness within the body, our fullest sense of connection with all of the universe is awakened, and the focus then becomes recognizing the highest good rather than personal pain or dysfunction.

Increasing the length of inhalations and exhalations and holding the breath are common in meditative breathwork. But manipulating the breath in this way can cause some anxiety, since many traumatic experiences are characterized by holding the breath or otherwise blocking its free flow. However, facing this anxiety by breathing mindfully into areas where fear has taken hold can put an end to suffering and replace it with a feeling of joy and deep well-being. The breath tends to open up the subconscious, and real transformation and integration often depend on giving up any resistance and surrendering to change. Extensive practice is often required to work through the increasingly subtle levels of resistance. As you progress through the various stages of spiritually oriented breathwork, it may take you into

the eye of the storm, but you will have the opportunity to develop the strength and courage to awaken to a more enlightened state, one in which you can meet whatever arises with a calm mind and a relaxed body.

I have spent a considerable amount of time close to nature, especially while living on the high seas, where my experience of free diving on coral reefs in the tropics disclosed the most about my respiration. When it came to holding my breath under water, I was totally outclassed by the Cuna Indian divers of Panama and world-record holders (imagine fifteen minutes!), but I was able to stay down long enough to sometimes spear some fresh fish for dinner. Over the years, each time I dove under, I was able to get a clear sense of my overall condition by the length of time I could stay down without running out of air. What had once been a momentary experience had, through mindfulness, become a practice.

When Ram Dass, born Richard Alpert, spoke of spiritual breathing back in the 1970s, he suggested that on the inhalation, we think of the power of God within us, and that when we exhale, we visualize the grace of God surrounding us. Meditative breathwork can indeed connect us with our true nature, whether we define that essence as God, spirit, the higher self, or primordial purity.

Six Types of Breathwork

Before deciding on a particular breathwork practice, you might want to consider the different ways you can work with the breath. Certain methods may be more suitable, useful, and enjoyable for you than others. Although some demand more effort or require successive stages of instruction, the choice depends on what resonates with the way you tend to learn and with what you specifically wish to gain from the practice, whether it's the release of physical, emotional, and mental restrictions or the development of more self-awareness, greater breath control, expanded physical abilities, a deeper vibrational connection with your core, or a more spiritual way of being.

1. **Basic conscious breathing techniques** are those that work primarily to enhance self-awareness. They are usually simple practices that require minimal physical effort, but necessitate

full attention on the breath. These gentle techniques, which individuals can easily learn to practice on their own, lead the consciousness into an expanded state of awareness of habits, feelings, and limitations. The aim is to help you break through any limitations and perform full, deep, conscious breathing in a natural, effortless manner.

2. **Controlled breathing techniques** are generally part of an intermediate or advanced stage of practice and require added effort and diligent practice to heighten awareness and develop the ability to modify breathing patterns. They are often pranayama practices in which there is greater focus on breath retention or the pause between breaths. These methods allow you to explore how the vital life-force energy interacts with the breath.

3. **Focused breathing** involves techniques for healing existing dysfunction and is often applied to tight or restricted areas of the body. The breath is used to create a space for healing pain and relieving tension by expanding, cradling, and softening the problem area. Focused breathing has a similar role in the release of emotional issues held in the body. This type of breathwork is often supported by touch and can be used during sessions of applied bodywork.

4. **Movement-supported breathing practices** combine physical exercise with breathwork in ways that increase awareness of the connection between the physical body and the breath. The movements can be subtle and meditative, such as those used in certain forms of yoga, qi gong, and Bagua, or more lively activities such as stretching, bending, bouncing, or group dancing. These practices are generally taught by a skilled instructor, who can also support the recipient when performing any difficult physical maneuvers.

5. **Touch-supported breathing techniques** can draw attention to the breathing process itself or direct the energy of the breath to specific areas of the body. Touch can be self-applied, as is the case when you place your hands on the lower belly to get a sense of how well you are using that part of the body to breathe. Touch can also be used by a practitioner in the course of a bodywork treatment to remind you to breathe into a painful or restricted area. No matter who applies the touch, gentle holding, rubbing, tapping, pulling, or pressing are most commonly used.

6. **Sound-supported breathing practices** use resonance and entrainment to stimulate healthier breathing. A variety of instruments, such as tuning forks, singing bowls, gongs, and electrical instruments, can provide harmonic vibrations, as can sounds initiated by the recipient. These might include vocalizations, toning, chanting, humming, sighing, laughing, or even crying. Beautiful or ecstatic music has a special way of uplifting the spirit and freeing the breath and can also massage the body and mind with its vibrations.

Any method of working with the breath brings energy into the body, so all of these techniques are useful and have a place in the realm of breathwork. In fact, many of the existing therapies, energetic movement exercises, or meditative practices that employ breathwork include elements of each of the six. It's which technique is emphasized that makes a form of breath therapy distinct. There is no firm rule about what works the best for any individual, since that can be discovered only through experience.

As with any practice, it is always possible to get stuck, unable to release what is holding you back. This doesn't mean that something is wrong with you or that it is the wrong practice. At certain times, you may just need more perseverance to break through limitations and judgments into a new world of possibilities. Reading about breathwork here just gives you an idea of what is contained within the wonderful frontier of breathing practices. Being fully involved in doing the practice is how real understanding and self-awareness comes.

Four Phases of the Breath

Just as there are differences within the various practices discussed in this chapter, each has its own language for describing what might be received or sent out during the act of breathing. From the standpoint of personal healing, the idea of breathing in uplifting energy and breathing out wasted energy seems to be the most predominant theme, especially when healing energy is breathed into problem areas of the body. In certain meditative or breathwork practices, the inhalations and the exhalations can be beneficial not only for the individual breather but also for anyone else around her. There are also specific meditation practices in which the intentions are reversed, such as with tonglen, in which you breathe in suffering and breathe out love and healing (see more in Chapter 10). Take a moment to ponder the accompanying table of the different intentions that can be made during the breathing cycle. Being conscious of these during your breathwork practice will enhance its effectiveness, especially if you choose intentions and language that resonate with you personally. You can certainly add your phrases to this list.

While Breathing

With the Inhalation:	With the Exhalation:
Take in good energy	Send out bad energy
Bring energy into the belly	Allow energy to spread around inside
Take in fullness	Let go of emptiness
Take in the positive	Let go of the negative
Pull into your center	Let go and relax
Call forth the pain	Let the pain be okay and dissolve
Witness any trauma	Let it all be small
Let fresh energy expand	Let go of negative energy
Bring in nourishing love	Let love spread all around
Bring fresh vital energy in	Send vital energy out with love
Feel sensations in the body	Allow feelings just to be
Bring breath into tight areas	Let the tension and blockages soften and release
Bring in vital prana energy	Let prana cleanse and release negative thoughts
Bring up any emotions	Let the emotions soften their hold
Feel any upsetting emotions	Relax, soften, and accept any feelings
Go into your issues and concerns	Let them melt away
Visualize light entering	Let light expand and flow outward
Bring vitality into your whole body	Let it rest there
Bring air and energy into body parts	Send it back out to the world
Imagine bringing in goodness	Let it spread within and around you
Focus on your core	Relax into spaciousness
Visualize suffering around you	Send out loving light
Take in the suffering of others	Send out goodness and love
Give blessings to your body	Transmit blessings to others

Remember the power of the pauses between the inhalations and exhalations. The two pauses provide a space for you to become aware of the message you really want to receive and send through the breathing process.

Meditating on this underlying vast space is like dipping yourself into the expanse of stillness within the inner ocean of your being, where the possibilities for self-realization are infinite.

A Compilation of Breathwork Therapies and Practices

Each of the following guided practices and facilitated therapies uses a variety of breathing techniques to bring the recipient to a state of wholeness. This includes practices such as conscious breathing, deep and rhythmic abdominal breathing, internal cellular respiration, yogic or pranic breathing methods, and many others. These breathwork practices may also use touch, visualization, spontaneous physical movements, exercises, postures, divine light, music, chanting, toning, mudras, and meditations to reeducate the body and mind. In some cases, the process used in one therapy seems only slightly different from that in another, but each has become an identifiable practice that you can choose to experience. Many are carried out in a group setting with an instructor or facilitators creating an comfortable and supportive atmosphere, but quite a few of the guided practices can also be accomplished on your own at home once you have learned them well. If group therapy is not your thing, depending on the particular therapy, it may be possible to arrange a one-on-one session, and in certain meditative practices, solitude is preferred. Except for one aquatic therapy done in a pool, most take place in a large space dedicated to providing the right ambience, with participants standing, sitting, or resting fully horizontal or in a partly reclined position. The duration of each can range from twenty minutes to almost five hours. A number of the practices are carried out with participants in a very relaxed state, whereas others engage the body in movement or exercises.

Although most of the following breathing therapies can be helpful for anyone simply searching for self-enhancement, many are especially suitable for those who have been traumatized by some life event. However, certain conditions may be contraindications to breathwork therapies. Depending on the particular therapy, they include chronic illness, drug addiction, major heart problems, abnormal blood pressure, pregnancy, recent surgery, cancer, glaucoma, some forms of epilepsy and asthma, and certain mental illnesses, such as bipolar disorder, depression, schizophrenia, or paranoid personality disorder. In these cases, it would be best to talk to your health care provider, as well as with the group facilitators, before proceeding with a particular breathwork therapy.

Anyone wishing more general information about breathwork practices can contact the International Breathwork Training Alliance at www.breathworktrainings.com. It is a consortium of professional breathwork schools, trainers, and practitioners that was formed to help promote breathwork as a vital healing modality for wellness.

Authentic Breathing®

Dennis Lewis, founder of the Center for Harmonious Awakening, has made significant contributions to advancing breath awareness through his books and teachings about developing natural, grounded breathing habits. His work, derived mostly from Taoist practices, explores the changes in inner alchemy and sensory awareness brought about by following the breath and listening to the body, which can lead to heightened sensory perception and greater self-knowledge. Slow, natural breathing, without the effort or manipulation that causes tension, allows the muscles to reach a state in which a person is relaxed, open, and more fully conscious. Lewis also emphasizes that emotions are strongly connected to the breath and the nervous system, so rather than repressing feelings, they must be released by the balancing, cleansing, and energizing qualities of the breath. Learning how to identify current breathing patterns and improve natural rhythms is considered an essential first step before more advanced breath-control work.

Authentic Breathing adheres to ten basic principles for opening up restrictions and breathing authentically in daily life: breathing through the nose, sensing the movement of slow breathing, relaxing the belly, letting the breath engage with the whole body, letting go more with the exhalation, making the exhalation long and slow, pausing to sense relaxation and increase awareness, inhaling only when it comes easily, sensing the space in the body, and feeling the mystery.

The practice of Authentic Breathing is intended to replace the harmful effects of habitual underbreathing by involving the whole body in the harmonious movement of the breath. This practice requires a good understanding of anatomy and the various phases of respiration, along with the desire to be on the path of self-discovery. The first step is to become aware of present breathing patterns, as well as the obstacles that inhibit the breath and their effects. It is essential to watch, sense, and feel without trying to change anything. The client is taught how to inhale and exhale fully within the three breathing spaces of the lower, middle, and upper chest. A strong, complete exhalation helps strengthen the diaphragm and creates room for a full inhalation, which will come in easily and naturally if simply allowed to do so. A variety of techniques, exercises, and meditations are then used to expand awareness. These include practices such as opening up the pause of spaciousness, metaphysical breathing, conscious breathing, six-sound healing exhalations, the smiling breath, the heart breath, the humming bee breath, the expanding time breath, and the boundless breath.

The benefits of Authentic Breathing may include the transformation of anger, the reduction of pain, an improved ability to relax, the release of tension (especially in the neck and shoulders), enhanced sexual pleasure, a positive effect on blood pressure, improved life-force energy, a boost to the immune system, the removal of toxins, a better self-image, and a sense of wholeness. By freeing the breath and allowing it to engage more fully with the body, the mind and the spirit can also be set free.

Contact: www.authentic-breathing.com

Breathing Coordination

One of the first to recognize the importance of proper breathing, Karl Stough gained new insights during the 1950s and 1960s through extensive research on exceptional Olympic athletes, opera singers, and patients suffering from debilitating respiratory disease. He recognized that a complete exhalation allows a greater intake of needed oxygen on the inhalation and that the air trapped in the lungs by restricted breathing could lead to illness. A complete exhalation can be encouraged by strengthening the diaphragm, which also allows the rib cage to expand, frees up adjacent body parts, permits the voice to resonate more fully, and teaches the body to let go of stress. Although there is no distinct modality called Breathing Coordination, a number of breathwork practitioners who trained with him are dedicated to keeping his principles available to those who wish to learn more about them.

Contact: www.breathingcoordination.com

Breath Mastery

Dan Brulé is a teacher and healer experienced in many forms of breathwork and healing arts practices,

such as those found in Medical Qi Gong, Prana Yoga, Zen, and meditation. One of the original advocates for breathwork as a therapy and the founder of both the Spiritual Breathing Movement and One Sky International, Brulé created his own breathwork training program, Breath Mastery, to help others learn breath awareness exercises and techniques for conscious breathing through presentations worldwide. This program offers breath-energy training, Chinese medical breathing practices, breath-awareness exercises, spiritually oriented breathwork, and an assortment of other conscious-breathing techniques. Ancient Eastern and modern Western methods teach average people how they can heal themselves and increase their potential through conscious breathing. The spiritual practices involve ways of using the breath as an agent of change.

These breath awareness and breathing techniques can be carried out for a variety of purposes, ranging from athletic performance to profound spiritual awakening. Initially, individuals practice breath awareness by paying attention, becoming witnesses, and observing the subtle details of the breathing process. An essential element is learning how to breathe in a conscious, connected, circular, and rhythmic way in which the inhalation is active, the exhalation is passive, and there are no pauses between the breaths. The ability to direct the breath into all three areas of the torso—lower, middle, and upper—must also be mastered. When the inhalation is directed into the heart and fills the entire breathing cavity, the head and the abdomen become connected by this space filled with loving energy, and the body, heart, and mind are unified. A long, deep, slow cleansing inhalation that connects the recipient to the sacred source can create a shift from one state of mind to another. The art of engaging with the exhalations leads to surrender and relaxation, which will help release negative thoughts, fears, and pain. Exploring what happens when breathing through the nose or the mouth or while making sounds is another important element of the practice. If these skillful steps are practiced without judgment, resistance, and attachment, the road to mastery of the breath will have few bumps in it.

Contact: www.breathmastery.com

Buteyko Method

Dr. Konstantin Buteyko was a Russian doctor and professor who, as a medical student during the 1950s, recognized a correlation between a patient's breathing and the severity of her illness. He also found that as a patient's condition worsened, her breathing rate increased in a manner similar to hyperventilation, in which the amount of carbon dioxide in the body is reduced, creating an imbalance that affects the level of oxygen in the blood and brain and can cause many types of disease. Continued research revealed that many seemingly healthy people chronically overbreathe. He proposed that health can be improved by slow, shallow diaphragmatic breathing through the nose, taking in a small volume of air with each breath. Breathing less frequently creates the proper levels of carbon dioxide in the circulatory system, which improves oxygenation of cells and tissues, calms the nervous system, and relieves stress, tension, and agitation. By 1985, Buteyko's breathing lessons had become a part of the Russian health care system, where they were used to treat a variety of breathing difficulties. Today, instruction in these techniques is also available outside Russia. His special breathing techniques have been clinically shown to benefit people with restricted airways caused by asthma and bronchial conditions, though many breathwork therapists propose different methods of balancing the breathing process. Contact: www.buteyko.info

Holotropic Breathwork™

Holotropic means "moving toward wholeness" and represents one of the first forms of breathwork established as a distinct therapy in the West. It was developed by Stanislav and Christina Grof between the 1960s and 1980s, and during this developmental period, it evolved from clinical studies on the therapeutic potential of psychedelic drugs into specially structured group workshops that integrate breathwork and elements of other healing therapies in a way that allows people to access all the aspects of their lives from which they have become disconnected. Since its inception, Holotropic Breathwork has progressed into a practice that uses deep, intensified, and somewhat rapid breathing coordinated with euphoric or ecstatic music and rhythms to induce nonordinary states of consciousness that mobilize the body-mind's spontaneous healing potential.

Underlying this therapeutic method is the belief that breathwork is the key element for reconnecting with unresolved issues and releasing all of their stuck energy. Its goal is to provide wholeness, healing, and wisdom through an often-cathartic process that will weaken the hold of traumatic psychological constraints and offer new possibilities for transcending habitual ways of perception. A session of Holotropic Breathwork combines sustained breathing, evocative music, and focused energy-release bodywork. It concludes with recipients creating artwork that reflects their experience, followed by a group sharing session. A specific sequence is followed, but since it is a very subjective journey, participants are encouraged to react in their own ways to the experience without expecting any particular result, simply allowing whatever needs to surface to do just that. Although this journey of self-exploration takes place in a group retreat setting, each individual is cared for by another participant, who acts as a source of loving support and encouragement. Trained facilitators supervise the process and interact with recipients as needed with touch, assisted body movements, and verbal intervention.

The techniques used are considered the catalyst for creating the nonordinary state of mind. Participants breathe more deeply and rapidly than usual for an extended period—up to four hours—while specially chosen, evocative music is played at a high volume. Although the preferred method of breathing is constant, deep circular breathing without a pause between the in- and outbreaths, participants may deviate from this. Initially, when they stray from this method, facilitators will remind them to keep up the rapid deep breathing. However, as the journey begins to deepen, maintaining this focus is not always possible, and when an altered state is reached, the breathwork is not so critical to the unfolding process. Participants have the option of receiving energetic bodywork, which is primarily pressure work on painful, tight, or blocked areas of the body rather than massage; chakra-holding energy work is also available. Responding to the needs of the breather and her changing energy, the facilitator will apply pressure to the painful area. The pressure creates resistance, which helps the recipient become more engaged with the cause of the pain. The breather can amplify the feeling by breathing into that area while pushing or tensing her body against the pressure of the facilitator's hand. These actions can stimulate painful feelings so that they intensify to the point at which the concentrated energy explodes, dissipates, and leaves the body, taking the cause along with the pain. A powerful energetic and healing release can happen at any time during a session, with or without bodywork. When an emotional component is involved, the release can be very cathartic, with the body and voice bringing forth unusual movements or powerful sounds. Fortunately for participants, the loud music covers up most of the distracting sounds made by other participants, so all are free to express themselves without fear of judgment.

Holotropic Breathwork can provide both psychological and spiritual healing that opens up and integrates an individual's shadow side. Some more involved workshops can last for days and may combine breathwork sessions with other techniques such as shamanic journeys, vision quests, meditations, and Gestalt Therapy, with periods of time off for relaxation and contemplation. The work has been the basis for therapeutic variations on the Holotropic process that have been developed over recent years.

Contact: Association for Holotropic Breathwork
International – www.grof-holotropic-breathwork.net or www.holotropic.com

Integrative Breathwork

In 1991, Jacquelyn Small, who was trained in psychology and social work, developed her own form of breathwork after teaching experiences in Holotropic Breathwork for several years with Stanislav Grof. Although it is very similar to the Holotropic process, Small has made some adaptations in creating Integrative Breathwork. Her approach grounds this method in the psychospiritual therapeutic work of integrating the ego personality with the soul, or higher self. The intention of the method is to produce a nonordinary state of consciousness in which a person can more directly experience the higher self and gain a more peaceful state of acceptance in dealing with life and its often-challenging conditions.

A session consists of a two-hour exploration of the self induced by a sequence of carefully chosen music that begins with an invocation inviting higher powers forward. In conjunction with the breathwork, some hands-on bodywork is used in the healing process, along with elements of soul-based psychology. Shadow work, psychodrama, movement with play, guided imagery, yoga, meditation, journal work, and expressive artwork are combined in a session. The process concludes with an open sharing session to help integrate any feelings that

came up during the breathwork. Since the breathwork is intended to access the cellular memory of suffering lodged in the body, each individual will have a different releasing experience. The Eupsychia Institute, founded by Small, carries on with training and healing using breathwork and soul-based psychology.
Contact: www.eupsychia.com

Kundalini Yoga Breathwork

Although a form of yoga rather than a type of therapy, this practice makes full use of the breath in conjunction with a number of meditative practices and movement exercises aimed at energizing the whole being. Kundalini, the energy of the coiled serpent residing at the base of the spine, can be an energetic doorway into the vast realm of conscious awareness through which a person can connect with his spiritual essence. Kundalini also represents a core connection and the potential for union with the divine universal energy that manifests in the body through the energy channels and the chakras. What really makes Kundalini Yoga different from other forms in which the breath is an integral part of the practice is the focus on the vital energy rising within the central channel.

Numerous types of Kundalini breathwork can be practiced. Some use slow, deep breathing, and in others, the breathing is quite rapid. Generally speaking, these yogic breathing methods are done while meditating either seated or in the lotus posture, though some are accomplished while standing, lying down, or performing various movements or asanas, such as the Sun Salutation, Eagle, and Camel. The Breath of Fire practice (rapid abdominal breathing combined with long, deep, relaxed breaths) is an integral part of the various exercises intended to awaken the kundalini energy at the base of the spine. The breathwork is often done in conjunction with body movements: twists, rotations, stretches, bends, and swings. Chanting and vibrational sounding are key elements in the practices. Kundalini Yoga, which has a significant connection with ancient tantric practices, is considered one of the most direct paths to awakening. However, it must be done correctly, for taming the serpent is not an easy task. Since a premature awakening of this powerful energy can be very unsettling, the initial guidance of an experienced practitioner is highly recommended.
Contact: www.yogibhajan.org

Merkabah Breathwork

The Merkabah (also spelled Merkaba) is a divine spirit body composed of two symmetrical, counter-rotating electromagnetic fields of light shaped as star tetrahedrons. These fields of light act as a vehicle for accelerating the process of ascension by transporting a seeker beyond time and space to the dimension of the unified energy of all creation. The Merkabah has been used by ascended masters to link with those reaching for the higher realms. After receiving instructions during a visitation from angels, Drunvalo Melchizedek combined this sacred geometry with breathwork to create a meditative process that activates the Merkabah, which surrounds the body, beginning at the base of the spine and extending outward. Once activated, this field is capable of carrying the consciousness directly to a higher dimension, maximizing the potential of the spirit and allowing the experience of unity with the divine. Bob Frissell, the founder of Breath of Life, was trained by Melchizedek and offers workshops as well as private sessions. Visualization of the Merkabah is used in other modalities, in particular the One Light Healing Touch bodywork practice.

Sacred Geometry of the Merkaba
Light Spirit Body with Counter-rotating Fields of Light

Tune into the higher realms with
Spherical Breathing.
(18 Stages)

As described in Frissell's book, *Nothing in This Book Is True, But It's Exactly How Things Are*, a star tetrahedron is made up of two interlocking tetrahedrons in a manner that resembles the Star of David, but three-dimensionally. The mental star tetrahedral field is electrical in nature, male, and rotates to the left. The emotional star tetrahedral field is magnetic in nature, female, and rotates to the right. It is the linking together of the mind, heart, and physical body in a specific geometrical ratio and at a critical speed that produces the Merkabah.

During a healing, the recipient carries out an intricate seventeen-breath meditation, which aids in imaging the rotating star tetrahedrons of the Merkabah within and around the physical body. Each stage of the breathing exercise proceeds in a deep, rhythmic way while meditating on the heart, carrying out specific visualizations, and performing eye movements and hand mudras. The first six parts of the meditative breathing process are intended to balance polarity, and the next seven reestablish the proper flow of prana through the entire body. Further breathing techniques are used for shifting the consciousness and opening the inner eye. The final eighteenth special breath is received from the higher self when the time is right for assimilation and integration. Contact: www.bobfrissell.com or
www.thespiritualcatalyst.com/articles/
what-is-the-merkabah

Middendorf Breathexperience / Breathwork

Professor Ilse Middendorf developed this therapy in Germany during the 1930s, influenced in part by the work of Moshe Feldenkrais. Her work is recognized as a major practice of somatic breathwork in Europe. The breathing education process employs a series of movement exercises that encourages the breath to come and go naturally within the body consciousness. The basic principles are that the breather must be fully present and must perceive the movement of the breath through sensations, rather than through thinking, imagining, or intuiting, although these are still helpful. The aim is not to control the breathing process, but to explore the perceptible dimensions of breath, which may reflect how people experience life itself.

The approach is gentle and nonmanipulative, and the practice emphasizes invigorating the inhalation and creating space for free movement of the breath within the cycle of inhalation and exhalation. This space can appear naturally during the pause, after which the next inhalation occurs spontaneously without force. The work also examines how people physically hold themselves, because involving only the upper body in breathing creates improper posture and tension. Therefore, Middendorf Breathwork strives to balance the body by engaging both the upper and lower body.

Individual sessions are accomplished on a massage table, and group sessions are done on the floor. Classes teach simple stretches, movements, and vocal sounding, which increase awareness of habitual patterns and help participants develop familiarity and skill with the conscious breathing that will rejuvenate every cell in the body. Practitioners use hand pressure, compressions, and gentle touch, though not massage, to encourage the unfolding of the client's breath. These stimulations, along with movement, enliven the breath and increase both body and breath awareness. Once a good sense of the way the breath and body work together has been developed, the recipient is gently stretched in order to create a space in which she can be guided into better posture and alignment, which in turn enhances the free flow and quality of the breath. The process also teaches clients to recognize that certain qualities of breath belong to specific energy centers, such as those in the solar plexus, lower belly and heart, and that the breath can flow in different directions—upward, downward, and horizontally. As part of an individual bodywork session, recipients can engage in a breath dialogue, a conversation that uses sensing rather than words to improve how they express themselves.

In more recent years, a special breath-experience movement program called Breathdance has been created at the Middendorf Institute in Berkeley, California. In this program, the breath is the source and initiator of all movement and expression, thus actualizing inner beauty and truth while enhancing self-expression. The process also helps recipients take responsibility for making the shift from doing or controlling to simply allowing their own creative resources to tackle any problems.
Contact: Middendorf Institute for Breath
Experience – www.breathexperience.com

Nishino Breathing Method / Sokushin Breathing

This method of cultivating energy was developed during the late 1970s by Japanese ballet instructor Kozo Nishino, who was also an Aikido and Kung Fu master. Nishino understood that energy is generated by respiration and nutrition and that the cells of the body will die without both. Cellular respiration, also called internal respiration, is the process that brings oxygen and the life-force energy to all the cells and organs of the body, and the Nishino Breathing Method uses breathwork and physical exercises to strengthen cellular respiration and functioning. This enhances the life-force energy and preserves and restores youth. Considering the number of times cells reproduce in a lifetime, keeping this activity vital is important for maximum longevity. The method consists of two primary parts: breathwork exercises that include Sokushin Breathing and a practice of energy exchange called Taiki. As a master of Aikido, Nishino had a good understanding of the inner workings of subtle energies, and his method reflects that knowledge.

Though it was developed independently, Sokushin Breathing, one of the basic exercises, is similar to some qi gong practices that are used to circulate energy throughout the body. The practitioner breathes in through the nose and visualizes earth energy coming in through the feet, rising to the lower dantien energy center in the abdomen, and being steadily propelled up the spine to the crown. After a gentle holding pause, the energy is allowed to settle back down the front of the body to the lower dantien, from which it is exhaled down to the feet and out the soles into the earth. This breathing method works to strengthen cell function, enhance vital chi energy, and restore youthfulness.

Taiki, the second component of Nishino, is a unique practice of implementing the smooth, efficient exchange of energy and information on a cellular and atomic level. Once a person has developed control of energy through the Sokushin breathwork practice, this exchange can take place not only within his own body but also between him and another person. The results can be quite entertaining. The practitioner who knows how to send energy can propel this life force outward to others without causing them any pain. This "blow of energy" excites the receiver's own cells and causes his body to move spontaneously—jumping, bouncing, dancing, or being flung away—while simultaneously smiling, singing, or laughing. It looks like an invisible force performing a magic trick. Similar types of energy mastery have been demonstrated by Aikido masters, who defend themselves without seeming to move. Studies of these practices have left logically minded researchers baffled. As with many aspects within the realm of subtle energy work, true understanding requires experiential knowledge, and the real aim of these practices is to cultivate personal energy and the pleasure of being alive so that any adversity can be overcome.

Contact: www.nishinojuku.com/english/e_top.html

Optimal Breathing™

This self-help breathwork training program was established by Michael White and includes a number of programs that are designed to create optimal breathing habits. Optimal breathing is the ability to breathe freely and naturally under all circumstances, whether at rest, work, or play. It is important for maintaining sufficient oxygen to fuel the brain, heart, eyes, organs, and cells of the body. Participants learn methods for developing coordination, depth, fullness, size, ease, and smoothness of breathing; ways to better use breathing; the kind of nutrition that assists proper breathing; how to cleanse and detoxify the respiratory system; how to protect themselves from pollution; and methods of resolving specific problems. Improving a person's ability to relax is also considered essential for optimal breathing. The program addresses many poor breathing patterns, such as shallow breathing, which may be caused by muscle tension, emotional stress, improper posture, obesity, contact with harmful chemicals, and an assortment of other environmental concerns. The techniques used are not the sometimes-strenuous breath-control exercises found in yoga, but rather more relaxed and natural ways of harmoniously coordinating the breathing process.

Contact: www.optimalbreathinginstitute.org

OxyGenesis Breathwork

This form of breathwork therapy focuses on correcting restricted breathing patterns, thereby expanding the capacity to live more fully. The therapy was developed during the 1980s by Lois Grasso, who had extensive experience with various conscious breathing methods and body-oriented therapies. This practice is intended as a self-healing method for rapidly clearing emotional baggage from the subconscious by using the power of deep abdominal breathing. It recognizes that laughter, crying, and yawning play an important part in emotional release and that restricting these natural processes can create unnecessary stress. When physical responses to emotions are stifled, as when crying children are told to stop acting like a baby, breathing becomes constricted. This unnatural holding of the breath prevents the release of the tension caused by the painful event that triggered the crying. Over the years, this pattern of holding the breath and the feelings becomes the habitual response whenever something stressful occurs. Of course, this is only one of the many issues that could create restricted breathing.

The therapy works with conscious connected breathing, a rhythmic process with no pause between the inhalation and exhalation, as a means to release chronic tension. It also incorporates percussive Acupressure, such as the tapping practice in the Emotional Freedom Technique, manual stimulation of tense muscles, and many other methods. Much of the work focuses on giving the body permission to release unexpressed physical and emotional energy. The overall goal of the practice is to make it more instinctive to breathe deeply and relax when faced with anything stressful, thereby reducing the likelihood of further negative effects from held tension.

Contact: Oxy Genesis Institute – www.oxygenesis.org

Pranayama (Ayurvedic Breathwork)

Pranayama, which includes a vast number of breathing practices and techniques that originated within the ancient Ayurvedic healing system of India, is primarily used to stimulate and store the life-force energy known as prana. Though it appears to be empty, cosmic space is actually filled with divine energetic potential and power that manifests itself in life forms as prana. Pranic energy permeates every being and can burn like fire to purify all. It is a self-energizing force that is closely tied with human consciousness; when we die, the breath and the pranic energy dissolves into the cosmic energy.

Prana is intimately linked with the breath, which serves to regulate its flow throughout the body, and proper breathing is considered the primary way of harnessing its power. Disease is believed to arise when prana is deficient. A person will then feel troubled, restless, confused, restricted, and stuck. The practice of pranayama allows individuals to strengthen this life-force energy and put it to use through regulating the incoming and outgoing flow of breath in conjunction with breath retention. As increased prana flows throughout the body, symptoms of disease will disappear. Since a person's state of mind is strongly affected by the level of energy within, a person will feel less disturbed and be more content when prana is enhanced or balanced. Pranayama can also influence attention. When breathing is irregular, the mind wavers; when the breath is steady, the mind becomes steady. In meditative practices, when the mind follows the breath, it will be drawn into stillness. Pranayama also energizes consciousness so that practitioners can become aware of information that lies dormant in the unconscious. Pranayama can be seen as a way to breathe light and truth into a space that allows all of life to be enjoyed more fully.

Most practices of yoga incorporate pranayama breathwork. Numerous breathing techniques are used to enhance a person's well-being by increasing, decreasing, or balancing the flow of prana within the body, the energy channels (nadi), and the chakra system. The flow of prana can have a significant healing effect on the physical level, especially on digestion, the immune system, the nervous system, circulation, and respiration. Some pranayama practices act to cool, steady, relax, and balance bodily functions and organs, whereas others can excite, energize, and heat them. There are also techniques that prevent leakage of prana from the body. Many of these practices produce the internal body heat known as the inner fire of purification, which works within the subtle energy channels to burn up waste and rid the body of toxins. Some practices are accomplished by using special vocal sounds, particular tongue positions, mudras (hand positions), head movements, body postures, and visualizations. The "right" practice depends on individual needs and skills at that moment in time; however, overall balance is the ultimate goal. Combining the practice of pranayama with yoga postures (asanas) will deepen the experience.

Besides linking the body, mind, and emotions, the breath is also a pathway to the subtle energy body. Certain practices in pranayama allows the practitioner to direct energy inward to the chakra centers and draw it up to the crown chakra, which is the space of pure consciousness and liberation. As the mind follows the breath in this meditative way, it will rise with the prana; over time, this can bring positive and peaceful changes to the mind, allowing a clearer understanding of the self and one's life purpose, mental and emotional relief, and inspired relationships with others. Yogic breathing also furnishes techniques for inducing awareness of the finer energy wavelengths that assist with centering. Many of

these advanced practices require special training and careful attention to the actual process, but once mastered, pranayama breathwork is considered the highest form of purification and self-discipline for both the mind and body.

The initial goal of pranayama practices is to develop deep, effective breathing that uses the diaphragm, upper and lower chest, and abdomen. Equilibrium between stagnant and active energies is very important, and slow, deep exhalations give the body more time to free itself of waste and blockages, creating more space for fresh energy to enter with a full inhalation. An interval of breath retention (kumbhaka) is the pause that refreshes, and provides a longer period during which energy can be absorbed and awareness awakened. Pranayama also includes techniques that move the various forms of prana known as vayus (wind energies) in particular ways. For example, a practice might include breathing in a high breath, exhaling a low breath, finding a middle breath, moving energy upward, spreading the breath and energy out into the whole body, or generating heat. The assortment of techniques available is quite extensive.

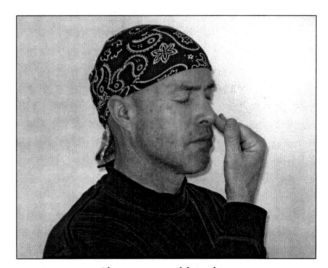

Alternate nostril breathing.

Yogic breathing techniques are divided into basic and more advanced, although some fall into both categories. Typical basic methods include bellows breathing, alternate nostril breathing, cooling breathwork, the soft humming breath, the hissing breath, skull shining, light sounding, and single nostril breathing. Advanced methods include bandha-lock breathwork techniques, ujjayi breathing, surya bheda (a special form of nostril breathing), bhastrika (forced rapid deep breathing), and an advanced energy-purification practice called samanu breathing. Most of the techniques, whether basic or advanced, aim to prolong the retention period between breaths. The deeper and slower the breathing and the more evenly balanced the inhalation and exhalation, the longer the pause will last. Some advanced yoga practitioners can enter an altered state in which breathing is so slow that they don't even seem to be alive.

Initially and during many practices, breathing through the nostrils instead of the mouth is considered optimal, because nose is designed to moisturize, warm, and cleanse incoming air. Energetic activity in the nose can also quickly trigger a reflex in the nearby brain that can cause a beneficial shift in consciousness. In contrast, breathing through the mouth can cause dizziness, nervousness, and emotional problems during practice. Some techniques call for breathing equally through both nostrils, and others use alternate nostril breathing, though specific practices may modify the way common techniques are carried out.

It is wise to get proper guidance in pranayama practices so that abilities can grow naturally and effortlessly. In time, more advanced and subtle techniques can be incorporated as skill and self-awareness develop. No matter what the practice, the keys to pranayama are correct posture, comfortable clothing, a peaceful setting, a good time of day, limited food intake before practice, and clear nasal passages. Breathing should be rhythmic throughout all the repetitions of the technique and never strained or forced. If yoga postures are incorporated into pranayama practice, props such as blocks, straps, bolsters, stretching bands, sandbags, and blankets may be needed for additional support.

Many forms of yoga are integrated with pranayama breathwork. Yantra Yoga and Tantra Yoga are two that put great emphasis on the breath. Yantra Yoga in particular uses breathing to guide the movements required when performing the various asanas. Tantra Yoga, on the other hand, uses the breath to help move the kundalini and other sacred energies. (See more on these techniques in Chapter 11.)

Quantum Breath Meditation

Because the practice of meditation and the breath are so deeply interconnected, they each can support the other in a very special way. Yogi Amrit Desai, a master

of meditation, who had already established his own form of yoga, created Quantum Breath Meditation to assist both beginning and experienced meditators in entering the deepest level of meditative awareness with tantric and breathing techniques that silence the restless mind. Working with the breath also creates a deeper connection between a person's pranic energy and the universal quantum field of energy in the realm of the divine. In addition to using his own practice of Amrit Yoga to relax the physical body, special techniques are employed to help the individual enter into a meditative state in which she is being rather than doing. The aim is to help participants learn how to tap into their deepest levels of consciousness and effortlessly enter a stress-free space in which awareness can expand in infinite ways and stress-related health problems can subside. (See more under Amrit Yoga in Chapter 11.)
Contact: Amrit Yoga Institute – www.amrityoga.org/more-teachings/quantum-breath.html

Radiance Breathwork®

In the 1970s, psychologist Dr. Gay Hendricks and his wife, Dr. Kathlyn Hendricks, developed Radiance Breathwork after years of experiencing and experimenting with a number of other methods, including Holotropic Breathwork, the Feldenkrais Method of Somatic Education, and Reichian Therapy. The word *radiance* in its title refers to the way people look and feel after the practice. Radiance Breathwork is a transformational process that uses movement, intense conscious breathing, and elements of body-centered psychotherapy to ease unconscious feelings out of the body and open up the energy channels.

During his research, Hendricks noticed that people with psychological problems tended to exhibit a sharp transition between the inhalation and exhalation, and he concluded that life trauma can interfere with a smooth breathing cycle. He also recognized the correlation between fear and poor breathing. He was inspired to find ways of breathing that would help individuals get past their own issues and their resistance to change. What was needed and what he created became a method by which individuals could manage pain, release stress and tension, build energy and endurance, handle emotions in a healthier way, prevent and heal personal problems, enhance concentration, improve physical performance, help with graceful aging, and facilitate psychospiritual transformation. Additional programs that combine techniques with activities were created to help with special concerns, such as trauma release, addiction recovery, treatment of asthma and respiratory disorders, sexual enhancement for couples, and better performance in sports.

The therapeutic training emphasizes creating a conscious breathing process, as well as an interpersonal connection among participants when carried out in a group setting. Elements of the process of enhancing conscious breathing include learning how to relax and listen, studying breathing mechanics and anatomy, sensing from the inside out, cultivating deeper full breathing, performing alternate nostril breathing, integrating the mind and body, increasing sensory awareness of the breath through movements, fine-tuning the whole-body breath, freeing the rhythm of the breath within the breath, breathing into more profound states of relaxation, tensing and letting go of the body, and generating a deep experience of streaming energy.

Sessions are performed on an individual basis or in a group workshop and last as long as two hours. There may be some initial preparation with teachings on helpful breathing exercises before the actual Radiance session begins. Then, the participant lies down and relaxes on a firm but comfortable surface and reviews her intentions. Any fears or questions can also be addressed at this time. The facilitator then leads the breather through the slow, comfortable style of breathing that is most appropriate for that individual, while helping her let go of conscious control. In some cases, a period of rapid breathing in deep gulps along with movement exercise may also be used. Music and bodywork are sometimes employed to help access the unconscious and trigger emotional release. The facilitator encourages the recipient to experience her feelings, move through them, and keep going, even if she feels fear, unpleasant emotions, or some other form of resistance, so that all the emotional material can come to the surface during the breathing process. The session continues as long as the client feels the need to work on unpleasant emotions. Once the emotional release has been integrated, slow breathing brings a feeling of being grounded and at peace. The Hendricks also developed a number of transformative body-centered methods to provide conscious living skills that can improve relationships. Contact: The Hendricks Institute – www.hendricks. com/newwp/wp-content/uploads/ Radiance_Preview.pdf

Rebirthing Breathwork Therapy

The word *rebirthing*, originally coined by Leonard Orr while experimenting with his breath in a hot tub, is found in descriptions of many different modalities and psychotherapies. However, it was through therapeutic experiences while recipients were immersed in tubs or pools that rebirthing got its name. Floating in the water, people often quickly connected to the womb-like environment and regressed to this earlier state of consciousness. Over the years, practitioners have adapted and modified the actual therapeutic process, and now it is not necessarily carried out in the water. Rebirthing has come to be a general term associated with various forms of bodywork or personal processing that bring about a release by connecting a person with past significant or traumatic events, such as may have occurred at the moment of birth. This experience lends itself to powerful emotional release, often with spiritual revelations.

Rebirthing: finding your inner child

Rebirthing Breathwork, a therapy developed by Leonard Orr between the 1960s and the 1970s, primarily uses the simple process of circular breathing to create an altered state of consciousness. In the early years of breathwork practice, some therapeutic methods, including Rebirthing Breathwork, used rapid rates of breathing similar to panting to create an altered state of consciousness and a strong emotional release. Although a powerful cathartic release can be quite beneficial, there was debate about how well any real transformation could be fully integrated, especially if an individual was somewhat neurotic. As the years passed, practitioners have become more aware of what really works to meet the needs of the individual and have adjusted their techniques accordingly. Today, recipients are guided through a process that relies on a relaxed, gentle, and connected circular breathing rhythm.

Whether in the aquatic version in which the recipient floats in warm water or on dry land, depending on the protocol, the client is encouraged to use deep inhalations and relaxed exhalations to consciously access primal emotions and the imprints, beliefs, and feelings acquired earlier in life. By connecting the mind and body through the breath, memories held in the cells of the body can be released, bringing about a profound release of blockages throughout the body's various systems. The role of the facilitator is to offer loving support, both verbally and through touch therapy. The rebirther often assists clients by making affirmations and calling attention to subtle changes in the participant's breathing to help her deal with issues as they arise. The client may go through many varied experiences such as vibrating, weeping, laughing, and moaning, but the facilitator encourages the breathing pattern to continue until the recipient's feelings moves through and out of the body. Powerful feelings of well-being and a sense of the vibrational flow of freed-up energy may emerge after past experiences, including the birthing process, are relived consciously. A more intense technique called compression therapy may be used to encourage a "second rebirth." In this method, the client is wrapped in blankets and other people press down on her body to simulate the compression found in the birth canal.

Throughout the process, careful consideration is given to revealing the unconscious defenses, inhibitions and patterns of tension that have become roadblocks to engaging with and enjoying life to the fullest. By connecting the recipient to the strength and courage of the true self, the breathwork allows the conscious processing of these unresolved issues. Once conscious, the issue can be neutralized and integrated by breathing through them from the space of safety and comfort created by the support of the practitioner. This release of unconsciously created illusion and false images enables the integration of energies that free a person from feeling like a victim, thus empowering new, healthy choices.

Contact: Rebirthing Breathwork International – www.rebirthingbreathwork.com

Shamanic Breathwork

The most powerful forms of therapy are often the ones that help individuals awaken to the realization that they can heal themselves by remembering who they truly are. Shamanic Breathwork represents a process that inspires reconnection with the inner healer by blending ancient shamanic traditions with new methods of breath therapy. Trained facilitators give support and assistance to participants, who journey into realms of discovery, often inner underworlds accessed in an altered, dreamlike state.

Although there are many different traditions and procedures for making the journey, the participant's use of deep, connected breathing is the ingredient that makes Shamanic Breathwork different from other traditional forms of shamanic therapy. A typical session begins with various rituals and ceremonies that might use smudging and invocations to spirit guides, power animals, or other entities. Through these activities, participants are inspired to surrender to the higher power within. Drumming often leads the journey, which may last for two or three hours. What unfolds is a highly individualized experience that is unique to each person involved. Shifts in consciousness may give rise to states of joy and bliss as well as to struggles with negative forces that may be attached to the soul. Facilitators may incorporate bodywork, energy work, guided meditations, soul retrieval, and extraction of intrusive entities, and with help from the loving hearts of spirit guides, they support the participants in traveling where they need to go. This may mean freeing them from all limitations, even at the cost of temporarily losing touch with their familiar identities. Fears may come as they enter the vastness of transcendence in the spirit realm, but in the end, the embrace of loving energies and the reconnection with a fuller sense of self will melt and transform the fears and put them to rest.

Linda Star Wolf, the founder of Venus Rising, is a shamanic practitioner who created her own version of breathwork known as the **Shamanic Breathwork™ Process**. She has also published a book about her work. Contact: www.shamanicbreathwork.org

Somato Respiratory Integration (SRI)

Somto Respiratory Integration is a form of breath-work developed by chiropractor Dr. Donald Epstein, also the creator of Network Spinal Analysis, for the purpose of helping the brain reconnect with the body's experiences by turning the attention within. The twelve-step process involves a series of guided and focused exercises intended to dissipate energy stored as tension, enhance structural flexibility, increase the feeling of safety within the body, and help increase internal awareness. If the body itself needs adjustment or shows recurring patterns of dysfunction, paying close attention to the spine may help resolve these problems. Specific exercises that link enhanced somatic awareness with the breath are integral to the process. Through focused attention on the gross and subtle bodies and on the movements and rhythms evoked by breathing, the recipient's awareness of existing tensions will increase. The exercises are recommended anytime an individual is overwhelmed by a particular symptom, is fearful, or feels disconnected from life.

Each guided exercise within the practice incorporates gentle, slow, conscious breathing synchronized with hand placement and body movement to create a connection between the breath and the body. Participants are usually either seated or lying on their backs, and the process starts with breathwork focusing on the upper chest, the breastbone area, and the navel and then moves on to other areas of the body. When the recipient identifies an area that imparts a sense of ease and connection, an intention is spoken, asking that this feeling spread to any existing areas of discomfort. In another exercise, the recipient first places the palms on an area of distress, breathes into it, and makes a sound, possibly a moan, that represents how that area would speak. Then the hands are moved back to a place of ease, and a pleasurable sound is made. This alternation encourages the problem area to resonate with its healthy partner. Once the breathwork exercises that make up SRI are learned, they can be practiced anywhere for self-healing. Contact: www.donaldepstein.com

Taoist and Qi Gong Breathing Practices

Over the centuries, both Taoist and qi gong methods of enhancing personal energy have assimilated the art of breathing into a broad range of physical exercises and meditative practices. The two are philosophically closely linked within the system of Chinese medicine. Although the principles of Taoism originated around 600 BCE with the teachings of Lao Tzu, the foundation of the practices probably was established centuries earlier with the Daoyin body-mind stretching exercises and Tu Na breathing exercises, which evolved into what is now called qi gong. These practices are very likely associated with the inner energy work known as Nei Gong. Since that time, many forms (called styles or schools) have been created, both as martial arts and as internal medicine, which is used to stimulate vitality and provide longevity. In recent years, Mantak Chia, the developer of the practitioner-applied form of bodywork known as Chi Nei Tsang, has been instrumental in spreading the teachings of the Tao in the West.

The Taoist perspective on health is very complex and involves many levels of subtle energy. However, what has evolved is a very simple, dynamic, and natural approach for enhancing well-being that recognizes a deep connection between breathwork and energy work. This healing way encompasses a variety of practices and therapies that work with the opposite but complementary forces of yin and yang, the three treasures, and the five elements. All Taoist and qi gong breathing practices revolve around the energetic essence of vital chi energy, which is considered essential to life and longevity. There is a strong focus on the meridians and the dantien energy centers, and the goal of all the practices is the balanced circulation of vital chi energy throughout the body.

Whether it's self-care practices or applied bodywork, the breath is the common denominator. Most of the traditional Chinese practices concentrate on using the breath to acquire, store, and send vital chi energy internally to the three primary dantien energy centers as well as to all the cells, organs, and systems of the body. Moving through the meridians and circulating throughout the body, the chi energy can stimulate the natural functioning of the organs, eliminate tension, and heal damaged tissue. The act of breathing in this way also massages the organs. The three key elements in many of these techniques are completely breathing out unwanted energies, fully breathing in new revitalized energies, and understanding that balancing the flow of energy throughout the body can provide good health and longevity. Most practices coordinate the inhalation and exhalation through the nose and mouth and use meditative attention and subtle physical movement to direct the energy into all areas of the body.

Some qi gong and Taoist breathing techniques, such as storing, sending, and nourishing energy, are discussed in the section on specific techniques later in this chapter. In general, storing energy refers to the practice of breathing into the abdomen in the area of the kidneys. Sending means directing the breath and chi energy internally into the various organs or weak areas of the body, as well as extending the energy externally to heal and nourish other people. Almost all of the Taoist and qi gong therapies that involve using the breath emphasize moderation, balance, harmony, and adherence to the laws of nature. Although there are many forms of practice, the actual differences between them are often very subtle.

Though all of the meridian pathways may be involved in these breathwork practices, the extraordinary energy pathways within the body, and especially the central channel, are essential. The central channel actually is made of up two extraordinary meridians—the conception channel in the front of the body and the governing channel on the back—that work together to form a circular flow. The practice called the Microcosmic Orbit creates a continual loop of energy by directing the breath and therefore the energy through these two channels, circling from the perineum up the back to the crown of the head and back down the front of the trunk to the navel and perineum. The complete opening of the flow through this orbit circulates, directs, and preserves the flow of chi through the other major meridians of the body. There is also a smaller orbit practice that takes place in the lower abdomen. In Taoist breathwork practices, warm-current breathing meditations act to open the Microcosmic Orbit by employing concentration and relaxation exercises. As awareness of chi is taken to a deeper level, the breath induces the chi to become more refined. Attaining the ability to direct the flow of chi through the Microcosmic Orbit is considered a prerequisite for any student who intends to study higher levels of Taoism.

To obtain enlightenment at the soul level is to reach the divine realm, which is the highest state of the Tao and contains the energetic frequencies of pure consciousness. One spiritual Taoist practice, called Jing, Qi, Shen, Xu, Tao, works with subtle energy to transform matter, energy, and soul essence within the kidneys, spinal cord, brain, heart, and soul. The aim of the practice is to move the frequencies of matter, energy, and soul progressively to the more refined realms through deep breathwork, specific placement of the hands, different visualizations of light, and chanting, all done in a sitting posture. The practitioner inhales deeply and then holds the breath while chanting and visualizing. On exhalation, silent chanting is performed while focusing on each vital area of the body. Initially, a series of breaths is directed toward the kidneys to produce jing energy. Next, the focus is on the spine behind the navel area to transform jing to qi. Attention then shifts to the brain and the crown chakra, where another series of breaths is done to transform qi to shen. While maintaining the seated position, the hands and attention are moved to the heart, and a series of breaths transforms shen into an even more refined form of cosmic energy called xu. The last phase of the practice transforms xu to tao (the ultimate force) by focusing on the soul temple, located between the physical heart and the heart chakra. This practice requires guidance from a master, and after it has been perfected, it should be done as often as possible.

Qi gong, which literally means "energy breathing exercise," correlates very closely with Taoist practices and has even a longer history in China as a method for maintaining health. Qi gong primarily works with the circulation of chi and sees the breath as the way to cleanse, balance, and energize the body, thereby maintaining inner harmony. In many practices, the inhalation tonifies deficient chi, and the exhalation reduces or disperses excess chi. Inhalation is most often done through the nose while concentrating on clearing away thoughts and relaxing the body. Visualizations of the flow, texture, and color of energy are also incorporated. Qi gong recognizes the same central channels and meridian pathways of energy as Taoist breathwork and uses the breath to heighten awareness of the practitioner's spacious inner core. Quiet meditation and contemplation are an integral part of the practices, enabling the participant to become more focused and attentive. Although qi gong can be accomplished in many positions, practicing while sitting is considered the most effective, and attention to details on how to hold the body during practice, whether standing or sitting, is essential to allowing a more relaxed state of being fully present. Certain exercises also involve focused body movements

Microcosmic Orbit
Great Heavenly Cycle of Chi
with smaller orbit, dantiens, key points, and related glands

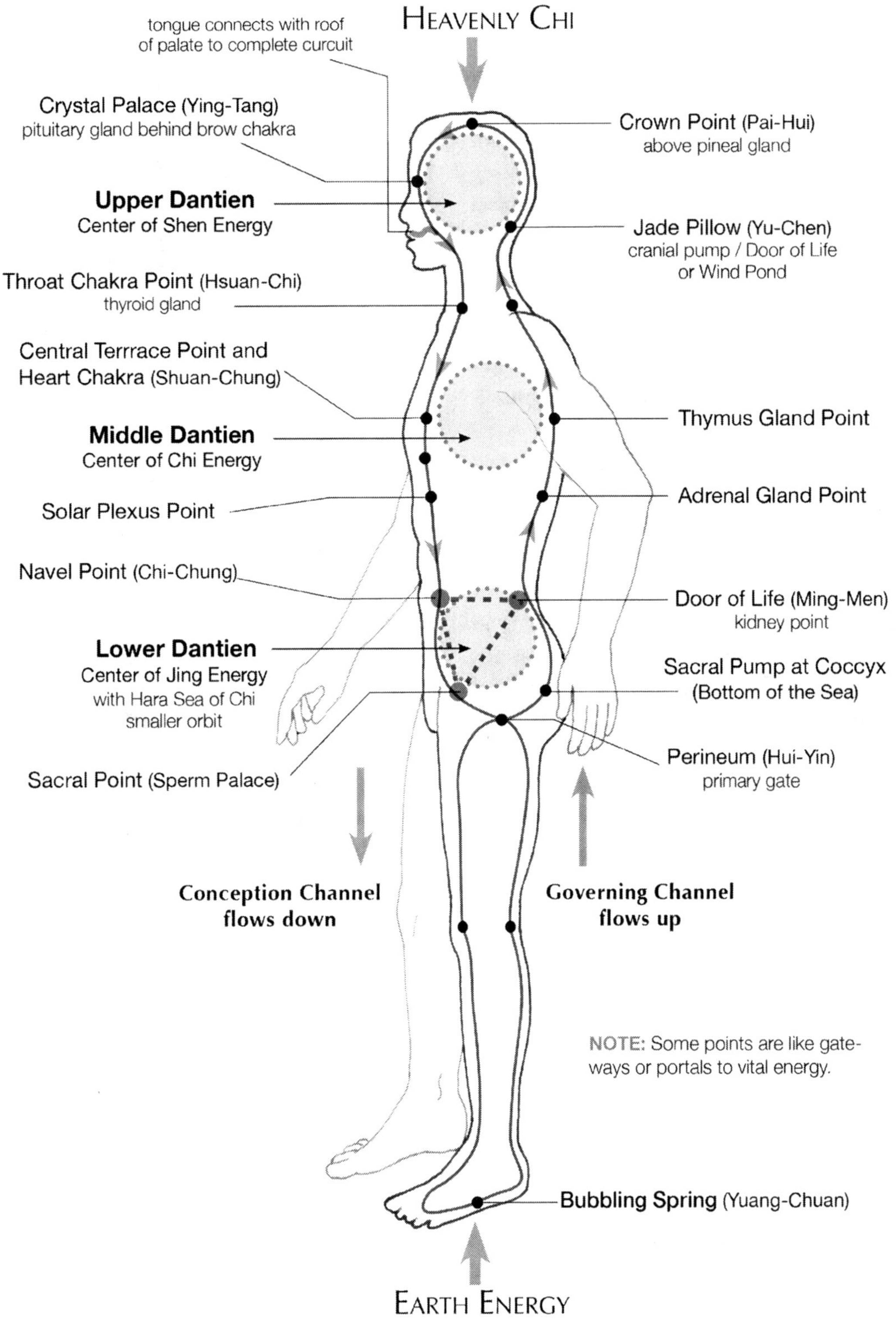

HEAVENLY CHI

tongue connects with roof
of palate to complete curcuit

Crystal Palace (Ying-Tang)
pituitary gland behind brow chakra

Upper Dantien
Center of Shen Energy

Throat Chakra Point (Hsuan-Chi)
thyroid gland

Central Terrrace Point and
Heart Chakra (Shuan-Chung)

Middle Dantien
Center of Chi Energy

Solar Plexus Point

Navel Point (Chi-Chung)

Lower Dantien
Center of Jing Energy
with Hara Sea of Chi
smaller orbit

Sacral Point (Sperm Palace)

Crown Point (Pai-Hui)
above pineal gland

Jade Pillow (Yu-Chen)
cranial pump / Door of Life
or Wind Pond

Thymus Gland Point

Adrenal Gland Point

Door of Life (Ming-Men)
kidney point

Sacral Pump at Coccyx
(Bottom of the Sea)

Perineum (Hui-Yin)
primary gate

**Conception Channel
flows down**

**Governing Channel
flows up**

NOTE: Some points are like gateways or portals to vital energy.

Bubbling Spring (Yuang-Chuan)

EARTH ENERGY

orchestrated to enhance a particular breathing technique, and self-massage may also be used. All of the different practices can be done alone, with a partner, or with a group. The distinction between different styles may be designated by language describing the way they are carried out—*internal or external, hard or soft, fast or slow, sitting or standing, moving or non-moving.*

When a person maintains a self-disciplined practice for a period of time, the techniques will become a permanent habit. It is important to remember that all should be accomplished without straining or creating any discomfort. Once the basic techniques have been perfected, the practitioner can take up deeper specialized meditative methods in which the breath and sounds are used to focus on the circulation of energy through other meridians, acupoints, the fascia, the endocrine glands of the hormonal system, and the internal organs of the body. A large assortment of breathwork and movement practices containing a variety of techniques for awakening, holding, and spreading energy to all areas of the body are available. Specific qi gong and Tai Chi self-care practices are discussed further in Chapter 11.

Tibetan Yoga of Breath and Movement

Tibetan healing practices combine elements from the indigenous Bön tradition with its shamanic roots, Ayurvedic practices from India, Chinese Traditional Medicine, and Buddhist philosophy. Different forms have been handed down secretly through the ages and have only recently been revealed to the West. Although the breath is used in a number of different ways in the Tibetan medical system, some specific Trul Khor breathwork practices from the Bön tradition are still used today and are taught by Tenzin Wangyal Rinpoche as the Tibetan Yoga of Breath and Movement. This energy-based approach is aimed at enhancing human potential, and, like many other teachings in the Tibetan Buddhist tradition, offers methods by which to purify the energy body and transform suffering. The Tibetan view of the energy body recognizes lung as the internal wind energy, somewhat equivalent to chi or prana. Lung is represented on the physical plane by the breath and is strongly connected to consciousness. Integral to Tenzin Wangyal Rinpoche's approach is the cultivation of lung through the Nine Breathings of Purification and five Tsa Lung exercises, which uses vital energy and nonconceptual experience to purify the body, speech, and mind.

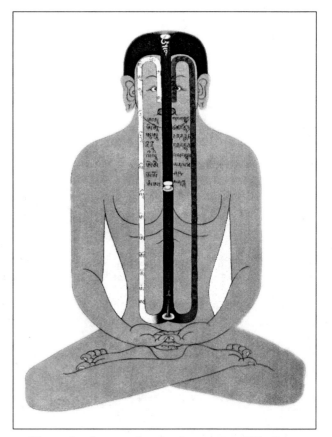

The paths of energy flow in the practice of Tsa Lung.

The central principle of these meditative practices is that the breath of awareness can help release limitations and blockages held in the karmic conceptual pain body. These negative narratives and their consequences are created when the thinking mind attempts to organize life experiences into a seemingly safe and secure reality, which hides the true nature of experience. By using the breath to invigorate the wind energy that purifies the misconceptions that cause suffering, the practitioner is assisted in entering a space in which wisdom and creativity are unleashed. Tenzin Wangyal Rinpoche suggests that participants place attention directly on the wind energy of the breath and on the body's sensations to calm the mind and sense the energy behind the stories they have fabricated about experiences. By catching the underlying wind energy, focusing the mind, exercising the body, and using the breath in specific ways, the habitual patterns of the conceptual mind can be released, emotional or mental afflictions alleviated, and the flow of subtle energy improved.

The **Nine Breathings of Purification** is a meditation for transformation that calls on the three primary sacred energy channels in the body. These primary channels are in the core of the body along the length of the spine, and the goal is to propel the breath and energy through them. While sitting erect in a relaxed posture on a chair or floor cushion, with the chest open and the hands at rest, the meditator rests in the stillness of the body, the silence within, and the spaciousness of the mind. Using alternate nostril breathing, visualizations, and the energetic movement of the breath through the three central channels, the meditator works through a sequence of subtle awareness exercises to purify and dissolve the three root poisons of anger, attachment, and ignorance. These poisons are the cause of all suffering and obscure the subtle wisdom energies and positive qualities that are available within the inner ocean of spaciousness that is every being's true nature. Purifying confusion at this deep level can have a positive effect on the perception and experience of life.

Further cleansing within these channels is accomplished through five **Tsa Lung** exercises. These practices work to release restricting patterns that can be manifested within the five chakras that are linked to the central channel. (Tibetan medicine assumes that there are five chakras, rather than the seven found in Ayurveda.) In these exercises, the focus, the breath, body movement, and the cultivation of natural awareness are used in a specific way to open the chakras. By focusing on the space within each chakra, a person can access the subtle energies and wisdom that reside there.

In Tsa Lung, the vital breath and mental concentration are integrated with particular body movements. In contrast to Indian styles of yoga in which the practitioner holds a pose with the body still, the Tsa Lung practitioner holds the breath still while parts of the body move in a prescribed sequence. Here, the participant uses the breath to enhance the flow of different forms of energy through the primary central channel and the two secondary channels on either side of it. Each of the exercises is designed to affect a specific chakra by using different forms of wind energy, known individually as upward moving wind, life-force wind, fire-like wind, pervasive wind, and downward-clearing wind. Each form of wind energy contains the five elements of earth, water, fire, air, and space, and the exercises direct these elements to the chakras and thereby brings balance and harmony within the body, mind, and spirit. Working with the wind energy also has a strong influence on the balance of each of the five elements. First, the seated practitioner inhales fully into the abdomen, leading the flow of prana up the left channel, down the right channel, and back up the central channel. Then, the breath is held while gently performing a specific sequence of body movements designed to open blockages and integrate the energy within the channels and chakras. After releasing the breath, the practitioner rests in open awareness. Although the exercises are not complicated, practicing them effectively requires a certain amount of stamina and resolve, since the breath must be held until the physical movement is finished. The psychological and spiritual benefits become more enhanced as continual practice takes the practitioner to deeper levels of awareness. Other forms of Tibetan Yoga are discussed in the section on yoga in Chapter 11.
Contact: Ligmincha International –
www.ligmincha.org

Transformational Breath®

As the name suggests, this form of breathwork therapy is capable of creating significant emotional, energetic, and spiritual change. Designed for personal empowerment, it was developed in the 1980s by Dr. Judith Kravitz, after she healed herself of throat cancer. Kravitz spent many years working in different forms of healing, including breathwork, and studying and experiencing other therapies, such as Rebirthing and Holotropic Breathwork, before she created Transformational Breath. This method recognizes that a person's breathing patterns—the quality of the breath and any restrictions in it—are affected by characteristic behavior, suppressed emotions, and life experiences, even some caused by circumstances at the time of birth. Transformational Breath is not intended merely to eliminate restrictive breathing patterns that can cause illness, but to clear and heal negativity in the subconscious mind and the cellular memory, thus awakening spiritual awareness and helping the recipient connect with her higher self and the energies and states she wishes to create. Intentional circular breathing and diaphragmatic breathing techniques are used to activate the body's wisdom and its natural healing response, which can stimulate transformative energy, increase awareness, and facilitate the acceptance of feelings.

The non-stop, fully connected, whole-body circular breathing used in Transformational Breath requires making only simple adjustments to the rhythm of the breath and, along with gentle bodywork and Acupressure can open up restrictive breathing patterns so participants can breathe freely in a flowing way, just as a baby does. Emphasis is placed on a deep, full inhalation, since this is how most of the nourishing energy and oxygen is taken into the body. Deep diaphragmatic breathing is considered an essential tool for treating disorders, and the therapy leads the recipient in stages through the process of developing this ability.

The Transformational Breath process can be orchestrated in a number of ways by incorporating a variety of elements. In addition to breathwork, tools used at some point in the therapy include verbal guidance, gentle but firm touch, music, sound healing (such as toning), kundalini exercises, body movement meditations, pressure work on certain emotional body points throughout the body (based on a special body mapping chart), affirmations, forgiveness exercises, laughter therapy, entrainment, and conscious invocations. All are designed to help participants relax, release, and listen internally, while increasing self-awareness, gaining better access to their fullest potentials, and raising their vibrations and level of consciousness.

Transformational Breath is generally carried out in a group setting, though private work may also be available. Sessions start with simple practices to help recipients analyze existing breathing patterns and then move on to instruction in the more specialized breathing techniques. Most of the breathwork is done with recipients reclining in a slightly upright, relaxed position. It begins by inhaling and exhaling through the mouth to open the lower chakra energy centers, which helps create a strong physical foundation; breathing through the nose primarily activates the upper, more spiritual chakras, and students graduate to it as their journey continues. As a team of facilitators circulates through the room, a watchful partner tends to a participant's needs while she engages in the breathing practices for about an hour. During this time, facilitators can apply nurturing touch to help participants surrender and release blocked energies and repressed emotions. Once a state of receptivity is reached, all sorts of sensations and feelings can surface, and in the final stages, positive affirmations help recipients embrace and integrate that which has arisen. There is then an energetic opening to higher levels of awareness and the self. Special practices

incorporate Partner and Mirror Breathing, Underwater Breathwork, counseling, and other forms of advanced breathwork. Transformational Breath can be very helpful for those suffering from a variety of chronic disorders, and additional sessions may be recommended for people with special issue or concerns. Workshops, group and private sessions, and training programs are now available worldwide.

Contact: Transformational Breath Foundation – www.transformationalbreathing.com

Vibrational Breath Therapy (VBT)

Vibrational Breath Therapy is a specially designed Prana Yoga practice, developed by Sri Bala Ratnam, that combines meditation on the heart center, the chanting of the primal sound of Om, and deep pranayama breathing. It is a regenerative process that works with the resonant vibratory frequencies of the physical, astral, and causal planes of existence to move individuals into a transcended state of being. By meditating, chanting, and breathing at a deeper level, a more natural state of health and well-being can be established.

In these practices, the sound of Om is focused sequentially into the chakras at the navel, throat, and brow, as well as into the neocortex of the brain and the causal energy bodies that are associated with the three planes of existence and their relative states of consciousness. The practice is designed to neutralize past emotional tensions and trauma while activating the heart center, opening the seat of the soul, and enhancing psychic qualities. A well-trained master leads the individual through this transformative process with encouragement and positive reinforcement. This divinely inspired discipline has been developed through years of devoted yogic training and is meant for those with the sincere intentions of looking inward for true healing.

Contact: www.adavic.org.au/PG-articles-vibrational-breath-therapy.aspx

Vivation®

As a young man, Jim Leonard always looked for a simple way of directly resolving emotional issues and achieving true happiness. In 1979, after years of study that included work with Leonard Orr (the "father" of rebirthing), he created Vivation, a physically pleasurable process for quickly healing any kind of emotion, pain, trauma, or experience. Vivation is a feelings-based skill. By connecting directly to the physical feelings in the body, negative thoughts about those feelings are bypassed, resulting in a much more honest and pleasurable experience. The result is an integration of feelings, bodily sensations, and life experiences. By embracing and making peace with every detail of life experiences, the recipient can naturally replace any internal turmoil with improved health and self-confidence, becoming immediately more effective, positive, creative, relaxed, enthusiastic, and happy. Although the healing process is not limited just to breathwork, it would not be possible without it.

Vivation is learned through seven sessions that each combine an hour of lessons and experiential exercises with an hour or two of coached Vivation work. The recipient is taught a number of elements that include circular breathing skills, breathing techniques to help bring body and feelings into conscious awareness, methods for complete relaxation, techniques to improve awareness to detail, and ecstatic integration. The process is intended to be enjoyable and allow receivers to quickly gain a new perspective on the entire human experience, thus clarifying what they most desire. As a straightforward way of producing integration, Vivation may be especially helpful for those who do not seem to have the discipline necessary for yoga and meditation or whose unresolved trauma has prevented them from progressing. After receiving the complete series of lessons, the client achieves autonomy with the process, and can be carry it out anywhere at anytime. It is said that there are no particular contraindications that would restrict anyone from undertaking this healing process.
Contact: Vivation International – www.vivation.com

Your Breathing Body

This compilation of meditative somatic breathwork practices was developed by Reginald Ray, who integrated many other spiritual modalities with his years of Tibetan Buddhist practice. Many of these ancient practices came through his own root teacher, Chogyam Trungpa Rinpoche, one of the first to bring Vajrayana practices to the West from Tibet. Some of these practices originated in India, where the enlightened siddhas and yogis taught them to laypeople from all castes of society. Ray's teachings, which are rooted in the higher tantric practices of the Vajrayana, are spiritual in nature and use the body and the breath as the pathway

to healing and transformation. The body mirrors the spaciousness of the universe, and the breath is like the wind blowing through this open space, melting away those issues that limit the practitioner's potential. The teachings are based on the premise that the body itself is the most trusted guide on the spiritual path and that breathwork can not only be used for stress reduction and better health but can also lead to deep self-realization. Meditation on the breath can calm the mind, increase nonconceptual awareness, and bring consciousness into a more spacious, embodied state.

Through his own deep experiences over decades, Ray has formulated, taught, and written about many liberating practices that use the sensations within the body as a doorway for self-awareness and spiritual awakening. To make some of these practices more accessible, a series of teachings and meditative breathwork practices has been compiled into an audio collection of twenty guided sessions that progress from simple initial practices to more subtle, advanced energetic levels of breathwork. The breathwork is done with participants either lying down or sitting in a balanced posture, and each of the meditative exercises can be done alone or with friends, spending as little as thirty minutes or as long as several hours.

The somatic breathwork practices include such topics as the ten-points practice, earth breathing, five levels of breath awareness, perineum breathing, threefold breathing, twelvefold belly breathing, cellular breathing, inner posture awareness, expanding the central channel, shamatha (calm abiding), dissolving with the outbreath, skull breathing, exploring the chakras, and the eight gates to emptiness. Each of these practices support participants in sensing, deep listening, visualizing, focusing, following, surrendering, and exploring their own embodied experience. Just reading about these practices will not have much effect. They must be experienced through active participation.
Contact: www.dharmaocean.org

A Collection of Specific Breathing Techniques

The breathing techniques used within the practices just discussed and many others as well have been developed simultaneously, consecutively, or separately over thousands of years in different parts of the world. Long ago, healers, yogis, monks, seers, gurus, holy men, and adepts from India, China, Tibet, South America, Egypt, Mesopotamia, and other places around the world created powerful techniques of breath control that would allow practitioners to improve physical abilities, overcome fear, heal illness, increase self-awareness, promote longevity, and attain enlightenment. Because of the close relationship between breath and the vital life-force energy called chi or prana, many of these practices can transform or transmute this energy, leading to the rejuvenation of body, mind, and spirit.

The primary techniques used by beginners are simple ways that help you listen to the subtle inner workings of your body and teach you how to breathe more deeply and continuously in a natural, spacious, and energizing way. Most are exercises that simply involve making small, subtle changes that help allow the breath and energy to circulate within more areas of the body. Some practices are also intended to help move the vital energy with and through the breath to places in the body where it can be stored and transformed. All are not only useful for simple relaxation or the reduction of dysfunction and stress but are also valuable ways of deepening your well-being on many levels. With practice, the subtle elements of breathwork become second nature, and with the energy that is generated, you can expand your sense of self, become more at home in the body, free the emotions, calm the mind, and nourish the soul.

Advanced practices involve more difficult techniques, often those used in yoga and meditation, that reveal much about the interrelationship of breath, movement, and posture. These often require much practice to master and usually should not be attempted until you are proficient in the simpler primary techniques. Many are intended as powerful ways of not only equalizing or retaining the breath but also controlling and raising the latent kundalini energy. Advanced breathing exercises are very powerful, and people can experience dizziness or loss of consciousness while practicing some of these techniques. Thus it's important to work initially with an expert teacher to avoid developing bad habits or using too much force. The keys are to relax, take it slowly, and be exceedingly mindful of the process. Remember that the life force dwells within the breath, and if you listen carefully, you may receive some inner guidance while doing advanced breathing techniques. At some point, you may find that the breath is actually breathing you rather than the other way around.

Practicing a bandha lock in full lotus.
PHOTO COURTESY OF WILLIAM GEISLER

The descriptions given within the following compilation of techniques are brief and intended to give only a basic sense of what is involved with each practice. The subtleties are best learned through a teacher. Because different instructors come from different lineages, you may find variations in how a technique is taught. In addition, there are only subtle differences between many of these techniques. Some are a specific part of a healing method, and others can be used as a complete therapeutic process in themselves. Combining several in a session is also possible.

Descriptive names are provided, sometimes with traditional names for each practice and information about its origin, purpose and the tradition of therapy in which it would likely be used. Although many of these practices come from ancient traditions, some have more contemporary origins and may or may not include elements of the older forms. No matter how they evolved or what system of healing uses them, these breathing techniques can be part of an effective practice that can benefit your health in a variety of ways.

Abdominal Breathing is one of the principal beginning methods for developing the slow, deep, deliberate breathing that is the foundation of breathwork, and it is part of a number of different methods of healing that include breathwork therapy. Though there are many ways of engaging the abdomen more fully in the breath cycle, this particular practice involves conscious control of the inhalation, a retention period, and a full exhalation. Besides improving the physical functioning of the muscles and organs involved in the breathing process and positively affecting the nervous system, this type of breathing helps move the life-force energy through the body. The abdomen is an important energy center in Asian medicine, so its condition is considered vital to energetic well-being.

Alternate Nostril Breathing is a calming yet energizing form of channel purification known in Ayurvedic Yoga as **Anuloma Vuloma**; a slight variation of this practice, done either with or without breath retention, is called **Nadi Shodhana**. This popular type of pranayama breathwork manipulates the flow of energy through the nadis, the subtle energy channels in the body, to create a balance between stimulation and relaxation. The practice involves a repeated series of soft and gentle inhalations and exhalations of equal length through alternate nostrils, with periods of breath retention. It is intended to balance the flow of breath through each nostril and thus to balance the energy flow within the nadis and between the left and right hemispheres of the brain. From the Tibetan point of view, this technique is used to lead the flow of energy through the right and left channels into the central channel, from which it can be sent to other areas of the body.

Balanced Breathing is the goal of many breathing practices rather than a specific technique. In this breathing style, the inhalation and exhalation are of equal duration and intensity. A variety of techniques, such as alternate nostril breathing, can help balance the breath.

Balloon Pumping Breath is a technique in which the reclining practitioner consciously expands the diaphragm while inhaling into the belly. The air, visualized as a balloon, is held for a moment in the belly. Then, using the chest and abdominal muscles, this balloon of air is moved back and forth between the chest and the abdomen several times in a pumping motion. This practice is used in many qi gong exercises.

Bandha Lock Breathing is the Ayurvedic three-part practice of increasing prana in specific areas of the body by contracting and holding certain muscles without strain. The prana is then available for dispersal to areas of the body where it is lacking. These pranayama practices prolong the period of breath retention and can be carried out seated in a centered posture or while performing Hatha Yoga asanas. The Jalandhara Bandha lock acts at the throat by tucking the chin firmly against the upper chest directly after the inbreath to extend the retention period. All is released on the outbreath. The Uddiyana Bandha navel lock involves abdominal lifts in the extended pause after exhalation. After several contractions, the practitioner relaxes and inhales slowly. The Moola Bandha root lock is performed by pulling up the anal sphincter muscle on the inhalation to retain energy in the perineum, a key spot. The lock is released slowly on the exhalation. A very advanced technique, known as the Kumbhaka lock, is not directed at any specific area of the body and is for adept yogis who already have control over the previous three types of retention. Each of these bandha-lock practices is repeated for a specific number of rounds.

Bell Breath is a technique that combines the soothing sounds of Tibetan bells with deep breathing. The frequencies of the audible tones created by the bells are meant to entrain the brain waves and heart rhythms. During the process, the individual closes the eyes and brings happiness to mind in order to help enter an alpha state. This meditative breathing practice, which is often combined with pleasurable visualizations, is beneficial for increasing subtle awareness of the internal body rhythms. The practice can be combined with energetic bodywork.

Bellows Breathing is an advanced Pranayama Yoga technique known in Sanskrit as **Bhastrika**. This powerful, energizing practice, which resembles a dog panting, is performed to raise kundalini energy by alternately heating and cooling the body through a series of rapid, rhythmic, and forceful breaths through both nostrils that pump the air in and out of the lungs; breath retention and bandha locks are also part of the process. While breathing, the emphasis is on the exhalation. This deep abdominal breathing practice is repeated many times and is the basis of other vigorous exercises that remove blockages, clear the mind, and stimulate the nervous and circulatory systems. A similar practice is found in both Chinese and Tibetan healing practices.

Belly Breathing is a technique in which attention is placed on the opening (expansion) and closing (contraction) of the abdominal area during deep breathing. Although it is primarily a simple sensing process used to expand breath awareness, there are many subtle aspects that can be incorporated into the practice. It originated in China, but has spread to other cultures.

Brahman Breathing is a yogic practice done while walking. Retention of the breath is avoided, and slow, steady, and deep inhalations and exhalations through the nostrils are carried out in rhythm with the steps, with the duration of the exhalation twice as long as the inhalation. This Ayurvedic practice is appropriate for older people or those who are recovering from illness.

Bhramari Breathing, also known as **Humming Bee Breath** or **Nasal Snoring Breath,** is a meditative Pranayama Yoga breathing technique that uses the vibrations of the sound created to soothe the nerves, calm the mind, and aid concentration. The practice is done while sitting in a yogic posture and involves inhaling quickly through both nostrils with a snoring sound and then making the soft buzzing sound of a humming bee in the throat during the slow, smooth, even exhalation, followed by a period of retention. The lips are gently closed with the teeth slightly apart, and the jaw is relaxed. There should be no sense of strain, but as the practice progresses, the volume of the buzzing bee sound should be increased. The practitioner tries to become one with the humming vibrations as they resonates in the front of the skull and fill the head, the heart center, and the whole body.

Body Breathing, also referred to as **Skin Breathing,** is primarily a visualization method similar to cellular breathing in which the participant imagines breathing in and out through the surface of the whole body as well as through the lungs. Physiologically speaking, an exchange of oxygen and energy does take place through the skin; in fact, a person would die if the skin were airtight. There are many variations in the practice of body breathing. One form asks the practitioner to follow the breathing process through both the lungs and the skin while paying attention to the exchange of prana between the environment and specific areas of the body. Two particularly important places to observe this exchange are the orifices of the head and the heart center. The breathing is done in a slow, gentle, and deliberate way, sometimes to the sound of music or out in nature. Extra attention is often given to the exhalation as the

breath and energy spread out from the body. The practice is helpful for consciously linking and integrating the respiration with the nervous system. It is also creates a powerful sense of harmony with nature when done in beautiful outdoor settings. This practice most likely arose in China.

Bone Marrow Breathing is an advanced meditative Chinese Nei Gong practice for cultivating internal power by absorbing cosmic energy into the bones. The intention is to cleanse and revitalize the bone marrow, replenish the blood, and develop power. The process channels energy with little physical exertion.

Brain Breathing, also referred to as **Head Breathing,** is a method in which the breath is sent into the brain to clear and energize the mind. This is a very subtle awareness practice with roots in Taoism.

Breath of Fire, also known as **Agni Prasana,** is an energizing pranayama practice similar to though different from the Bhastrika practice. Agni Prasana uses rapid pumping on the outbreath as the spine and body move and undulate. This practice is meant to charge the nervous system, and the tempo of the breathing accelerates as the session progresses. This technique is also used in Kundalini Yoga to help activate the serpent energy that resides at the base of the spine. A variation on this practice known as Kapalabhati is described below.

Breath Retention refers to the neutral phase integral to the yogic breathing process in which the practitioner pauses and holds the breath between inhalation and exhalation. This pause occurs twice during the complete breathing cycle and represents the time in which chi is absorbed in the body. Various techniques can be employed to lengthen the pause so that more energy can be absorbed. This technique is a primary part of Pranayama Yoga and other meditative breathing practices that invoke stillness and encourage awareness of the inner potential that is found within the space created by the pause.

Cellular Breathing is a subtle method that uses intention and visualization to absorb the external energy of the universe and breathe it into every cell of the body. The goal is to cleanse the energy fields, prevent energy drainage, and bring energy in for storage and circulation throughout the body. It is especially powerful when combined with Body or Skin Breathing and can have an energizing effect when combined with other methods of breathwork.

Centerline Breathing concentrates on breathing through the skin into the bones and the central energy channel at the core of the body. It uses the entire body with deep, full inhalations and forceful exhalations.

Central Channel Meditation Breathing, also known as **Channel Awakening Breath**, is similar to Centerline Breathing except that its focus is to bring energy into the internal energy centers through the three central channels near the spine. The practice is carried out in a variety of ways by different healing traditions.

Chakra Breathing is a fairly advanced meditative method of exploring the chakras linked with the central energetic channel by moving the attention up through each center. It begins by lying flat and taking deep breaths to release tension down into the earth. This is followed by using the outbreath to move energy down through the body to the feet, allowing divine light energy to rush in from above. Next, the practitioner sits up and breathes earth energy in through the perineum and permits it to radiate up the central channel to the top of the head. The focus then turns to each of the chakras, starting with the lowest and slowly progressing upward, entering the space within each chakra while breathing deeply into that area. At each center, the practitioner can explore how the potential of that chakra is manifested in the central channel. Once the crown of the head is reached, the practice is to relax into the space and feel the flow from the infinite earth to the infinite sky, noticing all the energy centers as part of the continuum. The practice has roots in India, although a similar practice that works with different energy centers is found in China.

Chakra Visualization Meditation is an advanced yogic breathing practice also known as **Samanu**. This visualization practice employs pranayama techniques to purify the nadi energy channels and the chakras. Samanu is a meditative energy-purification process used by very advanced yogis.

Chi Compression Breath is a qi gong method used to pack energy into the lower abdomen for storage. It is somewhat similar to natural abdominal breathing, but in this practice, the four stages of the breath are lengthened, and three locks are applied and held to enhance the capacity for energy storage. The whole cycle is more protracted and slower than many other breathwork exercises.

Chi Pumping Dog Breathing is a rapid-action technique that resembles a dog's panting breath. It tends to create heat that burns through blockages in the body and is often used in Reiki and other forms of energy medicine.

Circular Breathing is a term commonly used to denote the continuous, flowing breathing technique used to play certain wind instruments, such as a didgeridoo. However, here it refers to a precise, rhythmic way of breathing that facilitates better awareness and acceptance of a person's inner feelings. It is somewhat related to the Chinese Microcosmic Orbit practice. In circular breathing, the inbreath assists the rising motion of the energy, and the outbreath helps the downward flow. Simplified versions of this circular breathing technique practiced with focused intention and visualization can be used by a beginner. More advanced and involved stages of this technique require instruction and diligent practice.

Cleansing Breath refers to a Taoist practice that uses long exhalations to allow all the toxic waste and carbon dioxide to fully exit the body and to create more room for oxygen to enter on the inhalation. It can also promote relaxation by removing energy blockages.

Cobra Breath is a Tantric Yoga breathing exercise used to move kundalini energy up from the root chakra at the base of the spine to the crown chakra at the top of the head and thereby expand consciousness. This practice also helps rejuvenate all the organs and systems of the body. It is begun by sitting erect, contracting the muscles in the perineum, and pressing the tongue to the roof of the mouth. This posture is held while breathing in and feeling the energy rise up the spine to the crown of the head. On the outbreath, the perineum is relaxed and, with the tongue still touching the roof of the mouth, the practitioner contracts the facial muscles and makes a hissing sound like a snake. The more times this technique is repeated, the stronger the effect.

Color Breathing is a simple visualization technique in which the practitioner breathes colors into the body. It is believed that certain colors have a healing effect on parts of the body and that specific colors relate to each chakra.

Cone Breathing is a subtle balancing practice that focuses on imagining the breath moving in and out of the chakras through the cones of spiral energy that emanate from these vortices.

Conscious Deep Breathing, which can also be described as deep, slow breathing, is very much like abdominal breathing, which is incorporated into many of the practices mentioned here. It is primarily a beginner's method to calm and integrate the mind and body, but can also help create awareness of where blockages exist in the body. This practice is an integral part of a number of therapies.

Cooling Breath is a Pranayama Yoga practice known as **Sitali**. It is performed by inhaling as if sipping or sucking air into the mouth with the tongue curled and extended outward and then exhaling slowly through the nose. Another cooling technique, the **Hissing Breath**, known as **Sitkari** in Pranayama Yoga, involves inhaling through the mouth with the lips open and the teeth together while the tongue is rolled back against the lower front teeth. A hissing sound is made during the inhalation. This is followed by a long retention of breath and a slow exhalation through both nostrils. Both methods are intended to lower body temperature.

Digestive Breathing is a way of retaining the energies that enter the body through what is consumed by sending the breath down into the digestive organs. This Taoist technique is related to cellular breathing, in which the practitioner breathes into every cell of the body.

Dirgha Breathing is a three-part abdominal pranayama practice carried out while lying down. It involves deep inhalations and exhalations done in three stages that focus sequentially on the belly, the midsection of the rib cage, and the heart center in the chest. The emphasis of the

practice is on taking long, slow, deep breaths. If it is performed upward with the abdomen soft, it has a relaxing and cooling effect, but if done from the chest downward with the abdomen firm, it creates more heat and energy.

Dissolving with the Outbreath is a highly advanced meditative practice that allows a person to extend the outbreath into space and then follow it out, thus becoming more aware of the infinite vastness beyond the self. The practice starts in a sitting posture, resting awareness on the breath at the tip of the nostrils. The inbreath is allowed to come naturally, and then full attention is placed on following the outbreath as it dissolves into space during the gap before the next inbreath. Through a series of breaths, the practitioner gradually allows the self to go more deeply into this space and remain there as long as possible. Thus the self can be dissolved in the infinite space in which there is no breath.

Earth Breathing is a basic meditative practice found in various traditions that is performed to relax, heal, reduce stress, gain presence, internalize focus, and find peace. Earth Breathing aims to create a profound sense of letting go of resistance, leading to effortless relaxation, and can lead to deep spiritual discovery. The breathwork is done lying down or in a seated posture. The practitioner takes slow, deep breaths and extends awareness downward to the depths of the earth in order to connect with the earth energy and thus ground the body. This connection allows earth energy to flow up into the body. Keeping the flow going is the key to the practice. There are also more advanced and subtle energetic levels of this practice that work with the infinite warmth and essence of radiant love.

Embryonic Breathing is a special Taoist practice, also known as **Primordial Breathing** or **Umbilical Breathing**, that focuses on circulating the breath and chi energy within the core of the body. It is a relatively advanced method that strives to reactivate the electromagnetic circuitry associated with the primordial cellular breath delivered through the umbilical cord to the fetus inside the womb before birth brings air into the lungs. This highly refined meditation practice draws upon the primordial sea of energy contained within the surrounding electromagnetic field. As the exercise proceeds, the normal physical breathing process becomes increasingly subtle until it almost stops. However, breathing through other parts of the body and particularly the lower dantien center below the navel is enhanced as the direct connection with the cosmic chi is increased. This practice is possible only after diligent work to stabilize the mind and fill the body with vital chi. Practices such as the Microcosmic Orbit, which works through the central channel, may also encourage the vital energy to flow in a similar subtle manner.

Energizing Breath is a practice in which chi is sent into the lower abdominal energy center (dantien or hara) just below the navel in the area of the kidneys and stored there. The goal is to build up reserves of energy that can be used as necessary. It is often part of both Chinese qi gong and Japanese ki gong meditation practices.

Energy Gate Breathing is a type of qi gong breathing in which the attention is placed on the flow of energy in and out of the energy gates at the crown of the head, the perineum, the palm of the hands, and the soles of the feet. The practice uses visualization, intention, and sensing to activate, amplify, and sustain the stream of energy through the gates, and it is helpful for learning how to feel energy moving within. Natural abdominal breathing is performed as the attention is shifted to the various energy gates.

Expanding Light Breathing is usually done while standing with the eyes closed and the arms resting at the sides. The practice begins by inhaling slowly through the nose while vividly bringing to mind the sensations of a recent exhilarating life experience to recapture those feelings of happiness and vibrancy. On the inhalation and while spreading the arms out, a ball of light is visualized expanding and spreading outward from the heart in all directions. At the maximum point of extension, slow exhalation begins, and the arms are brought down a bit more slowly than the actual exhalation. Focus is then returned to a small central place in the heart and the arms are dropped completely. The process is repeated with additional attention paid to the feelings. As the exercise continues in a slow and rhythmic way, the practitioner opens up more and more and can sense the subtle breath and tingling energy penetrating the space within.

Focused Breathing and the one-pointed **Gazing Meditation** are similar practices in which the monkey chatter of the mind is stilled by breathing slowly while the attention is placed on a specific internal point, such as the third eye, or an external object, such as the tip of the nose or a candle flame. Its aim is to calm the mind, reduce anxiety, and improve the ability to meditate. This practice is found within a variety of breathwork practices from different spiritual traditions.

Fountain Breath is a simple, somewhat contemporary qi gong technique that can be used to mellow out and remove accumulated stress. It is done while standing with feet slightly apart and knees bent. The hands are raised in front of the body and stretched toward the sky during an inhalation that consciously extends up through the heart into the sky above. On the exhalation, tension is visualized as being released from the body while the hands are slowly lowered.

Ha Sound Breathing is a technique in which the practitioner makes the sound "Ha" while exhaling quickly. The practitioner usually performs it while standing in a relaxed manner with both hands on the abdomen and inhaling deeply. This internal cleansing method is beneficial for the digestion and for increasing energy, and is used in polarity work, some chakra work, and in the Huna practices of Hawaii.

Hong Sah Breath is a practice done to calm the mind. The practitioner first inhales through the nose while silently counting to ten and mentally repeating "Hong." The breath is held for ten counts, after which it is exhaled slowly through the mouth while "Sah" is repeated out loud. After a pause for ten counts, the process is repeated.

Kapalabhati, also known as **Breath of Fire,** is a pranayama technique in which the seated practitioner inhales and exhales deeply at least four times. The exhalation is produced by forcefully snapping the belly inward, whereas the inhalation is done by relaxing the abdomen so that the air can simply rush in without effort. This practice is beneficial in balancing opposite energies such as male and female or hot and cold.

Kidney Breathing is a Chinese practice done while sitting or standing and involves breathing into the area of the kidneys in the lower back, a place where much vital energy is stored. The areas in the front and the back of the lower torso fill on the inbreath and then relax on the outbreath. The intent is to nourish the kidneys and promote better functioning.

Kriya Neti Cleansing Methods are preparatory techniques used before breathwork. These Ayurvedic methods of cleansing the nasal passages enhance the effectiveness of any form of breathwork by removing any irritants and purifying the nasal structure. They also help purify the mind and improve circulation. Salt water, milk, or ghee are most often used, and they are applied in various ways to the nasal passages.

Kumbhaka is a method of breath retention used in pranayama practices to enhance breath control and create space for more internal awareness. There are two points of retention, one at the end of inhalation and the other at the end of the exhalation. Retentions are done for a specific length of time that is often extended as progress is made to more advanced levels of practice. It is often used in conjunction with the three bandha locks.

Kundalini Breath is a pranayama practice carried out to increase physical energy and enhance spiritual awareness. Although there are many different exercises, the following is a simple example. Standing with the feet shoulder width apart and the knees slightly bent, the practitioner raises the arms above the head while inhaling through the mouth. While exhaling quickly through the mouth, the arms are brought down to shoulder level and immediately raised with the next inhalation. Initially, the practice continues at a moderate pace for a few minutes; for further progress, the time and intensity can be increased. The practice is intended to awaken the flow of kundalini energy and raise it up the spine.

Lengthening (Long) Breath is part of many techniques that work on prolonging the breath. It is a slow, meditative breathing process found in many forms of therapy and practices such as yoga, Taoist breathwork, and qi gong.

Long Deep Breathing, a basic practice found in many healing traditions, is often taught first, since it increases awareness of the movement of the diaphragm. It consists of first filling the abdomen by inhaling the air downward and then consciously pressing the air into lower areas of the belly. After holding the breath for a short time while arching the back and expanding the chest, the diaphragm is contracted, squeezing out all the air. The practice is often done by inhaling and exhaling through the nose while in a sitting position.

Longevity Breathing is an advanced and specialized energetic Chinese Nei Gong practice primarily used by adept monks or advanced breathers to transform very fine levels of energy. This Taoist meditation practice can be accomplishing in a variety of ways, often incorporating visualization, chanting, and specific breath-holding techniques.

Lower Dantien Breathing is a form of qi gong meditation on the navel area that cleanses the energy and stores it in the lower dantien energy center. This breathing practice also works with energy centers located between the eyebrows and at the solar plexus.

Mindful Breathing is the guiding principle of most subtle breathing practices and is found in a wide range of breathwork methods. Mindfulness is basically the process of paying close attention to physical, mental, and emotional states, aware of subtle details and changes within. Meditating on the breathing process itself can encourage the development of self-awareness and when used as part of other healing methods, lead to energetic and spiritual enhancement.

Microcosmic Orbit Breathing is a fundamental meditative qi gong practice for awakening and circulating the vital breath through the energy channels of the body. The vital breath brings universal energy in from the earth through the feet and cosmic energy in through the crown, purifying the two primary energy channels in the body. Microscopic Orbit Breathing awakens the energy by using the breath to guide the energy in a circular flow from the perineum at the base of the spine up the governing channel on the back of the body to the crown of the head and then down the conception channel in the front of the body. The tongue touches the roof of the mouth to complete the circuit. The goal is to get in touch with the flow of chi energy, locate blockages in the channels that need to be opened, and ultimately release them. After mastering this technique, the simple act of concentrating on the navel area (lower dantien) or perineum will cause the energy to instantly flow through the orbit. Once this warm current of chi energy flow has become a permanent habit and the internal pattern of flow is assimilated by the body and mind, there is a natural tendency to maintain this circulation and dynamic equilibrium automatically. It is a prerequisite for higher forms of qi gong.

Moorcha is an energetic Pranayama Yoga practice of inhaling through both nostrils and then retaining the breath while applying a chin lock in which the head is tipped forward. The exhalation is done slowly through both nostrils. The practice is used for cooling and relaxing the body.

Natural Abdominal Breathing is a simple practice common to many forms of therapy, especially those taking the Taoist approach of feeling, recognizing, and observing how fully relaxed respiration affects the whole body. The practice is designed so that the practitioner maintains full awareness of the proper movements of the body during inhalation and exhalation. It is often called whole-body breathing because the breath is meant to fill the entire space within the body. Inhalation is done through the nostrils in a slow and smooth manner, engaging the diaphragm and allowing the rib cage to expand outward and the breath to extend downward. The exhalation is also done through the nostrils by releasing the breath in a long, slow stream in which the abdominal wall contracts inward and the diaphragm rises. A short, relaxing pause follows before the next breath. This is a good practice for beginners to use and is considered the way everyone should breathe throughout the day.

Ocean Breathing is a Taoist practice in which the standing practitioner breathes in deeply while making an "Ah" sound, stretching the arms out wide and visualizing the breath entering the heart. After a restful pause at the end of the inhalation, exhalation is accomplished in a natural way. These actions are repeated several times and can then be performed by breathing in through the nose without sounding. In the final round, the stretch is extended in order to open the rib cage by raising the arms and reaching over the head as if to greet the sky. On the exhalation, the arms are brought down, and the practitioner bends over from the hips and releases,

letting the arms fall toward the ground. This is a very calming and centering practice that could very appropriately be done on a beach by the sea.

Ocean, Sky, and Great Heart Breathing is a Taoist practice that is carried out to harmonize and amplify yin and yang and the three treasures of jing (earth), qi (humanity), and shen (heaven). It usually begins with fundamental exercises that help the practitioner become more centered and grounded. The practice itself involves a series of inhalations and exhalations done with the healing sounds of "Hiss," "Haaa," and "Heee," synchronized with specific physical movements. Each part of the exercise focuses on the activation and circulation of chi within the head, heart, belly, lungs, and central channels and is repeated a number of times.

Ola Breath is a technique used in various healing practices to reduce stress held in the body. To begin, the buttocks and rectal muscles are contracted and the stomach pulled in as the breath is drawn into the upper chest. Next, the head is dropped onto the chest and the entire body tightened while the breath is held. The head is raised and moved forward and a hissing sound is made during the exhalation as the body relaxes. The process is repeated.

Organ Breathing is an advanced Chinese Nei Gong technique done to help the practitioner breathe energy into the organs of the body, returning them to a healthier condition.

Palm and Sole Breathing is a method found in most Eastern traditions in which the practitioner concentrates on feeling the breath as it brings the chi energy through key entry and exit points on the soles of the feet and the palms of the hands. It is performed as a meditation in which energy is brought into the inner central channels from the earth and the sky. When divine heavenly energy is desired, the palms are turned upward; they are turned downward to receive the earth energies.

Perineum Breathing is one of the principal techniques found in many meditative and spiritual yoga practices. It is often included in breathwork therapies, since it is considered essential for providing an energetic connection throughout the whole body. The perineum, located near the anal sphincter, is a gateway to the subtle energy body and the earth energies. The breath can be used to move the subtle life-force energy up through the body to soften or dissolve energy blockages or physical discomfort. Perineum breathing can be used in a number of different ways, but awareness is always kept on the perineum while breathing up into the body. One method is to exhale body tension down through the perineum into the earth. In another practice, energy is breathed up from the earth while contracting the sphincter; the practitioner just relaxes on the outbreath. Working with the perineum also has a role in awakening the kundalini energy that lies dormant like a coiled serpent at this gateway. When released, it will rise through the chakras and unleash healing energy throughout the body.

Plavini Breathing or **Floating Breath** is an advanced air-swallowing technique of Pranayama Yoga in which the goal is to get more air into the belly without straining. Although the practice is frequently performed in water, it may also be done in a normal seated position on land. By maintaining a prolonged full pause and exhaling and inhaling slowly, a practitioner can float in water for an indefinite period of time. In either case, it is helpful in increasing the ability to breathe deeply in a relaxed way and can be beneficial when dealing with stomach and digestive problems.

Pranic Energy Breathing is a concentrated Pranayama Yoga technique to bring the energy into balance within all the chakras of the body. It is part of many practices that emphasize awareness of the central channel, chakras, and life-force energy.

Recapitulation, a breathing practice rooted in the ancient Toltec shamanic healing tradition mentioned in the writings of Carlos Castaneda, uses the recollection of repetitive emotional conflicts from the past to discharge residual emotional holding in the body that prevents clear action in the present. The actual technique can vary, but often involves remembering past events and recounting all the feelings they generated while breathing and moving the head and shoulders sequentially to the right and left during the inhalation and exhalation. The practice works to energetically bring elements of the recollected memories to the surface, where they can be processed and discharged from the body.

Reverse Abdominal Breathing is a fairly advanced variation of abdominal breathing that reverses the natural in-and-out movement of the abdomen during deep breathing. The abdomen is contracted inward toward the spine during the inhalation and relaxed outward during the exhalation. To further enhance the compression with the inbreath, the anal lock is applied when the inhalation is complete. This technique is useful for strengthening the respiratory muscles and for drawing the energy inward for storage. The practice has roots in both China and India.

Rhythmic Diaphragm Breathing uses full, deep abdominal breathing performed without pause in a flowing and connected manner while standing, sitting, or lying on the back or stomach. The practice is similar to circular breathing and is commonly found in Eastern healing traditions.

Shamatha Breathing is a Buddhist meditative practice, often considered advanced, that explores the qualities of attention by using mindfulness and one-pointed attention to enhance awareness and quiet the rambling mind. The breath is a very accessible tool, but once the practitioner is adept, other things can be used as the center of focus, such as a candle, a distant spot, or something as subtle as the vastness of space. The practice is usually done in a sitting posture with the eyes gently open, and there are four phases to a session. The practice starts with a series of breaths with the attention completely on the sensation of the breath coming and going through the nostrils. Once settled and gathering the perception of the breath at this location, attention is shifted so that 50 percent of the focus is on the breath and 50 percent on the surroundings. Next, a series of slow, deep breaths are taken with the attention on just the surroundings. This is followed by gentle breathing in all directions at once. The last part involves just letting go, with all the attention on the infinite space in all directions, working with any boundaries until you are lost in the vastness of space.

Shen Breathing refers to the subtle Taoist meditative practice of bringing cosmic or spiritual energy into a person's being. It focuses on sky energy rather than on earth energy. The practice emphasizes strong intention and employs visualizations.

Skull Breathing is a highly advanced practice from Thailand that involves the act of breathing into parts of the head. The aim is to experience the density of the energy in the head and its inner breath, which will enable the awakening of higher perceptions and a compassionate view of others and will allow contact with past and present karma. The practice starts with twelvefold belly breathing that uses full inhalations and exhalations accomplished while lying down. Then the practitioner moves to a seated position and repeats the deep breathing process with the focus on the nostrils. Once the practitioner is fully present to the entry and exit of the breath, skull breathing using the inner breath begins. The attention is moved to the center of the forehead, the third eye chakra, and a series of inner breaths that direct the energy from the nostrils to the third eye are slowly taken. Next, attention goes to the crown chakra on the top of the head and a series of peaceful subtle breaths are taken while simultaneously focusing on the nostrils, third eye, and crown of the head. Then the practitioner breathes into the center of the brain, falls into the empty space, and expands this open space so it fills the skull. The final step is done on the outbreath by sending the awareness and breath outward into infinity and downward through the central channel into all the centers and out of the perineum to the earth. In the end, there is simply a feeling of warmth, fire, and bliss as this space is explored. It is a very subtle but rewarding practice.

Skull Shining Breath is a Pranayama Yoga method of breathing, similar to Kapalabhati, which aims to cleanse the frontal part of the brain. It involves a series of light, long, relaxed yet deep inhalations and fast, forced, vigorous pumping exhalations through both nostrils as the practitioner makes an audible hissing sound and rapidly contracts the lower abdomen. Then, without any period of retention, the abdomen is quickly released so the air can flow in. This is immediately followed by another forceful exhalation. After the exercise is repeated three times, there is a rest period with normal breathing. This series of exercises is continued for as many rounds as possible to flush out stale residual air in the lungs and help increase lung capacity while cleansing the frontal lobes of the brain.

Small and Long Sip Breathing is a slow, deep, meditative technique found in practices of Chinese medicine that are intended to help stimulate and lengthen the breathing process. The practice involves the act of inhaling through the mouth as if the lips are sipping from a straw. This activity is performed for both long and short periods and is used primarily to cool the body.

Smiling Breath is the simple Taoist practice of using the inbreath and a smile to direct the inner smile into all the organs and parts of the body in order to alter the physiological and emotional state in a warm-hearted way.

Sound Exhalation Breathing is a technique in which audible sounds are made during a gentle, rapid exhalation to emphasize the release of unwanted energy or toxic waste. Different sounds are used depending on which feeling, organ, body part, or chakra is the focus. This simple technique is used in many breathing practices to increase vitality and dispel anxiety. Many variations of this practice have developed over the years. In a simple method, the practitioner taps the chest and makes a Tarzan-like "AAHH" sound during the exhalation. There is also an intricate science detailing the use of special vowels and seed syllables that are helpful in balancing the chakras. This technique has roots in Tibet, China, and India and is used by different vibrational healing therapies.

Spacious Breathing refers to the Buddhist meditation technique of whole-body breathing accomplished to expand inner healing potential. It develops and increases the ability to breathe into the three spaces of the upper, middle, and lower areas of the torso. In addition to simplified versions of this practice, there are more advanced versions in which the practitioner visualizes filling the spacious inner core with energetic light and luminosity.

Spinal Breathing is a Chinese meditative practice in which vital energy is drawn into the spinal area in order to benefit the nervous system and awaken the central energy channels that run behind each of the chakras. An assortment of healing therapies now use this practice.

Surya Bhedana represents an advanced Pranayama Yoga breathing technique in which a slow inhalation through the right nostril is followed by retention with a throat bandha lock; the air is then exhaled through the left nostril. The goal is to gradually increase the breath retention period as the exercise continues. This exercise is repeated to heat the body and remove impurities that prevent the flow of prana. There are several variations of this technique.

Swallowing Breath is a Taoist technique in which the practitioner breathes in, swallows the saliva, tucks the chin, and sends the breath down to the digestive tract, where it is held. It is intended as a way to collect the essence contained in the saliva and absorb vital energy.

Tantric Breathing includes a number of the intermediate to advanced energetic techniques mentioned here that are used in Kundalini Yoga and some forms of Buddhist meditation. Similar to kundalini practices, the science of tantra involves the awakening of the sleeping serpent (vital energy) that dwells at the base of the spine in the area of the sphincter muscle or perineum. Taoists describe this energetic point of origin as the sacral pump or the Bottom of the Sea. Tantric breathwork includes bandha-lock practices and methods of awakening kundalini and unleashing the energy in other areas of the body in a balanced way. The practices of tantra require a very subtle level of energetic awareness of the luminosity within the emptiness of self.

Ten Points Practice is a contemporary method, though likely with ancient roots, of finding the tension or pain and letting it go down through the body into the earth. This is done while lying down. The ten points are specific points of contact between the body and the ground. A practitioner can use visualizations and sensations in this practice; visualization is an act of imagination, whereas sensation relates more to an energetic felt sense, but both work on extending awareness. The breathwork is done slowly with the attention moving from one to another of the ten points of the body in contact with the ground and finishes by holding the attention on all ten points at once.

Tension Breathing is a simple basic exercise of inhaling while tensing all the muscles of the body, holding the contraction for a moment, and then exhaling while simultaneously releasing the tightness. It is intended to promote relaxation, remove tension, and allow the practitioner to feel the energy. It can be done while standing erect in a balanced position.

Threefold Breathing is a contemporary meditative process with three different phases that take on the task of opening the three centers in the body, expanding the breath in the six directions with multiple inhalations, and increasing awareness of portals in the body. Opening the centers is a simple practice of exploring the interior of the body by working with the lower belly, lower chest and upper chest and by feeling and visualizing each of these area as they are filled with the breath. First with the outbreath, the practitioner lets go of patterns of tension and constrictive emotions. Next, the focus is on breathing energy into the back of the lower belly near the kidneys in a slow, even, and full manner while placing the hands on the belly. Afterward, the breath is released back down into the earth. This is done a number of times to open this space as much as possible. Then the hands are moved to the sternum at the midchest and a full breath taken into the area of the heart, where all sensitive feelings reside. After breathing into this area, the fingers move to the upper chest at the collarbone, and the breath is propelled into the space near the spine. After a series of breaths at this location, this practice is finished by breathing deeply into all three areas simultaneously in order to connect them. The second phase of the process involves expanding each of these three areas of the body by focusing the inbreath in six outward directions and then working with multiple inhalations in a specific order and a deliberate manner. This section of the practice requires greater exertion. The method is to take one slow, deep, continuous inbreath, allowing a rush of energy to fill all the open interior space within the body before exhaling. The final phase explores the three portals, or subtle openings, corresponding to the three areas of the body used in the first phase, through which the life force can enter the body. By breathing into each portal, feeling the opening, and then exhaling into space, the practitioner can pass through the portal into the open space.

Transport Breathing is a highly advanced Taoist form of concentrated breathing that is used to transport chi to the organs and all other areas of the body. Its goal is to revitalize all bodily functions.

Tube Breathing is a yogic technique that focuses on bringing light into the energy center at the navel with the inbreath and expelling bad energy or waste on the outbreath. The exhalation can also be used to send good energy out to others in need.

Turtle Breathing, a very slow, relaxed, and balanced method of breathing used for energy absorption, is commonly found in Chinese Taoist Nei Gong training. It is sometimes accomplished while carrying out slow physical movements.

Twelvefold Belly Breathing is a contemporary practice in which focus is on the energetic subtle body within the physical body. The aim is to strengthen awareness of the nadi pathways and the central channel near the spine. This meditative practice uses mental stillness and vigorous breathing to help vital energy flow to every cell in the body. It involves a series of exaggerated breathing cycles with very full exhalations from the belly to remove stale prana and allow space for more energy.

Ujjayi Breathing is a body-heating Pranayama Yoga breathing technique, also known as **Victorious Breathing,** that helps the mind focus on the breathing by incorporating sounds made by contracting the vocal cords. This form of controlled breathing is a deep, steady, and slow practice with inhalation done through both nostrils while sounding "Sa" followed by bandha locks. When exhaling through both nostrils, the cooling "Ha" sound is made. Another bandha lock completes the practice. This exercise is intended to strengthen the nervous and digestive systems. Simple versions of this practice can be done by beginners; others are for more advanced practitioners. It is quite valuable for increasing awareness, balance, and spiritual focus.

Vase Breathing is a technique used for bringing energies into the navel chakra to ground the wind energy. A deep breath is taken into the abdomen and while it is held, the mind and the energy are guided down into the same area. Sometimes the "Ah" mantra is incorporated. It is part of the Tibetan Yoga practice of developing inner heat.

Vibratory Breathing is a principal Ayurvedic practice that uses many different healing sounds and sacred syllables, depending on the tradition being followed. Sounds are produced during a long, even, controlled exhalation, continuing until the lungs are completely empty. Practices most often use "Ah," "Ooh," "Hum," or "Om." The attention should be placed not only on the sounds but also on the feelings and vibrations that spread out and penetrate the body like a vibratory massage.

Viloma is an energizing and body-heating form of pranayama that focuses on the pause between deep inhalations and exhalations. It is divided into two stages: one pause after the inhalation and the other after the exhalation. The practice can also be combined with alternate nostril breathing. Although there are some variations, the practice is often done while lying down.

Vital Air Breathing is simply a term that describes the breathing in of the vital life-force energy for the purpose of healing, a technique used in some Pranayama Yoga practices and in other energetic breathwork methods.

Whole-Body Breathing represents the ultimate goal of many energetic breathing practices: being able to breathe completely in a full and yet natural way through every surface of the body. This ability is generally attained after practicing many other methods of increasing awareness of the breath, such as the Chinese Microcosmic Orbit or practices found in Tibet that use the three central energy channels in the core of the body near the spine. By engaging the whole body in the act of breathing, every cell and organ can be rejuvenated.

Breathe in the Wind

Since I've been a sailor all my life, it's natural for me to liken the breath to the wind. Your whole life as a sailor revolves around the wind and all its variations in force and direction, and paying close attention to the wind is like focusing on the breath, both of which are critical to survival. An old sea chantey contains the lines "Hi ho, the wind blows free, oh for the life on the rolling sea." These winds fill not only our sails but also our lungs with the fresh clean air we need to live and to function in harmony with ourselves and others. When things are variable with conditions in flux, our minds often toss, turn, and get restless. But when the winds come in full force like a deep breath from the inner ocean of our being, it gives us an immediate focus so we don't waver. The winds that blow around the planet are the chi energy of the earth, and the wind of the breath brings that energy to the body, heals on many levels, and blows away the mental cobwebs of confusion. The arrival of a fresh breeze, just like the taking in of a new breath, is a welcome thing.

CHAPTER 9
Energy Flow Is the Key

Energy permeates the universe, our world, and every part of every being, because it is the essence of all matter and the driving force of creation. It generates magnetic fields and holds atoms together. It sets in motion all activity. Its vibrations are manifested to us as gravity, electromagnetism, light, heat, electricity, sound, cellular communication, and the Internet.

However, throughout human history, energy has also been viewed from a spiritual perspective in which it is seen as the action of universal cosmic energy not only within the physical body but also within what is called the subtle body. This subtle energy unites the body and mind and affects the physical, mental, emotional, and spiritual realms of existence. It is the vital life force that we bring into our bodies every day, and we cannot maintain proper health unless it is balanced and flowing freely. This subtle energy has many names in healing traditions around the world—chi, qi, ki, prana, mana, ka, ruach, lung, pneuma, and barraka. When it is unable to flow freely, varying degrees of loss of function and ill health may result. Over the centuries, a number of methods of improving the flow of energy for better health were inspired by the wisdom found within the inner ocean of our energetic existence.

In humans, changes in this universal energy are most apparent when personal energy is accumulated at birth and dispersed at death. We arrive in this world with a certain amount of energy—our inherent energetic potential—but many factors influence our ability to make use of this vital life force during a lifetime. Our physical energy comes from the sun that shines, the air we breathe, the food we eat, and the water we drink. On the psychospiritual level, there are many different experiences that can energize us or can trigger a shift that enhances the flow of energy. They include moments of love or enhanced awareness, liberation from negative emotions and restrictive thoughts, acts of exceptional endurance, and times of spiritual enlightenment. On the other hand, energy can be depleted when we become physically exhausted, ill, anxious, depressed, sad, traumatized, frustrated, bored, or spiritually disheartened.

It's important to mention, however, that the same things that cause a deficiency of energy can be the impetus for intervention and improvement, and many of the body-work modalities of energy medicine and self-care yogic practices can shift us toward the positive by recharging and balancing our internal systems and expanding consciousness.

Awakening Awareness of the Vital Life Force

It is definitely easier for the pragmatic mind to understand energy when discussing how a car runs or how electricity powers the lights in our homes. However, it is much more difficult to conceptualize the subtle flow of vital energy within our bodies, which can extend from the cellular level to energy fields that extend far beyond our physical boundaries. During their lives on this planet, many individuals have had experiences, both in and out of the body, that strongly indicate the existence of this unseen vital life-force energy. Metaphysical experiences, such as those experienced by yogis, meditators, and medical intuitives, often come about through diligent, focused use of the spiritual healing arts. Revelations of various aspects and dimensions of the vital life-force energy can also come about through unprompted or spontaneous life experiences. They can occur in an altered state of mind, a time when the normal train of thought is momentarily suspended—moments of exhilaration, unusual duress, extreme adversity; a powerful sexual or loving union; when using psychedelic drugs; or during a near-death experience. These occasions can offer a life-changing experience that inspires a new way of perceiving the world around and within. But a very subtle incident can have the same effect—something that piques the imagination, changes a point of view, enhances perception, or gives new insight into the inner ocean of vital energy. Whether the event is quiet and peaceful or dramatic and emotional, it will be an opportunity to gain new awareness about the nature of existence.

Years ago, when I was receiving a massage from a favorite bodyworker, I had a profound, shaky, surprising, powerful yet loving, supportive, and awakening experience. About an hour into what was intended to be one of my regular two-hour bodywork sessions, I felt a very powerful energetic shift. I no longer remember what aspect of touch therapy was happening at the time, but I presume I was very relaxed. I was lying on my back when a sudden rise of energy came up from the "Bubbling Spring" at the soles of my feet. It quickly expanded upward to include my whole body. I was definitely caught off guard, and since it was so powerful, I cried out to my practitioner, asking if she realized that something amazing was happening and asking her not to leave me. She acknowledged my concern, and said she would make allowance for whatever followed. It very quickly felt as if I were levitating off the table as the rush of energy intensified. Soon I was crying and laughing hysterically. You might just say I had a very cathartic experience, but I found it so profound and powerfully energetic that I later called it a "prana burst," perhaps kundalini energy rising. My practitioner (who had experience with various forms of rebirthing) made some significant changes in her approach to the bodywork and became very supportive of my processing this very unusual and unsettling experience. There were many shifts in focus as the therapy proceeded that day. At one point, she worked with me on issues of forgiveness. In other moments, we focused on the energy in my perineum. I had very powerful visions and physical sensations of melting into another dimension of time and space. I later found out that this altered state had lasted about two hours, and that I had been on the table for four hours!

After I was slowly brought back to a fairly grounded state and had completed the session, I was still bubbling and vibrating with energy. Although it began to recede, I could intentionally call it up again to some extent for days afterward. I had another treatment by a different practitioner the next week, and the same burst of energy arose again, though not as intensely. Over the following weeks, I found I was able to activate this subtle energy through visualization and breathwork; I was becoming more familiar with my newfound friend. However, as with all powerful peak experiences, the sensitivity and heightened awareness eventually became more subtle and finally passed away. Although I found great emotional satisfaction from this event and my yoga practice was

enhanced, it wasn't until years later that I had any experience quite as powerful. Still, it provided a great release and a shift in consciousness that significantly enhanced my perception of life, energy, and spirituality. I am most thankful. This sort of experience might be considered a premature energetic awakening, yet it laid the groundwork for my really feeling subtle energy, and it gave me a glimpse of the unseen realms of my own existence.

Becoming aware of subtle energy and learning to work with it will not happen for most of us in such a dramatic fashion; it's often a slow process of learning time-tested ways of helping the body, mind, and heart experience its natural, balanced flow and the vitality it brings. When it comes to day-to-day living, cultivating chi is not intended to make us overly energetic, but rather capable of maintaining a state of equilibrium in which energy is neither deficient nor excessive. However, intense experiences sharpen our awareness of this vital life force, and actually feeling it arise in the body enhances our sensitivity. This sensitivity will be useful in all holistic self-care practices.

Physical and spiritual energy really cannot be separated. In children, the word *energy* describes not only its physical manifestations but also the exuberance and joy of a fresh new life. When we become teenagers, sexual energy opens up new dimensions of the word. As adults, embodied experiences teach us how our actions and emotions affect us both physically and metaphysically. As we grow older, life's trials and tribulations may sap our physical strength, but at the same time, reflections on change and the impermanence of life may rekindle spiritual energy and its expression in qualities such as wisdom and compassion. The alternative is stagnation. Sure, we all have times when our personal energy cycles into a low ebb, but without these periods of apparent weakness we wouldn't recognize the difference when we are energized and full of power. The more we can develop the ability to sense the vital life force and call on it for transformative change, the sooner we can bounce back and fall in love again with life and all the relationships that it brings us. By learning how to tap into energetic resources, we can age more gracefully and maybe live longer too.

The Divine Cosmic Connection

The universal cosmic energy that exists on the transcendent divine level actually pervades all life. It's not something far away in space, but the motive force that fills our bodies and all the other physical forms in the universe. The connection between the physical and the divine is occasionally imaged as something like a fiber-optic cable, but it is probably something more pervasive and omnidirectional that permeates all forms of reality even to the subatomic level. The connection is believed by some to come through certain portals or spirals of celestial influence that have a profound vibrational connection to a person's electromagnetic field and genetic template, which exist within the universal matrix that manifests in the ultimate realm of cosmic consciousness. A clear image of how this connection is achieved is difficult to come by and pretty much beyond language. Descriptions and interpretation come through the visions of intuitives and through the personal perception and experience of its effects.

The core of our being is a space deep within where we hold subconscious and unconscious energetic information and the wisdom that comes from our connection with the universal energy of the cosmos. Many healing practices, both ancient and modern, recognize that working with the energy currents within this core can align us with the subtle fields of consciousness that exist beyond the range of normal perceptions and bring in the heavenly and earthly energies. When the space within is open, cleansed of obstructions, and integrated with the energy fields, a deeper connection with our divine core essence and a clearer alignment with our greater creative purpose in life are possible. The effects of this cleansing and balancing are transmitted to every part of the body's energy anatomy.

When working on the cosmic connection, the focus goes deep within the subtle body—the energy anatomy that coexists with the physical body—often through a process that awakens divine love, higher harmonic vibrations, and soul purpose. The methods employed for this purpose may include engaging the subconscious, working through the luminous energy field, DNA restructuring, thought-field therapy, vortex healing, auric restructuring, multi-incarnational recall, soul retrieval, the ascension process, divine channeling, or light-body activation. These all initiate a transformative and integrative process that propels our consciousness beyond the realm of everyday life, allowing us to access subtle information that is otherwise obscure. Opening the doorway to the infinite space of enlightened potential

that exists within each of us can seem quite daunting and beyond the capacity of our seemingly limited abilities. However, there is really no need to be overwhelmed, for a connection to what at first seems unattainable can be accomplished in small increments by making some form of meditation, breathwork, energetic exercise, and somatic bodywork a more significant part of our daily life practice. At the same time, simple relaxation, letting go of all thoughts of striving, and living in a more loving manner will help us stay spiritually aligned, become more self-aware, and handle better what life throws at us as we move into these uncharted waters.

The Manifestations of Energy

The dynamics of subtle energy are very involved and exist on different planes from the material to the cosmic. The vital life force can manifest as resonant vibrations, light, love, subtle information, and transcendent forms of consciousness that bring into the physical body a sense of harmony, balance, and well-being. As studies in quantum physics have demonstrated, the relationship between matter and energy is mysterious and ever changing. All energy vibrates at different frequencies, and the highest frequencies are those of the divine energy of the universe. Different spiritual traditions have given it different names—the Higher Self, Brahman, Atma, Logos, the Tao, Nirvana, the Holy Spirit, Allah, the Omnipresent, the Great Spirit, the One, the Divine Light Body, and the Absolute Unified Field of Living Consciousness. Most of the time, we humans are unaware of the information contained within this unconscious realm until some radical event or twist of fate propels us into this sea of potential. It then becomes apparent that this subtle energy really sustains the whole of creation.

According to knowledge acquired throughout the ages by exceptionally intuitive people, the higher vibrations of universal energy are transmuted into a denser, more manageable form when it manifests within the human body. Personal chi is actually a relatively lower, less-refined frequency of divine energy that has crystallized in a human body, but this vital life-force energy connects us on a very deep level to the cosmic energy. The energy in the body, even at the subatomic level, is a microcosm of the divine energy that permeates and animates all life. Our primal attraction to the divine

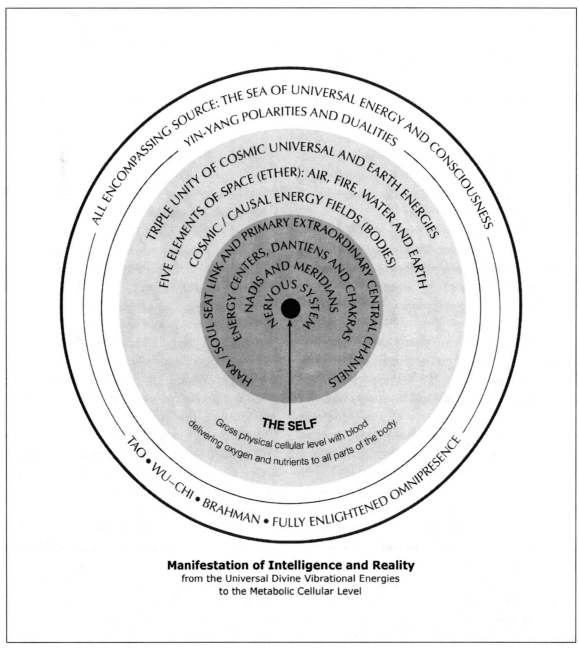

ALL ENCOMPASSING SOURCE: THE SEA OF UNIVERSAL ENERGY AND CONSCIOUSNESS

YIN-YANG POLARITIES AND DUALITIES

TRIPLE UNITY OF COSMIC UNIVERSAL AND EARTH ENERGIES

FIVE ELEMENTS OF SPACE (ETHER): AIR, FIRE, WATER AND EARTH

COSMIC / CAUSAL ENERGY FIELDS (BODIES)

HARA / SOUL SEAT LINK AND PRIMARY EXTRAORDINARY CENTRAL CHANNELS

ENERGY CENTERS, DANTIENS AND CHAKRAS

NADIS AND MERIDIANS

NERVOUS SYSTEM

THE SELF
Gross physical cellular level with blood delivering oxygen and nutrients to all parts of the body.

TAO • WU-CHI • BRAHMAN • FULLY ENLIGHTENED OMNIPRESENCE

Manifestation of Intelligence and Reality
from the Universal Divine Vibrational Energies
to the Metabolic Cellular Level

As small as we are within the great expanse of the universe, we are innately and deeply connected and need only remember, awaken, and integrate the magnificent subconscious possibilities within our inner ocean.

demonstrates that we remember this space of vast potential and that we need and desire a deeper connection with our source while we are on this earthly plane of existence. When we are drawn into the higher fields through energy work and become aligned with them, we can come to recognize a more transcendent and vibrationally refined level of energy that not only points to the existence of the divine source but also can lead to real transformation.

Depending on the information it carries, what it encounters, and the transformative practice being pursued, energy can materialize in varying forms and intensities. Knowledge from the ancient healing arts as well as new scientific revelations show that all energies, from the gross to the very fine, move by pervasive means that are not restricted to certain recognized pathways, but may show up as unique flow patterns with specific potentials. So we might perceive the flow of subtle energy as a coherent rhythm, a wave, a pulse, a synaptic signal, heat, light, photo emissions, or simply as vibrations. These flows can affect the nervous system, circulatory system, digestion, and metabolism in the physical body, as well as emotional, mental, and spiritual capacities. Where might the link between energy and the emotions and the mind be found? Certainly part of that path is within the nervous system, but perhaps not exclusively. Information contained in energy has a constant influence as it flows through us, and every aspect of our being, from subatomic particles to the higher energy fields that weave in and around us, contributes to that information. In short, life is a complex web of interconnection, much of it far beyond our conscious awareness. As our consciousness expands, this interconnection becomes more apparent.

It's fairly easy to see how physical energy enters the body with air, food, or sunlight. But how does the subtle energy that permeates the universe become part of us? On the one hand, there is a constant unseen exchange going on between us and the dimensions beyond our physical form, as if there were an umbilical cord of cosmic energy connecting us to the universe. On the other, the universal energy is already there deep within our inner ocean of innate potential. What we feel as personal energy is but a condensed portion of the universal, and our energetic consciousness is but a drop in the ocean of cosmic awareness. Because this universal energy permeates all life in an omnidimensional way, energetic healing can be approached from anywhere on the spectrum of its apparent manifestations—the physical, emotional, mental, etheric, or spiritual planes—and also multidimensionally. The energy we're predisposed to resonate with at birth, based on things like our genetic code, time of birth, and perhaps karmic influences from past lives, is subject to change throughout our lifetime. Environmental factors, such as solar rays, light, sound vibrations, and electromagnetic sources, have powerful positive or negative effects on our energetic state of being. And our physical status, emotions, personal relationships, and transformative life experiences have a continual, profound energetic effect that can block the flow of energy or transmit vibrations that stimulate the awakening of the vital life force and restore the body's healing mechanisms.

The Chinese, Tibetan, and Ayurvedic medical systems have the most complete conceptualizations of the ways in which the life-force energy actually manifests in the human body. The energetic healing practices within

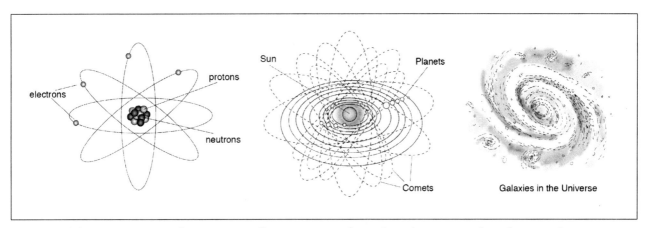

The macrocosm and microcosm of our existence, from the subatomic to the galactic realms.

each of these medical systems are grounded in their views of the qualities of subtle energy and its relationships with the physical. Although these practices come from different perspectives, the approaches to awakening and balancing the vital energies have many similarities, and their methods have been adopted by more contemporary energy medicine modalities.

In China, the Tao is a spiritual way ("way" is the translation of *tao*) or path modeled on the laws of nature and the essential elements of life. The Tao is considered to be the unified source of all life, which is pure, primordial, and boundless. Wu ji, the energy with which all things come and go, is seen as an alchemical tree of life and health, whose branches are the principles of the opposing yin and yang energies, the three treasures, and the five elements. The life-force energy is composed of the hereditary energy originally obtained at birth, which is present in the organs, energy channels, blood, and skin, and the lifelong energy received from food, air, earth, and nature.

Yin and yang represent the intrinsic polarity of energy, in which two forms are continuously balancing, completing and embracing each other.

The three treasures of the Tao, also known as the triple unity, reveal that the pure energy of the universe is composed of three different forms of energy known as shen, qi, and jing. Shen is celestial energy that comes from the heavens and all the planets and is considered to be the cosmic essence we are born with. It manifests in its own unique way as consciousness within each of us

and defines our true nature. Classical texts also discuss the possibility of absorbing harmonious energy from the universe and from the sun, moon, planets, and stars. Qi is the energy we acquire in life that comes in with the air we breathe. It is the vital force within the body's organs and energy channels (meridians), and supports the ability to function in an open-hearted way. Jing is the primal substance inherited from one's parents and is the vital sexual essence and the growth force underlying all consciousness within the body. It determines our patterns of behavior after birth. Jing comes from the earth, resides in the kidneys, and is acquired from the food we eat. These forms of energy give us the ability to protect the body, support and sustain movement, preserve the body's organs and fluids, maintain body heat, and support transformation.

Each of the three treasures is manifested within the five basic elements of fire, earth, water, metal, and wood from which the physical body is formed. These elements, sometimes referred to as the five phases, constitute not only the essence of our material world but also qualities of our inherent nature that need to be kept in balance. Each of the elements represents different qualities that affect our physical and energetic nature and ability to function in particular ways, and each is associated with a particular season, direction, climate, color, taste, emotion, sound, organ, and tissue. None exist separately, and true health comes when all are balanced and functioning harmoniously. In Chinese medicine, the five elemental phases are shown as a chart of cycles of production and conquest that demonstrates how the energy of one element can be

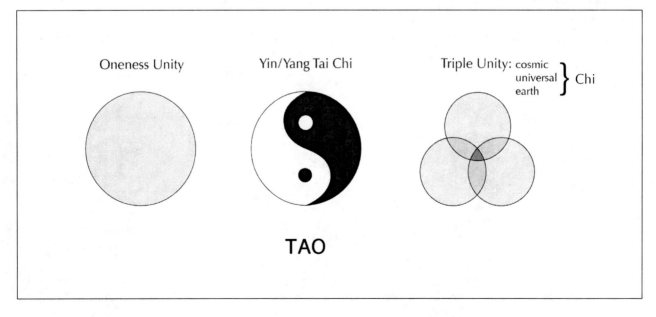

affected and transformed by the energy of another. In the production cycle, it is recognized that water produces wood, wood produces (feeds) fire, fire produces earth, earth produces metal, and metal produces water. In the conquest cycle, water conquers (puts out) fire, fire conquers (melts) metal, metal conquers wood, wood conquers earth, and earth conquers water. These relationships are apparent from close observation of nature.

The Taoist saying "As it is above, so it is below" reflects the idea that everything that exists on the heavenly macrocosmic level is displayed on the biological microcosmic level. Within the Tao, the laws of universal energy encompass a seemingly complex yet simple interrelationship between the flow of earth energy, the forces of cosmic heavenly energy, and the circulation of chi through the meridian pathways in the body.

In Tibetan medicine, the relationships and attributes of energy are a bit different, and the five elements are recognized as earth, water, air, fire, and space. Here, the earth energy reflects the apparently solid physical aspects of the body and constitutes balance and the feeling of being grounded. It is considered upward-moving energy,

since it rises from the earth. Water energy is that which is fluid, soft, comforting, calming, cleansing, and purifying. It is considered downward-moving energy because gravity makes it flow downward like a river to the sea. Fire energy represents that which is warm and inspiring, and it can manifest as the digestive energy in the organs around the navel. Air is considered to be pervasive-moving energy, since it exists everywhere in the body, and, like the breath, can blow away negativity, open, uplift and give vitality. (This makes sense when you consider how the winds of weather like those found at sea can free the spirit and cleanse the soul.) Space energy is that which is vast, open, and expansive. It represents the life-sustaining force that contains all other elements and is believed to be accessed through the heart chakra. It is space that allows all things, both positive and negative, to occur inside the body and to dissolve or be transformed.

In Ayurveda, the five elements are similar to those in the Tibetan system, except that ether takes the place of space. However, in this tradition, the vital life energy (known as prana) is said to manifest in five different forms, each of which has a particular way of supporting

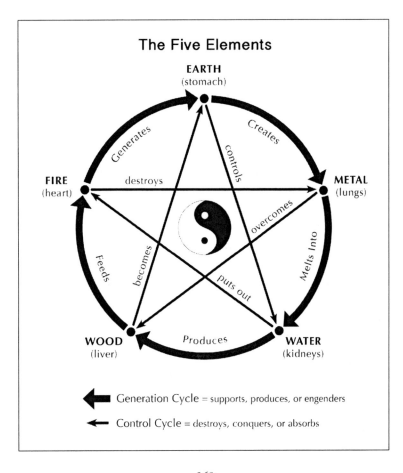

The Five Elements

EARTH (stomach)

FIRE (heart)

METAL (lungs)

WOOD (liver)

WATER (kidneys)

Generates · Creates · controls · destroys · overcomes · Melts Into · Feeds · becomes · puts out · Produces

Generation Cycle = supports, produces, or engenders

Control Cycle = destroys, conquers, or absorbs

life. Each of these vital airs relates to a particular area of the body and has a specific resonance, function, and movement; they are found within the different phases of the breathing cycle. Prana is the universal life force from the cosmos that is taken in with the inbreath. Udana is considered the connecting energy that affects spirit and matter and comes with the upward breath. Vyana is the spacious life force that gets circulated throughout the body in the diffused breath. Samana, the energy of bodily fire that helps digestion, assimilation, and metabolism, comes from the middle equalizing breath. Apana is the force that provides outward movement and assists in casting out waste with the outbreath. From the Ayurvedic perspective, all the currents of energy emanate from the chakras to sustain the force field of energy that our senses perceive as the physical body.

Though the perspective of these ancient healing traditions may differ, they all agree on one thing: the intrinsic connection of the divine and the human. This belief and the philosophy and practices arising from it have informed the many methods of healing that arose from or followed them.

Energy Fields and Energy Bodies

Gaining some insight into how the universal energy and cosmic intelligence arrive in all the cells of our body begins by looking at the energy fields that constantly communicate with and fuel what is called the human energy anatomy. These energy fields, which may actually be fields of living consciousness, extend from the cosmic to the physical level, and humans may very well be energy fields in physical form. The actual boundary between the human physical and energy anatomies and the energy fields is a matter of speculation, because they fluctuate as our physical, mental, and emotional conditions change. Since our link to the divine matrix of boundless energy and information is really all pervasive, the potential exchange of information extends beyond time and space. This is why distance healing is possible.

We may sense the vital energy that is inside and outside our physical bodies, but actually seeing energy fields is beyond the ability of most of us. Intuitive healers have given us images of these fields; they speak of radiant currents, vortexes of spirals and loops, light, or wheels within wheels that undulate with energy and create vibrations of harmonic resonance that can manifest

as both color and sound. Some say the fields are mystic golden spiral currents that emanate from the center of God. It may be that the fields of energy within the DNA (on the microcosmic level) and the galactic realm (on the macrocosmic level) take the form of a spiraling double helix that governs the progression of evolution. Another view is that the energy fields are whirling oval vortexes of energy that curve in space. These oval vortexes are also seen as electromagnetic resonance emanating from the center of the universe. Whatever the image, these fields of energy are believed to connect us to the omnipresent universal consciousness that contains not only the etheric matrix and genetic blueprint of all patterns of life but also the unlimited possibilities inherent in our as-yet-unperceived evolutionary potential. One thing seems to be true: as the horizons of modern science broaden, it seems likely that there will be a marriage between science and spirituality as it becomes more evident that consciousness is a form of energy, which is apparent in the simple realization that as we become more awakened, we become more vital.

The specific laws governing the undulations of the energy fields through all of creation remain something of a mystery, but quantum science has recognized the existence of arcs, helixes, spirals, waves, and vibrations that seem to adhere to the law of sympathetic resonance. Within the movement of energy, there appear to be wave phenomena that act as a system of feedback loops showing a deep interconnection between the subatomic and cosmic realms. In practical terms, this means that resonance is the basis of all form. The whole of creation can be seen as a dance of attunement, in which energy manifests as sacred sound currents, luminous beams of light, biophotons, and cosmic energies holding each other in a harmonic sphere of vibrations. The space that permeates the entire universe and all forms in it and makes the movement of energy possible may be the foundation of all existence. In any case, quantum physicists find that their interpretations of the dynamics of energy, form, and space are constantly evolving. What seems real from one perspective changes when contemplated from another point of view. So for now, we'll stop trying to conceptualize and just stay open to the infinite possibilities.

Although the universal energy can influence every aspect of human existence, there is a more direct connection to it through the energy bodies, which are energy fields that extend outward from the physical body; they are also referred to as biofields or auric fields. Each of these energy bodies is associated with an energy center in the subtle body, the energetic manifestation that is interwoven with the physical body. These energy centers influence specific spheres of functioning in the physical body. Therefore, any problem or imbalance within the energy bodies can cause dysfunctions or limitations in the areas governed by the energy centers. The energy centers, whether conceived of as chakras or dantiens, are part of the human energy anatomy discussed in detail below, but they are recognized as spinning vortexes of energy that can be portals to and from the biofields and energy fields beyond the physical form.

The radiance of the energy bodies close to the physical body can be seen as an aura of different colors by those with this intuitive gift. The biofield closest to the body is known as the lower etheric body and is associated with the first chakra near the base of the spine at the perineum. Expanding outward, the next energy body is the lower emotional body, connected with the second chakra at the sacrum. The third is called the lower mental body; it is related to the third chakra near the navel in the solar plexus. The fourth biofield is the astral body, which is connected to the heart chakra. This energy body and its corresponding chakra influence the ability to love and are important to overall well-being as the midpoint between the physically oriented chakras of the lower, less-refined energy bodies and the more refined, spiritual energy bodies connected to the higher chakras. The fifth biofield radiates even farther beyond the physical body and is considered the etheric physical template; it is related to the fifth chakra at the throat. The sixth biofield, known as the celestial emotional body, is associated with the sixth chakra at the third eye on the forehead just above and between the eyes. The seventh of the energy bodies is the ketheric or the causal mental body. It extends the farthest from the physical body and is connected with the crown chakra on the top of the head, which is considered a portal into the heavenly realms.

Beyond this seventh energy body are five other very subtle fields of energy called light bodies that have a deeper vibrational connection with the cosmic forces and contain more refined levels of energy relating to the soul's purpose. Each of these is said to relate to additional higher chakras that extend directly upward from the centerline of the physical body above the crown chakra. These light bodies—the soul star realm, the manasic realm, the buddhic field, the atmic realm, and the monadic realm—extend omnidirectionally beyond the human consciousness and illuminate our highest potential and spiritual purpose in life. These very subtle energy fields make up our innate capacity to become one with the universe and all the wisdom and insight it offers. Their conscious perception and integration requires a deep level of personal transformation, and only a few energy practices work with the subtle fields beyond the seventh.

The Human Energy Anatomy: Centers, Pathways, and Points

Although the actual flow of energy in each individual is constantly changing and will vary because of personal predispositions, conditions, and restrictions, we all have the same basic energy anatomy and the potential to open up all our energetic channels. Many ancient and even contemporary approaches to healing have a deep understanding of the flow of energy, but the most complete and detailed interpretations of the way it actually functions in the subtle body come from China, India, and Tibet. Japan and Korea essentially adopted the same perspective as the Chinese, but made some changes in how energy flow is perceived and influenced. The Near Eastern Kabbalistic view of energy is expressed in its Tree of Life, but no specific anatomy is outlined. Various indigenous shamanic or tribal cultures share the concept of a vital life-force energy, but again, do not provide a layout of energy centers and pathways. Contemporary healing modalities, such as Polarity Therapy or Eden Energy Medicine, have expanded the Chinese and Ayurvedic outlines of the energy anatomy to include the concepts of radiant currents, electromagnetics, polarities, orbs, and spheres of energy, but at the same time they share the same basic understanding as the older health care systems. Reflexology, which may have roots in Egyptian healing, speaks of a set of zones within the body that are associated with specific parts of the body, but this representation is not intended as a literal dissection of the pathways of energy flow. Recent quantum-science-based healing methods elaborate on particular pathways of flow and the energetic matrix within the human electromagnetic energy fields, but they haven't really created a new portrayal of the energy anatomy. So it seems that what developed in ancient times is still the clearest and most extensive description of the way energy flows and functions in human beings.

The Ayurvedic, Chinese, and Tibetan systems have certain similarities and some differences in how the energy anatomy is characterized. Ayurveda, developed in India, sees a primary core circuitry of central channels that connects us with the higher energy fields; a series of chakras, all of which are part of the subtle energy body; and a number of energy pathways known as nadis that contain an assortment of marma points. Each of these components has a direct effect on every system, aspect, and condition of the body and mind. Although healing energies can be activated by working on any of these components, the emphasis within most of the Ayurvedic healing practices is on the free flow of energy rising and descending within the three primary channels within the spinal area. From the Chinese perspective, there is less emphasis on higher energy fields. Instead, the focus is on three specific dantien energy centers; a highly developed system of pathways known as meridians; a vast number of points known as acupuncture points, acupressure points, or acupoints, which are used to activate a healing response in the body; and the circular orbit of energy through the vertical governing channel in a person's back and the conception channel in the front of the body. Chinese medicine does, however, share with Ayurveda the idea that the central channel plays an important part in transformative healing, although the particular practices employed are unique to each healing system. Tibetan medicine shares much of the Ayurvedic perspective, though it reduces the number of major chakras to five (and sometimes six) and employs methods stemming from its Buddhist heritage that emphasize the importance of purifying the body, speech, and mind. However, no matter how they diverge, all three healing systems recognize the existence of multidimensional realms of energy, core circuitry, energy centers, pathways, and points, all of which play an important part in our health, energetic state, and spiritual well-being.

Energy Centers Within the Body

The ancient healing systems all recognize the existence of energy storage or collection centers in the energy anatomy, though the way they are conceptualized is different. In Ayurveda, these centers are called chakras,

and there are seven major ones. Tibetan medicine combines the second and third chakras and the sixth and seventh for a total of five. The Chinese make it even simpler by identifying only three energy centers, which are known as dantiens. In each of these traditions, these centers are like spinning vortexes of energy that fluctuate according to physical, emotional, mental, and spiritual health. Many healing modalities help improve the functioning of these chakras by managing elements and conditions inherent within them; others work with these centers through their corresponding etheric fields. Each approach to awakening and balancing the body's energetic nature is viable and has a direct bearing on improving all our individual faculties and capabilities.

In the Ayurvedic approach, there are seven major chakras and numerous minor ones, each identified with a particular location in the physical body. Every one of the seven chakras has a number of essential attributes and qualities that directly affect physical, mental, and emotional behavior and functioning. Each governs certain aspects of consciousness and certain desires and obstacles related to particular behavioral characteristics. Besides the relationship that each of the lower five chakras has to the five elements of earth, water, fire, air, and ether, all have qualities that relate to a particular color, sound, organ, sense, shape, or plane of existence and are governed by a particular planet.

The first chakra, near the base of the spine at the perineum, is associated with earth energy and related to primal instincts, survival, security, and human potential. The second chakra is just below the navel. This center is linked with water and governs sexuality, relationships, pleasurable emotions, and metabolism. Above the navel in the solar plexus is the fiery third chakra, which regulates emotions such as fear and anxiety, personal power, growth, and identity. The fourth chakra is the important heart chakra, which offers passion, devotion, contentment, and unconditional love and compassion and is associated with the element of air. In the throat, the center of physical communication, is the fifth chakra, related to the element of ether. When the throat chakra is open, we can speak our truth. The third eye, or sixth chakra, in the center of the forehead just above the eyes, is associated with higher emotions, intuition, spiritual vision, and self-realization. The seventh chakra, the crown chakra on the top of the head, is the seat of nondual consciousness and can bring us into union with the cosmic forces of the divine realms. Each of the chakras is also associated with a particular gland.

Besides being connected to the primary central channel, each chakra includes cords, bundles, spirals, and pathways that spread inward through the body and outward into the surrounding fields of energy. Certain chakras, particularly those at the base of the spine and the crown of the head are powerful portals that connect us with the energies of both the heavens and earth. The chakra in the area of the heart has the capacity for giving and receiving love and compassion and acts as a bridge between the lower and upper chakras.

Just as in Ayurveda, the point of many Tibetan practices is to bring harmony and balance to the chakras. Although the tantric tradition recognizes six chakras, the usual focus is on five, which relate to the five forms of wind energy used in many Tibetan practices. (Wind, which is called lung in Tibetan, is one of the three primary bodily energies; the other two are tripa, or bile, and pekin, or phlegm). The root chakra relates to the downward wind, the functions of reproduction, excretion, and the element of water. The navel chakra is associated with the fire-accompanying wind, the function of digestion, and the element of fire. The heart chakra is

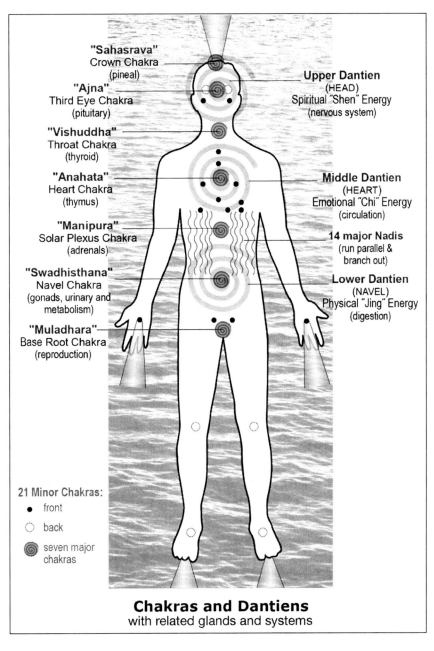

"Sahasrava"
Crown Chakra
(pineal)

"Ajna"
Third Eye Chakra
(pituitary)

"Vishuddha"
Throat Chakra
(thyroid)

"Anahata"
Heart Chakra
(thymus)

"Manipura"
Solar Plexus Chakra
(adrenals)

"Swadhisthana"
Navel Chakra
(gonads, urinary and
metabolism)

"Muladhara"
Base Root Chakra
(reproduction)

Upper Dantien
(HEAD)
Spiritual "Shen" Energy
(nervous system)

Middle Dantien
(HEART)
Emotional "Chi" Energy
(circulation)

14 major Nadis
(run parallel &
branch out)

Lower Dantien
(NAVEL)
Physical "Jing" Energy
(digestion)

21 Minor Chakras:
● front
○ back
◉ seven major
chakras

Chakras and Dantiens
with related glands and systems

linked to the all-pervading wind, love and compassion, and the circulation of the air element throughout the body. The throat chakra relates to the upward-moving wind, communication, and earth energy, and the crown chakra is associated with the life-sustaining wind and the element of space, which is the carrier of other elements. In Tibet, each chakra is also considered a psychic center and is associated not only with the five senses and five regions of the body but also with states of awareness. Each represents dimensions of wisdom applicable to our internal and external world. The goal of most practices is to disperse vital energy through the central channel to nourish and balance these chakras.

Chinese energy medicine works with three dantiens, also known as elixir fields, in the areas of the navel, chest, and head. They are connected to the conception vessel in the front of the body and the governing vessel in back, both of which are considered extraordinary meridians. The three treasures (primary forms of energy)—essence (jing), energy (qi), and spirit (shen)—reside in the dantiens. The Taoists say that these treasures are the energies of the earth, the human body, and the heavens with which each person is endowed when they are born into this world. The lower elixir field, behind and a bit below the navel, is the place where the essence energy of the earth is at home. It is associated with digestion and alchemically identified with the element of water. The middle elixir field, near the heart, is related to qi energy and the activity of the breath, circulation, emotions, pulse, and speech. It is associated with the element of fire, and its activities are similar to those of the Ayurvedic heart chakra. The upper elixir field, between the eyebrows, is associated with shen energy, the activity of the pituitary and pineal glands, and the nervous system. This dantien is alchemically identified with the embryo. The science behind the relationships between each of these centers focuses on the creation of harmony and energy flow.

In Chinese medicine, all the energy that is condensed from its ultimate divine form manifests in a fundamental way within the three dantien energy centers, each of which nourish the body and provide resistance to disease. Each of these three dantien centers reflects certain aspects of the emotions, the heart, and the spirit. In a way, they are like three minds within which each of the three treasures are stored. The upper dantien is considered the observing mind in which shen resides, though this

heavenly energy can also be stored in the heart. The central dantien is considered to be the conscious mind and stores qi, which relates to the air we breathe. The lower dantien, which is closely associated with the kidneys, is viewed as the mind of awareness and is vital to the storage of jing, or personal chi. Classic scriptures propose that jing, qi, and shen are so interrelated that they not only generate and cultivate each other but also can transform into one another. For example, practices that combine the breath with inward contemplation on the lower dantien help transmute the sexual essence of jing into the heart essence of shen. When all these centers work together in a balanced way, there is harmony and health.

The goal of all the Chinese Taoist energy work is to reverse the process of depletion, which is often caused by the demands of living in this world, by helping the dantiens work like burners, or furnaces, that purify and transform chi. The dantiens act as the storage centers that the extraordinary channels draw on for fresh energy to send to the major organ meridians. In the practices of qi gong, one aim is to gather the three treasures in the head to nourish the brain and raise the spirit energy.

Though the actual location, fundamental aspects, and qualities of these centers may be somewhat different from that of the chakras, the principle of replenishing the body, mind, and spirit is essentially the same. No matter what form of self-directed energy work, bodywork, or meditation is used, it's always possible to improve balance and harmony physically and energetically. When analyzing the seemingly different explanations and positions of the dantiens and the chakras, it becomes evident that there is no conflict between the two. If they are superimposed, it is apparent that the Chinese just created a simpler view than the Ayurvedic concept of the chakra centers, one that focuses on the head, heart, and belly as the most significant parts of our energetic anatomical makeup. (Coincidentally, Tibetan medicine sees these areas as three mental centers, each with its own type of consciousness.) The navel or second chakra appears to correspond to the lower dantien, the heart or fourth chakra to the central dantien, and the sixth chakra in the forehead to the upper dantien.

Because there is a deep, intrinsic energetic interconnection of the body, chakras, and energy fields, any modality or practice that focuses on healing by working on any of these dimensions will in turn automatically have a beneficial effect on the others. Therefore, any form of etheric energy-field work such as Reiki, Pranic Healing, or Polarity Therapy can be just as energetically effective as those that work with manual contact directly on the body. Personal self-care practices such as yoga and qi gong can cultivate a balanced flow of energy that permeates the energy centers, nervous system, and all the organs and cells of the physical body.

Pathways for the Flow of Energy

In the optimally functioning subtle body, the flow from the universal through the biofields to the cellular is balanced, open, and harmonious. The energy flows through pathways in the body like water running down to the sea. Some of these pathways are major rivers, whereas others are smaller streams or creeks. These rivers are part of a great network that loops throughout the body, circulating subtle energy to all its organs, tissues, and cells. Each organ uses this energy to carry out its primary function. Those in the upper part of the body provide for respiration and circulation, those in the middle of the body digest and assimilate, and organs in the lower body store energy and remove waste. The energy that circulates through the organs is also a form of cellular communication, connecting all the organs in the fundamental work of sustaining life.

The pathways are interconnected, so the condition of the flow in one can affect the flow in others. A blockage can cause energy to back up and prevent sufficient energy from moving forward; a weak organ that is unable to accept energy can create a dam. Just as in a river, the flow of energy can be dammed, blocked, and collect in pools, and any disruption in the flow can lead to detrimental physical symptoms. As with water, the flow of energy can change depending on the condition and behavior of the structures that it encounters, as well as with the cycles, tides, and natural rhythms present in the time of day, the season, or the weather. In addition, this flow of vital energy is affected by a person's mood, temperament, emotional state, and mental attitude. It has certain characteristic qualities, such as direction, force, rate, rhythm, and pulse, that can be recognized and manipulated. In addition, there are certain points along the pathways where energy tends to collect and where the flow can be influenced and balanced. They are similar to switches, and when certain adjustments are made there, the channel opens, and the current resumes its flow in a smooth and balanced way.

In Chinese medicine, the subtle pathways for the flow of chi are known as meridians. This extensive network, which runs through the whole body, is composed of twelve regular meridians, eight extraordinary meridians, and a number of connecting vessels and divergent channels, along with muscle and cutaneous channels. Most of them can be accessed through specific acupuncture or acupressure points, which can be used to influence the flow of chi for energetic healing purposes.

Each of the twelve primary regular meridians has a close relationship with a specific organ in the body, and they are organized into pairs of yin and yang channels that pass through both surface (exterior) and deep (interior) areas on both sides of the body, with chi flowing through them in a specific direction to the associated organ. For the most benefit, any massage or manipulation done on the meridians should follow the direction of the chi flow.

The eight extraordinary meridians, sometimes referred to as the strange flows, include a pair—the governing and conception channels—that are often referred to as the great central channel, for they play a significant role in certain powerful energy healing practices, such as the Microcosmic Orbit, that are vital to the well-being of the body and spirit. Since the governing and conception channels, which actually have more than one primary pathway, intersect at specific points in the pelvis and the head, these two circuits of energy are integrally connected. The other six extraordinary meridians are the penetrating channel, the girdling channel, two yin and yang linking channels, and two yin and yang heel channels. The extraordinary meridians play a different role from that of the regular meridians since they are not related to specific organs. They primarily function as a reservoir of energy for the regular meridians. Rather than providing a continuous, interconnected flow of chi, they allow it to flow in various directions between areas of excess and deficiency. When chi is abundant in the regular meridians, it overflows into the extraordinary meridians and then is returned to the regular meridians when needed. Except for the governing and conception channels, the extraordinary meridians do not have their own acupoints, but they do share some with the regular meridians.

The governing channel, referred to as the great father flow, runs from the tailbone and perineum up the back near the spine to the crown of the head. It regulates the six regular yang meridians. The conception channel, called the great mother flow, runs down the front of the body from the crown of the head through the lower energy center at the navel to the perineum and regulates the six regular yin meridians. Both of them are considered to be psychic meridians because of their close connection with the breath and the inflow of energies from the earth and the cosmos. The flow of chi in these channels is greatly affected by energy medicine, advanced forms of breathwork, and certain types of meditation. Releasing chi and directing it through these two channels generally has a calming, centering effect while also enhancing vitality.

Among the other extraordinary channels is the penetrating meridian in the abdomen, which helps store chi and has a regulating effect on the twelve primary meridians and prenatal and postnatal chi. The girdling channel, also called the belt channel, is the only horizontal meridian in the body. It encircles the waist, and works to balance the vertical flow of chi in the body. The two yin and yang linking meridians are known as the great regulator channels, and they control the energy that nourishes the body and defends against external pathogens that could cause disease. The paired yin and yang heel meridians primarily control physiological functions involving the ascent of fluids, the descent of chi, and general muscular activity.

A network of connecting vessels, branching off from the twelve regular meridians at specific acupoints, is a subsystem that helps distribute chi and blood throughout the body. Divergent channels also split off from the regular meridians to disperse chi to the face and head and to integrate other unconnected parts of the body into the overall meridian system. Muscle channels are groups of muscles, tendons, and ligaments that follow the paths of the regular meridians, and cutaneous channels are regions on the skin where superficial connecting vessels help provide positive chi that will repel disease-causing pathogens.

The beginning and ending points of the twelve regular meridians are generally in the hands and feet. However, the actual pathways taken throughout the body by each meridian is often a route that zigs and zags at different locations. It seems odd, though not impossible,

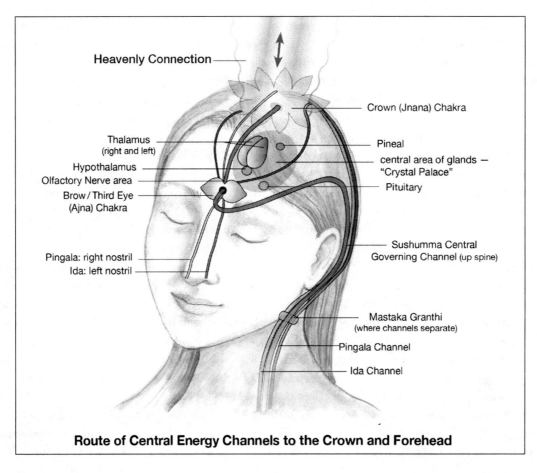

Heavenly Connection

Crown (Jnana) Chakra

Thalamus (right and left)

Hypothalamus
Olfactory Nerve area
Brow / Third Eye (Ajna) Chakra

Pineal

central area of glands — "Crystal Palace"

Pituitary

Pingala: right nostril
Ida: left nostril

Sushumma Central Governing Channel (up spine)

Mastaka Granthi (where channels separate)

Pingala Channel

Ida Channel

Route of Central Energy Channels to the Crown and Forehead

that energy would turn sharp corners, and therefore questions can arise about the accuracy of this portrayal of the pathways. Some practitioners, including Tetsuro Saito, the developer of Shinso Shiatsu, propose that meridians are not fixed but move and change size, quality, and location depending on the individual's actual energetic, mental, emotional, and spiritual state. These kinds of changes may also be true for the energy centers and energy fields. It's also possible that there are subtle kinds of energetic flow that are yet to be discovered. Even if the correct portrayal of these pathways is subject to change, the reality is that the activation and balancing of the flow of chi along these pathways is an established practice that has proven effective for many, many years. In each modality of Acupressure and Acupuncture, as well as self-care practices such as qi gong, the organs, body parts, and dantien centers can be affected in a positive way by cultivating energy that enhances vitality.

The pathways in the energy anatomy portrayed within the Ayurvedic system are also quite extensive, but are displayed somewhat differently. Here, the circulation of vital life-force energy, referred to as prana, flows through a vast assortment of nadi channels, fourteen of which are considered primary. These channels do not necessarily correspond to the pathways found in the Chinese system of meridians. Although the great central channel (sushuma) and the two side channels (pingala and ida) all extend from the perineum to head, as do the great central channels portrayed by the Chinese system, their actual pathway is imaged as undulating around and through the chakras. Chinese energy work focuses on cultivating the vital life-force energy to enhance longevity and the possibility of attaining immortality, whereas the Indian system concentrates on practices for purification and spiritual enlightenment, but each acknowledges the powerful energetic connections and possibilities inherent in these central channels.

The Ayurvedic pathways called nadis are intimately connected with the central channels as in Chinese medicine, but also with seven major chakras rather than three dantiens. The qualities and attributes associated with the chakras are more involved than those associated with the dantiens; however, the science behind the nadis channels and their marma points is less extensive than in the Chinese system. The emphasis of the various healing practices within the Ayurvedic system is on central core channels and the flow of chakra-cleansing energy within

them. This is reflected in the many meditative yogic practices that concentrate on the gate openings at the ends of the central channels and energy points at nerve intersections associated with the chakras. The detailed mapping of the pathways and points in the Chinese meridian system is not seen in the Ayurvedic approach, and there are definite differences in the number and distribution of the various pathways throughout the body.

Many of the practices used in Tantra or Kundalini Yoga, which were once kept as guarded secrets, employ techniques to awaken the dormant vital life-force energy and raise it up the central channel to cleanse the chakras and lead to heightened consciousness. In all of these practices, the universal energy can be accessed from the heavens and earth, directed through the energy centers, and distributed to different areas of body for the purpose of replenishment and nourishment. The actual way the energy circulates and the extent to which these practices use energy seems limitless and often goes beyond just the physical, mental, and emotional level to enhance our capacity to be more enlightened, spiritual beings.

In Tibetan energy medicine, which shares more of the Ayurvedic principles than those of the Chinese, there is little talk about meridians as such, although their existence is acknowledged. Most of the focus is on the central channel and practices that affect the chakras and the body, mind, and speech. In Tibetan energy medicine, the main central channel (known as the avadhuti or bu ma), recognized as the color blue, is accompanied by the white female channel (lalana or kyang ma) with life-producing and purifying lunar energies and the red male channel (rasana or roma) with obstacle-destroying solar energies. The red and white channels are on different sides in men and women. Each is considered equally honorable and an essential part of human nature, which has male and female qualities. Both side channels play a vital role in manifesting different forces and qualities that have a direct bearing on consciousness and behavior. All three run parallel to one another just in front of the spine; each runs through the chakras, and purified vital energy is circulated and dispersed in a particular manner through each of these channels to balance the chakras and enhance self-awareness. Unlike Chinese practices, there is very little use for or talk of other pathways in the body.

There are many similarities in how the Tibetan, Chinese, and Ayurvedic systems conceptualize the central channels, the connecting pathways, and actual path and direction of energy flow, but each taps into and circulates the energy in its own way. For example, in Chinese practices such as the Microcosmic Orbit, the energy runs in a circular fashion up the governing channel in the back and down the conception channel in the front. In the Tibetan practice of Tsa Lung energy rises up the left channel, descends down the right channel, and then rises up the central channel. In the Ayurvedic practice of Kundalini Yoga, the focus is simply on bringing dormant vital energy up the central channel from the perineum to the chakras and the crown of the head. However, the different practices of the three healing systems all have the same goal of cultivating and distributing more vital energy.

Energetic Pressure Points on the Body

There are a variety of therapeutically useful points where energy can be easily accessed by the hands of a practitioner, whether through an ancient or modern healing modality. The most comprehensive representation of these points is contained in Chinese medicine, which uses specific points along the various meridians that are related to the organs, tissue, body parts, and systems. The nature and effect of a point is determined by its exact location and the meridian it is on; special groupings are characterized by a particular relationship with a meridian. More than 2,000 points have been established, of which about 756 are used occasionally and around 250 are used frequently. When dealing with a specific problem, only a few points may be used during a treatment, but this varies according to many interrelated factors. As might be expected, expertise in choosing the correct point requires extensive training and many hours of practice.

The names of the points may reflect qualities, location, and ways in which the points are used. Each point originally had several different names, which, though exotic and enticing, often led to confusion about a point's correct location within the complex meridian system. After a numeric code was established, it became easier to look at charts that plotted point locations and determine which were most useful.

Since many of these points are about 1 to 3 mm in size and close to the surface of the body, often in a depression the size of a dime, access is usually quite easy. However, some are less obvious and may require the practitioner to explore the area to identify the exact location. All of the points are influenced by some form of manual contact. Although a certain amount of pressure is most commonly used, these points can be held, tapped, rubbed, compressed, stretched, and manipulated in ways that stimulate the balanced flow of energy. The chi accessed through these points can be tonified through firm, stationary pressure; dispersed by moving the pressure in clockwise or counterclockwise rotations; or calmed with light pressure. In Acupuncture, the angle at which the needles are inserted creates the same effects, and it is considered the most precise method for improving the flow of chi. Instead of needles, points may also be activated by light, magnets, crystals, moxibustion, sound vibrations, and electrical impulses.

Since the true cause of a problem in one part of the body may actually be in a different area, the choice of points used in Acupuncture therapy doesn't always seem to make sense; however, even if it appears counterintuitive, the choice is based on careful analysis. In the context of traditional Acupuncture, two points are often chosen, one close to the problem area and the other distant from it. For example, disease in the upper part of the body can be treated by selecting points in the lower part and vice versa. The yuan source points and luo connecting points are often used together; when treating deficient energy, a practitioner tonifies the yuan source point and disperses the luo connecting point. When there is excess energy, the process is reversed. However, the complete science of point work goes far beyond this general discussion, and the actual treatment and selection of points is based on the specific nature of the dysfunction or disease as it is present within a particular individual.

Certain forms of Acupressure, Acupuncture, and other energy-based modalities practiced in Japan, Korea, and other Asian countries may emphasize using only a limited number of the many available points, sometimes as few as twenty. Some use only specific points on just the extraordinary meridians or only points on the hands, joints, feet, spine, neck, head, or face. (The ears, tongue, face, and feet actually contain points that correspond with all the organs of the body.) There are also traditional energetic healing modalities, such as Japanese Shiatsu, that work directly on the meridians themselves rather than just through the points.

Points employed by other systems and modalities of healing may or may not intersect with points employed in Chinese Acupuncture and Acupressure. For example, the marma points of Ayurvedic medicine are on somewhat different channels of energy and are generally larger in size. Contemporary modalities such as Polarity Therapy, Trigger Point Therapy, Kured Therapy, Network Spinal Analysis, Craniosacral Therapy, Reflexology, Source Point Therapy, Touch for Health, the Emotional Freedom Technique, and certain forms of Applied Kinesiology have their own schematic representations and maps of the locations of points that will affect holding patterns and areas of tension. Many of the points trigger a healing reflex or energetic connection in the body that can relieve pain, remove blockages, and

increase the flow of fluids within the various circulatory systems. Some points are even found within the energy fields close to the surface of the body; they represent open portals through which the universal energies can enter the physical body.

When analyzing the various points on the body used by both traditional and contemporary modalities, it becomes apparent that certain groupings reflect a particular quality or purpose. The following list certainly does not cover all of the acupoints or reflex points, but simply provides an overview of the different basic types and their primary attributes.

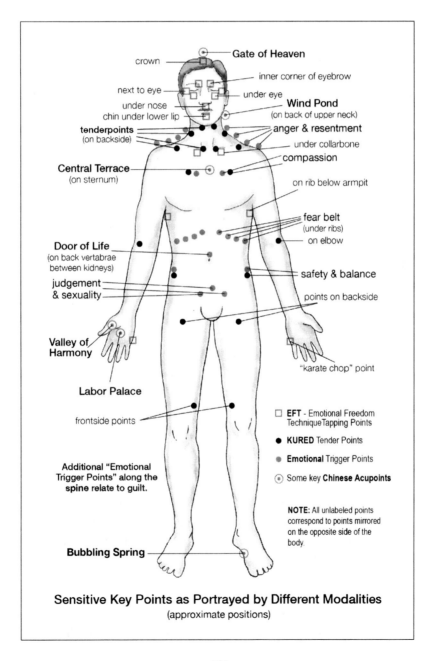

Sensitive Key Points as Portrayed by Different Modalities
(approximate positions)

- Acupoints – This is shorthand for what are also called acupuncture points, acupressure points, chi points, channel points, acu-holding points, or pressure points. They represent the myriad points along the meridians to which needles, hand pressure, or other implements are applied to influence the flow of vital energy.

- Alarm points – Although these twelve acupoints (called mu points) are located along a meridian on the front of the body that is not itself associated with any organs, they are useful for diagnostic purposes, because when they are painful, they indicate that chi has collected near dysfunctional organs in the chest and abdomen. Also in this category of alarm points are ashi points, which are not necessarily acupoints, but places where pain indicates an energy deficiency. Kured Therapy employs different tender points that correspond to typically sensitive areas of the body.

- Blockage points – Although this term can simply refer to acupoints that are blocked, it is also represents the hua tuo points (called jia and ji) on either side of the spinal column where nerves intersect. Each of these points connects through the nervous system to a specific organ, and when they are painful, they can often point out locations where nerve blockages exist.

- Cleft-xi points – These refer to the sixteen acupoints used to identify the condition of chi by observing the appearance of the skin at those locations. They swell and become sensitive when excess chi is present and are indented and painful when chi is depleted.

- Command points –These pertain to eight acupoints that are effective for treating the abdomen, back, head, and face.

- Confluent points – These are acupoints on the extremities that connect with either the eight extraordinary meridians or with the twelve regular meridians. Some of these points are very influential and can be used to treat disease in the corresponding tissues and organs.

- Connecting points – These are luo acupoints located where meridian channels split off in different directions. Fifteen points along the regular meridians act as switching stations to move energy between places where it is excessive or deficient. Connecting points are often used in diagnosis and have a strong effect when manipulated.

- Cranial points – These are points on the skull that are effective in enhancing the flow of cerebral fluids. They are often used in Craniosacral Therapy. Certain cranial points are also acupoints that are manipulated by other modalities to affect brain function.

- Distal points – These remote points are located away from the area of the body that exhibits symptoms of a problem. They are often very effective when held either by themselves or in conjunction with local points near the blockage.

- Emotional stress-release points – These represent often-sensitive neurovascular points above and around the eyebrows and mouth and above the center of the visceral cavity near the sternum. In certain therapies, they are held while the recipient performs a particular exercise. Tapping these points helps release emotions.

- Emotional trigger points – These sensitive points affect particular emotions in a positive way. They include points along the shoulder that relate to anger, points near the sternum that relate to love, points under the ribs that relate to fear, and points around the sex organs that relate to personal judgment.

- Etheric points – A select number of special source points just off the body are used in Source Point Therapy to activate healing within the body. They include the Diamond Point, the Golden Rectangle, the Navel Point, and a group of guardian energy points.

- Exit and entry points – These are the acupoints where the regular meridians begin and end. They are mostly in the toes and fingers, although some are in the face, chest and pelvis.

- Experience points – This term signifies a combination of acupoints that have been proven to be effective in treating specific disorders.

- Gateway points – Located on the extraordinary meridians, these are also known as gate acupoints or portals and include a few major, accessible, and useful points where meridians intersect the nerve roots, primarily at the top and bottom of the spine. The name also refers to those important locations from which energy can pass between the physical and etheric bodies.

- Glandular points – These include points associated with the seven glands that have a direct connection to the seven chakras and the metabolic functions of the body.

- Immunity points – These points near glands are useful for enhancing the immune system.

- Influential points – Since they have a strong relationship to the various organs, these points are used to treat diseases related to those organs.

- Intersection points – These key acupoints, which include crossing points, interface points, or hua tuo points, are found where two or more meridians intersect, and they represent junctions where the flow of chi comes together or divides as the different meridians converge or separate. Manipulation of these points affects all the meridians involved and is useful in treating related tissues and organs.

- Jin Shin Jyutsu points – These twenty-six safety energy lock points within the strange-flows circuitry of the extraordinary meridians are used in Jin Shin Jyutsu bodywork therapy.

- Luo points – These represent special passage acupoints that act as connecting bridges to equalize energy.

- Lymphatic reflex points – Also referred to as neurolymphatic points, they are used in certain therapies to stimulate the lymphatic system in order to remove toxins from the body. Most of these points, in shoulders, ribs, spine, and pelvic region, also have a strong effect on the nervous system.

- Marma points – These points on the nadi energy channels are used in the Ayurvedic system of healing. Although some correspond to those found in Chinese acupuncture, most have a different size, location, and characteristics.

- Meeting points – This is a group of eight hui points that are often combined with other acupoints to treat a specific problem.

- Nerve points – These neuroenergetic points are inherent to the nervous system. Some of them are closely related to acupressure points.

- Neurovascular holding points – These points are effective in stimulating the nerves and the cardiovascular system.

- Pivot points – This term refers to reflex points that are primarily within the pelvis. They are related to the symmetry and balance of the body.

- Pulse points – These diagnostic points are used primarily by practitioners versed in Chinese and Tibetan medicine to assess the rhythm and quality of the pulse of vital energy as it is carried by the flow of blood. Although many locations on the skull, spine, and feet can be used, the radial points on the wrist, where arteries are near the surface, are the ones most often used to ascertain a multitude of conditions within the body.

- Reactionary points – These constitute useful acupoints that are not necessarily located on a particular meridian. Certain practitioners who adhere to nontraditional methods of Acupuncture use these locations because of the beneficial reaction they provide.

- Reflex points – Not only do these points indicate a variety of conditions by responding to pressure in a particular way, but manipulating them can positively affect dysfunctional conditions in organs. Although reflex points are associated mostly with the practice of Reflexology, in which contact is made primarily on the feet and hands, a number of other therapies also employ distinct reflex points in their treatments.

- Shiatsu points – These are essentially the same as those used in Acupressure and Acupuncture, but in practice, a different assortment of up to one hundred or more are generally used to relieve tension and issues in the body. Many forms of Shiatsu actually focus on the meridians rather than on particular points.

• Special points – This signifies acupoints that are effective for revitalizing and treating illness and that have a strong synergistic effect on all organs.

• Spinal reflex points – These constitute special points along the spine that are effective in treating the nervous system.

• Spring points – These represent those acupoints with strong energy flow.

• Stream points – The flow in these acupoints, also referred to as river points, is not only ample but also nicely balanced.

• Symptomatic points – These are acupoints whose locations are closely associated with a particular symptom of an issue or illness. When contact on these points is painful, they may be called ouch points, and this often reflects the existence of an energetic blockages.

• Trauma points – These refer to locations on the body that not only hold trauma but, when treated, can help relieve particular acute or chronic conditions.

• Transport points – These acupoints at the ends of the four limbs of the body are also known as su points. Certain therapies work primarily on these points.

• Trigger points – These are points in the musculature where pain and tenderness caused by injury, strain, and stress are found. Often referred to as ouch or pain points, they are used in Myotherapy, Trigger Point Release Therapy, and an assortment of other forms of bodywork that address structural and functional issues. There are both primary key points and secondary associated satellite points; the satellite points, which are in a different area of the body, are activated by the key points. Compression on either type of point is commonly used to relieve the pain, and because some of these points correspond to shu acupoints, needling may also be used.

• Vita Flex points – These include the many specific reflex points used in Tibetan medicine to activate the flow of chi through the meridians.

• Vital points – This general term refers to acupoints that are not only very accessible but also provide good information about the actual energetic condition of different parts of the body.

• Well points – These acupoints are like pools or ponds of energy from which the vital life force readily springs up. This term is also used to signify sensitive points in the limbs or extremities of the body. In contrast, points in the trunk of the body, which are often larger in size and less tender, are considered lakes or seas.

• Yu points – These include an assortment of acupoints near the spinal column that are used to sedate energy.

• Yuan source points – These acupoints are yang points closely related to the circulation of fluids in the body and can be used to tonify the body's five yin organs. Each of the twelve meridians has a yuan source point.

Special Chinese Acupoints

The following is a list of some of the most useful pressure points on the body found in the practice of Acupuncture and Acupressure. They are often in areas where meridians intersect or near certain glands. The wonderful traditional names not only add a sense of romance but are very suggestive about what happens when these points are activated.

• Bottom of the Sea – This is considered the sacral pump that is near the tailbone; it has a direct effect on stimulating the rising of kundalini energy.

• Bubbling Spring – This point on the center of the soles of the feet acts as a gateway to the energies rising from the earth.

• Central Terrace – This spot on the chest near the heart has a strong effect on the feelings and the ability to love. It has a close connection with the heart chakra.

- Crystal or Celestial Palace – Located at the third eye near the pituitary gland, this point relates to wisdom and has a strong effect on spiritual insight.

- Door of Life – This point is on the spine between the kidneys and acts as a gateway to allow the surrounding vital energy to enter and accumulate in the lower dantien.

- Elixir Field – This point, at the intersection of different meridians in the area of the kidneys, relates to the sea of energy that can be stored in the lower dantien.

- Gate of Heaven – This spot, at the front of the top of head, is associated with the sixth chakra and represents the gateway to divine heavenly energies.

- Green Hammer – This is a point between the shoulders on the back that is related to and affected by the loads we carry through life.

- Jade Pillow or Jade Palace – This point, sometime referred to as the Wind Pond, is on the back of the head just below the cranial bones and both controls the breath and acts as a valve to regulate the flow of vital energy up the governing channel in the spine. Working on the point helps pump energy into the cranium.

- Labor Palace – Located on the palms of hands, this point is one of the minor chakras of the body and a key place from which to send and receive chi for healing.

- Medicine Palace – On the crown of the head, this point acts as the gateway for receiving enlightenment from heaven and for awakening mental resources. It has also been called the Window of the Sky. Some therapies call it the Meta Point and see it as a reflex point that enables more information to come into the brain.

- Shining Sea – This point, on the outside of foot above the heel, is very effective in treating the kidneys energetically.

- Valley of Harmony – Located between the thumb and the forefinger, this is a valuable point for the treating

symptoms involving the head, such as headaches, seasickness, or dizziness.

Working with Energy

Like many of our life processes, the flow of vital energy is unceasing, usually occurring without our knowledge and assistance. But by becoming conscious of its inner workings, we can enter into a partnership that will improve our health and our lives. When we learn to read its signals, we can take a proactive role in preventing our energy from becoming depleted or blocked. After all, we are the ones who get the signals that tell us something is wrong with its flow. Some people are more intuitive or skilled at perceiving energy, but we can all learn to activate and sense it. Once these skills are honed, we might even want to go on to help others.

Working with the hands is an easy way to begin sensing energy, and it is through the hands that most practitioners heal energetically. We instinctively place our hands on painful areas, but we can learn to mindfully focus and use that same energy. A simple method to activate the hands is to first shake them loose to remove any residual tension. Next, rub them together repeatedly to create heat and increase sensitivity. Once you notice a warm, tingling feeling, hold them a few inches apart and feel the sensations and subtle vibrations running between them. Slowly move your hands closer and feel the pressure on your palms as though you were pushing against an invisible balloon of energy that is constantly charged by the currents running through your hands. Do this while taking slow, deep breaths. Slowly increase the distance between your hands until the sensation is gone. Repeat the exercise, and try to change the size of the energy balloon and move it in different directions.

When you have a strong sense of the energy in your hands, rub them together again and place them on an area of your own body and see what you can feel. It is important to do this from a relaxed state of body and mind so that you can be aware of all the different sensations. Just relax and let the energy flow as it will. See what happens if you place your hands on the energy storage center just below the navel or on the heart center. It is good to finish by stretching and relaxing your hands and then closing your eyes and focusing internally on the way the whole body feels. By performing this kind of exercise over and over again, perhaps combining it with practices such as qi gong or pranayama breathing techniques, you can strengthen your ability to sense energy and its movement.

As your abilities increase, you will be able to play with the energy and strengthen your intuitive response to the various sensations that you feel. It's important to be receptive, surrendering to your perceptions without feeling any pressure to perform or straining to make things happen. Working with energy does not really require trying to do anything but just allowing what is always there to flow. Since all energy has the capacity to rise, descend, and dissolve into another form, it may seem to disappear, but it is really never lost and is always available. Like water flowing around rocks in a stream, its characteristics simply change depending on what it encounters. We just have to make a conscious connection to this vital life force so it can better serve our needs.

Once you have learned to activate energy, it is possible to transmit good vibrations to another living being.

You don't have to be a celebrated intuitive healer to be of service; energy healing is a natural human skill that can be effective even in small ways. Although you don't necessarily need to use your hands, they do help focus your attention. When you run energy through another person's body, there is really no way you can do harm. Energy has its own intelligence, and even if your technique is not quite correct or you try to move the energy in the wrong direction, the energy will usually go where it is needed. It's also hard to overload other people with energy, since they receive only what they are able to handle. Although energy work can really do no harm, it is possible that a recipient will become momentarily irritable, anxious, restless, or dizzy, because the body needs to adapt to the change in the energy flow and quantity. Even as a beginner, you can offer the healing power of energy to those in need.

Energy is felt, activated, moved, increased, diminished, balanced, and otherwise sensed in many different

...energy

Absorbing energy	Cultivating ...	Integrating ...	Repairing ...
Accessing ...	Decontaminating ...	Interlacing ...	Replenishing ...
Activating ...	Detecting ...	Interpreting ...	Restoring ...
Adjusting ...	Developing ...	Liberating ...	Sedating ...
Aligning ...	Digesting ...	Manipulating ...	Sending ...
Amassing ...	Directing ...	Mobilizing ...	Sensing ...
Amplifying ...	Dispersing ...	Moving ...	Scanning ...
Analyzing ...	Dissolving ...	Normalizing ...	Sharing ...
Applying ...	Distributing ...	Nourishing ...	Stimulating ...
Awakening ...	Elevating ...	Opening ...	Storing ...
Balancing ...	Emitting ...	Processing ...	Strengthening ...
Blowing ...	Enhancing ...	Projecting ...	Stretching ...
Breathing ...	Expelling ...	Pulsing ...	Sweeping ...
Bringing ...	Extending ...	Pumping ...	Swinging ...
Centering ...	Feeling ...	Purging ...	Throwing ...
Channeling ...	Focusing ...	Purifying ...	Tonifying ...
Circulating ...	Freeing ...	Reading ...	Tracing ...
Cleansing ...	Generating ...	Rebalancing ...	Transferring ...
Clearing ...	Guiding ...	Recharging ...	Transforming ...
Concentrating ...	Harmonizing ...	Reconnecting ...	Transmitting ...
Connecting ...	Holding ...	Regulating ...	Tuning ...
Conserving ...	Increasing ...	Rejuvenating ...	Unblocking ...
Controlling ...	Inducing ...	Releasing ...	Unleashing ...
	Infusing ...	Removing ...	

ways in all of the many realms of existence. Each of the words in the accompanying table can be followed by the word *energy*. If you are trying to become more aware of your own internal subtle energy and how it can be affected by intention and action, you might find these descriptive terms helpful. One method of contemplating them would be to read the list slowly and spend time visualizing and feeling the effect of each one as it applies to your vital energy and your ability to improve yourself and others.

The evidence is clear that we can take action to rejuvenate, improve our health, and increase the flow of energy by improving our habits and lifestyle and by performing or receiving energy work. Although good intentions are important, taking the initiative to actively participate in energetic practices that open up the wisdom in the body is important for good health. Disciplines such as Tai Chi, Aikido, Nei Gong, yoga, qi gong, enhanced breathing techniques, meditation, dance, and many other stimulating mind-body practices will help us by naturally infusing the body with energy. Many of us live in the mind, separated from the body, heart, emotions, or spirit, and these practices will help us become more centered and aware of the subtle internal connections within. As we become more embodied, aware, open, and eager to change, blocked energy will naturally tend to move toward release.

Both energy and breath are required for life, and the intimate connection between the two has been recognized for millennia. In fact, the Sanskrit word *prana* means both "energy" and "breath," with breath being considered simply the material form of energy. Since the body is also energy condensed into physical form, we can align and attune ourselves with the cosmic force through its carrier, the breath. As we breathe, we draw not only oxygen into the body but also the vibrations of the creative and healing power of the universe. A deep breath of fresh air simply makes us feel more alive.

The flow of energy sets life in motion, and the breath reminds us of this as it moves constantly through the body like waves of energy through the ocean. When breathwork techniques are used in a mindful way to enhance the cyclic process of respiration, it is possible to cultivate a balanced flow of vital energy and gain insight into its deep connection with the power of the universe. With the energy of the inbreath, we create a positive opening that brings all into the light of awareness; the outbreath is a negative contracting phase in which accumulated waste and stagnant energy are sent out. In between are two neutral phases, the pauses between inhalation and exhalation. The sense of fullness at the end of the inbreath and the emptiness at the end of the outbreath can allow us to experience both dimensions of this stillpoint in which inner perceptions of the all-pervasive force of energy can be experienced.

The breath and energy can revitalize the body, especially working together in an integrated practice. When the body is tense and resistant, energy is blocked, but breathing deeply signals the body to relax so the life force can run freely. The movement provided by certain practices and exercises are based in energy, but breathing fully while carrying them out can enhance their effects. Rejuvenating, enlivening practices such as yoga and qi gong generally combine breathwork and body movement—breath and energy working together in a meditative way—to enhance the cultivation of the vital life-force energy. These practices often incorporate meditative elements to help still the mind and body so that subtle sensations can be clearly felt. Simply practicing mindful breathing for a few minutes as a daily ritual—kind of like brushing your teeth—can also make a difference.

Bodywork and Energy

Because the different vibrational frequencies of energy can manifest in many ways, energetic healing must address energy on all levels—physical, mental, emotional, and spiritual. There are many avenues through which energy healing can take place. The vital life force fluctuates depending on an individual's experiences, and the amount, condition, and quality of the energy as it manifests within the energy fields, chakras, and pathways is always subtly changing. Being able to interact with and make adjustments to the state of this life force is what energy medicine is all about.

Though you certainly can practice energy healing on yourself, in the beginning, it might be more effective to have someone assist you in awakening your innate abilities. And there may be times when you need skilled professional intervention. Various energy-based healing therapies and spiritually transformative practices have been used in India, Tibet, and China for thousands of years, since the time of the early shamans, and today, these and many other forms of bodywork based on the science of energy medicine are available. They include modalities such as Acupressure, Acupuncture, Amatsu Therapy, Auric Healing, Bioenergetics, Chakra Balancing, Chelation Therapy, CORE Myofascial Therapy, Healing Touch Therapy, Huna Therapy, Insight Bodywork, Intuitive Energy Healing, Intuitive Energy Medicine, Jin Shin Do, Jin Shin Jyutsu, Kriya Massage, Kundalini Massage, Ohashiatsu, Polarity Therapy, Pranic Healing, Qi Gong Massage, Quantum Touch Therapy, Reconnective Healing, Reflexology, Reiki, Shiatsu, Thai Yoga Bodywork, Therapeutic Touch, Tuina, and Vibrational Healing Massage, to name just a few. Each has its own approach, energetic components, and particular techniques for awakening or stimulating the flow of the life force.

Because of the body-mind connection, energy is enhanced to some extent through all forms of bodywork regardless of its focus. Whether a practitioner helps you relax by releasing tension in a muscle, works on the circulatory or immune system, or assists in relieving trauma, the balance and flow of energy is enhanced on some level, and overall health is positively affected. However, the possibility of specifically improving the different energetic systems within your subtle body is increased when choosing one of the various forms of energy medicine, dispensed by a practitioner who is skilled in cultivating and transmitting energy. Energy medicine is not just for those with specific problems but is beneficial for anyone who wants to expand the overall potential of the body, mind and spirit.

The effects of energetic forms of bodywork are many and include clearing stagnant energy, breaking up or dissolving blockages that inhibit the free flow of healthy energy, generating increased quantities of nourishing vital energy, guiding and encouraging the circulation of the life force throughout the body, revitalizing both the energetic and physical systems, and creating inner peace and harmony by alleviating any emotional tension or conflicts. To accomplish this, the different methods of energetic healing use various combinations of breathwork, guided meditation, visualization, physical exercise, mental control, and attunements. In energy medicine's purest form, practitioners hold the highest vibration that can effectively interact with the client's energy and energy fields. As the recipient is entrained and attuned with the practitioner's higher vibrations, the

client's vibrations naturally rise to match those of the practitioner. The practitioner is able to direct universal energy into the recipient, sometimes to problem areas and sometimes by simply allowing the client's innate wisdom to guide the healing energies to where they are most needed.

Energy blockages often come from restrictions in the body and inhibit our ability to function as we should. For example, experiencing threats to safety sends impulses that stimulate the fight-or-flight response in the body, as does just worrying about imagined threats. Habitual and unconscious responses like these can get lodged in the nervous system, musculature, and abdomen as patterns of tension and armoring that constrict breathing and tie up energy that could be used for physical activity and mental processing. To counteract these limiting patterns, many energy-based modalities blend bodywork with breathwork, physical exercises, harmonic vibrations, or meditations. Some may include work on the physical plane by clearing blockages in the spine, fascia, circulation, or the nervous system. Many others concentrate on the energetic system by focusing on the network of energy pathways, the energy centers, the energetic biofield that surrounds and interweaves with the physical body, or even with the energetic blueprint in a person's DNA. Some use a psychospiritual process in which interventions repair and balance the flow of energy on the soul level. Certain modalities can also work to remove restrictions in a person's belief patterns. No matter what is altered in each approach, loving hands are the conduit through which energy moves, whether or not there is actual physical contact.

Over the centuries, the applied skills of dissolving, removing, and clearing blockages in the flow of energy and then generating fresh energy and guiding its circulation, have been found, lost, and rediscovered, and today the role of energy medicine is steadily becoming more recognized within the scope of conventional medical practices. For example, it is not unusual now to find Therapeutic Touch and Reiki being used in hospital settings to ease the pain and anxiety of patients and promote healing or to soothe those approaching the end of their lives.

Contemporary forms of practitioner-applied bodywork such as Applied Kinesiology, NeuroPhysical Reprogramming, Polarity Therapy, Reiki, Reflexology, Therapeutic Touch, Touch for Health, and the many other forms of energy medicine (and even certain forms of somatic psychotherapy) work in many different ways with many different aspects of the physical and subtle bodies: the fascia, nervous system and spine, acupoints, trigger points, reflex points, energy pathways, flow lines such as meridians, energy centers such as the seven chakras or three dantiens, the various layers of the energy fields, etheric gateways, energetic DNA blueprints, genetic codes, templates, the matrix, the calibration lattice, geometric grids, field currents, biosignatures, soul connections, and vortexes or portals of radiant light that connect the individual to the cosmic realm. Transformative healing can be accomplished energetically through various forms of touch: using pressure, tapping, and manipulations; working with reflexes and the pulse; scanning, sweeping, palpating, and stretching the body; running energy through the hands; and applying the vibrations of light, color, sounds, chants, tones, heat, electromagnetic currents, magnetism, pendulums, polarities, aromas, crystals, sacred symbols, and luminous cosmic rays. Practitioners may also call on guided imagery, soul retrieval, visualization, hypnotism, elucidations, affirmations, empowerments, attunements, spirit guides, ascended masters, deities, angels, and transomatic dialogue. The full spectrum of possibilities seems endless.

In addition, self-care practices, such as Tai Chi, Being in Movement, Self-Help Breema Exercises, Bagua Exercise Program, Aikido, Authentic Movement, Sensory Awareness, yoga, qi gong, self-massage, sound healing, and various forms of breathwork and meditation, are embodied methods that cultivate a balanced flow of energy within the body so that all of the cells, tissues, organs, glands, and body systems can work together harmoniously. Many of these practices work in stages, so the more you practice, the more you will benefit.

Two Powerful Ancient Practices

Two practices illustrate the way in which self-care practices can be used for energetic healing. Nei Gong and Yi Ren Qi Gong are forms of qi gong that demonstrate the power of an embodied, meditative energy practice that incorporates both breathwork and physical movement. Nei Gong has maintained its traditional form, whereas Yi Ren Qi Gong, whose roots are also in the distant past, was reestablished more recently. Just as

with the multitude of powerful yoga practices, both of these Chinese practices initially require the guidance of a master practitioner in order to fully grasp the essence and subtle aspects of the process.

Nei Gong is essentially an older version of qi gong as it is practiced today. It was developed thousands of years ago by Taoist monks in China and was probably the system described in the ancient publication on Chinese internal medicine often referred to as *The Yellow Emperor's Classic.* This text describes the complete science of energy flow and internal alchemy and teaches a system for feeling and developing subtle internal chi energy through blending breathwork, physical exercise, and meditative techniques. Nei Gong is very likely the primary foundation of Tai Chi, Bagua, qi gong and other internal martial arts and is closely related to the wisdom expressed in the *I Ching,* the book of changes. Various Asian bodywork modalities, such as Acupuncture, Amatsu, and Tuina, are based on this artful and scientific approach to energetic healing in which the main focus is on generating personal chi energy and guiding its circulation throughout the body. In Nei Gong, depleted energy is revitalized internally by the practitioner herself rather than by externally transmitting energy from one person to another, as would be the case in bodywork such as Amatsu therapy. In the practice of Nei Gong, a number of integral components each play a particular role in expanding awareness of the flow of energy and where it is being directed within the body.

Its primary component is breathwork, which is considered fundamental to all the other aspects of this practice because it can enhance self-awareness and help circulate the life-force energy within the body. Nei Gong breathwork includes such practices as breath lengthening, belly or organ breathing, breathing into the lower dantien energy center just below the navel, reverse breathing, spinal breathing, skin or cellular breathing, and circular breathing. The initial focus is on circulating chi along the regular and extraordinary meridian channels of the body. As this is happening, adjustments to alignment are made through subtle body movements that stretch soft-tissue fibers inward and outward along the meridians, giving the energy more room to move and affecting the rise and fall of internal energies within the energy channels. The practices also include activating certain points, absorbing and releasing energy, vibrating energy, and feeling or controlling the interconnections that exist. These techniques help dissolve any blockages in the flow of chi both in the external etheric energy body and in the three primary internal energy centers known as the dantiens. A part of the practice is the directly experienced act of controlling the flow of energy outward and the gathering of energy inward. An additional component involves working with the auric and etheric fields to gain better self-awareness and control, thus creating greater harmony with the universe. A very physical and sensitive energetic technique is used to generate and amplify circles and spirals of energy within the body through energetic emissions from the lower dantien. This is followed by practices that absorb chi from the upper, middle, and lower dantiens and project it inside or outside the body. Further energy work involves awakening and controlling the spinal energies, which is accomplished through the process of pumping internal energy up and down the spine.

In all of the Nei Gong techniques, the reliance on the dantien energy centers and the awakening and use of the right, left, and central energy channels near the spine are considered imperative to the cultivation of the free flow of the vital chi. All of its components are integrated to enable the development of psychic, clairvoyant, or mystical powers that signify the awakening of the spirit realm and the energy called shen.
Contact: Lotus Nei Gong School of Daoist Arts –
www.lotusneigong.net

Yi Ren® Qi Gong was originally created around 600 CE by Lu Tung-Pin, who also carried out celestial studies and began formulating Ample Reality Daoism. In recent years, Dr. Guan-Cheng Sun, a scientist and master qi gong practitioner, has been instrumental in reestablishing the practices of Yi Ren Qi Gong, which is based on the original practice of Nei Gong, but contains its own series of exercises for nourishing, balancing, strengthening, and harmonizing internal energies in the body and mind to develop energetic potential to the maximum. The underlying principle is that optimum health and consciousness are attained by learning and developing a number of skills to access vital energy and to employ it wisely. The components of the practice build upon each other by going to progressively deeper levels within the body.

In order to work with the vital chi energy, it is necessary to develop a body wisdom that is deeply sensitive to what is going on in the body physically, emotionally and energetically so that the needs of the organs can be known intuitively. The practice involves many different phases, all of which combine breathwork, physical movements, and meditations. Alternate sitting and standing slow-motion exercises along with active movements are used to bring the mind's focus to what needs to be healed, to build up energy, and to further help integrate the body, mind, energy, and breath while enhancing stillness, openness, and the awareness of the connection between the mind and energy flow.

The first component is learning how to access, feel, and develop energy rather than allowing it to dissipate, as often occurs when there are blockages. One way this can be accomplished is by infusing the body with earth energy, which can be held, circulated, digested, and used. Another technique involves energizing the heart. In both instances, cellular skin breathing is used to absorb the energy present all around. These practices are used to prevent energy drainage, protect personal chi energy, and cleanse the energy fields, while rejuvenating and replenishing chi. In order to cleanse the energy fields and prevent dysfunctions from occurring, unhealthy energies must be thrown off. This is particularly necessary whenever the disturbance comes from interaction with the energies of other individuals.

Another component is that of storing energy in the energy centers, each of which is associated with particular organs, glands, and meridians. The body wisdom is directed inward to detect the condition of the meridians, the dantien energy centers, or the energy gates in the body. Nourishing the third-eye energy center is considered essential for uniting the mind and body. Connecting to and circulating chi to change the direction of energy flow requires a clear focus in order to feel movements of chi while performing these exercises. A refreshing detoxification practice of circulating chi is used to help dissolve any potential illness.

A process called the Small Universe involves connecting the energy centers with the flow of chi, whereas another process, called the Large Universe, moves the chi beyond the centers through the twelve regular meridians that nourish the internal organs. A third process, called the Extraordinary Universe, activates the powerful extraordinary meridians, which act as an energy reservoir for the regular meridians.

Once the ability to circulate chi is acquired, deeper levels of practice are used to transform and digest the energy by moving it through the organs into muscles,

tendons, joints, and the bone marrow. Bringing the nourishing chi deeply into the body requires the ability to refine chi by transforming it into two very fine forms called rou chi and jing chi; an extremely refined level of digested chi is need to send chi into the bone marrow.
Contact: Yi Ren Qigong Center –
       www.yirenqigongcenter.com or
       www.iqim.org

Ultimately, the aim of both Nei Gong and Yi Ren Qi Gong is to provide a method for dynamic change through which we can adapt to life's circumstances and become more highly functioning people by understanding our internal energy flow and our energetic interactions with the world around us. However, just reading a description is not enough; they definitely have to be experienced to be really understood and appreciated.

Final Thoughts

As our body-mind becomes more energetically connected, vibrant, and able to resonate with the sacred source, we will become more empowered and enlightened in ways that help us alleviate all forms of dysfunction. There are beings who have shown us that it is possible to dwell in the pure energy of light and love, so it is not unreasonable to assert that this realm is available to anyone who is willing to seek it out. Contemplative practices designed to cultivate, awaken, integrate, balance, and align our hearts and minds will be vastly improved if we can bring into them an increased perception of the internal flow of energy in the body. Even if we are not spiritually inclined, energy work can improve our physiological condition, help resolve personal issues, and change our relationships with others. When we can learn to sense, feel, and visualize our vital energy, anything we do will have more authenticity and power.

Because energy is always changing, working with it is an ongoing process, but this work can integrate all of our fragmented parts into a unified whole that allows us to live life at our fullest potential with optimum health and consciousness. This union requires not only becoming more aware of and cultivating the internal subtle energies but also learning how to use energy wisely and how to celebrate the innumerable interweavings of energy flow that connect all beings and all levels of our existence. May we all tap into that pool of awareness so that we can come to live in harmony with the changes that will inevitably come our way.

CHAPTER 10
Making a Shift in Consciousness

The word *shift* implies a change, a new direction, and when we're talking about health and well-being, it could be the driving force behind positive action. We might ask ourselves: Are our perceptions and reactions healthy or do they lead to a state that invites dysfunction? The answer to that question might demand a shift in consciousness, a change in how we view ourselves and the world around us. If we can find a way to become more embodied—in other words, to rely on the body-mind connection—we can become more self-aware and more familiar with the subtle effects that people, things, and events have on the body, mind, and emotions. Perhaps our eyes will be newly opened to events or special moments that spontaneously awaken the insight and wisdom that makes life more enjoyable, loving, and worthwhile. When we can shift out of our habitual patterns of perception and behavior, it is possible to see the truth about who we are and the lives we meant to live. And when the blinders of limiting beliefs are removed, we can recognize the power that we have to heal ourselves and others.

A stupa monument decorated with the compassionate eyes of the Buddha.

Accessing the vast ocean of pure consciousness has been the goal of many who follow a spiritual path. From this spacious perspective, we can identify and ultimately transcend our limitations and discover new, creative ways to put to use the incredible potential we were each born with. Rather than staying caught in a web of limited possibilities, we can learn to lovingly embrace all that we encounter in life. We can become aware that all of our problems and worries can be an avenue to wholeness and learn how to use them instead of being used by them. This ultimate state, our inmost truth, is always present and accessible if we can only remove the mental beliefs and blockages that obscure our view of it.

Struggles and Obstacles

We humans are all born with the quality of openness and a sensitivity to the truth of an experience, but most of us had little instruction in how to carry this perception out into the larger world around us. At any stage of life, the longing to find love and acceptance is underneath every thought, word, and deed, and as children, the trial-and-error process of learning to act in harmony with the standards of a particular culture presented us with confusing issues. Our parents—our first teachers—were not always sensitive to our needs. Their own behavior often lacked the consistency that would keep our feet on the right path, and they passed down by example the dysfunctional habits they inherited or developed. Our mistakes and foolish attempts to do the right thing left us puzzled and disheartened. Developing the insight to see through all these outer influences would take years, and we each proceeded at our own pace. Actually, the process of learning the truth about anything is endless, and diligent work through a whole lifetime (or perhaps many lifetimes) might be necessary to harvest the deepest wisdom that will set the spirit free. In the meantime, we have to take a closer look at how things really affect us, because all of our experiences influence the thoughts, feelings, and beliefs that create the patterns of behavior we carry with us.

On becoming teenagers, we entered the domain of shifting hormones, maturing brains, and the burgeoning desire to escape from the restraints of family expectations, free to experience all that life seemed to be offering. This natural urge is a strong one, and, with luck, this growing process happens smoothly without unnecessary pain. Yet this isn't always the case. When our actions seemed to challenge our families and communities, we might have chosen to avoid and escape. But this can leave us with guilt, low self-esteem, sadness, and anger caused by the hurtful words and actions of ourselves and others. Rising passions and pressures mount and can make these years very trying for all involved.

When we were young, we often struggled in relationships with other people by taking things personally and reacting to problems with emotional outbursts that only temporarily soothed the ego. Certain situations became so overwhelming that we ran away without really facing them. If we were lucky, over time our peers and loved ones helped us learn new approaches that enabled us to handle life better and accept things as they were. However, even if we seem to have adapted and changed on the surface, inside we might still be carrying pain and wounds that we can't consciously admit to or are unable to deal with.

When we reached adulthood, certain experiences could stir up emotions and reactions that had not been fully resolved. This is especially true if a significant or traumatic event while we were growing up (and some would argue at the time of birth) threw us for a loop and got held in the body on an unconscious cellular level. The body-mind connection might then have shaped patterns of restricted behavior that drain energy, create unhealthy conditions, and even become an excuse for not being more responsible and successful in life. Some of us may even become emotionally addicted, clinging to these patterns and refusing to take a closer look at the root cause of the wounds, instead using them as the grounds for living life as a victim.

Considering the pressures and inconsistencies that arise in our lives as we respond to religious discourse, cultural discrimination, political tensions, dysfunctional families, and perplexing life experiences, it's easy to see why many people's hearts and minds become closed off. As time passes and these experiences become organized into a personal story, we each tend to develop and follow a set of patterns in our interactions with the world that may or may not improve our chances of becoming more aware and happier. If restrictive habits of behavior become ingrained within the mind and body, they constantly color the way we look at things, and the ability to perceive other possibilities becomes limited. The full recognition of our interconnection with others is hampered because we fear being hurt by them. Ignorance and troubling experiences just feed the fear and the sense of isolation, as do changes in our lives. We begin to judge ourselves, adding another layer to the belief that we can't live our dreams, and we implicate others in our failures. We might buy into the idea that an apathetic state is normal. This makes it even harder to break out of this trap of our own making and evolve into more self-aware and capable people. All of these thoughts and feelings are translated into the body and can't help but affect its functioning. Sadly, much of what constitutes ill health is determined by how alone, separate, misjudged, or afraid we feel.

However, all is not lost. There are means and methods to help us evolve, uplift our spirits, transform negative energies into positive opportunities, and allow each of us to become the person we meant to be. It is essential not only to recognize and rectify limiting patterns but also to work consciously to release any restrictions they have created. Life can be considered an ongoing learning process in which there is always an opportunity to adapt to situations as they really are and to find new ways of dealing with problems so that they don't stay with us. Sometimes this means recognizing that what was perceived as an unfortunate occurrence is really a blessing in disguise that simply requires more understanding; sometimes this awareness leads to deeper wisdom. We need not disregard the common sense we need to survive and the practical steps we might have to take, but developing insight into our issues can grace us with the ability to communicate more openly and love more fully.

So how does a person get beyond the impediments brought about by limiting attitudes, feelings, and beliefs? The first step is careful attention to the truthfulness of our perception of reality. To create a new path, we have to look inward and investigate the true nature of our wounds and learn to forgive ourselves and others. Since we are all imperfect beings, it is imperative to not reject imperfections, but to honor them as yellow lights on the road to transformation. Witnessing in this way can help us realize that pain and vulnerability will not destroy us and can give us the power to break free of a life defined by wounds and the fear of not being loved.

Some of us (particularly in the modern Western world) may need professional therapeutic intervention to help us break free.

As is evident from this book, there are a multitude of therapeutic approaches that can help us stop feeling like a victim of circumstances and awaken the innate healing potential and the ability to live fuller lives. Well-being can't help but improve when we tune in to embodied wisdom and listen to what it tells us about who we really are. But if the mind and its limiting patterns unconsciously hold us back, then a shift in perception is required to release its control. For some, this change might come spontaneously, but for many of us, contemplation and meditation can allow us to sharpen concentration and awareness, see through the actions of the ego, and awaken to the compassionate nature and healing power of the true self. As self-awareness grows and becomes aligned with something greater than ourselves, destructive patterns and emotions can be seen for what they truly are and lose their power and influence. The change in consciousness may be gradual, but learning to meditate lays the groundwork for further insight, and regular practice can help us break through conditioned reactions and also provide a sacred space in which to connect with the wisdom and healing energies that allow us to thrive rather than just survive.

Awakening Through Change

Shifts can come about spontaneously or intentionally, and life itself can become an agent of change, both positive and negative. During most of my younger life, I reflected deeply about things that might benefit my personal well-being, but had no real family or cultural context to support this exploration. I was neither aware of nor involved in spiritual practices such as meditation until much later on, when certain events propelled me in that direction. I wasn't an indigo child or someone with special psychic abilities, but from an early age there was always a strong mystical feeling connected with my dreams and my thinking about life. Although I could find temporary solace by venturing off alone into nature, especially on the water, I couldn't find an easy way to really resolve my deep emotional reactions to problems in my family. (Recognizing the problems others have, especially when it involves emotions, is often easier than looking inward to find your own truth.)

However, everything changed when I began to come of age during the significant revolution in consciousness brought on by the Vietnam War and the dawning of the Age of Aquarius.

The cultural upheaval and unrestrained experimentation of the 1960s were pivotal in propelling me toward new experiences that ultimately shifted my own consciousness. What started as a freestyle exploration of mind-altering indulgences, openness, cooperative living, and flower power soon evolved into a serious experiential search for the means of real transformation and the essence of the divine inner human potential. In time, this search led to holistic modalities and practices that have the power to change our perception of reality and guide us to a more balanced state of existence. For me, this included some amazing bodywork and breathwork experiences that provided what I can only call the powerful spontaneous combustion of a secret fire that gave me a glimpse of the amazing potential within the inner ocean of my being. Over the years to come, I continued to look for healing experiences and practices (such as yoga or qi gong) that would enhance my ability to become more integrated, connected, and free of doubt and that would interrupt my tendencies towards overly analytical thinking and unexplained sadness.

When my fear of being drafted into the army and possibly having to kill another human being was relieved by my number in the lottery drawing, I was able to move on to the next decisive period in my life. Realizing that my heart was not in college and discouraged by the state of the nation, I decided to take a trip to the Caribbean on my small sailboat. The next sixteen months of exploration was one of the most exciting and rewarding periods of rapid personal growth in my life. I soon realized I was definitely following my true life path and gained increasing confidence in my abilities. The experience of cruising on the ocean was mind-altering in a natural and elemental way and became the precursor to voyaging inward to the inner ocean that we all share.

Of course, it is true that crucial moments are not always happy ones, but they do still provide opportunities for positive change. Years later, I lost a boat on a reef. The experience was initially disheartening, but eventually it gave me the strength and determination to work harder toward my goals and take more responsibility for my actions. Being dumped for another by a lover was quite painful at the start, but I learned to look more closely at what goes on in personal relationships and how I actually and often unconsciously affect those around me. It also spurred me to look for deeper connections with those who matter most to me. Later in life, the experience of caring for a loved one suffering with cancer helped me to be more compassionate toward others, and the greatest gift is that she is still with us today. More recently, the death of a dear friend catapulted me into deeper soul searching and the recognition of the preciousness of life. It also stimulated me to reflect on how I could to handle my own inevitable passing with some sort of grace.

Many of life's most significant changes not only reflect the impermanence of our existence but in a way prepare us step by step for the final days and moments of our life. In each experience of change, the ego's attachment to what it perceives as stable is stripped away—a kind of mini-death—allowing us, if we choose, to dip our toes into the ocean of awareness, a space from which we can see beyond previous limitations. We can also learn much from the momentary and prolonged experiences that teach us about the subtleties and potentials of our true nature.

Life upon the sea presented me with many lessons and cultivated qualities and insights that could be carried over into other realms of daily life. Unlike living on the land, at sea there is no place to run to. You and your crew are literally in the same boat, and survival depends on careful observation, compassionate consideration, instinctive action, courageous decision-making, teeth-gritting determination, and efficient, properly timed action. When things don't work out as planned, you have to adapt and find new alternatives to resolve a particular situation. Being forced to meet your fate directly allows you to tap into a reservoir of strength you didn't know you had. You rapidly learn to accept things as they are and not let fear get the best of you, and any preoccupation with small problems or trivial issues disappears in a gale at sea. Rather than fighting with the sea, you really have to become one with it and learn how to best go with the flow.

Learning about what is important in life can certainly come through enjoyable and loving moments. We've all experienced this when we fell in love, whether with a person or a pet, a season or a song, a mountain or the mystery of life. In these moments, nothing matters but the present. We are blessed with a strong feeling of sacredness, which we will always hold dear in our hearts.

I was honored with several of these powerful visitations in my years at sea, and they had a strong affect on my perception of the universe and my place in it. On rare nights when the ocean is totally calm and the sky is cloudless, you see all of the stars above reflected in the ocean below. It's as if you are in the center of the universe, floating on a sea of stars, one with the cosmos of glistening light and soft darkness, where the darkness is but the carrier of the light. You are so small and yet so consequential. It's hard to tell if you are the macrocosm or the microcosm of the universe, for it seems as if the twinkling of all the stars speaks directly to the depths of your soul.

Another amazing nighttime occurrence happened only once in all my time at sea. My first mate and I were sailing along on the shallow Banda Sea between Australia and Indonesia when we saw ahead what appeared to be a glowing horizon and a long, golden sandy beach. It crept toward us faster and faster. After quickly consulting a chart to make sure there wasn't some kind of obstruction out there, we waited. Before long, the entire sea around us and as far as we could see was covered with this glow. We were spellbound by this miraculous transformation. Our logical minds soon realized we were immersed in a phosphorescent sea. I has previously seen varying amounts of phosphorescence, a phenomenon created as tiny bioluminous sea creatures move through the water, but nothing like this. As we scooped up a bucket of seawater to look the at thousands of points of light, a dolphin pranced by, appearing like the positive-negative reversal on a strip of film. It was hours later that we came through to the other side of this shining sea, gleaming in the dark of the night.

We never forget wondrous natural events like these, occasions that make us grateful to be alive, but even the small things in life can open up a more expansive view. This is exemplified by this thought: "See a leaf and realize the forest. See a wave and realize the ocean. See the eyes and realize the whole person." We often miss these moments because we just don't notice what's right under our noses. Many times every day, acts of kindness and the wonders of nature speak to our hearts, but we don't bother to listen because we're just too concerned with ourselves, too busy trying to insulate our little world, our plans, and our strategies from outside influences. But if we can learn to perceive every second of every day as a gift, a chance to explore more deeply the truth within, perhaps we can arrive at a new way of viewing everything offered, whether glory or misery, as a chance to see our place in the web of life.

The first step in shifting the consciousness towards staying in the present moment is recognizing how we react to and handle particular situations as they occur. Most of us have a conditioned tendency to react to an event in a certain way, but when we can pause and examine our initial thoughts and feelings before we act on them, we have a better chance of not being limited to a reflex response that doesn't always serve our best interests or that of others. A conditioned response might first show up as a feeling in the body, a tightness in the stomach or a rush of blood to the face, and it may be that the body's wisdom is offering us the chance to examine a response before it actually explodes in the mind or the mouth. As we inquire more deeply, we may learn that the reaction is based on the melodrama of our own story rather than on what is actually happening. If we can learn to use somatic self-awareness to recognized how we are controlled by the mental and emotional patterns that obscure the truth, we may understand how foolish that first response would have been, chuckle at ourselves, and let go of the conditioning behind it. The body's wisdom can direct us to the places in our inner world that need attention. It's hard work to sort through all of the misperceptions and illusions that precipitate the reactions, and it may be necessary to uncover new ways to make the shift in consciousness that honors and embraces who we are, that liberates us from the bonds of previously held constraints, and that opens our hearts and minds to the unconfined and compassionate nature of our true selves. Today, more and more of us are finding that a meditative practice can help us unravel the illusions and make this shift. Meditation can be the guiding star with which we navigate through the waves of stormy seas that life throws our way.

But what happens when the compass doesn't point to true north? The path to inner truth can send us on wild-goose chases in which what we thought we'd gained seems to slip away as we backslide into an old restrictive pattern of response. The wise ones would say this apparent twist of fate is a natural part of the process, because when we reach a certain level of intuitive or spiritual understanding about ourselves, new questions about who we really are and our true purpose arise from an even deeper place. This is just a sign that there is more work to

be done, and certain extremely difficult circumstances that really "rock the boat" often require a great deal of practice to face and then transform them. Since it seems there is no end to the process of unfolding awareness, we had better learn how to relax and enjoy the journey. Nobody said waking up was going to be easy, but it definitely helps to call to mind the insight and beauty of those rare spontaneous "aha" moments when you were able to glimpse the ultimate truth and the simplicity of noticing similar traces in everyday events.

Making the Shift Through Meditation

Although sometimes a shift in consciousness and an inner awakening comes spontaneously through life-changing moments or experiences (sometimes when we least expect it), the various practices of meditation were devised as more consistent ways of training the mind and clearing away all that obscures the true nature of body, mind, and spirit. By stilling the endless chatter of the mind as it chews on the past or worries about the future, we can learn to be fully present in what we are experiencing at any moment. Meditation is the very subtle art of being with an experience rather than doing anything about it, and from this state, we can become aware of the true nature of experience. Through gentle inquiry and deep listening, we can uncover the unconfined qualities of the awakened state—openness, love, compassion, creativity, joy, courage, and so much more.

By going deep within to the core of our being, we can enter an expansive space that allows remembering what has always existed but has been forgotten. When we put our attention on the vast space of this inner ocean, free of restrictive problems and issues, our souls can sing. It feels like finding true love, and indeed that's what we find. The tiny droplet of our consciousness merges into the inner ocean of awareness, and when you we're submerged in the depths of wisdom, there is less chance of being tossed about by the surface waves that crash over us in life. We may not always be able to stay in this inner space of refuge, but through practice we can keep coming back. Although what we are seeking is a natural state, uncovering it requires diligence and persistence in order to bring into being the real unfolding that is necessary for inner transformation.

From a more down-to-earth point of view, meditation helps us learn to integrate feelings and experiences that seem overwhelming instead of permitting them to create destructive patterns of behavior. It helps us understand that the realm of discursive thinking is not the place where the ultimate truth lies, since the nature of thought itself is conditioned and relative. The shift in consciousness aroused through meditation leads to a higher level of perception from which we can react from the heart, free of the contradictory influence of the thinking mind.

It's important to realize that we all begin at different levels of awareness, and a meditation practice needs to reflect where we are mentally and emotionally at any moment. Teachings might speak about ignorance and suffering and contrast them with the wondrous state that can be acquired through diligent practice. This often leads people into trying harder and harder to be a meditator without dealing directly with mental or emotional issues that can inhibit progress. When they try to leapfrog into a "higher" state of awareness, they get thrown back down to try to figure out what they overlooked. However, the process of awakening is exactly that—a process—and there are many stages to go through.

Troubling emotions, unconscious mental strategies, and nonstop judgments can prevent us from being fully present, feeling positive about ourselves, and honoring the essential sacredness of our being. Recognizing the real cause of our problems is critical to the process of letting go of the inhibiting attitudes and judgments they have caused. To do so, we may have to wake up from what Buddhist psychotherapist Tara Brach calls the trance of unworthiness. The practice of meditation helps us see through this illusion by investigating, recognizing, and allowing our problematic issues so that we no longer identify so strongly with fear or a sense of failure. Meditation gives us the chance to pause and ask what is happening, while at the same time inviting a feeling into a safe inner space of forgiveness and acceptance. Saying yes to the process and learning to recognize the love and compassion that are the true self will go a long way towards healing feelings of shame, guilt, and unworthiness. The pathway back home is often blocked by such thoughts, so self-acceptance is critical to releasing obstacles and developing love and compassion for ourselves. The fear of anything—being loved, being hurt, failing to measure up—can be embraced by the true source of love, which can bear witness to the hurt and give the pain a place of deepest truth in which to rest. It's like being the holder and the held at the same time.

However, there are times when simply allowing and accepting are not enough, and we may need professional counseling to unearth and uproot the causes and conditions that have made us who we are. The greatest gift to ourselves and to the world would be to seek that kind of help.

Meditation techniques are used in somatic practices that ask us to bring awareness to different parts of the body—for example, by imagining that we are breathing into a certain area—and a contemplative state of mind allows us to perceive the subtle movement or blockage of energy. Becoming mindful of physical sensations can point us back toward their causes, but sometimes just relaxing and bringing compassionate awareness to that area will cause a transformational shift. If we focus on the breathing process itself, its natural pauses are a moment of non-doing in which we can simply rest and look within. Meditation can help us become embodied, fully present in the unity of body and mind, and can lead to deep honoring of the body as the vehicle that allows us to practice.

Some people have the misconception that meditation is just a way to escape from reality, to abide in an empty state in which there is no thought or feeling. This is definitely not the case. Meditation does not result in sitting in isolation but in interacting more authentically and living more consciously in a human body. Meditation actually requires us to be more rather than less attentive, but that attention is directed at the truth of what we see in ourselves and in the world around us. Becoming more self-aware requires paying attention to the senses—examining their input rather than denying them—including the inner felt sense that connects us to the wisdom held within the body. Touch, sight, smell, hearing, and taste tie us to the physical world, but also offer us the spiritual opportunity to be fully present in every moment. This presence is a state beyond judgment in which the nose can locate all the blossoming fragrances, but accepts the reek of destruction; the eyes can see amazing things beyond imagination, but witness with compassion the suffering of others; the ears can hear splendid music, but also cries of pain; the hands can feel the heartbeat of a loved one, but wipe away tears of grief; the voice can speak words that express pain and pleasure in equal measure; and the body understands all of the wonders it holds, but accepts that we are not perfect. Meditation is not escaping into an empty void, but instead is conscious engagement with the world we live in.

Another fallacy about meditation is that when we come to see all the phenomena of life as just a passing dream, we will be free of any responsibility for the other figures in that illusion. In fact, when we begin to understand that every human being has the same potential to wake up that we do, we can't escape taking on even greater responsibility. We want all others to experience the same transformation, but we know that it is a personal one and that all we can do is hold the space for them by living according to its wisdom. As we begin to experience the qualities of an awakened heart and mind, compassion arises and flourishes, and we are compelled to dedicate ourselves to ending the suffering of all beings. (The Buddhist tradition even includes a vow—the bodhisattva vow—that pledges to do everything necessary to relieve the suffering of all sentient beings.) When joy emerges, we rush to share it. We use our own difficulties to internalize the absolute truth that we are just like all other beings in meeting the ups and downs of life. In short, we become spiritual activists, warriors of the heart.

Yet another myth is that once we have committed ourselves to practicing a spiritual path, all our worries are over. In fact, until we attain the consciousness of an enlightened master, awareness remains a relative thing. Much of what we are unaware is also not conscious to us, and it may be that this shadow side wants to stay hidden. No matter how diligent and sincere our practice is, we may still be held back by unseen inner entanglements and blockages. We might experience a spiritual crisis that sends us reeling into uncertainty; we might face the feeling of being stuck on the path, unable to see a solution. The only defense is the quality of perseverance. Deepening insight and increasing self-acceptance create conditions for those deeply held fears and beliefs to surface in the conscious mind, and then we can apply the instructions we have received to see through them as well. We can read about these kinds of struggles in the stories told about many masters and take hope and confidence from the fact that these human beings were eventually able to achieve what we are also seeking.

This final thought is not a myth: Meditation can open our hearts. Once we learn to see the splendor inside the true self, it is impossible not to recognize it in every other being. As we struggle with our problems, we can become conscious that others are up against exactly the same obstacles. We're all looking for the same things—love, joy, happiness, freedom from suffering, and peace of mind—but we're just coming at it from different directions. Learning to honor these struggles in all their diversity can help us resolve our difficulties in relationships with others and, by extension, with the world. If we can replace friction and conflict with understanding and compassion, enemies will become, if not friends, at least no longer strangers, and perhaps we can together craft a world ruled by love rather than by hate and fear.

The Practice of Meditation

Many, many practices for increasing spiritual awareness and transcending a conditioned existence have been passed on for thousands of year in different traditions. Some are very simple and appropriate for beginners; others require years of practice to distill their essence. The words of teachers from the various traditions speak across their surface differences, because the goal of most of the practices is the same: learning to uncover inner wisdom without being distracted by the confusion all around and within. For example, the wisdom of Buddhist teacher Pema Chödrön is very appropriate for beginning Western students of meditation, whether or not they are practicing in that tradition. She has a special way of talking about the emotional issues that are often the ones most in need of attention. However, discovering which practice and which tradition is the one that resonates has to be a decision that follows an honest evaluation of personal needs and propensities and a thorough examination of the authenticity of a teacher.

Meditation, bodywork, and breathwork are often partners in the healing process. Meditation is a key element in those healing therapies whose goal is the development of subtle sensitivities and increased self-awareness, and it is an integral part of many forms of healing, whether carried out through applied bodywork or self-care. Most practitioners of energy medicine or breathwork employ meditative techniques, such as visualization, mantras and chants, and concentration, to enhance their therapies. Yogic exercises and other movement practices are often used to work out the kinks after sitting in contemplation for long periods of time, and breathwork and energy work can be recognized in specific meditative practices. Particularly in approaches designed to improve concentration and still the restless mind, the breath is used as a focal point to which the attention can return after straying. Deep breathing can relax the meditator and soften tension in the body, which signals the mind to relax and let go. Some meditative breathing practices can ignite the inner fire and raise the vital energy in a way that purifies the energy anatomy.

Meditators are initially encouraged to find a quiet, sacred place where they can sit comfortably in the proper erect posture. The prescribed yogi position is half or full lotus; however, less agile folks can also sit on a mat in a simple cross-legged posture or kneel with the hips and buttocks elevated on a cushion or small meditation bench. Especially in the West, traditions are less strict, and it is possible to sit upright in a chair. The most common physical problem is developing tingling sensations or muscle cramps when sitting for prolonged periods of time. However, this can be minimized by learning a properly balanced and relaxed sitting position, by integrating periods of stretching or yoga into your practice, and by practicing for short periods before progressing to a longer time on the cushion. These kinds of body sensations can also be used as a part of the practice, and some forms contain releasing movements done with the body while seated or standing. Moving meditation can be performed while mindfully walking, running, or performing various activities, and, if necessary, you can even practice lying down. Even if you are not an advanced practitioner, it is possible to acquire benefits from short periods of meditation while riding on the bus or during a coffee break at the office.

Meditation hall at Wonderwell Mountain Refuge.

The mind has a tendency to wander, especially when confronting something painful, and the opposite habit of following after ideas or objects it finds pleasurable. The initial stages of meditation have been crafted to help people learn how to concentrate, avoid distractions, resist the constant intrusion of overwhelming feelings and emotions, and stabilize in these efforts. As the voice of the ego-mind is stilled, it may then become possible to inquire deeply into the nature of experience, the role of the mind in creating our stories about reality, and the unconditioned inner nature with which we all were born. It may become possible to touch in on the universal heart-mind in which all beings ultimately rest. As the personal self dissolves into this vastness, its healing power may shine through and melt away distortions and dysfunction.

Even though instructions on meditation can be found in books and videos, the personal attention of a qualified teacher can be a blessing in many ways. Nowadays, all over the world, it is relatively easy to find groups practicing different forms of meditation in health centers, spiritually oriented retreat centers, or even public buildings. In most cases, the leader first guides the meditation to help people get oriented and learn the basic elements. Once a certain degree of proficiency is reached, it is possible to maintain a contemplative or meditative outlook while living your life and doing common daily activities.

Meditation is similar to many energy medicine practices in that it does not necessarily rely on the recipient's intention to do its work, but a sincere wish to gain awareness and careful attention to every detail of practice can be very helpful. It's this that will carry you through the rough spots. What is important when approaching the practice of meditation is forgetting your own agenda and staying open to whatever arises. It may be beneficial to hold the intention to simply take a closer look at your thoughts and feelings and witness whether what goes on in the mind reflects your real core needs and desires. Once you have been guided through the initial stages and have established a strong foundation, it becomes easier to recognize and let go of the dictates of the mind and the concepts that block your view. It is also crucial to escape from the mind's habit of labeling experiences as right or wrong, good or bad. If you can just allow things to be as they are without judging them, you'll have the opportunity to examine their true nature and gain access to the wisdom that comes with recognizing what is really real. With experience, you may stop striving or trying to force something to happen and develop faith in the power of the practice to do what needs to be done. Your job is simply to stop thinking about yourself, let go, and stay open to whatever comes and goes.

The most important word in the phrase "the practice of meditation" is *practice*. All of the good intentions in the world are nothing without the experience. You can read a thousand books and listen to a hundred teachings, but until you sit down on the cushion, you will not feel the rising tide of the fullness of the inner ocean. The path of unfolding awareness is a lifelong process, but with better recognition of our fullest potential, along the way we can increase our ability to think clearly, have heartfelt compassion, and use our innate spiritual wisdom for the benefit of others.

Some Forms of Meditation

Various forms of meditation, each with subtle differences in practice, have been with us for thousands of years, especially as a significant part of the spiritual healing arts found in the East. All these forms of meditation are rooted in the mindful recognition of impermanence, the existence of a space of freedom beyond conditioned reality, and the possibility of the end of suffering.

Much of what has been said to this point, especially about the goals and effects of meditation, is drawn from these East Asian spiritual traditions, and the discussion will continue from that point of view. However, Judeo-Christian spirituality also has a long history of using active visualization and pure contemplation in an effort to enter a state of union with the divine. Over the millennia, Christian mystics have sought personal transformation through prayer and meditation, among them Augustine, Hildegard of Bingen, Francis of Assisi, Teresa of Ávila, Meister Eckhart, Thomas Merton, and, indeed, modern-day Quakers. Though you will have to go elsewhere for specific information about their practices, they are owed a deep bow of gratitude for holding this sacred space.

An in-depth discussion of all of the various forms of meditation is of course impractical, so it seems wise to focus on a few that have either wide acceptance or long histories. Even so, it is impossible to give more than the flavor of the forms discussed. But in truth, the effects of meditation cannot be gained by thinking about them but only through practice. Because many sprang from the same roots, they may vary only in subtle ways. Although all work to enhance awareness, each has a particular focus, an established process, and generally many stages of practice. All have been safeguarded in different lineages that extend back thousands of years, but most are still evolving to make meditation more accessible for people living in the modern world. Their function has been tested over time by many humans just like us, proving that the goal of awakening can be achieved. But only you can decide which one resonates with your heart and mind. The following comparison might help: some are like sitting by a cool mountain stream, and others are like sitting in front of a roaring fire.

Buddhist Meditation

Buddhism is a highly evolved, experiential system of spiritual practices directed toward the goal of enlightenment—a nondual state beyond the actions of the ego that cause suffering— as exemplified and taught by its founder, Siddhartha Gautama, honorifically known as the Buddha, "the awakened one." He is viewed not as a deity but as one who has shown the way. The teachings of the Buddha (the dharma) were initially transmitted in three turnings of the wheel of dharma, each building on the wisdom contained in the preceding ones. The first turning contains the Four Noble Truths, which acknowledge suffering, its causes, the possibility of its cessation, and the disciplines of the Eight-Fold Path to enlightenment. It offers four ideas whose contemplation will cause a person to practice diligently: the preciousness of a human birth, the impermanence of life, the results of actions (karma), and the defects of living trapped in habitual patterns of action and reaction. The refuge and renunciation practices arising from these basic perceptions are seen as the means for personal liberation from the world of causes and conditions known as samsara. The second and third turnings, which are referred to as the Mahayana approach, offered teachings on the lack of any solid, unchanging reality in all phenomena (often translated by the English word *emptiness*), the innate goodness of all beings and the qualities that arise from this true nature, and the role of compassion. Mahayana teachings and practices are grounded in the bodhisattva ideal in which a person pursues enlightenment not just for the self but for all beings, even if it means returning over and over to the relative world of samsara. The third group of wisdom practices, the Vajrayana, contains the extraordinary tantric methods that invite practitioners to connect directly and quickly with the essence of their being through purification practices, energy work and specific forms of meditation.

Buddhas are sprouting up everywhere.

As Buddhism spread from India to Tibet, China, and other Asian countries, different schools of practice developed, containing rich core meditation practices that focused on particular aspects of the original teachings and different sets of commentaries. The practices that emerged in Burma, Thailand, Sri Lanka, Laos, Cambodia and Vietnam, called the Theravada tradition, may differ somewhat from the Mahayana practices found in Tibet, Mongolia, China, and Japan, but all arose from the same teachings, and specific understandings and practices are widely shared. After the Muslim invasion of India in the eleventh century, Buddhism was mainly preserved outside its original home.

Buddhist meditation is designed to help people uncover the true nature, nature of mind, that has been obscured by the illusion that experiences have a solid, permanent, and independent nature and by the attempts of the ego to grasp on to them as if they will never change, which only results in suffering. (However, the teachings do not deny that the ego has a role in our ability to function in the relative world.) The actions of the ego are grouped into the three poisons—attachment,

aversion, and ignorance. By overcoming these poisons, beings can awaken to the natural state in which they are no longer operative, a state in which all is possible and from which unconfined capacities, such as wisdom, love, compassion, and healing power, are unleashed. Recognition of this true nature cannot be forced by doing or thinking; it is only when the conceptualizing mind is stilled or overwhelmed that awakening will dawn. Many of the meditative practices available in Buddhism are exercises in mindfulness and concentration designed to quiet the mind; others engage the mind in deep inquiry and contemplation on its true nature. Particularly in Vajrayana practices, the body (especially the subtle energy body) becomes an ally in these processes. Each of the primary Buddhist meditative practices has subtle variations, so people have a choice in which method resonates most strongly with them. In many instances, individuals practice one form as an initial practice or in tandem with another and then move on to more advanced practices.

Shamatha is a form of meditation in which a person mindfully observes whatever is occurring in the present moment. The first step is to quiet the mind so that thoughts do not interfere with concentration or create mental turmoil. The mind wants to do something, so this natural tendency is exploited by asking it to concentrate on an object, whether the breath, an external object, a visualized image, or a sound such as a mantra. As distractions arise, the mental focus is directed over and over again back to the object of contemplation. The breath is a convenient object of focus because it is always available, but care must be taken not to try to influence the breathing process; the objective is to allow the breath to flow in and out naturally and to simply observe. When working with an external object, suspend judgment and just notice what is there. This training eventually culminates in the ability to maintain focused attention for long periods of time and a state of calm abiding in the moment without judging or labeling whatever is occurring. This is still a dualistic state—there is a subject observing an object—which must ultimately be transcended. Shamatha is a prelude to almost all other Buddhist meditation practices.

Contact: www.samatha.org or www.buddhamind. info/leftside/lifestyl/medi/sam.htm

Vipassana, also referred to as insight meditation, is the gradual path of inquiring deeply into the nature of experience, impermanence, and the ways that past actions, both positive and negative, influence reactions. (In Tibetan Buddhism, *insight* has the additional meaning of the recognition of the nature of mind by gaining direct experience of its qualities.) Vipassana is one of oldest Buddhist meditation practice, attributed directly to the Buddha, and depends on the meditative concentration gained through the practice of shamatha. By focusing attention on the body, breath, feelings, or thoughts, the meditator can explore the nature of changing perceptions and go beyond mere intellectual understanding to experiential awareness. Some labeling of arising emotions or thoughts may be helpful, but openness and friendliness rather than judgment is essential. Suffering or discomfort, whether physical or emotional, is viewed as the opportunity to examine it more closely. Vipassana teaches students to pay careful attention to all life experiences and the ways they react to situations as they arise, and observation of conditioned responses to situations can lead the way to change. Contemplation of how emotional states motivate speech and action can illuminate the consequences of destructive emotions such as anger and greed and the importance of love and compassion. In Vipassana meditation, students train to ignore the impulse to grasp at false comfort and instead fearlessly dive into the inner expanse of the ultimate truth.

Contact: www.dhamma.org, dharma.org,
www.spiritrock.org, www.vipassana.com,
or www.vipassanadhura.com

Loving-Kindness (Metta) Meditation has been practiced since the time of the Buddha and has become popular in the West in recent years. Loving kindness can be described as the unconditional wish for the deep happiness of all beings, including the self. This form of training consists of radiating the energy of this wish of love equally to different groups of beings—the self, friends, strangers, enemies, and eventually the universe—with spoken phrases and mental imagery. The practices are designed to open the heart, allowing compassion to flow boundlessly, and to cut through the sense of separation between self and others. The newfound joy in the happiness of others can itself be the source of happiness for the person doing the wishing.

Contact: www.wildmind.org/metta or
www.sharonsalzberg.com

Tibetan Buddhist Meditation developed as a separate tradition as Buddhism spread out from India and found a home in Tibet, though not without a certain amount of struggle. Generations of enlightened masters preserved the Buddha's teachings in what became four major schools—Nyingma, Kagyu, Gelugpa, and Sakya—which each developed different perspectives on how to interpret and practice the teachings. These schools took many smaller practice lineages under their umbrellas, and there was also a certain amount of influence from the indigenous Bön religion. The idea of lineage is extremely important in Tibetan Buddhism, because passing the teachings down from teacher to student keeps misinterpretations from creeping in. However, as a result of the nonsectarian Rimé movement of the late nineteenth century, the teachings and practices of the different schools, though maintained as distinct, were shared and preserved by being transmitted to masters from other lineages. After the Chinese invasion of Tibet, exiled teachers began to take students from the West, and the new generation of teachers—Tibetans born in exile and classically trained Westerners—began exploring how to make the ancient teachings relevant to the modern world.

The Buddhism of Tibet, though based on the teachings of the Mahayana, also relies on the tantric practices found in the Vajrayana, particularly the use of imagery and practices of deity or guru yoga, in which the practitioner's mind and heart are merged with that of the teacher. (In Tibet, the seat of the mind is thought to be the heart rather than the brain.) The skillful means of Vajrayana lead the practitioner to a direct connection with the nature of mind, and therefore Vajrayana is seen as a direct and speedy path to awakening. However, much of the preparation work is carried out through what are called relative practices, such as shamatha and the sharp inquiry of vipassana, that are used to overcome all that obscures the true nature. All of the practices are grounded in the Mahayana concept of bodhicitta, the mind of enlightenment in which the motivation for any action is the awakening of all sentient beings.

Mahamudra (the Great Seal from the Kagyu tradition) and **Dzogchen** (the Great Perfection of the Nyingmas) are considered to be the highest forms of practice in Tibetan Buddhism. Though there are differences in approach and language, both work directly with the nature of mind and from the view that all beings are inherently buddhas, enlightened ones, and that all they must do is wake up to this fact. Shamatha and vipassana techniques are used in both, but from a different perspective; they act to overcome the attempts of the ego to dictate what is real and to signal the mind to release the perception of a self that has a substantial, independent existence. Working with negative emotions is an important part of both practice lineages, and the energy of these emotions is used in the process of transformation rather than rejected. However, the ultimate aim of both practice lineages is simply letting go into the openness and awareness undivided that is every being's deepest nature and then stabilizing in this state. Essential to this are instructions from the teacher about the nature of mind; in fact, the teacher, or guru, plays a pivotal role in all of the practices. As Vajrayana practices, both Dzogchen and Mahamudra rely on visualizations, mantras, and devotional practices focused on fully enlightened beings who embody the qualities of the natural state and evoke the practitioner's identical innate qualities. Many of these practices engage the subtle energy body, and the Mahamudra tradition contains a group of advanced practices known as the Six Yogas of Naropa that work with different human states—waking, dreaming, sleeping deeply, dying—as a path to awakening. The mind cannot think its way into the natural state, but through study and contemplation of its qualities and then the direct experiencing of them, the meditator invites buddha nature to make itself known.
Contact: www.mahamudracenter.org, www. pundarika.org, or www.tsegyalgar.org

Lojong is a set of practices that train the heart and mind in bodhicitta, the spirit of awakening that causes the practitioner to strive for enlightenment not only for the self but for the sake of all sentient beings. This practice was brought to Tibet by the Indian sage Atisha in the eleventh century CE, set down in its present form by Geshe Chekawa in the twelfth century CE, and practiced in all schools of Tibetan Buddhism. The essence of Lojong is reliance on a set of slogans that provide guidance in realizing ultimate and relative bodhicitta, taking difficulties into the path, measuring progress, maintaining discipline, and using the practices as a way of life. The slogans offer positive remedies to offset the conditioned ways of thinking and behaving that lead to suffering, and the practice creates the conditions for compassion to arise. They are often practical advice, such as "Don't wait in ambush" or "Don't confuse the worldly for the spiritual," but their meanings run much deeper than their simple language. A number of commentaries give insight into these deeper meanings, among them Jamgön Kongtrül's *Great Path to Awakening*, Pema Chödrön's *Always Maintain a Joyful Mind*, and Dilgo Khyentse Rinpoche's *Enlightened Courage*. The most well-known of the Lojong practices is tonglen, the meditative process by which a person exchanges the self for others by breathing in suffering and breathing out the energy of love as a powerful, though counterintuitive, act of compassion. Although contemplation of the Lojong slogans may be accomplished during meditation, they are pithy, powerful reminders of the importance of motivation in each thought, word, and act, and they are actually meant to be actively carried out under any circumstances in day-to-day life.
Contact: www.pemachodronfoundation.org/ articles

There are many other forms of Tibetan meditation that work with the spaciousness of the ocean of our inner awareness and incorporate practices involving extensive use of the breath in conjunction with particular movements of the body. The practice of Tsa Lung as found within the indigenous Bön Religion is one such energetic practice that is discussed in Chapter 8.

Zen Meditation is a Mahayana form that came to Japan in the twelfth century CE from the Chan Buddhism of China. Several distinct schools of practice developed, but all emphasize zazen ("seated meditation") and walking meditation as the most important avenue to enlightenment (satori). Zen Buddhism, like other Mahayana traditions, understands that all beings are buddhas, a fact that they can only experience themselves. From the Zen perspective, enlightenment can only be attained through direct insight, in which conceptual thinking and words cannot confuse the process. The personal guidance of a teacher is critical to the practitioner's progress, because the teacher is responsible for directly transmitting knowledge to the practitioner; as can be imagined, lineage and the purity of transmission is of fundamental importance in the Zen tradition. Teachings do not always rely on language, and may be as simple as a whack on the head or pointing at the moon in response to a question. The rigorous practice of Zen became better known in the West in the 1950s and 1960s through the writings and teachings of D.T. Suzuki and Shunryu Suzuki, and Zen was celebrated by beat poets such as Allen Ginsburg and Gary Snyder.

The practices of Zen include concentration exercises to still the mind, such as following the breath and awareness during walking meditation, formless seated meditation in which the mind is observed without judgment, and the contemplation of koans. Koans are puzzling statements or questions—a classic example is "What is the sound of one hand clapping?"—which cannot be answered by the conceptual mind but can precipitate an intuitive understanding of the nature of mind; they are used by teachers as a way of communicating with and testing students. Chanting is also an important part of Zen practice; the Perfection of Wisdom Sutra is frequently chanted as part of the daily liturgy, and chanting is also used to connect with the bodhisattvas who are dedicated to the awakening of all beings. In its purest form, Zen meditation is just sitting without any goals or any expectations, instead resting in absolute stillness and the spaciousness of the original mind.
Contact: www.zen-buddhism.net

Hara and Core Star Meditation

This contemporary form of meditation, which draws from both the Ayurvedic and traditional Chinese healing traditions, is a subtle process of visualizing the luminous life-force energy of all realms of the universe and drawing it into the human body. Its goal is to revitalize and cleanse a person's energy so that she becomes centered, peaceful, and in harmony with all of life. The practice creates a deep connection with the sky above and the earth below through the hara line, which is a central subtle-energy channel that runs "inside" the energy vortices (chakras) and has great influence on what is manifested through the chakra system. It passes through the lower dantien energy-storage center, the core star, and the soul seat (higher heart) in the upper chest and then out through the crown of the head to the soul star and beyond as an omnidirectional connection with the realm of divine love. Connecting with the hara line through this transformative meditation practice results in deeper alignment with intentions, divine essence, and soul purpose in life. The core star, or inner radiant essence, is a place deep within the subtle energy body (often portrayed as located in the center of the physical body) where there is a profound connection between an individual life and the divine universal nature of existence. Becoming centered there is the ultimate goal of this practice. The soul seat is a place of deep calm within, a subtle, multidimensional space that contains all possibilities and is beyond all polarizing energies and dualistic inclinations. The hara line, the soul seat, and the core star constitute the subtle, bioplasmic, universal link between the finer resonant frequencies of the divine energy fields and a person's energy anatomy (the seven auric fields, the chakras, and the energy channels, or nadis). In a sense, this divine high-frequency energetic essence is distilled into a form of pranic energy, which is diffused throughout the physical body. Since the innate creative and healing energies that well up from the core star deep within each person are often clouded by the grosser energies of restrictive thoughts and feelings, pure insight can be obscured on a conscious level. The Hara meditation works to counter this tendency by enhancing the uncluttered flow of pure divine healing light and awareness through the energy anatomy.

This guided meditation is performed with eyes closed in a relaxed standing posture after the practitioner has taken measures to become grounded. A series of focused visualization exercises in conjunction with deep breathing aligns the consciousness with higher powers through different locations along the hara line.

The earth energies are first connected with the lower dantien energy storage center, and then this connection expands up through the soul seat in the heart center and beyond the crown to the soul star and the heavens. The meditation proceeds in stages with focusing, breathing, and visualizations to enhance the perception and recognition of this line of divine light energy that exists deep within the core. The final stages of the meditation focus on the core star within the central abdominal core of the body; according to certain intuitives, this is where the connection to the eternal divine and real creative insights are manifested once the hara line is in total alignment with the higher energy fields.

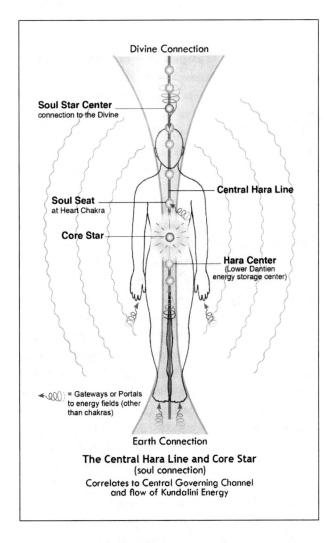

Divine Connection

Soul Star Center
connection to the Divine

Central Hara Line

Soul Seat
at Heart Chakra

Core Star

Hara Center
(Lower Dantien
energy storage center)

= Gateways or Portals
to energy fields (other
than chakras)

Earth Connection

The Central Hara Line and Core Star
(soul connection)
Correlates to Central Governing Channel
and flow of Kundalini Energy

The practice is often directed by intuitive energy healers, sometimes with the help of spirit beings. It works to energetically flush out all impurities and replace them with an upwelling of more advanced light energy. This new flow of energy from the divine realm has the capacity to transform dysfunctional thoughts and emotions and to expand awareness of a person's pure essence and soul purpose, which is oneness with the cosmos.

Contact: www.wingmakers.co.nz/Hara_Line_And_
    Core_Star_Medatation.html

Hindu Meditation

In the Hindu tradition, the goal of meditation is moksha, or liberation from the samsaric cycle of rebirths; the final stage before moksha is samadhi, a transcendent state of awareness in which the conscious is expanded beyond the dualistic and conceptual realm of mental understanding. Meditative techniques help the practitioner reach this place from which they can release into moksha. Meditation in the Hindu tradition is intertwined with yoga—not just the embodied practice of Hatha Yoga, but all eight branches, including pranayama breathwork—since these practices progressively prepare the body, still the mind, and open the heart. Meditative aids include visualizations (such as illuminating colors and light), sounds (chants and mantras), mudras (sacred hand positions), one-pointed concentration (gazing), especially on the third eye or a candle flame, and devotional practices. Various pranayama techniques work with the flow of vital pranic energy, directing it through various channels to the chakras and subtle energy bodies. Hatha Yoga exercises help the meditator sit for longer periods of time, and different meditation techniques may be combined with the postures. Many forms of yoga, especially Bhakti Yoga, rely on the visualization of deities such as Shiva or Krishna, and devotion to these enlightened beings stimulates devotion to the divine nature of all beings, including the self; many times, the heart is offered as a symbolic act of dedication. Sacred vibrational sounds are intended to melt away the endless chatter of the "monkey mind" and bring the whole being into resonance with harmony, balance, and unity, qualities inherent in the divine.

Meditation is the essence of most forms of yoga, such as Bhakti Yoga, Dhyana Yoga, Kriya Yoga, Kundalini Yoga, Siddha Yoga, and Tantric Yoga. Various practice lineages, often working with Ayurvedic healing practices, have preserved and continue to teach the means to maintain a continuous state of flowing energy and concentration that clears away the cobwebs and clouds of everyday perception and ultimately gives rise to the state of bliss and unity with the highest reality. (See more in the section on yoga in Chapter 11 and the section on pranayama in Chapter 8.)

Symbol of the sacred sound of Om.

Kundalini Meditation is directed at kundalini, the fiery life-force energy often portrayed as a serpent goddess that lies dormant in its home at the base of the spine. When it is awakened, it can be an agent of powerful spiritual change as it rises through the central energy channel and permeates the chakras and energy anatomy. The experience of kundalini rising can feel like a powerful wave crashing onto the shore or a smooth dive into the ocean of life-force energy. This can happen spontaneously under certain circumstances, and if the recipient of its power is not prepared, it can be troubling and overwhelming and can leave her quite lost and perhaps emotionally disturbed. However, when experienced through guided meditation, the awakening of kundalini can manifest as a state of mystical ecstasy with new insights, though this state can only be maintained with practice. Kundalini Meditation reflects the belief that the purpose of life is to achieve cosmic consciousness.

This life-force energy cannot be forced to wake up, but Kundalini Meditation, which has elements similar to pranic healing and tantric practices, can invite such an occurrence. The guided practice proceeds slowly in stages with great focus and attention inward to specific areas of the body. The awakening comes as a result of the participant's consciously and mindfully using the breath in conjunction with yoga asanas, visualizations, sounds, and techniques

for cultivation of prana. A variety of mental and sensory exercise may also be included. This form of meditation is considered a powerful way of quickly expanding consciousness, but it can take time to fully integrate the changes, which the intellect is often powerless to grasp. No words can express the essence of the revelations that occur when entering the uncharted territory of the mystical realm. Contact: www.kundalini.org/meditation.html

Transcendental Meditation® (TM) was transmitted by Maharishi Mahesh Yogi, and is based in the ancient Ayurvedic tradition of India. It became very popular during the 1960s and 1970s after the Beatles embraced it as a spiritual path. The aim of TM is to enhance physiological balance and body-mind integration through a simple program of postures, chanting, and pranayama breathing exercises. By developing a state of resting in alertness in which the practitioner can settle inward beyond thought to the peaceful level of consciousness that is the true self, these practices strengthen pure awareness and restore the knowledge and experience of higher states of consciousness.

TM does not attempt to train the mind through concentration, but uses the continuous chanting of a mantra (given to each student individually by a teacher) to overcome the conceptual mind's tendency to control things, thus allowing the practitioner to simply, naturally, and effortlessly transcend thinking and enter a state of alert restfulness. Certain sacred phrases or words can also be repeated out loud or silently. Just focusing on the chanting is a relatively easy way to keep from being distracted and prevent the mind from wandering. Contact: www.tm.org

Mindfulness-Based Stress Reduction (MSRB)
Mindfulness meditation practices have become widely available today and have been shown to be helpful in calming the mind, reducing stress, easing chronic pain, and improving health. They teach techniques for focusing on the experience of the present moment—the thoughts, feelings, sensations that are occurring—by simply noticing whatever happens without repressing or judging anything. One of the most available programs is the Mindfulness-Based Stress Reduction program

developed by Dr. Jon Kabat-Zinn at the University of Massachusetts Medical School. This method uses the increased awareness provided by mindfulness practices to reduce personal suffering, whatever its cause, by drawing on a person's deep inner resources. Rigorous scientific research has shown not only a reduction in physical and emotional symptoms and improved immune system functioning but also specific changes in the brain's circuitry caused by the repeated meditation practice.

At the heart of MSRB is a form of meditation from the Buddhist tradition in which the participant mindfully observes the breath. Participants commit to an eight-week training program that includes formal instruction and daily practice. They are guided in techniques for scanning the body, a sitting meditation using the breath as the focus of attention, and sitting and standing yoga. The instructional materials include information on bringing mindfulness into relationships, mindful communication, and working with pain. Each week's program also includes suggestions and informal practices for mindfulness in daily living.
Contact: www.umassmed.edu/Content.aspx?id=41254
    or www.palousemindfulness.com/
    selfguidedMBSR.html

Taoist Meditation

Taoist meditation is a relaxed, practical, and unstructured form of meditation. It is considered to be more like heightened observation than the rigid silencing of the mind. No force is used to bring stillness into play; whatever happens is simply observed without any interference. It encourages letting things be as they are, often with reference to the way things exist in nature. They primarily work with the process of generating, cultivating, transforming, and circulating vital chi energy internally, in order to promote better health, enable more personal power, and enhance the possibility of longevity. Once this is accomplished, it is possible to transmit this energy to others to increase their well-being.

Taoist meditation primarily teaches methods of using the breath, circulating chi through the major meridians, reducing energy leaks, and developing radiance by absorbing both cosmic chi from the universe and primal energy from the earth. These energies are often mixed, stored, and dispersed throughout the body to places it is needed. The process works to balance dualistic nature of reality, the opposites of yin and yang, and the male and female energies, while harmonizing the five basic elements of life—wood, fire, earth, metal, and water.

A classic method of refining and circulating chi is known as Microcosmic Orbit meditation. It involves using intention and breath to move internal vital energy in a circular fashion through the primary governing and conception channels located between the perineum and the head. It draws abundant energy up from the sacral area into the crown of the head and then returns it to the lower dantien energy storage center in the navel; from there, it can be distributed to the meridians associated with the major organs of the body, thereby delivered needed energy to them. The meditation also works in stages to cultivate the golden elixir of immortality through a practice that begins in the lower abdomen, moves to fill the primary channels, and culminates in the midbrain. This form of self-healing meditation also has a number of more advanced practices. (See more on this and other Taoist meditative techniques in Chapters 8 and 11).
Contact: www.1stholistic.com/meditation/hol_
    meditation_taoist_meditation.htm or
    www.energyarts.com/taoist-meditation

Finding Wholeness

Finding wholeness requires removing the many veils that cover up our true aspirations, potential, and soul purpose. Change is a natural part of life, and we will all leave this earthly plane someday. While we are here, being able to go with the flow and allow changes to happen will prevent our being bound up by limiting perceptions.

We humans are really spiritual beings in a physical body. The essence of our true loving nature is revealed in a baby's eyes, for her consciousness is not long gone from the sea of awareness from which she came into this world. The depths of this inner ocean are free of surface commotion, and once we dive into that stillness through meditation, we know that the deep-blue refuge is always there no matter the conditions are like on the surface. Rather than being spaced out by the entanglements of the world, we become spaced in to a state of inner knowing and witnessing. The more we can surrender and dive into this realm, the more insight we can acquire. To maintain this journey through the practice of meditation requires a balance between diligence, relaxed effort, and surrender to the vast realm of the universal consciousness. From that perspective, the ego will continue to express itself, but will no longer run the show. The intent of all elements of meditative practice is to become the subtlest expression of the self, in which there is only spacious, awake, and radiant consciousness, free of any qualities of craving, clinging, or aversion.

CHAPTER 11
A World of Self-Care Healing Practices and Exercises

In this chapter, we'll look at self-directed transformative practices, enjoyable exercises, and movement therapies you can carry out to help you move along the path to wholeness. They include forms of yoga, qi gong, martial arts, dance, physical movement exercises, nutrition, aquatic therapies, kinesthetic exercises, self-massage, sensory awareness practices, vibrational experiences, and integrative forms of play. All are embodied practices that call on you to use diligence and attentiveness in an active and conscious way.

Movement is fundamental to life in a healthy human body, and many of these practices have a movement component, whether it is physical or the subtle coursing of energy. Since the physical and the energetic combine in the act of breathing, awareness of the breathing process and the movement of energy are frequently an intimate part of these self-care practices as physical activity is mindfully synchronized with the breath.

Many of these practices initially require the guidance of an experienced instructor to teach you the fine points of the method. Instruction generally takes place in a group setting, often in a large room in a holistic health center or yoga center, and sometimes in in a swimming pool. Some require minimal training to perfect quickly, whereas others may require involve years of discipline to master. Most of these activities can be performed for as little as twenty minutes or as much as a number of hours on a daily, weekly or monthly basis. Whether you want to simply enhance physical performance or desire an experience of spiritual transformation, success will come through diligent practice and by keeping your attention focused inward so you can become more embodied and conscious of the deep pool of awareness that it already there inside.

If you've read any other parts of this book, you're familiar with the way the word *practitioner* has been used: a professionally trained therapist performs the techniques contained in a modality. However, in this chapter, you are that somebody. So expect to see *practitioner* used to describe the person actually carrying out the practice.

Taking the plunge into tropical waters is a fun way to take care of yourself.

Self-care practices and exercises require individual initiative and discipline to establish a regular practice. However, once you begin, the welcome feelings of increased vitality, balanced emotions, and the simple joy of being alive will provide the motivation to continue. All of the practices and exercises mentioned here support the increased self-awareness that can become part of your daily life. They usually do not entail any hands-on bodywork or massage applied by a practitioner; however, some of the healing practices, particularly those with Eastern origins, are part of a complex system and may include some elements of bodywork described in Chapter 6. Making these self-rejuvenating practices an integral part of your life can provide an inexpensive way for preventing blockages or dysfunctions that may lead to disharmony or illness. Self-care practices also enhance the ability to be a better bodywork practitioner assisting others in the healing process. Since improving yourself is really a prerequisite for helping others, anyone wanting to be a healer would be wise to take up some of these practices.

Aerobics to Yoga

Aerobics and Aqua Aerobics
Aerobics is a simple but vigorous exercise program that enhances basic fitness and energizes the physical

body. This enjoyable form of exercise was developed during the 1960s and is usually done in a group while moving to lively music. It's a fun, effective, and safe way to get in shape. An instructor demonstrates the arm, leg, and core exercises and stretches and leads the participants through sets of repetitions. Sessions usually begin with warm-up movements, continue with more vigorous exercises, and finish with relaxing moves that cool participants down. Appropriate for any age or ability, it is ideal for conditioning the cardiovascular system, increasing metabolism, and helping with weight reduction.

Aqua Aerobics is a more fluid form of aerobic exercise carried out while standing chest deep in a swimming pool. Just as with regular aerobics, movements are performed rhythmically, sometimes to music. The aquatic version is particularly beneficial for pregnant women, senior citizens, and those recovering from an injury. The support and natural resistance of water makes it a relaxing yet effective way to remove stress and tone the body.

Contact: www.livestrong.com/aerobics or
www.livestrong.com/sscat/water-aerobics

Aikido

In those films showing a venerable Asian man repelling a number of attackers without any apparent movement, the hero was probably an Aikido master who had perfected the ability to harmonize his energy with the universal ki (the Japanese name for the life-force energy). Aikido is an ancient, powerful, and formerly secret Japanese martial arts practice that was brought into the light by Morihei Ueshiba during the mid-1900s. Though considered one of the martial arts, it relies on ki energy within the meridian pathways and energy fields of the body rather than aggression to disarm an opponent. The goal of this highly disciplined "peaceful path" is mastering the self by stilling the mind and remaining present in the moment and centered in the body.

A variety of exercises are used to cultivate awareness, release fear, and increase flexibility, strength, and coordination. All movement is synchronized with the breath and accomplished from a grounded state of meditative concentration and mental and physical balance. Like other martial arts, physical training include holds, locks, pins, throws, blows, breakfalls, rolls, and escapes. More important is learning to use ki, which is delivered through fluid, three-dimensional circular or spiraling

motions from rapidly changing positions. Instead of developing physical strength to throw or resist punches, the practitioner trains to anticipate the attacking movements of opponents and then softly diffuse, disrupt, or counter this energy. Masters in this art have been known to defeat a competitor without ever striking a blow. Beginners practice techniques, such as the unbendable arm, to learn to calm the mind and connect more strongly with the energy within. Mastery takes years of training, but there is much to be gained from even the earliest stages of this practice.

Practicing Aikido can nurture the control, calmness, and self-confidence that will help anyone deal harmoniously with life's stressful situations and resolve conflict without force. For example, an elder Aikido practitioner was preparing to catch his bus home one evening. Just as he was boarding, a young man pushed by him, shouting that he was looking for a women who had deserted him and that he would kill anyone who got in his way. The old practitioner slowly entered the bus behind him. The only available seat was next to highly agitated man, who looked ready to explode at the least provocation. As the practitioner sat down beside him, the young man pulled out a gun, and it was clear that he hoped his aggressive actions would provoke someone into fighting with him. The old man sensed the anguish beneath the hostile behavior, and instead of responding fearfully to the young man's explosive energy, he began to speak as a friend about relationship problems. In the absence of resistance, the angry fellow eased up and put the gun away. As the old man continued speaking softly, the younger man relaxed more and more, much to the relief of the other passengers. Because the wise master used the Aikido principle of blending with the other's energy, a potentially lethal situation had been defused. At the next stop, the young man left the bus muttering nothing more than discontent with his situation.

Contact: www.aikido.com

Aquatic Exercises

Aquatic exercises depend on the support and fluidity provided by water in practices that are helpful for relieving stiffness and improving range of motion. Like Aqua Aerobics, these practices can be used as part of a rehabilitation program for those with disabilities, including neurological impairments. The following is a sample of available self-care practices; forms delivered by practitioners can be found within the section on Aquatic Therapies in Chapter 6.

Contact: Aquatic Exercise Association –
www.aeawave.com or Aquatic Therapy &
Rehab Institute – www.atri.org.

BackHab, developed by Ruth Sova, is a program of walking carried out in a pool that uses different strides to improve the balance and coordination of all parts of the body. When the whole body functions well, problem areas will automatically benefit. As its name indicates, BackHab was developed particularly for people with back problems or disabilities involving mobility. Participants learn to identify the cause of pain, how lifestyle contributes to it, and how to resolve it. Once this integrated exercise program is learned through classes with an instructor or videotapes, it can easily be practiced at any time.

Contact: www.ruthsova.com/backhab.htm

Burdenko Method is a system for conditioning, training, and rehabilitation based on water and land exercise programs. It was developed by Dr. Igor Burdenko and designed to develop balance, coordination, flexibility, endurance, speed, and strength in everyday life and sports activities. Working in water decompresses the body and avoids the force of gravity, which helps restore the body function. The method focuses on promoting proper alignment and incorporates exercises performed on different planes, in different directions, and at varying speeds to enhance basic movement patterns. Sessions integrate both land-based and water-based techniques, using a systematic progression of exercises based on the individual's needs.

Contact: Burdenko Water & Sports Therapy
Institute – www.burdenko.com

Halliwick Concept is a healing therapy formulated by James McMillan and his wife, Phil, in the early 1950s that employs water activities to teach primarily people with physical challenges or learning difficulties how to swim and move easily. A ten-point program works with balance control, movement, and mental adjustment and is performed paired with a facilitator. Games allow the facilitator to hold or cradle the client in the water and systematically and progressively teach balance and postural control. The activities are designed to guide the client through progressively more sophisticated rotational control to increase strength, mobility, and stability while decreasing any pain. The client is required to react and eventually predict what is needed to improve his neurological and musculoskeletal systems.

Contact: www.halliwick.org,
www.halliwick.org.uk, or
www.hermitage.ch

Water Pilates / Aquapilates is the Pilates exercise program adapted for use in a pool. Water provides a helpful antigravity medium for this series of movements, which focuses on flexibility, range of motion, musculoskeletal spinal alignment, and postural awareness. It also incorporates controlled breathing and abdominal strengthening techniques. There is more about Pilates in the section on Dance and Movement Therapies in this chapter.

Contact: www.aquapilates.net or
www.poolates.com

*Women on a remote island in the Pacific
make music by drumming on seawater.*

Water Yoga is the practice of performing flowing Vinyasa or Hatha Yoga poses while partially submerged in warm water. As with traditional yoga, its aim is to develop body-mind awareness and balance through movement coordinated with full breathing and long exhalations. Water is a very supportive medium that allows people of all levels of flexibility to enjoy fluid movement in all directions. Freed of the restrictions of gravity, participants find it easier to let go, relax, and receive the benefits of restorative poses. The temperature of the water and the time spent in it are the keys to providing a successful experience. This therapeutic form of practice is usually done in a pool of warm water while standing, floating, or supported by props. However, for those with a background in yoga, it is a fairly simple task to adapt certain movements to swimming in a pond or lake. Although not every asanas can translate to the water environment, modified back bends and spiral twists are quite possible while floating in deep water. Contact: www.wateryoga.net

Bagua Exercise Program

Bagua, more often referred to as Yin Style Bagua (YSB) or Bagua Zhang, is an ancient Chinese exercise and martial arts program for cultivating internal chi that was reintroduced by Dong Haichuan during the early to mid 1800s and passed on during the 1900s by Dr. Xie Peigi, who also played a part in the spread of the Tuina and Bagua Bodywork modalities. The exercises that are part of the Bagua Exercise Program combine meditations, moderate physical movements, breathwork, and the vibrations of eight healing sounds to open the flow of chi in the body's meridians and organs. The exercises are designed to promote self-regulation, improved strength, and healing, and they are closely associated with Nei Gong and qi gong.

The practice includes exercises in storing chi, practices involving the three dantiens (Chinese energy centers in the body), spinal passes, organ-strengthening poses, and methods of maintaining health. Movements are done in a slow, deliberate manner in conjunction with deep breathing and focused intention to produce a relaxation response, a stronger awareness of the vital life-force energy, and an enhanced ability to cultivate chi and direct it to where it is needed. There are twelve guided meditations, which are the most demanding since they require difficult postures while balanced on the knees. These exercises are only one part of the larger system of Bagua, which includes hands-on bodywork and martial arts practices that incorporate movements learned from animals, circle-turning techniques, and martial arts attack methods that use point striking. (See Bagua Bodywork in the section on Energy-Based Therapies in Chapter 6.)
Contact: Academy of Chinese Martial & Cultural
Arts – www.academychinesearts.org or
www.energyarts.com/bagua-zhang

Being in Movement®
Mindbody Education (BIM)

Being in Movement was developed by Paul Linden as a way of making the core elements of Aikido (a nonviolent martial art) more easily taught and learned. BIM includes both movement instruction and hands-on bodywork. It is an empirical, educational process that examines the self in the world, looking at interactions among musculoskeletal structure and function; movement planning underlying actions; thoughts, feelings, and beliefs; task performance; and ethical behavior. BIM models and teaches people the skills of logic, language analysis, clear definitions of terms, and evidence-based thinking.

One focus is overcoming the distress response. When people are challenged or threatened, the natural tendency is to constrict or collapse the body, attention, and movement. However, that response results in unnecessary strain and fatigue, creates feelings of powerlessness, and interferes with free, effective action. By learning how to open and balance their breathing, muscles, posture, and movement, people can develop an expansive physical and mental state of relaxed alertness, power, and kindness. This state of mind-body integrity is the key to handling any of life's challenges effectively.

BIM teaches empowerment through a specific process. The first step is to identify a challenging and/or threatening event in the client's life. Then the instructor helps the student identify the body responses to the practice stimulus, which will usually be contractive or collapsing. Next, the student is taught how to create a mind-body state of expansiveness, and practice using that space as a means of managing the practice event. The process is repeated with a graded series of increasingly intense stimuli until the original life situation has been mastered. BIM focuses on themes such as: relaxation—comfort and ease in breathing, posture, and movement, along with centered ways of dealing with pain and stress; personal growth—learning to sense the body foundations of emotional and spiritual states by moving toward a way of living based on awareness, power, and love; task improvement—efficient, injury-free, confident functioning in areas such as music, sports, computer use, pregnancy, or daily life activities; trauma work—reclaiming the body after physical or sexual abuse, surgery, injuries, or other overwhelming events; conflict resolution and assertiveness—creating

a body state of nonviolence, confidence, and strong boundaries as a foundation for effective ways of dealing with difficult situations.
Contact: www.being-in-movement.com

Breathing Practices – See Chapter 8

Budokon®

Yoga has often been integrated with other self-healing modalities to produce some unique forms of bodywork therapy. One such hybrid practice, known as Budokon, was developed around 2002 by martial arts and yoga master Kancho Cameron Shayne. Budokon combines Hatha Yoga, meditation, and certain elements of martial arts to stimulate strength, balance, and harmony in the body and mind. Its practices help practitioners uncover resistance and weakness and awaken to the true self through focused self-observation. It uses controlled movement to stimulate the cardiovascular system and eliminate toxins, along with meditations that enhance the ability to be more mindful in the present.
Contact: www.budokonuniversity.com

Chua K'a Bodywork™

Chua K'a Bodywork was created by Oscar Ichazo, who founded the Arica School® where Chua K'a Bodywork is presented as a two-day intensive group training. Chua K'a is deep bodywork done on oneself that enables the body to evolve to its highest degree of sensitivity and awareness. The impact of life experiences creates networks of muscular tension (pain) that are remembered fears. Working the tissues with precise hand and finger positions and a stick called a K'a, participants learn to transmit energy and heat to the bones, removing the tension. When physical tension is released, psychic tension is released as well. The complete Chua K'a Bodywork procedure consists of a uniquely detailed and comprehensive massage of the body, followed by a rolling of the skin (Skin Rolling), and ending with the application of the K'a stick.

The Arica School® was founded in 1968 by Oscar Ichazo as a School of Wisdom and Knowledge and has been offering programs and trainings worldwide since 1970. The website contains overviews of the school, Oscar Ichazo, the Arica System, training information, and articles. (Chua K'a Bodywork and The Arica School are trademarks of Oscar Ichazo, used with permission.)
Contact: Arica Institute – www.arica.org

Dance and Exercise Programs

The instinct to dance has been with humans since the dawn of time. As well as an enjoyable form of exercise, dance is a creative and energetic way to relieve stress and express deep feelings. In addition, dance can be a sacred form of celebration and a means to connect with the inner self. Dance is a great way to learn to love the body, and the therapeutic benefits for both the body and mind are far reaching. Most of the programs included here focus on helping people improve self-esteem and body image and deepen insight into patterns of behavior. This can disclose new options for coping with problems and improving self-expression. Since many of the dance therapies are done in a group setting, it is also a great way to connect with other people.

Movement and dance both permit direct experience of the self through the body; this kind of consciousness requires intensifying awareness of the sensations of the body through direct attention and intention. The recognition that dance and movement could also be therapeutic arose in the 1930s with the work of Marian Chace. Initially, it was considered a powerful tool for stress management and the prevention of physical and mental health problems. Since then, many others have developed different methods that enhance personal spontaneity, creativity, and self-awareness. The number of available movement-based therapies has exploded in recent years, and organizations such as the American Dance Therapy Association and the World Dance Alliance have been established to support and promote these offerings, as well as to maintain standards of excellence and competence within the field. In the more clinical psychological methods of Dance Movement Therapy, students are specifically trained and recognized as a Dance Therapist, Registered (DTR). After additional hours of clinical work, they are awarded the title of Academy of Dance Therapist, Registered (ADTR). Practitioners of other forms of dance therapy often have extensive dance experience, whereas in forms based on yoga, teachers are trained in their respective field.

As distinct from the modalities described in the Functional Movement Therapies section of Chapter 6, those presented here are different in that the instructor or trainer rarely incorporates hands-on bodywork, instead performing an educational role. Rather than being one-on-one sessions with a practitioner in a clinical setting, they tend to be carried out in a group process and may incorporate elements from a variety of therapeutic modalities. Many of the following forms of movement therapy are easy to learn, but others require more diligent practice. Some focus primarily on resolving dysfunctional physical, emotional, and mental issues; others are dedicated to reeducating the body through enjoyable dance.

Dancers in Bali not only tell a sacred story but also demonstrate how diverse dance can be around the world.

People who have suffered physical abuse and who therefore have personal-safety issues during close interaction with others may want to consider the effects this kind of group activity could have. However, many facilitators are very aware of concerns about personal boundaries, and some of the therapies are actually designed to reduce this kind of fear and will guide participants slowly through the process of transforming and releasing any inhibitions.
Contact: American Dance Therapy Association – www.adta.org, World Dance Alliance – www.worlddancealliance.net, or WDA-Americas – www.wda-americas.net

Authentic Movement (AM) was formulated as a method for personal development through a meditative and expressive dance practice that reveals the true self and brings joy to movement by following the direction of inner impulses. It was created in the 1950s by dancer Mary Starks Whitehouse and further developed by Janet Adler and Joan Chodorow. The process approaches dance and movement therapy from a Jungian perspective, and emphasizes movement as a means of communication. This practice of self-directed exploration calls on deep sensing of the self, inner listening, compassion, and acceptance, and the movements can trigger powerful feelings from childhood or infancy. The heart of the practice is conscious awareness of where movement arises in the body. A deeper recognition of the felt sensations of unconscious impulses leads to better perception of the physical aspects that reflect personality. This method of movement basically allows the dancer to sink in deeply and expand out fully.

This relatively simple practice can take place in a group or with just two people; one person moves, while another witnesses the movement. Those who move rest in a comfortable position, close their eyes, and wait without any conscious effort for a sensation or energetic impulse to arise from deep within. They then allow the feelings, thoughts, images, or memories that emerge to lead them into movement. Allowing the movement to arise spontaneously rather than trying to control it shifts the body naturally out of old and less effective patterns of activity. It is critical to maintain a nonjudgmental attitude, accepting the movement and the self behind it exactly as they are. Meanwhile, the witness simply observes mindfully without judgment, noticing how these movements affect her personally. If she chooses, she can move and make physical contact with the other person. Here, both individuals have the opportunity to see, hear, and feel the other. When the session ends, both the witness and the mover discuss their experiences. In a group session, pairs of participants work together. Besides being a good form of exercise, AM can be a useful tool for connecting with others through movement and stillness.
Contact: www.authenticmovementinstitute.com

Biodanza, founded by Rolando Toro Araneda during the 1960s, integrates music, intentional movement, and authentic interaction into a form of group therapy. Based on rituals that celebrate the sacredness of life, Biodanza, which means "dance of life," is intended to stimulate a sense of community while awakening individual consciousness and the sense of being alive in the present moment. Stimulating music provided almost entirely by acoustic instruments is considered the key ingredient for accessing primal emotions and the natural expression of the true self. Most groups are composed of about twenty people, though there have been sessions with more than a hundred participants. Gradual physical contact within the group provides a deeper sense of connection with others, and as the session progresses, each individual learns to recognize others' needs for either space or contact. Classes are very active and energizing, but by no means are they as vigorous as an aerobic exercise class, for the movements can also be quiet and gentle. Biodanza has an emotional component that uses biological rhythms and the pulse of the beating heart to facilitate the exploration and expression of individual creativity, vitality, sexuality, deep feelings, and spiritual transcendence. Biodanza is suitable for all ages and can also be performed in the water. Advanced classes, not appropriate for beginners, are also offered.

Contact: www.dev.biodanza4uk.com or
www.biodanza.us

Chakradance nourishes the true self through a blend of free-flowing movements and specific frequencies of sound provided by tones or evocative music. This healing practice, created by Australians Natalie Southgate and Douglas Channing, uses dance to explore and revitalize the seven primary energy centers in the body, known as the chakras, by removing blockages and opening up the flow of vital energy within the body. The music is designed to resonate with each chakra, progressing from the root chakra up to the crown chakra. Chakradance also brings the collective energies of the group into play to make the process enjoyable. Moving with eyes closed or covered with a mask in a room lit only with candles, dancers are encouraged to connect with the feelings and sensations that make up their inner worlds. They may then find that memories stored in the muscles awaken and release. Each dance can allow different insights that are later

expressed by creating a personal mandala drawing. This freestyle practice usually lasts for about two hours and is intended to provide a joyful sense of inner exploration that can be spiritually freeing. Longer dances are also done for special occasions. Other variations of chakra dancing have also been created by individuals involved in different spiritual practices.

Contact: www.chakradance.com

Contact Improvisation (CI), a system of improvisational movement danced with a partner, was founded in 1972 by dancer Steve Paxton, who celebrated nontraditional dance movements in his choreography. Contact Improv, as it is often called, is performed without dialogue or music by two people who always maintain a shared point of contact as they constantly move and explore touch, momentum, friction, and shared weight. Dancers play spontaneously with space as they learn to fall, roll, slide, counterbalance, lift with minimal effort, and respond to individual boundaries while still feeling connected. The emphasis is on touching the partner in ways and positions that not only give the

Enjoying Contact Improvisation.

sensations of a moving body massage, but create a spontaneous and mutually supportive way of enjoying each other. The dancers need to be responsive to their surroundings and aware of not only their own balance and breath but also that of their partners. The experience helps the participant learn how to allow and respond to unexpected movement and also how to relax the whole body and surrender to the support of another. Dances can be done in pairs or in a large group.
Contact: www.contactimprov.com/
　　　　whatiscontactimprov.html or
　　　　www.contactquarterly.com/
　　　　contact-improvisation

Continuum Movement is designed to help participants sense themselves as the fluidly moving beings they were in the watery environment from which they evolved. The body itself is defined by the movement of fluids within it, as blood, cerebrospinal fluid, lymph, and other fluid elements create a circulating communications network that speaks with the body's wisdom. Dancer Emilie Conrad, joined by Susan Harper, developed Continuum Movement during the 1960s as a way to help a person support the intimate connection between brain function and the body's cellular intelligence by using a combination of movement, breathwork, sound, and meditation.

This form of movement education teaches exercises that resemble yoga, but are carried out with an undulating, wave-like motion that enhances the flow of fluids in the body. Instead of using a set linear routine, the practice is a form of free improvisational expression with an emphasis on creating space and making unpredictable flowing movements that will stimulate the mind and the nervous system. Participants also learn specific breathing and tonal sounds that help create different effects on the body and mind. Combining breath, sound, and wave-like movement stimulates inner sensations and evokes a rippling effect that resonates with the body fluids and touches into the essence of flexibility, fluidity, and wholeness.

Harper has developed her own program, Continuum Montage, that combines Continuum Movement with dream work and practices that awaken awareness, heighten perception, and bring embodiment into being.
Contact: www.continuummovement.com or
　　　　www.continuummontage.com

Coordination Patterns™, also known as the **Wetzig Technique**, was developed by choreographer and movement researcher Betsy Wetzig during the 1970s, building on previous research into neuromuscular tension patterns. She recognized that the qualities of certain movements, which she identified as thrust, shape, swing, and hang, were correlated with specific personality archetypes that predict how a person communicates, creates, and learns. She combined these elements into Coordination Patterns, which can be used to improve physical, mental, and emotional functioning. Wetzig then developed ways of working with these patterns in an exercise program aimed at encouraging movement and mind to work as one.

The four Coordination Patterns describe personality as it is expressed in movement. Everyone is predisposed at birth to a certain pattern, and in these patterns, they exhibit the lowest neuromuscular tension levels. Although each individual uses all of these patterns, one usually dominates, and simple neurological tests are used to determine a person's patterns. Coordination Patterns training offers many easy exercises to help participants learn how to understand and develop the patterns and how to encourage a specific pattern to emerge or recede as necessary. Correctly applied, these exercises can lead to better physical movement and can enhance the practitioner's ability to discern the effects of the patterns on the self, on others, on relationship, and, indeed, on the whole world. This work relies on the body-mind connection to create a balanced, full, and healthy life.
Contact: www.moves4greatness.com

Core Connexion Transformational Arts® approaches dance as a moving meditation and a healing art. It was founded by Eva Vigran and is a synthesis of different forms of dance, martial arts, and meditation. The practice is intended to lead to creative expression from the core of the body by connecting it to breath and sensation. There are no steps to follow. Instead, participants follow musical themes, imagery, and suggestions. Guided though unstructured dance movement is used to inspire awareness and insight into the nature of the self and the way a person responds to the world. The movement is also used to affirm the feeling of being alive, help people get in touch with their bodies, and activate the life-force energy. Contact: www.coreconnexion.net

Dance of Liberation®, a healing dance experience created by Parashakti, helps allow inner creativity to break free from emotional, mental, and spiritual blockages. Although it is based in the shamanic tradition, the ritual dance actually weaves together the wisdoms from various traditions. Blindfolds are used to help provide a sense of mystery, enabling individuals to go deeper inward while dancing with a group of people to evocative music that often incorporates percussion and drumming. Individuals learn to feel the energetic interconnection of the whole group. Guides assist the dancers through the process of moving in the dark. Contact: www.parashakti.org

Dances of Universal Peace were the vision of Sufi teacher Samuel Lewis, also known as Sufi Sam, who was trying to find a way to promote peace worldwide. Conceived in the late 1960s, these events are simple, meditative, joyous circle dances that use the sacred phrases, chants, music, and movements of spiritual traditions from around the world to bring people together for open-hearted celebration and spiritual renewal that promote understanding and compassion. As people join hands in a circle, they perform a variety of dances and walking practices simply to create a joyous connection of heart and soul among all involved. Although originally based on Sufi traditions, over the years a growing number of movements and steps from many world traditions have been included in the Dances of Universal Peace. Dances can be held in many venues—schools, churches, retreat centers, peace gatherings—and at an assortment of different cultural events. In addition to circles that meet regularly, the dances are often done at seasonal ceremonies or during significant life passages. All the dances are open to everyone and to all ages. Contact: www.dancesofuniversalpeace.org

Dance Your Bliss is a transformative body-centered movement therapy created by psychotherapist and movement educator Rachel Fleischman, who was looking for a therapeutic approach that brought the body into traditional psychotherapy. Workshops help participants craft a dance of self-discovery, intended to celebrate their inner strengths and improve their lives. The process employs a body map to examine the inner world each participant has created, and expressive movement techniques guided by intuitive therapists help the dancers access the inner wisdom contained in the body and consciously connect with the true self. Each workshop is designed around individual needs without stipulating any specific steps. The practice can be done as a simple workout, but is more rewarding when the intention is a joyful experience of release for body, mind, and soul. Contact: www.dancingyourbliss.com

Dancing her bliss.
PHOTO COURTESY OF WENDY SICHEL

Dancing with Pain® is a holistic form of pain management taught to people suffering from chronic pain and to health care professionals through live and multimedia classes, workshops, and lectures. Journalist Loolwa Khazzom developed this therapeutic method based on the results she achieved through dancing during her own search for relief from pain. Rather than focusing on the pain itself, classes help participants learn how to dance comfortably from the places in the body that feel good. These movements can create new neural circuits that can alter, suppress, or even replace the pathways through which pain has been registered and can awaken the positive healing energy of pain-free movement. This method utilizes a feedback system

that encourages people to consciously tune in to their bodies and maintain attention there. The process takes courage and may not work for all forms of chronic pain, yet with patience and perseverance, relief may be possible. No previous dance or meditation experience is required, and even those who do not live with pain may find the process transformative.
Contact: www.dancingwithpain.com

Danyasa™ is a flowing movement practice that was created at the Costa Rican Danyasa Eco-Resort by its founder, Sofiah Thom. A fusion of Vinyasa Yoga and dance, Danyasa is taught in the resort's Bamboo Yoga Play studio and works with the principles of alignment found in the bamboo plant to provide flexibility, strength, rootedness, and openness. By experiencing the body as strong, supple, and sensual, participants learn how to express these inner resources and how to move through life with confidence, courage and presence. During the practice, which can take place with large group in a variety of natural settings, participants are encouraged to listen to their bodies while being guided through the movements by the facilitator. Expressive arts are part of the Danyasa experience, and various workshops use exercises in drawing, journaling, creative writing, and supportive dialogue.
Contact: www.danyasa.com or
www.sofiathom.com

5Rhythms®, developed during the 1970s when its creator, Gabrielle Roth, worked at the Esalen Institute, ushered in the era of ecstatic dance. It is a rhythmic and spirited moving meditation that allows practitioners to enter highly emotional and spiritual states. The goal in this style of dancing is to enable the dancers to open into their full creative potential by freeing themselves on every level. 5Rhythms facilitators call on vibrant music to accompany a journey that explores the way things naturally move and change as reflected in patterns of nature; just as a wave breaks on the shore, so does a surge of new feelings arise within a person. Roth recognized five kinds of motion that represent states of being: flowing, staccato, chaos, lyrical, and stillness. These can be danced alone or in sequence

to form a Wave. Although each participant in this group event is stimulated to dance with complete freedom of expression, the facilitator may direct participants to focus on a certain aspect of the body in movement to encourage creativity and self-awareness. Classes teach the basic elements of the five rhythms, and workshops delve deeper into 5rhythm maps, which are based on Roth's mandala of healing. 5Rhythms home base is at the Moving Center in New York City, but 5Rhythms workshops, classes and dance practices have spread worldwide, and video classes are available through Sounds True.

Over the years, Roth's work has inspired the creation of many other forms of dance movement therapies. 5Five Rhythms techniques have also been combined with Biodanza to create a more interactive group experience.
Contact: www.5rhythms.com

Finding ecstasy in 5Rhythms.

Folk Dance refers to traditional forms of dance that have been performed for many years as an integral part of many different cultures. Some are used for storytelling, and others have a more spiritual purpose. They are usually performed in a group and are a lively way to celebrate community. Folk Dance is also a great strategy to connect with past traditions within a local culture and to meet friendly people when traveling abroad. These dances are often taught at special dance camps held in various locations around the world.

Free Dance events, also referred to as Dance Free, represent the kind of gathering that originated in the 1960s. Free Dance is a very loose, undisciplined practice designed for enjoying life, releasing tension, and freeing self-expression. They promote the use of freestyle movements that help people release on many levels. Lively, rhythmic music is played, and participants need only get into the swing of things as they feel motivated. Free Dance can be a good activity for people who like to express themselves without restraint through the body in an open, accepting group environment.

Jazzercise, created in 1969 by Judi Missett, was one of the first exercise programs to make improving physical fitness enjoyable. A therapeutic method disguised as an entertaining group exercise experience that combines lively music with rhythmic dance movements, Jazzercise effectively improves physical flexibility and boosts cardiovascular functioning. Moves taken from yoga, Pilates, hip-hop, and kickboxing are fused into dance movements that are completed in a one-hour session. Jazzercise has grown in popularity and is offered in school programs and community fitness centers worldwide.

Journey Dance™ is a playful and intuitive method of using movement to discover and celebrate the god or goddess within. In 1997, Toni Bergins created this high-energy dance and fitness program as a means for personal growth and spiritual transformation. From her background in DansKinetics, yoga, and shamanism, Bergins designed a group journey of prayer and celebration by using dance as a spiritual practice that fosters inner strength, interaction, and creativity. Classes combine guided sequences of improvisational dance movements, elements of theater, ritual, sensual imagery, creative visualization, and vocalization to awaken the energy of transformation and inspire inner balance. Music with careful weavings of specific songs helps enliven the journey. Classes can be experienced in a daily fitness session, weekend workshop, or weeklong retreat.
Contact: www.journeydance.com

Kijo Body Meditation was created by Shelly Ross, a professional fitness trainer and shamanic medicine woman, as a complete workout for the body, mind,

emotions, and spirit. *Kijo* is the Hungarian word for snake and represents the mystery in all beings. Classes use powerful but easy-to-follow choreography that embraces all types of dance movements, shamanic healing principles, affirmations, and resistance training to build physical strength and self-confidence. Live music is produced with rattles, drums, and crystal bowls. For those seeking deeper meditative work, nine floor poses are used to open and align the hip, spine, and head, while settling the mind into a trance-like alpha state. Classes are open to everyone, and no experience with dance or meditation is required. In addition, special public ceremonies are offered at key spiritual times of the year, such as equinoxes and solstices. A fitness program is available for those who simply want to build stamina, and private shamanic healing rituals can address individual concerns.
Contact: www.wisewomanradio.com/interviews/ross.html

Kivo® Dance is a playful movement and vocalization practice developed by musician and dancer Lis Addison. *Kivo* combines the words *Kinetic* and *Voice*, and it blends conscious tribal dance with sound healing. Group workshops use rhythmic chants and playful heart-opening dance movements to create an ecstatic and spiritual experience. Attention to the vibrations of the human voice is considered important for connecting with the inner world and the higher self, and the movements create a state of embodiment. An attitude of inquiry about both the inner and outer aspects of presence is key to the practice. This practice is a fun and inspirational experience that is appropriate for all ages and abilities.
Contact: www.lisaddison.com/kivo

Kundalini Dance is an energetic self-healing journey through the chakras. By mixing free dance, meditation, and ritual, participants can gain insights about the body, mind, and soul that can lead to personal awakening and transformation. Developed by Leyola Antara from Australia, this practice calls on rhythmic beats and tantric and shamanic healing methods to lead participants through the seven chakras. It also incorporates a process to help clear old, stagnant emotional energy; this can provide a deeply cathartic experience. The overall goal is to bring insight and clarity about limiting beliefs while supporting the awakening of higher consciousness. Contact: www.kundalinidancetrainings.com

Nalini Method is a complete fitness experience that blends Pilates, yoga, aerobics, and strength and resistance training into a dynamic workout. Rupa Mehta created this movement program both for personal training and as an energetic activity that can be shared in a group setting. Its goal is to build physical strength while enhancing flexibility, improving endurance, increasing body awareness, and establishing better posture and body alignment. Class sizes are limited so that participants can receive personal attention, and any class with more than twenty students is facilitated by two teachers. Contact: www.nalinimethod.com

Nia (**Neuromuscular Integrative Action**) is a fusion of Tai Chi, yoga, and dance that allows individual participants to do their own thing, but in an orchestrated fashion. It was developed in 1983 by Carlos AyaRosas and Debbie Rosas as a way to condition the mind as well as the body. Its main principles are to have fun and to move with a sense of rhythm, mood, and skill. Though conceived as a total body workout, the exercises focus primarily on stretching and strengthening specific muscles. A typical session begins with deep-breathing exercises and meditation. Then barefoot participants move to stimulating music, combining heart-pumping kicks and punches adapted from the martial arts with free-dance floor work, all designed to increase body awareness and sensory perception. Although there are 52 specific moves, dancers are invited to vary the movement in their own ways and to adapt the choreography to their own bodies. The routines vary from class to class, but visualizations and simple vocalizations are usually an integral part of this energetic workout. More advanced training, with progression through different levels indicated by different colored belts, is also available. Contact: www.nianow.com

Odissi Dance is one of the oldest surviving forms of classical dance from India, dating back to the first century BCE. Over the centuries, different schools developed, including Mahari and Gotipua. The Mahari tradition was performed by the female devas in temples, whereas Gotipua was a style in which young boys dressed up in female clothing to perform female roles. The Odissi dances were held in high esteem by Indian nobility, but British rule brought the dances to near extinction. After independence, there was a slow revival of this tradition.

The graceful, fluid, and rhythmic movements of these dances are used to act out a story, accompanied by traditional music played on instruments such as the madal, tabla, bamboo flute, metal cymbals, sitar, and tanpura. The themes are exclusively religious in nature and often tell tales about Radha and Krishna. Most of the postures are created by contortions of the head, bust, and torso, and specific hand positions, or mudras, are an important component. In recent years, there has been a revival of this form of music and dance due in part to the work of dancers and teachers Guru Kelucharan Mohapatra and Guru Deba Prasad Das. Though not intended as a particular form of therapy, Odissi Dance, much like belly dancing (another classical art form taught in the West), can be a very rewarding and enjoyable learning experience. Contact: www.srjan.com

Paneurhythmy was formulated during the 1920s by Peter Deunov, the self-realized Bulgarian spiritual master known as Beinsa Douno. The word *Paneu-rhythmy* means "universal-beautiful-rhythm." It is intended for daily use by groups (some very large) as a tool to promote a healthy body, mind, and spirit and harmony in the individual, community, and cosmos. Its three strands of movement, specially composed music, and song gently balance the activities of the right and left brain. Paneurhythmy is danced outdoors in the early morning from the first day of spring, the time when the earth is most productive, until the first day of fall, when it is time for inner work to begin again. Early morning practice is critical, because at that time the earth is the most receptive and more vital energy is available for participants' bodies to absorb. The free-flowing, rhythmic dance takes place in a circle that moves counterclockwise with loving intent, attuning to the

cosmic rhythms and the pulse of the earth. It is said that the exercises have been brought down from the divine world to help humans in their evolution. The energy received through the dance assists participants in uniting with nature, opening their hearts to all that is living, refining their life purposes, and blossoming into their highest potential.
Contact: www.paneurhythmy.org

Pilates Therapy, also known as the Physical Mind Method, is a form of physical conditioning that employs a variety of exercises to produce lean bodies without using aerobics or weight lifting. It was developed during World War I in England by Dr. Joseph Pilates, a boxer, gymnast, and wrestler who had healed his childhood ailments with various holistic practices and physical exercises. After contributing his physical-healing methods to the war effort, he brought his work to America, where it became a popular movement exercise for dancers, performing artists, professional athletes, and screen stars, who found the strengthening and stretching movements invaluable both for rehabilitation and improving performance in their lines of work. It has since evolved into a method of strengthening core muscles and developing balanced alignment through working against resistance and using slow, controlled movements, set breathing patterns, and self-awareness. Pilates work focuses on centering, alignment, coordination, concentration, relaxation, stamina, and flowing movements.

Each exercise targets certain muscles and is done in a specific, balanced way that emphasizes not only correct muscle usage but also how to move from a stable central core. Through repetition, the student develops self-awareness and learns how to move consciously in a smooth, rhythmic way that helps elongate the muscles; many of the movements are similar to those in yoga. Although exercises progress sequentially from easy to more advanced forms, instructors will first analyze the client's movement patterns to detect any functional and structural problems and then design a program that fits those particular needs. Today, this movement therapy uses a variety of workout equipment, such as kinetic balls, a trapeze table, a spine corrector, tensioning springs, and a special universal reformer

tool. Pilates is considered one of the safest forms of exercise, because individuals can work, often without unnecessary exertion, at their own pace by themselves in a small space or in a larger room with a group of other participants.
Contact: www.pilatesmethodalliance.org

Sacred Circle Dancing is becoming very common worldwide. The dances come from many different cultural traditions and have evolved into forms that are primarily spiritual in essence and often honor Mother Nature. Sacred dances performed in a circle are emotionally uplifting and encourage bonding among participants, and there is a stimulating and energetic quality to this form of group movement. Participants in Sacred Circle Dances may join hands for certain movements or move on their own in the circular formation. Dances often tell a story or epitomize a transformative process that encourages a sense of unity and harmony. The actual movements can be quite diverse, and the accompanying music quite melodic.

Sacred circle dancing at Neskaya Movement Arts Center.

Shake Your Soul® and **SomaSoul®** were created by Daniel Leven, the co-founder of DansKinetics (now called YogaDance), to awaken joy, reduce stress, find freedom in movement through the wisdom of the body, and enliven the soul. Using his experience in yoga, qi gong, African dance, modern dance, and dance movement therapy, Leven has refined his approach to healing and transformation to include yoga, movement, mindfulness, dance, and psychotherapy that incorporates elements from the Laban Movement Analysis, Gestalt Therapy, and Body-Mind Centering approaches. Connecting creativity and spirituality, this dynamic movement and fitness therapy provides a framework that allows participants to tap into their natural rhythms and the human urge to dance. As dancers perform guided movements to the beat of the music, each session works to integrate the emotional and physical in an open-hearted and body-centered way that brings a sense of wholeness. The training is available to dancers, fitness professionals, yoga teachers, and individuals of all shapes, sizes, and ages. In addition, the Leven Institute of Movement Therapy, which was established in 1990, offers SomaSoul, a somatic training program for those interested in a career in health and healing.

Contact: The Leven Institute of Movement
Therapy – www.leveninstitute.com

Soul Motion™ is a conscious dance practice designed by choreographer Vinn Arjuna Marti to allow the language of the dance to become a dialogue between the soul and the dancer. During this practice, individuals are invited to investigate the inner world of imagination and to relax into creative and authentic expression. Accompanied by a wide variety of music, barefoot dancers explore different styles of movement as they relate to the self, a partner, the group, and life activities. Classes can be large or small groups, and the shared community developed through the process supports individual transformation. Soul Motion is a co-creative process that works with perceptions and presence to encourage authentic responses to the world around by gaining access to the wisdom of the body through direct movement experience.

Contact: www.soulmotion.com

TaKeTiNa is a process of using rhythm to develop physical and emotional balance. In 1970, Austrian musician and composer Reinhard Flatischler created this movement practice, and he and his wife, Cornelia, continue to refine and expand this meditative experience, which has now found its way into drama schools, hand drumming classes, corporate training programs, pain management clinics, and therapeutic practices worldwide. TakeTiNa is always done in a group, whose size can range from just a few to one hundred or more. It is conducted in a circle as facilitators in the center beat on a large drum. This direct experience of movement begins with simple, repetitive steps; then, the tempo shifts to constantly varying cadences, causing the dancers to come out of rhythm with the sound. As they find the beat again, balance is restored and perception deepened. Entrainment with the rhythms can have physical effects as well, including integration of the left and right hemispheres of the brain and positive impacts on the cardiovascular and central nervous systems. Members of the group support each other by joining hands and sending energy around the circle, and pairs or small groups are sometimes formed for individual practice and sharing. The process is a tool for personal growth and transformation, since the lessons learned can be applied to daily life, allowing people to stay focused and relaxed no matter what life throws at them.

Contact: www.taketina.com

Vajra Dance was taught for the first time in the West during the 1990s by Chogyal Namkhai Norbu, a Tibetan Buddhist teacher now living in Italy. It is a spiritual practice that uses a mantra known as the Song of the Vajra, tantric chants, meditation, and movement to integrate and harmonize the energies of the body, speech, and mind. A ceremonial Vajra Dance is performed on a mandala that depicts the relationship between the qualities of the individual and those of the world in which he lives. Participants dressed in colorful costumes dance in a circle while maintaining the natural awareness and spaciousness nurtured through meditative practices.

Contact: www.dzogchen.ro/vajra-dance

Yoga Dance®, originally referred to as **DansKinetics**®, uses dance and yoga in a rhythmic, meditative way to cleanse the emotions, dissolve stress, and uplift the spirit by transporting participants into a state in which healing can take place on many levels. This fun, exhilarating, and liberating experience is carried out with a group of participants in an open space that provides plenty of room to move.

Some of the classes combine yoga and breath-centered movement with classical dance steps and rhythms provided by music from many cultures. In other classes, participants perform a chakra dance that stimulates the seven main energy centers. Its movements can range from wild and extravagant to slow and meditative, and individuals are invited to open the flow of energy from the base of the spine to the crown of the head and back down to the earth. They can also dance their animal archetypes and spirit prayers. This rejuvenating and inspirational form of dance is for all ages with or without yoga experience. Daniel Leven, the co-founder of this expressive form of movement therapy, which was developed at the Kripalu Center for Yoga and Health, also includes other forms of somatic movement therapy in his training programs.

Contact: Kripalu Center – www.kripalu.org or
The Leven Institute of Movement
Therapy – www.leveninstitute.com

Yoga Trance Dance®, first developed in 1994 by Vinyasa Flow Yoga instructor Shiva Rea, fuses yoga and dance into a vibrant, high-energy workout experience. This practice is suitable for all ages and is offered in workshops at retreat centers worldwide. It was designed as a dynamic way to enhance range of motion, release energetic blockages, boost cardiovascular strength, and create a more positive relationship with the body. The experience takes the practitioner into ecstatic depths through natural movement, intuition, and creativity through yoga, dance movements, meditations, chants, and breathwork. Classes begin with a flowing style of Prana Yoga led by the instructor and then transition into free-form dance that evokes creativity and freedom. The session is completed with moving meditations and chants. The goal is for participants to experience the joy of dancing in a way that fills them with rejuvenating life-force energy.

Contact: www.shivarea.com

Zumba® **Fitness** is a Latin-inspired dance and fitness program that blends the dynamic beat of international music with a variety of easy-to-follow moves. During the 1990s, Colombian aerobics teacher Alberto "Beto" Perez forgot the music for his class and had to improvise with salsa and merengue music. The rest is history, as he moved to the United States and launched a company to license the Zumba method and train teachers. Besides the basic high-energy Zumba fitness program, there are programs exclusively for kids, active older participants, weight loss, strength training, body sculpting, and those who simply want the experience of a lively encounter with a group that can exceed more than one hundred people. The Zumba program currently offers six different types of classes, which include one that is practiced in a pool as an aquatic Zumba party. Though the benefits of aerobic exercise are well proven, Zumba can be done for the pure joy of movement.

Contact: www.betoperez.zumba.com or
www.zumba.com

Daoyin Therapy / Do-In

Daoyin Therapy is a comprehensive method of self-healing that may have been in use in China at the time of the Yellow Emperor, but can definitely be traced back to Chinese qi gong practitioner Daoyin An Qiao around 200 BCE. Taoist monks developed this exercise program by observing how people touched and cradled injuries, and it became a yogic practice that was adopted by Buddhist practitioners after Bodhidharma brought Buddhism to China in 530 CE. After spreading to Japan, Daoyin evolved there into a self-care practice known as Do-In. It has progressed over the ages, and in its present form Do-In was taught in Japan by Masaichi Enomoto; however, Michio Kushi was instrumental in promoting its practices as well as those of macrobiotics throughout the world.

Daoyin consists of self-massage, breathwork, mental concentration, and movements of the body that influence the circulation of chi and blood and that help prevent disease. Daoyin, sometimes considered a specialized form of qi gong with a unique ability to mobilize the vital life-force energy, is thought to have qualities superior to other forms of Eastern self-healing methods, because it uses certain standing and sitting postures to cure specific illnesses and advanced devotional meditation practices to cultivate perfection and union with the supreme Tao. Daoyin is also similar to Tai Chi in that it involves soft, slow, and elegant movements to promote the free flow of chi in the meridians of the body.

The practice of Do-In employs self-massage and Makka Ho stretching exercises (similar to Hatha Yoga postures) that incorporate abdominal hara breathing and meditation to quiet the mind and increase self-awareness. The exercises are fairly easy to learn and with practice, people can actually feel the energy under their hands, which will help increase their effectiveness as practitioners when applying the hands to heal another. A Do-In self-massage uses Shiatsu techniques that restore the flow of chi along the meridians by tapping, squeezing, rubbing, and pressing at various points along meridians over the whole body. This gentle form of self-massage is guided by the breath and can be done while sitting, twisting, crouching, or standing. In addition, the feet may be massaged by using the hands to apply deep pressure to specific points on the soles. (For more information on Makka Ho, see that heading in this chapter.)
Contact: Dragon Gate Chi Gong Daoyin Therapy –
    www.daoyintherapy.com.au,
    www.daoistcenter.org/daoyin.html,
    www.rianvisser.nl/shiatsu/e_doin.htm, or
    www.faqs.org/oc/Overcoming-Digestive-
    Problems/Soothing-do-in-massages.html

Diamond Approach

A precise training method for an inner journey of transformation and self-realization, the Diamond Approach was developed by Ali Hameed, who is commonly known as A. H. Almass. It incorporates both ancient Mahayana Buddhist spiritual teachings and modern transpersonal psychology. The Diamond Approach recognizes that these are two interconnected perspectives on human consciousness that can help open a person to a deeper understanding of her true nature. This method uses inquiry to explore that true nature through guidance that leads to a direct understanding of the soul's purpose. By investigating the essential structure of the ego, reality, and the universe as a whole, it is possible to reveal underlying insights that make it possible to objectively penetrate the patterns and structures of perception so that a person will not be bound by limitations that inhibit further self-realization.

The Diamond Approach recognizes that the fundamental characteristics of true nature manifest in five basic, connected yet boundless dimensions: emptiness, pure nonconceptual awareness, pure presence, pure universal love, and the dynamic dimension responsible for all our activities and ability to function. Reality as a whole is seen to have a structure based on the dimensions of true nature, and the Diamond Approach appreciates that spirit itself is structured and yet timeless and unfolding. The aim of this approach is to bring awareness closer to the dimension of pure presence and the heart closer to the dimension of pure universal love. Awakening those qualities will enable anyone to develop to her fullest potential.

Through a meditative process of self-inquiry into true nature, it is possible to explore the mental constructs and dualistic tendencies of the underlying psychological ego structures that constitute personal identity and that can create the primary obstacle to spiritual development. This self-inquiry allows the recipient to discover the patterns of behavior and barriers that influence her experiences in all stages of the inner journey. The deeper someone goes inside, the more fundamental and basic are the structures she encounters. This psychological exploration into the awakening of spiritual insights is currently accomplished primarily through group retreat programs and is of limited availability in only a few locations.
Contact: Ridhwan Foundation – www.ridhwan.org

Dream Therapy

Dreams have been used in a therapeutic way since ancient times. Many indigenous tribal or aboriginal people still use dream analysis to gain spiritual guidance in daily life, and Tibetan Buddhist monks practice a form of dream meditation or Dream Yoga to increase inner awareness. In more recent times, the psychic intuitive Edgar Cayce used his dreams to assess and treat many of his patients, and his approach became one of the most well known in the field of contemporary alternative healing. Today, a number of holistic health care professionals provide training for those who desire a better understanding of their dreams. Although some dream therapists focus on interpreting and increasing awareness of the dream world, other forms of dream work are intended for advancing the ability to recognize and apply the wisdom contained within dreams to improve a person's overall health. In addition, the more meditative practices of Dream Yoga are intended to enhance self-awareness and spiritual development. (See more on Dream Yoga in this chapter.)
Contact: www.mydrsy.com/about.html or
    www.hgi.org.uk/archive/sleepanddream2.
    htm#.U1g-PChLrdk

Egoscue Method

Egoscue is a do-it-yourself stretching therapy developed by Peter Egoscue to improve posture and provide pain-free mobility and balance in daily activities, such as standing, sitting, and moving about. It can also be used by professional athletes to alleviate pain, rehabilitate dysfunctions, and improve overall performance. The Escoscue Method employs isolated and strengthening exercises and a series of gentle stretches that are specially designed to correct dysfunctional postural alignment patterns; no hands-on manipulations are involved. Initially, the exercises can take an hour or more, but eventually the whole routine can be done in about twenty minutes. The therapy can be learned through instructions provided online or from a video; a visit to one of the clinics can yield a program customized to specific needs.
Contact: www.egoscue.com

Exerssage

Exerssage is a combination of exercises and self-massage that tones the facial muscles and reverses the effects of aging and injuries. It uses a yoga practice called Star Face integrated with the breath to release tension from the jaw and the muscles and nerves of the face, head, and neck and to improve the circulation of blood and oxygen. Twenty-four cranial and facial yoga postures and a contouring self-massage set to rhythmic sound that guides pulsating pressure on acupressure points make up the experience. Additional exercises are used to reshape the eyelids and tone the chin and neck. Both sound and intention are used to create a better connection to the vital organs of the body. It is considered an alternative to facial surgery or Botox, since it is a natural way to recondition the muscles of the face.
Contact: www.wisegeek.com/what-is-exerssage

Gyrotonic Expansion System® (GXS)

GXS is a energetic movement program developed by Romanian ballet dancer Juliu Horvath that is designed to create a balanced skeletal support system while increasing range of motion, strengthening muscles and ligament connections, and stimulating the internal organs and nervous system. It incorporates elements of Tai Chi, Kundalini Yoga, gymnastics, swimming, dance, and ballet, so that major muscle groups can be worked interdependently in an integrated, energetic manner.

Gyrotonic Expansion is done by strapping the feet and hands into a specially designed exercise machine that offers more than one hundred circular, three-dimensional patterns of movement. All movements begin at the spine and follow the natural energy lines in the body to build both internal and external strength. The flowing, undulating, spiral, and circular motions involved in the process are natural ones and are done with no interruption. Each exercise is synchronized with a corresponding breathing pattern and is performed either rhythmically or as an expression of a melody. This exercise program is popular with dancers, athletes, and people with spinal injuries.
Contact: International Headquarters –
www.gyrotonic.com

Homeopathy

Homeopathy is a gentle and natural form of health care whose principles have been used in many parts of the world for more than 200 years. It was popularized in the 1830s in Germany when Samuel Hahneman took up its study. As allopathic practices became more dominant during the early 1900s, this form of therapy fell out of favor, but in recent decades, studies showing its positive effects have brought homeopathy back into the mainstream of alternative medicine. Lithotherapy, a branch of homeopathy that employs essential elements found in rock minerals to stimulate certain enzymes in the body was developed in France during the 1970s.

Homeopathy is based on the law of similars, which means that if a substance produces a certain set of symptoms in a healthy person, when those symptoms are exhibited as part of a disease process, the remedy will be a diluted dose of the same substance. Symptoms can be emotional as well as physical. Homeopathic remedies deliver energetic information to the body's own self-healing mechanism rather than intervening biochemically. Therefore, even extremely diluted preparations can have great effect. They are available in several levels of potency and are taken only until the patient starts to improve. Remedies are usually derived from plants, flowers, or minerals, and during the course of their preparation, any toxic side effects are carried off and the power of the healing ingredients amplified. As underlying symptoms rise to the surface, different remedies may be necessary, and chronic conditions may take substantially longer to improve. The goal of Homeopathy is to provide the body with what it needs to naturally overcome the energetic imbalances that are causing the symptoms of disease.

The homeopathic practitioner begins with an in-depth interview with the patient to evaluate all aspects of a person's health. This is followed by careful research to select the most appropriate remedy for the individual's physical and emotional constitutional type and the symptoms involved. Specific instructions are given to the client about the use of each remedy, and further consultation with the practitioner may be scheduled to evaluate the body's response and any physiological changes. Homeopathy has proved to be quite effective for treating a number of acute ailments or dysfunctions, and information is available that allows individuals to set up a homeopathic first aid kit for personal use.
Contact: www.homeopathic.org

Integrative Yoga Therapy (IYT)

Kripalu Yoga teacher Joseph LePage developed Integrative Yoga Therapy in 1991 after experiences with a variety of healing modalities. IYT combines yoga, meditation, guided imagery, pranayama breathwork, and Yoga Nidra with recent insights in body-mind health research to provide a way for individuals to free prana blockages, release the hold of stress, and enhance well-being and their connection to the spiritual realms. Like many other holistic modalities, it works on the physical, emotional, and spiritual level to reach the feeling of wholeness that the free flow of vital life-force energy can provide. Group support and sharing are part of this integrated healing approach.

Sessions often begin with a guided body-awareness journey that takes participants through the entire body to help them feel and interpret energy flows and patterns. The facilitator then selects the particular asanas most appropriate for a participant's specific conditions. Each asana is synchronized with the breath and is performed in an open, compassionate manner, inviting thoughts and feelings about a condition to come to the surface. Each pose is followed by the appropriate counterpose. There is constant use of meditation, mudras, visualization, guided imagery, deep relaxation, pranayama breathing, and dialogue,when needed. The facilitator never imposes any intended results, but waits for self-generated developments to arise within the participants.
Contact: www.iytyogatherapy.com

Interplay

Interplay, developed in 1989 by Cynthia Winton-Henry and Phil Porter, is an experiential practice that helps people learn how being fully present in the moment can make life can seem more like play than like work. The practice makes it possible for individuals and communities to become more creative, innovative, spontaneous, aware, adaptable, intuitive, trusting, and able to deal with difficulties in a manner that doesn't get in anyone else's way. Participants work alone, in pairs, in threes, or as a group to understand the joy of improvisation, using playful exercises in physical movement and contact, words and storytelling, song and silence. Live music is provided when appropriate. Interplay is now being used by educators, artists, health professionals, religions, and corporate organizations, and is offered at locations all over the world.
Contact: www.interplay.org

Kentro® Body Balance

Angelika Thusius created the Kentro Body Balance method of centering movements after years of observing and analyzing the fluid movement of people in twelve countries, especially elders who move with ease and grace into old age. Kentro is designed to prevent, reduce, and eliminate pain and stiffness in muscles and joints that influence posture. This program does not push the body to correct posture. Instead, participants learn gentle exercises that help them move from the pelvis, the powerful main center of the body. As a result, the entire body reshapes itself into natural strength and limberness while engaging in daily activities, such as preparing food, sitting at the computer, and raking leaves. Kentro enlivens the naturally joyous and resilient expression of person's true nature.
Contact: www.kentrobodybalance.com

Laughter Therapy

Laughter is the simple and natural physical expression of positive emotions, and it has long been recognized that a sense of humor can carry a person through difficult situations. The ability to laugh during stressful times is beneficial for physical and mental health, since it eases tension and uplifts the spirit. The most well-known advocate of this activity as a form of therapy is Norman Cousins, a journalist and health educator who publicized the use of laughter as part of his program to counter life-threatening health problems in the 1970s and 1980s. Medical research has also shown a correlation between laughter and positive biochemical changes in the cardiovascular, immune, and endocrine systems of the human body. Although laughter is taken for granted as simply a naturally enjoyable act, deliberate ways to achieve this emotional release have been developed around the world.

Laughter is contagious.

A laughter session is generally carried out in a group to induce the contagious chain reaction that everyone is familiar with. All participants have to do is laugh continuously for an extended period of time. Even if it is hard to find something to laugh about, an initial period of just faking it will tend to shift into great, big belly laughs. A number of practitioners of healing modalities have incorporated the "practice" of laughter as part of their therapy, and East Indian doctor Dr. Madan Kataria, known as the giggle guru, developed Laughter Yoga as a club movement in 1995.
Contact: www.laughteryoga.org

Makko Ho Exercises

Makko Ho, an integral part of Do-In Therapy, is a series of easy-to-follow, energy-based exercises put together in Japan by Shizuto Masunaga, who also developed his own form of Shiatsu. The series is also used as a self-healing practice in some forms of Shiatsu Therapy. Although these exercises are different from those used in qi gong or Tai Chi, they too are based on an understanding of the five elements and the meridian system. Each of the basic set of six simple exercises aims to remove blockages and increase the flow of chi through

specific pairs of meridians in the body. The full sequence covers the whole body and all of its organs. It is also a self-diagnostic tool that enables practitioners to improve not only the function of the organs but also related emotional and mental states. The goal of Makka Ho is to help people become more aware of the body-mind connection, enhance vitality, and prevent or inhibit the development of disease.

The exercises are learned through an instructor, who first takes a student slowly through one exercise at a time, allowing time for full integration of the details of the movements. Then, the movements can be linked together in a continuous sequence at the practitioner's own pace. Students are encouraged to hold strong intention and awareness of the breath throughout a session, feeling how the breath changes bodily sensations. The act of exhaling is emphasized, since that is the time when the body releases waste products. Observation of the way the mind and emotions respond to any tension already present in the body is also key. The instructor monitors progress until the participant become proficient, after which the exercises can be easily performed for a period of about twenty minutes at home on regular basis.
Contact: www.endthetrendnow.com/makko-ho

Martial Arts

Although many of the martial arts grew from the desire to defeat enemies by increasing personal power, at their core these practices emphasize cultivating inner strength, flexibility, and resilience, all of which have many other applications throughout life. The keys to success in each of the practices are enhancing self-awareness and activating and learning to control the vital life-force energy through balanced movement, breathwork, and mental concentration refined by meditation.

It is difficult to pick out the true origins of the martial arts from the existing legends, but most trace their beginnings to the Shaolin Temple in China. It was during the sixth century CE that the legendary Da Mo, known as Bodhidharma in India, arrived at the temple and started teaching the monks to defend themselves against attacking pirates. This training, as well as the teachings of Chan Buddhism, soon spread across the Far East, eventually evolving into various schools with different styles of practice.

Martial arts can be classified as either soft or hard, internal or external, and yin or yang, but all are primarily ways of training the mind and body to work together. By cultivating a quiet, unwavering mind and inner strength, a practitioner can choose to softly yield to obstacles, just as water in a river flows around the rock it encounters on the way to the sea, or confront them with vigorous power and swift action. Although most of the martial arts train practitioners to act both defensively and offensively, some, such as Karate, place more emphasis on attacking, and others, such as Aikido, rely on softly blending with and diffusing the opponent's energy. To be successful at either approach requires extensive training in increasing, balancing, and using the energy within the hara (Japanese) or dantien (Chinese), the energetic center in the lower belly. Personal cultivation of chi has always been paramount in the practice of the martial arts, and complete mastery of these disciplines takes years of rigorous practice. Although the practices can generate great physical power, their real intention is to break through the self-imposed limitations that obscure a person's true potential. It's interesting to note that many of the traditional Asian bodywork healing modalities evolved out of the need to treat injuries sustained by martial-arts practitioners during combat.

Most people associate martial arts with practices from China and Japan, such as Kung Fu, Jujitsu, Tai Chi, Karate, and Aikido, but there are also a number of skillful movement arts intended for combat, defense, sports, self-development, or spiritual enhancement found in other cultures around the world. These include such practices as Korea's Taekwondo, Malaysia's Pentjak Silat, Brazil's Capoeira, India's Kalarippayattu, Greece's Pankration, and Escrima from the Philippines.

Meditation

Many different forms of meditation have been employed since ancient times by monks, yogis, and spiritual adepts, and these practices are incorporated into a number of holistic healing therapies, as well as into breathwork and yoga. Today, mindfulness-based meditation has become recognized as a way to reduce the stress that can negatively affect health. Other practices, particularly in the Buddhist and Hindu traditions, lead meditators into experiencing their true nature. In the Judeo-Christian tradition, the goal might be uniting the soul with the Creator. The result of these deep practices can be a clear sense of a connection with all beings and a strengthening of compassion for the self and others. Meditation not only empowers the individual, but its effects reverberate throughout families, communities, and the world.

Joining a facilitated meditation group is an easy way to learn these transformative practices. However, they can be practiced on a daily basis almost anywhere—a quiet sanctuary in a room at home or a serene space outdoors. Once a meditator learns to overcome distractions, it is even possible to practice sitting on a park bench or walking down the street in the middle of a city. However, most people find it beneficial to alternate between a regular home practice and a weekly visit to a local meditation group, where they can obtain guidance to help them progress through more subtle levels of practice. (A longer discussion about meditation will be found in Chapter 10.)

Naturopathic Medicine

This form of alternative health care incorporates a wide range of therapeutic methods that will effectively remove barriers to the body's own self-healing abilities. Although naturopathic doctors, or naturopaths, may use both traditional and conventional methods to make diagnoses, the therapeutic approach is based on natural procedures and substances. Six principles help define Naturopathy: nature has the power to heal; the whole person must be treated; treatments must be noninvasive and natural; healing is only possible by identifying and treating the true cause of disease; prevention is the best cure; and doctors are most effective as teachers. As well as training in anatomy and physiology, naturopaths also study physical medicine, nutritional and botanical medicine, homeopathy, physical manipulation, hydrotherapy, psychology, counseling, and Acupuncture. A treatment program may include diet and lifestyle changes and use fasting to rest and cleanse the body systems and stimulate metabolism. A naturopathic doctor can incorporate herbal remedies, special nutritional supplements, and homeopathic remedies as part of the therapy. With its emphasis on education and prevention, naturopathy seeks to motivate the individual toward better health and recognizes that the body, mind, and spirit must all be engaged in meeting this goal.

Contact: American Association of Naturopathic
Physicians – www.naturopathic.org

Nutritional Approaches

Although it's well known that proper exercise and a balanced diet are essential to good health, today's fast-paced lifestyles have changed people's eating habits in ways that often lead to nutritional deficiencies. In addition, mass production of many foods makes avoiding preservatives, chemical additives, and foods containing harmful pesticides, hormones, or genetically modified ingredients a daunting task. The consumption of large amounts of impure fats, poorly processed oils, and dairy products creates congestion and stagnation in the body's systems that restricts the quality and flow of blood and other vital fluids; it also leads to chronic inflammation, obesity, and cardiovascular disease. From the Chinese-medicine perspective, the production of the excessive heat that is part of an inflammatory response can literally suck energy from other parts of the body where it is needed.

The healthy human body requires plenty of pure water and the right amount and combination of vitamins, minerals, amino acids, and unsaturated fatty acids, as well as proteins, antioxidants, enzymes, and friendly bacteria. Proper nutrition also helps prevent disease by invigorating the immune system and increasing the ability to combat stress. Although most of the necessary elements are found in a healthy, balanced diet, there are many supplements and medicinal herbs that can make up for any deficiencies. A number of dietary programs have been proposed over the years, and many have accomplished their goals; however, it is wise to closely examine those without a holistic approach.

Fortunately, there is a growing awareness of the need to avoid so-called junk foods and to rely instead on organically grown, minimally processed foods. The sustainability and locavore movements, the rise in farmers' markets now found in many communities, and renewed interest in labeling foods that are genetically modified are some of the ways people are taking steps to improve their choices. There are also a number of practices and therapies that use nutrition to prevent potential problems or to resolve existing dysfunction. Whether centuries old or relatively modern, most of these therapies suggest specific changes in diet, as well as dietary supplements, to develop stronger bodies, cleanse impurities, and help balance energy production, all without producing any problematic side effects. Many also offer advice about lifestyle factors that can be the cause of health problems. People with chronic health issues may need a customized "prescription" that combines diet, exercise, stress management, and appropriate nutritional supplements to help them live healthier, happier lives. As many have already realized, any of the following nutritional practices can be adopted as a regular part of daily life.

Herbal Therapy, also known as Phytotherapy or as Kampo in Japan, has probably been in use since the time of hunters and gatherers. Most indigenous cultures around the world lived close to nature and learned which plants were useful through a long process of experimentation. This information has been passed down through the generations by folk healers, and using herbs was one of the few methods for treating disease until the modern era. Therapeutic herbal practices varied depending on what was locally available; however, practices that developed in China, Japan, India, and the Americas had many similarities.

Herbal Therapy is the science of restoring health with medicine derived from herbs and plants; it can be delivered by the external application of body wraps and poultices or the ingestion of infusions, decoctions or tinctures. Today, herbal teas or tinctures are the methods most often used. Asian health care systems emphasize the importance of proper diagnosis before prescribing herbal remedies and have made an art out of studying a patient's history and carefully examining the tongue, pulse, and abdomen. Herbalists from other traditions have adopted this approach as well, because a full picture of the patient's condition is critical to choosing the appropriate herbal formulation for a particular condition, one that will also support the body's own natural healing mechanisms. Many complex herbal remedies are compounded for a specific purpose, though simpler ones can be used for the general purpose of creating more balance and harmony or as a preventive measure. Contrary to the popular belief that anything natural can't be harmful, herbs do have detrimental and sometimes life-threatening side effects, especially when combined with other medications. Therefore, consultation with a professional herbalist would be wise before embarking on extensive use of herbal remedies.

Contact: www.herbs.org or www.americanherbalistguild.com

Macrobiotics describes a philosophy and a holistic approach to diet that was introduced to the twentieth-century world by George Ohsawa and Michio Kushi from Japan, though its principles are followed in other cultures. It stresses eating foods that grow in the same environment in which the diner lives; changing foods as the seasons change; and basing diet on the grains that the majority of human teeth are designed to process. Vegetables, beans, and nuts are integrated into this grain-based diet, and fruits, fish, and animal products are eaten occasionally. In keeping with its Asian origins, Macrobiotics combines foods to balance their yin and the yang qualities. It is primarily seen as a way to prevent disease by maintaining optimum health, but macrobiotic dietitians can use a variety of diagnostics to determine the diet necessary to combat certain disease conditions. Macrobiotics got a lot of bad press when individuals took this practice to the extreme by limiting their diets to brown rice, which created severe nutritional deficiencies. However, the food pyramids that are produced by organizations such as the United States Department of Agriculture now recognize the importance of a grain- and vegetable-based diet. Like the disciplined practices required by many spiritual traditions, following a macrobiotic diet can lead to the peace of mind that comes from living and eating in harmony with the universe.

Contact: Kushi Institute – www.kushiinstitute.org

Nutritional Supplements and Probiotics can be useful for maintaining good health when people don't meet the nutritional needs of the body because of poor eating habits. Supplements include vitamins, enzymes, minerals, amino acids, fatty acids, fiber, antioxidants, probiotics (which introduce friendly bacteria into the digestive system), teas, herbal extracts or tinctures, immune-system boosters, blue green algae and spirulina, and the so-called super foods found in nature, such as blueberries, goji berries, green tea, or dark chocolate. Some work directly to influence biochemical processes in the body, and others are targeted at preventing disease or improving overall functioning. Supplements can be taken in a powdered form that is put in a drink or as tinctures or pills. The kind of supplementation used by bodybuilders and some professional athletes has proven to have many detrimental side effects. Indeed, any supplement can be damaging to health if used improperly. Although anecdotal evidence of their efficacy is widespread, few clinical studies validate the benefits of the use of supplements except in specifically diagnosed conditions.

Progressive Muscular Relaxation (PMR)

PMR is an anxiety-management technique developed by Edmund Jacobs in the 1930s. Its simple, self-administered muscle relaxation techniques are designed to counter the physical changes that anxiety triggers by inducing a relaxation response that will calm the body and mind. PMR uses the principle of the pendulum—when an object in pulled back in a certain direction and then released, it will move in the opposite direction—to release tension, pain, and stress from the body.

The method involves the two-step technique of tensing and releasing muscles; it can be done at home while standing, sitting, or reclining, and takes only a few minutes to perform. The first step is to focus on a particular muscle, inhale, and tense the muscle by tightening and squeezing it without moving any other part of the body. Tension can be felt as the position and breath are held for a few seconds. On the exhalation, tension is gently released and attention is focused on the subtle changes that occur. After a short period of relaxation, the process is repeated, working systematically with muscle groups throughout the body, starting with areas of minimal tension and working progressively into those areas with greater tension. The process is completed by tensing and releasing all the muscles of the body together. It is important to coordinate the breathing in a slow, deep way with the tension-relaxation cycle. The practice will quickly reduce the physical effects of anxiety, while also offering the practitioner a way to rediscover the distinction between relaxation and tension in the various muscle groups.

Contact: http://www.essenceofstressrelief.com/ progressive-muscle-relaxation.html or http://www.anxietybc.com/sites/default/ files/MuscleRelaxation.pdf

Qi Gong (Chi Gong)

There are three kinds of knowing: the intellectual understanding that comes from the mind, the truth that the heart is grateful for, and the gut feeling that understands harmony and balance. So too, the ancient Chinese practice of qi gong recognizes three inner energy centers in the head, heart, and belly, known as dantiens. Working with the dantiens helps practitioners cultivate chi (spelled "qi' in modern Chinese), the universal life-force energy that permeates the body, mind, and spirit. One translation of *qi gong* is "mastery of the universal life energy," and part of the practice is learning to become proficient in circulating balanced energy between the dantiens and all parts of the body through the energy meridian system. Qi gong is based on the premise that suffering, disease, and even ignorance are caused by imbalances, blocked meridians, or insufficient energy circulating in the body, but the strong and balanced flow of this internal energy can lead to perfect health, a long life, and great happiness. These effects are achieved by consciously observing what happens internally, enhancing the ability to relax, opening blocked meridians, releasing stale or damaged energy, and filling the resulting free space in the body with the free flow of fresh energy. Qi gong also is said to support the development of inner peace, spiritual powers, and immortality.

The origins of Qi gong go back thousands of years. Around 2700 BCE, when traditional Chinese practices were first defined as a system of healing during the reign of the Yellow Emperor. *The Yellow Emperor's Classic on Internal Medicine* speaks of an earlier form of qi gong called Nei Gong. (See Chapter 9 for more on Nei Gong.) Healing exercises in the form of a dance were known to be used by tribal people during the Tan Yao period around 2400 BCE. It was at that time that the legendary practitioner Peng Tzu reportedly lived hundreds of years because of his practice. Over the years, the practice of qi gong was also referred to as Tu Na, which means "focused breathing," and a variation of the practice was called Daoyin, which means "to use the mind and physical movements to lead and guide the circulation of chi." Qi gong and other forms of energetic healing were influenced by many elements: the *I Ching* (also known as *The Book of Changes*), the philosophy of Taoism established by Lao Tzu, the five element theory, the principles of balance between yin and yang, Confucian philosophy, the influx of Buddhism after 200 CE, and the idea of righteous conduct as an essential ingredient for uniting with the inner nature. Although it is difficult to determine the specifics of techniques

used during ancient times, the original intention of qi gong as found in the practices of Nei Gong seems to be primarily to increase longevity, an aim that very much interested the Chinese. As the influences of Buddhism came into the practice, qi gong became a more spiritually oriented form of self-enhancement, but retained its energetic fundamentals.

By the first century CE, during the period of the Eastern Han Dynasty, Buddhist temples taught many forms of meditative qi gong practices. It was also during this period that the famous Taoist Jun Quan incorporated the movements of animals into the practice. The Shaolin school, one of the most ancient Chinese training academies and well known for its development of martial arts practices such as Kung Fu, produced other forms of qi gong. These newer forms were first practiced at the school in the sixth century after the great Indian Buddhist teacher Bodhidharma (Da Mo) arrived and became motivated to teach after witnessing the terrible physical condition of the monks, who spent all their time meditating and copying scrolls while living under the threat of attack by roving bandits. Bodhidharma was not only the founder of Chan Buddhism (later known as Zen in Japan) but also established the principles that led to internal exercises known as the Eight Pieces of Brocade and a practice called "the art of breath of the enlightened ones." Both are composed of stationary and moving exercises accompanied by breath control. The Wudang school in the mountains in the heart of China also developed a style of qi gong known as Wudang Qi Gong, a method of relaxation, rehabilitation, and invigoration based on easy-to-learn techniques of breathing, movement, concentration, and relaxation that meld the body and mind into one. This Taoist style is based on the cycle of the five elements and awareness of the core through the attentive observation of the body and emotions. Over time, the practices created by different schools displayed three primary purposes: spiritual development, physical health, and martial arts. Certain schools focused on ways to prolong life, others emphasized training the heart and soul, and some helped practitioners search for their true natures. As health practices, various forms of qi gong taught individuals how to recover from dysfunction and were used as a form of applied bodywork.

The vast array of qi gong exercises employ contemplative movements that are coordinated with the breath and combined with concentration on the three dantiens, in particular the lower dantien, which is considered the area where chi is stored. The power of qi gong comes as the energies of heaven and earth are joined together within the body, releasing energy blockages, encouraging the body's natural healing ability, and giving the practitioner the discernment to see through the seeming safety of habitual patterns of behavior. Constant practice leads to enhanced receptivity and helps practitioners cultivate the three treasures of qi (internal life-force energy), jing (essence), and shen (spirit). In its simplest form, qi gong uses physical effort, with the mind involved to some degree. At the intermediate stage of practice, the mind and body are used in equal measure. As the practice goes deeper, the mind becomes critically important and is actively involved in circulating chi through very subtle movements and breathing carried out from a deeply relaxed and meditative state. However, all levels of practice are aimed at cleansing, gathering, and circulating chi energy. When the flow of energy is balanced and properly activated, the body, mind, and spirit can be revitalized, making it possible to live in harmony with the rhythms of nature and the dynamics of human consciousness.

Qi gong can be described as either internal or external, depending on how the chi is used. External qi gong, also referred to as chi emission, represents the act of transferring chi energy from one person to another. Only after a practitioners have become proficient at developing, cultivating, and balancing chi internally will they really be able to help others. Some of the therapeutic practices of applied bodywork discussed in Chapter 6 offer good examples of external qi gong; a number of energy-medicine modalities such as Reiki use the same type of energy transmission. In these methods, the therapist corrects chi deficiencies blockages in the recipient by using strong mental focus and specific arm movements to send energy from the practitioner's energy center out through his hands. In effect, the practitioner externalizes and projects his own chi to effect changes in the patient's surrounding energy field, energy centers, or internal meridian pathways. Since chi tends to go where it is needed, external chi healing will transmit vital energy without actually touching the recipient. When strong chi is flowing freely, it is harder for any disease to take hold.

When qi gong is practiced as a form of self-care, it is called an internal exercise and can include hard or soft practices. Both kinds of practices are designed to cultivate chi; hard practices act on three levels of the physical body, transforming the tendons, bones, and skin, whereas soft internal practices affect the mind and spirit, with less attention on the body.

The internal practice of qi gong requires slow, purposeful movement coordinated with the breath. When performed in a standing position, a relaxed stance with the knees slightly bent is recommended. Numerous exercises that incorporate different steps are employed to cleanse, recharge, strengthen, circulate, and disperse chi within the body. Body movements can be simple and subtle, without much observable activity, or more dynamic, with a variety of motions that include twists, shakes, twirls, and swings that contract, unwind, and stretch the body. Slow, deliberate movements done with very little physical effort make it possible to become more aware of the subtle feeling of the chi energy and its movement. In some of the basic practices in which the arms are raised slowly upwards in the act of gathering chi, the movement can be imagined as being supported by the rising tide of the ocean, thereby allowing the body to respond like a loose piece of seaweed. The dynamic movements are designed to regulate the flow of chi through the meridians, redistribute stagnant or deficient chi, balance the yin and yang, and regulate the five elements of earth, metal, water, wood, and fire that correlate with the internal organs. When performing the dynamic exercises, it is essential to remain relaxed and not strain.

Breathwork techniques may vary, but breathing is mostly done through the nose, is often full and depth while remaining gentle and rhythmic, and may involve movements of the belly. The techniques range from simple circular methods of deep abdominal breathing to the use of micro- and macrocosmic orbits, in which chi is visualized and sent with the breath through the governing and conception energy channels that extend along the front and back of the trunk. Another specific breathing exercise involves swallowing air to cleanse the internal organs and enhance the circulation of chi throughout the body, thereby strengthening the immune system and granting peace of mind.

Qi gong practice is a meditation in motion in which the practitioner tries to empty the mind and allow internal awareness to strengthen. Visualizations help focus mental attention and are often directed toward the lower dantien, the place where the energies of the earth and heaven are mixed and stored together in a big ball of energy. The practitioner must be fully present in the moment, observing the subtle movements of the flow of energy. If thoughts come up, they are acknowledged and invited to fade, as the practitioner continues to focus on the breath. Affirmations of oneness with the universe can be expressed silently or out loud. As sensitivity to chi increases, there is a shift in the body-mind consciousness, creating a space in which the practitioner is centered and able to move freely. By engaging the mind with the body and the breath, qi gong helps the practitioner return to the source of primordial energy from which everything emerges, a place in which he can find the best prescription for healing.

Internal healing also may use sounds. A significant practice known as the Six Healing Tones works to stabilize health by using six healing tones that deliver energy to each of the organs, along with standing and moving meditations that strengthen the muscles and start a process of internal alchemy in the body. While always striving for correct pronunciation, the sounds are spoken loudly to quickly detoxify the organs, softly to cleanse them, or silently to replenish them. Each healing sound is specific to an internal organ, but all can be used if no clear cause of an illness can be identified. All of these sounds are part of the ancient Taoist Tu Na breathing methods that work vibrationally to cleanse the body of turbid chi and are used in qi gong.

Two qi gong stances used for cultivating chi.

Qi gong can be performed while standing, walking, sitting, or lying down. Practices can be done alone or in a group for short or long periods at any time of day, although it is considered preferable to start the day right by practicing in the early morning. It is easy to learn and simple to perform anywhere, although it initially requires proper training. The complete set of exercises offered by a master instructor will probably consist of a beginning moving form, a meditative nonmoving form, and a condensed form used for more advanced students. The simple moving form takes only about twenty minutes to perform and includes some visualizations and affirmations that help the practitioner absorb energy from the earth, sun, moon, and heavens. The meditative nonmoving form focuses on the regulation of the nervous system and the spirit and, once learned, can be performed whenever and wherever the need arises. It is important to keep the training slow, relaxed, and within the practitioner's physical capabilities to avoid creating pain through overexertion. The intention to relax is an essential aspect of the learning process, and its guiding principles are to be kind, to speak with reason, and to act from the heart. Although some practices can take years to perfect, many benefits can be realized at the onset, and the energetic response to continued practice can have a significant effect on balancing body systems, enhancing the immune system, strengthening metabolism, and preventing disease. The key to advancement in qi gong is regular practice.

Today, there are over two thousand individual qi gong exercises, and new styles of practice are constantly being created. Since many forms use similar postures, movements, breathing techniques, visualizations, and methods of mental training, the actual differences in their essence is often quite subtle. Training in numerous forms are presently available at schools around the world. In the West, established classes may be available even in small towns. The forms that use simple, smooth, and subtle focused movements and stretches in concert with the breath are the ones most widely taught, but no matter how simple or complex the exercises may be, they all focus with simplicity, naturalness, and effectiveness on the energetic process of integrating the body, heart, mind, and spirit.

A number of practices have made significant contributions to the spread of qi gong in the West. They encourage exploration and expression of the body's innate wisdom by helping people become more aware of what is happening deep within. The practice known as Diamond Qi Gong, an intense and graceful form of Tibetan Buddhist healing, was brought to the West by Tibetan nun Lama Fo Fu in 2003. The traditional Taoist/Buddhist practice of Fan Teng Gong, which is short for Dao Yuan Fan Teng Gong, offers a tranquil way to develop intense inner warmth and helps practitioners radiate more light and dissolve blockages. This method of inspiring positive changes in health was only recently brought out of secrecy and employs meditation exercises during which the hands are moved to different energetic points on the three dantien energy centers. The Dao Yuan School of Qi Gong, founded by master Guo Bingsen and Edith Guba in Germany, reestablished this practice to help people improve their energy levels by changing the state of mind from doing to being. Guigen Qi Gong is a complete system of medical qi gong developed during the late 1900s at a hospital in Beijing by Dr. Xu Hongtao based on his research and treatment of people with stress-related conditions. The practice of Pangu Shen Gong, developed by Master Ou Wen Wei and also referred to as Mystical Qi Gong, is both a modest and advanced form of tantric Buddhist and Taoist training that uses a simple yet powerful set of qi gong energy exercises to achieve good health through the prevention of and recovery from disease and enhancing spiritual development. Spring Forest Qi Gong, developed by Master Chunyi Lin, has gained in popularity in recent years. The exercises used in this practice are oriented toward helping Westerners and those new to qi gong learn the basics of the practice and easily learn how to feel the chi energy almost immediately. Wuji Hundun Qi Gong is an ancient form of Chinese health maintenance that was handed down by Duan Zhi Liang of Beijing, China. It consists of a blend of inner (Nei Qi) and outer (Wei Qi) energy-cultivating techniques with roots in the martial art of Kung Fu. Yi Ren® Qi Gong is a complex form of Qi Gong practice that originated around 600 CE, fell into obscurity, and was recently reestablished in a healing system created during the 1990s by Dr. Guan-Chen Sun. The practice aims to cultivate a growing awareness of the flow of energy within the physical body and mind as well as between individuals and their environment. Yi Ren Qi Gong works to enhance the power of direct knowing by integrating chi with the intuitive mind and the network of internal organs, the muscles, and bones,

which helps participants identify different energy interactions and recognize the kind of energy that nourishes their innate abilities. (See more about Yi Ren Qi Gong in Chapter 9.)

Contact: The National Qigong Association – www.nqa.org, www.masterfofu.org, www.develop.qigong-uk.eu, www.pangushengong.org, www.springforestqigong.com, www.wujiproductions.com/what-is-wuji-qigong-2, or www.guigen.com

Self-Bremma Exercises®

This self-care practice is part of the comprehensive system of Breema Bodywork that Malicheck Mooshan brought from a village in the Kurdish Mountains in the Middle East. Just like its applied-bodywork component discussed in Chapter 6, the exercises are beneficial for the muscles, bones, and joints, but they also teach the art of being present, which helps with physical, mental, and emotional balance and harmony. This extensive collection of exercises is designed to help a person focus on expressing herself through movement by increasing the vital energy in any given moment and increasing receptivity to that which is most beneficial in her life. The practice is safe, nurturing, and energizing, and the movements are natural and rhythmic. Rather than being carried out with force, the exercises are performed using the relaxed weight of the body.

Of the assortment used, one particular practice, the Kidney Charge exercise, is similar to the Chinese qi gong practice of revitalizing chi. This is done by sitting comfortably with the soles of the feet together, the spine straight, and the breathing deep and slow. After a few breaths, the practitioner collapses forward on an exhalation and brings the arms behind her, brushes them in a circular pattern over the back a few times, and then vigorously slaps the palms on the lower back above the kidneys for three or more full breaths. After this, the body is relaxed and returned to an erect seated position. This short practice can be done at any time of day and is useful for relieving feelings of fatigue.

Contact: The Breema Center – www.breema.com

Self-Massage

The practice of self-massage is a very accessible and inexpensive way of encouraging the healing process, preventing dysfunction, and promoting inner well-being. A sore spot in the body draws attention to itself, and there is a natural instinct to rub it; however, learning specific techniques can provide a more therapeutic outcome. In addition to using helpful tools such as backscratchers, tennis balls, toe spreaders, and wire head massagers, there are a number of hands-on practices that can be easily learned in a relatively short period of time. Most of the methods offer a variety of benefits, including loosening the muscles, lubricating the joints, increasing circulation, and revitalizing chi energy.

A simple head massage tool.

Many modalities of practitioner-applied bodywork—Chi Nei Tsang, Ai Chi, Asclepius Therapy, Reiki, Bagua Bodywork, Hoshino Therapy, Anma Massage, Reflexology, Kunye Massage Therapy, Shiatsu, and Jin Shin Jitsu among other—include practices of self-massage that are taught to clients to perpetuate the effects of a bodywork session. Chinese and Japanese methods of self-massage generally incorporate techniques from Acupressure, Tuina, the Taoist healing methods of Daoyin and Wu Chi, and qi gong. These practice primarily focuses on enhancing the flow of chi energy for better health and longevity.

Although different techniques are used in the traditional forms of self-massage discussed below, the variations among them are often very subtle. Most can be accomplished in a relatively short time (between fifteen and thirty minutes) while sitting, standing, or lying down in a comfortable quiet place. It is also possible to do short versions while out and about or during a break at work.

Demonstrations of how these practices are carried out can be seen by searching for their names on YouTube, bing.com/videos, and other search engines.

Abhyanga Self-Massage, just like the practitioner-applied version, is an integral part of the Ayurvedic therapy that originated in India. As with many other methods used in Ayurvedic healing, this self-massage is used to cleanse, detoxify, and purify the body while enhancing the flow of vital pranic energy. It is distinctive in its reliance a liberal amount of the most appropriate warm oil is lovingly massaged into the body. The practice is preferably accomplished in a clean, quiet, warm setting where personal hygiene can be attended to. Many choose their own bathrooms for this purpose, but any facility that is comfortable will work as long as towels are handy.

The oil is applied with a combination of long, clockwise, circular strokes and vigorous fingertip massage movements that start at the head and work progressively down over the whole body. The amount of pressure varies depending on the sensitivity of the particular body part and what intuitively feels right. Loving affirmations support the self-nurturing process. An Abhyanga self-massage relaxes and revitalizes the skin and muscles while improving circulation, enhancing the immune system, and slowing down the aging process.

Qi Gong Self-Massage sometimes accompanies qi gong meditative movement exercises and can be very helpful after sitting for long periods in meditation. Like other qi gong practices, self-massage focuses on activating chi energy in the body. It can be done while sitting, standing with knees relaxed, or lying down, preferably wearing loose clothing that won't restrict movement. As a warm-up, the hands are rubbed together to increase their sensitivity to the flow of energy. Chi activation exercises include patting the sides of the head, squeezing and pressing different parts of the body, swinging the arms, slapping the body, and brushing and shaking.

Shiatsu Self-Massage, primarily used in Japan, was publicized outside that country by Toru Namikoshi. It has similarities to the Chinese and

Taoist methods of self-massage, but makes use of fingertip and thumb pressure on a variety of specific acupoints all over the body. Unlike practitioner-applied Shiatsu, the individual is limited to areas that can be reached with the hands. The hoku point, located in the valley between the thumb and index finger is useful for treating headaches, neck pain, and other problems in the upper body.

Taoist Self-Massage is part of a larger therapeutic system that includes various techniques to dispel negative emotions, relieve stress, and strengthen the senses, internal organs, and nervous system. A variety of methods can be used; some focus on acupoints, whereas others work with pain points or various muscle groups, and movements of the hands can be gentle, moderate, or vigorous. The simple daily practice, accompanied by slow, deep breathing, can take ten to twenty minutes to complete.

A seated session often starts with a short meditation followed by rubbing the hands together to warm them and to activate the chi. Techniques can vary with each part of the body, and the hands can be open or loosely held in a fist. When the hands are open, pressure is usually applied with the fingers, although the thumbs or palms can be used. During the treatment and especially on each out-breath, the attention should be focused on the flow of energy running along the arms and down the fingertips. Types of contact include pressing, tapping, combing, slapping, popping, pulling, rubbing, and squeezing; vibrating and circular hand movements can also be used. The sequence starts with acupoints all around the head followed by those on the upper neck, and continues down over the rest of the body. If more attention is needed in a particular area, extra time is taken there. Treatments conclude with a relaxing period during which the hands are held over the lower dantien energy center near the navel to promote the storage of the chi.

Tui Mo Self-Massage, found in Tuina and Qi Gong Medical Massage, is considered an effective means of preventive health care, but it can can also help treat specific illnesses. The bodywork focuses on activating the chi by giving attention to various pressure points located on meridians on the head, face, neck, shoulders, chest, abdomen and other extremities. Either hand can be used alternately or both can work together in techniques such as rubbing, holding, pinching, pressing, dragging, and squeezing. The sequence begins with pressing or dragging movements on both sides of the forehead and rubbing the palms on both temples. Specific points along the body, each having a particular effect, are then engaged, with the amount of pressure and the type of hand movement varying with location. Sometimes the finger or palm pressure is stationary; other times, back-and-forth, sweeping, or circular motions are applied.

Wu Chi Self-Massage comes from the practice of Tai Chi. It has roots in Taoist practices and is also found in Tibetan Yoga. Rather than using the hands, it involves a number of slow, subtle body movements that massage the internal organs. It is usually accomplished while sitting in a still, meditative, upright position.

Sensory Awareness (SA)

Charlotte Selver created Sensory Awareness after studying with German bodyworker and educator Elsa Gindler, who had healed herself of tuberculosis through breathing exercises. During the period from 1910 to the 1930s, Gindler was instrumental in the establishment and growth of many somatic practices and psychotherapies; a number of her students went on to develop their own healing practices, which have now become well established worldwide. Gindler's work on the development of presence and her ways of creating relaxation, which emphasized paying attention to the breath, were revolutionary for that time. Selver's Sensory Awareness, which Alan Watts referred to as living Zen, was brought to the United States in 1938 and influenced many disciplines, such as Gestalt Therapy, and the work of Moshe Feldenkrais, Wilhelm Reich, and Fritz Perls. Sensory Awareness was designed to help individuals become fully present in the here and now. Rather than a therapy that uses a structured series of movements, physical training, or a particular recipe for healing, SA uses quiet alertness and simple conscious inquiry to bring about healthy changes without strain or effort. The teachings aim to enhance perceptions and restore the unity of mind and body by simply observing and allowing what is natural for each person.

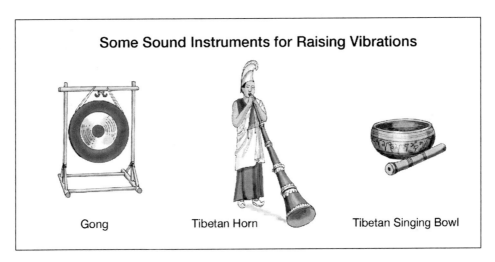

Some Sound Instruments for Raising Vibrations

Gong   Tibetan Horn   Tibetan Singing Bowl

Sensory Awareness avoids repetitive mechanical techniques. Instead, it relies on spontaneous, self-generated movements to remove restrictions in the body. By approaching each action in a sensitive, thoughtful, and joyful way and gently focusing on the breath and sensing how this and other subtle movements feel within the body, an individual can relieve tension, loosen restrictions, and improve balance, flexibility, and coordination. By removing the effort to make something happen, this simple practice creates a very subtle shift in consciousness in which body awareness is increased and the recipient gains a direct perception of unity in mind and body that goes beyond intellectual understanding. In this endeavor, Sensory Awareness is similar to many forms of meditation. Selver was also instrumental in the establishment of applied therapies such as Sensory Reeducation and Esalen Bodywork, which are discussed in Chapter 6.
Contact: www.returntooursenses.com

Shinkiko

Shinkiko is an ancient spiritual form of Medical Qi Gong modified by Dr. Masato Nakagawa, who was also responsible for the creation of Chickwando. Although similar to qi gong in its breathing exercises, flowing body movements, and postures, this meditative healing process uses shinki, a high-frequency healing energy, to remove stagnant energy and raise the level of consciousness. Shinkiko is based on the close relationship between the nonphysical world of energy and the divine spirit, and its aim is to enhance the vital lifeforce energy without physical touch by synchronizing the recipient's vibrations with the healing vibrations of divine cosmic energy. Energy revitalization leads to better physical functioning and body alignment, heightened intuition, and an open heart. When all parts of the body are aligned and the heart is full of vibrational harmony and love, any dysfunction or illness naturally dissipates. Practitioners claim to be able to tap into a limitless amount of universal energy through resonance with the high vibration of its cosmic source. Contact: www.shinkiko.com/english/

Sound Healing Practices

When at sea, the sound of the wind is music to a sailor's ears, for wind is what is needed to propel the boat across the water. The sound of rain falling soothes the farmer, who knows that crops will grow. The sound of the bus coming relieves the commuter of worries about getting to work on time. The sound of food being poured into a cat's bowl is cause for much rejoicing and rubbing of ankles. Sound provides relief and joy and inspiration, but certain sounds have proven to have a resonance that takes people beyond emotions to deep inner healing.

Sound therapy is an increasingly popular way to enhance well-being, and the resonant harmonic frequencies produced can have a positive effect on health. Some forms of energy medicine assert that each part of a healthy body vibrates at a certain frequency and that disease occurs when the body is out of tune. The body can be brought into harmony and thereby heal itself through the subtle entrainment that occurs when the body synchronizes with the vibrations present in certain sounds. Certain sounds can change a person's mood in minutes, and others can influence the structure of the body. Inspirational prayer or songs can cleanse and enliven the spirit by bringing to human ears the music of the celestial spheres.

Sound healing can take on many forms from the simple acts of groaning, humming, or singing to the prolonged chanting of "Om." Pulsed sounds can break up patterns and release blocked energies, whereas sustained sounds can help integrate, sooth, and restore natural rhythms. A variety of instruments, such as tuning forks, crystal bowls, singing bowls, drums, and the human voice, can be used at home to create the sounds that heal.

Contact: Sound Healing Research Association –
    www.soundhealingcenter.com,
    www.healingsounds.com, or
    www.globalsoundhealing.net

Chakra Toning subtly aligns and balances the inner energy centers. This practice is not difficult to learn, although it may be helpful to receive some training. Synchronized with the breath, a sequence of pure vowel sounds arising from deep inside are toned, prolonged for as long as possible, and directed into the chakras. The practice usually starts with the root chakra at the base of the spine and works upward to the crown of the head. Different traditions assign different tones to the chakras, but the most common are "uuuh" for the root chakra, "oooo" for the sacral chakra, "oohh" for the navel chakra, "aahh" for the heart chakra, "eehh" for the throat chakra, "aayy" for the third eye chakra, and "eeee" for the crown chakra. The pitch of the tones gets higher as the practice moves up through the chakras. Each of these sounds relates to and stimulates a particular gland that activates the organs in that area and are sounded for a few minutes before moving on. Seed syllables associated with each chakra can also be used: Lam, Vam, Ram, Yam, Ham, Om, and Ah or silence, moving up from the root chakra to the crown chakra.

Contact: www.http://www.the-energy-healing-
    site.com/chakra-tones.html

Chanting and Mantras use the voice in songs of praise or supplication. A mantra can be a single word—Om, the primordial sound of the perfection of the universe, or the name of a deity, such as Krishna—or a series of sacred words, such as Om mani padma hung, which usually cannot be translated literally. The chanting of mantras is a devotional practice that dates back to early Hinduism, but many different spiritual traditions rely on the use of sacred sound to unite supplicants with a loving presence, however that may be defined. It is said that a mantra carries with it the vibrations of all who have ever chanted it, adding to the power of its use. Some mantras dedicated to certain sacred beings are believed to have specific effects. For example, for Tibetan Buddhists, when the mantra of Green Tara is recited one hundred thousand times, all obstacles, including disease, can be overcome. The Hindu Ganapati prayer to Ganesh fulfills the same purpose. In Christianity, hymns and prayer praise the name and the works of God and request assistance in daily life. Visualizations often accompanies the chanting of mantras, especially in tantric practices.

*A unique type of chanting in Bali—
the Monkey Chant.*

Although mantra recitation can be carried out as a mental activity, audibly chanting the sacred sounds engages the body, speech, and mind in an activity that can carry participants into a sacred space full of the heart-warming feelings of love and devotion. Group chanting is a ritual part of spiritual practices in Hinduism, all schools of Buddhism, Jainism, Sikhism, Taoism, Christianity, and aboriginal cultures. The effects of group chanting can be very pronounced as space is filled with sound, allowing the participants to simply rest

in its vibrations. Kirtan, the ancient Indian style of call-and-response chanting, was introduced to the West by Kriya Yoga practitioner Paramahamsa Yogananda in the first half of the twentieth century as a practice for personal healing and transformation. One of the first of many to popularize kirtan is American Krishna Das. After spending years in India immersed in Bhakti Yoga with his guru, Neem Karoli Baba, the former rocker came home and developed a style of chanting that fused traditional songs of praise with Western harmonics and rhythm. Numerous other spiritually oriented performance artists have created melodic forms of chanting that have a strong, vibratory, and quite enchanting effect on their audiences.
Contact: www.krishnadas.com or
www.healing.about.com/od/chanting/

Harmonic Overtone Chanting, also known as throat singing, is a style of singing in which special techniques allow some of the unheard overtones contained in all sound waves to become audible. The peoples of Mongolia and Siberia were probably the first to use this style, whose history stretches back through time, but it can be found in Africa, the Middle East, and North America. The practice was also adopted by Tibetan Buddhist monks, who concentrated on drawing out the low pitches in continuous ritual chanting. One of the first Westerners to see the possible effects of overtone singing was German composer Karlheinz Stockhausen. He composed a performance work, *Alphabet für Liège*, to demonstrate the effect that sound could have on matter, even down to the atoms of the human body; it used twenty-eight distinct overtones to provide harmonics that resonated with the brain in a way that provides a healing psychological change. More and more musicians discovered the effects that harmonic overtones could add to their work, and it can be found in most genres of modern music.

Jill Purce, an Englishwoman who studied with Stockhausen and introduced him to the work of Hans Jenny, the scientist who experimented with the ways powders and liquids reacted to sound vibrations, had spent her early years investigating the spiraling flow of labyrinths and contemplative traditions using the voice and sound. She chanted for many years with Tibetan monks and other overtone singers and became convinced that sound, and especially the voice, could produce a healing effect. Purce went on to create a sound healing practice, The Healing Voice, through which she teaches Mongolian overtone chanting to groups. It may take time for participants to master the art of overtone chanting, but its effects can be felt early on and it can become a daily spiritual practice. By entraining with the vibrations of the overtones, the chanter can enter an altered state that melts the mind into a new sense of awareness, brings harmony and vitality to the body, and energizes the spirit. Purce also conducts shamanic group healing ceremonies that use pure sound, chanting, breathwork, visualization, and movement to create healing mandalas. She has a special interest in families and has created special rituals to honor the ancestors and heal ancestral lines.
Contact: www.healingvoice.com

Stretching / Callanetics

Stretching is one of the most natural ways for people to release tension, yet many do not realize the value of simple stretching techniques that can easily be learned and then carried out on a daily basis. When done correctly, stretching exercises can help repattern the physical structure of the body in a beneficial way. This practice often involve some form of stretching of isolated body parts, as well as resistance movement patterns. It is wise to listen to the body when practicing such exercises to avoid any unnecessary injury. Stretching in the shower is a great tonic for people who are stiff in the morning. There are certain types of equipment that can assist in stretching the body, including rubber balls of various sizes and inversion tables that can suspend the body in a position that helps stretch and lengthen the spine and release compression.

It would be impossible to list all of the many exercise programs based on stretching. One example would be the simple practice of Callanetics developed in the 1970s by Callan Pinckney for the purpose of pain relief. It incorporates stretches that use very small muscle contractions, which are carried out very slowly and gently while breathing naturally. Pelvic curling rotations are a key element of the exercise. The hour-long workout uses arm swings, leg exercises, sitting stretches, and circular pelvic rotations all done in a specific way that benefits alignment and balance.

Contact: www.callanetics.com

Tai Chi

A relaxing form of meditation in movement, this collection of subtle energy-balancing exercises, also known as T'ai Chi Chu'an or Taijiquan, comes from ancient China, and like many other martial arts, its practices were originally developed by monks as defense against bandits or warlord. The literal translation of *Tai Chi* is "supreme ultimate fist." Taoist monk Chang San Feng is credited by some as formalizing it into a internal martial art in the thirteenth century. Subsequently, different masters created their own styles, but of the four basic styles of Tai Chi—Chen, Yang, Wu, and Sun—that have been handed down through the ages by various lineages, the Yang style is the one often used today. The practice was prohibited during some periods of Chinese history, but these restrictions haven't applied since the last century, and today many people in China can be seen doing their forms in parks or courtyards each morning or performing in competitions.

Instruction in Tai Chi is now widely available, and it is practiced for its health-giving effects rather than for combat. Although the movement appears soft, passive, and yielding, Tai Chi taps into the vast quantity of energy that can be gathered from the heavens and earth and recirculated through the body, sometimes directed with great precision in the active movements that mirror those found in combat. Like the breathing and stretching exercises of Daoyin and Tuina that are integral to its practice, Tai Chi is based on the Taoist principle that life is a balance between the opposing forces of yin and yang. Each movement works in harmony with the breath to remove blockages and restore the flow of chi by balancing the energies within the practitioner. Its aim is to allow each person to become a master of internal energy, a warrior of the heart, powerful yet compassionate and moving with centered, effortless action and inner strength.

A key element in the practice of Tai Chi is focusing awareness on the energy storage center in the belly (the lower dantien), where the centers of gravity and balance are located. Relaxed attention and sensitivity to balance and body weight help create the fluid movement characteristic of this practice. There are both long and short forms of the exercises in which a sequence of slow, effortless movements and held postures, each with its own evocative name reflecting the motion of animals or movements found in nature, are performed in a rhythmic manner synchronized with deep abdominal breathing. Once the tranquility of mind evoked by practicing the uninterrupted series of exercises is internalized, it will reverberate throughout the day, flowing like a never-ending river. The gentle movements of Tai Chi makes it suitable for older people and those who are less flexible. The practice, which heals by strengthening the practitioner rather than treating specific dysfunctions, can increase circulation, flexibility, balance, and mental focus and can resolve health problems caused by stress.

Contact: Institute of Integral Qi Gong and Tai Chi – www.nccam.nih.gov/health/taichi/introduction.htm or www.tai-chi.com/

Tai Chi Me is a related practice known as "the middle softness" that originated in China during the 1700s. Its different exercises include solo postures, push-hands practices with partners, and weapons training. People were once secretly trained within particular families, but a condensed form of the practice is now available worldwide. The training primarily helps develop a person's balance and reduce the chances of injuries from falling. The short form of Tai Chi Me has thirty-seven postures and during practice, the participant's body flows without interruption from one to another while maintaining a state of mindfulness. It is a flexible dance of push and yield, done in a circular motion, which is intended to participants become more centered in life. Training starts with solo work and then moves on to exercises with partners.

Yamuna® Body Rolling (YBR)

Yamuna Body Rolling uses different air-filled balls of a specific size, density, and resistance to release restrictions held in the body, increase circulation, reeducate muscles, stimulate bones, increase flexibility, and improve overall body alignment and functioning. It is a somatic self-care practice created by Yamuna Zake, who also developed the practitioner-applied therapy called Yamuna Body Logic. (See the section on Structural Therapies in Chapter 6.)

The body-rolling exercises are usually taught in a group setting; individual participants learn how place the balls on the floor and how roll the body over them in a variety of flowing exercise routines that have been designed for different parts of the body. The pressure created as the body sinks onto the ball helps release muscle tension and subtly massages internal organs. Each movement is done with attention to the breathing process. During classes, the facilitator's hands may contact the client's body above the spot where the ball has been placed, either on the floor or against a wall. This allows the practitioner to experience the effects of the ball on both sides of the body at once. The ball can also act as a fulcrum when applying sustained traction outward and away from the center of the body, resulting in an equal release, from front to back and side to side that helps bring core muscle groups into balance. The session proceeds in a specific order, covering most of the body, freeing up the joints, and allowing previously restricted energy to flow. The exercises resemble a relaxed form of yoga in which the body takes up different positions that stretch and work muscles and organs in a therapeutic way. Once a student learns the exercises, the practice can continue at home.

Contact: www.yamunabodyrolling.org

Yogalates

This is not a coffee drink consumed before doing yoga, but a fluid exercise program guided by a facilitator that combines Iyengar Yoga and the conditioning exercise of Pilates. Yogalates was developed by Louise Solomon as a low-impact, easy-to-learn method of building up core strength by combining the flexibility gained from yoga with the stability established in Pilates. The process relies on a continuous flow of motion by using deep breathing and continuous circular movements between various yoga poses. Although it is primarily a blend of just yoga and Pilates therapy, some Shiatsu bodywork can be included. The exercises are intended to create increased range of motion, relaxation, strength, and body awareness through the inward focus developed by these practices. The only equipment needed is a towel, floor mat, and a Pilates Thera-Band® that creates resistance. Certain asanas are repeated a number of times while breathing deeply and inhaling and exhaling with each movement. Although Yogalates is most often done as an exercise practice on dry land, it has been adapted into a form of fluid aquatic therapy.

Contact: www.yogalates.com.au

Yoga

The ancient practice of yoga is part of a system of self-liberation based on the principles of conscious living that likely originated before the earliest written languages were established. Yogic postures have been found on statues dating back to at least 5000 BCE, and the first Hindu scripture to mention yoga, the *Rig Veda*, is dated to around 2500 BCE, though this date is disputed. It describes yoga as part of a healing tripod of body, mind, and soul contained within a sacred science of life, components of which evolved into the Indian healing practice of Ayurvedic medicine. Yoga comes from the Sanskrit word *yuj*, which literally means yoke, but in this case represents the union of this healing tripod and the science and art of conscious living. Modern usage tends to equate the word *yoga* with physical movement, but many traditional forms are carried out from within stillness. Physical forms of yoga are carried out with specific body movements and positions, known as asanas, and are intended to provide numerous physical and spiritual benefits.

What is called the early Vedic period ended around 1000 BCE when the publication of the *Upandishads* ushered in the Pre-Classic period. These scriptures concentrated on the inner focus of yoga. The Epic period arrived around 600 BCE. It was during this time that the *Bhagavad Gita,* poems telling the story of Krishna, were published. This was followed, around 500 BCE, by the Classical period of philosophy, the time when Buddhism, Jainism, and six orthodox schools of Hindu yoga philosophy were established.

It wasn't until the second or third century BCE that Indian sage Patanjali systematized the practice of yoga. In his *Yoga Sutras,* he defines yoga as the cessation of thought waves in the mind and the means of finding the freedom to choose an inner connection with the divine self. He expressed yoga as a spiritual exercise, a sadhana, for purifying the body and mind and developing concentration, which leads to a thought-free mind and a state of nondual consciousness, or samadhi, in which distinctions between subject and object disappear. A total of 196 sutras, each representing different threads of yoga, convey how personal effort and experience can provide the spiritual knowledge that will help practitioners go beyond the ordinary human condition. The eight branches, or paths, of yoga he formulated join forces to help people reach of the goal of liberation from habitual patterns of reaction and awaken to self-realization, inner peace, and enlightenment.

Bhakti Yoga illustrates the devotional and ritual path of the heart in which uniting with the divine can clear away the dust of imperfection and can call forth a transcendent state of consciousness.

Hatha Yoga, also known as the yoga of will power, prepares the body for spiritual realization by creating a body of light through the practice of meditation, pranayama, asanas, and cleansing practices. All forms of physical yoga are included under this heading as means of purifying the body and creating the conditions for self-realization.

Jnana Yoga is the four-fold philosophical path to enlightenment through hearing, contemplating, and experiencing the teachings and cultivating virtues, including the discernment that distinguishes the real from the unreal and the detachment that makes pain and pleasure equal. This wisdom allows practitioners to see the difference between fleeting pleasure and abiding truth.

Karma Yoga relates to the active life path in which compassionate action of body, speech, and mind and service are used to transform the world.

Kundalini Yoga is the practice of awakening the vital life force and psychic powers with the guidance of a guru. The goal is to remove all obstacles to full liberation through a series of controlled practices.

Mantra Yoga refers to the practice of chanting sacred sounds and chants that help still the mind and bring a state of clarity.

Raja Yoga is the royal path to the higher states that can be obtained when the mind is refined through practices that prepare it for transcendence into pure consciousness.

Tantra Yoga relates to working with the body as a temple through the union of opposites, dynamic stillness, the breath, and the awakening of the kundalini energy that is a direct route to liberation.

Patanjali further describes the practice of Raja Yoga as having eight (ashta in Sanskrit) parts or limbs (anga); thus, it is also called Ashtanga Yoga. These limbs outline the ways in which the body and mind can support the practitioner on the path to enlightenment. They represent the original formulation of Ashtanga Yoga prior to what later developed as the modern Ashtanga practice by Pattabhi Jois.

Yama outlines restraints that, when followed, will help develop self-control. The practitioner is asked to renounce violence, lying, stealing, improper sexual relations, and avarice. Living in accordance with these principles will result in an ethical life in which the practitioner's outer relationship to the world reflects the inner values being cultivated.

Niyama presents observances and conduct that a practitioner should follow. It follows after Yama, because adhering to the restraints of Yama generates the energy to practice Niyama. Patanjali suggests that there are five observances: purity of body, speech and mind; contentment; diligence in spiritual practices; study of the self and of the soul; and surrender to God. Other traditions include virtues such as modesty, generosity, faith, mantra recitation,

The practice of Asana Yoga.
PHOTO COURTESY OF WILLIAM GEISLER

and remorse for misdeeds. Abiding by these virtues creates positive habits of behavior. Both Niyama and Yama represent moral and ethical directives rather than commands.

Asana offers a physical method to keep the body healthy and in harmony, thus rendering it a fit vehicle for the soul. Its postures, or asanas, entail precise movement into different body positions, which are held for differing periods of time. This general description has given rise to many different forms of practice that carry out different aspects of its basic intention.

Pranayama emphasizes the role that breath plays in maintaining a healthy body and mind. It includes a variety of breathing practices, ranging from the simple to the complex, that energize the body and help the practitioner learn how to manipulate and control the flow of prana, or vital life-force energy, through the pathways and portals of the body.

Pratyahara literally means "withdrawal of the senses," but it can be experienced as liberation from the mind's habit of attachment or aversion to the external objects perceived through the senses. Directing the mind inward, away from sensory perception, can be assisted by controlling the flow of vital energy to the sense organs and restraining from actions that would create distractions. It is often used in the early stages of developing concentration in meditation and emphasizes the practice of pranayama.

Dharana trains the mind to concentrate on a single object, such as a particular part of the body, the breath, a candle, a sound, a mantra, or a visualization. The mind can also be focused with kriyas, exercises in visualizing inner light, colors, and sounds. By constantly returning to the object of meditation, the practitioner can gain mastery over the wandering mind.

Dhyana is meditation characterized by effortless concentration uninterrupted by distractions. The practices of the first six limbs prepare the body and mind for entering this state in which the senses are withdrawn from objects of distraction, the mind is stilled,

and the practitioner rests in a state of pure awareness. It is still a dualistic state, because the consciousness is aware of an object, the act of meditating itself.

Samadhi represents the state of perfect union in which the individual soul becomes one with the supreme universal consciousness. It is a nondual state of bliss and joy in which any separation of experience into subject and object is transcended. The attainment of samadhi is the ultimate spiritual aspiration of the eight-fold path of yoga.

Yoga has spread far beyond the land of its origin. At the World's Fair in Chicago in 1893, a grand collection of leaders of the world's religions gathered for the first time. Swami Vivekananda, the only Hindu present, made a very eloquent speech about yoga that sparked the interest of many. The teachings of Krishnamacharya during the 1930s and 1940s, a time when British rule in India was in decline thanks to the selfless, nonviolent work of Mahatma Gandhi, had a widespread impact on the world. In addition to reviving the practice of the Hatha Yoga sequence of asanas, Krishnamacharya established a school in which he taught a number of individuals who would become instrumental in the worldwide spread of yoga as it is known today. His son, T. K. V. Desikachar, developed his own approach, believing that practicing was more important than the style of practice and that all teachings should respect the individual and individual needs and abilities. Krishnamacharya's only female student, Indra Devi, became the first woman to bring the teachings of yoga to the West in the 1960s. She taught yoga in Mexico, Argentina, and then in the United States, where she established the first American yoga center in California. She remained an important figure in the dissemination of yoga until 2002, when she passed away at the age of 102. B. K. S. Iyengar, a student of Krishnamacharya who recovered from childhood frailty by practicing yoga, had a significant impact on the spread of yoga, particularly in the United States, through teachers that he trained and his book, *Light on Yoga*. A proponent of precision and proper alignment in the practice of asanas, he also popularize yoga by introducing supportive props and creating therapeutic postures that helped treat specific ailments. Another famous student, Sri K. Pattabhi Jois, firmly believed that all could live long and healthy lives through the practice of yoga. He primarily focused on the teachings of Vinyasa Yoga, which emphasizes developing heat and strength by fluid movement through a series of asanas synchronized with deep breathing. Since the 1960s, yoga has become a part of modern culture; nowadays, all sorts of people include a yoga practice in their daily lives. Although many people use yoga simply for physical fitness without exploring the fuller dimensions of these practices, an ongoing shift in consciousness is awakening them to the ocean of possibilities it offers.

The physical practice of Hatha Yoga, which uses breathwork and various movements and postures (asana), was originally created to help enable the individual to practice meditation for longer periods. Many different forms of yoga have evolved over the centuries in parts of the world other than India, including practices that combine a series of body movements and postures with mudras, chants, mantras, visualizations, devotions, meditations, energizing techniques, and breathing exercises to help rejuvenate all parts of the body, mind, and spirit and to expand human capacity and the potential for enlightenment. Although the different styles of Asana Yoga may be different in technique, sequence, timing, and area of focus within the body, the common denominator is increasing the vital prana energy flow through the use of very specific mental and physical exercises, many of which have been established by disciplined and devoted adepts over centuries. From another perspective, today the practice of yoga is recognized as being useful in resolving emotional problems, correcting dysfunctions, and healing disease.

Although the word *yoga* causes modern seekers to think of Asana or Hatha Yoga, many of the other forms don't use any physical movement at all, instead making the meditative practices that cultivate awareness a way of living and being. This can have many therapeutic benefits. Since health and consciousness are interconnected, yoga can help address the root cause of disease by enhancing this mind-body connection. If people are physically ill or stressed out, their feelings, thoughts, and consciousness will reflect this imbalance. By creating physical, mental, emotional, and spiritual balance through the practices of yoga, it may be possible to reverse symptoms such as high blood pressure caused by stress and handle the energy of the emotions more compassionately.

Group yoga practice.

Over the millennia, hundreds of forms of yogic practices have been created, and the listings below describe only some of them. Coverage has been limited to those that are the most respected and also the most available through well-trained teachers in the West. Many of the practices are not necessarily the traditional forms of yoga that evolved in India. Some come from the Far East, and some are contemporary forms created by practitioners who have synthesized different wisdoms into unique ways of carrying out these revitalizing practices. Some are spiritually oriented, emphasizing meditative practices that include ways of using the breath, visualizations, sound, and the vital life-force energy. Others present the diverse ways of performing physical asana movements and postures. All will help practitioners learn to cleanse body and mind in the sea of physical and spiritual well-being.

The descriptions cannot provide a total picture of what is involved with each practice, and their length depends on the amount of information available rather than any judgment about their significance. Each can be explored initially by experiencing it under the guidance of a skilled instructor, realizing that individual facilitators of each type of yoga may teach the same practice in different ways with variations in emphasis and focus. When choosing a class, look for an instructor who is gentle, respectful and honors a desire to learn. Since training during practice can lead to injuries, beginners might want to consider asking the teacher not to be overly forceful in making adjustments.

Contact: American Yoga Association –
> www.americanyogaassociation.org,
> www.yogajournal.com, or
> www.nccam.nih.gov/health/yoga

AcroYoga® is a relatively new and playful formulation that combines acrobatics with basic yoga positions. The positions used range from simple to complex and require a trusted and supportive partner, since some of the poses require flying through the air to rest in a supported posture. AcroYoga often looks like some kind of circus act, and a certain level of physical strength is required. At certain times, Thai Massage may also used to encourage an even greater release.

Contact: www.acroyoga.org

Acu-Yoga for Self-Healing™, developed in the 1970s and 1980s by Dr. Michael Reed Gach, Ph.D., combines yoga with healing contact on acupressure points while stretching various muscles and meridian pathways. It applies knowledge of the chakras and Traditional Chinese Medicine's Acupressure Therapy, which validates yoga as a tremendously healing spiritual path. Acu-Yoga is based on the premise that yoga postures naturally stimulate specific acupressure points to free and balance the flow of vital life-force energy in all areas of the body for self-healing, a process that is also aided by the release of muscular tension provide by both yoga and Acupressure. This naturally leads to a healing experience of oneness.

Acu-Yoga is a fully integrated form of yogic therapy combining yoga postures with meditations, breathing techniques, mantras, and mudras. For instance, there are numerous yoga postures that stretch the neck muscles to open meridians and twelve pressure points around the neck, known as "Windows of the Sky," which can influence the fifth chakra and the thyroid gland and open the flow of energy between the spine and cranium. Controlled deep-breathing exercises performed while holding poses and the deep relaxation that immediately follows also contribute to self-healing.

Contact: www.acu-yoga.com

Amrit Yoga, developed by Yogi Amrit Desai, combines inner stillness with outer action by bringing the awareness developed through meditation to the physical practice of Hatha Yoga. Vigorously performing asanas with strong internal focus helps engage the mind and the emotions, enables the alteration of unconscious karmic patterns, and empowers a deeper integration of body, mind, heart, and soul. Meditating on the breath is a key ingredient of the practice, since the breath acts a bridge to connect personal energy with the universal field of energy. Combining breathing with focused attention is a powerful tool for restoring bodily functions, releasing blockages in prana energy, creating a sense of unity and harmony, and connecting with the spirit.

Contact: www.amrityoga.org

Ananda Yoga was founded by Swami Kriyananda, based on the teachings of his guru Paramahamsa Yogananda, and emphasizes relaxing into the yoga postures. It incorporates yoga philosophy and asanas, pranayama breathwork, meditation, and specific energizing exercises. The primary goal of Ananda Yoga is to enter a continuous state of heightened awareness that can raise consciousness and create the conditions for inner happiness.

Contact: www.expandinglight.org/anandayoga/

Anatomic Yoga concentrates on the science of anatomy and physiology behind all postures. Students learn about the biomechanics of the muscles, tendons, joints, and ligaments as they apply to exercise, form, and function. They also study the fundamentals of pranayama and the ways in which the different asanas work on the lower and upper chakras. This knowledge can then be used in the performance of asanas.

Contact: www.discoveryyoga.com/AnatomicYoga.
> htm

Anusara Yoga, whose name means "flowing with grace," is based on the belief that all beings are intrinsically good. Anusara was formulated by John Friend in 1997 and incorporates a mix of elements from Hatha, Iyengar, Siddha, and Tantra Yogas. The practice emphasizes the opening of the heart

through a Vinyasa flow style practice with challenging poses and an emphasis on physical alignment; props are used as necessary. Although the practice can be lighthearted and fun, it is not easy. It is primarily for those interested in both physical and spiritual well-being and intends that lessons learned in class are brought into daily life.
Contact: www.anusarayoga.com

Arhatic Yoga is a synthesis of various yoga practices, purifying breathwork exercises, and meditative techniques that was created by Chinese-Filipino spiritual Master Choa Kok Sui, the founder of Pranic Healing bodywork. Arhatic Yoga is designed to heighten spiritual development by activating the chakras and balancing their negative properties, safely awakening the sacred fires of kundalini energy, and neutralizing negative tendencies that keep the soul from being in charge. The practice is intended to allow people to pursue spiritual development without retreating from worldly affairs. Daily challenges and interactions are considered part of the learning process. Initial levels of practice use meditation and breathwork to purge negativity from the energy body and provide a solid foundation for kundalini awakening. Intermediate practices include meditations that energize the chakras and prayers that enhance divine love, all of which provide a deeper connection with the higher self and develop stillness and awareness. The most advanced level of practice is the attainment of the Golden Body and enlightenment itself.
Contact: www.arhaticyoga.org/

Ashtanga Yoga, also known as Ashtanga Vinyasa Yoga, was formalized by Sri K. Pattabhi Jois in the first part of the twentieth century. Pattabhi Jois learned the practice from his teacher, Krishnamacharya, one of the first to recognize the value of combining breath with movement in yoga. Pattabhi Jois's form is a set sequence of asanas performed in the Vinyasa style, in which each movement is closely linked with the breathing and flows rhythmically into the next, taking the body from one posture to the another without rest. An intense and vigorous practice, Ashtanga Yoga generates heats, strengthens the body, and activates the flow of prana, thus

strengthening, aligning and purifying the entire body and mind. Participants are guided step by step in a clear, precise manner through a series of progressively more difficult levels of practice.
Contact: www.ashtanga.com

Bhakti Yoga, one of the original eight major branches of yoga, is a practice of adoration and devotion that creates a direct and loving relationship with the divine by softening the heart and removing the egoistic habits and reactions that cause suffering. By surrendering to the will of the divine, each individual is able to find a sweet path to a deep, transcendent, and blissful state of consciousness. This complex and rigorous yoga of meditative absorption and surrender requires consistent and conscientious practice to awaken of the divine that is always present in the heart. Chanting and prayer are integral elements. Both Sri Swami Sivananda and American-born chant master Krishna Das have contributed to the spread of Bhakti Yoga in the West.
Contact: www.bhakti-yoga-meditation.com or www.yogajournal.com/practice/2661/

Bikram Yoga, often referred to as Hot Yoga, was created in 1971 by Bikram Choudhury. It uses only a specific sequence of twenty-six asanas considered to heat the body, and they are repeated in a very warm (95 to 105 degrees) room. Postures combined with breathing techniques are generally quite intensive and physically strenuous as they vigorously work to warm, stretch, and tone the muscles. This form of yoga is popular with people who want a real physical workout. An aquatic version of this practice performed in warm water has also been created.
Contact: www.bikramyoga.com

Circus Yoga is a nontraditional form composed of acrobatics, partner yoga, clowning, circus skills, group games, and an assortment of creative dance and movement. It is intended to foster a playful connection and better communication among a group and to develop ways to entertain others with unique feats of physical prowess. The practice is considered suitable for individuals of all ages and skills.
Contact: www.circusyoga.com

Dahn Yoga is a body-mind training method that combines deep stretching exercises, meditative breathing techniques, and energy-awareness training. Dahn Yoga had its origin in Korea and is described as "the study of the prime vital life force energy that is the basis of all forms of life." This systematic practice of energetic healing is intended to help participants experience the body and its innate healing powers by strengthening the fundamental life force through exercises that open the energy meridian pathways. It was reformulated by Ilchi Lee as a natural form of self-care that helps prevent and treat common illnesses. The objective is attaining the highest possible level of personal potential in which the energy within and union with the earth energy can be felt.
Contact: www.dahnyoga.com

Dream Yoga extends the practice of yoga beyond normal waking hours. Many indigenous cultures around the world have placed great emphasis on the power of dreams and considered them messengers from the spirit world, offering guidance in daily living or during times of trouble. The Australian Aborigines relied on the Dream Time for advice on living in harmony with nature. Native Americans contributed insights from dreams to the decisions of councils of chiefs. Malaysian "dream people" created wood carvings to represent the wondrous stories revealed in dreams. In contemporary times, psychotherapy and body-mind therapies have focused on the importance of dream interpretation, and the study of lucid dreaming has expanded. However, in the context of yoga, more focus is placed on recognizing the underlying awareness that exists even while sleeping than on deciphering the messages found in dreams. Among the many yogic traditions found in India, China, and Tibet, as well as in practices in Islamic and Christian traditions, there are numerous approaches aimed at transcending the self, whether the individual practitioner is awake, sleeping, or dreaming, including different practices of Dream Yoga. Although there are distinctions in each path to the ultimate truth, the goal of awakening is essentially the same.

Although yogis, lamas, and gurus do see significance in the content of dreams, the practice of Dream Yoga explores ways to expand conscious awareness of the deeper dimensions accessible from the state of dreaming or deep sleep. In Tibetan Buddhism, the practice of Dream Yoga employs specific techniques before and after falling asleep so the practitioner can learn to equate the illusory quality of dreams with the dream-like drama that constantly distorts the nature of experience. A contemporary form of Dream Yoga, known as Integral Deep Listening, supports these ideas with an emphasis on lucid living and the inclusion of multiple perspectives on the process of becoming free of illusory dreams and one with the divine true nature of existence
Contact: www.dreamyoga.com or
www.integraldeeplistening.com

Embodyoga® is a Vinyasa Yoga practice developed by Patty Townsend that fuses together mind-body centering practices, breathwork, Hatha Yoga, and Tantra Yoga and emphasizes an exploration of the body from the cellular level to the subtle energy body. It stresses keeping the spine free of blockages that would impede the flow of prana along the central channel during the practice of asanas. The somatic process of Embodyoga incorporates a variety of practices including asanas, pranayama, pratyahara (the practice of turning perceptions inward), dharana (one-pointed focus of consciousness), and dhyana (meditation). All work to diminish ego control and invite the practitioner to enter within and discover the innate wisdom that can see all illusion as it is. Imagination, visualization, and sounding are also used in a way that allows the separation between subject and object to fall away.
Contact: www.embodyoga.com

Forrest Yoga is a relatively intense and physical style of Vinyasa Yoga that was formulated by Ana Forrest. The practice incorporates elements of Native American healing and places emphasis on abdominal bodywork and breathing. It involves a vigorous sequence of asanas that are intended to build up heat to sweat out toxins, release stored emotions in the body, provide a deep connection with the heart, and heal psychic wounds. This style of yoga often appeals to students who want a strong emotional and physical workout.
Contact: www.forrestyoga.com

Guru Yoga, sometimes referred to as **Deity Yoga**, is a devotional Buddhist Vajrayana practice in which the practitioner strives to merge body, speech, and mind with that of an enlightened master or fully awakened being such as the Buddha. The true object of Guru Yoga is none other than the meditator's own ground of being; the teacher is simply the embodiment of the qualities of that primordial purity that an ordinary person may find difficult to recognize in herself. The practice involves visualizations, the requesting and receiving of blessings, and refuge vows. The inspiration provided by the practice and the guidance of the teacher are key ingredients to forward movement on the path to full awakening.
Contact: www.palyul.org/eng_teachings-guruyoga.htm

Hatha Yoga, also known as the yoga of will power, contains the physical practices that prepare and purify the physical body and the mind for higher meditation practices. All forms of physical yoga—for example, Ashtanga, Vinyasa, or Iyengar—fall under the heading of Hatha Yoga, but in modern times it has come to mean a practice of simple asanas done slowly and gently. Pranayama breathwork is often included, and more traditional styles may bring in purification practices and meditation. This is a good form for beginners and is appropriate when a person wants to wind down from a period of stressful activity. Although it deals primarily with the physical aspects of yoga, the practice can also create conditions for self-realization.

Inner Fire Yoga, also known as **Tummo**, is an intensive method used in advanced stages of Tibetan Vajrayana practices working with subtle energy. Along with other meditation techniques, the practice incorporates visualizations to connect with internal energy, free up trapped energy, and redirect the energy of seemingly destructive emotions. Energy is generated, stored in the navel area, and then distributed through the energy channels of the body. Although the practice can generate enough body heat to melt ice, its true goal is purification so that the meditator can rest in the empty space of awareness in which the mind is free of conceptual divisions. In Tibet, the practice of Tummo has

enabled accomplished yogis and monks to live and meditate for long periods of time in cold mountain caves wearing only thin cotton garments. Similar experiences of creating this mystic fire have been found in the advanced practices of Kundalini Yoga. The practice of Inner Fire Yoga has also been shown to slow down body metabolism by undetermined mechanisms that have puzzled researchers. The practice of Tummo is not to be taken lightly. If the individual is not properly prepared and the energy not skillfully guided, imbalanced and even psychotic episodes can occur.
Contact: www.thoughtbrick.com/meditation/tummo-meditation-depth-guide/ or www.holistic-guide.com/tummo-yoga/

Insight Yoga, created in the 1980s by Sarah Powers, blends meditative Buddhist practices with Yin/Yang Yoga and transpersonal psychotherapy. The practice uses a combination of meditative Yin poses, which are held for a long period of time, and flowing, active Yang movements from Viniyoga, Ashtanga, and Iyengar teachings to enhance the flow of energy through the meridians and deepen insight into the natural state of innate awareness. Breathwork, visualizations, mindfulness meditation, self-inquiry, dialogue, and extended periods of silence are all employed to bring about a state of inner balance and psychospiritual transformation.
Contact: www.sarahpowers.com

Integral Yoga is a term that can refer to two things. The first is Sri Aurobindo's spiritual teachings about unifying all parts of one's being with the divine; it is a yoga of synthesis that harmonizes the practices of Karma, Jnana, and Bhakti Yogas. During the early twentieth century, Sri Aurobindo wrote several books, among them *The Life Divine*, *The Synthesis of Yoga*, and *Savitri*, describing his system of purna or "complete" yoga, also sometimes called supra-mental yoga. He collaborated with Mirra Alfassa, a Frenchwoman who came to one of his retreats and eventually founded his ashram and became the spiritual guide for the community. He called her The Mother, since he considered her an incarnation of the Mother Divine.
Integral Yoga ™ also refers to a gentle and meditative form of Hatha Yoga, created about a half

century ago by Swami Satchidananda, that combines various yogic practices to stimulate a transformation that enables spiritual unity. This system puts equal emphasis on the use of pranayama breath control, meditation, asanas, and deep relaxation. It also includes a specially formulated set of kriya exercises and chanting.
Contact: Integral Yoga Institute – www.iyiny.org

Ishta Yoga, developed during the 1960s by Alan Finger, is a restorative form of Hatha Yoga that combines asanas, pranayama, chanting, and meditation into a physical and spiritual practice to preserve health and wellness by opening the energy channels and providing an avenue to self-awareness. This slow-paced style of yoga, also known as the yoga of synthesis, emphasizes yogic breathing and embraces elements of a variety of styles, such as the slow pace of Sivananda Yoga, the relaxed movements of Viniyoga, the careful alignment found in Iyengar Yoga, and the rigorous poses of Ashtanga, though not its continuous movement. Ishta Yoga is safe for all ages and offers a personalized approach that helps students learn the poses and modifications that are right for their own self-development and empowerment.
Contact: www.ishtayoga.com

Iyengar Yoga is a method named after its well-known developer, B. K. S. Iyengar, who wrote the landmark books, *Light on Yoga, Light on Pranayama,* and *Light on Life.* This form of Hatha Yoga practice emphasizes proper body alignment and symmetry of asana postures with attention to detail. The asanas are practiced in a specific sequence and timing that has a cumulative effect on the body. Rather than constant movements between asanas, poses are held and then repeated several times. A variety of props such as blocks, straps, and pillows are used to compensate for any lack of flexibility and provide more comfort during the various poses, making the practice more accessible to those who have trouble performing certain asanas. Once a certain level of mastery has been achieved with the asanas, additional pranayama breathwork and meditation are incorporated. This refines and amplifies the effectiveness of the postures by enabling the mind to become meditatively absorbed with all the parts of the body. Although it tends to focus on refining only particular asanas, most of which are not very strenuous, Iyengar Yoga can nevertheless be quite invigorating and may be beneficial for those with chronic pain and back or joint problems.
Contact: www.bksiyengar.com

Jivamukti Yoga is a form of Hatha Yoga that also cultivates deep listening by working with healing sounds, chanting, and music to attain individual liberation of the soul. The practice incorporates the elements of devotion, compassion, meditation, and service found in the *Yoga Sutras* of Patanjali. In this yoga, the physical exercise in performing asanas is less important than the goal of enlightenment. The practice of Jivamukti, which means "liberation while living," was established by David Life and Sharon Gannon and emphasizes how to apply yogic philosophy to daily life. This practice is also distinguished by strict adherence to a vegetarian diet.
Contact: www.jivamuktiyoga.com

Jnana Yoga or **Advaita Vedanta Yoga** is the yoga of wisdom and represents the direct path to self-realization. Its meditative self-inquiries clear away the delusions of the mind (maya) and allow the experiencing of the transcendent, nondualistic truth (brahman) that is always present within. By using techniques such as Neti Neti to repeatedly discard illusions in an active way, Jnana Yoga allows its practitioners to realize that all doubts, fears, and worries no longer present a problem. It is the most difficult of all yogas and must be practiced for a long time to reach its goal. Discerning the truth behind that which seems real requires great self-control and the perfection of meditative concentration, as well as devotion and discipline. But that truth is the means of liberation and the route to happiness.
Contact: www.yoga108.org/pages/show/
55-jnana-yoga-introduction or
www.yogasatyananda-france.net/
pages/en/jnanayoga-en.php

Karma Yoga, also referred to as **Buddhi Yoga** or the yoga of service, is the practice of correct action and selfless service; it represents the compassionate way of life called for in the ancient Hindu *Bhagavad Gita.* The concept of karma is often misunderstood, but it primarily concerns the fact that every action, every word, and every thought plant the seeds of future positive or negative action, speech and thought. By practicing compassionate service, the quality of compassion is strengthened and will arise spontaneously in future situations.

Kayakalpa Yoga contains ancient techniques traditionally used by the siddhas (adept meditators) of India to enhance the life-force energy and prevent disease. Its objectives are to improve physical, mental, and spiritual well-being, and through the same practices, to maintain youthful energy and appearance, improve quality of life, and promote longevity. The practice involves a series of special short movement exercises that stimulate the flow of energy in the channels and chakras. Kayakalpa Yoga is one part of a larger transformative therapy developed by Dr. Raam Pandeya. (See Kayakalpa in the section on Special in Chapter 6.)
Contact: www.kaya-kalpa.org

Kid's (Children's) Yoga brings basic Hatha Yoga practice to children in a gentle, supportive, nurturing way that helps them reduce tension and make a healthy shift into adulthood. Most younger children have flexible bodies that become stiffer as they internalize the tensions of daily life, and yoga is a wonderful way to prevent the development of physical constrictions that can be detrimental to cognitive abilities.

Kripalu Yoga is a style of Asana Yoga, that combines asanas with meditative practices that develop awareness, concentration, and absorption. It was originally established by Kundalini Yoga master Amrit Desai, who named this style, as well as the Kripalu Center for Yoga that he founded in 1985 and named after his guru Swami Sri Kripalvanandji. Desai left the center, relinquished the Kripalu name, and is no longer associated with the practice and the center. The practice as it exists today uses both active and restorative poses and is more spontaneous and flowing than other styles of yoga. Attention is placed on the subtle flow of prana through the asana postures and meditations, which moves the practitioner into deeper levels of

body-mind awareness. Proper breathing synchronized with each movement is emphasized throughout the practice. Compared to other styles of yoga, the postures are held for longer periods of time. This gives participants the opportunity to explore and let go of any emotional or mental blockages. The practice is composed of three stages in which the individual first learns to do short poses synchronized with proper breathing, followed by extended and demanding poses that work with meditative practices to develop better awareness of thoughts and emotions. In the final stage, the postures and meditation are combined to create what is called a meditation in motion, in which movements flow spontaneously from one posture to the next. Kripalu Yoga allows individuals to work within the limits of their own physical abilities and advises always listening to the body during practice.
Contact: www.kripalu.org/article/375

Kriya Yoga contains ancient pranayama breath-control techniques and, like Kundalini Yoga, is practiced to create inner fire that can purify personal karma. Eight nose-breathing practices and six purification practices use breath control to rein in the mind and open the flow of prana up the primary channels within the spine through the chakras. Bandha locks, mudras (sacred hand gestures), mantras (sacred sounds), and Bhakti Yoga devotional practices are also part of the practice. The yoga is done in six stages, each progressing gradually towards higher kriya levels. Kriya Yoga is taught through a strict lineage to keep true to the once-secret form that was revived during the 1860s by Mahavatar Babaji Mahara. The practice was later brought to the West by Paramahamsa Hariharananda and Paramahamsa Yogananda, who became famous for his book, *Autobiography of a Yogi*. The lineage of teachers continues to this day with the latest Paramahamsa (a title of highest distinction) being Paramahamsa Prajnanananda. The practice can only be learned by direct transmission from an authorized master.
Contact: Kriya Yoga International – www.kriya.org/ or www.prajnanamission.org/

Kundalini Yoga, also referred to as **Laya Yoga**, provides a powerful spiritual practice that can promote personal transformation and liberation. Kundalini is the primordial cosmic energy that lies dormant at the base of the spine, and the practice strives to awaken a higher state of energy and consciousness by tapping into this subatomic divine energy that pervades the infinite universe. Through the ascent of kundalini energy, the negativities and obstacles to full liberation in all the chakra energy centers are gradually transformed, melting away karmic condition and creating a state of unity with the divine. This process of awakening kundalini is best learned in stages through a series of controlled practices that are experienced with the guidance of a master. Guided practices incorporate specific asanas, mental focusing, pranayama breathwork, mantras (special words or phrases), mudras (hand positions), chakra work, meditations, visualizations, kriya techniques, bandha locks, and various tantric practices, including sexual union. Certain sound healing techniques such as gong sounding, toning, and ecstatic music are also incorporated into the practices. Most of the exercises work not only to enable the open flow of pranic energy but to instill a balanced, relaxed state of expanded awareness and a transcendent state of spiritual unity. This practice originated with the warrior class in ancient India, and Yogi Bhajan, Gurmukh Kaurkhalsa, and Sri Anandi Ma were all instrumental in perpetuating the teachings through different lineages.

Kundalini can also be activated spontaneously by unusual or significant life events, such as a near-death experience, and the emergence of this energy can be quite unsettling for the unsuspecting. Many cultures have seen this arousal as something worrisome or detrimental, since it can manifest with violent physical effects and emotional states that mimic psychosis. However, the daily practice of Kundalini Yoga taught by a master allows a gentle and safe progression toward awakening, rather than uncontrolled spontaneous occurrences. Any disorientation is then recognized as the valuable unfolding of the truth of the mystery of existence, and the unsettled ego is immersed in a sea of unlimited love, wisdom, and compassion. The energy can also be transferred from the guru to the disciple through a Shaktipat initiation, which establishes a unique spiritual bond that enhances the transmission of further embodied spiritual knowledge and wisdom.
Contact: www.3ho.org/kundalini-yoga or
   www.kundaliniresearchinstitute.org/
   What%20is%20KY.htm

LifeForce Yoga is a simple, contemporary form of yoga used to manage physical, mental and emotional disorders through practicing compassion and working with the vital life-force energy. Founded in the West by Amy Weintraub, it offers strategies to enhance the sense of well-being without changing a basic yoga practice. The daily practice is intended to lessen feelings of separation, one of the most significant causes of depression. By developing an authentic sense of connection to the self and others, life can be embraced more fully. LifeForce Yoga does not require any particular form of asana practice; it is intended as a supplement to any style of yoga.
Contact: www.lifeforceyoga.net

Mantra Yoga uses the repetitive recitation of tones, call-and-response chants (kirtan), and the sacred sounds of mantras to help focus the mind and create a state of clarity and stillness within. A mantra is a word or a phrase that carries powerful energetic vibrations, and the continual repetition of a mantra can heighten concentration on and union with the enlightened presence it represents. In the practice of japa, divine names such as Rama or Krishna are recited over and over again to help to still the mind. Certain specific sounds can also be directed at the seven chakras for energetic and spiritual healing.
Contact: www.theyogasanctuary.net/tips-mantras.
   html

Mega Yoga, a new adaptation of yoga for overweight people, uses specific poses that are beneficial for weight control. Megan Garcia created Mega Yoga as an enjoyable weight-loss program that can be used by any person who desires a more comfortable and healthy life.
Contact: www.megayoga.com

Nada Yoga is also called the yoga of sound and refers to the practice of using the vibrations of sounds to tune the chakras, calm the mind,

influence disease processes, and create a sense of self-realized wholeness. The source of sound can be the subtle, often-inaudible vibrations of energy flowing internally or the external frequencies of evocative music or vocal toning. Practitioners can begin by listening to external sources of sound or by using their voices to create tones and then listening carefully for the internal sounds to emerge. This meditative practice requires deep concentration that gently leads the mind into a relaxed state of awareness of the emotions and energies within. Guru Swami Nada-Brahmananda, a great master of Nada Yoga, was instrumental in the teaching of this practice.
Contact: www.spiritsound.com/nadayoga.html or
     www.russillpaul.com/articles/article/
     1162814

Nyasa Yoga is the practice of projecting the divine into the body in a ritual that transforms the body into a sacred space. Through meditation and conscious touching, the practitioner instills the qualities of sacred sounds or images within different parts of the body. As the practitioner focuses on an image, feeling, or sound, allowing it to fill the mind, the fingers or hands are placed in sequence on a series of sacred points on the body; the touch may include circular rubbing and can be accompanied with verbal affirmations. The union of physical sensation and spiritual activity transmits holiness to that part of the body. More simply, the same process can be used to send light and healing to damaged parts of the body and mind. This form of yoga can be very nurturing and a great way to honor the divine within the body in a joyful way.
Contact: www.drbpsahi.com/nyasa_yoga_healing.
     html

Okido Yoga is a dynamic style of yoga, developed in the mid 1900s by Dr. Masahiro Oki, that combines elements of yoga, Chinese Taoism, and Japanese Zen. A form of Zen Yoga, the practice stresses the natural state of balance between the opposites of tension and relaxation, hot and cold, and stillness and movement. Keeping these in balance also requires the simultaneous balancing of the mind, so that bussho (the Japanese term for buddha nature)

can also be cultivated. The practice involves a series of flowing asana movements intended to balance, energize, and purify the core strength of the mind and body. A synthesis of Zen and Hindu meditation practices known as Meiso Yoga, which employs controlled breathing, relaxation, and the strengthening of the lower dantien (the energetic point of physical equilibrium located below the navel), is an integral part of the practice. All these aspects work to release blockages so that the body and mind can be revitalized energetically. The yogic exercises found in this form of movement meditation are either hard (tensing) or soft (relaxing), and different practices for soft warming or hard strengthening are often used at different times of the day.
Contact: www.okidoyoga.org.uk/

Partner (Couples) Yoga is simply the practice of Hatha Yoga poses done in by two people who move together in a way that provides mutual support and the physical sensation of touch. When couples, whether or not they are romantically involved, practice in this way, trust and communication can be strengthened in an enjoyable and beneficial experience.
Contact: www.partneryoga.net/

Polarity Yoga is an energetic form of yoga that is part of the practice of Polarity Therapy. It features a series of fast-moving, flowing asanas that are synchronized with the breath to balance the nervous system and expel negative energy currents stuck within. Polarity Yoga is based on the five elements of earth, water, fire, wood, and metal, and the exercises support each element by stimulating the zones in the body that are related to that element on the energetic level. In this practice, the distinctive loud sounds of energy release called Ha breaths and movement are used on the exhalation to help expel negative energies. These simple and gentle exercises are always completed by holding the sunrise asana used in the practice of sun salutations. The practice is suitable for individuals of any skill level, since classes are designed with the individual participants' needs in mind.
Contact: American Polarity Therapy Association –
     www.polaritytherapy.org

Power Yoga is a vigorous, fitness-based approach to Vinyasa-style yoga. It is primarily a Western interpretation of the Ashtanga style of practice, although it does not follow the traditional set sequence of poses. Classes can vary widely, but all emphasize strength and flexibility and see yoga mainly as a way attain a full-body workout. This rapid, flowing style of yoga requires self-discipline and endurance, since the poses are held for long periods and are often done in a heated room. Although, as in other styles of yoga, there is focus on the unity of the body, mind, and spirit, this rigorous workout is mainly targeted at people who are already quite fit and want to increase stamina to another level. Variations of Power Yoga have been almost simultaneously created by a number of individual Western practitioners, including Baron Baptiste, Byran Kest, and Beryl Bender Birch.
Contact: www.baronbaptiste.com,
www.poweryoga.com, or
www.power-yoga.com

Pralaya Yoga is a form of Hatha Yoga developed by Robert Boustany to create balance by isolating and embracing the weakest areas of the body. The practice addresses injuries and imbalances associated with athletic training, surgical complications, or chronic misalignment. A series of poses are used to develop maximum physical functioning and the best energetic alignment by placing uniform pressure over a joint, on the spine, or in other parts of the body. The spine is always kept relaxed and long. The goal is to maintain open energetic pathways, even in the face of adversity, by cultivating a quiet, attentive presence and a strong sense of acceptance that will help prevent and melt away any emotional or mental blockages.
Contact: www.pralayayoga.com

Prenatal Yoga provides an ideal way for women to stay in shape during pregnancy. This gentler form of yoga incorporates the deep breathing and relaxation techniques that may be helpful during the birthing process. Poses that are particularly beneficial for the relief of lower back pain are included. A similar practice known as Postnatal Yoga helps women who have already given birth recover muscle tone, balance and coordination. Newborns are welcome to attend this gentle practice.

Purna Yoga integrates the spiritual aspects of yoga, precise Iyengar alignment-based asanas, meditation, and pranayama, and includes instruction in nutrition and yogic living. Its goal is to help participants discover a feeling of deep harmony between their bodies and spirits, become able to live from the heart, and develop the mental, emotional, and spiritual awareness that facilitates personal growth and a more enlightened view of reality. Emphasis is placed on the importance of creating good karma in daily lives. The first stage of practice is enhancing realization of the divine. Other stages of the practice guide participants in surrendering to the universal soul that does not recognize any separation between beings and rejecting all obstructions to the path of total transformation. Various levels of practice are provided for those with different levels of experience.
Contact: www.purnayoga.com or
www.adhyatmik.org/activities-
and-projects/purna-yoga/

Qi Flow Yoga, a movement practice that is intended to awaken the joy of being, employs elements of breathwork, energy work, qi gong, Tai Chi, and Yin Yoga. This body-based practice was developed by Eckhart Tolle's teaching partner, Kim Eng, as a way to bring peace, vitality, and conscious presence into each moment. Eng is a counselor and spiritual teacher who also developed Presence Through Movement workshops that focus on the integration of mind, body, and spirit. Her Qi Flow Yoga practice helps participants cultivate the flow of chi energy and release the mind's controlling activity by applying mindful presence and pure attention to body movement. In this short yoga practice, rather than thinking about the process, the mind simply rests on the inhalation and exhalation of the breath and on feeling the chi flow while moving slowly through a series of yoga and qi gong postures. The continuous sequence of meditative movements done in harmony with the breath helps cultivate and circulate chi, sending it to where it is most needed. Audible sounds can occasionally help the process

along. Although the practice is ultimately done in its complete form, participants can take more time doing those parts that resonate most. This gentle, grounding form is easy for beginners with limited experience in yoga.
Contact: Qi Flow Yoga – www.soundstrue.com or www.eckharttolle.com/about/kim/

Raja Yoga represents the royal path of mental union accomplished through concentration and control of the mind to defeat lust, greed, anger, delusion, pride and envy. This is accomplished by meditating on directing the life force to bring the mind and emotions into balance so that attention can be placed directly on the divine. As the life force energy is directed through the central channel along the length of the spine, the awareness is focused on the third eye, a point located at the center of the lower forehead. The intent is to awaken the consciousness to a transcendent state of well being.

Restorative Yoga is the name commonly given to a style of practice that uses props to support practitioners, an approach that was developed by B. K. S. Iyengar. Restorative Yoga classes consist of floor poses held passively for several minutes while the practitioner is supported by props such as bolsters, blankets, and pillows. The poses used include asanas designed to move the spine in all directions, such as inversions; poses that work on the abdominal muscles to enhance the movement of body fluids and stimulate and sooth the internal organs; and movements that encourage the flow of prana through the body. Savasana (corpse pose) is held for a long period of time at the end of the session to enhance a deep relaxed state.
Contact: www.restorativeyoga.org

Sadhana Yoga Chi is a disciplined practice used to still the mind and unite the vital life-force energy with the body, mind, and soul. Although this form of yoga is based on elements of Vinyasa, Ashtanga, Yin, Power, and Restorative Yogas, participants are encouraged to freely practice other systems of yoga and holistic healing. Sadhana Yoga, developed by Doug Swenson, seeks to enhance health and fitness, clear the mind, and fill the heart with peace

and harmony. A variety of smooth and gracefully connected Vinyasa-style movements are generally used to increase the energy flow that is promoted by the individual yoga postures. Sadhana Yoga Chi can work at a levels that is appropriate for either beginners or advanced students and combines both hard and soft forms of strengthening work. In addition, adjustments are made to each yoga posture to enhance the individual's level of comfort and energy. The complete practice embraces proper diet, body cleansing techniques, and ways to feel a direct connection with the natural flow of the chi energy.
Contact: www.sadhanayogachi.com

Sahaja Yoga is a form of meditation used to find peace within by tapping into the divine energy of love embodied by Sri Mataji Nirmala Devi, who offered the practice to the world in 1970. The practice is one of self-realization though the action of kundalini energy. Initiations are offered freely to groups and individuals; through a simple process, the kundalini energy is encouraged to arise gently and naturally. Further techniques for using the energy to manifest the wisdom of the chakras and to connect with the true self are offered free of charge through worldwide centers.
Contact: www.sahajayoga.org

Seniors Yoga, adapted to the particular needs and abilities of older students, is a simple, gentler form of Hatha Yoga that has gained popularity in recent years. It is beneficial in supporting the aging process by not only helping to maintain resilience and flexibility but also by strengthening the immune system and revitalizing the body and mind.

Shadow Yoga is a contemporary freestyle innovation, developed by Natanaga Zhander, that is rooted in the practice of classical Hatha Yoga. The emphasis is on preparing practitioners for further advancement in the practice of yoga by dissolving sheaths or shadows, the frozen energetic behavioral patterns caused by energy blockages that can prevent reaching the steady, undistracted state that allows insight through yoga. The energy is freed by bringing light to these blocked areas with deep

breathing and skillful physical activity. A series of varied positions and fluid movements adapted from yoga, Indian dance, martial arts, and even the animal kingdom are used to enhance the flow of life-force energy, which can liberate the mind from projections and fluctuations. After three preliminary standing forms, the practice continues with a combination of asanas, inversions, kriyas, mudras, bandhas, pranayama, and pratyahara.
Contact: www.shadowyoga.com

Shiva Yoga is the practice of awakening the third eye (sixth chakra) located within the forehead, whose physical manifestation is the pineal gland. In the mystical Hindu tradition, the third eye is the gateway to the inner vision of supreme reality, and the pineal gland is considered to be the organ of cosmic consciousness. The goal of Shiva Yoga is to enhance inner vision to gain access to the innate wisdom that all beings possess but rarely recognize. By opening the third eye to cosmic insight, it is possible to transform inhibiting and limiting desires into the brilliant awareness of true inner nature. The practice is one of gazing at and worshiping the lingam symbol of the Hindu god Shiva along with the chanting of mantras. This concentrated gaze generates psychic heat, which stirs the pineal gland to produce psychic light and intuitive knowledge. Although the method and techniques used in this form of yoga are simple, the practice requires years of dedicated training with a sincere and experienced teacher. Richard Matthews brought the practice to England after training for over thirty years with Shiva Yoga master H. H. Mahatapasvi Sri Kumaraswamiji.
Contact: www.shivayoga.net/technique

Siddha Yoga is based on the Hindu spiritual traditions of the Vedanta and has been taught by Bhagawan Nityananda and his student, Swami Muktananda, who brought the practice to the West. In the past, many great yogis, known as siddhas, practiced by themselves for years in remote natural areas to gain insight. The aim of Siddha Yoga is to help practitioners realize the inner divine self so that all suffering can be eliminated. The practice involves meditating on and worshiping the inner self to recognize that it is there that the divine actually dwells.

Siddha Yoga incorporates silent meditations placing the attention on the flow of the breath and a mantra, along with the transformational practices of chanting, selfless service, and awakening kundalini. Today, the practice is often accomplished at a satsang, where groups of devotees can meet and become initiated and trained in various levels of practice by a master.
Contact: www.siddhayoga.org

Sivananda Yoga is a relaxed form of Hatha Yoga based on the spiritual teachings of Swami Sivananda. In 1957, he instructed his devoted disciple, Swami Vishnudevananda, to bring the teachings to the West, and the International Sivananda Yoga Vedanta Centre was established in Montreal, Canada There are now branches around the world. The practice puts emphasis on full yogic breathing, and the training aims to increase vitality and decrease the chance of disease by providing the practitioners with the proper amount of exercise, breathing, and relaxation. Asanas, pranayama, positive thinking, and meditation are essential to the practice of Sivananda Yoga. Participants are also encouraged to eat a vegetarian diet and live according to the principles of yoga philosophy. Although the program often includes a practice of twelve basic asanas, the actual sequence of the practice will vary with each instructor.
Contact: www.sivananda.org

Structural Yoga Therapy is a holistic style of yoga developed during the 1970s by Mukunda Tom Stiles that works therapeutically to correct bad postural habits and increase joint freedom and flexibility. Exercises for muscle strengthening are followed by classic yoga asanas. Pranayama breathing is incorporated to support the restorative process. The practice can be adapted for individual needs and is beneficial not only for those with alignment and mobility problems, but also for students who want to enhance their abilities to live fully with vitality.
Contact: www.yogatherapycenter.org

Surat Shabda Yoga, also referred to as the path of light and sound, is an ancient Hindu spiritual practice with Arabic influences that relies on celestial sound currents to raise consciousness. The practice

combines sacred celestial sounds, mantras, chants, devotional music, pranayama breathing techniques, meditations, and simple asana postures to dissolve blockages, enhance the senses, increase vitality, and assist practitioners in merging with the divine energy of the cosmos. While performing only those asanas that support and promote the process of meditation, individual practitioners engage in pranayama to slow down breathing and metabolism, permitting them to meditate with a clear mind. Students are also trained to sit comfortably with eyes closed and focus on an imaginary point just in front of the eyes while repeating the mantra of their choice. The goal of this practice is to internalize what seems to be external through concentrated, focused attention.
Contact: www.healthyliving.azcentral.com/surat-shabd-yoga-7817.html

Svaroopa® Yoga aims to enhance inner opening by using precise alignment in carefully selected poses and the meticulous placement of props to release tension and energetic blockages in the deepest layers of the body. The goal is to maximize the body's potential by releasing tension without excessive exertion. In practice, the emphasis is on opening the spine by beginning at the tailbone and moving progressively upward through each section of the spine while performing supportive warrior poses. Advanced classes explore ways to use the body while keeping the spine open. The physical changes experienced through this release can permit a profound shift in consciousness and recognition of the participant's true potential.
Contact: www.svaroopayoga.org

Swara Yoga is an ancient pranayama practice in which the continuous flow of breath through one nostril creates a sound on which to rest the awareness. Its goal is to help practitioners reach a level of concentration that enables them to realize cosmic consciousness. This tantric practice associates the breath with the activities and phases of the moon, sun, planets, seasons, and time of day, and the breathwork helps the practitioner understand the nature and effects of the element on the body and mind by observing the different patterns of breath.

Although in the distant past, Swara Yoga was used to gain an understanding of the governing forces of the universe, it is now considered a way to free beings from the negative influences that inhibit heightened awareness.
Contact: www.swarayoga.org

Taoist Yoga, founded on the ancient Chinese art and science of healing, involves numerous energetic and meditative practices in which the body moves in a deliberately slow and easy way to increase the flow of vital chi energy, release restrictions, and enhance longevity. Most practices reflect the core principles found in the traditional Chinese system of healing: the meridian energy system, the forces of yin and yang, and the five primary natural elements. Practices emphasize channeling, moving, and storing the energy in the lower abdomen (the dantien energy center, connected with the kidneys), as well as distributing energy to those areas of the body, including internal organs, whose energy needs replenishing. The goal is to revitalize body functions, deal with negative emotions, balance and harmonize the internal flow of energy, and learn how to better communicate with the forces of nature and the universe. In general, this style of yoga is gentler and easier to learn than those found in the Indian practice of Asana Yoga. Although both use the breath as an essential part of the practice, the techniques of Taoist Yoga are essentially less strenuous with more emphasis on natural breathing. They also focus on breathing energy into and through the different energy pathways.

Practice sessions often start with simple warm-up exercises to connect, stretch, and relax the body, quiet the mind, and awaken the energy systems for the actual series of practices, which progress from a basic level to those that are more advanced. The vast repertoire of exercises, done in a meditative way with the full force of concentration directed inward, are carried out from standing, sitting, or reclining positions; healing sounds may also be used. The Iron Shirt practice is a standing posture that works to ground the practitioner while strengthening physical structure and posture; twelve basic movements are used to stretch the meridians. A breathing practice known as the Microcosmic

Orbit is employed to strengthen the flow of energy through the primary conception and governing energy channels located at the front and back of the spine and circulate it from the perineum to the crown of the head. Advanced practices transform and refine energy and then send it to different parts of the body. This includes the practice of balancing and refining sexual energy by uniting it with the heart and bringing it into the higher energy centers. An ancient bone-breathing method, known as Bone Marrow Nei Gung, is used to guide energy into the bone marrow and thereby prevent premature aging. Numerous other practices act as a form of inner alchemy to transform the body, mind, and spirit. Taoist practices are closely related to the practice of qi gong and include self-massage that incorporates particular strokes and acupressure. (See more in Chapter 8 and other entries in Chapter 11).
Contact: www.universal-tao.com/article/esoteric. html

Tibetan Yoga has a vibrant history as a spiritual practice, and Tibetan medicine has developed its own approach to prevention, healing, and the promotion of longevity through fusing early practices from other areas—Traditional Chinese Medicine, Taoism, Ayurveda, qi gong, and traditions of the indigenous Bön religion—with the tenets and practices of Buddhism. Tibetan Yoga practices are generally designed to unite the body and mind and rely heavily on the influence of the subtle energy body. Although Tibetan Yoga does not have the same relationship to the cosmos found in Ayurvedic Yoga, many of the yogic exercises aim to enhance the flow of energy within the body by calling on universal energy from above and earth energy from below. Tibetans combined two of the seven chakras found in the Ayurvedic system and work with just five chakras. They also have their own theories about the five elements and how they affect the physical body.

Tibetan Yoga practices are an integral part of a larger spiritual system that has been passed down since the Indian mystic Padmasambhava came to Tibet in 747 CE, following a succession of Indian teachers who first brought the teachings of the Buddha to Tibet. Padmasambhava (also known as Guru Rinpoche) emphasized tantric ritual, devotion, and

yoga. Each of the four main lineages of Tibetan Buddhism have developed different approaches to integrating the physical and spiritual forms of yoga into their paths.

Kum Nye Yoga practices are found in different forms in the different schools of Tibetan Buddhism, though not all have been brought to the West. As taught by Tarthang Tulku, Kum Nye is a relaxing style that uses an array of subtle yet powerful movement exercises to transform negative patterns and release emotional and physical tension held deep within the body. The practice combines slow movement, asanas, breathing exercises, visualization, and meditation to strengthen the flow of energy and release tension that is manifested as blockages in the chakras and energy channels. These activities nurture and heal by stimulating energy, sharpening the senses, connecting with feelings, providing inner balance, and enhancing awareness. The basic breathing and movement exercises are well suited for all ages and physical abilities, but more advanced levels of exercise require further guidance. The exercises are especially beneficial for those who sit in meditation for long periods of time.
Contact: www.kumnyeyoga.com or www.tibetanyoga.org

Tantra Yoga is closely allied with the teachings of the Buddhist Vajrayana path to awakening, which emphasizes using difficulties and negative emotions rather than trying to eliminate them. All of the paths of Buddhism initially offer techniques to help students develop meditative concentration and sharp insight into the true nature of the practitioner and the reality constructed by the conceptual mind. Vajrayana methods include numerous advanced transformative energy practices that work to enhance awareness by refining the impure energies in the body, and the meditative practices of Dzogchen and Mahamudra train the practitioner to rest in the natural state of nondualism.

Tantras are ancient texts detailing secret, esoteric methods of attaining enlightenment that were usually transmitted only directly from teacher to student; their teachings are also seen in certain forms of Ayurveda Yoga. Tantra Yoga has often been misinterpreted by an over-enthusiastic focus on its sexual aspects. Although it is true that some tantric practices work with the blissful union of the male and female, tantric practices are designed to transform all energy into a spiritual form. In general, the practices work within and through the psychophysical body using the energy system of the subtle body to create energetic harmony that supports clear insight and the fullest realization of the nature of mind.

One of the best-known Tantra Yoga practices comes from the Kagyu lineage, whose enlightened teachers include Tilopa, Naropa, Milarepa, and Gampopa. Naropa created a series of practices known as the **Six Yogas of Naropa**. They include tummo (the yoga of inner heat), gyulü (the yoga of the illusory body), ösel (the yoga of clear, radiant light), phowa (the yoga of transference of consciousness), milam (the yoga of the dream state), and bardo (the yoga of the intermediate state). These highly spiritual practices deal with the five essential components of tsa (energy channels), lung (wind energy), drö (psychic heat), tigle (essense), and sem (mind). Each has the potential to support the mind and body consciousness to enable inner liberation from negative forces through meditative practices referred to as wisdom activities.

Contact: www.tibetanmedicine-edu.org

Yantra Yoga, known in Tibetan as **Trul Khor**, came to Tibet during the eighth century when Padmasambhava arrived from India to further the spread of Buddhism. Guru Rinpoche had learned Yantra Yoga from Humkara, a Nepalese sage. Vairocana, an adept disciple of Padmasambhava, recorded and translated the text on Yantra Yoga and then trained others, who passed it down orally through the centuries. During the 1970s, Dzogchen master Chogyal Namkhai Norbu passed teachings on to several Westerners, and Lama Lobsang Palden, who was fortunate enough to secretly receive these teachings in Tibet after the Chinese invasion,

brought the practice to the United States. Yantra Yoga works to integrate the profound essence of the Dzogchen teachings with the body, speech, and mind of the practitioner.

This form of Tibetan Yoga employs a combination of body postures, movements, pranayama breathing, mantras, visualizations, and meditation techniques that influence the movement of energy in the body. The practice is basically easy to understand, but can take a lifetime to master. Unlike many other traditional yoga practices, Yantra Yoga postures are not held, but quickly flow into the next. Because breath and energy are so closely associated, the breath is intimately connected with each movement. Many Yantra Yoga asanas are similar to those of Hatha Yoga, but they are assumed in a much different way. In addition to a preliminary set of training exercises, the practice uses five series of asanas, and each series works with a different characteristic of the breath to influence the movement of subtle energy through the chakras and energy pathways. Both short and long forms of this practice can be followed. It is considered essential to move without tensing, straining, or struggling. The goal of Yantra Yoga is to purify the mind, body, and spirit for healing and in preparation for spiritual transformation. Since the practice is quite intense and physically demanding, Lama Lobsang also developed and teaches a form of bodywork, known as Yantra Yoga Massage to help practitioners who have difficulty accomplishing the movements. (See more in Chapter 6.)

Another form of Trul Khor is known as **Tsa Lung**, a simpler practice of that was originally used in the indigenous Bön tradition and later influenced by Vajrayana teachings carried to Tibet from India. The difference between the two forms are very subtle. Both practices work to purify negative energies that obscure the nature of mind through the systematic use of breathwork, visualizations, movement, mantras, and mental exercises that enhance the flow of energy and internal awareness. In Tsa Lung, breath and mental concentrations are integrated with particular body movements

done while sitting. Unlike practices in Hatha Yoga, in which practitioners hold a pose with the body still and the breath flowing, asanas are held during a pause in the breath, this form of Tibetan Yoga holds the breath still while the body (See more in Chapter 8.)
Contact: www.yantrayoga.org or
www.ligmincha.org

TriYoga, also referred to as **Kali Yoga**, is a flowing practice that incorporates a Ashtanga and Kundalini Yoga and rhythmic pranayama breathwork fused into a dancelike flow of asanas performed to the accompaniment of music. Tri Yoga was created by Kali Ray to increase a person's level of energy physically, mentally, and spiritually, while creating mental clarity and heightened awareness.
Contact: www.triyoga.org

Viniyoga™ is a gentle form of yoga created by Sri T. Krishnamacharya and T. K. V. Desikachar that uses asanas, pranayama, chanting, meditation, ritual, and relaxation methods to enhance physical, mental, emotional, and spiritual development. In this practice, the function of each asana is stressed, and each is repeated a number of times. Movements follows a sequence that is led by the breath. Viniyoga has a more relaxed approach to the placement of the body than Iyengar Yoga and is performed at a much less vigorous pace than either Ashtanga or Power Yoga. Viniyoga modifies the postures to meet the particular needs of the individual student.
Contact: American Viniyoga Institute –
www.viniyoga.com

Vinyasa Yoga, also known as **Flow Yoga**, emphasizes generating heat and strength through precise, fluid, and continuous movement synchronized with deep breathing. This active style, which is also incorporated into other forms of Asana Yoga, moves quickly from one pose to another rather than holding each for a long time, and asanas are connected by a recurring sequence of movements that are carried out during a single breathing cycle. Each pose is usually followed by the appropriate counter-pose to promote proper balance. Beginning series are designed to stretch and strengthen the muscles for

increasingly challenging asanas and pranic practices such as bandha locks. Because the breathing that accompanies its motion is continuous, Vinyasa Yoga places greater importance on the flow rather than on correcting alignment in poses, though adjustments are made as necessary. However, classes can vary between slow and fast moving, depending on the teacher. The steady breathing and flowing movements Vinyasa Yoga help signal the mind to relax and can release blockages in the energy system of the practitioner. Classes are often begun and end with devotional practices, some honoring the contributions of Pattabhi Jois.
Contact: www.yogawiz.com/types-of-yoga/
vinyasa-yoga.html

Yin Yoga is an inwardly focused, slow-paced style of yoga practice strongly influenced by the traditional Chinese practice of working with the energy meridians. It was introduced to the West by martial arts grand champion Paulie Zink, along with Yang Yoga and the full range of Taoist Yoga techniques. Yin Yoga uses soft, gentle seated and reclining poses that are held for a long period of time and is designed to stimulate the joints rather than muscles, increase the circulation of vital fluids, improve flexibility, and energize the meridian system by enhancing the flow of chi. It directs the attention, which is usually focused outward, into a compassionate inner inquiry into the contents of the body, mind, and heart. Yin Yoga is often done in preparation for meditation. The practice also uses active, invigorating Yang-style poses, which are held for short periods of time. This form imparts the felt sense of the body to practitioners through enhancing inner awareness and embodying the awakened primal energy and helps them stay with each experience as it arises. Yin and Yang Yogas contain new postures, variations of traditional asanas, and the opportunity for insight that make it a relaxed and enjoyable practice appropriate for many Westerners.
Contact: The Yin Yoga Institute –
www.theyinyogainstitute.com or
www.yinyoga.com

Yoga Nidra was derived from tantric practices of conscious sleep and Dream Yoga by Swami

Sivananda, and during the 1960s, his disciples spread the practice of Yoga Nidra. Swami Satyananda Saraswati modified the original by combining it with Western relaxation practices, and several other variations have also been developed. Yoga Nidra leads a practitioner into a state of deep consciousness between wakefulness and sleeping in which there are no images, which is what differentiates it from practices that work with dreams themselves. However, within this state, awareness is active, so the practitioner can witness the activities of the body and mind free from the clouds of confusion and, from this vantage point, see through the illusions and purify negative karma. The practice begins by completely relaxing the body through mental scanning, breathwork, and visualization. Then awareness is placed on the heart chakra, the doorway to the state of Yoga Nidra, and the practitioner simply lets go into that space and rests in the stillness within. This state is maintained until thought returns, no matter how brief that time may be; diligent practice will lengthen the period of silence. Yoga Nidra is in itself a spiritual path, but it can also be used to prepare a practitioner for further exploration of the awakened heart and mind. A Westernized version, **iRest Yoga Nidra**, developed by psychologist Dr. Richard Miller, author of *Yoga Nidra: The Meditative Heart of Yoga*, has been used with good effect to treat returning military suffering from post-traumatic stress disorder.

Contact: www.yogawonders.com/yoga-nidra, or
www.swamij.com/yoga-nidra.htm, or
www.irest.us

CHAPTER 12
Ripples From My Inner Ocean

The Winds of Fate

One ship drives east and another drives west
With the selfsame winds that blow;
    'Tis the set of the sails
    And not the gales
That tells them the way to go.

Like the winds of the sea are the winds of fate
As we voyage along through life;
    'Tis the set of the soul
    That decides its goal
And not the calm or the strife.

—*Ella Wheeler Wilcox*

At a very early age I was blessed with the sound of the sea calling me through the bedroom window. It was "a wild call and a clear call that could not be denied." I lay in my bed wondering where the sea could take me, and my imagination was stimulated by my father's tales of pirates, storms, and faraway islands. My childhood dreams of adventure finally became real, and I was able to escape the confines of life at home and sail out alone in search of the mysteries beyond the crests of the waves. My connection to the sea became stronger as I realized the freedom and sense of wonder that were mine out on the water. The joy of watching a sunset or dolphins at play and feeling the wind on my face were my delight. But it wasn't always smooth sailing, and even as a boy, I learned to give the sea the respect it deserves.

I will always remember one childhood experience. A friend and I loved to go down and play on Maine's rocky coast when big storms came in. It was a challenge to see how close we could get to the breaking waves as they crashed on the rocks, sending geysers of water high in the air. One day we were playing at the top of a cliff, forgetting that bigger waves periodically come further in than their smaller brothers. Suddenly we were in the

grasp of a giant, thundering breaker that covered us and dragged our little bodies toward the sea. Our fingernails dug in, and when the wave finally receded, we were only a few feet from the edge. In no time flat, we removed ourselves from the area and breathed a sigh of relief at our close call. It was one of those life lessons: Don't mess with Mother Nature.

I am profoundly grateful for all I have learned throughout my life, and particularly from the seagoing lifestyle. Probably the most important lesson was learning to be flexible enough to see all the possible solutions that would help me adapt to changing situations. I also had my eyes opened about the value of cooperation, persistence, patience, courage, and kindness. It seems to me that a life lived according to these principles can't help but lead to deep well-being and happiness not only for ourselves but for the others around us.

Whether to hold or change course in the face of uncertainty is a constant part of all our lives. We never really know how a situation will pan out or how a person will respond to our actions, and it just might be that we can't have it our way after all. So the success of any venture or, for that matter, a personal relationship often depends on our ability to adapt. When weather conditions make a sea crossing difficult, a sailor must use every tool at his disposal to keep his vessel working effectively, sometimes taking a new course to the next destination. When a group project fails to reach its goal, it's the flexibility of each participant in reconsidering previous viewpoints that allows a different approach to be imagined. When a loved one grows angry, careful listening and a willingness to compromise can save the day. The situations are endless, and the circumstances constantly challenging.

It's not only mental flexibility that helps us adapt to change but also being flexible in the body. For a sailor, letting the body relax and go with the flow is important during rough sea conditions. The ocean swells and rising waves require the body to be limber, fluid, and flexible in order to maintain balance, stay centered, and be comfortable. The same applies to the ups and downs of any situation. The best course of action depends on realistic responses to a situation as it actually is, and sometimes our habitual patterns of seeing and reacting get in the way. When a relaxed and flexible body is free from the tension and stress that trigger these responses, the mind and emotions can take a hint from the body and relax into the new state of affairs. This more enjoyable way of being can also open the door for intuition to chime in with some advice from the heart. It's the body-mind connection hard at work making things better for all.

I had many opportunities to contemplate flexibility when sailing around the world. On one occasion, my first mate and I spent what seemed like an eternity attempting get around the often-stormy southern coast of Africa. Because of the distance between the limited number of ports that could provide safe haven and the frequency of the gales that swept the area, it was necessary make sure there was enough time to get to the next harbor before a gale hit. One time, we decided conditions were good to go, but abandoned all pride and turned back when the next forecast challenged the wisdom of that decision. On a longer crossing from the mainland of the United States to Bermuda, we encountered a four-day gale. The prevailing winds were such that we had to completely give up on that destination and instead make our way down to the Bahamas, far off our intended course.

Other twists and turns in my life experiences also taught me about adapting to changes and creating new opportunities for learning. Sometimes it became clear that staying with a job, a partner, or a spiritual teacher wasn't getting me where my heart told me I needed to go, and I left all that I knew to embark on a new life path. Even if that new course initially took me down a road of regrets, I eventually learned that every moment in the journey, no matter how discouraging, is really a teacher and that it may be best to enjoy the infinite possibilities inherent in uncertainty rather than to just tolerate conditions or struggle to arrive at a preconceived destination. Other times, that new path was dictated by events beyond my control, so I just had to figure out how to make the most of it. Being propelled in a new direction often has a way of prompting us to find new opportunities for growth and inspiration.

Sailing safely on the high seas or the sea of life absolutely depends on the members of the crew working together to achieve a common goal, not just with half-hearted efforts but by continually striving to do their very best. Cooperating with other members of the sailing community is also paramount, and not only when another boat is in trouble. World cruisers are some of the best comrades around, because they all realize that survival ultimately depends on being willing and able to lend a helping hand to anyone they encounter. The sharing of information is the primary mode of cooperation—whether it's knowledge about distant ports or the best place to buy good vegetables—and if you need advice or a helping hand to figure out why the engine won't start, someone will be at your side. This collaborative way of relating to others can extend to our relationships with anyone anywhere. The old saying "we are all in the same boat" reflects the idea that we share many of the same life experiences and that we are equally deserving of care and assistance. It's an unwritten law of the sea to give assistance to another when the need arises, and the world would be a different place if it were the law of the land as well.

Persistence is the quality that allows forward motion when the way is long and hard, when good intentions, skill, and insight are not enough, though sometimes it can become just a matter of endurance to make it through. It often is inspired by a worthy cause, whether it's the eventual arrival at some paradise island or the attainment of good health or greater self-awareness. Persisting against all odds does have to be tempered with discernment, good judgment, and wisdom or it becomes stupidity. But persistence can be a true friend when we have to complete a difficult task, such as sailing against the current, finishing a long project, or staying with a demanding self-care practice.

Patience definitely goes hand in hand with persistence and is certainly required when the end seems far off. It once took me more than seven exhausting hours to sail only half a mile in a fickle wind to get into port after being at sea for a week. Another time, I spent five days drifting in a calm without a working motor before the wind returned. In many life situations, patience is tested when things don't go our way. It seems to be something we have to learn by experience as we realize that all the fussing and fuming doesn't anything but wear us out, especially when we become impatient with another person who is wrestling with her own problems. By being persistent, we can still get our needs met, but it may just take longer than we had hoped. Looking at the situation realistically, relaxing, and accepting things as they are makes life easier. I often try to apply this lesson when driving in city traffic or dealing with a demanding relationship.

It's easy to understand the part courage plays at sea, especially when encountering severe storms or taking on the challenge of sailing blindly in fog through a shipping channel. But it also takes courage to express our hidden truths and personal feelings and to recognize and accept ourselves as we are, imperfect and often vulnerable, wrestling with doubt, shame, and fear. It can also be difficult to find the courage to permit intense feelings of joy that we may feel we don't deserve. Courage seems to be a necessary quality when attempting to boldly bound forward into the great unknown, and when courage is powered by love and the glimpses of wonders we get through special "aha" moments, anything seems possible.

Kindness is a simple quality that doesn't always come easily, especially when we're stressed or feeling tired and separate from the people around us. Experiencing the kindness of others can teach us the value of kindness and motivates us to be kind in return. The warmth and affection of the Pacific islanders, not only to children and elders but also to a stranger like me, had the distinct effect of promoting that quality in me. Returning the favor to everyone I encountered on foreign soil helped open doors to people's homes and hearts, allowing more sharing of what matters most.

There are probably many places were it's possible to find communities where these qualities are apparent, but I found them in abundance on the remote North Pacific island of Kapingamarangi, where about five hundred Polynesians live. The island is part of the Federated States of Micronesia, which was a U.S. trust territory after World War II, so the islanders have long been aware of the products and technology of the modern "first world." However, they had the courage and wisdom to hang on to their simpler traditional ways. Their fishing boats have outboard motors, but the sails are always on hand for times when there's no money for gas. Since the arrival of the occasional supply vessel is unreliable, they grow what crops they can in the meager island soil. Activities such as building a new house or launching a boat are the shared responsibility of the community. Every child has many "mothers" and is loved and cared for by all the women within the community. The islanders consider themselves an extended family, and when my

first mate and I arrived, we were adopted into the clan. Before we left, our new brothers and sisters helped us write a thank-you note in the Kapinga language, which we posted on message boards on the island. When we sailed off, the beach was lined with people waving and waving until we were out of sight. It was kind of like leaving home.

The diversity that I encountered on my global travels also worked its magic. Respecting diversity honors cultures and people who are different and undercuts unworthy assumptions or prejudice. Instead, we are able to see how these qualities I have been talking about operate in the very different lives of the people all around us. Our lives may seem separate, but the reality is that we all are at our best when things like patience, courage, flexibility, and most especially kindness are expressed in all our actions. What amazing lessons we can learn as we begin to see the ways that people from different cultures express and live out these qualities in many and varied ways. It can change our perspective. It can open our hearts.

Our Life's Work

This book started with an enumeration of the problems facing our world today. Modern civilization seems to be less civilized than ever before—so many stressed-out people running around with no regard for others, completely out of touch with their bodies, hearts, and souls. If you agree with me that change is necessary, we must each take up the challenge of spiritual activism. What does this mean? For me, spiritual activism means using every means possible to develop a healthy body, mind, and spirit and then taking the wisdom gained out into the world. As Mahatma Gandhi said, "We must be the change we wish to see in the world." The seeds of discontent with the status quo have been planted, so now we must plant the seeds of hope.

Real change for the better comes from a change in human nature, from an inner shift in consciousness that is then mirrored in outer actions. It seems that our lives can definitely improve when we risk a deeper exploration and understanding of who we really are. As we break through into the light of awareness, the rewards can spread in many directions. But we need tools—agents of change, the "weapons" of the spiritual activist—to make dreams a reality.

We might start by redefining the word success. Many problems in the world are caused by our being motivated by things that don't really serve us or the common good. The misplaced and self-centered emphasis on personal success—big houses, fancy cars, fantastic vacations, money to burn—regardless of how others are affected has taken many people down the wrong road. Would it not be wiser to measure success by the good we have done, by the people who love us, and the people we love? My car has a bumper sticker on it with a quote from Jimi Hendrix: "When the love of power is replaced by the power of love, then the world will be a better place." It's certainly a place to start. Rather than viewing success as a trickle-down theory from above, it is time to recognize it as a trickle-up theory from deep within each of us who share this planet. If the goal is to bring our highest potential as loving human beings to fruition, the vibrations of this uplifted spirit may just help entrain others with a more open-hearted way of living.

It may sound hokey, but love really does conquer all. We are each the cause, effect, and cure for all that happens to us, and love is the most important thing in our toolbox. As we go through life, we come to realize that there are many kinds of love: love of self, love of family and friends, and the unconditional love that embraces all. But how we are able to perceive and feel love depends on how open we can be to it. It sometimes seems like there's a battle going on between the mind and the heart, and if we become closed off to love through hard times, it can be difficult to receive it, let alone give it. Those hard times may be personal experiences that bring us pain and cause us to hide out in secret places deep inside, or they might be actions of others that reinforce our feelings of shame or unworthiness. As has been pointed out many times in this book, when these feelings are held in the body, their effects are reinforced. Being a warrior of the heart means "conquering" these suppressed feelings, biased thoughts, and outdated or useless beliefs by freeing ourselves from their hold. By taking time to relax, listen, and allow pain and unresolved issue to surface from within, while at the same time taking refuge in the loving and compassionate presence of the spirit, we can create a new story that, over time, will heal any fear and bring warmth and loving presence to the body, mind, and emotions. Learning to deeply appreciate our good qualities and thoughtfully accept our flaws with the firm resolve to do our best to overcome them—in other words, self-love—is the first part of spiritual activism. When we can let go of what inhibits us and resonate more with the innate goodness we have within, it seems possible to connect deeply with our life and the lives of others.

The love of truth is another kind of love, and when we recognize the truth of our potential as loving human beings, we can uphold this same capacity in others. As we see every person's potential for what it truly is, we can help them heal by providing the acceptance and forgiveness that we have given to ourselves. We can learn to love our enemies and treat violence as a symptom of an illness that needs preventive care or healing. Since I seem to be quoting enlightened beings, here's one from Martin Luther King, Jr.: "Darkness cannot drive out darkness; only light can do that. Hate cannot drive out hate; only love can do that." When violent behavior is met with love and compassion, aggression dissipates as the "bad guys" realize that though the action cannot be tolerated, someone sees the human being behind the deed.

Compassion is love in action, and it understands that what we perceive as our own limitations are shared by others. Acts of compassion can be seen throughout society, but there is still much to be done, one person and one act at a time, until our world is ruled by the heart rather than by competition, greed, and hatred. When we treat each other as equally worthy and divine, the conditions that lead to strife and war won't have a chance to arise. Although our capacity to act with unconditional love and compassion increases in stages as we grow older and wiser, each of us is capable of spreading good will at any time to some degree. As wisdom and healing skills grow stronger, it is important to apply them in ways that work both for ourselves and for others.

Awareness is the tool that allows all change, and wisdom is its fruit. The search for peace and harmony can take many paths and is often confronted with confusing obstacles. Through awareness, we can realize what binds us to suffering and what resonates deeply within our head, heart, and belly. Knowing where we want to go and what we must do to get there will help us find and sustain the joy, true happiness, and bliss that make life worth living. To be an adept and seaworthy traveler means being constantly vigilant and attentive to every detail, for we know not how changes or blessings will come.

Spiritual activism also means taking responsibility. Responsibility for what is the question. In every culture, the immediate family is where we get our first lessons in responsibility. As we grow older, we become accountable to our friends, our school, our community, and our country. Our struggle for individual happiness, autonomy, and independence becomes entangled with our responsibility to society. With all the tribulations and conflicting tensions that develop as we try to meet these responsibilities, it's no wonder we tend to give up on our own dreams and aspirations and even our path to enlightenment. Although we may find solutions that seem to work, we might also feel denied or disconnected. Some of us are lucky and determined enough to find an occupation that resonates with our heart and soul, but too often the really important job of recognizing our true potential is neglected for the so-called good of the outer world. Being cooperative and of service to others is by no means a bad thing, but it is necessary to find a balance between different kinds of responsibility. And when we can find a way to honor our responsibility to developing our true self, we will gain the love and wisdom that we can transmit to our friends, family, community, country, and the whole world. Sounds like a tall order, but there are many examples throughout history in which individuals who attained a significant degree of self-realization have been instrumental in changing the course of history for the better. This kind of change also comes from grassroots efforts, and today with the Internet, one person's voice can have a far-reaching effect as a good idea resonates positively around the globe. It may take some devotion, but we can all do our inner work while still being actively involved in the outer world.

Motivation is essential to any endeavor. Sometimes the discipline and motivation to make an effort is dictated by a sense of obligation and responsibility. Survival is also a strong motivator, and when ill health strikes, it can act in this way, forcing us to make changes that we may never have been able to contemplate before. Life at sea certainly provides experiences in which survival inspires action without hesitation. When I was sailing along in a small boat off the north coast of Jamaica, the line that hauls the mainsail up and down got jammed near the top of the mast, making it impossible to get the sail up higher so that we could hold course against the wind and current that were driving us in the wrong direction. We were desperately low on food, and it was crucial that we get into port that morning. When dawn came, we found we were drifting too far to the west, away from land. I had just one crew member with me, but he was seasick and unable to do much of anything. So I had to climb the mast while the boat was rolling badly in rough seas to make the necessary repairs by myself. I eventually did succeed in completing the task, though badly bruised, and was able to raise the sail all the way up and drive the boat to windward into port. I definitely learned that being motivated by a desire to survive can give the extra strength required to complete the hardest tasks.

But motivation also comes from a heartfelt calling to enhance our own well-being. It comes from love, curiosity, or the desire for openness, freedom, and wisdom. By calling on these reasons for action, we can gain the staying power necessary to carry out a practice that may require considerable time and effort to achieve beneficial results. The effects of practices such as those found in this book—better health, increased vitality, greater ease, joy in living—and learning to trust our own capacity to heal and grow can inspire us to further action and outweigh any difficulties we might encounter. In the end, motivation is ultimately about being drawn to something that feels worthwhile. When we are motivated by something that really resonates with the body and mind, we can be more naturally committed, no matter how difficult the task. We can continue wholeheartedly along the path that leads us to developing further intuition, increasing our capacity to awaken our innate healing energies, and realizing that we are already spiritual beings in a vast ocean of pure consciousness. And as we find joy and happiness, there is a natural inclination to pass them on to others.

Obstacles As Opportunities for Transformation

Life is full of cycles within cycles that create special moments in which the right conditions are present for us to transform obstacles into opportunities for making better choices. If we're lucky, unresolved issues kindly return to our consciousness to give us another chance to deal with them. The trick is to be aware of when this is happening so that we can take advantage of the moment. True transformation may demand a series of integrative experiences that build on each other.

Change requires envisioning new ways of being. Sudden flashes of insight can free us from our limited perspective, and we may find ourselves in a realm of unknown possibilities, a place of transformation far beyond our comfort zone. This experience can be either very awe inspiring or unsettling. We may fear that transformation will strip away all the defenses we have erected to hold pain at bay. It may scare us more than living in a habitually dysfunctional way. But when we realize that opening to the confusion and fear that precede a life-altering experience can propel us forward into a better world, we will likely find the courage to proceed. Those who are brave enough to enter the dark reaches of their subconscious and unravel the secrets within their soul will surely find the bliss that resides underneath the surface turmoil.

We all encounter obstacles when striving to accomplishing something, and we will all have times when we get stuck trying to figure things out. We might not have the right skills to get a certain job, enough money to buy a house, or strong enough love to maintain a relationship. We might be trying hard to be a better person, only to find we don't always do the right thing. On a deeper personal level, we might not have the insight to see what is limiting our potential. Not only does our perception of reality get distorted by painful life experiences, but our beliefs and opinions can get in the way of recognizing the truth of the matter, making our predicament hard to resolve. We may need to deconstruct some concepts and stories—those we tell ourselves and those that others tell us—to change our distorted viewpoint and reclaim our authenticity. It is also natural to encounter resistance when attempting to deal with sensitive issues. Richie Havens once sang about paradise being a hard place to find. Although the song rings true, it is heartening to know that paradise is right here waiting to be discovered.

One of the primary obstacles we face is that things are not always what they appear to be. This was apparent in an incident that happened in the Strait of Malacca, which runs between mainland Malaysia and the islands of Indonesia. It's an area that historically has been home to ruthless pirates. One day, my first mate and I were sailing up the Strait when we spotted a distant vessel making a turn in our direction. A boat full of men headed directly toward us, and our minds raced, trying to figure out what to do. But when the boat got so close we could make out the men's faces, it suddenly turned.

The men waved and headed off in a different direction, much to our relief. We later found out the truth of what seemed to be an act of aggression. The men were not pirates, but fisherman who were not having any luck catching fish. Local custom blames a bad spirit onboard, and the solution is to drive the boat straight at another vessel and throw the bad spirit onto the other boat by turning sharply. The fishermen could then continue on with the delighted expectation of an improved catch. Our first impression certainly had been influenced by what we mistakenly thought was true.

First impressions are just stories that we believe without knowing the whole truth. They often have more to do with how we perceive and react to things than with reality. They are a form of judgment, and we can use moments like this to recognize this activity in ourselves and begin to understand how it limits our actions and reactions. When we only have part of the truth, it can turn into a self-limiting belief that will require a shift in perspective and awareness.

A tendency to be competitive can also hold us back from authentic interaction with our world. When everything is viewed in terms of how it can benefit us, our family, or our business, we glorify conquest and the battles it requires. This takes us further and further away from the place of loving and accepting things as they are and connecting with others as equals. It adds to the separation between ourself and others. If only we could focus instead on supporting, promoting, cooperating, and allowing for solutions that benefit all, we might be able to create positive change through this kind of skillful action.

Many of us carry around feelings of unworthiness and low self-esteem that limit our ability to accomplish what we desire and leave us hopeless. This leads to much unhappiness, especially when the pain of neglected or unfulfilled aspirations are held unconsciously on a cellular level in the body as well as in the psyche. It is essential that we face these feelings and learn the truth about the their causes, perhaps with the assistance of healing practices or counseling. This kind of pain can propel us into discovering new dimensions of ourselves that can help us resolve the problems we face. When we dissolve any resistance to viewing ourselves as amazing human beings, our burdens can disappear. We might even begin to recognize that pleasure and pain are a continuum and that each offers opportunities for transformation and self-realization. Pain may be inevitable, but, as the wise ones say, suffering is optional. Eventually we can come to appreciate the wisdom in all our life experiences, and learn to laugh in the belly and awaken in the heart.

Let's face it. Taking responsibility for all that happens in life requires a fair amount of diligence, and laziness can easily enter the picture. We are all creatures of habit, and it often takes extra effort to get ourselves out of our comfort zone and take on a healing practice. Celebrating the body's new health and vitality can energize us into making the extra effort.

We also tend to overlook the small problems that create an underlying current of discontent, for it is usually the big ones that grab our attention and compel us to deal with them. When I reflect on my past, I can vividly recall the times I lost a boat on a reef, was left by a woman, had a significant injury, or suffered the loss of a dear friend. I was forced to spend much time contemplating their effect on me and absorbing their lessons. But the little, nagging, day-to-day issues in personal relationships and inner dilemmas have a cumulative effect that we don't even notice until an argument, a fight, or war of some kind breaks out. Wouldn't it help to become more attentive and responsive to these small problems each time they arise within and around us?

Aging presents its own obstacles if we buy in to the idea that stiffness, aches, and pains are an inevitable part of growing older. They may emerge more frequently, but complaining about them just increases their power to drag us down. There are still plenty of happy and healthy older people who stay active and live life to the fullest right up until the moment they pass. If we take care to listen to our bodies, decrease stress, and increase joy, it is possible that we can not only survive but thrive as we age.

All of these constraining concepts and beliefs have an energetic quality and leave their signatures on the body. They not only affect our health and well-being but also inhibit the possibility of transformation. When their hold is released from the body, mind, and spirit, it might just bring a life in which we all are greater than we dreamed of. What we now call magic will become a normal, everyday experience.

What seems very important to me is finding what truly helps us become more present in every moment, whether it's awareness of obstacles or of the possibilities in them. We must continually remind ourselves that there is always buried treasure beneath the surface of our inner sea. Thich Nhat Hanh says, "Each moment is an occasion to live deeply and happily in peace." When all of our parts—our body, mind, emotions, intuition, heart, and soul—are awakened and act harmoniously, we can say "Yes!" free from attachment to an outcome and full of the strength, power, and love that has always been within us. We can't control the winds of fate, but we can always adjust our sails and keep ourselves headed in the right direction.

Bringing It All Together with the Fabulous Five

We humans are creatures with a body and a mind, and we use both to perceive, feel, and express emotions. But we are also beings permeated by energy, whose radiance enlivens the physical and communicates with our spirit. All our parts are influenced by each other, and only when all aspects of our being are integrated and working harmoniously together at their fullest potential can we attain optimal health and well-being. By treating, preventing, or releasing any dysfunction, bringing something fresh and worthwhile into the body, and allowing the emergence of previously hidden healing capacities to fill the heart, reclaim the body, pacify the mind, and uplift the spirit, we can use this body-mind connection to our greatest advantage. And by tapping in to, cultivating, and revitalizing the vital energy and the wisdom held in the body, we can become more present, integrated, self-aware, and open to a dynamic reality free from the chains that bind us to unhappiness and ill health. Diving deep into our inner ocean can bring us to a more embodied state in which we have a conscious connection with the self as a unified whole.

Most (if not all) of the bodywork practices discussed in this book demonstrate the power of the body-mind connection. But when we examine how this power is being activated, there seems to be a complementary combination that covers all bases. I like to call this the "Fabulous Five." Each component is powerful in itself, and though every practice won't contain all of them, it seems as if there are traces of the subtly interconnected Five peaking through every method of healing.

May I present to you the Fabulous Five: body sensing, physical movement, breathwork, energy work, and meditation. Body sensing allows us to feel the body's reactions to stimuli, whether it's touch or something happening internally. This felt sense can also deepen our perception of the role that the mind and emotions play in creating that felt sense and how, in turn, the body affects the emotions. Physical movement is any physical activity, whether slight or exaggerated. It may enhance physiological and psychological performance, keep us more aligned and centered, and increase balance, harmony, and the flow of vital energy. Breathwork includes any kind of conscious breathing practice that employs mindful participation, concentrates on the body as a whole, and acts as an avenue for further self-awareness. It can also be a focused process that releases restrictions and imbalances and helps us develop a deeper sense of presence, unity, and subtle energy flow. Energy work involves any experiential practice that helps cultivate a balanced flow of the vital life force. It doesn't matter if it is some form of energy medicine applied through the hands of a practitioner or a self-care discipline. Meditation is the component that brings each of the other four into clear view by using contemplative practices to deepen self-awareness and permit the arising of our innate capacity for wholeness. Each of these five components is always available to us and can be used to some extent even when we're sick or injured.

The actual practice can be a simple one. Just think about rubbing a towel over your body after a shower and then stretching. If you coordinate the breath with the physical movement and meditate on the energy flow within, then you have just accomplished the simple act of combining the Fabulous Five in one harmonious practice. How about some ecstatic dancing? Consciously breathing in sync with the body movement while focusing the mind inward on the felt sense of the movement and the flow of vital energy instantly becomes another such practice. You can find the same combination of elements present in many modalities of bodywork or self-care practices. When you analyze the practice of yoga, qi gong, or many other movement modalities, it becomes evident that the Five work in concert with each other to release impediments and open our eyes to what we treasure most within. Paying close attention to what happens internally and energetically during these experiences can bring about real transformation and the natural arising of more self-awareness as the wisdom held in the body becomes revealed.

By staying curious and maintaining full presence in the body as a whole, we can become more embodied and connected to all that inspires. When we mindfully focus inward on the feelings and sensations in the body while using the breath to access the flow of energy within the body, any controlling dysfunctional emotional and mental patterns of behavior loose their hold as they are replaced by open-hearted awareness of a more authentic state of being. When the mystical or magical elements inevitably arise from within and wash through our body, mind, and soul, the previously limiting aspects of our being will dissolve away into a sea of pure loving potentiality.

As we make the effort to become more open, learn to connect with the wisdom held in the body, hold a space for the mind to melt into the breath, and awaken the energetic life force, it's possible to be filled with the love and compassion that is always within us. As this new strength and freedom unfold, it will be easier to see how everything that happens in life is not only worthwhile but also a means for transformation and enlightenment. When we take up the challenge to expand the potential for peacefulness, happiness, and truth, they can become the ultimate blessing for which we may give continual praise. When we move further into exploring the unknown within, we may come to feel more at home in the body and realize that we are just spirit having a human experience, one in which we breathe in more love and breathe out more compassion to the world.

Seeking Happiness

I once had a friend who jokingly asked me if I was having a good time living the hard life or a hard time living the good life. I responded that I didn't believe these could be the only possibilities. Instead, we can hold the intention of having a great time living a happy life. Happiness isn't some fleeting emotion, but a state of mind in which we're not overwhelmed by the waves crashing around us. On my first cruise to the tropics, we placed a Meher Baba quotation—"Don't worry, be happy"—in plain view on the boom gallows as an inspiring idea to keep in mind. We found it to be a wonderful mantra.

I don't pretend to be someone like Meher Baba, but the following are some phrases that I find helpful to keep in mind when trying to make each moment happier for myself and the people around me. They are all simple, helpful things that we already know are really good to do, but often forget about or take for granted.

Stretching in a beautiful natural setting.

1. *Play like a child without being too serious or self-ish.* Some people talk about the need for fore-play, well how about the idea of a relationship in which both people are forever playing, enjoying each other as they move through life.

2. *Stay close to the rhythms of nature, for this feeds the soul.* Our attraction to nature is really precious and a natural tendency for many of us. No wonder people want to live near the sea, by a river, or on a hill with a spectacular view. Those living in the city really appreciate those vacations in the country.

3. *Eat healthy food and drink pure water.* If we honor the nutritional needs of the body, it will support us with more energy and harmony.

4. *Listen to pleasant or evocative music and sing sometimes.* Rhythmic sounds and melodies provide vibrations that feed the soul and free the heart. Music brings people together worldwide.

5. *Get plenty of physical exercise and maintain a balanced posture.* Dancing, swimming, riding a bike, or just walking all strengthen the body and enhance the flow of energy.

6. *Strive for early detection of any potential problems before they become chronic.* Being proactive prevents detrimental issues from developing.

7. *Take time to breathe deeply in rhythm with the beat of your heart when you feel stressed, tense, or just very busy.* The breath is a carrier of the vital life force and is the most available way to cultivate energy and transform your point of view.

8. *Keep an open beginner's mind, receptive to new insights.* A curious, humble, and inquiring mind will give you and other people the benefit of the doubt that we all deserve. Never presume that you are unworthy.

9. *Talk less and listen more.* Really listening to what's stirring inside can be powerfully healing. Deep and silent listening to others allows them to express what may otherwise remain unsaid if your comments or impatience to speak interrupt their thoughts.

10. *Be genuine about what you feel.* When you express what is true for you, others will be free to do the same.

11. *Follow your passion with activities and work that resonate deeply with your heart and soul.* Finding joy and bliss is our birthright and spending your time with something or someone you love will bring inspiration and fulfillment.

12. *Worry less about the past and future and strive to be more conscious of the present.* Worrying about a situation will not change the result. Now is the only time we have to live fully and become more aware of what is true.

13. *Laugh more at yourself and with others.* Humor is a magical force that can release any feelings of tension or loneliness while bringing comfort and a feeling of freedom.

14. *Keep good company with like-minded friends and teachers.* We are all products of our relationships, and if they are inspirational and supportive, our true potential can be nurtured.

15. *Honor diversity and be active in service to others without the expectation of reward.* Knowing we

have been helpful to everyone we encounter can make our hearts sing.

16. *Express gratitude for even the small things.* As we appreciate the beauty and wonder of all that exists, they become blessings that naturally feed the heart and soul.

17. *Allow magical moments to arise.* The possibilities are all around us, and if we're open to them, they can blossom.

18. *Hold space for others to grow and overcome their difficulties.* By giving others this gift, their inner ocean of potential can expand. Remain truthful when providing constructive criticism.

Happiness is something that we each have to define for ourself in consultation with the wisdom of the body and the yearnings of the heart. This emphasis on the self may appear to conflict with our desire to help others, but when each and every one of us gives life and voice to positive feelings and energy, we send out into the world the harmonic vibrations of unconditional love that can work miracles. Even if we are the recipients of negative words or emotions, our own attitude can reflect the good back to someone who may very well be in distress. After all, can we be truly happy if those around us are in pain? We can all learn to grow in love from people, things, and events that touch the heart, and receiving from another's heart enhances our ability to give from the heart. We will treasure such tender moments our whole life. Does love correspond to happiness? Maybe not, but it doesn't seem that happiness is possible without love. Perhaps we can rewrite the phrase "falling in love." Instead, let's devote ourselves to rising in love together.

A Final Blessing

The evolution of humankind seems to move along in stages at a pace that is rapidly increasing. The agricultural age lasted for thousands of years. The industrial age covered less than two hundred years. In recent decades we have been rapidly moving through the information age. Are we now about to shift into a new age of expanded consciousness that recognizes our interconnection and is filled with insight, harmony, and balance? I believe that this shift is already happening as our discontent with the status quo propels us to take up the challenge of positive change.

As each of us changes for the better, the world around us will change. Our capacity as humans definitely seems to evolve as we dive deeper into the inner ocean of our awareness, only to discover the limitless potential that is right under our noses. When we open the floodgates to the sea of opportunity, dive into the divine blissful source we all share, feel the passion and joy of the mystery, and commit to sharing what we learn with all beings, we can help each other find a real port of refuge in the inner sanctum of the heart, where everything feels so right.

This book and its many complementary therapies, practices, and techniques are my heartfelt attempt to share some worthwhile and inspiring information that people can use to heal the body and uplift the spirit. Many of these practices have been a powerful blessing in my own life, and I sincerely hope that they can help others chart their own true course in life. This book was a challenge and a labor of love, and in the end, I accomplished something I never thought possible.

It all comes down to what we make of our experiences, and turning all challenges into opportunities for blessings can go a long way in creating not just a fleeting sense of satisfaction but a state of real, lasting happiness. With the courage to dive into the vast inner ocean of our being, we can arise washed free of our ills, embodied and illumined with the light of wisdom. By always aspiring to do what we love, we can build upon those revealing, inspiring, magical moments and integrate their essence into our daily lives.

May the radiant overflow of your heart and the cosmic giggle within your inner ocean of awareness tickle your fancy from now to eternity.

May the winds of love blow through your soul as you rise to the surface with new insight from the inner sea of potential and possibilities.

May you forever find yourself swimming in oceans of love and rivers of rapture.

Appendix: Complementary and Alternative Health Care Resources

American Association of Acupuncture and Oriental Medicine (AAAOM)
P.O. Box 96503 #44114
Washington D.C. 20090
866-455-7999
www.aaaomonline.org

American Holistic Health Association (AHHA)
P.O. Box 17400
Anaheim, CA. 92817
714-779-6152
www.ahha.org

American Holistic Medical Association (AHMA)
23366 Commerce Park, Suite101B
Blackwood, OH. 44122
216-292-6644
www.holisticmedicine.org

American Massage Therapy Association (AMTA)
500 Davis Street, Suite900
Evanston, IL. 60201
847-864-0123
877-905-2700
www.amtamassage.org

American Organization for Bodywork Therapies of Asia (AOBTA)
1010 Haddonfield-Berlin Road, Suit 408
Voorhees, NJ. 08043
856-782-1616
www.aobta.org

Associated Bodywork and Massage Professionals (ABMP)
25188 Genesee Trail Road, Suite 200
Golden, CO. 80401
800-458-2267
www.abmp.com

Association for Comprehensive Energy Psychology (ACEP)
349 W. Lancaster Avenue, Suite 101
Haverford, PA. 19041
Mobile Office 619-861-2237
www.energypsych.org

Association for Research and Enlightenment (ARE)
215 67th Street
Virginia Beach, VA. 23451
800-333-4499
www.edgarcayce.org

Institute of Noetic Sciences (INS)
101 San Antonio Road
Petaluma, CA. 94952
707-775-3500
www.noetic.org

International Alliance of Healthcare Educators (IAHE)
11211 Prosperity Farms Road, Suite D-325
Palm Beach Gardens, FL. 34410
561-622-4334
www.uiahe.com

International Association for Energy Healers (IAFEH)
PO. Box 1904
Tualatin, OR. 97062
503-454-0469
www.iafeh.com

International Association of Healthcare Practitioners (IAHP)
11211 Prosperity Farms Road, Suite D-325
Palm Beach Gardens, FL. 33410
561-622-8273
800-311-9204
www.iahp.com

International Society for the Study of Subtle Energies and Energy Medicine (ISSSEEM)
2770 Arapaho Road, Suite 132
Lafayette, CO. 80026
303-425-4625
www.issseem.org

National Center for Complementary and Alternative Medicine (NCCAM)
National Institutes of Health
9000 Rockville Pike
Bethesda, MD. 20892
301-519-3153
888-644-6226
www.nccam.nih.gov

National Certification Board for Therapeutic Massage and Bodywork (NCBTMB)
1901 S. Meyers Road, Suite 240
Oakbrook Terrace, IL. 60181
800-296-0664
www.ncbtmb.com

National Certification Commission for Acupuncture and Oriental Medicine (NCCAOM)
76 S. Laura Street, Suite 1290
Jacksonville, FL. 32202
904-598-5001
www.nccaom.org

Novato Institute of Somatic Research and Training
1091 Calcot Place, Suite 412
Oakland, CA. 94606
510-261-4570
www.stillnessinmotion.com

Index

A

Abbott, Lynn 264
Abela, Pietro 268
Abhyanga 146, 164
Abhyanga Self-Massage 435
Ackerman, Dr. John 155
Acoustic Touch System 293
AcroSage 261
AcroYoga 445
Active Isolation Stretching 46
Active Release Techniques 36
Acu-Light Color Therapy 156
Acupressure 147
Acupressure for Anyone 150
Acupuncture 152
Acutaping 88
Acutonics 293
Acu-Yoga for Self-Healing 445
Addison, Lis 419
Adler, Donna 105
Adler, Janet 414
Advaita Vedanta Yoga 449
Advanced Energy Healing 213
Advanced Integrative Therapy 133
Aerobics 409
Agni Dhatu Therapy 262
Agnisar Kriya 128
Ahsian, Naisha 241
Ai Chi 95
Ai Chi Ne 95
Aikido 410
Akabane Method 155
Akashic Field Therapy 262
Akashic Record Analysis 262
Alchemia Reiki 247
Alchemical Bodywork 133
Alchemical Synergy 134
Alexander, Doug 48
Alexander, Frederick 66
Alexander, Gerda 68
Alexander, Ron 88
Alexander Technique 66
Alfassa, Mirra 448
Almass, A. H. 424
Amador, Vincent 248

Amanae Transformational Bodywork 134
Amanohuna 213
Amatsu Therapy 160
Amma, Sri 236
Amma Therapy 161
Ampuku 128
Amrit Yoga 445
Ananda Yoga 445
Anandi Ma, Sri 451
Anatomic Yoga 445
Anderson, Kathryn 231
Animal Bodywork 263
Anma Massage 161
An Qiao 204
Antara, Leyola 419
Anti-Aging Facial 102
Anusara Yoga 445
Applied Kinesiology 263
Applied Physiology 162
Applied Resonance Therapy 264
Aqua Aerobics 409
Aquacranial Therapy 95
Aquatic Exercises 410
Aquatic Integration 95
Aquatic Proprioceptive Neuromuscular Facilitation 96
Aquatic Relaxation Chamber 96
Aqua Wellness 105
Araneda, Rolando Toro 414
ARC (A Return to Consciousness) 268
ARCH (Ancient Rainbow Conscious Healing) 213
ARC-Work 268
Arhatic Yoga 446
Armitage, John 250
Arnold, Ute 297
Aromatherapy 77
Aromatherapy Salt Glow 102
Arvigo, Dr. Rosita 124
Arvigo Technique of Maya Abdominal Therapy 124
Asana 443
Asclepius 96

Asclepius Therapy 96
Ashi Acupoint Meridian Qi Gong 184
Ashiatsu Oriental Bar Therapy 269
Ashtanga Yoga 446
Ashton, Debbie 103
Asian Rasul 100
Assagioli, Roberto 316
Aston, Judith 67
Aston Kinetics 67
Aston-Patterning 67
Astrological Consultation 305
Atisha 402
Attunement Therapy 214
Aura Soma Care System 84
Auric Healing 214
Auricular Acupuncture 155
Aurobindo, Sri 448
Authentic Movement 414
Autogenic Training 305
Autonomic Response Testing 267
Avicenna 273
Awareness Release Technique 213
Awareness Through Movement 69
AyaRosas, Carlos 420
Ayurvedic Therapy 162

B

Bach, Dr. Edward 78
Bach Flower Therapy 78
BackHab 411
Bad Ragaz Ring Method 97
Bagua Bodywork 167
Bagua Exercise Program 412
Bagua Zhang 167
Bailey, Alice 222
Balinese Massage 36
Bamberger, Dr. Lynn 180
Bamboo Fusion 78
Bandler, Richard 314
Baptiste, Baron 453
Barber-Hancock, Dr. Flo 114
Barnes, John 45
Barral, Dr. Jean-Pierre 129
Barrie, Louise 74
Bartenieff Fundamentals 71

Bartenieff, Irmgard 71
Bartlett, Dr. Richard 231
Barton, John 265
BART Therapy 275
Bassett, Dr. Andrew 81
Basti 128, 166
Batu Jamu Massage 79
Baum, Brent 138
Beaulieu, John 294
Becker, Dr. Rollin 113
Beetz, Dr. 82
Bee Venom Acupuncture 155
Behavioral Kinesiology 265
Being in Movement 412
Belavi Face Lift Massage 102
Belot, Helen 253
Benedicte, Meg 257
Benham, Christopher 218
Benjamin, Ben 36, 52
Benjamin System 36
Bergins, Toni 419
Berry, Al 265
Berry, Lauren 37
Berry Method 37
Be Set Free Fast 134
BEST (Bio Energetic Synchronization Technique) 167
Bhagavan, Sri 236
Bhajan, Yogi 175, 451
Bhakti Massage 168
Bhakti Yoga 446
Bhosle, Dr. Ram 188
Bi-Aura 214
Bikram Yoga 446
Bindegewebs Massage 39
Bindu 165
Bingsen, Guo 434
Biodanza 414
Biodynamic Craniosacral Therapy 113
Biodynamic Massage 124
Bioenergetics (Bioenergetic Analysis) 168
Bioenergy Therapy 215
Biofeedback 79
Bio-Geometric Integration 111
BioGeometry 269
Bio-Kinesiology 265
Biokinetics 110
Biomagnetic (Magnet) Therapy 81
Biomat Therapy 82

Bioresonance Feedback Therapy 82
Bioresonance Therapy 82
Biosonic Repatterning 294
BioSync 37
Bio-Tuning 294
Birch, Beryl Bender 453
Bloom, Bernadette 222
Bodhidharma 204, 423, 427, 431
Body Alignment Technique 135
Body Baths and Showers 97
Body Compresses 99
Body Management 265
Body Memory Recall 135
Body Mind Centering 67
Bodynamic Analysis 306
Body Packs / Fango Therapy 100
Body Scrubs 100
BodySpeak 268
Body Talk 169
Body Wraps and Hot Packs 100
Bohm, Dr. David 113
Bone Setting 206
Bone Toning 295
Boreh 36
Boustany, Robert 453
Bowen Technique 38
Bowen, Thomas 38
Bowenwork 38
Boyesen, Gerda 124
Brain Gym 266
Brainwave Optimization 270
Brazilian Light Energization 215
Breast Massage 271
Breathdance 337
Breathing Coordination 333
Breath Mastery 333
Breath of Life 336
Breema Bodywork 169
Brennan, Barbara 215
Brennan Healing Science 215
Brine Baths 97
Brockman, Howard 218
Brown, Dr. Sue 111
Bruder, Leslie 54
Brulé, Dan 333
Brunschwiler, Arjana 107
Bruyere Energy Medicine 217
Bruyere, Rev. Rosalyn 217
Buddha Maitreya Soul Therapy 85
Buddha (Siddhartha Gautama) 399

Buddhist Meditation 399
Buddhi Yoga 449
Budokon 413
Budzek, Jeffrey 38
Budzek Medical Massage Therapy 38
Bulbrook, Dr. Mary Jo 221, 223
Burdenko, Dr. Igor 411
Burdenko Method 411
Burmeister, Mary 172
Burnham, Bruce 102
Burnham System 102
Burroughs, Stanley 201
Buteyko, Dr. Konstantin 333
Buteyko Method 333
Butterfly Touch Massage 168

C

Callahan, Roger 143
Callahan Technique 143
Callanetics 439
Cameron, Dr. Clark 255
Cangemi, Lilia 101
Carey, Donna 293
Carver, Willard 110
Cataldo, Arthur 213
Cathiodermie (Hydradermie) 83
Cayce, Dr. Edgar 232, 271, 424
Cayce/Reilly Massage Therapy 271
Chace, Marian 413
Chair Massage 271
Chaitow, Boris 48
Chaitow, Dr. Leon 50
Chakradance 415
Chakra Toning 438
Champissage 165, 271
Chang San Feng 204, 440
Channing, Douglas 415
Chanting and Mantras 438
Charcot, Jean-Martin 274
Chauffour, Dr. Paul 53
Chavutti Thirumal Massage 166, 272
Chelation Therapy 217
Chi Gong 430
Chikly, Bruno 280
Chikwando 170
Childre, Doc 312
Chi Nei Tsang 125
Chinese Energetics 207
Chi Po (Pai), Dr 203
Chiropractic Therapy 110

Choa Kok Sui, Master 240, 446
Chodorow, Joan 414
Chogyal Namkhai Norbu 176, 198, 422, 458
Chogyam Trungpa Rinpoche 349
Chopra, Deepak 163
Choudhury, Bikram 446
Christopher Method 218
Chua K'a Bodywork 413
Chubinsky Method 83
Chubinsky, Vladimir 83
Chun Do Sun Bup 174
Chunsoo 175
Chunyi Lin, Master 434
Circus Yoga 446
Cirolia, Laura 320
Clinical Acupressure 149
Clinical Flexibility and Therapeutic Exercise 38
Clinton, Asha 133
Cohen, Bonnie 67
Cohen, Michael 243
Cold Laser Therapy 88
Collier, Kim 79
Colon Hydrotherapy 126
Colonic Irrigation 126
Color and Light Therapy 84
Connective Tissue Massage 39
Conrad, Emilie 416
Constitution Acupuncture 155
Contact Improvisation 415
Contact Reflex Analysis 265
Continuum Montage 416
Continuum Movement 416
Coordination Patterns 416
Core Beliefs Psychotherapy 306
Core Connexion Transformational Arts 416
Core Energetics 307
CORE Myofascial Therapy 39
Core Structural Integrated Therapy 39
Couples Massage 272
Cousins, Norman 426
Craig, Gary 137
Cramer, Patricia 297
Cranial Osteopathy 53
Cranial Structural Integration 114
Craniosacral Therapy 112
CranioSomatic Therapy 114
Crenotherapy 100

Croibier, Alain 130
Cryotherapy 100
Crystal Gemstone Facial 102
Crystalline Therapy 85
Crystal Resonance Therapy 241
Crystal Therapy 85
Cupping 154
Custis, Tim 142
Cymatic Therapy 295
Cyriax, Dr. James 51, 111

D

Dahn Yoga 447
Daily, Dr. Charles 137
Dale, Dr. Theresa 284
Dalton, Dr. Erik 115
Dance Free 418
Dance of Liberation 417
Dance Programs 413
Dances of Universal Peace 417
Dance Your Bliss 417
Dancing with Pain 417
DansKinetics 422
Danyasa 418
Daoyin An Qiao 423
Daoyin Therapy 423
Davidson, Dr. Stephen 53
Dayana 41
Day, Christine 134
Deep Tissue Massage 40
Degriefing Therapy 307
Deity Yoga 448
DeJarnette, Dr. Major 114
DeLany, Judith (Walker) 50
De La Warr, Dr. George 89
DeLucrezia, Nancy 51
Dennhofer, Maire 214
Dennison, Dr. Paul 266
Dennison, Gail 266
Desai, Yogi Amrit 340, 445, 450
Desikachar, T. K.V. 443, 459
Detox Foot Baths 97
Detzler, Robert 255
Deunov, Peter 420
Devageet, Swami 237
Devi, Indra 443
Devi, Sri Mataji Nirmala 454
Dewe, Bruce 202
Dharana 443
Dhauti 128

Dheeraj, Shantam 200
Dhondup, Dr. 200
Dhyana 443
Diamond Approach 424
Diamond, Dr. John 265
Diamond Qi Gong 434
Dicke, Elizabeth 39
Diepold, Dr. John 144
Dilgo Khyentse Rinpoche 402
Divine Clairvoyant Channeling 218
Divine Energy Healing 258
DNA Activation 256
Doi, Hiroshi 247
Do-In 423
Dolphin-Assisted Therapy 94
Dolphin Dance Healing 101
Dong Haichuan 167, 412
Dorje, Lama 118
Dosick, Ellen 319
Douche Shower 97
Doula Therapy 286
Douno, Beinsa 420
Dowsing 86
Dream Yoga 447
Duan Zhi Liang, Master 434
Dubro, Peggy 220
Dull, Harold 107, 195
Dunning, Jo 242
Dyer, Rev. Louisa 320
Dynamic Embodiment 68
Dynamic Energetic Healing 218
Dynamic Spinal Therapy 114
Dzogchen 402

E

Ealy, Dr. C. Diane 237
Early Intervention Therapy 55
Eddy, Dr. Martha 68
Eden, Donna 219
Eden Energy Medicine 219
Educational Kinesiology 266
Edu-K 266
Egoscue Method 425
Egoscue, Peter 425
Eight Constitution Acupuncture 155
Einstein, Albert 81
Electro-Acupuncture Diagnostics 156
Electro-Acutherapy 156
ElectroCrystal Therapy 85
Embodyoga 447

EMDR Therapy 308
Emery, Kevin 251
EMF Balancing Technique 220
Emotional Freedom Technique 137
Emotrance 308
Endermologie 86
Endo-Nasal Therapy 156
Endo, Ryokyu 193
Energetic Integration 56
Energy Interference Patterning 221
Energy Medicine (EM) / TYLEM 221
Energy of Life 148
Energy Psychology 309
Eng, Kim 453
Enomoto, Masaichi 423
Epstein, Dr. Donald 116, 343
Erdal, Dr. 185
Erickson, Dr. Milton 274
Ericksonian Method 274
Esalen Massage 40
Esogetic Colorpuncture 156
Esoteric Healing 222
Essential Energy Treatment 277
Etheric Pulse Therapy 222
Eutony 68
Exercise Programs 413
Exerssage 425

F

Facials 102
Facilitated Pathways Intervention 114
Fan Teng Gong 434
Faraday, Michael 81
FAR Infrared Therapy 87
Fascial and Membrane Technique 130
Feinstein, David 220
Feldenkrais Method of Somatic
    Education 68
Feldenkrais, Moshe 69
Finger, Alan 449
Fitzgerald, Dr. William 185
Five Element Acupuncture 157
Five Rhythms 418
Flatischler, Reinhard 422
Fleischman, Rachel 417
Fleming, Tapas 150
Flotation Repatterning and Flotation
    Therapy 103
Flow Yoga 459
Fluidics 108

Fluid Moves (Aquatic Feldenkrais)
    103
Fo Fu, Lama 434
Folk Dance 418
Foot Fitness 63
Ford, Debbie 318
Ford, Dr. Clyde 141
Formative Psychology 309
Forrest, Ana 447
Forrest Yoga 447
Four-Hands Massage 272
Fox, Dustin 293, 296
Frank, Dr. Victor 267
Franklin, Ellen 293
Free Dance 418
Fremming, Grethe 268
Friend, John 445
Frissell, Bob 336
Fukushima, Kodo 160
Functional Fascial Taping 88

G

Gabrielsen, Ole 248
Gach, Dr. Michael Reed 445
Gagnon, Alice Brown 307
Gail, Jeffrey 282
Gallo, Dr. Fred 309
Gan Jin Osho 189
Gannon, Sharon 449
Gaomo 155
Garcia, Megan 451
Garshana 147
Gattefosse, Rene-Maurice 78
Gauthier, Irene 283
Gendai Reiki 247
Gendlin, Eugene 310
Gendlin Focusing 310
Gentle Bio-Energetics 168
George, Alexander 104
Gerber, Dr. Richard 209
Gerdes, Lee 270
Geriatric Massage 272
Geshe Chekawa 402
Gestalt Therapy 310
Giammatteo, Dr. Sharon 41
Gilbert, William 81
Gindler, Elsa 436
Glum, Dr. Gary 50
Goff, Rebecca 95
Golden Spoons Facial 102

Goodheart, Dr. George 264
Gordon, Nancy 218
Gordon, Richard 242
Graham, Douglas 279
Grant, Laurie 213
Grasso, Lois 338
Graston, David 87
Graston Technique 87
Green, Will 40
Gresham, Lansing 275
Grigore, Dr. Gabrielle 186
Grigorian Organic Spa Reflexology
    186
Grinberg, Avi 311
Grinberg Method 311
Grinder, John 314
Griscom, Chris 233
Grof, Christina 334
Grof, Stanislav 334
Gua Sha 87, 155
Guba, Edith 434
Guigen Qi Gong 434
Guinot, Rene 83
Gumenick, Neil 157
Gunther, Bernie 40
Gurunam 223
Guru Yoga 448
Gurwitsch, Alexander 82
Gyrotonic Expansion System 425

H

Hahneman, Samuel 425
Hakomi Integrative Somatics 318
Hakomi Method 311
Halliwick Concept 411
Hameed, Ali 424
Hammam Therapy 103
Hammond, Mary 218
Hancock, Dr. Dallas 114
Hanna Somatic Biokinetics 70
Hanna Somatic Education 69
Hanna, Thomas 69
Hara and Core Star Meditation 403
Hara Bodywork 127
Hardee, Ruthie 269
Hariharananda, Paramahamsa 450
Harmonic Overtone Chanting 439
Harmonyum 223
Harper, Susan 416
Hartmann, Silvia 308

Hashimoto, Dr. Keizo 291
Hatha Yoga 448
Hatsumi, Dr. Masaaki 160
Hauschka Body Compress Massage 99
Hauschka, Dr. 99
Havlic, Dr. C. Harold 267
Havsboel, Rolf 268
Hawaiian Hot Stone Massage 280
Hayashi, Dr. Chujiro 245
Hayes, Patricia 251
Hay, Louise 232
Healing Dance 104
Healing Touch for Animals 263
Healing Touch (HT) Program 223
Healing Touch Spiritual Ministry 272
Healing Voice 439
Health Kinesiology 266
Heart Energy Awareness Release Technique 213
Heart Math Therapy 312
Heartsong, Beloved 228
Heart & Soul Healing 224
Heartwood 41
Hecker, Hans-Ulrich 88
Heckman, Dr. Claude 47
Heller, Joseph 70
Hellerwork 70
HEMME Approach 41
Hendricks, Dr. Gay 340
Hendricks, Dr. Kathlyn 340
Hendrickson, Dr. Tom 41
Hendrickson Method 41
Hendrix, Dr. Harville 312
Hensel, Thomas 251
Herbal Therapy 429
Hikmat Healing 273
Hindu Meditation 404
Hippocrates 96, 273
Hiskoliya Massage 284
Holoenergetic Healing 273
Holographic Memory Release Technique 137
Holographic Memory Resolution 138
Holographic Repatterning 187
Holographic Sound Therapy 295
Holotropic Breathwork 334
Homeopathy 425
Horvath, Juliu 425
Hoshino Amma 170

Hoshino Therapy 170
Hoshino, Tomezo 170
Howard, Nina 102
Howe, Linda 263
Howell, Dr. Dean 116
Howell, Neva 222
Huang Ti 203
Hua Tuo, Dr. 201
Huatuojiaji 201
Hubbert, Paul 295
Huma Somatic Psychotherapy 74
Huma Transpersonal Bodywork 74
Humkara 458
Huna Kane Temple Massage 279
Huna Therapy 278
Hunt, Dr. Helen LaKelly 312
Hunter, Dr. Neva 234
Hurley, Dr. John 118
Hyakuten, Inamoto 248
Hypnotherapy 274
Hypnotrance 274

I

Ibn Sina 273
Ichazo, Oscar 413
Ideokinesis 70
Imago Relationship Therapy 312
Indian Rope Massage 166, 272
Indigo System 80
Indonesian Body Wrap 100
Indonesian Massage 36
Infratonic Sound Therapy 295
Ingerman, Sandra 291
Ingham, Eunice 185
Inner Fire Yoga 448
Inner Focus 224
Insight Bodywork 170
Insight Yoga 448
Integral Deep Listening 447
Integral Yoga 448
Integrated Awareness Therapy 275
Integrated Energy Therapy 225
Integrated Kabbalistic Healing 275
Integrative Body Psychotherapy 313
Integrative Breathwork 335
Integrative Eclectic Shiatsu 191
Integrative Grief Therapy 307
Integrative Manual Therapy 41
Integrative Reflexology 186
Integrative Yoga Therapy 426

Interplay 426
Intuitive Energy Healing 226
Intuitive Energy Medicine 227
Ionization Therapy 104
iRest Yoga Nidra 460
Iridology 157
Irmansyah Effendi 250
Ishikuro, Iris 249
Ishta Yoga 449
Isometric Massage Therapy 42
Isometric Muscle Balancing 42
Iyengar, B. K. S. 443, 449, 454
Iyengar Yoga 449

J

Jacobs, Edmund 430
Jaffe, Dr. Carolyn 266, 276
Jaffe, Dr. Robert 213
Jaffe-Mellor Technique 276
Jahara, Mario 105
Jahara Technique 104
James, Tad 319
Jamgön Kongtrül 402
Jamison, Lynette 96
Janov, Arthur 315
Jazzercise 419
Jelm, Christopher 248
Jelm, Jeannine 248
Jing, Qi, Shen, Xu, Tao 344
Jin Kei Do Reiki 247
Jin Shin Do 171
Jin Shin Jyutsu 172
Jivamukti Yoga 449
Jnana Yoga 449
Johnson, Dr. Ranae 289
Johrei Massage 173
Johrei / Vajra Reiki 247
Jois, Sri K. Pattabhi 443, 446, 459
Jones, Lawrence 60
Journey Dance 419
Jun Quan 431
Junyu Wu 207

K

Kabal, Dr. Herman 96
Kabat, Dr. Herman 55
Kabat-Zinn, Dr. Jon 406
Kahi Loa Ho'okhi (Mana Healing) 279
Ka-Lei Therapy 173

Kali Yoga 459
Kamadon, Alton 233
Kampo 429
Kam Yuen, Dr. 207
Kaneko, Dr. DoAnn 161, 191
Kapalabhati 128
Kapke, Barry 170
Karim, Dr. Ibrahim 269
Karma Dhauti 166
Karma Yoga 449
Karni, Dr. Zvi 140
Karuna Ki Reiki 248
Karuna Reiki 248
Kase, Kenzo 88
Kataria, Dr. Madan 427
Kati Basti 128
Kato, Dr. Kyoshi 117
Kaurkhalsa, Gurmukh 451
Kayabhyanga 147
Kayakalpa Therapy 277
Kayakalpa Yoga 450
Keleman, Dr. Stanley 309
Kellogg, Dr. John 127
Kelly, Dr. Charles 317
Kenku Jutsu 115, 161
Kentro Body Balance 426
Kerali 285
Keralite Massage 166, 272
Kest, Byran 453
Khazzom, Loolwa 417
Kiai 174
Kiatsu Ryoho 174
Kid's (Children's) Yoga 450
Kijo Body Meditation 419
Kinesio Taping 88
Kinesis Myofascial Integration 42
Kinetic Awareness 71
Kinetic Voice 419
King, Gisele 231
King Solomon Healing 227
Kipp, Donald W. 180
Kiradjee Massage 278
Kishi, Akinobu 189
Kivo Dance 419
Klinghardt, Dr. Dietrich 267
Kneipp, Sebastian 105
Kneipp Therapy 105
Knott, Margaret 55
Kobido 102
Kodo Massage Therapy 278

Kolden Techniques 278
Komitor, Carol 263
Komitor Healing 263
Komyo Reiki Kai 248
Kondanna 170
Konno, Jun 95
Korean Hand Acupuncture 157
Korean Hand Massage 186
Korean Massage / Korean Martial
    Therapy 174
Korean Sasang Healing System 159
Koren, Dr. Tedd 111
Koren Specific Technique 111
Kosmed Therapy 88
Kousaleos, George 39
Kravitz, Dr. Judith 347
Krieger, Dr. Dolores 256
Kripalu Massage 43
Kripalu Yoga 450
Kripalvanandji, Sri Swami 450
Krishna Das 439, 446
Krishnamacharya, Sri T. 443, 459
Kriya Massage 175
Kriyananda, Swami 445
Kriya Yoga 450
Kriya Yoga Bodywork 175
Kuan Yin 231, 251
Kumaraswamiji, H.H. Mahatapasvi
    Sri 455
Kum Nye Yoga 457
Kundalini Dance 419
Kundalini Massage 175
Kundalini Meditation 405
Kundalini Reiki 248
Kundalini Yoga 450
Kundalini Yoga Breathwork 335
Kunye Massage Therapy 176
Kunz, Dora Van Gelder 256
Kurashova Re-education 43
Kurtz, Ron 311
Kushi, Michio 423, 430
Kwon, Dr. Dowon 155

L

Laban Movement Analysis 71
Laban, Rudolph 71
Ladara 285
Lad, Dr. Vasant 163
LaHo-Chi 228
Lakhovsky, Georges 83

Lamm, Mark 37
Lamm Therapy 37
Lao Tzu 204
Laozi 204
Laser Therapy 88
Laskow, Dr. Leonard 273
LaStone Massage 90
Laughter Therapy 426
Laughter Yoga 427
Lavin, Ron 235
Laya Yoga 450
Leahy, Dr. Michael 36
Lee, Dr. Jema 155
Lee, Ilchi 177, 447
Lee, Michael 72
Lee, Ping 192
Lee, Shar 118
Leflet, Dave 41
Leif, Stanley 48
Lenair Healing Technique 229
Lenair, Rhonda 229
LENS (Low Energy Neurofeedback
    System) 80
Leonard, Jim 348
LePage, Joseph 426
Leven, Daniel 421, 423
Levin, Dr. Jeff 135
Levine, Dr. Peter 141
Levry, Dr. Joseph 223
Levy, Dr. Peter 50
Lewis, Dennis 332
Lewis, Samuel 417
Li Chu Kuo 204
Liebchen, Kay 88
Life, David 449
LifeForce Yoga 451
Lifestream Massage 62
Lightarian Reiki 248
Light Body Activation 229
Lilly, Dr. John 103
Lin, Banya 177
Linden, Paul 412
Ling, Pir Heinrik 61
Lio Wan So 205
Liquid Sound 105
Lithotherapy 425
Lobsang Palden, Lama 198, 206
Lojong 402
Lombardi, Ethel 249

Lomi Lomi Massage (Hawaiian Bodywork) 278
Long, Max 279
Looyen, Ted 43
Looyenwork 43
Louise, Suzanne 227
Lovestream Touch 230
Loving-Kindness (Metta) Meditation 401
Lowen, Dr. Alexander 168
Lowe, Whitney 52
Low Level Laser Therapy 88
Lubeck, Walter 249
Luminous Energy Field Healing 230
Lungtok Tenpai Nyima 198
Luscher, Dr. Max 84
Luthe, Dr. Wolfgang 305
Lu Tung-Pin 204, 388
Lympho-Fascia Release 280
Lypossage 44
Lyu Ki Dou 105

M

Machado, Auntie Margaret 279
Macrobiotics 430
Macrobiotic Shiatsu 191
Magnetic Acupressure 148
Magnetic Field Therapy 81
Magnified Healing 231
Mago Energy Healing 177
Mahamudra 402
Mahara, Mahavatar Babaji 450
Maharishi Mahesh Yogi 405
Maitland, Geoffrey 117
Maitland Mobilization Techniques 117
Makko Ho Exercises 427
Manaka, Dr. Yoshio 158, 292
Manaka Yin Yang Channel Balancing Therapy 158
Mandel, Dr. Peter 156
Manners, Sir Peter 295
Mantak Chia 126, 343
Mantra Yoga 451
Manual Articular Approach 130
Manual Lymphatic Drainage 281
MAP (Medical Assistance Program) Therapy 313
Marantz, Benjamin 261
Marcher, Lisbeth 306

Mardana 148, 165
Mariel Reiki 249
Marma Chikitsa 177
Marma Massage 165, 177
Marmapuncture 158, 165
Marpa the Translator 197
Martes, C. J. 263
Martial Arts 427
Martin-Neville, Dorothy 258
Marti, Vinn Arjuna 422
Masayuki, Dr. Saionji 120
Masunaga, Shizuto 193, 427
Mathebula, Carol 298
Matrix Energetics 231
Matsumoto, Kiiko 128
Mattes, Aaron 46
Mattes Method 46
Matthews, Richard 455
Maury, Dr. Margaret 78
McCann, Don 61
McClure, Virnala 275
McConnell, Jenny 88
McConnell Taping 88
McCraty, Dr. Rollin 312
McKenzie Method 115
McKenzie, Robin 115
McLean, Terri 283
McMillan, James 411
McMillan, Phil 411
McTimoney, John 112
McTimoney Method 111
Meagher, Jack 60
Mechanical Link 53
Medical Intuitive Therapy 232
Medical Massage 44
Medi Cupping 154
Meditation 428
Meeker, Lloyd Arthur 214
Mega Yoga 451
Mehindra 258
Mehra, Dr. Lajpatrai 285
Mehta Face Massage 271
Mehta, Rupa 420
Meiso Yoga 452
Melchizedek, Drunvalo 336
Melchizedek Method 233
Mellor, Judith 276
Men Baozhen 167
Menpa Phuntsog Wangmo 176
Mensendieck, Dr. Bess 72

Mensendieck Remedial Therapy System 72
Mentastics 75
Mentgen, Janet 223
Merkabah Breathwork 336
Merudanda 165
Merudanda Spinal Massage 115
Meshew, Margie 196
Mesmer, Franz 81
Metamorphic Technique 282
Metamorphosis 282
Mezger, Dr. Johann 61
Mezieres, Françoise 72
Mezieres Method 72
Microcosmic Orbit 406
Middendorf Breathexperience / Breathwork 336
Middendorf, Ilse 336
Miller, Claire Marie 186
Miller, Dr. Richard 460
Milliken, Dr. Tulsi 221
Mills, Deborah 254
Milne, Dr. Hugh 120
Milner, Kathleen 250
Mindell, Dr. Amy 315
Mindell, Dr. Arnold 315
Mindfulness-Based Stress Reduction 405
Mineral Salt Bath 97
Mines, Dr. Stephanie 142
Misono, Isai 128
Missett, Judi 419
Mitchell, Dr. Fred 44
Mitchell, Dr. Steve 250
Mitchell, Karyn 250
Mitsu, Mieko 247
Mobilization with Movement 117
Mochizuki, Shogo 103
Mo, Dr. Haeng-Yong 174
Mohapatra, Guru Keluchuran 420
Mongolian Cluster Massage 282
Mongolian Koyashai Massage 283
Mongolian Milk Back Massage 283
Moon, Dr. 155
Moore, Ivy 251
Mooshan, Malicheck 169, 434
MORA 82
Morse, Dr. Beverly Kitaen 313
Morter, Dr. Ted 167
Moxa 179

Moxibustion 154, 179
Muktananda, Swami 455
Mulligan, Brian 117
Mulligan Techniques 117
Multi-Incarnational Recall 233
Murai, Jiro 172
Murley, James 200
Muscle Energy Technique 44
Muscle Resistance Testing 266, 276
Myers, Thomas 42
Myofascial Release 36, 45
Myomassology 283
Myopathic Muscular Therapy 47
Myopractic Muscle Therapy 47
Myoskeletal Alignment Techniques 115
Myotherapy 62
Myss, Carolyn 226, 232

N

Nabhi Basti 166
Nada-Brahmananda, Swami 452
Nada Yoga 451
Nadi Swedana 107
Nagarjuna 163
Nakagawa, Dr. Masato 170, 437
Nalini Method 420
Nambudripad Allergy Elimination Technique 149
Nambudripad, Dr. Devi 149
Namikoshi Shiatsu 191
Namikoshi, Tokujiro 190, 191
Namikoshi, Toru 191, 435
Naprapathy Treatment 48
Narendra, Mehta 271
Naropa 197, 402, 458
Nasya 166
Native American Healing 283
Natural Hot Spring (Mineral) Therapy 97
Naturopathic Medicine 428
Nauli 128
Navach, Dr. Joseph 155
Nei Gong 387
Nelson-Hannigan, Mary 90
Nelson, Mike 96
Nelson, Sue 96
Nelson, William 80
Neo-Reichian Therapy 314
Nerve Mobilization 48

Nester, Nancy 224
Neti 166
Netra Tarpana 166
Network Spinal Analysis 116
Neural Manipulation 130
Neural Systems Kinesiology 266
Neuro-Biofeedback 79
NeuroCranial Restructuring 116
Neuro-emotional Technique 138
Neuroenergetic Kinesiology 267
Neuroenergetic Release 180
Neuro Energetic Repatterning 180
Neurofascial Release Therapy 53
Neurofascial Therapy 47
Neuro-Linguistic Programming 314
Neuromuscular Massage Therapy 48
Neuromuscular Reeducation 50
Neuromuscular Techniques 48
Neuromuscular Therapy American Version 50
Neuromuscular Therapy St. John Method 50
Neuromusculoskeletal Therapy 50
NeuroPhysical Reprogramming 284
Neurosomatic Therapy 49
Neuro-Structural Bodywork 51
Neurotherapy 285
Newman, Dr. Charles 237
Newsum, Dr. Lawrence 110
Nia (Neuromuscular Integrative Action) 420
Nimmo, Dr. Raymond 49, 112
Nimmo Receptor Tonus Method 112
Nims, Larry 134
Nine Breathings of Purification 346
Nishino Breathing Method 337
Nishino, Kozo 337
Nityananda, Bhagawan 455
Niyama 442
Noetic Balancing / Noetic Field Therapy 234
Nogier, Dr. Paul 155, 185
No Hands Massage 286
Nolte, Dorothy 75
Nonviolent Communication 314
Nuad bo Rarn 195
Nutritional Approaches 429
Nutritional Response Testing 267
Nutritional Supplements 430
Nyasa Yoga 452

Nyatri Tsenpo, King 196

O

Ochs, Dr. Leonard 80
Odissi Dance 420
Ogden, David 96
Ogden, Pat 318
Ohashiatsu 181
Ohashi, Wataru 181
Ohsawa, George 430
Okada, Mokichi 247
Okazaki Restoration Massage 182
Okazaki, Seishiro "Henry" 182
Okido Shiatsu 191
Okido Yoga 452
Oki, Dr. Masahiro 191, 452
Oldfield, Harry 85
Oncology Massage 286
One Brain System 267
One Light Healing Touch 235
Oneness Blessing 236
Oneness Deeksha 236
Onsen Muscle Therapy 51
Onsen Technique 51
Optimal Breathing 338
Opto-Crystal Therapy 85
Orgone Therapy 314
Orgonomic Therapy 139, 314
Orr, Leonard 341
Ortho-Bionomy 236
Orthopedic Massage 51
Oschman, James 209
Osho 237
Osho Illumination Therapy 237
Osteopathic Manipulation Therapy 52
Ott, Rolf 114
Ou Wen Wei, Master 434
Overly, Richard 168
OxyGenesis Breathwork 338
Ozone / Oxygen Therapy 89

P

Padabhyanga 166
Padmasambhava 197, 457, 458
Page, Ken 224
Pain Release Phenomenon Technique 118
Painter, Jack 55
Palmer, B. J. 110
Palmer, Dr. Daniel 81, 110

Panchakarma 164
Pandeya, Dr. Raam 277, 450
Paneurhythmy 420
Pangu Shen Gong 434
Panisset-Curcio, Kimberly 215
Panisset, Mauricio 215
Pannetier, Pierre 238
Panthermal Treatment 106
Panti, Don Elijio 124
Paracelsus 81
Parashakti 417
Park, Gui-Dai 174
Park, Jae Woo 150, 158
Parnell, Aaron 73
Parness, Dr. Alix-Sandra 224
Partner (Couples) Yoga 452
Patanjali 441
Pauls, Dr. Arthur 236
Pavek, Richard 139
Paxton, Steve 415
Pearl, Dr. Eric 243
Pediatric Acupuncture 159
Pediatric Massage 274
Pediatric Remedial Massage 159
Pema Chödrön 397, 402
Peng Tzu 203, 431
Penman, Anne 159
Penman Laser Technique 159
Perelandra System 313
Perez, Alberto "Beto" 423
Perls, Fritz 310
Perls, Laura 310
Peterson, Karen 150
Pet Massage 263
Petteway, Robert 47
Pfrimmer Deep Muscle Therapy 53
Pfrimmer, Therese 53
Phaigh, Richard 51
Phenomenal Touch 54
Phipps, Toshiko 190, 191
Phoenix Rising Yoga Therapy 72
Photon Sound Beam Therapy 89
Physiatrics 55
Physical Mind Method 421
Physical Therapy 54
Physioacoustic Therapy 296
Physiohelanics 237
Phytotherapy 429
Pien Ch'ueh, Dr. 204, 287
Pierrakos, Dr. John 307

Pierrakos, Eva 307
Pilates, Dr. Joseph 421
Pilates Therapy 421
Pinckney, Callan 439
Pinda Swedana 107
Piradara 195
Pizhichil 166
Pod Experience 101
Pohaku Welawela Lomi Lomi 280
Polarity Therapy 238
Polarity Yoga 452
Polish Brossage 100
Popp, Dr. T. A. 82
Porter, Phil 426
Positional Release Therapy 60
Position Therapy 177
Post-Surgical Therapy 44
Postural Integration 55
Power, Ellavivian 234
Powers, Sarah 448
Power Yoga 453
Prajnanananda, Paramahamsa 450
Prakritik Chikitsa 166
Pralaya Yoga 453
Prana Chikitsa 166
Pranassage 183
Pranayama 443
Pranayama (Ayurvedic Breathwork) 338
Pranic Healing 240
Prasad Das, Guru Deba 420
Pratyahara 443
Pregnancy or Prenatal Massage 286
Premaratna, Ranga 247
Prenatal Therapy 282
Prenatal Yoga 453
Primal Therapy 315
Primus Activation Healing Technique 241
Probiotics 430
Process Acupressure 149
Process Oriented Psychology 315
Progressive Muscular Relaxation 430
Proprioceptive Neuromuscular Facilitation 55
Prudden, Bonnie 62
Pryanta 241
Psychic and Spiritual Renewal Counseling 316
Psychophysical Integration 75

Psychosynthesis 316
Psychotronics 89
Pulsating Energy Resonance Therapy 83
Pulse Reading 287
Purce, Jill 439
Purna Yoga 453
PUSH Therapy 56
Pyves, Gerry 286

Q

Qi Flow Yoga 453
Qi Gong 430
Qi Gong Medical Massage 183
Qi Gong Self-Massage 435
Quantum Biofeedback 80
Quantum Breath Meditation 340
Quantum Energetics 242
Quantum-Touch 242
Quantum Vortex Technology 257
Quimby, Phineas 232, 234
Quispe, Don Manuel 230

R

Radiance Breathwork 340
Radionic Therapy 89
Radix 317
Raheem, Dr. Aminah 149
Rainbow Reiki 249
Raindrop Therapy 89
Raja Yoga 454
Raktamoksha 128
Raku Kei Reiki 249
Ram Dass 329
Rand, William 248, 251
Rangdrol, Tobin 296
Rapa Yad Bioenergy Healing Technique 243
Rapid Eye Technology 289
Rasayana 166
Ratnam, Sri Bala 348
Ray, Dr. Barbara Weber 249
Rea, Shiva 423
Rebirthing Breathwork Therapy 341
Reconnective Healing 243
Reflexology 184
Regression Therapy 317
Reich, Dr. Eva 168
Reich, Dr. Wilhelm 139, 314
Reichian Release Therapy 139

Reiki 244
Reilly, Dr. Harold 271
Remann, Micky 105
Renner, Kamala 133, 175, 247
Reposturing Dynamics 73
Resonance Repatterning 187
Response Therapy 255
Restorative Yoga 454
Risley, Nancy 252
Robertson, Arthur 249
Rocha, Mara 173
Ro Hun Therapy 251
Rolf, Dr. Ida 57
Rolfing Structural Integration 57
Rolf Movement Integration 58
Rosas, Debbie 420
Rosenberg, Dr. Jack Lee 313
Rosenberg, Marshall 314
Rosen, Marion 73
Rosen Method 73
Rosquist, Dr. LaMar 118
Rossiter, Richard 58
Rossiter System 58
Ross, Shelly 419
Roth, Gabrielle 418
Rubenfeld, Ilana 289
Rubenfeld Synergy Method 289
Ruby, Margaret 221
Ryan, Wade 247
RYSE 252

S

Saam 159
Sacred Circle Dancing 421
Sacro-Occipital Technique 114
Sadhana Yoga Chi 454
Sahaja Yoga 454
Saint Germain 250
Saito, Tetsuro 192, 377
Salsa Massage 58
Samadhi 443
Samvahan Vibrational Massage 188
Sangye Gyatso 198
Saraswati, Swami Satyananda 460
Satchamar 228
Satchidananda, Swami 449
Satir, Virginia 222
Sattavavajaya 166
Sauna Therapy 106
SCENAR Therapy 81

Schlade, Pamela 241
Schrei, Bob 254
Schroter, Aman 107
Schultz, Dr. Johannes 305
Schwind, Dr. Peter 130
Scotch Hose Massage 98
Scott, Dr. Jimmy 266
Scrivner, Jane 90
Seaman, Tom 253
Seemorg Matrix Work 133
Seichim Reiki 249
Seichim, Seichem, Sekhem, SKHM
    and SSR 252
Seifukujitsu 182
Seiki Soho Therapy 189
Seitai 117, 161
Sekhem-Seichim-Reiki 253
Self-Bremma Exercises 434
Self Healing Experience 229
Self-Massage 434
Selver, Charlotte 40, 58, 436
Seniors Yoga 454
Sensorimotor Psychotherapy 318
Sensory Awareness 436
Sensory Reeducation 58
Sensory Repatterning 74
Sen, Wesley 280
Serizawa, Dr. Katsusuke 193
Seva Stress Release 150
Seven Element Theory 162
Shadow Process Therapy 318
Shadow Yoga 454
Shake Your Soul 421
Shamanic Breathwork 342
Shamanic Breathwork Process 342
Shamanic Healing Methods 290
Shamatha 400
Shamballa Healing Tools 86
Shamballa Reiki 250
Shambhala Pyramid System 86
Shapiro, Dr. Francine 308
Shatkarma 128, 165
Shatkriya 166
Shayne, Kancho Cameron 413
SHEN Therapy 139
Sherwood, Dr. Jonathan 173
SHE (Self(s) Healing Experience) 229
Shewmaker, Diane 253
Shiatsu 189
Shiatsu Anma 191

Shiatsu Self-Massage 435
Shima, Dr. Miki 155
Shinden Jutsu 128, 161
Shinkiko 437
Shinki Ryoho 174
Shinso Shiatsu 192
Shirobhyanga 165
Shirodhara 165, 291
Shirodhara Nasya 291
Shiva Yoga 455
Shodhana 166
Shonishin 159, 274
Shulman, Jason 275
Siddha Yoga 455
Sills, Franklyn 113
Silva, Dane 280
Simons, Dr. David 62
Singleton, Aaron 148
Singleton, Sue 148
Sitz Bath 98
Sivananda, Sri Swami 446, 455, 460
Sivananda Yoga 455
Six Healing Tones 433
Six Yogas of Naropa 458
Skeele, Rebecca 234
Skildum, Sandra 278
Skille, Olav 296
Skinner, Joan 74
Skinner Releasing Technique 74
Small, Jacquelyn 335
Smith, Chris 144
Smith, Dr. Fritz 121
Smith, Linda 272
Sneehana 166
Soft Tissue Release 59
Sohn, Dr. Robert 161
Sohn, Tina 161
Sokushin Breathing 337
Solomon, Louise 441
Soma Bodywork 59
Soma Neuromuscular Integration 59
SomaSoul 421
Somatic Emotional Psychotherapy
    309
Somatic Exercises 70
Somatic Experiencing 141
Somato-Auricular Therapy 155
Somato Emotional Release 140
Somato Respiratory Integration 343
Somatosynthesis 141

Soma Veda Therapy 59
Sombat Tapanya 195
Somé, Sobonfu 308
Songtsen Gampo, King 197
Sonopuncture 159
Sotai Exercises 292
Sotai Ho Massage Therapy 291
Soul Focused Healing 254
Soul Lightening Acupressure 149
Soul Memory Discovery 319
Soul Motion 422
Sound Healing 292
Sound Healing Practices 437
SourcePoint Therapy 254
Southgate, Natalie 415
Sova, Ruth 95, 411
Spa Therapy 106
Spinal Joint Mobilization 117
Spinal Touch Therapy 118
Spiral Release Bodywork 142
Spiritual Acupuncture 177
Spiritual Healing Massage 254
Spiritual Response Therapy 255
Spiritual Restructuring 255
Sports Massage 60
Spring Forest Qi Gong 434
Stapleton, Amba 183
Stapleton, Don 183
Steam Bath Therapy 98
Stein, Diane 251
Stewart, James 74
Stibal, Vianna 256
Stiles, Mukunda Tom 455
Still, Dr. Andrew 52
St. John, Paul 49, 50
St. John, Robert 282
Stockhausen, Karlheinz 439
Stokes, Gordon 267
Stone, Dr. Randolph 238
Stone Massage Therapy / Hot Stone
    Massage 90
Stone Therapy Massage 90
Stough, Karl 333
Strain & Counterstrain Technique 60
Structural Awareness 75
Structural Energetic Therapy 61
Structural Foot Balancing 297
Structural Yoga Therapy 455
Sturrock, Gaye 283
Suchikarma 159

Su Jok 150
Su Jok Therapy 157
Suma Chien 204
Summerfield, Phoenix 253
Summers, Elaine 71
Sun, Dr. Guan-Cheng 388, 434
Sunshine, Shari 296
Sun Szu-Miao 204
Surat Shabda Yoga 455
Sutherland, Dr. William 53, 112
Suzuki, D.T. 403
Suzuki, Shunryu 403
Svaroopa Yoga 456
Swara Yoga 456
Swedana 107, 165
Swedish Massage 61
Sweigard, Dr. Lulu 70
Swenson, Doug 454
Swe-Thai 196
Swiss Shower 99
Syntropic Insight Bodywork 296

T

Tachi-Ren, Tashira 229
Taegeuk 159
Tai Chi 440
T'ai Chi Chu'an 440
Tai Chi Me 440
Taido, Yoshida 117
Taiki 337
Taikyo Shiatsu 192
Takamori, Seiji 247
Takata, Mrs. Hawayo 245
Takatsuno, Michael 56
TaKeTiNa 422
Talladas 124
Tantra Yoga 457
Tantric Dakini Approach 194
Tantsu Tantric Shiatsu 195
Taoist and Qi Gong Breathing
    Practices 343
Taoist Meditation 406
Taoist Self-Massage 436
Taoist Yoga 456
Tao Shiatsu 193
Tapas Acupressure Technique 150
Tapihritsa 196
TARA Approach 142
Tarthang Tulku 176, 457
Taws Method 59

Taws, Stuart 59
Tellington-Jones, Linda 263
Tellington TTouch 263
Tempaku, Tamai 189
Tenzin Wangyal Rinpoche 346
Tera-Mai Reiki 250
Tesla, Nikola 83
Thai Herbal Compress 99
Thai Massage 195
Thai Yoga Bodywork 195
Thalassotherapy / Algo Therapy 107
Thayer, Stevan 225
The Radiance Technique 249
Therapeutic Touch 256
Theta Healing 256
Thie, Dr. John 202, 264
Thom, Sofiah 418
Thomson, Donna 254
Thoth 233
Thought Field Therapy 143
Three-in-One Concept 267
Thusius, Angelika 426
Tibetan Buddhist Meditation 401
Tibetan Cranial 118
Tibetan Medicine 196
Tibetan Point Holding Acupressure
    150
Tibetan Pulsing Healing 200
Tibetan Universal Massage 200
Tibetan Vita Flex Therapy 201
Tibetan Yoga 457
Tibetan Yoga of Breath and Movement
    346
Time Line Therapy 319
Tobar, Hugo 266
Todd, Mabel Ellsworth 70
Tohei, Koichi 174
Tompkins, Raven 241
Tom Tam 201
Tom Tam Healing System 201
Tonglen 402
Tong Ren Healing 201
Tonpa Shenrab Miwoche 196
Total Body Modification 267
Touch and Breathe 144
Touch for Health 202
Townsend, Patty 447
Toyohari Meridian Therapy 160
Traditional Chinese Medicine 203
Trager Approach 75

Trager, Dr. Milton 75
Transcendental Meditation 405
Transformational Breath 347
Transformational Kinesiology 268
Transformational Reiki 250
Trataka 166
Trauma Touch Therapy 144
Travell, Dr. Janet 62
Trembath, Michael 188
Triane, Sol Ta 230
Trigger Point Release Therapy 62
Tripodi, Jonathan 135
Trisong Detsen, King 197
TriYoga 459
Trul Khor 346, 458
Tsa Lung 347, 458
Tsubo Therapy 193
Tui Mo Self-Massage 436
Tuina 205
Tulsi Biofeedback Imaging System 221
Tummo 448
Tummo Reiki 250
TYLEM 221

U

Udvartina 147
Ueshiba, Morihei 410
Unani Tibb Medicine Therapy 273
Underwater Pressure Massage 99
Unergi Therapy 297
Unified Field Therapy 257
Upledger, Dr. John 112, 129, 140
Uranda 214
Urine Analysis 289
Uro Basti 128
Usui, Dr. Mikao 245
Usui Reiki Ryoho 245
Usui/Tibetan Reiki 251
Utt, Richard 162

V

Vairocana 206, 458
Vajra Dance 422
Valnet, Jean 78
Vamana 128
Vandergrift, Charlotte 42
Varisara 128
Vascular Autonomic Signal 155
Vass, Dorothy 55

Veltheim, Dr. John 169
Versendaal, Dr. Richard 265
VIBE Healing 83
Vibrational Attunement Massage 296
Vibrational Breath Therapy 348
Vibrational Healing Massage Therapy 297
Vibro Acoustic Therapy 296
Vichy Shower Massage 99
Vigran, Eva 416
Villoldo, Dr. Alberto 230, 291
Viniyoga 459
Vinyasa Yoga 459
Violet Flame Reiki 251
Vipassana 401
Virechana 128
Visceral Manipulation 129
Vishesh 147
Vishnudevananda, Swami 455
Visionary Acupressure System 148
Visionary Craniosacral Approach 119
Vivation 348
Vivekananda, Swami 443
Vodder, Dr. Emil 281
Vodder, Estrid 281
Voll, Dr. Richard 156
Vortex Alignment 135
Vortex Healing 258
Vunkuwa Massage 298

W

Walaski, James 52
Walker, Dr. Scott 138
Wall, Vicky 84
Walsh, John 150
Wang Shu He, Dr. 204, 287
Wassertanzen 107
WaterDance 107
Waterman, Dr. Robert 234
Water Pilates / Aquapilates 411
Water Yoga 411
Watson, Dan 228
Watsu Therapy 107
Wei Chi Healing Reiki 251
Weinman, Ric 258
Weintraub, Amy 451
Wei Po-Yang 204
West, Cameron 95
Wetzig, Betsy 416
Wetzig Technique 416

Whiltshire, Annie 259
Whiltshire, William 259
Whitehouse, Mary Starks 414
White, Michael 338
Wieder, Dr. June Leslie 295
Williams, Bill 59
Williams, Dr. Louisa 267
Williams, Ellen 59
Wiltsie, Charles 44
Wine, Zhenya Kurashova 43
Winton-Henry, Cynthia 426
Wirkus, Mietek 215
WISE Method 258
Woga 108
Wolf, Linda Star 342
Woonki Acupuncture 177
Wordsworth, Chloe 187
WOW Processing 320
Wrights, Machaelle 313
Wu Chi Self-Massage 436
Wudang Chi Gong 431
Wuji Hundun Qi Gong 434

X

Xie Peigi, Dr. 167, 412
Xu Hongtao, Dr. 184, 434

Y

Yama 442
Yamaguchi, Chiyoko 248
Yamamoto, Shizuko 191
Yamuna Body Logic 63
Yamuna Body Rolling 440
Yantra Yoga 458
Yantra Yoga Massage 206
Yellow Emperor 203, 431
Yin Fu 167
Yin Style Bagua 167
Yin Yoga 459
Yi Ren Qi Gong 388, 434
Yi Zhi Chan Tuina 205
Yoga 441
Yoga Dance 422
Yogalates 441
Yogananda, Paramahamsa 439, 445, 450
Yoga Nidra 459
Yogassage 183
Yoga Trance Dance 423

Yom, Dr. Tae Hwan 155
Yongdzin Tenzin Namdak 198
Yoo, Dr. Tae Woo 157, 186
Young, Gary 89
Young, Michael 45
Your Breathing Body 349
Yuen Method 207
Yumeiho Taiso 121
Yumeiho Therapy 120

Yun, Jae "Johnny" Kwon 174
Yuthog Yonten Gonpo the Senior 197
Yuthog Yonten Gonpo the Younger 197

Z

Zake, Yamuna 63, 440
Zarlen Therapy 173
Zeigler, Patrick 249, 252
Zen Body Therapy 193

Zenith Omega Healing 259
Zen Meditation 402
Zen Shiatsu 193
Zero Balancing 121
Zhander, Natanaga 454
Zhenjiu 152, 179
Zink, Paulie 459
Zone Therapy 184
Zumba Fitness 423

About the Author

LeCain W. Smith learned early in life that his personal path to awakening was through bodywork and the breath. He has since spent untold hours on a massage table, carrying out "experiential research" under the hands of many skillful practitioners. He has also been the grateful recipient of generous instruction in yoga, qi gong, and breathwork practices. In between, he managed to fit in a six-year circumnavigation of the globe on his sailboat, write two books on nautical themes, produce a video about his travels, and, as a licensed sea captain for more than forty years, teach others maritime skills. "Captain Lee," as friends around the world know him, returned from his adventures on the world's oceans committed to diving into his inner ocean, that realm of innate wisdom he knew he could enter by making the body and breath his partners in discovery. Although he is not a practitioner of any specific modality, his heartfelt desire to help others experience true healing inspired him to make a lengthy research trip around the United States, interviewing practitioners and developers and uncovering hidden gems of bodywork and breathwork modalities. He returned to gather all the information he had collected over a lifetime of experiences on land and sea—holistic healing methods, energy medicine, and revitalizing self-care practices—into the present volume. If this endeavor changes the life of only one person, he will consider it a success. A Maine native, this sea captain, weather intuitive, yacht surveyor, and carpenter now spends most of his time on Maine's downeast coast, although the siren song of travel is hard to resist. He is always ready to hop on a massage table at a moment's notice or share his treasure chest of information. You can contact LeCain at 7innersealee@gmail.com or go to his website, www.windroseaway.com.

CPSIA information can be obtained at www.ICGtesting.com
Printed in the USA
BVOW04s0802280814

364348BV00010B/3/P